The Butcher of Pakistan

The True Story of a Medical Terrorist, Corporate Healthcare Greed, and a Corrupt Legal System

Eric Deters

Bulldog Media, Inc.
5247 Madison Pike
Independence, KY 41051

Distributed by:

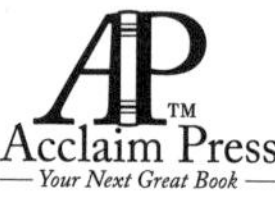

P.O. Box 238
Morley, MO 63767
(573) 472-9800
www.acclaimpress.com

ISBN: 978-1-956027-24-2 | 1-956027-24-6
Library of Congress Control Number: 2022936939

First Printing: 2022
Printed in the United States of America
10 9 8 7 6 5 4 3 2 1

This publication was produced using available information.
The publisher regrets it cannot assume responsibility for errors or omissions.

Contents

Dedication

"Honor and shame from no condition rise.
Act well your part: there all the honor lies."
—Alexander Pope

This book is dedicated to the 580 Durrani victims Deters Law represents.

This book is dedicated to all the attorneys, expert witnesses, nurses and support staff who played a role and continue to play a role in the battle for the victims of Durrani.

This book is dedicated to all the creditors who trusted in me in the cause so our pursuit of justice would not fail.

This book is dedicated to all the informants who came forward.

This book is dedicated to my wife, Mary, and our family who prayed for and supported me through thick and thin: my mother-in-law and father-in-law, Becky and Jerry Zimmerer, our children, sons-in-law and grandchildren: Cory, Erica, Cooper, Caroline, Charlie Ann, Chad, Rylee, Raygn, Rhett, Cole, Cameron and Parker.

This book is dedicated to my friends, fans and supporters who recognize I am not the villain, but the unyielding advocate for justice for the Durrani victims.

This book is dedicated to the jurors who voted against Durrani and for our clients.

My gratitude for all is immeasurable.

I believe Divine Providence chose me for the role I have played in this story. I am grateful for the strength and determination God gave me to fight on.

Justice

"Justice is truth in action."
—Joseph Joubert

Al Pacino is one of my favorite actors. He separates himself from other thespians by his passion. His passion displays itself in his roles. In every movie Pacino stars, there is a moment during the film he unleashes an extraordinary verbal tirade or inspirational speech. In *The Scent of a Woman,* Pacino stood and delivered a defense for his young friend, Charlie, in a student assembly. In *The Devil's Advocate*, Pacino nearly convinces the audience to see the world from "his" point of view, the devil himself. In *City Hall*, as the Mayor of New York, Pacino delivers a eulogy at a young black boy's funeral which stirs the soul. My favorite Pacino movie moment is in, *And Justice for All.* As criminal defense attorney, Arthur Kirkland, a small-time lawyer in Baltimore, Pacino finds himself defending a judge for rape. Kirkland disdains the judge. Pacino's character cares. He cares about his clients. However, he is no simple idealist. He is also pragmatic. Most of all, he cares about justice. He knows justice and the law do not always meet. What transpires during his opening statement is one of the best moments ever in a courtroom drama. I'll leave it for you to watch.

If anyone is asked what justice is, their response will include various variations of truth, fairness and what is right. A misconception by the general public is justice equals law. Nothing is further from the truth. Being in the law business for over thirty years, I've witnessed injustice too many times in the Court, in politics, in public policy and in life. The money machine promotes injustice. By this book, I hope to shed light on injustice in this country.

My life motto is borrowed from a quote from Theodore Roosevelt: "Aggressive fighting for the right is the noblest sport the world affords." I believe this. I practice this. It's not always easy, but it is always worth it.

If Durrani operated on you, your child, your family member or friend, it may not be too late to pursue a claim against Durrani and the hospital where he performed the surgery. If you want your matter reviewed, please send an email to eric@ericdeters.com. Also, if you know any information regarding Durrani or any hospital where he operated, please contact me as well.

INTRODUCTION

"I was born for a storm and a calm does not suit me."
—Andrew Jackson

This book chronicles a true and original story of a medical terrorist, corporate healthcare greed and a corrupt legal system. Initially, I arranged for someone else to write it and gave them all the materials necessary. However, it became impossible to relate the story I lived for a decade to someone else and expect them to do it well. As the old saying goes "when you want to do something right, do it yourself." So I did. Only I know all of this story. The purpose of this introduction is to outline the parameters of the book.

I'm not a Shakespearean prose writer. My style is choppy and blunt, more Hemingway while failing to be Hemingway. Regardless, I believe I succeed in narrating the story in readable fashion.

This story covers every possible legal process and issue imaginable. This book should be standard reading in every law school in America.

I chose *Acclaim Press* as the distributer. *Acclaim Press* is a small Midwest publisher that published two prior books I wrote. I admire Doug Sikes and *Acclaim Press,* and I trust them. I'm allowed editorial freedom including naming the book, the politically incorrect to many, "*Butcher of Pakistan*." A New York editor I engaged to proof the book immediately suggested a title change. Not on my life. Durrani is the Butcher of Pakistan. You will learn how he earned the name.

As reflected by photos inside these pages, this book condenses a thousand banker boxes of information. The prologue will whet your appetite for what is in store.

Most of the chapters are short for a reason. I wanted to divide the material well for the reader. Several chapters in the end are long in order to share with the determined and interested reader more detail of the hospital and insurance company conduct. It remains incomprehensible.

This is not a political tale, but what occurred is squarely seated in the politics of a court system, and my views and actions that make me a pariah in both major political parties. I am a conservative libertarian and populist who supported, and still supports, President Donald Trump. This makes me persona non grata to establishment Republicans and liberal Democrats.

I also apologize in advance—this story contains no false modesty. I hate false modesty. It is a form of a lie. Modesty is a virtue. False modesty is a lie. It is simply a fact that what I and my legal team achieved in this cause is exceptional and unique. This is a "one of a kind" story in American legal history.

I have thought of and strategized every hour of every day and night for over ten years about the plight of the Durrani victims and how I could secure them justice. This book is another move towards that goal. My conscious is at peace; I have attempted everything possible for these victims. It still has not been enough. Those responsible for Durrani victims' plight should be shamed for eternity. This story is a blemish on the soul of medicine and American justice. By purchasing this book and spreading the word, you will help us in the shaming.

As epic as this story is and as amazing as the anecdotes are, you will not learn of hundreds of more stories until the litigation is final. The reason is this must be drafted so we don't care if our enemies in the litigation read it. They will read it.

I want to stress in the phony world of "frivolous lawsuits," this story does not involve car accident whiplash cases. This story involves unnecessary spine surgeries.

I republish entire letters or emails in their entirety when doing so simply works best. I assure you, those entire letters or emails are worth every word.

Also, when I use "I", it is sometimes meant to be "we" or "Deters Law." All decisions which require the past or present owner of Deters Law to make, they made.

Reading this story, you may conclude one could expect evil from a surgeon, the hospitals, their lawyers, and law firms. But for the court system to collaborate in their corruption is a new level of wicked.

During these events, I believe, and others close to me believe, that my life has been in danger. Why the concern? Because of the powerful evil interests I fight with reckless abandon. The publication of this book will increase their animus towards me. These interests always work to suppress these stories from ever being told.

Leonidas ordered one Spartan back to Sparta to inform Sparta and all of Greece of what occurred at Thermopylae. If Leonidas never sent Dilios, no one would have ever known the story. It is why I wrote this book. If I never undertook this project, it would never be known and that would be a tragedy. The entire country needs to know what happened. The book uses the public record documents and "behind the scenes" accounts.

No one will sue me for defamation, because this is all true. My wife worries no one will believe the story. The main basis of all the facts came from my own personal experience, emails, letters, documents, depositions, and court transcripts.

A multi-episode and multi-season documentary is being produced from this book. Look for it in over a year. Please also check out butcherofpakistan.com for more information, photographs and videos.

I refused to sign a confidentiality and non-disparagement agreement on settlements in this matter. I sent an email refusing to sign the Cincinnati Children's non-disparagement agreement while stating: "There will be disparagement."

Dr. Abubakar Atiq Durrani is only referred to as "Durrani" based upon a legitimate issue whether or not Durrani graduated from medical school. Regardless, he does not deserve the title "doctor."

I'll never be world famous, but at least I know I played a lead role in the most incredible medical/legal story ever told. As Durrani victim Nick Battista told me: "It is a mortal wound to the reputation of the medical and legal community."

If the events described in this story occurred in Los Angeles, Chicago, New York, Philadelphia, Miami or a state or jurisdiction without Ohio's unfair laws and systems, the cases would have settled the first year for an extraordinary amount of money. It's unfortunate for the victims.

The local Cincinnati, Ohio media as a whole ignored this story except when reporting on any action against me. I hope a thoughtful, national journalist will cover our collective plight. I predict they will. Nothing against *Erin Brockovich* and *Dark Waters*, but this story surpasses both in the struggle factor.

Prologue

"Aggressive fighting for the right is the noblest sport the world affords."
—Theodore Roosevelt

This is a true story. It's also a story that is not over. The story must be told before too much time passes, and the uncertainty when this story will be over. For the victims of Durrani, it will never be over. The world must know now what happened to the victims of Dr. Abubakar Atiq Durrani. Unlike the stories you hear in the news regarding a surgeon performing horrific procedures or performing acts of sexual deviancy on patients, this story involves much worse compounded evil.

From 2005 to 2013, Durrani performed unnecessary spine surgeries on unsuspecting victims in Cincinnati, Ohio hospitals. The hospitals knew he performed these unnecessary procedures, but they craved the money Durrani generated. Durrani's insurance company, Medical Protective, refused to pay the victims. I fought and continue to fight an epic battle unlike any other in the history of American law. The Ohio court system, led by the corrupt Chief Justice Maureen O'Connor, refused to provide the victims timely trials. The Kentucky Bar Association and Ohio Disciplinary System would do all they could to aide Durrani by assailing me at every turn.

This saga covers a thousand victims and a thousand anecdotes including the following:

1. A federal grand jury indicted Durrani for healthcare fraud. Rather than face a federal jury, Durrani fled the United States to Pakistan.
2. Seventy-nine men and women died waiting for their trials. More will sadly follow.
3. At the rate trials are scheduled, trials will be going on for twenty more years.
4. Deters Law won a record number of verdicts, including the largest in Ohio history for a medical malpractice case.
5. Durrani allowed his German Shepherd dog, "Hank," to hang out in his lobby and patient rooms. Patients contracted MRSA. "Hank" had MRSA so bad his veterinarian demanded Durrani not allow "Hank" around other animals or people. According to the veterinarian records, "Hank's" penis dripped with pus as a result of his MRSA infection.
6. A "whistleblower" against Durrani at Children's Hospital, Dr. Charles

Mehlman, is pursuing a lawsuit against Children's Hospital over their retaliation against him.

7. During this battle, I was suspended, retired, went broke, served time in jail for contempt fighting for trials, was banned from the Courtroom, banned from the Courthouse, considered suicide out of spite and frustration, fought two state bar associations, betrayed by friends and family, including my father, my brother and the Hamilton County Prosecutor, had the IRS criminal division sent after me, almost lost my arm and nearly died from a staph infection, and yet kept the trust of 580 clients, financed the battle by borrowing and paying back millions and to this day I still stand.
8. One of my most important assistants in this cause is Sarah Jones York, a Cincinnati Ben-Gal Cheerleader, who was fired as a teacher for a relationship with a student. She is now married to him and they have three children. She famously sued thedirty.com for defamation and won her trial. I successfully represented her in both her criminal and civil case.
9. Warren Buffett of Berkshire Hathaway owns Durrani's insurance company, Medical Protective and Chuck Holbrook, another critical character in the story, flew to Omaha, Nebraska to lobby him for the victims. The attempt failed.
10. Chuck Holbrook contacted Dog the Bounty Hunter about traveling to Pakistan to grab Durrani. We sent a similar message to Erik Prince of Blackwater.
11. A Cincinnati mass shooting outside and during our first federal trial targeted a federal judge in the same building as our trial. The shooter decided he could not pass the front door check point, so he shot up a bank across the street.
12. One of the trial lawyers for the Durrani victims, Fred Johnson, may have been murdered.
13. Our lead trial lawyer, Alan Statman, also represented the chief witness against Pete Rose.
14. One of Durrani's partners threatened to sniper shoot Dr. Tayeb, Durrani's employee who turned against him.
15. The law firm Deters Law is now owned by Glenn Feagan, whose family were mobsters in Newport, Kentucky in the 1950s and '60s led by enforcer "Screw" Andrews. My grandfather, Bud Deters, editor of the *Kentucky Times Star*, secured on the cleanup Newport Committee against the mob. Today, Glenn and I, united in this cause, chuckle at the irony.
16. We have set a record for affidavits of disqualification against corrupt judges. We filed forty total against Maureen O'Connor and Judge Mark Schweikert from December 15, 2017 to November 21, 2019.

In the history of jurisprudence, no group of citizens in America suffered more incomprehensible injustice than the Durrani victims:

1. All the pain, suffering and misery from unnecessary spine surgeries.
2. Judicial corruption born from medical industry money.
3. In American history, no judge ever sealed jury verdicts. The Ohio judges sealed the Durrani victims' verdicts.
4. The victims have faced unjust Ohio laws including what is called the statute of repose and limitations on damages. All of this is explained in the book.
5. In ten years, there have only been fifty-six trials (580 clients)
6. Seventy-nine men and women have died.
7. The ordeal forced forty victims to file bankruptcy.
8. The ordeal forced countless foreclosures, evictions and lawsuits against Durrani's victims.
9. Despite obvious bias, Judges refused to remove themselves.
10. A corrupt judge entered a gag order against us speaking out.
11. Local media failed to cover the story based upon the hospitals being one of their leading advertisers.
12. We have faced countless unfair Court rulings, which are detailed in the book.
13. The Ohio court system coddled Durrani.
14. Healthcare companies, Medicare and Medicaid approved the unnecessary surgeries and then have sought reimbursement through what are called medical liens on the settlements we obtain. We sued them all on this issue.
15. The state court refuses reputation, credibility and impeachment evidence common in all trials.
16. The state court withholds the truth of Durrani's absence.
17. The state court refused BMP-2 increased risk of cancer evidence. You will learn about BMP-2 in the book.
18. The state court refused one filing number for the massive Court filings, which increase our court costs based upon the clerk charging $1 per page. If we file a twenty-page brief in five hundred cases, it costs $10,000. Our clients must pay these costs.
19. The victims will be gravely prejudiced if one of our experts die or quit and since this litigation will cover twenty more years; it will happen.
20. The state court ordered us to pay all the court costs even before cases were resolved. This has never occurred in American legal history.
21. The state court sat on post-trial motions for over a year. This delayed the appeals of our victories by two years.

22. Medical Protective, Durrani's insurance company, makes no offers on any cases.
23. Covid delayed trials for a year and a half.
24. Estates and bankruptcies throw our clients into the probate court and bankruptcy court bureaucracy.
25. We pay millions to try case after case, including out-of-town experts flying in for every trial.
26. The bar associations investigate all the baseless bar complaints the Durrani team file against us and ignore all the ones we file.

David v. Goliath has nothing on this story.

From 2005 to 2013, Durrani performed unnecessary spine surgery on over a thousand unsuspecting victims. The hospitals knew and looked the other way for the oldest reason since Judas took thirty pieces of silver. The destruction to the bodies, minds and lives of Durrani's victims is unquantifiable. While refusing to succumb to all the obstacles, power and corruption, I would nearly lose my arm, all I owned, my liberty, my law license in three states, and nearly my life.

The litigation would pit me, nicknamed "The Bulldog" and my "merry band" of loyal "nicked" people as I referred to them, against Durrani, the largest medical malpractice insurance company in the country and the largest employers, largest hospitals and largest attorney defense firms in Cincinnati, Ohio.

It is my hope this book and story grabs the attention of the entire country, and pressure from every direction crashes down upon those responsible for all the harm. I must secure and define the malignant legacy of the Butcher, the hospitals, their lawyers, the Ohio and Kentucky Court systems, Maureen O'Connor, Mark Schweikert, and all the rest.

The profits of this book will be shared with all the Durrani clients of Deters Law, because it is their collective story and needs to be told in a collective manner. It is my greatest honor to do so with their permission and support.

THE BUTCHER OF PAKISTAN

Chapter 1
JAILED

"No man in the wrong can stand up against a fella that's in the right and keeps a coming."
—Texas Ranger Bill McDonald

No man possessed more contempt for another man than I possessed for Judge Mark Schweikert. On September 13, 2019, we faced off at a contempt hearing.

Schweikert, old, gray-haired and wearing glasses, glared down from the bench at me, Eric Deters. Ten years earlier, Chuck Martin, a writer for the *Cincinnati Enquirer*, nicknamed me "The Bulldog" for my tenacity in fighting for clients. Always in trouble with the Kentucky Bar Association for my brash, unconventional style, which included publicly stating my distaste of the entire legal system, I still worked as a retired lawyer in the small-town Kentucky law firm that bore my name, Deters Law.

I stood up from the counsel table wearing a black T-shirt. The front bore a quote of Gladstone Ohio's Chief Justice Maureen O'Connor used in a law review article "Justice delayed is justice denied." The back of my shirt bore a list of fifty-two names who died at the hands of a spine surgeon named Durrani. The number of deceased victims at the time of this book publication rose to seventy-nine names. I wore the shirt in contempt of Judge Schweikert. With my shaved head, goatee and defiant attitude, I appeared more like Bruce Willis in *Die Hard* than a one-time practicing attorney. My law firm's shorthand for Schweikert became "Reich", owing to the judge's treatment of our clients and Deters Law. I bestowed this Nazi reference upon him. He earned it and deserved it. I once told him in an email I would ensure the world would forever equate "Schweikert" with "corrupt judge."

This hearing, which took place in the old marble courtroom in the Hamilton County Courthouse on Main Street in downtown Cincinnati, was the culmination of years of mutual disdain. Age fifty-six at the time, I publicly blasted Judge Schweikert, the Kentucky Bar Association, colossal sized law firms, and the entire legal system. I now faced up to six months in jail from allegations of violating Schweikert's gag order in over five hundred medical malpractice cases, which dragged on for nearly a decade.

Two weeks earlier, dozens of Durrani victims and I protested on the courthouse steps to demand timely trials for the victims of Durrani, a once much-touted Cincinnati spine surgeon.

From 2005 to 2013, Durrani performed thousands of fraudulent spine surgeries that left his patients with physical and emotional scars, crippling injuries and permanent debilitating pain. His radical operations killed several of his victims. Durrani harmed so many patients with such obvious intent, several who worked with him considered him "a medical terrorist." I publicly declared him "The Butcher of Pakistan."

The region's hospitals where Durrani brought in millions in revenue knowingly ignored Durrani's conduct. I filed over five hundred lawsuits against them. Durrani's malpractice insurance company, Medical Protective, promised their physician clients to fight every victim's claim to the bitter end.

I coordinated and guided the legal battle for the victims and for Deters Law, the law firm I founded twenty years earlier in Northern Kentucky which is across the Ohio River from Cincinnati. Our main law office rests in a town of 20,000 called Independence, Kentucky. We also leased office space in downtown Cincinnati.

After a decade, the Durrani malpractice cases remained untried before juries. Schweikert refused to allow group trials and only heard one case at a time. Meanwhile, fifty-two of our clients died waiting.

For half an hour, I pled my case against contempt. I argued the demonstration on the courthouse steps occurred after courthouse hours with the blessing of a local judge while Schweikert vacationed in Florida. I argued I never violated the gag order, because our protest focused on obtaining timely trials for the hundreds of Durrani victims—not the merit of the cases. In other words, we protested Schweikert. I posted a video of the protest on my Facebook pages, where I enjoyed over 50,000 friends and followers.

"Every day, your Honor, we get e-mails from Durrani's patients who have been disabled and can no longer work. Evictions, heating and air conditioning turned off. I'm the victims' advocate. I deal with these over five hundred people every day. Think about that. Five hundred and eighty people and their plight. And Durrani preyed upon the low socioeconomic group. And I deal with that. I deal with that every day," I argued.

While I asked for mercy, I never crumbled. To the contrary, I stared straight at Schweikert and in a stern voice called him evil.

Schweikert falsely claimed I tried to prejudice future jurors. "From your statements today, there is no question in my mind that your attitude and your intent is to disrupt this court's efforts to provide fair and impartial justice to these parties. So, it's the order of the court that you serve a period of fifteen days in the Hamilton County Justice Center. And further that you remain there until these things are removed from your Facebook page."

What a wisecrack. Schweikert never made any effort to "provide fair and impartial justice" to the Durrani victims.

Silent, I never begged or shed a tear as I accepted my fate. I drew my hands behind my back. Handcuffed, a sheriff's deputy escorted me out of Schweikert's courtroom. While being sentenced to jail is usually shameful, I felt nothing but pride.

Chapter 2
JEFF POTTS

"If you falter in times of trouble, how small is your strength."
—Solomon

When Jeff Potts visited the offices of spine surgeon Dr. Abubakar Atiq Durrani, neither he nor his wife Cheri, planned for another operation on his scarred back. Then forty-six, Potts underwent three lower back surgeries following the day his high school coach sent him late into a lost-cause football game as a sophomore running back. "He took all the first-string guys out and put me in. The defense ran right through our line and hammered me. I heard a snap in my back as I crumbled to the ground." Potts remembers.

The spinal column is the most important and most abused structure in the human body. It consists of thirty-three individual bones called vertebrae stacked on top of each other to support and protect the spinal cord all the way from the brain to the tail bone. The vertebrae for identification are numbered and divided into regions: seven cervical (neck), twelve thoracic (mid back), five lumbar (lower back), sacrum (connecting spine to hips) and coccyx (tail bone). The cushioning gel in between the vertebrae are discs. Nerves branch out from both sides of the spinal cord to every part of the body, sending signals back to the control centers of the brain. Wear and tear on the spine, aging, injury and surgical errors result in walking problems, numbness, pain and even paralysis. The spine is not to be trifled with, and every honest and competent spine surgeon informs patients that surgery is the last resort. No one's back is ever the same after surgery.

After the football injury, a lumbar laminectomy, an enlarging of the spinal canal to relieve pressure on the nerves, solved Potts' lower back problem for ten years until the strain of his work as an HVAC worker caught up with him. With all the stooping, crouching and lifting of heavy equipment, Potts reinjured his lower back, leaving him in excruciating pain and causing him to limp on his right leg. Two failed back surgeries followed, then spinal injections, steroids, physical therapy, massage therapy and a nerve stimulator implant. Potts took the powerful narcotic Oxycontin. With Oxycontin, Potts could crawl out of bed in the morning and walk the family dog a block and half before returning home.

In 2009 Purdue Pharma, under pressure to control the epidemic of opiate addiction raging across the country, changed the Oxycontin formula so pills could not be crushed for snorting or injection, which delivered a more potent high for addicts. The new formula failed to control Potts' pain.

At a loss for an alternative, Potts' primary care doctor referred him to a pain specialist, Dr. Zeeshan Tayeb, at the Center for Advanced Spine Technologies (CAST), wholly owned by Durrani. Tayeb recommended the full array of techniques Potts and his wife already tried: spinal injections, steroids, a spinal stimulator, physical therapy, and a product Tayeb sold not covered by insurance. Tayeb told the Potts it worked "like a fountain of youth." Tayeb ordered another battery of tests, including a MRI. Discouraged by this consultation, Potts and his wife Cheri took the information back to their primary care physician. The primary care doctor recommended the MRI.

The same day Potts had the MRI scan, the CAST office called and informed Potts he required surgery. CAST scheduled an appointment for Potts with Durrani. At age forty, the middle eastern Durrani possessed gray hair and a mustache. "Durrani hurriedly examined Jeff and then turned around in his chair, took a disk from his nurse, put it in his computer and popped Jeff's scan," Cheri said. "He pointed to the screen and said, 'That's what's wrong and I can fix it.'"

"The scan showed a cross section of Jeff's lower spine or lumbar region. The nerve roots extended out of the left side of the spinal canal looked thick and healthy like a shoestring," Cheri said. "But the nerves extending out of the right side appeared withered and thread-like. I thought this explained his pain and why he drags his right foot."

The Potts never viewed the image again. To this day, the Potts question whether it reflected Potts' spine or another patient. Durrani "sold" them on surgery. "He kept saying, I can fix you, I can fix you," Potts recalled. "I almost fell out of my chair with joy."

On October 15, 2010, while being rolled to the operating room, a "really bad feeling" fell over Potts. Durrani assured Potts the minimally invasive procedure would mean Potts would be up and walking the next day. "He told me he had just done the same surgery on someone that morning, and that patient was already walking," Potts recalls.

Durrani originally scheduled Potts' surgery at the UC Health's recently opened West Chester Hospital. There Durrani could schedule an operation any time he wanted. The $117 million facility opened the year before in an upper-middle-class suburb north of Cincinnati. The hospital struggled and needed Durrani's revenue stream. Potts' insurance would not cover the surgery at West Chester Hospital so the operation took place at Good Samaritan, a long-established and respected downtown Cincinnati hospital where Cheri Potts worked as a nurse in the neonatal intensive care unit.

Surgery began at 9:45 a.m. and two hours later, Durrani declared the surgery a success to Cheri. After waking, Potts experienced excruciating pain for the next eight hours. When Cheri visited Potts in the recovery room, "he looked awful, was pale, sweaty and clammy. He kept moaning about his stomach. He held his abdomen and cried. His blood pressure and heart rates elevated and he ran a fever," Cheri remembers.

Over the following three days, Potts progressed without incident. On the day of discharge, a nurse changed the dressing on his right flank wound where Durrani inserted his scope. The nurse noted the skin "pooched" around the incision, and a small amount of yellow green drainage stuck on the dressing, both signs of infection. Good Samaritan still sent Potts home around 2 p.m. By 7 p.m., Potts felt "bad all over." Cheri Potts tried and failed to reach Durrani by phone. By 5 a.m. the next morning, Potts groaned in pain and could not move or leave his bed. By 11 a.m., and still unable to reach Durrani, Cheri called an ambulance.

When Potts arrived at Good Samaritan's emergency room, the doctor removed the right flank dressing and stool and gas escaped from the incision. The surgeon on duty performed an emergency exploratory abdominal surgery. This surgeon discovered Durrani punctured Potts' bowel twice during the spine surgery.

The surgeon repaired the damage by removing twelve inches of the lower intestine and reconnected the bowel. Potts remained hospitalized for the next twenty-five days and would take months more to recover at home on IV antibiotics. Cheri used over two hundred hours of her vacation pay to care for Potts including bathing him, dressing him and changing his bandages.

Durrani obviously botched Potts' operation. As they learned more, the Potts questioned if Jeff even required the surgery.

Chapter 3

Deters Law

"Fight's commenced! Get to fightin' or get away!"
—Wyatt Earp "Tombstone"

On October 1, 2011, the Potts family drove south on Kentucky Route 17, the four lane road through the heart of Kenton County towards Independence, Kentucky. They ran late as a result of an accident on the interstate. They worried being late would make a poor first impression at our first meeting.

Cheri hoped their visit to my law office would be more productive than their dealings with John D. Holschuh Jr., past president of the Ohio State Bar Association and one of the alleged top personal injury lawyers in the Cincinnati region. Holschuh failed to impress Cheri. Holschuh gathered all the information, then sat on the case for eleven months before informing the Potts he would not pursue it further. Holschuh told the couple perforation of the bowel was a normal risk for any lower spine surgery and it would cost his law firm $50,000 to find an expert medical witness who would testify in their favor. The message the Potts received: their case was not worth Holschuh's time or money. Holschuh would be one of many Cincinnati lawyers who turned down Durrani cases before I began taking them. Holschuh's judgment of the Potts case would be embarrassingly wrong.

Cheri refused to give up against Durrani. She believed Durrani would injure and kill other patients. She chose to find another lawyer. She Googled Durrani's name and the word "attorney" and up popped a link to me. The fact I advertised myself as "The Bulldog" peaked her interest. My slogan? "If you need a bulldog, call The Bulldog."

My website warned readers to avoid Durrani, "The Butcher of Pakistan."

As a host on the 50,000 watt local Cincinnati radio station 700 WLW and later on other smaller stations, I developed a following. On the radio, I railed against Durrani, local and national politicians and the legal system. I represented several clients who accused Durrani of injuring them with fraudulent surgeries, I hoped the publicity would stir up more.

As the Potts's car rounded the final curve toward my office, Cheri recalled commenting to Jeff in a positive fashion on the modesty of my law building. Unlike Holschuh's office, located on the 27th floor of a glass-and-granite high rise in the heart of downtown Cincinnati, I practiced out of a one-story brick building with a simple sign out front. Converted from a 1960s bank building, the office still featured the drive-through portico.

Inside our single glass entry door is a small lobby with two chairs and an end table. An old sliding-glass teller window opened into the front office. At each end of the old check writing counter I placed ceramic busts of Jefferson and Lincoln. On the walls of the lobby hung tributes from my radio and legal career by way of newspaper clippings and magazine covers.

One of my staff members slid back the teller window to greet the Potts and directed them to enter through the door on their right. Once inside, the Potts found themselves in the midst of ten staffers working the phones and computers at desks walled in by file cabinets and stacks of banker boxes.

Jeff turned to Cheri, smiled and said, "This is my kinda guy."

Chuck Holbrook, a handsome man in his late forties who once worked as a Hollywood creative representative, greeted the Potts. Chuck once successfully crashed an Oscars ceremony. He now worked for me as my chief client liaison. Chuck also became my best friend and staunchest supporter. Grateful for the job I gave him, Chuck looked up to me as a big brother. Chuck apologized to the Potts for my being called out of the office, sat down with them and patiently took down all their information. Chuck told the Potts he had no doubts I would take their case. Chuck possesses outstanding people skills and knows how I want clients treated. He became a reliable extension of me. He once interacted with radio fans online for thirty minutes as me until I arrived at the event. In addition, I already put out the directive to the staff: "If anyone contacts us about Durrani, we take the case."

Skeptical of the visit based upon my absence, several days later Cheri heard me "ranting and raving" on the radio. "It was like he was screaming," she said. "But that was before I realized that's just how he talks."

Cheri told Jeff she thought I was "loud and opinionated," not lawyer-like at all. Jeff responded, "He's the guy I want. If he's loud and opinionated, I want him to be loud and opinionated for me."

In the following months, Cheri communicated with me via text and sometimes phone. I impressed her by always answering her queries within minutes. "If he was busy, it might be with a quick yes or no. But he would always get back to me in more depth within a day."

I would soon meet the Potts at a Durrani media press conference.

Chapter 4
Press Conference

"I have never insulted man or woman in my life, but if you knew what a wholesome regard I have for damn liars and rascals, they would be liable to keep out of my way."
—Wild Bill Hickok

On February 23, 2013, I prepared for a press conference featuring twelve Durrani clients and their families who milled around my waiting room in my Cincinnati, Ohio law office. When Chuck Holbrook pointed out Jeff and Cheri Potts to me, I walked over and introduced myself. I thanked them for coming to the press conference even though they asked not to be interviewed by the media.

I leased space on the fourth floor of the Spanish style exterior building where Fox 19 News also called home. The space is in what is known as Queensgate and lies blocks from downtown. It's right off Interstate 75. Radio stations Realtalk 1160 and 1360 Oldies also leased space there. I made Realtalk my home after WLW, then used 1360 to broadcast my show for ClassX Radio. This provided a perfect situation for me. I could do my radio show then check on things at the Cincinnati office. After paying rent for a year, I stopped paying rent based upon cash flow. I told the landlord I would move. The landlord preferred I stay because the building already had a leasing problem and the landlord worried about the appearance of too many vacancies. I would stay there four years rent free.

Our twelve clients attending the press conference included: Jacob Feltner, Josh Roy, Brenda Shell, Barbara Hensley, Crystal Pierce, Julie Martin, Tim Marshall, Stephanie Herrin-Threm, Carol Wilson, Jason Romer and David Scott.

I held this press conference for revenge against Mike Lyon, Durrani's Medical Protective Insurance handpicked lawyer, for his fighting over the meaning of language in a release on two Durrani cases I recently settled with Cincinnati Children's Hospital. Before the cases I now had, I pursued two cases against Durrani and Cincinnati Children's and settled them. Durrani personally escaped the "noose" on those two cases. Mike Lyon found a friendly judge to interpret the language in the release with Children's Hospital to dismiss Durrani from the cases. It would prove fortunate in the long run, because my guard would forever be up against the scoundrel, Mike Lyon. I never trusted him again.

This press conference would now lead to Mike Lyon's "client" Durrani and his "real client" Medical Protective being hit with a legal tsunami in the form of hundreds of lawsuits. Mike Lyon won the release battle, but Durrani and Medical Protective would now have a war. It would have never happened, but for Mike Lyon's conduct in those two cases.

The Judge who ruled in Mike Lyon's favor, Pat DeWine, is the son of Ohio

Governor, Mike DeWine. At the time, Pat DeWine served as a Hamilton County Common Pleas Judge. He would later become an Ohio Supreme Court Justice. While Judge DeWine considered the release issue, Mike Lyon's frat boy like partner, Brad McPeek, served on Pat DeWine's fundraising committee. Pat DeWine's own "friends" called him Deweenie behind his back.

Reporters from three of the four local TV stations showed up at the press conference, but no one from the *Cincinnati Enquirer*, the only daily newspaper in town. I believe I landed three stations because the courthouses were closed for President's Day. The media rarely cover medical malpractice cases before a verdict. "It's my opinion this is an exception," I told the media. "Dr. Durrani has performed unnecessary surgeries, not just according to our spine expert, but Tri-State treating orthopedic and neurosurgeons who have dealt with his patients after his surgeries. This is unheard of in medical negligence cases. In depositions, local doctors are testifying under oath that Durrani performed unnecessary surgeries. They recognize Durrani is a threat to the public. This is an important public policy issue. As a public service, the media and the press have an obligation to report on this story."

My career in law and my past career in politics gave me media experience. I know what stories the media should cover or want to cover. A threat to public safety deserves their time and attention.

None of the expert depositions in the cases I handled so far, came from doctors at any of the six hospitals where Durrani performed his surgeries. These hospitals included two of Cincinnati's largest employers: Children's Hospital Medical Center, which ranked second in the region with nearly 20,000 employees, and UC Health, a division of the University of Cincinnati, with 12,000 employees and four in-patient facilities, including West Chester Hospital where Durrani now operated. Good Samaritan, Christ, Riverview, Deaconess and Jewish also allowed Durrani to operate. Durrani also operated at a surgery center called Journey Lite.

All of these hospital systems advertised heavy in the local media market to cultivate their image as exceptional healthcare institutions with the exception of Riverview out of Dayton. Children's boasted in ads of being named among *U.S. News & World Reports*' top pediatric hospitals in the nation. Although Durrani still operated at West Chester at the time of my press conference, UC Health's media page touted the hospital's HealthGrades ranking as one of America's 100 Best Hospitals for Spine Surgery in 2012 to 2013 and in the nation's top ten percent for spine surgery 2013. "This achievement is truly a direct reflection of our entire organization's commitment to quality and is indicative of the exceptional and highly specialized care that West Chester Hospital provides."

These hospitals love their hospital rankings with *U.S. News World Report*. You will never find a phone number for the rankings. They use a company out of North Carolina named RTI. After much effort, we finally reached RTI, but they weren't interested to hear what we had to say. I put together a package of information and sent it to them. The next year, Children's dropped from #2 to #3 in the national Children's Hospital rankings. I only hope I caused the drop.

At the press conference, I announced I filed seven new cases in the morning against Durrani. I invited the media to interview my clients about their experiences. I knew the media preferred to interview victims, not lawyers. My clients shared compelling stories. All of them divulged a story similar to that of Potts. Durrani lied about their conditions and claimed he could "fix them as good as new" with a simple surgery. Instead, their conditions only worsened and they sought other surgeons to relieve their suffering.

When the news stories aired that night, our law office phones rang off the hook the next morning. By the end of the week, I represented one hundred and fifty clients against Durrani and local hospitals. Before the press conference, few of Durrani's victims even questioned their treatment. If they suffered complications or pain after surgery, Durrani apprised them it was "normal" and the healing process takes a year or more. If victims sought a second opinion, other surgeons remained silent witnesses. No one suggested contacting a lawyer.

My greatest accomplishment in my professional life is the press conference led to saving thousands from the scalpel of Durrani. When the news broke about Durrani, patients began cancelling surgeries. I received emails and phone calls thanking me.

With one hundred and fifty new clients signed up, I required an action plan. Calls had to be taken or returned. Clients must complete all the forms and provide the information necessary for us to represent them. I made a quick assessment on each case to determine if a lawsuit could be filed in time and when it must be. We chose to take no chances and when possible, filed within a year of the surgery. We chose the press conference as a "triggering event" for many clients to begin the one year statute of limitations based upon most not realizing what Durrani wrought upon them. We also tried to file within four years of their last surgery to meet what you will learn is the statute of repose. Many facts affect these deadlines including continuing treatment. Ohio law also requires an affidavit of merit by a qualified orthopaedic surgeon before filing at the courthouse.

Every member of my staff assisted in signing up clients. Staff met them in the office if victims could drive in to either the Cincinnati office or to Independence. Chad Fuller, my 19-year-old son in law, and Chuck Holbrook, drove day, night and weekends to countless houses around the tristate. Chuck first trained the young Chad how to meet and talk to clients, then cut him loose on his own. Bonds would form with all staff and the victims. One client, Dorothy Rose, an elderly victim, liked Chad so much, she fancied giving him her car she no longer drove.

Every lawyer and paralegal became part of the drafting team. I held drafting parties after hours and paid $300 extra to each lawyer and staff member for every lawsuit drafted. The format of the background and claims never altered. However, the individual circumstances of each client differed.

We achieved the impossible. By the end of 2013, we filed hundreds of lawsuits, and all lawsuits included an affidavit of merit from a qualified surgeon.

Chapter 5
Informants

"We stand at Armageddon, and we battle for the Lord."
—Theodore Roosevelt

As I hoped and expected, the press conference not only raised awareness among Durrani's patients, but brought information from hospital staff who worked with Durrani.

Many believe my use of publicity as ill advised, but I knew what I was doing. Having the press conference and news coverage warned the public, gave us clients and provided informants with inside information. I still use this method. Without inside information, we would have never been able to hold hospitals accountable, because the law protects the internal reviews of the doctors. This means that despite a hospital's internal investigation and reviews proving there is a "bad doctor," the public never is allowed to know. It is absurd. It is also the law. We soon unraveled the Durrani tale against two hospitals: Cincinnati Children's and West Chester.

I received the following email from Melissa Dowler on July 29, 2013:

> You need to look into complaints about Durrani at Children's Hospital. His lawyer is not telling the truth or Durrani is not telling his lawyer the truth (Cardinal Rule Number One). He has on record at least once complaint that I am aware of for making sexist remarks to staff. "You do not need food or sleep all you need is sex."

He was very powerful but the most despicable "professional" person I have ever encountered.

He offered a nurse at West Chester Medical Center 10K if she would give him a blow job and stare him straight in the eyes while doing it. (EWWW) not for any amount of money... YUCK. He thinks he is God's gift to women. When he left Children's Hospital (I am sure they asked him to) he was having an affair with his Physician's assistant. I understand that his wife wanted or wants to leave him but if she did she would have to go back to Pakistan. I am wondering who then would take care of the penguins he has at his house?? He has also told people that he has something he wears over his penis to enlarge it. No wonder the poor guy is messed up overcompensating for his micro penis.

I would look into a nurse that worked with him. I have no idea if she continued her association outside of Children's Hospital with him but I know she is still friends with him on Facebook. She is there under ____________________________. She has gotten married since I knew her. She is made of the same greedy cloth he is. I understand she was clocking in 80 hours a week and most days not in her department before 11 am. It was suspected that she was coming in at 5 am and clocking in and leaving to run her own business. She packed her stuff up 2 weeks after being hired there and took up shop behind closed doors in his office. He hired her out of the waiting room (She is quite pretty) when her son was a patient of his.

I got suspicious of her character and in 2007 I looked her Medicaid Waiver program she participates in and found that in 2006 she was paid over 96K!!!!!!!!!!! while working 80 hours at CCHMC (impossible). She no doubt is involved in fraudulent activity and probably learned it from him. She ran her own private business behind closed doors in his office and turfed all of her work to _______________ who was Durrani's administrative assistant (also on Facebook). ________ had NO IDEA how to do her work... she was good at getting everyone else to do it for her ___________

Interesting enough, ______ suddenly quit CCHMC before all this latest regarding Durrani and federal charges hit the fan. I am wondering what she knows about this since she scheduled all of his surgeries... or at least at one time did when he worked at CCHMC. I think she left before all this happened because it is quite odd that she did. Her husband is a respiratory therapist at CCHMC and they are not rich by any means to live off of one income. (Oh unless she is getting Durrani money somehow).

There are "spine nurses" that do case management at CCHMC that could fill your ears regarding Durrani... as they did mine. I was around him very briefly. I did not want to be associated with him and had no idea he was doing what is in the media. I just knew his character was someone I would never associate myself with. He is DRAMA and loves it. I guess he finally has his wish.

We legally recorded many of the conversations of witnesses as they contacted us. Ohio and Kentucky is referred to as a one-party state, which means you are allowed to record the conversation without informing the other party. This begets honesty and candor. One of the informants who came forward, Krissy Probst, worked as the administrative assistant of Durrani. She turned Durrani into Children's administration because of his affair with his physician's assistant, Jamie Moor, now Jamie Lewandowsky. Probst claimed Durrani would leave surgeries and permit young, inexperienced assistants or "fellows" finish the operation while having sex with Jamie in his office. Probst saved everything on her computer. We sent what is known as a discovery request to Children's and warned them not to delete anything. Children's sent us four banker boxes of emails Krissy Probst saved. I personally sat down in my living room floor for a week and read every email and document in those boxes. I eliminated the relevant from irrelevant and categorized them by topic and witness. The emails helped us corner Children's Hospital and West Chester Hospital. Without Krissy Probst contacting me, it would have never happened.

Durrani scheduled multiple spinal fusions a day. A spinal fusion is an eight-hour procedure in many cases. Most surgeons schedule one a day. "He would do two at once," Probst told us. "He would start them both at 7:30 a.m., and so he would run from room to room. Or he would leave and his surgical fellow would do the other one." Durrani and the hospitals generated extra revenue, but patients paid the price.

"If an operating room wasn't available," Probst said, "he would go above our business director and go directly to the OR supervisor and get a different room by claiming the surgery was an emergency. Other surgeons might leave the operating room for a short period and return, but Durrani would leave for four or five hours, sit in his office, and then come and check on things when he decided he wanted to."

This, too, would become a Durrani modus operandi: claim the surgery an emergency.

According to Probst, Durrani told staffers at Children's he was born a Prince back in in his native Pakistan. Probst, friends with Durrani's wife Shazia, told us Shazia's family paid for Durrani's medical school training and Durrani sent money back to Durrani's family in Pakistan. All the travel expenses for Durrani's speaking engagements and attendance at conferences were paid by Medtronic, the maker of the BMP-2 bone grafting material sold under the name Infuse. Durrani used BMP-2 in his spinal fusions without patient consent and often without following FDA guidelines. More on BMP-2 later.

We gave Krissy Probst's name and contact information to the U.S. Attorney and they interviewed her. We disclosed Probst as a witness, but David Brittingham, Children's attorney, wouldn't produce her for a deposition. She would no longer talk to us after Brittingham spoke to her and threatened her with a HIPAA violation.

When Probst's deposition happened by force of subpoena, Probst's damning stories about Durrani changed in the conference room at the Cincinnati law office of Dinsmore & Shohl, Cincinnati's largest law firm with hundreds of lawyers.

Fifteen minutes into the deposition, our attorney produced the transcript of her phone call to the firm.

ATTORNEY: Now previously we talked about that you spoke to our office and you said you told the truth?

PROBST: Correct.

ATTORNEY: Okay, I'm handing you your statement from that office.

Probst's demeanor changed as our attorney slid the transcript across the conference table in front of her.

PROBST: I don't have a statement from that office.

BRITTINGHAM: Have you ever seen this document?

PROBST: No.

Brittingham requested to go off the record. Brittingham then held an improper thirty-minute break with Probst. Probst would spend the remainder of the deposition attempting to backtrack from her recorded statement. This is why you record statements.

I contacted Joe Deters, Hamilton County Prosecutor, to prosecute David Brittingham for suborning perjury on the Probst matter. Suborning perjury is knowingly supporting and assisting perjury. Brittingham should've been charged, but no charges ever came. I would later find out why. I'll share later.

A former operating room nurse at West Chester, Vickie Scott, sent an email to me claiming Durrani had other surgeons performing his operations at the hospital while documenting them in the operating room records as his own. When nurses complained about the practice to their supervisor, the supervisor told them it was up to the nurses to ensure the records were accurate, not Durrani. This nurse and others also complained Durrani would sometimes have his current mistress, Beth Garrett, who replaced Jamie Moor, assist during his surgeries even though she had no reason to be in the operating room.

Elizabeth Dean, one of the original patient access representatives at West Chester, described every area of the hospital as a "ghost town" before the arrival of Durrani in 2009. West Chester's net loss in 2009 was $13.3 million. In 2010, Durrani performed 534 surgeries at West Chester and the net loss dropped to $5.2 million. Over his four years at West Chester from 2009 to 2013, Durrani performed a total of 1,823 surgeries, an extraordinary number. In the entire state of Ohio, Durrani ranked second in Medicaid/Medicare billing.

On July 27, 2013, Elizabeth Dean sent me the following email:

> Mr. Deters,
>
> My name is --------- and I was one of the original patient access representatives at West Chester Medical Center, which is now West Chester Hospital, starting employment------ there before they opened the doors for business. I had my responsibilities within the hospital including Durrani cases and completing financial reports for the CFO, Mike Jeffers. I was also included in most corporate meetings regarding the processes for the ------ performed by Dr. Durrani in the testing area of the hospital and was the actual Patient Access Rep that registered and spoke with all the Durrani patients.

Before Durrani began to practice at West Chester Hospital, every area of the hospital was a ghost town. Considering it was a new hospital, it was still not picking up revenue like it should have. We were required to ask for all copays when the patient arrived just to keep the numbers up as much as possible.

I quit in the midst of the crazy atmosphere. I was considered terminated because I did not complete the final two weeks of my leave notice. The new Access Representative Manager was Lisa Davis, who was also the Office manager of Dr. Blankenburg of Hamilton, who was charged with child molestation along with his twin brother. She pushed me into the driver seat in most of the Durrani corporate meetings because I was the one who designed the patient flows for the hospital. I was the one who waited on most the Durrani patients, and I have a five-year history as a medical biller with University Internal Medicine Associates. I know the hospital needed the money. I reviewed the final numbers from Mike Jeffers each month and also logged all payments received on the surgery cases. They did not give us raises for 2010 and were struggling as a new hospital. They let go all the original CEO and corporate employees once the hospital was bought by UC and appointed the ER physician as the new CEO. Their excuse was they wanted to have the hospital ran by physicians. After all the original corporate employees and their visions of honesty and integrity were gone, the hospital became something different that I didn't want to be a part of.

I thought that my knowledge would help to get these patients what they deserve, which is a relief. The hospital did know Durrani's history of being banned from other hospitals and were desperate to survive. I no longer have the UC email account, but there were emails between Mike Jeffers and myself to prove that I did see the figures and the amount of money coming in. You have my permission to verify if I was an employee at the hospital during the times I have mentioned. I'm not one to step forward, but I have heard many of Durrani's patients' stories first hand and have checked them in as inpatients and outpatients. It made me so sad that I couldn't help them or tell them to find another dr. I feel this would be helping all of them. It just wasn't right.

On August 3, 2013, Sean Rider sent me this email:

> Hey, I've been following with interest the whole Durrani case. I've had the displeasure of working with him at West Chester, and lol when I saw the news. I read the transcript and email of the 2 informants and can say they are right on when they describe him. I can't speak to the billing issues because I wasn't involved on that side, but he was one of the most inappropriate, sexist, pompous surgeons I have met. The patients standing up for him really don't know the guy. He may have had decent bedside manner, but otherwise he was a real a-hole. He was having sexual tirades with a female sales rep, his employees, and god knows who else. There was also talk that he belonged to some "playboy club" which was some sort of sex

club. I wonder if they have a playboy club in prison!? I'm just glad I don't have to work with him again. Good luck with the case.

On August 2, 2013, Vickie Scott sent me this email:

> I worked at West Chester in OR and many nurses went to OR Management (Elaine Kunko, Denise Evans), Risk Management (Jill Stegman) about Durrani and his practices. No one did a thing. It was brought to the then acting OR Assistant Manager Elaine Kunko's attention that Durrani (because the way cases were scheduled) was making it appear in OR records that he was doing all the procedures. The response was to get the nurses together and say make sure your documenting is correct. But there were many steps that had to be taken in the computer record to change the Primary Surgeon and no one ever in-serviced the staff to make those corrections. I am glad someone is taking this man down and West Chester Hospital, they try to present to the community that it is this stellar, first class, award winning place, but Durrani is an example of the priority in that Hospital. $$$$$.
>
> By the way, West Chester's current perioperative Director, Kathy Hayes came from Children's, word was Durrani got her the job. The hospital also hired an OR Manager with less than 2 years OR experience and had only been a nurse since 2009. Can bet he did not have the experience to see or even have knowledge to know the unethical practices of this surgeon. Just saying…
>
> Forgot to mention the OR manager the 29 year old Mark Tromba was hired because the current CNO (Chief Nursing Officer) Patrick Baker had worked with him before in another hospital, Tromba was not a manager. Patrick Baker is a wolf in sheep's clothing, bad guy. The whole group of upper management Jack Talbot, Tom, Ron, they were all told about problems in the OR. Poor Dr. Joseph, well seemed intelligent, clueless. Baker is really running the place. Every single manager has been replaced since he got to that hospital. Replaced with friends of his (Patrick Baker) or individuals easily manipulated!

Feeling safe as the hospital's top revenue producer, Durrani verbally abused staff at the hospital. He referred to women in the X-ray department as "whores" and "puntas." He made sniffing sounds implying someone smelled. He embroidered his X-ray apron with the word "Daddy."

On March 6, 2013, Tammy Benzinger, manager of volunteers at West Chest Hospital, sent an email to five administrators: "Today I was at the surgical desk and an employee stated to me that Durrani is going to get himself into a lot of trouble. He called an employee 'Mexican" all the time and had just called another employee a Jew. As part of the management team, I felt I needed to pass this information along to the team. Thanks, Tammy."

Gerry Goodman, the former interim nursing director of the operating room at West Chester, gave sworn testimony regarding her experiences with Durrani. Durrani's surgical partner, Dr. Nael Shanti, operated on Durrani's patients alone and Durrani billed them illegally under his own name.

"They would be doing three cases simultaneously," Goodman said. "One patient had a deep, deep problem. She developed some post-operative bleeding in the recovery room. Durrani went ahead and proceeded to do another elective procedure while this patient was being attended to by other people."

Vendors of medical devices often accompany surgeons in the operating room. Durrani always had a representative from Medtronic during his surgeries. "They go in for a variety of reasons," Goodman said. "One is to help measure and guide what products you use, and the other is sometimes to upsell. I mean these guys are always hawking their wares."

"Complaining to hospital administrators failed," Goodman lamented. "No one ever got back to me. I was told pretty much that he was making money, that they needed to make the money, and therefore I really shouldn't be bothering them so much."

Other informants from West Chester reported Durrani kept patients under anesthesia for an unsafe amount of time. Durrani would have patients put under by an anesthesiologist and line the patients up for their surgeries. Witnesses testified Durrani once left a surgery in progress to bid on a Lamborghini on eBay. Durrani also offered money for sex from women staffers.

Dean, Scott, Rider, Probst, Dowler and Goodman "broke the dam" on the hospitals. Based on their information, I drafted a long list of names to request depositions.

Chapter 6

Spine Surgery

"First, do no harm."
—Hippocratic Oath

What does every American expect from their surgeon? They expect the truth, honest information, the necessary tests, a full explanation of their condition, and how the surgery will resolve or relieve that condition and other alternatives. Americans expect surgeons not to attempt anything beyond their ability and skill. They expect a referral to anyone else necessary. They assume their needs and care will come before any financial consideration.

Durrani failed on all counts.

What does every surgeon expect from every patient? The patient should be honest, answer all questions honestly, provide all information needed, follow the surgeon's advice, ask proper questions, and report any and all relevant condition changes.

Durrani's victims thoroughly fulfilled their obligations. This included answering in writing Durrani's ten-page intake form, which covered every imaginable topic and issue.

What is involved in every surgery? Risk of death, infection and failure weighs on the minds of the patient and their families; risks of anesthesia; pre-operative testing/doctor consults; scars, pain after surgery, hospitalization, pain in recovery, physical therapy, possible infection, missed work for patient, stress, anxiety and fear; inconveniences; financial stress; post-operative testing/doctor consults; radiology exposure from all radiology before and after surgery and post-operative medication.

Having any surgery is a serious matter. Having a spine surgery is a most serious matter.

What is involved in a spine surgery? Everything mentioned above for a surgery, but more. There is risk of paralysis, increased risk of nerve damage, pain because it is the spine, permanent restriction in range of motion, and arthritis.

Durrani's victims had other issues in common. Most already consulted with other spine doctors who informed them surgery was not an option. When they met Durrani, he seized on their despair with promises of "fixing" them. No one pushed back on Durrani's hopeful prophecy. Fear fueled the fraud.

Durrani would misrepresent the radiology to his victims. While a radiologist would report no issues, Durrani would document severe issues. Durrani would report these serious issues to the victim's primary care physicians, who also trusted Durrani. Durrani would usually recommend surgery after one consult. Durrani would not obtain and review the victim's prior records. Durrani would also scare the hell out of his victim's by informing them their "head would fall off", literally. They would "be in a wheelchair" or they would be "paralyzed" if they rejected his surgery proposal. Durrani rarely recommended alternatives to surgery including non-surgical measures. Durrani also always chose the most extensive procedures.

When a patient visited Durrani, they filled out a form that describes everything. He generally didn't do a physical exam and would order radiology films such as MRIs. The MRI would document mild or no stenosis. Durrani would immediately write a letter to the primary care physician stating the patient suffered from severe stenosis and surgery was the only option. The clients never saw these records. They only saw the record that they filled out. They never saw radiology reports. When Durrani ordered an MRI, he told patients their MRI showed severe stenosis and they believed him. Durrani pulled this off for years.

The very back of Durrani's form asks the patient to mark whether they desired to discuss surgical options or non-surgical options. Most victims left this blank or marked both. Patients were open to non-surgical or surgical. Durrani always chose surgical.

Chapter 7
PATIENTS

"If you are going through hell, keep going!"
—Winston Churchill

From 2005 to February 2013 and before my press conference, Durrani patients had no way of knowing of Durrani's fraud.

When patients suffered issues, Durrani told them "It takes a year." When they sought second opinions, those surgeons never shared Durrani's bad reputation and practices. Doctors are aware patients have a year to sue them if they "deviate from the standard of care and cause harm", so Doctors are also trained to explain it "takes a year" to heal up.

None of the victims possessed knowledge of what the hospitals knew about Durrani. The hospitals concealed it all. Hospitals knew Durrani was committing fraud, but they kept silent while he contained to operate. When victims heard about thirteen lawsuits from the press conference, victims thought to themselves "maybe this is why I have had problems." The clients never saw or reviewed their medical records or radiology. They never read what Durrani documented in their chart. Remember, this was before MyChart.

Durrani's victims suffered through an unnecessary spine surgery, the ultimate betrayal of a doctor. All the victims deal with severe pain management issues. Some turned to illegal drugs to stop the pain when legal medication failed. I never judged them. Durrani preyed on victims of the lowest social economic group. The majority of our clients are poor and old, on Medicaid and Medicare. Victims faced evictions, divorces, bankruptcies and debt on top of all the pain.

There is a state bar association rule in Ohio and Kentucky that forbids an attorney from giving money to a client. It's called champerty, and it's an allegation you're buying their loyalty. I violated this rule with Durrani and other clients a thousand times and never gave a damn. When a client contacts you and they need to buy school clothes or are in desperate need for groceries, sometimes you just do the right thing. One client's pet dog meant so much to them, I paid for the lifesaving surgery. Christmas time always brought client requests. I always treated these requests with dignity. Imagine the embarrassment of having to make these requests. I never denied one rational request. Many promised they would never ask again. Most would. They had no place else or no one else to ask. I ignored or denied a few extraordinary requests such as "I would like a new car." I would buy them a used one. Large defense firms' clients do not need financial assistance to survive.

From the beginning, we held monthly "Support Group Meetings" at the Holiday Inn in Covington, Kentucky to update the clients in person. Covington is located directly across the Ohio River from Cincinnati and after Louisville and Lexington, is Kentucky's third largest city. We rented a large room and provided food and drinks for the clients. The room was set up in theater style seating with a podium at the front. We provided a rundown of the litigation status, and then open the room for questions. I have cried in front of the group many times listening to their plights and trying to express how much I care about them.

We have busted third parties attempting to attend the meetings. Chuck Holbrook once caught someone from the Ohio Disciplinary Counsel staking out our meeting. As always, they worried more about what I was doing as opposed to justice for the victims. We also send out regular email updates.

In order to keep so many clients satisfied, communication is critical. Some clients are good with email updates, others need face to face contact. We provide both.

In these meetings, everyone is raw and real. We laugh, cry, shout and cuss. I open up to the clients and provide an atmosphere where clients can express their emotions. Many have attended one meeting and are not able to attend another simply because the visual devastation is too much. They observe the pain, wheelchairs and victims walking sideways. I have carried all of this for ten years. It weighs heavy on me every day.

Alyssa Jackson had her first surgery by Durrani at Children's at age thirteen. In 2006, after Durrani inserted a rod that bent and caused further damage to her spine, Alyssa returned three years later to have the rod removed. Heavy pain medication and steroid injections helped Jackson through college and the next seven years of her life. In 2016, Jackson saw Dr. Robert Bohinski at the Mayfield Clinic, a prestigious private clinic in Cincinnati, to obtain relief from her constant pain.

In a twelve-hour surgery, Bohinski removed twelve pieces of damaged hardware from Jackson's spinal column. The pieces rubbed against her bone while her nerves coiling around them like roots. Durrani fused her spine incorrectly and it could not be altered. Bohinski shaved down the bone to prevent further rubbing on the nerve endings. Alyssa still suffers pain daily. She switched to physical therapy to control her symptoms and no longer receives steroid injections. Her first job after becoming a nurse would be at Children's Hospital. "Compared to other Durrani patients, I'm doing very well," she said.

Joshua Kauffman walks like a seventy-year-old man and finds it impossible to sit longer than thirty minutes without pain radiating down his legs. His entire back is scarred from the spine surgery that Durrani performed in 2007 at Children's Hospital when he was only twelve years old. Every day is a struggle. He worries about his future.

Durrani's post-operative care left much to be desired. When seventeen-year-old Ben Thaeler developed an infection at the incision site a month after his surgery, Durrani insisted it was an allergic reaction and sent him home. His mother insisted otherwise. Durrani finally reopened the incision and discovered the infection. Three more surgeries followed to eliminate its source. Suspecting Durrani's surgery had been ill advised, his mother took Ben to the Mayfield Clinic for evaluation. The surgeons at Mayfield removed all of Durrani's hardware, including an unattached rod which nearly ruptured his spinal cord. Five surgeries later, Thaeler, now twenty-nine, still suffers severe pain and nerve tingling.

For those already battling health issues, Durrani usually worsened their conditions. At the time of her surgery, Mary Mauntel was a happy seven-year-old Down Syndrome little girl with a small but growing vocabulary and the ability to speak to her parents. The family's primary care physician referred Mary to Children's Hospital to have Durrani evaluate her. Durrani told the family Mary needed emergency spine surgery or her head would fall off.

Mary's real problem was simply psoriatic arthritis, a condition caused by one knee being bigger than the other. Durrani severed Mary's vocal cords during the surgery and she never spoke again. Her parents deal with violent outbursts because Mary has no way to communicate. The poor angel is trapped in a voiceless world created by the demented Durrani.

Karen Taylor suffered back pain from her scoliosis. Even so, she became an avid equestrian and worked five jobs: realtor, massage therapist, part-time bookkeeper, rental property manager, and small items sorter for UPS. At her first appointment with Durrani, Durrani told her she necessitated immediate surgery or life would soon relegate her to a wheelchair. One operation turned into five to fix what Durrani messed up on one. Durrani pierced her spinal cord with one screw and tore open her aorta with another. After her surgeries, Taylor became incapacitated and wheelchair bound. She lost all five of her jobs and became completely disabled.

Chapter 8
The Butcher

A man like Ringo has got a great big hole, right in the middle of himself. And he can never kill enough, or steal enough, or inflict enough pain to ever fill it.
—Doc Holliday "Tombstone"

The law firm's investigation into Durrani's background produced massive evidence of lies and fraud. In a medical malpractice case, a lawyer usually fails to find anything nefarious in a doctor's background. We found a smorgasbord buffet of deceit on Durrani. Durrani lied consistently about his background and credentials beginning with his birth year. On his application for his Ohio medical license, he used August 29, 1967. On a temporary certification to the Ohio Medical Board and his passport, he listed 1968. On the majority of other documents, including his resume and an Ohio speeding ticket, he used 1969.

From 1976 to 1983, Durrani allegedly attended LaSalle High School in Multan, Pakistan and moved on to a "pre-medical" education at Governor's College in the same city. Both schools ignored requests to confirm Durrani's attendance.

From 1986 to 1991, Durrani claimed on his applications for medical licenses in Kentucky, Ohio and Texas to have attended the Army Medical College in Islamabad, later known as the National University of Science and Technology (NUSTI). Durrani gave three different dates for his graduation: 1990, 1991 and 1995. All three dates fall after his claim to have passed the National Board of Medical Examiners test in Cairo, Egypt in September of 1990. NUSTI informed my office by email they have no record of Durrani as a student or alumnus.

In verifying Durrani's license, the Ohio Medical Board file stated Durrani graduated on December 1, 1990 from a different medical school—Bolan Medical College at the University of Baluchistan. Bolan happened to be his father's employer. The elder Durrani worked as a clerk and computer operator according to postings on social media. In a deposition, Durrani would deny ever attending Bolan or knowing how the Ohio licensing board obtained this information. Regardless, records reflect Durrani allegedly received his Pakistani medical license on November 3, 1991.

From 1991 to 1996, there's a five-year gap in Durrani's resume, although Durrani would later claim when the Kentucky medical board questioned him about this gap, he completed an internship and residency at Nishtar Hospital in Pakistan during this time. There's no mention of either in any of his Ohio medical records. Durrani left Nishtar off all his resumes.

Durrani married his wife Shazia in 1995 and after his marriage, he trained in orthopedic oncology at the Royal National Orthopedic Hospital in Middlesex, England from August 7, 1996 to February 6, 1997. Durrani later claimed in a deposition he spent four years there. True or not, a highly respected doctor at Royal National recommended Durrani to Dr. Alvin Crawford, a pediatric spine surgeon at Children's with an international reputation.

In 1997, at the invitation of Crawford, Durrani began a fellowship in pediatric spinal surgery at Children's Hospital. Crawford searched for a protégé to follow in his footsteps as head of the pediatric spine surgery program at Children's and Durrani became the chosen one. Meanwhile, Durrani failed his U.S. licensing exam in 1998 in Nevada.

From July of 1998 to December of 1998, Durrani attended a pediatric orthopedics and scoliosis fellowship at Texas Scottish Rite Hospital in Dallas. Hospital officials reported to the Ohio and Kentucky medical boards his irregular attendance. Also while at Texas Scottish Rite, Dr. John Herring, caught Durrani falsifying information for a research paper Durrani planned to present at an International Orthopaedic Conference in Canada. Being Durrani's supervisor, Herring ordered the paper withdrawn. From January 1 to June 30 of 1999, Durrani attended an orthopedic oncology fellowship at the University of Florida in Gainesville. They, too, reported Durrani's irregular attendance to the Ohio and Kentucky boards. It seems Durrani suffered from an irregular attendance problem.

From July 1, 1999 to June 30, 2003, Durrani completed his residency training in orthopedic surgery at the University of Cincinnati under Dr. Peter J. Stern, Chairman. On his evaluation form of Durrani, Stern graded Durrani an average student.

On October 16, 2000, Tracy Newton, ironically represented by me, filed a medical malpractice lawsuit against Durrani and others. At this time, I knew nothing of Durrani. The Newton case settled during trial. Tracy tragically lost her leg. In 2004, Durrani lied to the Ohio Medical Board about this lawsuit. Ohio's Special Activity Certificate in 2004 asks in question #17: *Have you been a defendant in a legal action involving professional liability (malpractice)....*" Durrani lied. He marked no. He knew it was not true. He would later lie about being sued in sworn testimony and then claim when proven a liar it was no big deal because he was only named as a resident. Lies upon lies would be the normal for Durrani.

On January 3, 2001, Durrani received a Physician Notification Letter from Ellen Witsken, Associate Director Health Information Management Department of Cincinnati Children's Medical Center. The letter stated: "*the listing below represents records of discharged patients that are incomplete and in need of your attention.*" *It continued:* "*failure to compete these records within thirty days will result in automatic suspension of all non-emergency admitting and clinical privileges.*" Durrani was seventy-two days late on two cases. This notice would be the first known issue of Durrani's practice of not completing his records. Durrani would fail in his record keeping over and over, year after year.

On April 12, 2002, Casey Pflum filed a medical malpractice lawsuit against Durrani and others at University. Again, I filed the lawsuit. Durrani lied about the Casey Pflum lawsuit the same as he would Tracy Newton's. The Pflum lawsuit also settled.

On July 1, 2002, Durrani began his last years as residency at University of Cincinnati. He would be Chief Resident. It's of no consequence, but Durrani touted it as if it was.

On August 16, 2002, James Johnson filed a lawsuit against Durrani. Again, Durrani would lie about this in 2004 to the Ohio Medical Board.

In 2003, Durrani became a Medtronic consultant. This means for advocating and using Medtronic products, Durrani received money. This is a dangerous and prevalent practice in corporate healthcare. In 2003, Durrani began negotiating his contract with Cincinnati Children's Medical Center. He reached terms of a salary of $250,000 a year plus more based upon his revenues. Again, incentives breed corruption for the dishonest.

On February 28, 2003, Robert Ferrell filed a medical malpractice lawsuit. Durrani lied about this too in 2004 to the Ohio Medical Board. On the heels of this lawsuit, on April 11, 2003, Robert Hughes sued Durrani. Durrani would now forget all five lawsuits when the Ohio Medical Board asked him if he was ever sued.

It is true Durrani in these five lawsuits, as a resident, was not the main target of the malpractice. When I began taking Durrani cases in 2013, I never even remembered Durrani as a Defendant in these cases. As a Defendant, one might think Durrani's memory would be better.

On June 30, 2003, Durrani's residency ended at University of Cincinnati. His Ohio temporary license ended the same day. On July 1, 2003, Durrani received a temporary Kentucky Medical license. From August 1, 2003 through July 30, 2004, Durrani began a spine surgery fellowship at the infamous Leatherman Spine Institute, University of Louisville.

The *Wallstreet Journal* profiled Leatherman and its spine doctors as a "spine surgery mill." Dr. Charles Mehlman, a Cincinnati pediatric spine surgeon, who plays a role in our story, claimed this fellowship changed Durrani into a money hungry monster. Durrani craved what the Leatherman surgeons acquired: money, planes, yachts and multiple mansions. Dr. Keith Wilkey, our spine expert, actually attended this same program a year before Durrani and experienced a chance encounter with Durrani. While Wilkey walked in the rain and found himself being soaked in an unexpected storm, Durrani stopped his car, picked Dr. Wilkey up and gave him a ride. Of more relevance, Wilkey knew how Leatherman trained and while an eccentric place, knew Leatherman never trained surgeons as Durrani performed.

Durrani never practiced in Kentucky again. He claimed to the Kentucky Medical Board for years he held privileges at a Kentucky hospital. In 2011, St. Elizabeth Medical Center in Northern Kentucky near Cincinnati rejected Durrani's request for privileges. Children's inadvertently placed Dr. Crawford's recommendation to St. Elizabeth in the box of emails they sent to me. Dr. Crawford only marked "good" on Durrani's form. Dr. Wilkey told me this is a red flag because everyone always marks excellent.

On May 17, 2004, Durrani signed his contract with Cincinnati Children's. Dr. Alvin Crawford would begin protecting Durrani the rest of Durrani's time in Cincinnati.

Although all of the above probably convinces you Durrani is a diabolical liar, here's more in summary fashion:

1. There is a discrepancy on how long he trained or studied in London.
2. He lied about being a visiting professor at Children's Hospital in Philadelphia.
3. He lied about his credentials on a seminar flyer at West Chester.
4. He has lied repeatedly about his credentials on self-promotion internet publication.
5. He lied about being the Director of Spine Surgery at West Chester, a position that never existed.
6. He lied about being the editor or board member of the *Orthopaedic Research Society.*
7. He lied about being a member of the Orthopaedic Medical Association.
8. He lied about being a member of the International Neurofibromatosis Association. It does not exist.
9. He lied about being a member of the Spinal Deformity Study Group.
10. He lied that he never applied to and was denied privileges at a hospital. He was denied privileges at St. Elizabeth Medical Center.
11. He lied about his hospital privileges never being suspended. They were at Children's and West Chester.
12. He lied about his family's wealth and status.
13. He lied about being a consultant for Globus Medical.
14. He lied about being a consultant for Wright Medical.
15. He lied about his patents being for minimal invasive spine surgery.
16. In his 2018 deposition, he denied being divorced from Shazia Durrani, despite a September 15, 2014 Final Judgment Entry of Divorce.
17. He lied on his Ohio and Kentucky Medical Applications whether or not he was ever charged with a crime. On July 4, 2009, Shazia Durrani filed a complaint against him in Mason Municipal Court, Warren County, for Misdemeanor First Degree Assault. This charge was pending when he filled out the application. Shazia struck Durrani with a stiletto heel.
18. Durrani's name does not appear now on the active doctors in Pakistan

under the Pakistan Medical and Dental Council (PMDC). The PMDC held a meeting on October 23, 2017 and sent a warning December 14, 2017. Durrani denies all this.

19. He lied about being the physician to the Saudi Royal Family. On December 11, 2009, Durrani's lawyer filed a Motion to Continue a hearing in his Mason Criminal case where it stated: "Dr. Durrani is the physician to the Royal Family of Saudi Arabia and has been called to serve the Royal Family."
20. He lied about belonging to the Ohio Medical Association.
21. He lied about being a visiting professor at Army Medical College in Pakistan in June of 2005.
22. He lied about being a member of the Florida Orthopaedic Association. It doesn't exist.
23. He lied about why he left Cincinnati Children's Hospital.
24. On January 7, 2010, he was asked this on his Kentucky renewal license: "Since you last registered, to your knowledge, have you become the subject of any criminal investigation or are any criminal charges pending against you?" *No.* As of January 7, 2010, the charges were still pending.
25. On March 14, 2011, on an Ohio Medical Board form he was asked: "Have any malpractice awards been paid by you or on your behalf for acts occurring in any state other than Ohio?" He answered no. That was a lie.
26. On April 19, 2012 he conducted a seminar by himself at West Chester. We have the flyer. He claimed on that flyer that he was an Assistant Professor at UC and Children's. He was neither.
27. On December 6, 2012, the Ohio Medical Board form he filled out asked: "Have any malpractice awards been paid by you or on your behalf for acts occurring in any state other than Ohio?" *No.* That was a lie.
28. Durrani posted online on January 25, 2017 and January 26, 2017 a self-promotional bit. He falsely claims: "Dr. Atiq Durrani holds plenty of other respected titles e.g. Assistant Professor at the department of Orthopaedic Surgery, University of Cincinnati, Ohio – Staff Affiliate at the University of Cincinnati, Ohio – Courtesy Staff at Bethesda and Good Samaritan (Tri-Health), Cincinnati, Ohio – Courtesy Staff at Mercy Hospital Mt. Airy, Cincinnati, Ohio, The Jewish Hospital, Cincinnati, Ohio and at Fort Hamilton Hospital, Cincinnati, Ohio."

He did not hold any of those positions as of January 25 or 26, 2017.

29. He claimed he attended American University.
30. He claimed on his resume he was the Editor or a Board Member for the *Clinical Orthopaedics and Related Research*. He never was.
31. He claimed he was a member of the American Academy of Orthopae-

dic Surgeons. (The organization which board certifies.) He was expelled from that organization June 16, 2014.

32. In 2008, he claimed hospital staff privileges in Kentucky. He lied. He did not have them.
33. In 2009, the law firm for Children's Hospital, Dinsmore & Shohl sued him for legal fees Durrani owed them for work on a patent. He never reported this on forms to the Kentucky Medical Board and Ohio Medical Board when questions asked for this information.
34. On the State Board applications when they asked, "have you ever been sued for anything else besides medical malpractice," he answered no. Dinsmore & Shohl sued him for fees from legal work.
35. He claimed to be "America's Top Orthopedists, 2011." He did not list an organization that gave him that award and we have searched and can't find anything indicating that he has received this award. His name was not found under an Ohio or Kentucky search.
36. According to *MagCloud*: Atiq Durrani added high honor to his sterling resume when he was awarded the Award of Honor in Orthopaedic Surgery by the National Institute of Medicine in 2013. The award is the latest in a long string of awards which renowned spinal surgeon Atiq Durrani has received in his career, including being named one of America's Top Orthopedist in 2011. In addition, Atiq Durrani was a Whitecloud Award Nominee for best Clinical Paper in 2010 and has been awarded several prestigious fellowships and trusteeships." That's not true.
37. According to *Professional On The Web*. Renowned spinal surgeon and founder of CAST (the Center for Advanced Spine Technologies), Atiq Durrani has earned a reputation as a consummate professional and a man of unimpeachable moral fiber. Atiq Durrani has been the recipient of a slew of awards and accolades in his distinguished career, including being named one of America's Top Orthopedist in 2011 and being given the Award of Honor in Orthopedic Surgery by the National Institute of Medicine in 2013. Atiq Durrani's pioneering techniques have made many of his spinal surgeries into outpatient procedures." That's not true.
38. According to *Word Press*: Written by Dr. Durrani as declared on August 12, 2013: "As a leader in orthopedic medicine, Atiq Durrani has made monumental achievements in his field of research and practice." "Atiq Durrani is revolutionizing the field of medicine in a way that has never been done before, making him a leader in his field. Atiq Durrani has now established some of the most advanced orthopedic procedures in history and around the world. Atiq Durrani's work is being read, taught, and replicated all around the world." That's not true.
39. Written by Dr. Durrani as declared on August 3, 2013: "The research of

Atiq Durrani is the leading research in the field of orthopedics." That's not true.

40. Written by Dr. Durrani as declared on July 29, 2013: "Atiq Durrani's achievements are known world-wide as the latest in orthopedic procedures and research. Atiq Durrani has developed the most advanced spine program in the world, making his work the leading research in the field. Atiq Durrani is revolutionizing the field of orthopedics and orthopedic surgery. As he continues to excel in his area of specialty, Atiq Durrani gains more recognition around the world. Atiq Durrani is at the forefront of his career, and is changing the way orthopedics is being performed by doctors from all over the world." That's not true.
41. Written by Dr. Durrani as declared on July 27, 2013: "In 2005, Atiq Durrani was named a Trustee at the University of Orthopedic Research and Education Foundation." That's not true.
42. "Atiq Durrani was also awarded the Award of Honor in Orthopedic Surgery by the National Institute of medicine in 2013." That's not true.
43. His application for Licensure to the Kentucky Board of Medical Licensure included many discrepancies.
44. He reported he had a South Carolina License. Not true.
45. He did not timely complete the Kentucky HIV/AIDS education Kentucky.
46. The Postgraduate Medical Education form completed by Children's Hospital Medical Center was not sealed or notarized.
47. The Postgraduate Medical Education form completed by Texas Scottish Rite Hospital for Children was not sealed or notarized.

The Courts would exclude nearly all of this from evidence at the trials. Court or no court, the hospitals in Cincinnati either failed to obtain all of this information or they chose to ignore it all. None of Durrani's victims knew any of it.

Chapter 9

The Bulldog

"Tomorrow is the most important thing in life. Comes into us at midnight very clean. It's perfect when it arrives and it puts itself in our hands. It hopes we've learned something from yesterday."
—John Wayne

I enjoy Shakespeare. He stands alone as a wordsmith. He once wrote: "What is past is prologue." It is true. I am the product of all of my "prologue", which prepared me for the Durrani litigation. Although not an overly religious man, I believe divine providence called me to represent these victims.

I want to begin with my family. I'm married to Mary Zimmerer who has lived the entire Durrani battle with me. As you read this story, you will marvel how our marriage survived. To the chagrin of my enemies, it has. We have six children, three each from our prior marriages. From oldest to youngest: Cory, Erica, Charlie Ann, Cole, Cameron, and Parker.

From 2013 through today, I found comfort in my family during the struggles. Cory tragically died in a car accident at the age of 21. A bright light snuffed out. Charlie Ann married Chad Fuller. They have three children: Rylee, Raygn and Rhett. Charlie Ann and Chad bless us by involving us in the angels' world. I am "Pop Pop" and Mary is "Mimi." Parker earned the nickname "Funcle." Chad owns his own company, Crimson Ground Services. Charlie Ann is a "stay at home" mother. Erica married Cooper Bowen. They are both lawyers. Their angel, Caroline, brings us more joy. Cole lives and works for Peloton in Colorado. Cameron works for his father's company and is pursuing a cyber security degree. Parker owns and operates his own yoga studio, Parks Yoga. We love and support our children and grandchildren, and they love and support us.

No one needs examples to know how family is everything, but they counterbalanced all the stress I suffered during the Durrani litigation.

After graduating from Northern Kentucky University's Chase School of Law in 1986, I joined my father's law firm, Deters, Benzinger and LaVelle, the largest in Northern Kentucky.

Although I began at my father's firm as a general practitioner, it soon became clear to me my temperament and passion fit helping people, not representing banks, hospitals and insurance companies. I preferred representing people.

Born with a passionate gene inherited from my Scots-Irish mother who grew up in Harlan County, Kentucky, I have fire in my blood. I love my Harlan roots and my good luck hat remains after thirty years, my Harlan County Green Dragons ball cap. I'm quick to temper and quick to calm again. I also vacillate between tougher than a pine knot and choking up tears. My motto is a quote from Teddy Roosevelt, which hung in my Uncle Jerry's office: "Aggressive fighting for the right is the noblest sport the world affords." I believe this maxim and I live it.

I grew up being allowed only to watch television shows like *The Waltons* and *Little House on the Prairie*, John Wayne and *Tarzan* movies and sports. Good versus evil, right versus wrong, standing up for the little guy, empathy and compassion.

I'm quick to claim I'm a sinner, not a saint. I have made mistakes and I have flaws. I'm at peace in knowing the good in me and my actions far outweigh the wrong. I detest snobs, mean people and the self-righteous.

I loathe bullies—always have and always will. I have a great sense of empathy born in part out of having a younger brother, Seth, who lives with cerebral palsy.

I grew up with six brothers and four sisters. My brothers and I earned wages by completing farm chores: cleaning out horse stalls, putting up hay, painting fences, bush hogging, mowing, tending to the tobacco crop, building fence, taking care of cattle and building barns. Chores on the farm began at 8 a.m. during the summer and ended at 5 p.m. or later. We worked six days a week and rotated the Sunday duties. This meant once a month, we worked thirteen straight days. I remember beginning work on the farm at eight years old, rolling hay bales close to a wagon so a man could throw them on a wagon. At thirteen, I would do thirteen straight days once a month, six days otherwise. During school months, we worked after school and always on Saturday. The boys' "dormitory" was an addition to the original house heated only by a wood-fired boiler we kept stoked or froze to death.

Barring all television during the Lenten season, my mother wrapped a purple ribbon around the television with a knot we couldn't untie and retie without her knowing. We never watched Saturday morning cartoons. We worked. We watched *Disney* on Sunday night. Mom required a family rosary every evening after dinner during the months devoted to the Blessed Virgin Mary, May and October and for every tornado warning. As we reached our teens, Mom disallowed speaking to boyfriends and girlfriends on the phone, although we boys would walk over to Dad's horse barn office at night to escape detection and call our girlfriends.

As a child, I was cursed as a bed wetter. I kept my bedwetting a secret throughout my years at St. Cecelia Elementary School until sixth grade. One of my Dad's Sunday school students, who worked on our family farm, found out I wet the bed and told his little brother, my classmate. To avoid the embarrassment, I bought time by bribing my classmate with lunch snacks and picking him on my kickball team since my team always won. Despite being the smartest and most popular kid in my class, as an eleven-year-old boy, I feared ruin. These events to this day make me aware how something can really affect a child. I soon made a decision that altered my life. I would leave St. Cecilia by applying to Covington Latin, where students skipped the seventh and eighth grades and entered high school at twelve and graduated at fifteen. This would remove me from St. Cecilia before my classmates discovered my embarrassing secret.

I passed the entrance exam and gained admission at Covington Latin. Although I entered Covington Latin for my own reasons, I credit the school's rigorous classical instruction for a good education. However, I would never repeat it if given the choice. I found it the longest four years of my life.

I earned average grades at Covington Latin School even when studying four hours a night. Mischievous, I battled Gary Whittle for earning more detention than anyone else in class. I graduated at age fifteen and attended St. Thomas More College in Northern Kentucky, now Thomas More University, where I majored in history and minored in business administration.

In grade school, I read every biography in the St. Cecilia library. My love of biography and history continued through high school, college, law school and beyond. I developed a love of so many historical figures from Lincoln, Churchill, Teddy Roosevelt, Andrew Jackson, and Martin Luther King, Jr. I have an extensive biography collection.

I admire our Founding Fathers. I admire Martin Luther King, Jr.'s use of peaceful protests and his movement that created change. Leonidas gave up his life to give Greece three more days to prepare for Xerxes. I enjoy American, Greek, Roman, and European history. Truman is another hero, he would refer to Plutarch more than cabinet members for wisdom. As in real life, with staff and clients, I enjoy those who are "nicked" or suffered and overcame. I find it comforting in the Bible God used flawed men for important causes, as he has used me in the Durrani cause.

During college, I became famous for the field parties I threw at the family farm. I became the social director for my fraternity, an Eric Stratton in *Animal House*. To this day, everyone remembers the field parties I threw in the spring and fall. We called them "Bladder Busters." We put bands on hay wagons and kegs of beer on trucks.

Despite the mischief, I never crossed a line that would wreck my life, hurt anyone or send me to jail. I believed from an early age I was chosen to do something worthy in life, and several near death incidents reinforced that belief.

At age fifteen, while riding in a new Berlinetta Camaro owned and driven by Alan Smith, a high school buddy, we missed a sharp turn on a country road and slammed into a tree. Alan hurt his knees and Dave Ison broke his neck. Thankfully, Dave survived. I failed to wear a seatbelt, so I hit the dashboard and windshield. Thankfully, I only suffered a bruised kidney, which kept me in the hospital for a week. When I saw the car later, I couldn't believe I survived.

In my late teens, while bush-hogging a back field at the family farm, the tractor began to tip over. Somehow, I managed to jump off and when it failed to tip over, jumped back onto the tractor without falling and being ground up by the bush hog.

Another time, my brother Thad spread gravel from a moving dump truck. Suddenly, the rear left wheel of the truck hit a hole and the truck bed twisted and spilled eight tons of rock to the side where I stood on the running board. Thad shouted my nickname at this time: "Squirrel!" I froze and barely missed being buried under eight tons of rock.

At twenty-three I suffered a strange cardiac event. If I never drove myself to the ER, I would have died. I received the last rites over that one. I'll never forget looking up in a daze at the ER doctor. He grabbed his head with his hands and exclaimed: "I can't believe we are losing him." They would later determine I simply had a rare short circuit. No heart issues. The priest sent to deliver me my last rites appeared to be ninety years old (think the classic old Italian priest). He began the ritual and since I had consciousness, he asked for a confession. So here I am at twenty-three, thinking to myself, what do you know that I don't. Am I dying? I had no interest in confessing all my sins to this stranger. Then I made the call. I decided, heck if this is it, I'm cleaning my soul and going to heaven clean as a whistle. So I gave the old Italian priest all of it. I mean all of it. I'll never forget it. He hurriedly completed the rites and left as if he had just saved a complete heathen.

Although I learned the value of hard work at an early age, my upbringing wasn't without its privileges. As a front-page article in *The Kentucky Post* in 1984 titled "Non-Trivial Pursuit" pointed out, the Deters family: my father Charlie, Uncle Jerry and Grandfather Bud exerted a "sweeping influence" over Northern Kentucky institutions, from hospitals, colleges, banks, real estate, and political and religious leadership.

In May 1986, at twenty-one, I graduated from law school and joined Dad's firm. I passed the Kentucky Bar exam in October of that year, the Ohio Bar a year later, and the Florida Bar in 1988. For at least a year, I found myself the youngest lawyer in Kentucky.

After becoming an associate partner, then equity partner, at Deters, Benzinger & LaVelle, I began my own firm in 1999 and began doing things my way. I not only thought outside the box, I created a whole new box.

To stop an estranged husband from stalking and harassing one of my clients, I wrote up a legal warning on my letterhead and asked Chuck Holbrook to show up at the man's front door one night dressed in a black leather jacket, black boots, and black hat. At my direction, Chuck said to the guy, "My boss wanted me to hand deliver this letter and make sure you got it. I trust I won't have to be back." And then Chuck left. We found out later from his wife the guy peed his pants. He never bothered her again. Hand delivering a letter like this was and is perfectly legal and ethical. Of course, other lawyers would never do it.

Chuck and I would use the hand delivery letter practice another time for the girlfriend of a Vice President of Cumulous radio. Her stalker never bothered her again, either. This VP couldn't believe everything they tried for a year failed and I solved their problem. I never billed him, hoping he would put me on air. He never reciprocated the favor.

I brag I live on naps. Everyone around will support my contention. I have a theory when you're tired, if possible, sleep. Who works well tired? So I take naps including in the morning if up all night, always in the afternoon like a kindergartner, always early evening. I figure if I stay up until 3 or 4 a.m. and take two hours sleep, it's not short sleep, it's a long nap. This allows me to work sixteen to eighteen hour days. And I do.

I'm fortunate I am able to recalibrate myself with a nap, movie, dinner, lunch, workout, short drive or a visit with my grandchildren. I never need a week on a beach.

Outworking opponents means long hours. To boost my energy and immunity, I take countless vitamin and herbal supplements. I've never missed more than an afternoon of work due to sickness during even my most stressful years. I'm fifty-eight, so I'm proud of this personal accomplishment. I have never suffered from one chronic ailment—not one full day of work missed sick. Rather than drink coffee or soft drinks, I use NoDoz, which I joke is "pure grade" caffeine. I enjoy the caffeine without the sugar of soft drinks. I never developed a taste for coffee or tea.

My phone is critical. It never leaves me. Ever. I text and email all day, evening and night to staff, clients, family and friends so much that I make at a breakneck speed countless decisions every day and get ninety percent of them right. Jeff Bezos preaches how you never have all the information you need, so you gather all you can, and decide. He's right and that's how I operate.

My law practice included handling every conceivable legal matter. This experience gave me broad insight. While car accidents and medical malpractice cases became the majority of my work, I handled criminal cases, domestic cases, real estate transactions, wills, and probate.

I'm in the process of writing another book called: *Armed with a Righteous Cause*, in which I detail incredible stories from my legal career. I have also written a book about my brother Seth, called *Seth*, I still need to publish. In addition, I have published three other books: *Pioneer Spirit*, a true Kentucky High School basketball story better than *Hoosiers*; *Saving Grace*, a true story about a woman who killed her attacker; and *Willie: Great American*, Bill Cunningham's biography.

In 2006, *The Kentucky Post* wrote a story about me with the headline *"He's King of Taking Cases to Trial."* From 1998 to 2005, I had nineteen trial verdicts, more than any other lawyer in Northern Kentucky. Many lawyers fear taking a case to trial because of the expense, fear and unpredictability of juries. Not me. Before my eventual suspension and retirement as a lawyer, I thrived on the challenge and lived for the courtroom adrenaline rush.

Two years later, a front-page story in the *Cincinnati Enquirer*, under the headline "*Courtroom Bulldog – Lawyer Eric Deters Fights Hard*," earned me the "bulldog" moniker I would turn into an advertising tool. *The Enquirer* story detailed my community's year-long battle to move a proposed jail site from my backyard in Independence, Ky. to the city of Covington. It was a group effort. I was one of the leaders. "He filed lawsuits, organized and rallied hundreds of irate homeowners and sparred with the fiscal court," the story said about me. "He also made sure the media showed up to cover the melee."

My bravado in the jail battle caught the attention of popular WLW talk radio host Bill "Willie" Cunningham, who asked me call in to his show almost daily for updates on the jail battle while he played the theme music from *The Godfather* in the background, a humorous reference to Ralph Drees' power and influence in Northern Kentucky. The Kenton County Judge Executive and the region's largest builder, Ralph Drees, chose the jail site we fought. Cunningham introduced me to the station's program director, Darryl Parks, who had been impressed with my on-air performance with Willie. I dared to ask Darryl Parks for a shot as a host and he gave it to me.

For four years, I filled in for Cunningham and others in evenings and on weekends, holidays and vacations. Rick Walburg, Wille's producer, used "Bulldog" to identify me for radio. I embraced it. I thought a bulldog represented strength and determination, and I could not have a better name for the law business. In addition, the bulldog is a favorite among dog owners, the mascot for the Marines, mascot for the United Kingdom, and mascot for hundreds of colleges, high schools and recreational teams.

I created Bulldog Nation and Bulldog Mafia all with bumper stickers, t-shirts, hats and sweatshirts. I give them away. I have trademarked the following: Bulldog Nation, Bulldog Mafia, Witty & Wise, Radio Superbity, American Jury, Judge Bulldog, and Oracle Status. I have more future plans for the brand.

All of this drove my enemies nuts with jealousy.

There is a lawyer referral service called Martindale Hubbel. They track "hits" on lawyers. One week, out of all the 1.5 million lawyers in the country at the time, I was the number one searched lawyer.

Cincinnati *City Beat* magazine ranks everything in the city by voters. In the past, I received the most votes as the best lawyer and as the "biggest troublemaker." I beat out Cunningham for that title. One year, *Cincy Magazine* chose me as one of Cincinnati's most interesting people. One year I finished behind Chris Collingsworth and George Clooney as the most popular Northern Kentuckian.

In 1993, I finished second to Ben Chandler as Outstanding Kentucky Young Lawyer by the KBA. Ben was elected Attorney General that year. I know Ben, as we both were sworn as Kentucky lawyers the same day. Ben would later serve in Congress from Lexington, Ky.

I fought an official MMA cage fight against a police officer twelve years my junior to benefit disabled veterans. I lost. The fight broke a record for attendance at Indiana's Dearborn County Fairgrounds. To this day, it remains one of the stupidest things I've ever done.

By the time the Potts arrived at my office in Independence, I lived David v. Goliath. I boasted offices in Northern Kentucky and downtown Cincinnati, a law firm with twenty lawyers and a hard-working support staff of eighteen. My willingness to challenge those with power and influence and my unconventional tactics both inside and outside the courtroom, made powerful enemies whose vengeance would come at me just as I began the long battle for Durrani's victims. I used my public platform to level the playing field against the powerful, and the powerful resented every bit of it.

The editor of a Highland County, Ohio newspaper once told me to keep doing what the old Irish journalist Finley Dunne professed: "*comfort the afflicted and afflict the comfortable.*" I would do my best.

Chapter 10
THE DEVASTATION

"Never, never, never, quit."
—Winston Churchill

Three life factors affect our happiness: relationships, finances and health. Durrani destroyed all three. If someone suffers from severe health problems from an unnecessary spine surgery, it affects their finances, then it affects their relationships.

Jason Romer worked in public relations and sales for a small cell phone startup when he saw Durrani in 2011 for back pain at the urging of his wife. On Romer's first visit to the office, Durrani declared Jason needed emergency surgery. Durrani promised it would be a simple, arthroscopic procedure, a laminectomy to remove part of the bone in his vertebra to relieve the pressure on his spinal cord.

When Romer woke from surgery, "I knew immediately something was wrong with my right leg. It was mostly pain, but when I tried to walk on it, it was like it would just shut down." Three months later, Romer required more back surgery, an emergency spinal fusion. "They just kept pumping me with more Oxycontin, and then they put me on Xanax," Romer remembers. Romer would never work again and he now walks with the help of a cane. His wife, unable to deal with it all, left him.

At forty-four, Romer is on disability and living at home with his parents. "How do you like that in your mid-forties?" he said. "Once my mother and father are gone, I don't know what the hell is going to happen to me." His right leg swells and bursts into blisters due to a damaged nerve condition called Complex Regional Pain Syndrome. "Believe it or not, I've come a long way in the past eight or nine years. I have finally accepted that this is what I can do and this is what I can't do. I can't push myself too hard or I will be right back to where I began."

Parents of children butchered by Durrani suffer guilt. They trusted the Cincinnati Children's Hospital brand. I remind them it is understandable they trusted the brand. The fault lies with Children's.

Many Durrani victims fell victim to opiate addiction from either Durrani's over-prescribing their medication or left them in such pain after surgery they turned to street opiates for relief. Sherri Lynn Allen, forty-four, claims Durrani hooked her on Percocet after a spinal fusion surgery which left her in dire pain with no feeling in her left leg from the knee down.

Forced to use a walker after surgery, Allen fell into a deep depression and contemplated suicide. She lost her job, her husband, her home, and twice placed herself and her two small children in an emergency shelter. At one point, her colon ruptured from the pain medication shutting down her digestive system. A surgeon removed a foot of her colon. Determined not to use pain medication, she showed up at a detox clinic and declared, "I need your help." Drug-free for three years, she earns straight As in nursing school.

Robert Masters thought his life was ruined after a car accident and two botched surgeries Durrani performed on his neck. The pain and medication prescribed by Durrani spun Masters into a black hole of depression and drug dependence that drained him of energy and any interest in life.

After missing days of work, he lost his job as a city sewer inspector. He soon lost his Christian faith. With his anger near the boiling point, he lost his high school sweetheart and wife of twenty-two years.

The couple divorced, but stayed in touch for the sake of their sons. Robert eventually rediscovered his faith and a new philosophy of life: "live every day I can to the fullest." In 2013, he returned to the operating room and a new surgeon repaired the hardware Durrani left poking out of his neck. After two years, Robert and his wife reconciled and remarried.

Paul Baker, a self-employed electrical contractor earning $200,000 a year, saw Durrani for a sciatica problem he learned later could have been solved with physical therapy. Durrani lied and told Baker without surgery Paul would end up in a wheelchair. After the operation, Baker suffered so much pain he could no longer perform electrical installations, lost his business and his ability to support his family.

Rather than taking the pain pills prescribed by Durrani, Baker turned to alcohol. This led him through four different jobs and cost him his marriage. Baker sobered up and earned his associate degree in electro-mechanical engineering. He returned to work as master electrician for a non-profit agency in Cincinnati that does repairs and remodels for low-income homeowners. Sober, he still suffers from pain if he "moves a certain way."

"No one who hasn't had the experience can truly understand the psychological toll of being a victim to a fraudulent surgery that leaves you more impaired and in pain than before you placed your trust in the medical system," said fifty-four-year-old Katie Prater. Prater taught in an inner-city school in Columbus, Ohio and served as a senior master sergeant in the Air National Guard. In 2011, Durrani literally screwed Katie's skull to her neck during an operation in 2011. Unable to turn her head, she is in pain from the base of her neck and the right side of her face and shoulders. Katie laments, "Slowly, as the days go by, and you are dealing with the aftermath suffered at Durrani's hands, you begin to lose sight of who you are, and lose all confidence, slowly withdrawing into isolation, and not having the energy to do what you normally do. You go through what seems like a never-ending grief process, where you mourn the person that you were."

Sabrina Cain, our videographer and photographer, relates a common theme expressed among the hundreds of clients she interviewed and photographed. Durrani seemed "a savior" prior to their surgeries. When asked what they missed most about their old lives, the majority struggled through tears to give their answers. Each video Sabrina produced, scarred her. "I would leave work but still suffer from knowing all that I knew. All of the victims wanted someone to help, someone to listen, and justice. Eric took on all that for them. For over five hundred victims."

Sabrina believes she suffers from post-traumatic stress disorder from photographing and videotaping over four hundred Durrani victims. She photographed the clients' back scars. All of them can be viewed on butcherofpakistan.com. As a result of all her photography and video interviews, I gave her the name of the Durrani victims' angel.

The last question we always ask at trial of our clients is what they miss the most prior to Durrani? The thought in our client's mind immediately triggers emotion for the jury to hear and witness. The question carries the victims back to a better time in their lives and it's heartbreaking.

Chapter 11

The Victims

"Noble souls, through dust and heat, Rise from disaster and defeat, The stronger."
—Longfellow

Every one of the Durrani victims suffered in unimaginable ways. It's impossible and unnecessary to relate the details of all their stories. This book can't contain all of the carnage. In the back of the book, we have listed a summary of each of our five hundred and eighty clients, so no one is left out. All the victims' stories have common themes. It is critical you understand the incomprehensible magnitude of the harm to place in context the subsequent treatment of them by the legal system.

In 2007, Macy Acord enjoyed her life as a four-year-old active little girl despite challenges when she met Durrani. Born with Goldenhar syndrome, Macy met all gross motor milestones. She used the G-tube for medications and her tracheostomy remained capped during daytime hours. Macy suffered from scoliosis due to multiple vertebral anomalies related to the Goldenhar syndrome, but Dr. Alvin Crawford monitored it prior to Durrani.

Approximately one month after Macy's first surgery with Durrani, the growing rod construct broke through her skin. Macy underwent four further surgeries in the following two weeks due to another hardware breakage and wound infection (MRSA) so severe it required IV antibiotics at home.

A year later, Macy experienced severe complications related to the spine instrumentation placed by Durrani. After complaining of neck pain, imaging proved the hardware broke loose. Macy endured another revision surgery with Durrani. A couple days after surgery, Kelly Martin, Macy's mom, noticed Macy's difficulty moving her left leg. Durrani attributed this to swelling and promised it would resolve. Durrani sent Macy home from the hospital. The neurological issues only progressed at home. Macy suffered incontinence and her bladder and paralysis worsened. Kelly drove Macy to the ER, where imaging indicated kyphosis and a spinal cord injury due to a spinal fracture with significant cord compression. Macy required two more surgeries with neurosurgeon Dr. Kerry Crone.

Macy endured eight surgeries, seven of those surgeries due to complications from the first. The fifth and sixth surgeries resulted in paralysis requiring extensive inpatient rehabilitation. Macy suffered right vocal cord paralysis after the fifth surgery.

Durrani performed nine unnecessary surgeries on Gayle Bachmann, which fell under the time frame of Durrani's suspension. Several loose screws cause Gayle severe pain.

Despite all the suffering, Phyllis Bechtold endured; she fought through with an indomitable spirit. Phyllis brought our legal team so many baked goods over the years, we all gained "Bechtold pounds."

During a sports physical exam at her primary care physician's office, Mackenzie Bender measured a spine curvature of seven degrees. By the fall of 2010, her curvature progressed to thirty-seven degrees and she obtained a referral to an orthopedic surgeon at Shriners Hospital. Shriners recommended bracing her until she finished growing. Mackenzie saw Durrani for another opinion and he recommended a "new" procedure called Spine Stapling. He performed surgery on Mackenzie on March 9, 2011. Spine Stapling is considered experimental and should have never been used on Mackenzie. It caused her severe pain and issues as she grew into adulthood.

Doris and Gerald Botner, an elderly couple, both had Durrani surgeries. Doris had two surgeries and Gerald had four surgeries with Durrani. Gerald's surgery resulted in hardware failures and revision surgeries. Mr. and Mrs. Botner both tested positive for MRSA after their surgeries and after they were exposed to Durrani's dog, Hank. Gerald Botner passed away May 1, 2018.

Sabrina Cain interviewed James Brown at his home. She captured a glimpse of his day on video. When James went outside, he wouldn't be able to get back up the stairs for hours. James had no furniture in his living room and giant black garbage bags full of his clothes lay on the ground. He sat in an old broken grey office chair, his only furniture. When he stood up from the broken chair, Sabrina taped his limited range of motion. He could barely stand. He shook and grabbed onto the window for balance.

After Sabrina told me about James' condition, we took him living room furniture. James Brown passed away days before his scheduled trial.

Joseph Davis attended the support group meetings decked out in Cincinnati Reds gear. He sent frequent emails to staff nearly every day, expressing gratitude and praying for us.

Ollie Deaton's son put Durrani up against a wall when he realized Durrani mistreated his mother. The rod Durrani placed in her back protruded from her butt and caused a bad infection. Ollie died before she got her justice.

Prior to Durrani, Deb Doyle loved to work. Since the surgery, her life feels hopeless. She has moments that overwhelm her to the point of suicide.

In 2012, Darrell Earls enjoyed being an active husband, father, brother, and pastor of a church. He lost everything after Durrani's surgery. He battled MRSA, which he contracted from Dr Durrani's surgery and several other dangerous infections, which caused the amputation of his toes. Darrell Earls died waiting for justice.

Durrani left Robert Ellington with a cantaloupe-sized mass sticking out of his side. Durrani told Robert it was a hernia. A surgeon told Robert it was not a hernia and it was caused by Durrani's surgery, cutting the nerves and muscles when doing his incision. Robert passed away on March 4, 2016. Weeks later, Connie, Robert's wife, who also suffered at the hands of Durrani, passed away on March 18, 2016.

Severe stress from the unimaginable pain Durrani caused during surgery resulted in Tony Falkner suffering a stroke and dying.

On August 6, 2008, Neil Favaron suffered a motor vehicle accident. The neurosurgeon told Neil he did not need surgery. Because Neil continued to have back pain a family member referred him to Durrani. At the first appointment, Durrani recommended Neil have immediate surgery or he would be paralyzed for the rest of his life. Durrani misdiagnosed and exaggerated the MRI to scare Neil into having surgery.

Prior to surgery, Neil had a bright future ahead of him. As a marine veteran, Neil promised his best friend to be his best man in his wedding. Durrani's surgery prevented Neil's ability to be the best man.

Neil passed away at the young age of thirty-five while struggling through severe pain up until his last breath.

At thirteen, Jade Hamby had no previous medical history other than jaundice as an infant. According to Jade's mother, Desiree Payton, they were referred to Children's after an urgent care visit for a sports physical indicated scoliosis. Desiree remembers Durrani informing her the scoliosis was an 82-degree curve and that Jade would "handle surgery better now." When she asked Durrani about possible complications, Durrani told her no complications.

Jade suffered a severe spinal cord injury during surgery caused by Durrani. Desiree remembers Durrani informing her she needed to be strong for Jade and not to cry in front of her and to leave the room if she was going to cry. Once Jade awoke from surgery, the first words to her mother were "Hi Mommy, I feel weird," and "Am I taller?" Her mother left the room, so Jade would not see her cry. Desiree also remembers Durrani telling her "it's just something that happens, and it happened to your child" and telling Jade whatever she wanted for Christmas, Durrani would purchase. As if that would "even the score."

With an unstable spine, Desiree knew Jade still required surgery. In 2009, Dr. Agabegi took over Jade's care and performed a posterior spinal fusion.

Unfortunately, it was too late. Jade's life completely changed after Durrani's surgery. Jade suffered through constant hospitalizations and nursing home admissions. She suffered from a chronic bone infection, colostomy and urostomy due to bowel and bladder issues, chronic pressure ulcers, mental health deterioration and a tracheostomy. In May 2018, sepsis took her life. For ten years, Jade laid in a bed. Her life over.

Durrani performed three unnecessary surgeries on Karen Johnson. After one of the surgeries, Karen suffered from dislodgement of hardware that adhered to right kidney and caused an obstruction. This caused her right kidney to be completely non-functional, which resulted in its removal.

Durrani performed surgery on Sarah Juergens on three separate occasions. We could not reach her to discuss her case. Chuck Holbrook and Chad Fuller drove to her home to check on her and called the police to do a wellness check. Police found Sarah deceased.

Prior to surgery, Valarie Kopp rode her own Harley and worked as the director of Aces & Eights Harley Owner's Group. She would ride her Harley, wearing full leather seeking adventures. Post-Durrani surgery, she tries to get through the day. Her life destroyed by Durrani.

Durrani paralyzed Adrian Lilly. He lay in his bed in pain until he died. I visited him in his home days before he passed. I felt the anger and pain from his mother towards Durrani, the system, me, all of it. It's a moment when you feel as if you failed. Adrian's case had a statute of repose or time problem, but that changed nothing regarding what Durrani did to him.

Heather McCann, a beautiful blonde, fell for Durrani's scare tactics. She now has a permanent kink in her neck. Prior to surgery, Heather aspired to become a model. Durrani ruined those dreams.

Kyra McClendon is one of the many young athletes Durrani performed an unnecessary procedure on while he worked at Children's.

Kevin McDonald is Durrani's last patient he performed surgery on at Children's Hospital. He performed surgery on Kevin on March 7, 2009. Kevin suffers in pain every day.

Durrani operated on Tonia McQueary ten times at nearly every hospital where he practiced including Christ Hospital, Riverview, Journey Lite and West Chester.

After Jill Millis' surgery with Durrani, it took her six months to learn how to walk at a rehabilitation hospital.

Donna and Gordon Rister attended nearly every meeting. The scars left by Durrani on Donna, like most of his victims, were simply horrific. He operated on Donna's back top to bottom. She walked around with an erector set like cage around her back and neck. I gave Donna a hug on a Thursday evening at a meeting and she passed away the next Monday. When Gordon received a check from a hospital settlement, he offered it back to me to help the cause. I thanked him but declined. Gordon is unable to speak of Donna without crying.

Theresa Robbinson-Woods, despite her debilitating condition caused by Durrani, attended protests and other clients' trials.

Prior to Durrani's surgery, Carol Ross worked as a cocktail waitress. In her client video interview for the office, Carol tried through tears to extend her arm out to hold one single piece of paper. Durrani took her livelihood and her joy in life. "Hotdogs! Do you know how many hotdogs we have to eat in one month?" Carol yelled, as she shared her frustration now that she is unable to support herself.

Mike Sand saw Durrani for one leg being slightly shorter than the other, not a back issue. Durrani immediately told Mike he needed surgery. Not only did Durrani not resolve the leg issue, Durrani destroyed his back. Dr. Lee Greiner of Mayfield testified for Mike Sand. Dr. Greiner testified under oath Durrani lied and misdiagnosed the leg issue. Dr. Greiner testified even if Durrani diagnosed the leg issue properly, which he did not, Durrani performed the surgery on the wrong level of the spine to correct the issue he claimed.

Dr. Greiner, when the Durrani ordeal began, told me all the Cincinnati spine doctors "were behind you." It made me feel empowered. Lee Greiner, at my request, performed a surgery for Becky Breitenstein for free. A screw Durrani place was lodged near her aorta. At any time, it could puncture the aorta and she could bleed out. Becky never had the money or insurance to pay for the surgery. Greiner did this for me.

Durrani nearly killed Steven Andrew Schultz in the operating room. Steven lost too much blood and spent eight days in the ICU. Durrani told him to buy the book, "*Don't Sweat the Small Stuff.*"

Elaine Waxler is a sweet elderly woman who suffered through seven unnecessary surgeries by Durrani. She lives with her brother, Bill Wolder, also a victim of Durrani. Elaine is fragile, as she walks around with a cane, completely hunched over. Elaine still comes to all the meetings.

Durrani brutalized so many young victims. Below is a letter to me from a mother, who carries guilt for trusting Children's Hospital and Durrani.

Dear Eric,

Our family would like to thank you for your commitment to see this through, for the passion that fuels your heart and soul. You have been a voice so greatly needed, a light that has shown when we only felt darkness, a power that has carried us when we did not have strength to continue.

You are the voice, of all that have felt powerless, when wrong should be the only right! Our fight has been your gift of service and tireless desire, to see that those wronged, are made right, again!

Is there enough words to truly express all that you have done? You have led us into the battle and fought by our sides never giving into defeat, no matter how the direction the battlefield was laid out. You led us in directions, safely and strongly protecting us from the lies, deception and of those disconnected and uncaring to our case.

When we are taught to trust in those that are educated and in power to make decisions for the best interest of health and wellbeing, we submit and release that power with trust and respect that all will truly be made for the right and our best interest. Everything that our family believed and trusted about those in control and power has been lost. We will never truly believe that our best interest and care is what makes the difference, instead we are left with doubt and mistrust.

In 2008, we trusted in the name and foundation of a very loved and respected, Cincinnati Children's Hospital. I offered openly and freely my child, based on that trust that only her health and best interest was at the heart for her healing and care at that establishment. We were handed a doctor, a smile and handshake that our child would never hurt or feel pain again, that she was in the best hands and to never worry, Durrani would fix my daughter and that you could trust him.

And so we believed, and trusted...

Today, our life has carried the shadows and the devastation left behind. As a parent, I wonder what I could have done different? The dreams that a parent hopes for their child never came to light. Instead my daughter fought a continuous pain, depression and addiction, that took her far from the direction and path for truly living her life. Battles with pain, leading to self-medication and self-destructive behavior, leaving to years lost and never regained. Incarceration, relapse, addiction, depression- that is the nightmare that haunts my daughter and our family. The shadows that we carry every day, left behind from a hospital, their doctor, his smile and handshake, are the scars that are forever bedding in our souls.

We cannot change what has been, only the direction that we go. My daughter has learned to live one moment at a time. She is forever imprisoned by the scars that show on her body, the pain that is never ending and the refusals by other doctors to help her. The scars of Durrani run deep and forever, like a tattoo branded on her back. My daughter just turned 29, she was 16 years old when she met Durrani.

I do not wish this pain, burden or life on anyone, but the years my daughter has lost, imprisoned by her pain and addiction, with off and on years behind bars, should be a pain that is felt by those that closed their eyes, and a man that had no conscience for the lives and years lost to line their own pockets.

Eric, thank you so very much for all the fight, the support and continuous caring for so many, but mostly being our voice, when we could not be heard. You and your amazing staff will always be the new reminder of the fight those scars now stand for!

This is a comprehensive summary of Durrani's fraud and malpractice on the victims:

1. Victims had prior surgeries by other surgeons.
2. Victims had incomplete, inaccurate or improper consent forms. Many even no consent form.
3. Most had operative reports dictated late.
4. Most had either BMP-2 and/or PureGen or both used without knowledge or consent and used without the proper cage.
5. Durrani misrepresented the radiology.
6. Durrani misrepresented their conditions both pre-op and post op.

7. All underwent one or more unnecessary spine surgery. A few leg and shoulder surgeries.
8. All are worse off since Durrani's surgery.
9. Durrani represented if they did not have the surgery they would be "paralyzed" or "die" or "in wheelchair" or "head would fall off" type statements.
10. They have difficulty finding care including prescription drug therapy.
11. They trusted Durrani and the hospitals.
12. Durrani never reviewed their prior records.
13. They sought non-surgical solutions.
14. Treating doctors support their claims.
15. Many primary care doctors were recruited by Durrani and the hospitals to refer to Durrani.
16. The C1-C2 EDS patients' surgeries were experimental by Durrani's own admission at a seminar. He misrepresented the outcomes.
17. Many had surgeons or assistants of Durrani they did not know perform their surgeries.
18. Durrani rarely attempted conservative therapy first.
19. Most after surgery had the need for:
a. Hospitalization
b. Treatment for infection
c. Corrective surgery
20. They all have a permanent injury and a scar under the Ohio statute qualifying for a permanent injury.
21. The EDS victims now have a "kink" in their neck.
22. Durrani never fully explained the risks of his surgery.
23. Durrani always made statements: "good as new" or "I can fix you."
24. Durrani bullied and preyed upon the victims.
25. The parents of the children carry guilt because they trusted Durrani and the hospitals.
26. Durrani would usually recommend surgery the first or second visit.
27. Victims all have suffered some financial difficulties.
28. Durrani seized upon pre-existing conditions to perform surgeries.
29. Many victims became addicted to narcotics.
30. Not one local spine doctor supports Durrani as an expert.
31. Dr. Durrani misrepresented patients' recovery: "be up next day" or "back to normal."
32. The billing for BMP-2 and PureGen was concealed.
33. Many of the fusions failed.
34. Insurance often times rejected payment based upon "experimental."
35. Durrani lied in operative reports and in his consult notes. He would send the PCPs letters with false representations such as: "they are doing great."

36. The patients never saw these records, notes, operative reports or itemized bills.
37. Many of the patients try to live a normal life.
38. The C1-C2 EDS patients have swallowing issues.
39. Durrani never gave options other than surgeries.
40. Many had a spine surgeon prior to Dr. Durrani inform them there were no further options.
41. Many had surgeries at levels not consented to or informed about.
42. On C1-C2 EDS patients, Durrani falsely claimed they had a "pannus" or inflammation in the radiology.
43. Durrani's legal counsel and their experts claim Durrani has a better understanding of the radiology than the radiologists.
44. Durrani performed surgeries he was not trained to do.
45. Durrani misrepresented in children the severity of their scoliosis or kyphosis. He would not use bracing.
46. In every BMP-2 victim, they have an increased risk of cancer.
47. Durrani performed surgery on high-risk patients without explaining it to them: smokers, elderly and overweight.
48. Many of the BMP-2 patients have ectopic bone growth.
49. Many have a broken screw or hardware.
50. Most had multiple surgeries.
51. Many of the times on the intraoperative reports are lies.
52. Durrani's radiology misrepresentation include:
    a. Spinal Stenosis and grades of it
    b. Spondylolisthesis
    c. Scoliosis Measurements
    d. Kyphosis Measurements

The following is a summary of all the issues Durrani victims suffered: worse pain, constant pain, depression, suicidal, swallowing issues, retrograde ejaculation, disabled, paralyzed, evicted, foreclosed, bankrupt, lost income/jobs, lost career, scars, decreased mobility, decreased flexibility, decreased quality of life, headaches, worsened precondition, leg/arm numbness/tingling, guilt, anxiety, loss of consortium, drop things, can't drive, permanent injury/pain, activities can't do, need to sit down frequently, unable to ride in cars at length, increased risk of cancer, loss of sleep, arthritis, missed school, humiliation, muscle spasms, need for narcotics, muscle relaxants, heating pads, physical therapy, need for cane, loss of strength, psychologist, walking issues, need for help, decreased social life, need for anti-depressants, pain doctors, endured surgeries, anti-inflammatories, infections, injections, more medical treatment, corrective surgery, decreased sex, marital stress and loss of insurance.

Chapter 12

Dr. Keith Wilkey

"An army of deer led by a lion is to be feared more than an army of lions led by a deer."
—Chabrias

Dr. Keith Wilkey grew up in Dayton, Ohio. He graduated from Ohio State in 1985 with a biochemistry degree. In 1989, he graduated first in his class from Wright State Medical School.

After Wright State, Wilkey trained at Brooke Army Medical Center in San Antonio, Texas, where he completed his internship and residency. Internship and residency is time a doctor must spend after medical school actually training by doing. Fellowships are simply additional training. From 2004 to 2006, Wilkey fellowship trained at the Leatherman Spine Institute in Louisville, Kentucky. Wilkey then practiced in New York and Illinois before coming to Oxford, Ohio.

In 1991, Wilkey served in Desert Storm in the Marine Corps as an orthopedic surgeon. In 1998, he obtained his Board Certification in orthopaedics. Board certification is a process a doctor goes through to receive an extra "stamp of approval" from his peers in a specialty. He remains a member of the national orthopedic organizations American Academy of Orthopaedic Surgeons and North American Spine Society.

David Andrew, an attorney friend, called me one day and asked me to represent a friend of his, Dr. Keith Wilkey. David had a conflict and he thought I would be perfect for Wilkey's case. It was a case against McCullough-Hyde Hospital in Oxford, Ohio, north of Cincinnati.

An orthopedic spine group recruited Wilkey to Oxford, Ohio. After Wilkey arrived, Wilkey tried to make changes and improvements, but his new partners balked. They fired him and yanked his hospital privileges. The hospital sent out several of Wilkey's cases for what's called an external review, and the external review supported Wilkey. His employers buried the positive report and never gave it to Wilkey's attorney or anyone else.

I represented Wilkey in the case against McCullough-Hyde Memorial Hospital in federal court in Cincinnati before Judge Michael Barrett. I met Judge Barrett for the first time during the Wilkey trial. Judge Barrett and his staff would tease me for all the foam core blow ups I used. I used nearly a hundred documents on blown up foam core rather than use an electronic format. I had blow-ups scattered everywhere in the courtroom, but I kicked the other lawyers' ass also all over the courtroom. The case settled for $300,000 in the middle of the trial, after Judge Barrett looked at the witness involved in hiding the report and said, "don't leave town." Unfortunately, Wilkey filed bankruptcy as a result of what McCullough-Hyde did to him.

When I began signing up Durrani cases, I remembered my client Wilkey and contacted him. Wilkey informed me he knew Durrani when they both trained at the Leatherman Spine Institute in Louisville and knew Durrani to be well trained. Mike Lyon always used the phrase "exquisitely trained" when he would describe Durrani at trial. I always believed a woman exquisite, not a doctor. Wilkey began as a skeptic, thinking a look into the surgeries would be unnecessary, but reviewed them as a favor to me. What he reviewed shocked him and Wilkey called me and said, "Eric, these are not just unnecessary surgeries. This is fraud." He began signing the affidavits of merit we needed to file lawsuits.

For a negligence/medical malpractice case, the harmed party must prove by the preponderance of the evidence (tip the scales, greater than 50%) a doctor deviated from the standard of care and the deviation caused harm to the patient. It's a national standard of care and the harmed party must have an expert testify on the issue.

Once the standard legalese from background, qualifications and claims had been established in the affidavit of merit, we would insert the specific facts from each case from the nurse review of all the records. Under Ohio law, an expert must either teach medicine at an accredited college or practice over 50% of their time in their field. After Wilkey reviewed the medical records and radiology, he signed the prepared affidavit of merit. Wilkey cut no corners. He literally looked at all the radiology films and the medical records of every case he reviewed. He also refused to sign off on several cases. Wilkey told me even a fraud sometimes performs a necessary surgery in the correct manner.

Wilkey moved to St. Louis after his McCullough-Hyde experience. Chuck Holbrook drove a U-Haul truck full of Durrani boxes to Wilkey in St. Louis. The boxes filled up an entire room in Wilkey's office. Wilkey would give his first depositions in Durrani cases in St. Louis. Bob Winter, soon to be introduced, and I made the six hour drive to St. Louis. As Durrani's lawyer took Wilkey's deposition, Wilkey held up just fine.

The following is the statement we used before each deposition of Wilkey. It will provide you the comprehensive information Wilkey reviewed.

On The Record
Statement or Plaintiff Exhibit For
Dr. Wilkey Depositions

This is to supplement past discovery where applicable, to supplement what Dr. Wilkey will rely upon in all trials and applies going forward to every deposition Dr Wilkey gives in the Dr Durrani litigation. Because Dr Wilkey will be testifying as one of our experts in all cases, the facts on which he bases his opinions and the opinions he gives on credentialing and retention apply to all cases. The only variables will be the dates of our clients treatment and surgery and new information we add from ongoing discovery. In addition to everything produced in discovery, the following is an update of all binders now reviewed and relied upon by Dr. Wilkey:

BINDERS:

1. Binder of Durrani Depositions (new)
2. Dr. Durrani Background – Criminal Information
3. West Chester Surgery Schedule (new)
4. The Case Against West Chester #1
5. The Case Against West Chester #2
6. The Case Against West Chester #3
7. The Case Against West Chester #4 (new)
8. West Chester/UC Health Trial Exhibit List
9. Children's Hospital E-mails
10. Children's Binder 9-27-14 (Also same Children's Hospital #1)
11. Children's Hospital Binder #2 (new)
12. Documents Produced in Journey Lite Discovery – Volume #1 (new)
13. Documents Produced in Journey Lite Discovery – Volume #2 (new)
14. The Case Against Hospitals Binder #1 (new)
15. The Case Against Hospitals Binder #2 (new)
16. BMP-2 Binder
17. Dr. Wilkey Excerpts from West Chester Signed AOMS
18. Bruce Podrat Deposition (new)
19. Dr. Wilkey McCullough Hyde Lawsuit (new)

Pursuant to the Notices of Deposition, all these materials have been sent to defense counsel in compliance with the Notices of Deposition.

Dr. Wilkey has been sent and reviewed these materials. For all his opinions, he relies upon these facts and evidence. He stands by the opinions disclosed in these materials and his affidavit of merit except where distinguished at his deposition.

During his deposition, Dr. Wilkey may not recall every fact or opinion, but for disclosure purposes they have been disclosed and he does rely upon them.

The purpose of this statement is to ensure full disclosure so you are free to ask any question you like from these materials.

All of this avoided the defense lawyers' attempt to exclude Wilkey's testimony for not disclosing everything. It comprised of dozens of four-inch-thick binders.

Wilkey also met with many of the victims in our Cincinnati law office and examined them to help his testimony. Mike Lyon actually filed a baseless Ohio

Medical Board Complaint against Wilkey on these exams. The Board dismissed it.

Dr. Wilkey would later work at the Reno VA Hospital and then in New York, near Buffalo.

There is no one more important and valuable to this cause than Dr. Keith Wilkey. Without him, I couldn't have succeeded. To his great credit, Wilkey believes it his duty to the medical and orthopaedic profession to fight this battle with me.

Dr. Andrew Collier would also be a great assistance to our cause. He reviewed cases and signed affidavits of merit on cases when Dr. Wilkey couldn't complete the reviews. We agreed Dr. Collier would not testify, but the affidavits of merit helped us.

Chapter 13

The Bulldog Meets the Butcher

"I'm your huckleberry."
—Doc Holliday "Tombstone"

By November 29, 2011, I had visited enough large defense firms in downtown Cincinnati over the years that I knew what to expect on my first visit to Lindhorst and Dreidame in the Scripps Center Tower on Walnut Street. All these law firms had an expansive main lobby, marbled floors, high ceilings, modern art deco furniture, and chrome plated elevators.

On the twenty-seventh floor which Lindhorst occupied sat the smiling, well-dressed receptionist behind a high marble-top desk. With an over-sized conference room, over-sized conference table and comfy chairs, I would soon sit opposite Durrani. The court reporter at the end of the table would carefully transcribe every word Durrani and I exchanged—my questions and his answers. A serving table held coffee and cups, a platter of cookies and iced bowls with bottled water and soda. These law firms always monogrammed the cups, coasters and glasses with the name of the firm.

Mike Lyon represented Durrani. He declared himself the top medical malpractice attorney in Cincinnati. His "peers" voted him to Ohio's "Super Lawyers," an honor bestowed by the advertising spent on "Super Lawyers." I always mock the "Super Lawyers."

In *Cincinnati's 2022 Top Doctors*, Lindhorst bought an ad for Mike Lyon. It reads as follows:

PERSONAL INJURY MEDICAL MALPRACTCE: DEFENSE

Michael F. Lyon, Esq. named to the Super Lawyers list since 2004, the Top 50 in Cincinnati and Top 100 in Ohio for the past 10 years, is a Diplomat of the American Board of Trial Advocates, Fellow of the International Society of Barristers, and past president of the Ohio chapter of the American Board of Trial Advocates. Lyon was the first Ohio lawyer to attain the rank of Diplomat of the American Board of Trial Advocates, which requires a minimum of 100 jury trials.

Mr. Lyon has taken more than 220 medical malpractice trials to verdict in 15 different cities throughout Ohio and northern Kentucky and represented physicians in the Ohio District Court of Appeals and Supreme Court of Ohio more than 65 times. The firm's ability and willingness to take cases to verdict is its most critical asset for physicians in need of defense.

In addition to preparing and trying cases, the medical legal team of Lindhorst & Dreidame, which includes Super Lawyers honorees James F. Brockman and Paul J. Vollman, prides itself on helping physicians and their families navigate the trauma, stress and anxiety stemming from a medical malpractice case that goes to a jury trial. This combination of trial experience and personal support for physicians and their families has helped earn the firm its impressive 90+ percent success rate.

Lindhorst & Dreidame represented Durrani and The Center for Advanced Spine Technologies (CAST), the insurer, Medical Protective, owned by Warren Buffett's Berkshire Hathaway. Lindhorst assigned at least ten attorneys from their firm to the Durrani cases. Working with Mike Lyon the most would be Jim Brockman and Paul Vollman. Laura McCluskey from Lindhorst assisted early on, but soon took a job at Medical Protective. Joining Lyon from another law firm would be another so called "Super Lawyer," Paul W. McCartney of Bonezzi, Switzer, Polito, & Hupp. McCartney represented Durrani in all cases dated prior to January 1, 2009 and Lyon all cases dated after. River City Insurance employed McCartney on a policy Children's bought when Durrani left Children's.

Children's Hospital Medical Center would be represented by Dinsmore & Shohl and a half dozen attorneys, including David Brittingham, another claimed Ohio "Super Lawyer," Thomas Kemp and Allison Knerr. West Chester Hospital, a subsidiary of the University of Cincinnati's UC Health division, would be represented by three different law firms, including Dinsmore & Shohl, Frost Brown Todd and Rendigs Fry. Frost Brown Todd assigned their leading health care attorney, Walter E. Haggerty Jr., one more Ohio "Super Lawyer" and Bill Paliobeis. Rendigs Fry assigned Karen Carroll and Jeff Hines to the Durrani cases. Dinsmore & Shohl assigned Marilena Walters, Melissa Korfhage and Mary Jo Pullen. There were so many Super Lawyers among the defense teams that I created my own satirical moniker of "Super Duper Lawyer." Charlie Lester, a lawyer friend and I even incorporated the name in Kentucky. Charlie and I became the only "Super Duper Lawyers."

Dinsmore & Shohl boasts 217 Cincinnati area lawyers and 761 national. Frost Brown Todd has 140 Cincinnati area lawyers and 529 national. Taft Stettinius & Hollister claims 133 Cincinnati area lawyers and 650 national. Keating Muething & Klekamp has 122 Cincinnati area lawyers. These represent Cincinnati's four largest law firms. We battle them, Rendigs, Lindhorst and Bonezzi every day in the Durrani litigation.

Good Samaritan Hospital would have Mike Foley as counsel. David Calderhead and David Lockemeyer represented Christ Hospital. Taft represented Durrani on appeals. Russell Sayer served as their lead lawyer.

I had never met Lyon or Durrani in person. All I knew at the time about Lyon is he recently lost a record Hamilton County verdict in a cardiology case. David

Lockemeyer told me about it and claimed Lyon was unprepared for the trial. These defense lawyers enjoy talking about each other behind each other's backs. I would later learn Mike Lyon actually keeps a running record of his cases on a resume. How he phrases his defeats is comical. He would state: "They demanded $1,000,000, but they only won $500,000."

I met Lyon in the waiting room and he escorted me into the conference room. Lyon looked like a mortician. While we chatted briefly in the waiting area, the first thought that came to mind is how much Lyon looked like Grandpa in the old *Munsters* TV series. He groomed his long white hair back from his widow's peak. Two large fleshy ears and bushy eyebrows were attached to his head.

Our first case scheduled for trial in January 2014 involved a young mother, Crystal Pierce, debilitated by a Durrani fraudulent spine surgery. Another spine surgeon performed a second surgery to remove the screw in her vertebra which left her in agonizing pain. The deposition I would take was for the Pierce case.

With everyone in the conference room, Lyon re-entered the room with Durrani. Durrani wore a brown silk tailored suit, a starched white shirt and brown tie. He possessed an unassailable air of conceit. He impeccably trimmed his hair and mustache. He manicured his nails. Durrani smiled and chatted with me before the deposition began. Durrani acted as if he held no hard feelings toward me and simply considered me a misguided lawyer doing my job.

In 2009, Crystal Pierce worked as an IRS tax examiner. She visited Durrani to seek a second opinion for the intense pain and tingling down her right arm triggered whenever she turned her neck.

Pierce's original surgeon, Paul Cohen of Mayfield, fused two of the vertebrae in her neck to give it more stability, advised against further surgery and suggested physical therapy. Pierce sought a second opinion. Pierce heard about Durrani from her mother-in-law. Durrani not only recommended further surgery, he told Pierce she risked being paralyzed if she didn't have two procedures to fix the problems in her neck caused by Cohen. During the days prior to the second surgery, Durrani urged Pierce to have someone stay at home with her to call 911 in the event of an emergency.

Within weeks, Durrani operated on Pierce at Christ Hospital and fused the two vertebrae above her previous fusion with screws and used the synthetic material BMP-2. BMP-2 stimulates bone growth to fill the gap between the vertebrae usually where a cushioning disc has been removed. BMP-2 is so toxic the FDA requires it be used only in conjunction with a metal cage to keep the material from seeping outside the area of application.

Two days after her neck fusion, Durrani took Pierce to surgery again at Christ for a second procedure, a laminoplasty, this time widening the spinal canal in her neck to relieve pressure on the spinal cord. He inserted a metal plate with four tiny screws, each no longer than the width of a pencil, to keep the separation in place.

Pierce felt intense pain after the second surgery, but Durrani declared the operation a success and told Pierce the pain was simply a normal part of the healing process. Pierce visited her pain doctor, Dr. Carl Shapiro, who performed a scan and found one of the screws Durrani inserted pressed against her "dura" the membrane that surrounds the spinal cord and contains the spinal fluid. Dr. Shapiro explained the impinging screw worsened her condition and urged its removal.

Durrani insisted Dr. Shapiro didn't know what he was talking about and told Pierce he placed the screw in perfect position. Durrani accused Pierce of being an Oxycontin addict who simply sought more medication. The pain required Pierce quit work. Pierce scheduled an appointment with her original surgeon, Dr. Paul Cohen, who removed the errant screw. Her condition improved immediately and she no longer needed her pain medication. Unrelated to our story, years later Dr. Cohen died in a tragic snow ski accident.

Throughout the deposition I took, Durrani treated Pierce's accusations as simply a "misunderstanding" between surgeons. Using my "country lawyer" style, I lured Durrani and Lyon into underestimating me. Lyon quoted Shakespeare in Court during irrelevant moments and out of context. Since I can cite Shakespeare myself, this always made me laugh. I would think to myself "this jury doesn't give a damn about Shakespeare." Lyon also favored words like "efficacious" when effective worked as well. Remember *Laverne and Shirley*? I believe a lawyer in a jury trial should speak as normal as possible for the best communication. If Laverne and Shirley wouldn't understand the word or phrase, don't use it. I have a vocabulary. I simply choose not to use it when it is unnecessary.

What follows are actual deposition exchanges:

DETERS: Okay. Crazy question just popped in my head. Have you er —-- have you ever been treated for any medical condition or psychiatric condition that involves mental illness?

DURRANI: Not so far.

DETERS: Okay.

LYON: Maybe after this deposition. (Laughter)

DETERS: You can blame me for your mental illness. (More laughter.)

Durrani refused to admit he terrified Pierce into surgery or botched it. I sought to gain an admission the screw he left impinging on the dura around her spinal cord deviated from the standard of care.

DETERS: If a board-certified orthopedic spine surgeon would say that the screws were constantly indenting the dura and the dura mater is quite sensitive to the pain, what would be your response to that?

DURRANI: That is their opinion.

DETERS: Is it true if a screw indents the dura, is it quite sensitive to pain?

DURRANI: The dura is sensitive to pain.

DETERS: So, if a screw was in it, it would cause pain?

DURRANI: There you are misquoting the facts. The screw we are talking about is not a pedicle screw. These are tiny five-millimeter screws that are –

DETERS: So, this screw wasn't in the dura?

DURRANI: It was not in the dura.

DETERS: But if it was, it would cause pain?

DURRANI: It would cause pain, correct.

DETERS: And it would cause pain every time she moved her neck if it was in the dura?

DURRANI: If it was in the dura, correct.

DETERS: It is certainly possible that some of her pain is from the irritation of the dura from the protruding screws. And it's your prior testimony that if the screws were in the dura, that would be medical negligence, correct?

DURRANI: I did not say that.

LYON: Objection.

DETERS: Would a screw in the dura be a deviation in the standard of care?

DURRANI: The answer is true.

Bingo. While Durrani denied the screw was in the dura, we knew the screw was in the dura and could prove it through the MRI, Dr. Cohen and Dr. Shapiro. If we proved it, Durrani now admitted it malpractice. Putting on any case at trial is the placing together pieces of the puzzle until you have a finished puzzle. I knew I could now complete the puzzle.

I sensed Durrani lost his privileges at several facilities, including Christ, based upon his beginning his own surgery centers in Cincinnati and Northern Kentucky. I wanted proof. Durrani's squirming in his chair during my next line of questioning reinforced my belief:

DETERS: With respect to Christ Hospital and Children's Hospital, why don't you have privileges there now?

DURRANI: Because we moved. Our practice location used to be at the old Deaconess Hospital. When that closed, we moved our practice north, and now all our surgeries are done at (University of Cincinnati) West Chester (hospital) because my office is up — is way up north.

DETERS: Why did you move to West Chester? Why did you start –

DURRANI: It's a business decision.

DETERS: Just a business decision?

DURRANI: Uh-huh.

DETERS: Okay... You made a business decision to start the Center for Advanced Spine Technologies instead of practicing in the local hospitals. Why did you make that business decision?

DURRANI: I was a University and Children's Hospital employee. I left the employment and I started my own practice. That was a business decision.

DETERS: But why?

DURRANI: It was a financial decision because I did not want to take the financial package the University was offering me at that point.

DETERS: So, you decided that you could make more money starting your Center for Advanced Spine Technologies versus working at those hospitals?

DURRANI: It was the financial aspect… one of the decision makers.

In time, I learned Durrani lied about it being a "financial decision."

Chapter 14
The Butcher is Arrested

"I've never killed a man who didn't deserve killing."
—Wild Bill Hickok

You rarely hear of doctors being arrested for crimes related to their medical practices. It is usually for other reasons.

On July 23, 2013, two hours before sunrise, agents of the FBI and DEA pulled their dark SUV into the circle drive of Durrani's six-bedroom, five-and-half-bath brick McMansion at 4800 Bethany Road in upscale Warren County, Ohio. Officially, Durrani resided there with his wife Shazia and two teenage children.

Durrani's home sprawled across five acres. His home rested just a ten-minute drive from the local country club and the premier amusement park in Southwest Ohio, Kings Island. Durrani purchased the home with ill-begotten gains.

In front of Durrani's house ran a double walkway separated by a long reflecting pool with three small fountains gurgling. Durrani once hoped to purchase penguins for his kids. To accommodate the flightless birds, Durrani installed a saltwater pond in the backyard. Durrani discovered no zoo would sell penguins to him, so the penguin dream died.

After agents rang the doorbell, Durrani's wife answered, sleepy and irritated. Shazia told the agents they would find her husband at the condominium of Beth Garrett. Garrett, twenty-nine, worked as Durrani's administrative assistant and became his latest mistress. Durrani bought her a condo. The agents apologized for the intrusion on Shazia, and headed to Garrett's.

A DEA agent friend of mine on scene described to me what follows. Dressed for work, Durrani came out with his hands up. When an agent announced to Durrani he was under arrest on charges, Durrani acted as though they had the wrong man. He insisted he had been cooperating with the FBI in an investigation of "Eric Deters and his Bulldog Nation" for calling him 'The Butcher of Pakistan.' "You should be arresting him, not me," explained Durrani. The agents looked at each other with bewilderment and amusement, then arrested Durrani. Durrani insisted he worked with the FBI to charge me with a hate crime for violating his civil rights as a permanent resident of the U.S. On the contrary and unknown to Durrani, my clients and I collaborated with the local office of the U.S. Attorney in the investigation of Durrani.

We provided the Assistant United States Attorney, Tim Mangan, all the evidence we compiled against Durrani. When we began reviewing these cases, we realized the common themes of the improper use of BMP-2, lies regarding radiology films and unnecessary surgeries. Tim Mangan convened a grand jury and began calling our clients to the grand jury. For example, Dana Setters, who suffered a kinked neck from a C1-C2 level surgery, testified.

The United States government hired an expert out of Peru to testify on what is called a false panus. Durrani would intentionally obtain a film with the neck positioned a certain way to create the "condition." The surgeon from Peru is apparently the premier expert in the world on the issue. These patients suffered from "Ehlers-Danlos Syndrome." It's an elasticity in their weak neck muscles. Durrani is the only surgeon in the country who performed this surgery on this condition. The United States focused on these cases for an indictment. Durrani referenced in a video he developed this surgery with a Baltimore surgeon. We contacted the Baltimore surgeon, and he told us he never heard of Durrani.

In public, I kept referring to Durrani as the Butcher of Pakistan. Mike Lyon and Durrani filed a baseless bar complaint against me for doing so. It was dismissed. The more they complained, the more I called him the Butcher of Pakistan. Once in Judge Steven Martin's courtroom, they complained to Judge Martin of my label. I told Judge Martin that if Durrani was from England, I would call him the "Butcher of England." Durrani just happened to be from Pakistan. I hold zero animus towards the Pakistani people, but to their government and leaders, I hold plenty. My use of "Butcher of Pakistan" is a proper and deserved harsh description of Durrani.

The same day DEA arrested Durrani, DEA also seized the computers and records at CAST and shut Durrani down.

The agents secured a thirty-count federal indictment for Medicare and prescription fraud. The grand jury charged Durrani with bilking Medicare of millions of dollars by offering his patients spine surgery as their only option; scaring them into risky procedures with a false claim they would be paralyzed or have their heads fall off their spines in a car accident; ignoring or failing to read the reports from radiologists; exaggerating or lying about the results of those reports; injecting patients for pain in areas where patients had not complained of pain; scheduling patients for surgery before awaiting the results of alternative treatments, and often dictating his operative reports and patient records months after the actual treatment. When Durrani finally submitted his reports, he lied about the patient's diagnosis, the procedure performed and the instruments used during the operation. Durrani's surgical assembly line resulted in his not bothering to create reports specific to each patient. He used templates.

What follows is the detail of the chronology of the criminal charges:

On July 22, 2013, the U.S. Attorney filed a Federal Criminal Complaint against Durrani for false statements regarding to healthcare matters and fraud.

On July 25, 2013, the DEA arrested Durrani. At his first appearance in Court, the Court ordered Durrani to notify all his clients of his criminal charges. By

Order of the presiding federal judge, Durrani posted in his office and sent a letter to his patients warning them of the criminal charges. The Cincinnati media covered Durrani's arrest.

As a result of Durrani's arrest, Lyon canceled Durrani's deposition scheduled for August 10, 2013.

On August 7, 2013, Durrani was indicted on five counts of 18 U.S.C. §1035, entitled False Statement related to Health Care Matters, and five counts of 18 U.S.C. §1347, entitled Health Care Fraud. Thirteen of my clients testified before the federal grand jury.

On August 19, 2013, I wrote to Lyon asking whether the depositions of Durrani scheduled for August 22, 2013, and August 29, 2013 would take place. Lyon canceled the depositions.

On August 22, 2013, Durrani in a letter to patients announced the criminal charges against him.

On August 28, 2013, Glenn Whitaker, Durrani's criminal attorney, in a federal pleading on Durrani's behalf titled "Motion to Modify Conditions of Release" stated: "Durrani is not a flight risk…" Durrani also offered up his wife's and children's passport in an attempt to convince the Court he would never abandon them."

On October 16, 2013, Durrani was further indicted by the grand jury with a Superseding Indictment as follows:

- nine counts of 18 U.S.C. Sections 1347 and 2 ("Health Care Fraud")
- nine counts of 18 U.S.C. Section 1035
- three counts of 18 U.S.C. Sections 1347 and 2
- one count of 18 U.S.C. Section 1035 (a)(1)
- one count 18 U.S.C. Sections 1341 and 2 (Frauds and Swindles)
- one count 18 U.S.C. Section 1035 (a)(2)
- eleven counts 21 U.S.C. Section 841 (a)(1) ("unlawful distribution of a controlled substance") and 841(b)(1)(C)("Penalty subsection.")

On November 6, 2013, Medical Protective advised Durrani of the upcoming jury trial of *Pierce v. Durrani* set to begin January 6, 2014. Durrani signed a "no consent" form with Medical Protective blocking any settlement of any case. Medical Protective would later receive federal court approval to settle Durrani cases without his consent.

On November 25, 2013, a federal judge held a Final Pre-trial for Durrani's federal criminal trial. Durrani waived a speedy trial. The court set a new trial for August 14, 2014. Durrani later lied under oath at a 2018 deposition about the speedy trial issue. He claimed he never waived and wanted his "speedy trial." He waived.

According to the U.S. Attorney's office, Durrani's surgeries accounted for $12 million in charges billed to Medicare over a three-year period from February 2010 to late January 2013. Durrani also signed prescription forms and he authorized employees to fill in the blanks. During his numerous visits to Pakistan, Durrani's staff would fill in prescriptions and Durrani would prescribe controlled substances to his patients while outside the U.S., both felony violations.

At 7:30 a.m. of Durrani's arrest, Bruce Whitman, a local defense attorney, received a call from Lyon. At the behest of Lyon, Whitman scheduled to meet Durrani to discuss the ongoing FBI investigation into his medical practice. Durrani's arrest happened before the meeting. Whitman knew Durrani would be in the lock-up in the federal courthouse in downtown Cincinnati awaiting his bond hearing. Whitman agreed to represent him at the hearing.

After my DEA friend called me to give me the Durrani arrest news, I wept with joy. I told everyone in the office the news and drove home to share the news with Mary. I gave her a hug, cried some more and said, "It's over." Once arrested, I knew Durrani would have to plead guilty to something. We would have a defendant in our medical malpractice trials sitting there guilty of a felony.

Federal magistrate Stephanie K. Bowman held Durrani's bond hearing the morning of his arrest. Whitman showed up with Durrani and represented to Bowman that Durrani wasn't a flight risk despite the fact he returned to Pakistan three or four times a year to visit his parents and siblings. Durrani also insisted at the hearing his father was dying of cancer and he wanted to return to Pakistan to see him.

The red flags for holding Durrani included his frequent Pakistani trips and his father's condition. Pakistan also refused to honor any U.S. extradition orders since 2011 when U.S. Navy SEALS, acting without Pakistan's knowledge or consent, stormed Osama bin Laden's secret compound in sight of Pakistan's military academy and killed him.

Bowman fell for Whitman's argument. She ordered Durrani not to leave the tristate area. She released him without an ankle bracelet and gave an order for Durrani to turn over his passport despite Durrani possessing the money and connections to obtain a fake passport.

Durrani then dismissed Whitman and retained Glenn Whitaker, a high-profile white-collar criminal defense lawyer in Cincinnati. I reached out to Whiteman and Whitaker and suggested we might work out a deal for leniency in the criminal case in exchange for Durrani testifying against the hospitals. They never responded. To this day, it makes no sense to me.

What follows is the letter I sent to Whitman on August 5, 2013 and to Whitaker on August 20, 2013:

This letter is to request the following on behalf of my client. The request is made solely by me in my capacity as counsel for over 300 of his former patients.

It is not being made with the consent or even knowledge of any state or federal authority.

1. Dr. Durrani's both consent and give instruction to all his available insurance carriers to settle the claims we have filed and/or tender all his limits to do so.
2. To fully cooperate with the federal investigation and provide any and all information he has regarding Children's, West Chester/UC Health and Journey Lite to both us and all state and federal authorities.

If he fails to oblige by these requests, we will be asking the sentencing Court on behalf of our over 300 clients to consider not only his conduct leading them to us, but his refusal to attempt to make amends and assist them as they seek being made "whole" as much as possible. Furthermore, if he fails to do these things, I assure you all or most our clients will be at the sentencing hearing to speak. I'm confident the Court will limit the number who speak, but allow all to attend.

I know you know how doing or not doing these things plays into federal sentencing.

Dr. Durrani cannot win a criminal trial with my client's testifying. Any jury will loathe Dr. Durrani upon hearing their stories. Good luck with attempting to make a medical malpractice battle with expert testimony out of a criminal trial. Furthermore, the witnesses coming forward from West Chester alone will convict him. Despite his public statements, I'm confident he will soon realize what I ask for is a better route for him.

I believe it malpractice for Whitman and Whitaker to ignore my requests. They both did.

In my opinion, every defense lawyer in America would welcome working out a proposal which might have resulted in no jail time. It's simple arrogance and wanting the criminal case to proceed as far as possible so they could bill Durrani as much money as possible. This happens every day in America.

The afternoon of Durrani's arrest, two dozen former patients of Durrani and their families gathered in our waiting room in our downtown Cincinnati office waiting to be interviewed by the local news media. The victims assembled at my behest for a press conference. I recorded a video in the office parking lot explaining the significance of the arrest.

Stephanie Herrin-Threm appeared on WCPO-TV and explained Durrani's surgery limited the range of motion in her neck. *"Driving has become a real challenge for me,"* she said. Dana Setters sat on a leather sofa with her husband Craig by her side with her two-year-old daughter Tatum at her knee. *"My head leans to one side. I can't drive. I can't play with my little girl or lift her up,"* Setters lamented.

Herrin-Threm explained, *"We're after justice. We want to see him stopped."* Setters chimed in with *"the arrest was the best news we all could get today."*

The news detailed I filed malpractice suits against Durrani on behalf of one hundred and fifty clients. The story concluded with Lyon defending the besieged doctor. *"He's exquisitely trained. He's been practicing in this town since 1990. He's never paid a penny in a medical malpractice case. Ever. Nor has he ever had a serious complaint by any hospital, risk manager, or employee. So here we are."* All lies.

Within weeks from the arrest news, I represented another three hundred clients and within a year over five hundred clients. More hospital nurses and staff began to contact my office with complaints about Durrani, but no doctors. Every member of our law team swung into the sign up and filing mode again.

After two press conferences, we now had over five hundred clients.

Chapter 15
My Arm

"Life is full of chances and changes, and most prosperous of men may in the evening of his days meet with great misfortunes."
—Aristotle

In November 2013, my arm in the right shoulder area ached. My right arm is the same arm I dislocated playing football. I remember crying and begging for pain medicine as I sat in the ER waiting room with the dislocation.

Years later, I woke up in the morning with a red and inflamed shoulder too painful to move. I drove to St. Elizabeth Medical Center where the emergency room doctor ordered an x-ray, examined the arm and announced my arm was locked up or "frozen", and I should simply exercise it and all would be fine.

I left the hospital and drove to the office. As the day dragged on, I became sleepy and delirious. I called my primary care doctor, Troy Schumann, also my fraternity brother from college. Troy asked me if I would like an orthopedic referral. I sensed urgency for myself and requested Troy order an MRI as soon as possible. I explained to Troy the orthopedic would want an MRI first. Troy arranged for an MRI for late afternoon the same day. The last memory I have is stepping out of the car with Mary, who drove me to the testing site in Edgewood, Kentucky.

At the completion of the MRI, we drove towards home. Mary's phone rang. Based upon the MRI results, Schumann ordered me to the hospital for emergency surgery. I had a severe staph infection.

Since we found ourselves near home and a minute from Schumann's office, an ambulance met Mary and I at his office. The ambulance sped me off to the St. Elizabeth Medical Center, the same place which in the morning told me my shoulder was "frozen."

At the hospital, Dr. Giewe, a young orthopedic surgeon, greeted us. He informed Mary that without immediate surgery, I would lose my arm in twenty-four hours and probably my life. The staph infection reached the bone in the shoulder.

Mary consented to the immediate surgery conditional upon after the surgery, they would transfer me to University Hospital in Cincinnati. Dr. Giewe removed part of my right bicep and trapezius muscle with all the infection and transferred me as requested.

At University, Dr. John Wyrick took over my case and performed five more surgeries on my arm over ten days. I not only lived, I kept my arm.

Late November 2013, ice, snow and cold racked Cincinnati. The anesthesiologist came to see me in my hospital room with an interesting revelation. She informed me my vocal cords rested congenitally further in my throat than normal. Intubation required a special tool. She told me "I don't know how St. Elizabeth put you under." I have this vision of St. Elizabeth jamming a tube down my throat trying to place it. Regardless, Dr. Giewe did a fine job. The anesthesiologist recommended I purchase a medal to wear to alert any future surgeon of my condition in an emergency. I now jest this is the reason for my "golden" voice.

The doctors preferred I stay longer, but I couldn't take being cooped up in a hospital bed any longer. Too much to do.

I ran the Durrani litigation from the hospital. Attorney Debbie Nelson helped with taking depositions in my absence. A staff member tried to lead a rebellion and two clients, David Scott and Stephanie Herrin-Threm, discharged me. Both of their cases would turn out poorly after leaving us. Herrin-Threm died of cancer before her trial and her lawyers recommended to her husband a $50,000 settlement. He accepted. David Scott, who we moved mountains for, left us after I refused his demand to give him a significant sum of money.

On Thanksgiving Eve, I told two University residents if they refused to release me, I would throw a chair through the window and break out. They released me. I arrived home and hit the couch. One reason they allowed me to go home is for sixty days, I would have antibiotic through an IV and a box I would carry on my waist. Vancomycin saved my life.

As I laid on the couch during Thanksgiving, I enjoyed seeing my grandchildren, Rylee, Raygn and Rhett. My health is of great anxiety to my children, because their mother died of cancer at thirty-three when they were eight, seven and five years old. Being home eased their minds, too. Mary stayed with me every day at the hospital worrying. She still worried.

I could not lift my right arm above my head. With the IV in my arm and a box around my waist, I went back to the office after Thanksgiving. My scar today remains a foot long, but I have my arm. If I never insisted on the MRI, I would have lost my arm and life. Always fight for your own care.

Chapter 16

Durrani Flees

"Cowards die many times before their deaths;
the valiant never taste of death but once."
—William Shakespeare "Julius Caesar"

On December 21, 2013, a Saturday morning, I worked alone at my Independence office desk with the battery-operated pump attached to my belt and the IV line running into my right arm delivering a continuous infusion of antibiotics.

Weeks after being released from the hospital, I prepared for the Crystal Pierce trial, the first of the Durrani malpractice cases to go to trial. Three weeks away, all the facts and evidence had to be nailed down, organized and massaged into its simplest form for presenting to the jury. Ginger Dietrich, a nurse who worked for me, prepared an outstanding nurse summary of the entire case. I used it to prepare everything.

The most important case in my twenty-seven years of practicing law, I had to win. I borrowed more than three million dollars and would need more. Results matter when you need money. I used all my cash and mortgaged every asset I could during the Durrani litigation. Unless I showed in the courtroom the Durrani cases were winners, I would fail.

Filing malpractice suits is expensive. Unlike defense attorneys who bill by the hour and receive their pay no matter how long a case goes on and regardless of the outcome, victim lawyers receive no pay until there is either a settlement or a jury award paid. The process takes years. Meanwhile, the expenses mount. As mentioned earlier, before the lawyers of victims file a malpractice suit in Ohio, they need an affidavit of merit from a qualified expert attesting to the case's merit. Those cost about $10,000 each for a spine case. Multiply that by the 580 clients we represented, and the sum comes to $5.8 million. Millions more must be paid for staff, expert witnesses, testimony, and court filing fees. The price tag for justice doesn't come cheap.

On this Saturday, my cell phone rang. No matter how occupied, I never ignored my phone. Of all people calling me that morning: Mike Lyon.

"Eric, I just want to let you know Durrani fled the country and he's back in Pakistan. I just found out from Durrani. He called me." Lyon sounded disingenuously distraught.

I sensed something awry. If Durrani skipped the country on fraud charges, why contact Lyon—his insurance company's lawyer—rather than his criminal defense attorney?

I also thought "thanks Judge Barrett and Magistrate Bowman" for not ensuring Durrani would not flee. One would believe the two of them would "make up for it" with maybe some guilt action. They never have.

The FBI later discovered Durrani obtained a fake passport, traveled to Mexico and then Brazil before flying to Pakistan. Durrani left behind his wife and two teenage children without a word. Durrani bragged for years of his connections to Pakistani intelligence. He also claimed to be part of Pakistan's royal family, even though the country abolished its monarchy in 1956 and became a republic. But who knew? "Durrani" like "Patel" in India and "Smith" in America, is one of Pakistan's most common last names. Plenty of Durrani's serve in Pakistani government. All I know, he should have been held in custody or monitored.

Knowing these claimed connections, for a year after Durrani's flight, I kept all our outside home lights on every night and looked under my truck every morning. As if they wanted me dead, these two steps would save me.

Lyon expressed his sincerest "regrets" to me Durrani would "no longer cooperate and participate in the litigation, so your insurance coverage for your clients has gone away." Lyon spoke about the $42 million in coverage on Durrani and CAST from Medical Protective Insurance, the nation's largest and oldest malpractice insurance firm. Lyon spoke not with regret, but passive aggressive glee. Having leveled Durrani with an indictment, I saw the flight as a Lyon and Medical Protective counter measure.

I kept my mouth shut and allowed Lyon to finish babbling.

"I'll call you back at one this afternoon," Lyon said. *"I'll have more details for you then."*

I immediately phoned Trisha Morley, my court reporter, and asked her to meet me at the downtown Cincinnati office. When Lyon called at 1 p.m., I didn't share with Lyon that Morley transcribed our conversation. I needed an excuse for using the speaker phone for the recording without raising Lyon's suspicions. What follows is our conversation:

LYON: How are you doing?

DETERS: Well, I wanted to tell you something. My right arm, I cannot use it except to like, prop it up on a table and write. I can't lift it or anything, so I got you on speaker—

LYON: That's all right. Better be careful, man. You better take some time to get that rest because you know what infections are like; they're still in you.

I asked if Lyon had any more details about the circumstances surrounding Durrani's flight.

LYON: I'll just tell you exactly what happened. I had not heard from him for about nine — I had not seen him for about nine days, and I really kind of left him alone. I usually hear from him every day, every day.

DETERS: Uh-huh.

LYON: And so about — after about seven days, I sent him a couple emails and said, "How you doing..." blah, blah, blah; he sent me back a couple emails simply saying, "you know, I'm just — I'm kind of depressed. I'm really not, you know, communicating with anybody..." blah, blah, blah; you know, I left the guy alone.

Then last Thursday morning I emailed him. I said, "I need to talk to you about this trial that's coming up. We need to get together and start getting ready..." blah, blah, blah. He emailed back, said, "I'll call you tonight on your home phone. What's your home phone number?"

Now, he never called me on my home phone, and you know, who uses their home phone anymore?

DETERS: Right.

LYON: And so, I gave it to him, and about 11:00 Thursday night, he called me and informed me that he's in Pakistan.

DETERS: Wow.

LYON: That's it; and I did not—you know, I did not ask him the circumstances, needless to say, but I did inform him that as an officer of the court, I needed to immediately inform the U.S. Attorney, the marshal and the judge, which he said, "Fine." And I told him I would do that the next day, and you know, that's it; and then the next day I called Glenn (Whitaker) (Durrani's criminal defense lawyer) at home that evening and informed him.

DETERS: So, he called you before he called Glenn?

LYON: Yeah, he didn't call Glenn. He hasn't talked to Glenn.

Lyon elaborated Durrani now operated at a clinic in Lahore, Pakistan. I asked Lyon if he knew if Durrani planned to return. Lyon said he didn't ask. We agreed it unlikely since Durrani would immediately go to jail on his flight warrant and remain there until his criminal trial and certain conviction.

Lyon claimed he spoke to Durrani's wife and she was unaware Durrani left the country. I thought no surprise there, with Durrani living with Beth Garrett and Durrani offering up his wife's and children's passports if the judge allowed him to travel to Pakistan.

LYON: I felt so sorry for her. She just -- almost had a heart attack on the phone.

DETERS: I could imagine; and her children, too.

LYON: Yeah. She thought they were going to get arrested. I said, "That's not going to happen. You're not going to get arrested." Don't--you know--

DETERS: Yeah, they didn't do anything wrong.

The conversation then turned to the legal implications for the hospitals involved in the case and what happens to their liability with Durrani absent. Not far into the discussion, Lyon made a bizarre admission about his handling of another doctor's malpractice case involving the same insurance company.

LYON: Now I just had a trial in Lima, Ohio; the one I told you about. I told you— (the client) was in Hawaii. Now, I told him not to come (to the trial). I didn't want him there because he was a weird and goofy guy, and I just took a risk and I didn't have him come. Now, if he had said, "Look, I'm not coming, screw you" (and refused to cooperate with his own defense), (Medical Protective) would have been in a position to say, "Fine, we'll defend you, but we're not going to cover you."

I wondered to myself if Lyon advised Durrani to flee the country in order to protect the insurance company's $42 million? As Durrani's insurer, Medical Protective, not Durrani, paid Lyon's legal fees. My transcribing this phone call would be my single wisest act in the litigation. It would help save $42 million in insurance coverage for our clients. To this day, it's the only recording of a lawyer I have ever made in forty years.

Lyon tried to persuade me to delay the Pierce trial until a court decided whether Medical Protective remained liable for Durrani in his absence and his "failure to cooperate." Lyon promised a lawsuit in federal court to clarify the issue. The suit asked the court to rescind Durrani's Medical Protective's malpractice policy by claiming Durrani breached the insurance contract by fleeing the country and not cooperating in the defense of the claims.

Lyon recruited Stan Chesley to take me out to lunch and convince me not to try the Pierce case. Chesley, a Cincinnati lawyer who rose to national prominence in the 1980s as a pioneer in major class action suits, asked me to lunch at the *Table* restaurant in downtown Cincinnati, "Why are you going to trial, Eric? You know there's not going to be insurance coverage for Durrani."

I told Chesley I was not concerned about the insurance issue, and I would try the Pierce case.

Federal Judge Timothy Black later ruled against Medical Protective by finding Medical Protective needed to show in each malpractice case whether or not Durrani's lack of cooperation hurt their defense. More on Chelsey and that later.

Chapter 17

Tayeb and Shanti

"One man in the right is a majority."
—Andrew Jackson

Dr. Zeeshan Tayeb left CAST in November 2013 after the feds swooped in. Born and raised in Cincinnati, Tayeb wanted to return to his hometown after completing medical school at Wright State University in Dayton, Ohio and a fellowship at the Nexus Pain Center in Provo, Utah. He arrived to work at CAST in 2009 as its pain and rehabilitation specialist. Once there, Tayeb soon realized Durrani wasn't interested in providing patients with pain management, physical therapy or any other first-line therapies prior to surgery, only after surgery.

When it hit the fan about Durrani, we learned Tayeb ran to the feds. I believe it an act of self-preservation. Durrani instructed Tayeb to place pain injections in the wrong place so patients would still suffer pain and choose surgery. Tayeb did it, too. How evil?

We planned to "turn" Dr. Tayeb and another Durrani employee, Dr. Nael Shanti. Shanti, Durrani's employee spine surgeon, left for North Carolina. Johnny Armstrong, my brother-in-law, was a patient of Tayeb. Johnny lined up a meeting between Tayeb and I at a middle eastern restaurant in Clifton in Cincinnati, called the *Mediterranean.* I met with Tayeb around Thanksgiving in 2013, and Dr. Tayeb began spilling all the beans. He contacted Shanti and Shanti spilled more beans. I met Tayeb at the *Mediterranean* many times over the course of a year.

Tayeb claimed when he turned against Durrani, Dr. Schneeburger, a former South African Special Forces soldier who served as Durrani's general surgeon, threatened him with a sniper shot when Tayeb least expected it.

Tayeb told Durrani's attorneys during his subsequent deposition Durrani never waited to determine if pain injections or other alternatives worked before scheduling a patient's surgery:

"Other orthopedic places that I had looked at, you know, prior to CAST, an individual would go through a certain amount of conservative care, and then after a certain amount of the workup had been done, they would refer the patient over to the surgeon. This was a little different, something I wasn't used to, or at least nothing that I had gone through during my training. People were coming into the surgical practice at CAST and only being referred back the other way on an as-needed basis. It was as though everyone who was walking needed to be cut on in some way, shape or form whether it was needed or not."

Tayeb testified he often heard from his patients Durrani told them "I can fix that" with a surgical procedure. Durrani told patients they would be paralyzed if they didn't allow him to operate as soon as possible. Durrani forged ahead with surgeries, while ignoring or not requesting an MRI of the patient's affected region.

Kimberly Kelly, a former X-ray technician at West Chester Hospital, confirmed Tayeb's testimony. Kim wrote in an affidavit she witnessed on more than one occasion Durrani's medical orders for Tayeb to place the steroid injection below the actual pain level stated by the patient. The treachery didn't end there. Kelly testified Durrani's operative reports on patients would claim he performed a "thorough discectomy" for a herniated disc only to have the same herniated disc appear on the next radiology report.

Shanti, Durrani's junior partner and operating assistant, testified to Durrani's fraudulent surgeries. Shanti testified Durrani ordered him to perform spine operations on patients when the radiology films clearly showed they weren't necessary.

Shanti testified Durrani always bragged he could receive whatever he wanted from West Chester based on his revenue volume. Durrani would order Shanti to do a surgery and Shanti would look at the films and say to himself, "I don't know why I'm doing surgery on this person."

We only received this information from Shanti by agreement to leave Shanti alone. Otherwise, not only would we have never received the information, but he would also have defended his conduct and Durrani's. Regardless, Wilkey refused to sign affidavits of merit against Shanti.

As the physician delegated to visit Durrani's patients after surgery, Tayeb testified patients were often left in worse condition but patients believed as Durrani told them, "All was fine." None of Durrani's patients ever mentioned BMP-2 or PureGen to Tayeb. Durrani used the materials without patients' knowledge or consent. The grafting materials often left such a thick, boney overgrowth in Durrani's patients Tayeb found it impossible to insert a needle into their spinal column to relieve their pain.

We believed with Tayeb and Shanti's testimony, Medical Protective would settle. We were wrong. As we would learn, nothing mattered.

Chapter 18

Crystal Pierce

"Let us have faith that right makes might, and in that faith, let us to the end, dare to do our duty as we understand it."
—Abraham Lincoln

On January 6, 2014, Judge Ethna Cooper scheduled *Pierce v. Durrani* for trial. After overruling Mike Lyon's request for a trial delay, Judge Cooper assigned the trial to Visiting Retired Judge Guy Guckenberger. Hamilton County uses a lousy system that allows retired judges to double dip and work as visiting judges or "pinch hitter" judges. The lazy judges send trials to the Visiting Judges. Joe Deters, Hamilton County Prosecutor, shared stories with me all the time and spoke how lazy the judges in Hamilton County were.

Mike Lyon based his continuance request on a morning call from Walt Haggerty informing him of the recorded call between Lyon and I. I contacted Haggerty and Brittingham and told them about Lyon's call to me. I believed it was in their clients' best interest to assist me in keeping the $42 million of insurance in play. They agreed, but then turned around and alerted Mike Lyon. I now added Haggerty and Brittingham to the Lyon "no trust" list. They preferred cozying up to their fellow defense lawyer rather than working with me to keep the $42 mil lion as part of a settlement with their clients.

When I'm fully prepared for a trial, I actually have a metaphysical experience. I feel what I imagine a great athlete feels knowing he or she is prepared and ready to dominate. You're prepared. Everything's organized. The other side sits at the opposing counsel table. You're waiting for the judge to walk out. I feel the power wash over me and I know I'm going to win.

The Hamilton County Courthouse is a 100-year-old, nine-story building. Senator Warren G. Harding of Ohio dedicated the courthouse. Harding later became President. The courtrooms are grand and imposing, with ornately coffered high ceilings, limestone and granite walls and wood crafted for the judge's bench, witness stand, jury box and audience pews.

Personnel from several tristate hospitals and support staff for both legal teams packed the audience for the Pierce trial. Defense attorneys for the hospitals sat in the pews to determine who would win round one between Deters v. Lyon.

During the jury selection process, called voir dire, I learned not to be anti-physician. The medical profession is held in too high esteem. As an example, I told the Pierce jury how I chose not to sue St. Elizabeth over my arm issue. The Pierce jury turned out to be bright and educated including three business owners, a business manager and an accountant. The foreman was Bob Schneider, the husband of the former Republican Speaker of the Ohio Assembly, Michelle Schneider, who I would later learn is a fan of mine.

During a jury selection break, my brother-in-law, Johnny Armstrong, who was sitting outside in the hallway, overheard Lyon talking to the hospital defense attorneys about me. *"He's vicious. I can't do anything. He's just too vicious,"* complained Lyon. That made me smile. I wasn't vicious. I just wasn't taking any of his crap. They spoke in front of Johnny, not knowing who he was.

Lyon claimed on the record he didn't know where Durrani was, but he believed him to be in Pakistan. Lyon claimed Durrani couldn't receive a fair trial in the United States. I believe Lyon told Durrani to disappear. We would later file suit against Lyon on this issue.

I believed the jurors deserved to know of Durrani's criminal indictment and his flight to escape prosecution and civil liability. He chose to flee. He chose not to attend the trial. At the pre-trial hearing, Judge Guckenberger ruled he would instruct the jury Durrani simply chose not to attend. We could not inform them of more.

Guckenberger refused to sanction Durrani for his refusal to appear for his trial. If Crystal Pierce failed to show, the Court would dismiss her case. Durrani failed to appear and nothing happened to him.

Despite one juror having heard of Durrani's issues during jury selection, Mike Lyon left him on the jury. Of course, when defense attorneys commit malpractice, their clients never take any action against them.

During the week-long trial, I relied on a time-honored legal maxim: keep it simple. Abraham Lincoln once said, *"Find the path to a person's heart and you will find the road to their logic."* This is true at all times. Appeal to the jurors' hearts to reach their brains. Never allow the defense to pull you into the weeds. Give the jury a compelling narrative. It's also important to keep it visual. I prepared large medical record "blow ups" and utilized an overhead projector for views on a large television screen.

I stressed to jurors an unnecessary spine surgery, even if it failed to result in permanent harm or death, is a brutal assault on a patient's body. It's stressful, painful, costly and takes months of recovery before a patient can return to work and return to a normal life. Besides the surgery itself, the patient must have all the pre-operative testing, physical exams and radiology imaging. Patients must line up insurance coverage, time off from work, and have someone drive them to and from the surgery. Even if the operation is a success, there's physical therapy. A surgery leaves both physical and emotional scars. Victims deserve compensation and the perpetrators deserve to be punished.

I called two witnesses during the Pierce trial. Wilkey testified that Durrani failed to meet the standard of care. Crystal Pierce testified Durrani lied to her regarding the necessity and urgency of the surgery and she found herself worse off from the surgery.

With his crew cut and glasses, Wilkey appeared and sounded authoritative and credible. Wilkey agreed to defer payment on his Durrani case work until I secured settlements. Wilkey waited for his pay. He would send me bills on each case. He told me: "Pay me when you can."

Wilkey testified by video for the Pierce trial based upon his unavailability for trial. This means we recorded Wilkey's testimony prior to trial and played it to the jury on a television screen during trial. This is common due to experts' schedules. At this video deposition, Lyon got out of line, I stood up, banged my fist on the table and I think darn near caused Lyon to wet his pants. He never got out of line again at the deposition. As always, these events are edited from the deposition and the jury never sees them.

From the witness stand, Pierce told her story simple and sympathetically in her quiet voice. She grew up in Winton Place, an inner suburb of poor residents north of Cincinnati and began working in the dietary department of a retirement community at age fifteen.

Pierce graduated from high school and trained and worked as a Certified Nurse Assistant. At age nineteen, she landed a job at the Internal Revenue Service. She began as a mail clerk at the same Northern Kentucky processing facility where her mother worked. In four years, Pierce worked her way up to tax examiner. After her surgeries with Durrani, Pierce was in too much pain to work full-time. She tried part-time work at the IRS from 2010 to 2012 before quitting altogether.

While she testified, the jury noticed thanks to Durrani, Pierce could not turn her head.

I chose not to discuss money with the jury. I showed the jury the lost income and medical bills, but I did not ask for a sum of money for pain and suffering. I told the jury in closing, "If you decide in Crystal's favor, all I ask is that you're fair. However, if you want to sock it to them, do it."

I chose not to call to the witness stand two other physicians who treated Pierce before and after her Durrani surgeries, Cohen and Shapiro. Each asked a small fortune to testify. With their medical records entered as evidence, the records alone documented scathing things about the quality and outcome of Durrani's operations. Lyon's stipulation to these records was another malpractice.

I saw nothing "super" about this "super lawyer." Lyon later admitted this mistake. Lyon used this silly "box reference" about placing evidence in a box. As I would point out, I not Lyon, filled the box with evidence. Lyon would discuss the judge calling "balls and strikes" in his attempt for a baseball analogy. He memorized the jurors' names too, which I find creepy. During the course of the Pierce trial and all future Durrani trials, Lyon also had the habit of falling asleep during trial and jurors noticed. He also texted Durrani from his table. How do we know? We saw the texts.

Durrani gave a deposition in the Pierce case. The one I described earlier. It was not by video, only in writing. I could have used it, but decided to force Lyon to read into the record. A deposition is allowed to be read into the record. Lyon would only call two witnesses, Patrick McCormick, an Ohio orthopedic who I destroyed on cross examination, and Durrani. Lyon read Durrani's deposition. I stood at the podium reading the questions and Lyon sat in the witness chair reading Durrani's answers. I believe this played out well for us.

In his closing argument, Lyon took issue I failed to call Cohen and Shapiro.

LYON: This case completely lacks the expert testimony that one would need for you as the jury—this is the key—what tools you need; you need those tools, and you don't have them. When you open up that box, there will be no treating physicians, there will be no doctor. Why isn't Dr. Cohen here? "$13,000? I can't afford it." That's just an attempt to appeal, once again, to your sympathy and to create another side show in this case of side shows.

Dr. Cohen, Dr. Shapiro, two individuals who treated her, they are not here. Neither one of them are here to say she can't work, she can't do this, can't do that. They are not here. It's just one after another of an excuse as to why they don't have the probative evidence in the box that they need.

I knew instantly what my rebuttal would be.

DETERS: Well, it takes lot of nerve, Mike, and I believe that you got Chicago roots; Chicago is a tough town. I like Chicago. It's my wife's favorite town. Good place to visit. The nerve—the nerve to stand up here and say, "Huh, where is Cohen?"

He's not here. Of course, we know we got all his medical records that Dr. Wilkey reviewed.

Where is Shapiro? Of course, we know we have all his medical records that Dr. Wilkey reviewed, and they speak for themselves. And you also heard about the $13,500 to get (Shapiro) here.

It takes nerve to make that an issue, when… WHERE is Durrani!?

The jury broke out laughing. Amy Plewke, a staff nurse in our office sitting in the audience, let out a loud laugh with the jury.

It wouldn't be my last laugh at Lyon's expense. During his closing argument, Lyon told the jury our case was simply about winning money and that's all Crystal and I cared about.

LYON: They just picked the mud up and they throw it on the wall and they say give us money. That's what this case is about. Nothing specific, nothing precise, no science, no medicine, just statement after statement after statement, hollow, hollow statements, all in an attempt to win a lawsuit. That's all this is…

I told you there was a home plate umpire in this case, and it's Keith Wilkey. It's clear. Every ball and strike he called here, he called it to help me. Every ball and strike he called in this case he did it to try win a lawsuit.

My rebuttal finished Lyon off:

DETERS: He has the nerve to say we just want a big verdict. Did I ask for one? I didn't even give you a number. I said, "be fair." Now, I admit, if you want to give a big verdict to send a message to Durrani, let him hear it…

You know what, it really boils down to, do you believe her? If you believe Crystal Pierce when she says Durrani says you will be paralyzed if you don't have this surgery, we win all claims. Do you believe that? And guess what, unlike the good people in this medical community that, if a lawsuit is filed against them would take the stand and defend themselves, he elected not to be here…

Lyon is accusing us of trying to say anything to get a verdict. Oh, but he doesn't; all this song and dance he just gave you? Listen, you should vote for us because we want to win and he doesn't.

The jury now began deliberation. I never won a verdict in a malpractice case where the jury deliberated only a few hours. Longer deliberations usually meant the jurors were trying to settle on an award amount for the victim. The jury continued for another hour, then another and another. Seven hours elapsed before the jury returned to the courtroom to deliver their verdict.

The jury foreman handed the verdict to Judge Guckenberger. He perused it and gave it to the bailiff, Judy Walters, who read it aloud to the courtroom. We won a verdict for a total $1,040,000.00.

Pierce and I both broke down in tears. I won my all-important first Durrani trial. It would also be my last trial as a lawyer.

Chapter 19

My Style

"Be the hammer, never the nail."
—Unknown

In 2012, I first drafted and posted everywhere what I called "*My Secret*." Read "*My Secret*" which follows and ask yourself if this is a lawyer you would want to hire and ask if lawyers you have hired followed this:

A prosecutor the other day asked me my "secret" for having so many clients. They admitted they were impressed. I said I shouldn't tell you my "secret", but I know no one else will do what I do anyway, so I'll go ahead and tell you my "secret." I want the world to know so you will want to hire me too. So here is my "secret" which I do not want to be a "secret."

1. I give out my phone number and email address to everyone and anyone including on the radio and encourage people to text and email me 24/7/365 with any legal question or case, big or small. Then, I back it up by responding. It blows people's minds. It requires a commitment on my part and toleration on my wife's part. Christmas. Super Bowl Sunday. I'm there. Rapid response. Not only does no lawyer do this, since I'm an attorney of note, it impresses the hell out of people. I do the same on all social media sites.
2. I embraced the Bulldog brand. How many lawyers have a brand? I do. What's the brand? The Bulldog will fight for you. Who wants a lawyer who doesn't fight for you? No one.
3. I don't worry about being paid on every case or every hour of work. Build relationships.
4. I have guts. Is there anything wrong with trying to help someone by "swimming upstream"? No.
5. I perform competent and excellent work. There is no substitute for just doing a damn good job. I have redoubled my focus on this in 2013 by emphasizing it with my entire staff and all my partners. I get angriest at myself if I, or we, fall short.
6. I think outside the box? No. I make an entire new box. I'm blessed with an innate ability to come up with creative and original ideas and plans to help clients.
7. I care. I just give a damn. I get sick in the guts when I lose. I put myself in my client's shoes. The law school and bar association preach: "it's not

personal", "I'm just doing my job", "don't get personally involved", etc. It's a bunch of baloney. Care. Give a damn. Personally.

8. I know for a fact no lawyer outworks me. It is physically impossible to work longer then I do.
9. My opponents always underestimate me. They think I'm just a radio personality with a law license who isn't serious. In "Devil's Advocate", Al Pacino recommends: "Never let them see you coming." The very brash and national defamation lawyer in "the dirty dot com case", the day after trial, admitted he got licked. He never saw it coming.
10. I use the media, my radio show and my widening social network as the great equalizer against the power I fight. It helps. They fear it. Why do I share? Makes no difference. Lawyers I know just don't have it in them to do what I do. I'm glad. More business for me.

I venture a guess you would love to hire an attorney with these maxims and policies. The Kentucky Bar Association hated my rules.

Then there are my Facebook Rules:

My Facebook policy. I have posted this before, but it has been a while. I see Facebook as a chance to connect with both people I truly know and casual acquaintances too. I'm not going to know or meet all of you. Some keep their "friends" very closed. I choose not to on Facebook for several reasons. I developed fans from radio and law. Why not interact with them? I enjoy the platform where I can share my life and entertain, inform and inspire. I have a few rules:

1. I'm never mean to my Facebook friends.
2. I expect my Facebook friends not to be mean to me or my other Facebook friends.
3. Disagreeing is fine. The minute you're nasty. Blocked. Why should I give anyone a shot on FB at me? It's FB "friends." It's not FB "enemies." It should be fun.
4. I share personal events, but never too personal.
5. I won't allow perverted sex-oriented posts. If you see one, it is only there because I haven't seen and deleted it yet.
6. Tag and or share rule. So long as your tag or share is something my FB friends would enjoy or would like to know I don't mind at all you tagging and sharing. I also want to help you. BUT don't abuse the privilege. I don't want the sunglass sellers!! Lol. Feel free share any of my posts. The honor is all mine.

I also FB because I want to be able to respond quickly to my core friends, fans and supporters to anything. I FB because it's been a great source of legal business to the law office which I manage and work—The Deters Law Office.

I also have proven for years, that if you are a FB friend, radio fan, client of the office, friend, etc., you get 24/7/365 access to me by text 859-250-2527 or eric@ericdeters.com.

Never hesitate. If I don't respond right away, I'm napping, sleeping or dead.

Finally, if you see me out, please introduce yourself to me as a FB friend. I enjoy it. It's fun. Please don't begin by saying—"You don't know who I am, do you?" Pet peeve of mine. Just introduce yourself.

Thank you for your FB friendship. Be oracles, not jackwagons. Be witty and wise, not stupid and dumb. Work until you die. God. Capitalism. Constitution. You're probably a sinner, not a saint. Me too. Don't be self-righteous. Carpe diem!

These two guidelines give my friends, fans and clients something free and valuable: access to me and someone who will try to help them.

Chapter 20

The Kentucky Bar Association

"Now remember, when things look bad and it looks like you're not gonna make it, then you gotta get mean. I mean plumb, mad-dog mean. Course if you lose your head and give up then you neither live or win. That's just the way it is."
—Josey Wales

During each year as an attorney, my relationship with the entire legal profession worsened. Rather than remain silent about all the shenanigans, I spoke up and out. Soon the KBA came calling.

Entering Kentucky's system of lawyer discipline is what I imagine crossing the river Styx to be like. After a lawyer responds to a complaint in writing, the bar's trial commission holds a hearing and votes on the guilt and punishment. The matter moves to the full Board of Governors and then the Kentucky Supreme Court. If the chief bar counsel agrees with an automatic reinstatement, the accused lawyer serves the suspension and goes back to work. If the bar counsel opposes automatic reinstatement, the lawyer must apply for reinstatement to the KBA's Character and Fitness Committee. From the Committee, the matter also proceeds to the Board of Governors and Kentucky Supreme Court.

In 2011, Kentucky Bar Counsel brought over a dozen charges against me. The hearing on them occurred over two days at the Commonwealth Hilton in Florence, Kentucky. Prior to 2011, I never faced any serious discipline. In other words, from 1987 to 2011, no issues. In 2011, I became Mr. Rule Breaker? No. In 2011, my jealous lawyer enemies hated I always landed the high-profile cases.

My trial commissioner was Frank P. Doheny, a partner at Dinsmore & Shohl and a stodgy mean man if ever one existed. Kentucky Bar Counsel chose him for me. After a two-day hearing, Doheny issued a twenty-one page report in which he recommended a one hundred an eighty day suspension. The report went into detail on everything the establishment hated about me. The report claimed I violated several rules, including contacting clients already represented by other attorneys, my claiming bias on the part of Grant County Judge Stephen Bates during one of my radio broadcasts and my accusing several of a conspiracy on the location of the new jail location in Independence, Kentucky.

I fired off a response to the media. "Those baseless charges against me do not include dishonesty, a crime, theft, malpractice, harm to a client, moral turpitude or any shameful act. They are nitpicky nothings."

While my long battle to keep the new jail out of my own backyard in Independence led to my radio career and a burgeoning legal practice, it also laid the foundation for much of the bitterness against me in powerful circles. Not long after I began leading the fight against the jail site, I was slapped with a $22,000 fine for filing a lawsuit in Campbell County Circuit Court. A so-called Rule 11. This came from a new judge who recently left the U.S. Attorney's office. I could not believe it. My law school classmate, Deanna Dennison, would prove a prophet. She called me, expressed support and then said, "Watch, now every lawyer will file a Rule 11 against you." They did and do.

In a *Cincinnati Business Courier* story, I publicly blamed my disciplinary woes on the jealousy of "cuff-link wearing" lawyers in Kentucky "who want to neuter The Bulldog." The story ended with me saying, "I have not, nor do I expect to lose, one client over this, because my clients love me. I don't golf. I don't go to bar association functions. I fight like the dickens for my clients." I never lost a client.

When the public learns you have these battles, every disgruntled client takes a shot. Every jealous two-bit lawyer takes a shot. There is only one path to survival. Fight.

I harbored plenty of reasons to suspect the attacks were personally and politically motivated. Large law firms dominate the bar associations in all states. In addition, in Kentucky and Ohio, I battled these large law firms every day. My lawyer and political friend Larry Forgy called it a "cabal" against me. The trial commissioner in my first suspension, Frank Doheny, was a partner in Dinsmore & Shohl out of Louisville, the same Cincinnati firm which represented Children's Hospital in the Durrani cases. I actually interned at Dinsmore in Cincinnati during my junior year in college, working as a "go-fer" who made copies and delivered documents. Jerry Kearns, the head of the tax department, made me stand in the rain waiting for his wife to drop off his electric pencil sharpener. I formed my opinions early regarding these lawyers.

I appealed Doheny's decision to the Board of Governors. Larry Forgy and I argued my case. The Board agreed with us on all the charges except a few and rather than a one-hundred-and-eighty-day suspension, recommended a sixty-day suspension. The Kentucky Supreme Court followed with a sixty-day suspension. Kentucky Bar Counsel, Linda Gosnel, objected to my automatic reinstatement and forced me to apply for reinstatement. In fifty-two days, I went through the entire process. The Character & Fitness Committee approved me 3 to 0. The Board of Governors 13 to 0 against me. The Kentucky Supreme Court 7 to 0 for me. Bar Counsel kept coming and I faced another sixty-day suspension. They objected to my automatic reinstatement again.

In one of the most hypocritical policies, the KBA punishes lawyers who defend themselves against bar complaints. Lawyers trained to argue and fight are expected to not fight. If you do, they punish you more.

I would never get my Kentucky license back. Because the Ohio and Florida bar associations had reciprocal relationships with Kentucky, I would be suspended in those states as well. Rather than fight my case in Ohio, where I never suffered any formal complaints, I chose to retire so I could continue as a paralegal at Deters Law. My fall from legal grace happened a week after I won the Crystal Pierce trial.

Other lawyers and clients saw the opportunity to pile on while I was vulnerable. I had to fend off a steady stream of new complaints after my suspensions. Even a local restaurant sued me by claiming falsely I ran up a $10,000 bar tab bill and stiffed them. I don't drink. The Kentucky Bar's Character and Fitness Committee continued to find fault with my social media posts criticizing local politicians, attorneys, and judges.

As a result of these legal battles with the bar associations, I decided to transfer my law firm's ownership to my then eighty-five year-old Dad. I did not have to do this, but I decided it best.

A later chapter details my KBA battle in greater detail. I simply needed to set the table chronologically about my circumstances. Under the rules approved by the Ohio Disciplinary Counsel in 2013, I was not permitted to sign pleadings or represent individuals in any court proceedings. I consulted with my father daily and observed all the rules.

Nevertheless, the state disciplinary counsel that answers to the Ohio Supreme Court, launched several probes into the firm's operation. None resulted in a formal disciplinary charge. We always diverted time and energy to fight these complaints. Our complaints against the defense attorneys and judges in the Durrani cases were "stayed" while the Durrani cases were pending. It was an abuse of power and selective prosecution of us. The rule states any discipline involving a pending legal matter is stayed or frozen until the matter is over. The Ohio Disciplinary Counsel applied this to our complaints against them, but not theirs against us.

I saw the firm I spent decades building shrink from eighteen lawyers in 2013 to four in 2016. My suspensions and retirement forced me into the role as the firm's strategist and coordinator. I no longer argued for them at trial.

In the all-consuming Durrani cases, I found other lawyers to send into the courtroom in my stead.

I would like you to ponder a lawyer or lawyers you may know who you believe corrupt and wonder how they have never been suspended or disbarred. I bet you know at least one. In Northern Kentucky, there is a lawyer named Keith Johnson who date raped a woman and pled guilty to a crime. No suspension. A prosecutor named Linda Tally Smith was having sex with a detective in the middle of an investigation of a murder. She put in writing she knew other cases would be suspect based upon his lying. She said nothing. She did nothing. The KBA never suspended her day. Robert Poole practiced law years while under criminal charges. Robert Poole actually advertised under my name on Google after my suspension to try to grab Durrani cases. He's now a convicted sex trafficker. Of all the lawyers I know who I wouldn't trust to park my car, only I received this ridiculous prosecution from the KBA.

When I received my suspension in Ohio, it was one week after I won the Crystal Pierce trial. I had to retire from Ohio for various reasons. I never suffered any discipline problem in Ohio. Based upon reciprocal discipline with Kentucky, Ohio suspended me. Ohio had a rule that a suspended attorney could not work in a law firm while suspended, if it's the same law firm that I worked as an attorney. This means I couldn't work for Deters Law as a suspended lawyer. The solution to this was for me to retire. I had two choices: not work on the Durrani cases and leave the law firm, or retire my Ohio law license and keep working on the Durrani cases. Retiring was the only solution to allow me to continue with Durrani cases. The KBA forced me to give up my license in Ohio. Since then, Kentucky has adopted this same rule. It's the "Eric Deters" rule.

Finding lawyers who would fight proved difficult. On July 20, 2014, I sent the following email to every lawyer and staff person in my office. I believe you will find it amusing:

"Can I for the love of God have one lawyer with guts and balls?!! One?! One?! Who can speak up and out??!! Fight? Argue? Show some passion?! Not get ran over?! I don't understand it. I don't want any damn replies. I try and try. I show and show. I preach and preach. Guess what? This is a profession which depends upon these things. Clients want and expect these things. It's not about getting the hell along with evil!!! It's about defeating evil. When God wanted to throw Lucifer out of heaven, he chose Michael the Archangel with a sword of fire! Many of you would have said God be nice to Lucifer. Just ask him to leave. If God called on You the Archangel you would have asked Lucifer: please go pretty please. Everyone say a rosary and novena if you're Catholic and any other prayers if you're not that I get reinstated soon before it's too damn late. If my boss said. Go get EM. And that involved no ethical or legal issues (speaking the hell up, doesn't). I would say awesome. Charge!!! But no… Let's be mamby pamby. You may want to tune into my radio show Sunday where the topic is only good bad ass guys (and gals) protect us from the bad ass bad guys. Wussy good guys lose. Always."

You may not believe it, but I am unlike any lawyer in the country. No lawyer in the country thinks and acts like this:

1. I hate lawyers.
2. I loathe large defense firms.
3. I told the bar association off.
4. I publicize all the lawyer secrets such as scaring criminal defendants to grab a bigger fee.
5. I truly care about people and clients.
6. I act in my own financial detriment to fight for clients.
7. I'll publicly attack a judge.

There is constant and continuing harm the KBA and the media inflicts upon me by causing the public, who do not know the facts, to assume "Eric must have done something really awful." No, I have not. Everyone knows a false allegation can harm for a lifetime. When anyone states I was disbarred, it really stings, because I was not. There was no basis for disbarment and the KBA never requested it.

Not one single time have I ever opened the mail receiving a bar complaint and said to myself: "Damn, I'm in trouble." To the contrary, every time, I knew I should have had nothing to worry about because they were always bullshit. The KBA used the bullshit.

Another harm inflicted by the KBA and the media, is causing individuals and scoundrel lawyers to try and take advantage of what they believe is a weakened state. I would be sued by any least slighted client, or they would file a bar complaint. I chose my only option, stay strong and fight back. I would not allow them to destroy me like the vultures they are. I'll not detail them here, but I either beat every one of them or paid a nuisance settlement like $5,000 to $10,000 to simply avoid spending my time defending or trying a case when I had no time to do so. I am also very proud that every single time Deters Law committed malpractice, we admitted fault and told our insurance to pay. It's impossible for a law firm not to make a mistake now and then. I assure you law firms, like doctors and hospitals, never admit it. I have. We have.

Chapter 21

BRENDA SHELL

"Those who dare to fail miserably can achieve greatly."
—Robert F. Kennedy

Brenda Shell developed scoliosis as a child. In 1971 at the age of sixteen, Shell underwent her first spine fusion and had rods placed to straighten her curved spine. After college, she began a career as a secondary school biology and anatomy teacher. In 2007, her sister in law recommended Durrani for her pain. Another spinal fusion prolonged her teaching career three years.

In 2010, Shell returned to Durrani complaining of numbness in her left leg. After a cursory examination and an MRI, Durrani informed her she required emergency surgery for loosened screws from her previous surgery. Shell preferred waiting for the end of the school year. Durrani insisted: "If those screws go through your skin, you're going to be in a lot of trouble." Durrani performed not one, but three more surgeries. Shell never returned to the classroom.

Shell preferred Christ Hospital for her next procedure. Durrani insisted on West Chester Hospital. Durrani never informed Shell that he lost his privileges at Christ.

When Durrani performed the first of three surgeries on Brenda, he never adjusted the screws. Without Shell's consent, he removed one of the discs between her vertebrae. In the process, Durrani cut the nerve cord to her left leg. After the procedure, Durrani bragged to Shell's husband John the procedure went as planned. Shell knew otherwise. She couldn't lift her toes and the front of her feet, a condition known as foot drop. She couldn't walk without dragging her foot and tripping. Shell could no longer feel when her bladder was full and suffered from urinary incontinence.

Durrani claimed Shell had a hematoma, a build-up of blood between the dura of her spinal cord and a vertebra compressing the nerves to her leg. Durrani scheduled another surgery at West Chester to resolve this. This time Durrani nicked the dura, the covering around the spinal cord, and exposed her for an infection of her spine and brain. Not long after the surgery, Shell became incoherent, lethargic and developed a life-threatening case of spinal bacterial meningitis.

Neither Durrani nor the hospital informed Shell of the infection. Durrani claimed Shell must have suffered a stroke. The hospital began her on IV antibiotics. Durrani whisked her off to her third surgery in three weeks to remove the infectious material in her spine.

After the third surgery, Shell lay in bed for four weeks unable to walk or control her bladder. Durrani insisted she return home. Another doctor at the hospital told her to stay put. Durrani insisted on her discharge to a nursing home, but Shell refused. Shell later checked in to the Drake Center, the region's premier center for long-term acute care and rehabilitation. There she learned about her meningitis and began the long road to recovery.

Five weeks later, Drake sent Shell home with IV antibiotics for the next six months. She completed a year-and-a-half of physical therapy to overcome the paralysis in her left leg and foot. Shell has no feeling in her bladder and must catheterize herself to drain her urine. She walks with a brace on her left leg and uses a cane. Keeping her balance is a challenge. She has fallen numerous times, once breaking an arm and another time suffering a tear to the rotator cuff in her shoulder. Shell is in constant pain.

Bitter is an understatement for Brenda Shell.

By 2014, Shell required assistance to walk to the bathroom. Her son encouraged her to go to the Mayfield Clinic. Shell knew one of her former students who worked at Mayfield, so she agreed. Brenda sent her medical records over to Mayfield and received a call from Dr. Robert Bohinski, a neurosurgeon at the clinic. He recommended surgery to repair the damage left by Durrani.

Bohinski repositioned the misplaced screws in her spine but the severed nerve cord to her leg could not be repaired. Bohinski also informed her BMP-2 engulfed her spine. Shell had no clue what BMP-2 was and what that meant. Not approved by the FDA except for use in the lower spine, the FDA also required the material be used only in conjunction with a small metal cage inserted into the spinal column to keep the bone growth confined to where it's needed. Bohinski told Brenda her spine was an absolute mess. BMP-2 spread everywhere, but Bohinski couldn't do anything about removing it.

The Shells hired John Holschuh, the same lawyer Potts once hired. They grew unhappy with his effort.

In 2013, John Shell saw a newscast about my taking cases against Durrani, "It seemed like he was kind of a fighter for the underdog. He didn't mind taking on cases where he was fighting uphill," said John. He checked out Deters Law online and called me.

Chapter 22
Butler County

"Success is not final, failure is not fatal; it is the courage to continue that counts."
—Winston Churchill

I never cared for my youngest brother Jeremy, who also is an attorney. He's ten years younger than me. Besides being the typical spoiled, youngest child of a large family, he's the classic trouble making, lazy, never done anything conniver. He's insecure and spent his entire adult life manipulating his way by screwing over others including family members. This story is not about him, but I'll share one story to make the point. My brother Jed gave Jeremy a job as an attorney. Jeremy, out of forty plus lawyers at Deters, Benzinger & LaVelle, found himself dead last in every evaluation category. Jed gave Jeremy a "lifeline" before they fired him. Then in the "dead of night," Jeremy stole Jed's largest client. I also do not believe he's ever tried a case to a jury. Despite my concerns, my Dad and I decided to allow Jeremy's two law partners, Jeff Fichner and Wes Williams, to try the second case against Durrani, Brenda Shell.

Although they were former prosecutors, neither Fichner nor Williams possessed any experience with medical malpractice cases. I believed I could coach them to victory. I knew they tried cases. I tried a case against each of them when they were prosecutors, won one and lost one.

This would be our first case in Butler County, a predominantly Republican region north of Cincinnati. Judge Guy Guckenberger still would not permit the jury to be told of Durrani's arrest and flight to Pakistan. Judge Guckenberger was assigned all the Butler County cases, because the elected Judges of Butler County were too lazy to handle them.

Long-time Butler County Sheriff Rick Jones appears on *Fox News* and other shows. He's an anti-illegal immigrant champion. He also refused to allow his deputies carry Narcan to revive victims of opioid overdoses. Jones' philosophy? If they want to die, let them. I agree with Jones on most issues, but not that one. He also recently jumped on the mandatory vax train.

I prepared the case for trial and created a blueprint for the strategy. Fichner and Williams ignored my advice regarding two jurors. One was a nurse. Based on her answers during questioning, they thought the nurse would be a good juror. As an experienced trial lawyer, I know jurors lie. You don't want a nurse on a malpractice jury because they are part of the health care system. Nurses may have issues with doctors, but when push comes to shove, they close ranks. They will cut a doctor slack. The other juror was a middle-aged white conservative libertarian male, I would have loved to talk politics with him outside a courtroom, but they lack compassion. He became the foreman. Chuck Holbrook served as my eyes and ears in the courtroom. He and I texted and he passed on my thoughts to Jeff and Wes. I suppose they knew "best." Jeremy sat in the courtroom, too, during the trial. I imagine he vetoed my suggestions.

Wes and Jeff gave the shortest opening in history for a malpractice case, losing the opportunity to teach and educate the jury. Brenda made a gaffe as well. When Shell testified, having endured the loss of her teaching career, pension benefits, medical bills and more, Shell blurted out: "I'm just tired of being broke." Frustration leads to mistakes.

The jury deliberated seven hours. Judge Guckenberger prepared instructions for the punitive damage phase of the trial expecting another Pierce like win. Mike Lyon even turned to Karen Carroll and stated: "Well, when we lose, we will appeal." When the jury returned to the courtroom, to the shock of all, they announced a 7 to 1 defense verdict.

Over the next several days, I unloaded to my Dad about Jeremy, Wes and Jeff. I couldn't believe a jury rejected Brenda's claim. How could any jury vote for a doctor not present in the courtroom. Regardless, I concluded the Wes and Jeff experiment. I searched for a new option. Later, I only blamed Butler County.

I decided to match up my daughter, Erica, a recent graduate of Chase Law School who passed the Ohio Bar, with someone. I would sit with them at the counsel table.

On December 19, 2014, I received an email from Matt Hammer. Matt claimed he passed the July 2014 Ohio State Bar Exam and was sworn in as an attorney on November 17, 2014. He held a law license for a month. He claimed to have experience trying criminal cases in Toledo under a Legal Intern Certificate. He concluded in his email he would "love any opportunity to gain even more experience." I would give it to him.

Hammer wrestled at Moeller, the Catholic high school on Cincinnati's more conservative northeast side, and graduated from the University of Dayton. He graduated from the University of Toledo College of Law and lived and practiced out of his parent's basement.

In his email Hammer said, "Man I'd love to work for you." I replied, "Okay, interview Sunday 1:00, Fox 19 office." He came in the conference room looking like a wrestler with glasses. I immediately liked him and assumed he had fight in him. I looked at this young kid and said, "If I were to ask you to try a big case tomorrow, what would you say?" He responded, "Let's do it." I replied, "You're hired." The interview lasted minutes. While other young lawyers in my office seemed scared of their own shadow, this kid answered how I would have answered.

To help mentor Hammer, I accepted an offer of assistance from Ben Maraan, a Cincinnati lawyer whose background was in real estate and business law. The same age as me, Ben Maraan's loyalty proved to be unflinching. He would play an important role in reviewing and signing Durrani filings, handling scores of depositions and assisting in all the Durrani trials from then until now.

Chapter 23

Greed Over Patients

"Nonsense, I have not yet begun to defile myself."
—Doc Holliday "Tombstone"

Qui Tam is the shortened version of the Latin phrase "qui tam pro domino rege quam pro se ipso in hac parte sequitur", meaning, "who sues in this matter for the king as well for himself. A Qui Tam Claim is a False Claims Act claim that allows a private person, known as a relator, to prosecute a lawsuit for the government and receive a reward if successful in assisting receiving money for the government.

A relator receives twenty percent of what the government recovers. When you hear of a whistleblower lawsuit, it is really a qui tam. It must involve government money, such as Medicare or Medicaid.

We used all the information we uncovered and filed a qui tam claim against West Chester Hospital.

On October 9, 2015, the Department of Justice issued a Press Release. It is worth placing here in its entirety to reflect what West Chester allowed to happen relative to Durrani.

Cincinnati-based West Chester Hospital and its parent company, UC Health, have agreed to pay $4.1 million to settle allegations that West Chester Hospital violated the False Claims Act by billing federal health care programs for costs associated with medically unnecessary spine surgeries, the Justice Department announced today.

"Hospitals have a responsibility to ensure that services provided at their facilities are medically necessary and appropriate before they bill federal health care programs for those services," said Principal Deputy Assistant Attorney General Benjamin C. Mizer, head of the Justice Department's Civil Division. "When providers charge for medically unnecessary services, we will aggressively seek remedies under the False Claims Act."

This settlement resolves allegations that West Chester Hospital knowingly submitted claims to Medicare and Medicaid for hospital charges related to medically unnecessary spine surgeries performed between 2009 and 2013 by Dr. Abubakar Atiq Durrani, a surgeon from Mason, Ohio, who had admitting privileges at West Chester Hospital. Durrani was arrested in July 2013 and charged with health care fraud violations relating to allegations that he performed medically unnecessary spine surgeries on patients residing in Ohio and Kentucky. Following his arraignment, Durrani allegedly fled the United States and remains a fugitive.

Medicaid is funded jointly by the states and the federal government. The state of Ohio and commonwealth of Kentucky paid for some of the Medicaid claims at issue and will receive approximately $72,000 of the settlement amount.

"Federal health care programs cover only those procedures that are medically necessary," said U.S. Attorney Carter M. Stewart of the Southern District of Ohio. "The U.S. Attorney's Office is committed to pursuing providers that seek payment for unnecessary medical procedures."

"Any time greed replaces medical necessity as the primary factor in performing invasive procedures and surgeries on Medicare and Medicaid patients, our most vulnerable citizens – the elderly, disabled, and economically disadvantaged – are imperiled," said Special Agent in Charge Lamont Pugh of the Health and Human Services Office of Inspector General (HHS-OIG). "Medical businesses and physicians who unnecessarily place patients at risk to boost profits will be held accountable for their actions."

The civil settlement resolves a lawsuit filed under the whistleblower provisions of the False Claims Act, which permit private parties to file suit on behalf of the United States for false claims and obtain a portion of the government's recovery. The civil lawsuit was filed in the Southern District of Ohio by former patients of Durrani and is captioned United States ex rel. Scott, et al. v. Durrani, et al. As part of today's resolution, the whistleblowers will receive approximately $800,000 from the federal share of the settlement.

This settlement illustrates the government's emphasis on combating health care fraud and marks another achievement for the Health Care Fraud Prevention and Enforcement Action Team (HEAT) initiative, which was announced in May 2009 by the Attorney General and the Secretary of Health and Human Services. The partnership between the two departments has focused efforts to reduce and prevent Medicare and Medicaid financial fraud through enhanced cooperation. One of the most powerful tools in this effort is the False Claims Act. Since January 2009, the Justice Department has recovered a total of more than $25.2 billion through False Claims Act cases, with more than $16.1 billion of that amount recovered in cases involving fraud against federal health care programs.

This matter was investigated by the U.S. Attorney's Office of the Southern District of Ohio and the Civil Division's Commercial Litigation Branch, with assistance provided by HHS-OIG. The claims resolved by this settlement are allegations only and there has been no determination of liability.

Chapter 24
A Promise

What the lawyer needs to redeem himself is not more ability, but more courage in the face of financial loss and personal ill will to stand for right and justice."
—Louis D. Brandies, U.S. Supreme Court Justice

We filed a lawsuit against Mike Lyon and his law firm, alleging their role in Durrani's flight and attempt to void insurance coverage. At the date of publication it remains active.

After this lawsuit and my suspension, Dad and I met for breakfast with Mike Lyon and Brad McPeek at Covington *First Watch* on a weekday morning. We requested the meeting.

At breakfast I asked Mike if he knew what George Washington and Robert E. Lee had in common? Mike replied with a look of perplexity. I responded that while the outcome of one ended in victory and one in defeat, they both kept their armies and cause alive. I told Lyon no matter what, I would keep the Durrani litigation alive until we won. I have kept my word eight years from this breakfast.

If a radiologist in Cincinnati is sued for missing cancer in a screening, do you know how easy it is for the radiologist to find a Cincinnati radiologist to defend him? Easy. All the spine surgeons, all the neurosurgeons, and all the radiologists in Cincinnati, and Lyon has not been able to find one in the Cincinnati area to defend Durrani. We counted sixty-one spine surgeons in Cincinnati during our litigation against Durrani. Not one has served as an expert for Durrani. Considering the Cincinnati hospital networks are involved, it should be easy to find one. Instead, Durrani's defense team brings experts from California with a few exceptions. Their "experts" try to defend the indefensible. They end up looking like buffoons.

I want to embarrass to the world some of the experts who have come and gone defending Durrani's fraud for money:

1. Robert Biscup
2. Joseph Raymond O'Brien
3. Warren D. Yu
4. Dahari Brooks
5. Nandan Lad
6. Michael K. Rosner
7. Faheem Sandhu
8. Jason Sheehan
9. Charles Cobbs

10. Scott Thomas Dull
11. Kevin Yoo
12. Joel R. Meyer
13. Dennis Whaley
14. Jerome Barakos
15. Paul Kaloostian
16. Sigurd Berven
17. Patrick McCormick
18. Mark Younis
19. Mario Ammirati

While they must recruit "whores," we use the same three experts for every trial. Our experts are unassailable. When they hire a new expert, Lyon and his cohorts do not inform them of Durrani's plight of indictment and flight. Imagine their experts' shock when they hear this first at the deposition or trial testimony. They don't inform them of these facts so the experts will not reject the review.

At a hearing to discuss trial settings, Judge Guckenberger's bias shined through. Erica Deters, Cooper Bowen, Matt Hammer, and Ben Maraan argued for our clients. One of the issues argued involved Durrani not being a doctor and the recent media surrounding the issue. Judge Guckenberger actually expressed concern to Erica whether or not she and Deters Law were concerned Durrani would sue us for defamation. Hysterical. If Durrani filed one, he would have to file it and pursue it in the United States. He would have to come back.

The hospital's and Durrani's attorneys requested a contempt hearing on the media coverage as a gag order violation. Since it involved me personally, I asked permission to address Guckenberger directly. He granted my request.

At a break, I offered the defense lawyers a simple deal: we would remain forever silent for the rest of the litigation and the issue would be dropped without ever discussing the issue with their clients; they refused. All the hospitals and Durrani need to know their lawyers refused that deal in 2015.

At the judge's bench, thirty lawyers gathered, I seized my chance. I informed the Court of the proposed deal and how they rejected it. I looked across at Mike Lyon on the other side of the bench and quoted Shakespeare and Shylock from the *Merchants of Venice* and compared Lyon and company to Shylock and his desire of a "pound of flesh." I used this, knowing Lyon believed he owned the sphere of Shakespeare. As I roasted Lyon, Lyon slithered away as a timid combatant to the counsel tables. He wanted no part of the exchange. He said nothing in response.

Also at this hearing, Lyon claimed on the record he did not know where Durrani was, but believed him in Pakistan. Really? Lyon also stated Durrani fled because he did not think he could receive a fair trial. Guckenberger would never sanction the conduct.

Chapter 25

TIM MARSHALL

"Not only so, but we also rejoice in our sufferings, because we know that suffering produces perseverance; perseverance, character; and character, hope."
—Romans 5:3-4

Erica Deters, my daughter, and Matt Hammer, would try our next case. I sat at counsel table and assisted. The trial took place in February 2015. Tim Marshall, a morbidly obese man in his fifties, saw Durrani in July of 2012 for a second opinion for his severe back pain. While a previous surgeon urged Marshall to hold off on surgery until he lost a good portion of his four hundred pounds, Durrani told him "there was nothing to fear." He insisted on an immediate procedure to relieve Marshall's lumbar spinal stenosis, a narrowing of the spinal canal compressing the nerves from the lower back into the legs. Durrani had no business operating on Tim Marshall, weighing four hundred pounds.

Durrani operated on patients contraindicated for surgery: obese, smokers and elderly. While surgeons forced patients to quit smoking before spine surgery, Durrani didn't care if they smoked. Smoking affects a fusion surgery in a negative way.

On July 25, 2012, Durrani performed a decompressive laminectomy on Marshall at West Chester Hospital. Durrani removed the roof of the vertebra to create more space for the nerves. Without Marshall's consent, Durrani used a bone grafting material PureGen to fuse the weakened vertebra. PureGen has the same function as BMP-2. PureGen is processed from stem cells harvested from human donors. It mimics the regenerative ability of youthful tissues by increasing the concentration of stem cells available to repair tissue and build bone.

Similar to BMP-2, PureGen is rife with dangerous side effects, including the risk of bony overgrowth in and around the spine which can compress nerves and cause intractable pain and muscle spasms. PureGen never received approval from the FDA for any use, because the clinical trials of the biological drug were terminated in 2011 by its maker, Alphatec Spine of California. Alphatec used fraudulent claims and financial incentives for doctors to expand PureGen's use while stalling FDA regulators. Only after their surgeons, including Durrani, implanted PureGen in thousands of patients, bringing in millions of dollars to Alphatec, did they withdraw PureGen from the market.

For three years, Durrani implanted PureGen in his patients and profited from it through a kickback scheme. Durrani became the owner of what is called a Physician Owned Distributorship or POD. Durrani named his POD Evolution Medical. Durrani, through Evolution Medical, would sell PureGen to West Chester. Durrani would use PureGen in surgeries allowing West Chester to upcharge it. Alphatec, Durrani and West Chester all made money. The patients never knew. We hired an expert on this practice, Dr. Scott Lederhaus from California who would testify to the unethical nature of this practice.

Without FDA approval and without patients' informed consent, the implantation of PureGen was nothing short of battery and fraud. In many patients, PureGen worsened their pain. Patients with PureGen implanted in the cervical spine of their neck often attested to difficulty in swallowing and a nagging choking sensation in their throats. Other patient complaints included changes in the tone and volume of their voices and a chronic cough.

In a 2016 report, the U.S. Senate Finance Committee found surgeons with a physician-owned distributorship (POD) performed nearly twice as many fusion surgeries (94% more) as non-POD surgeons. Overall, hospitals that permitted their surgeons to have PODs performed twenty-eight percent more surgeries. The result: unnecessary surgeries.

During surgery, Tim Marshall coded twice on the operating table and twice after surgery. Marshall spiraled into kidney failure and shock. During the operation, Marshall lost more than six pints of blood. After the surgery, Durrani gathered the family members including Marshall's wife Michelle, a retired nurse, her sister Debra and her husband and told them "everything went fine."

Debra asked, "Is he in any pain?"

Durrani answered jovially, "No, he was the one who caused me pain."

On their way to visit Marshall in intensive care, Michelle and Debra ran into Dr. Daniel Tanase, head of ICU at West Chester.

Tanase asked Michelle quietly, "If your husband's heart stops again, do you want us to resuscitate?"

Dumbfounded, Michelle said: "I'm sorry. You must have the wrong patient."

Tanase persisted. "Your husband is the sickest patient we have in this hospital right now."

Michelle protested again. "No, sir. You're wrong. I just talked to the surgeon and he said everything was fine."

Tanase took the two sisters to Marshall's room and showed them Marshall on life support struggling for life. Durrani lied to them.

Debra urged Michelle to contact a lawyer, but she chose to focus on Tim first. For the next ten days, Marshall lay in a coma with his breathing supported by a ventilator and his kidneys by dialysis. Several weeks later, West Chester sent him to the Drake Center where Tim "learned to walk and talk all over again," said Michelle. A day later, Marshall was sent back to West Chester Hospital with a high fever and drainage from his surgical wound. A serious infection threatened his life.

Durrani's junior surgical partner, Shanti, performed a surgery the next day. Before the operation, Michelle overheard Shanti tell another doctor that "he was tired of cleaning up Durrani's messes." After weeks of recovery and rehabilitation, Marshall went home, but continued to need antibiotics by IV.

During a follow-up visit to Durrani's office, Marshall returned to the hospital a third time for an extremely low blood cell and platelet count. Marshall contracted MRSA, or a Methicillin-resistant Staphylococcus Aureus, a type of bacteria now resistant to many of the antibiotics used to treat ordinary staph infections.

After a visit to the hospital to see Marshall, Michelle, her sister and brother-in-law stopped at an Applebee's in Florence, Ky. for dinner. The server overheard their conversation and told them a similar story about her nephew's botched spine surgery. The boy's surgeon? Durrani. Jaws dropped around the table. The server urged them to contact me if they wanted a lawyer. Serendipity at Applebee's.

I suspected Marshall contracted MRSA during his interactions with "Hank," Durrani's beloved German Shepherd. Durrani allowed Hank to roam the lobby offices and patient examining rooms at CAST. Michelle remembered watching Durrani walk down the hallway at CAST petting Hank before entering the room where Tim waited for a follow-up exam. Durrani removed Marshall's bandage and began to examine the surgical wound.

"Don't you need gloves?" Michelle asked him.

Durrani said, "Oh, no. I'm fine."

Based on many of Durrani's patients contracting MRSA infections and interacting with Hank, we asked Mike Lyon for Hank's veterinarian records. Lyon declined. We then found out the name of Hank's veterinarian and subpoenaed the records from his office.

Hank's vet records detailed Hank suffered from MRSA so bad, pus dripped out of his penis. The vet informed Durrani not to allow Hank around people or animals. The veterinarian insisted Durrani bring Hank in the back door, so Hank did not interact with any other pets or people. Durrani allowed Hank to mingle with his patients knowing Hank's condition. This is one of the countless examples of Durrani's complete disregard for his patient's well-being. Are not a terrorist's actions intentional?

Gerald Botner and his daughter Nancy both developed MRSA after surgeries by Durrani and exposure to Hank. Doris Botner, Gerald's wife, remembered Durrani "took that dog everywhere." His office receptionist at Deaconess Hospital "would take him for walks" during the day. Durrani always spoke to Hank in German, the language Hank trained in.

The Marshall trial would be the first time Erica and I would be in a trial together. It would yield some amusing moments.

During a pre-trial hearing, Judge Guckenberger announced he denied our request for grouping the Durrani cases together. In response, I quickly passed Erica a handwritten note on yellow legal paper:

This has to be said — "Your honor, your email said we would have four or five trial teams. We had our teams come today. Now we aren't doing this. I don't understand. The defense are all of Cincinnati's largest firms. They can do this if you make them. You said you would."

Erica folded the note in half, wrote in big letters on front of it, and handed it back to me: "DAD, SHUT UP. XOXO" While it might anger some dads, I found it funny.

Judge Guckenberger "recruited," with the assistance of Chief Justice O'Connor, a group of retired judges to help try Durrani cases. Judge James Brogan was one such recruit and Judge Guckenberger assigned the Marshall trial to him. A retired appeals judge, while not having trial experience, Judge Brogan knew the law. Right away, we liked him. You could tell he would be fair. That's all we wanted.

Right out of the gate, Lyon objected to my sitting at the counsel table with Erica and Matt. Brogan overruled the objection. During the trial, Brogan allowed me to assist Erica and Matt as any judge would allow an assistant.

At breaks, Judge Brogan enjoyed talking and sharing stories with everyone.

Erica caught Lyon privately coaching Durrani's wife, Shazia, on her testimony. When Erica protested, Lyon claimed it all was perfectly fine because he wasn't representing her at trial. Erica complained to Brogan. When Brogan called Lyon out on coaching a witness, Lyon then claimed he represented Shazia and Erica breached their client-attorney privilege. "There was definitely shady stuff going on," Erica told me. Shady. Sketchy. Unethical. You name it. It applied to Mike Lyon.

Erica and Matt performed well under my guidance. During the trial, Tim suffered a medical condition and an ambulance took him from the courtroom to the hospital.

We would learn the Marshall jury as the least serious jury of all time. They picked their foreman based upon the woman going to the bathroom after they first sat down for deliberations. When she came back, they said, "Okay, you're the foreman." They thought this method of selection hysterical. After the trial, a juror actually complained Erica chewed on her pen, her nervous habit. It pissed me off. Let's not worry about Durrani being present, by golly a lawyer chewed on a pen.

The trial took two weeks. During the middle of trial on March 2, my brother Jed died from complications of advanced kidney cancer. He was fifty-four. I received a text message with the news from my sister Celia while in the courtroom. I became emotional and I told Erica, who also wept. Brogan expressed his sympathy as did defense lawyer Karen Carroll. Mike Lyon never said a word.

Jed was the fourth child and the second oldest boy in our family. I was close to Jed and my older brother Thad growing up. Jed became the epitome of a Kentucky country lawyer. He'd go in to work at 8 a.m. in the morning and return home at 2 p.m. and tinker on his tractors.

Jed's hobbies included woodworking, restoring old tractors and automobiles, hunting, fishing and tree farming. He was a "good ole country boy" and an avid supporter of the NRA. He proclaimed himself the head of the Southern Kenton County militia. He drove his military personnel carrier in parades. He only lasted six months after his diagnosis. In his honor, the Kentucky General Assembly renamed a three-mile stretch of Old Madison Pike through Independence "Jed Deters Memorial Highway."

After Jed's death and despite my cash-strapped world, I picked up the tuition for my nephew Lucien's Catholic schooling. Without anyone knowing, including Lucien and his mother, I borrowed money to pay for Lucien's four years at Covington Catholic High School. Yes, this is the "famous" Nick Sandmann's high school. Lucien would graduate near the top of his class and attend the University of Dayton in Ohio. He plans to be an engineer.

The jury in Marshall needed only four hours to reach a defense verdict. I knew it was a bad sign when their deliberation only lasted four hours. It was a long and miserable drive of 50 miles up Interstate 75 from Independence, Kentucky to Hamilton, Ohio to hear the news. When the jury heard of Durrani's flight in the post-verdict interview, all of them felt bamboozled.

Erica and Matt showed promise during the Marshall trial They listened to me. I prepared the witnesses. I prepared everything and they executed well in the courtroom.

After two trials, I had enough of Butler County. Not only did the juries suck, but just driving all the way to the courthouse and back took over an hour, even if no traffic. My son Parker, who worked in the office helping Chuck Holbrook, would get a ticket nearly every damn time he drove there. Once he received speeding tickets back-to-back days. No one would be happier not going to Butler County than Parker.

Chapter 26

BMP-2 and Puregen

"All that is necessary for evil to triumph is for good men to do nothing."
—Edmund Burke, Father of Conservative Thought

We tried another trial in Butler County, the Laura Kranbuhl-McKee case. This client shockingly simply did not want her trial. She didn't care. We had to "twist her arm" to do it. Next in line, we could not move her trial. We laid guilt on her about the team and other clients needing her to step up. Judge Tim Hogan, a retired federal judge, would preside. Ben Maraan and Matt Hammer would try this case and do the best they could under the circumstances. Erica no longer wanted to try Durrani cases. Trials are not for everyone and losing Marshall upset Erica. Laura would not even open her mouth to speak when she testified. We sat a chair next to the jury box so they could hear her. It remains one of the most bizarre events we ever experienced at a trial.

On the morning of the trial, Judge Hogan entered an Order in our favor on nearly every issue. Ben, Matt and I looked at each other with shocking amazement. When Judge Hogan kept repeating himself with clear dementia issues at the outset of the trial, Mike Lyon and Walt Haggerty asked us at a break to agree to a mistrial. We refused based upon Hogan's Order. They only wanted a mistrial based upon the Order. Then at the end of the trial, Judge Hogan reversed his entire pretrial order. We couldn't believe it and we lost the trial.

When we reported what Haggerty and Lyon said about Hogan to Hogan, he misunderstood and filed a bar complaint against us. Hogan no doubt suffered from dementia.

What's the definition of insanity? Doing the same thing and expecting a different result. Well, we were slow to recognize our "insanity." Learning from our losses, we decided to try one more time with one of our strongest cases, Julie Martin. Martin worked three jobs: full-time at a Citibank call center, part-time as a Wal-Mart cashier and managing a handful of rental properties.

In 2005, Martin suffered from lower back pain which worsened until her family doctor could no longer prescribe enough pain medication to control it. A colleague at Citibank recommended Durrani to Martin whose CAST clinic was in Erlanger, Ky. literally one minute from Citibank. Martin decided to stop there on the way to work.

In November of 2011, Martin visited Durrani, who used his fraudulent tricks. He obtained an X-ray at the office, showed it to Martin and said, "Oh my gosh, were you in an accident?" Martin welcomed to know the source of her pain. "I could see one vertebra in my lower back was collapsed and the two above the collapsed vertebra were slanted," said Martin.

Durrani warned Martin she could be paralyzed if the condition worsened or she suffered an accident. Then he reassured her, "We can get you all fixed up, you'll be like new!" The remedy? A spinal fusion surgery. He promised Martin she would spend one night in the hospital before going home good as new. Martin readily agreed to Dr. Durrani's plan.

What Martin did not know at the time is a spinal fusion is one of American medicine's most controversial procedures. It means removing the damaged or degenerative disk that acts as a rubbery cushion between the vertebrae to allow flexibility for bending. To stabilize the spine, surgeons fill the gap left by the missing disc with bone grafts taken from the patient's hip, the traditional method. More experimental and controversial surgeries implant a synthetic material like BMP-2 or PureGen between the vertebrae to spur growth and connect the bones. The average cost of a single spinal fusion ranges from $14,000 to $26,000. This is only the surgeon fee.

According to a 2006 study published by doctors at Dartmouth Medical School, the U.S. has the highest rate of spine surgeries in the world, particularly on the lumbar or lower back area of the spine despite having no real difference in the rate of back problems compared to other countries. The rate of lumbar fusion alone, Durrani's favorite procedure, nearly quadrupled in the U.S. in a single decade, from three per 10,000 Medicare enrollees in 1992 to eleven per 10,000 in 2003. In 2003, Medicare spent over one billion dollars on spine surgery with lumbar fusion accounted for almost half the total. At the same time, rates of lumbar spine fusion varied dramatically across U.S. regions, depending on what part of the country a patient lived in. Researchers found no significant difference among regions in the rate of lower back problems, just spine surgery.

The Dartmouth study concluded: "The underlying causes of the international and regional variations found in rates of spine surgery are unknown. Potential factors include lack of scientific evidence, financial incentives and disincentives to surgical intervention, and differences in clinical training and professional opinion."

According to a *CBS News* analysis of Medicare data in 2014, the number of spinal fusions in the U.S. continued to climb, a seventy percent increase between 2001 and 2011, making them more frequently performed than even hip replacements. The growth is excused as improved technology and an aging population who wants greater mobility. It has sparked a debate on whether many of the surgeries are necessary, especially on degenerative or arthritic conditions of the lower back that can be treated with cheaper alternatives that have lower risks. The financial incentives for performing spinal fusion include surgeons can earn five times as much as they can with less risky alternatives. Hospitals benefit from the added revenue stream.

In 2010, a *Wall Street Journal* investigation found another financial lure for performing spinal fusions: the kickbacks and consulting fees that medical device companies pay surgeons for using their products. Medtronic, an Irish company and the world's largest maker of spinal implant products paid Durrani as a medical "consultant," sent him on free medical junkets around the world and bankrolled his fellowship training program for surgeons at Children's Hospital.

Medtronic is also the manufacturer of BMP-2 bone grafting material Durrani used in many of his surgeries. The FDA claims BMP-2 should never be used in patients under the age of eighteen because their bones and skeletons are still not fully developed. Durrani used BMP-2 on scores of young patients at Children's without their knowledge but with the full knowledge of Children's administrators. He also used it on all areas of the spine, young or old.

BMP-2 stands for Bone-Morphogenetic Protein-2, a protein found in the human body in small doses and necessary for the healing and formation of bones. As a genetically-engineered form of the protein, Infuse is more technically known as rhBMP-2 for "Recombinant Human" BMP-2. Implanting BMP-2 with a saturated sponge induces new bone formation and can be used for the treatment of broken bones that are slow to heal or for fusing together small gaps in bones. Once fused with the bone, in a matter of days, BMP-2 cannot be removed from the body.

Studies show BMP-2 can have up to thirty-five different adverse effects in patients, including an increased risk of cancer and even death. The most common are bony overgrowth in and around the spine, painful inflammation of the nerves, acute swelling of surrounding tissue, and retrograde ejaculation, a male condition in which the semen flows backward into the bladder instead of emerging through the penis during orgasm. Several of our clients suffered from this bizarre and embarrassing condition. Other side effects include complications of fetal development in pregnant women, problems with cancer treatment, bowel and bladder dysfunctions, respiratory failure and excessive bleeding.

Durrani implanted BMP-2 fraudulently into the spines of thousands of patients at Children's Hospital and West Chester Hospital with the full knowledge and blessing of its administrators, who were more vested in the revenue that BMP-2 brought to their facilities than the safety of their patients. Hospitals tracked its use as they tracked everything. Hospital administrators bought, stored, and distributed large quantities of BMP-2 and marked up its cost on patient bills.

Administrators also knew their informed consent forms for patients made no mention of BMP-2 or its many risks. Gerry Goodman, interim director of the operating room nurses at West Chester Hospital, reported the absence of patient consent to a variety of administrators, including CEO Kevin Joseph, M.D., and COO George Caralis. They ignored her complaints. After repeatedly complaining to Caralis, he told Goodman she was just being "an emotional female."

Documents from Children's Hospital reflect Medtronic paid Durrani $60,000 in 2008 alone for his services. Both Durrani and Medtronic refused to disclose how much money Durrani received over the years from Medtronic for consulting fees, attendance at conferences, fellowship training, and "experimental" use of BMP-2 in the operating room. A Senate investigation in 2012 revealed Medtronic paid out $210 million to surgeons like Durrani across the country for consulting, royalties, and other arrangements between 1996 and 2000.

More than other surgeons, Durrani often had a sales representative from Medtronic assisting in his surgeries at both Children's and West Chester hospitals. The representatives guide the surgeon in the use of the company's products, but they also influence the scope of the surgery, encouraging more use of their products whether they are needed or not. Hospitals look the other way because the salespeople save them the money for training their own surgical assistants and because use of their products adds to their bottom line by marking up the price for patients. Durrani was especially close to one sales representative associated with Medtronic, David Rattigan. The two had a falling out when Durrani learned Rattigan tried to move in on Jamie Moor.

Because of its many side effects and risks, BMP-2 was approved by the FDA in 2002 for use only in adult patients with degenerative disc disease of the lower spine and only after non-surgical therapies had been tried for a period of six months. Respected medical journals like *Spine* were careful to publish research that pointed out the many risks of BMP-2 and its limited benefit for patients. Medtronic found other ways to promote their product in the medical community. The company turned for help to a well-known orthopedic surgeon at the University of Wisconsin, Dr. Thomas A. Zdeblick, who developed the cage for implanting Medtronic's BMP-2. Zdeblick is paid a royalty for every fusion surgery in the nation that used Medtronic products.

The July 1, 2008 FDA Bulletin to hospitals and doctors included the following:

This is to alert you to reports of life-threatening complications associated with recombinant human Bone Morphogenetic Protein (rhBMP) when used In the cervical spine. Note that the safety and effectiveness of rhBMP in the cervical spine have not been demonstrated and these products are not approved by FDA for this use.

Since the safety and effectiveness of rhBMP for treatment of cervical spine conditions has not been demonstrated, and in light of the serious adverse events described above, FDA recommends that practitioners either use approved alternative treatments or consider enrolling as investigators in approved clinical studies.

Patients treated with rhBMP in the cervical spine should know:

- the signs and symptoms of airway complications, including difficulty breathing or swallowing, or swelling of the neck, tongue, mouth, throat and shoulders or upper chest area
- that they need to seek medical attention immediately at the first sign of an airway complication
- that they need to be especially watchful 2 -14 days after the procedure when airway complications are more likely to occur
- FDA has approved the use of two rhBMP's for well-defined medical conditions in limited patient populations
- rhBMP-2 (contained in lnFuse Bone Graft) has received premarket approval for fusion of the lumbar spine in skeletally mature patients with degenerative disc disease (DDD) at one level from L2-S1

Durrani or the hospitals never provided information to a single Durrani patient and no Court has ever allowed this fact in the trials. It's outrageous. BMP-2 should only be used at the lowest level of the spine and never on children. Durrani used it on everyone and everywhere.

All the hospitals concealed BMP-2 and PureGen from their bills. They would describe BMP-2 and PureGen simply as "miscellaneous" on the bill.

Soon after he became editor-in-chief of *The Journal of Spinal Disorders and Techniques*, Dr. Thomas Zdeblick began publishing articles touting the benefits of BMP-2 and underplaying its many risks without revealing his financial ties to Medtronic. At one point, Zdeblick's journal declared that Infuse/BMP-2 "may become the new gold standard in spinal fusion surgery" over traditional bone grafts taken from the patient's hip.

The 2012 Senate investigation found Medtronic hid payments to the authors who wrote favorable journal articles about BMP-2 and secretly participated in drafting and editing those articles, usually to downplay the side effects of BMP-2 and to exaggerate the risks and pain of using the patient's own bone for grafting. Medtronic reaped billions of dollars from its bribery and deception — $700 million to $900 million a year — before insurance companies and government programs began declining payment for BMP-2 in 2007 after complaints from doctors and patients came pouring in.

With the revenue stream for BMP-2 drying up, Durrani turned to another product for use in his fusion surgeries: PureGen. Developed jointly by Alphatec Spine of California and Parcell Laboratories of Delaware, PureGen concentrated stem cells collected from live donors. Stem cells have the special ability to develop into different types of cells and can help repair damaged tissue and build bone. PureGen can lead to excessive bone growth around the spinal cord, compressing nerves and causing patients intractable pain, paralysis, spasms, and limb cramps.

In 2011, with the FDA's approval, Alphatec began three clinical trials with PureGen limited to 50 adult patients undergoing surgery for degenerative disc disease. The company soon terminated all three trials without releasing or publishing the results. The company still marketed PureGen without a valid FDA license to spine surgeons, including Durrani, who was an early adopter of the product. The FDA classified PureGen as a "biologic" drug derived from human or animal proteins and like vaccines, fell under the FDA's licensing process. Alphatec argued instead PureGen was simply human tissue and did not require FDA approval.

The dispute with the FDA was still ongoing when the company began aggressively pitching the product to spine surgeons with deceptive claims for its safety and effectiveness. While the FDA limited PureGen's use to just fifty patients during trials, Alphatec boasted in its 2012 annual report that Alphatec had been implanted in over 3,500 patients. Finally, under pressure from the FDA, Alphatec quit shipping PureGen in February of 2013.

With the help of West Chester Hospital administrators, Durrani found a way to use the unapproved drug at a handsome profit to himself. West Chester began purchasing PureGen in October of 2011 from a local distributor, Innovative Medical Consultant, through its sale representative Thomas Blank. As Rattigan did for Medtronic, Blank often assisted Durrani during surgeries with PureGen.

In May of 2012, Durrani decided he wanted in on PureGen. Durrani formed his own physician-owned distributorship, Evolution Medical, and with Blank marketing, Durrani began selling Puregen to West Chester and other hospitals by February of 2013. A year before, the Senate Finance Committee warned of the dangers of physician-owned distributorships and helped pass a bill outlawing "kickback" schemes whereby physicians "double-dipped" by using the same medical devices they sold to hospitals.

To hide his illegal activities, Durrani never disclosed to his patients he used PureGen. With the help of West Chester Hospital, the drug never appeared on their medical bills. Even if a patient looked at their detailed itemized bill, they wouldn't see it. As with Medtronic's BMP-2, West Chester officials looked the other way because they earned a markup on the use of the drug.

My clients reported a long list of harmful side effects from Durrani's use of PureGen. All found their pain worsened. Those who had it implanted in the cervical or neck area of the spine attested to a chronic cough and difficulty in swallowing liquids or even their own saliva. Many patients described a choking sensation along with changes to the tone and strength of their voice. Those who had it implanted in the middle and lower spine reported increased pain, difficulty with walking, numbness and tingling in their lower extremities and decreased flexibility in their back.

Darrell Earls, a minister who had PureGen implanted in his lower spine, wrote in his client narrative that "even after two corrective surgeries, I continue to have limited use of my left leg. The pain is ever-present. I am easily fatigued and have severe pain after brief tasks such as cooking dinner, preaching a sermon, even making a bed. Bending over is so painful and produces such instability that my family helps put on my socks and shoes. I require a cane for ambulation, due to left leg weakness and limited range of motion."

Duane Pelfrey, who had PureGen implanted in his neck, wrote that there is "pressure on my throat making it unbearable to swallow meds and food. Loss of range of motion in my neck and stiffness in back. The pain is so severe that I can no longer sleep lying down. I have to sleep sitting up. The pain in my neck is unbearable most days. The pain runs between my shoulder blades into my chest and throat and side of my neck."

A patient has a right to determine what happens to his or her body and the preservation of that right requires the patient be informed when a bone growth product, that causes irreversible harm, is placed in his or her body.

Wilkey in reviewing all the cases was more than comfortable testifying PureGen caused our clients throat issues. Wilkey saw the causation connection. Wilkey performed in all his reviews his own *Daubert* study. *Daubert* is a U.S. Supreme Court case which outlines the requirements of a scientific assertion before it may be used in Court. The Court would not allow Wilkey to testify to these issues.

According to Medtronic's package insert for BMP-2 as well as other industry literature, the following risks are associated with the use of BMP-2:

a. Male Sterility
b. Cancer
c. Increased progression of cancer
d. Suffocation of the cervical region
e. Bone fracture
f. Bowel/bladder problems
g. Loss of spinal mobility or function
h. Change in mental status
i. Damage to blood vessels and cardiovascular system compromise
j. Excessive bone mass blocking the ability to treat pain
k. Damage to internal organs and connective tissue
l. Death
m. Respiratory problems
n. Disassembly and migration of components
o. Dural tears
p. Ectopic and exuberant bone formation

q. Fetal development complications (birth defects)
r. Foreign body (allergic) reaction
s. Gastrointestinal complications
t. Incisional complications
u. Infection
v. Insufflation complications
w. Neurological system compromise
x. Non-union
y. Delayed union
z. Mal-union
aa. Change in curvature of spine
bb. Retrograde ejaculation
cc. Scars
dd. Tissue and nerve damage
ee. Itching
ff. Pain
gg. Hematoma
hh. Anaphylactic reaction
ii. Elevated erythrocyte sedimentation rate

Injury Percentages:
a. Ectopic Bone Growth-63%
b. Inflammatory Neuritis-15%
c. Osteolysis/Subsidence-13%
d. Acute Swelling-7%
e. Retrograde Ejaculation-2%
f. 85% of time, BMP-2 implanted in off-label use

Durrani never explained a single one of these risks to a single patient.

Durrani and the hospitals repeatedly used BMP-2 in these non-FDA-approved manners. It's called "off label." The problem is if it's "off label" and not an approved normal use, you must inform the patient. Durrani, nor the hospitals, ever informed the patients.

Medtronic's fraudulent scheme was successful and resulted in a revenue stream ranging from seven hundred to nine hundred million dollars per year.

The Spine Journal began receiving complaints from doctors around the country who were pointing out contradictions between papers published by doctors with financial ties to Medtronic and other data involving BMP-2 complications.'

Senator Baucus stated, "Medtronic's actions violate the trust patients have in their medical care. Medical journal articles should convey an accurate picture of the risks and benefits of drugs and medical devices, but patients are at serious risk when companies distort the facts the way Medtronic has. Patients everywhere will be better served by a more open, honest system without this kind of collusion."

Senator Grassley stated, "The findings also should prompt medical journals to take a very proactive approach to accounting for the content of the articles along with the authorship of the articles and the studies they feature. These publications are prestigious and influential, and their standing rests on rigorous science and objectivity. It's in the interest of these journals to take action, and the public will benefit from more transparency and accountability on their part."

Major findings of the Senate investigation include:

a. Medtronic was involved in drafting, editing, and shaping the content of medical journal articles authored by its physician consultants who received significant amounts of money through royalties and consulting fees from Medtronic. The company's role in authoring or substantially editing these articles was not disclosed in the published articles. Medical journals should ensure that any industry role in drafting articles or contributions to authors is fully disclosed.
b. Medtronic paid a total of approximately $210 million to physician authors of Medtronic-sponsored studies from November 1996 through December 2010 for consulting, royalty and other arrangements.
c. An e-mail exchange shows that a Medtronic employee recommended against publishing a complete list of adverse events, or side effects, possibly associated with BMP-2/Infuse in a 2005 Journal of Bone and Joint Surgery article.
d. Medtronic officials inserted language into studies that promoted BMP-2 as a better technique than an alternative by emphasizing the pain associated with the alternative.
e. Documents indicate that Medtronic prepared one expert's remarks to the FDA advisory panel meeting prior to BMP-2 being approved. At the time, the expert was a private physician but was later hired to be a vice president at Medtronic in 2007.
f. Medtronic documents show the company successfully attempted to adopt weaker safety rules for a clinical trial studying BMP-2 in the cervical spine that would have allowed the company to continue the trial in the event that patients experienced severe swelling in the neck.

In response to the various controversies surrounding BMP-2/Infuse, including a June 2011 article in the *Spine Journal*, the Yale University Open Data Access (YODA) team reached an agreement for Medtronic to provide full individual participant data from all their trials of rhBMP-2 and allow unrestricted independent re-analysis of this data.

The YODA study involved research teams from two universities: the University of York and the Oregon Health and Science University.

The review focused exclusively on the use of BMP-2 in patients undergoing spinal fusion surgery for treatment of degenerative disc disease, spondylolisthesis, or any other relevant spinal condition.

The three main objectives of the study were: 1) to examine the potential benefits of BMP-2, 2) to examine the potential harms of BMP-2, and 3) to assess the reliability of the published evidence base.

Medtronic submitted data from seventeen studies, including twelve randomized controlled trials (RCTs).

In total, the YODA study analyzed the data from 1,409 participants.

Though the results showed moderate success with fusions as a result of BMP-2, the study found that BMP-2 results in several different complications including: arthritis, implant-related events, retrograde ejaculation, wound complications, and neurological, urogenital, and vascular events.

In regard to the alleged tampering with the peer-reviewed studies by Medtronic, the YODA study found only two out of twenty peer-reviewed journal publications reported a comprehensive list of all adverse events that occurred during the studies.

Furthermore, the way in which adverse event data was presented in the literature was inconsistent, and the rationale for presenting some adverse events but not others was rarely clear.

The study concluded for the period up to twenty-four months after surgery, treatment with BMP-2 increases the probability of successful fusion but this does not translate to clinically meaningful benefits in pain reduction, function, or quality of life. The small benefits in these outcomes observed from six months onward come at the expense of more pain in the immediate post-operative period and a possible increased risk of cancer.

Even more relevant to the case against Durrani and the Hospitals is the YODA study's conclusion that, "[i]t is very important that these findings are expressed clearly and discussed with patients so that they can make informed choices about the type of surgery they would prefer." Never.

The YODA study concluded that Medtronic "misrepresented the effectiveness and harms through selective reporting, duplicate publication, and underreporting."

The YODA study further concluded that Medtronic was involved in drafting, editing, and shaping the content of medical journal articles on BMP-2 authored by its physician consultants who received significant amounts of money through royalties and consulting fees from Medtronic. The company's significant role in authoring or substantively editing these articles was not disclosed in the published articles.

Medtronic paid a total of approximately $210 million to the physician authors of Medtronic-sponsored studies on BMP-2 from November 1996 through 2010 for consulting, royalty and other arrangements.

An email exchange showed that a Medtronic employee recommended against publishing a complete list of adverse events or side effects possibly associated with BMP-2 in a 2005 *Journal of Bone and Joint Surgery* article.

Medtronic officials inserted language into studies that promoted BMP-2 as a better technique than an alternative procedure by overemphasizing the pain associated with the alternative procedure.

Medtronic's actions violated the trust patients have in their medical care. Medical journal articles should convey an accurate picture of the risks and benefits of drugs and medical devices, but patients are at serious risk when companies distort the facts the way Medtronic has.

When asked how he got his Medtronic grant, Durrani responded, "You apply to the Medtronic's corporate and say this is what we want to do, like everybody else in the country applies, and then they come and evaluate the thing and say, "Okay, we think it's worthy. We'll give you the grant."

In regard to his role as a Medtronic consultant, Durrani stated, "If there are certain products that they help us in developing, then they will come to us for a certain consultant role for a certain product development."

Durrani also stated, *"I was involved in the development of the minimally invasive spine instrumentation."*

Durrani gave conflicting reports on his financial relationship with Medtronic. Medtronic's website has no information regarding their relationship with Durrani. Durrani also gave conflicting reports on how much compensation he received from Medtronic for his consultation services. In one deposition, Durrani stated in response to an inquiry as to how much payment he received, *"It's a standard compensation. Again, it's on the website, how much they've paid us."* In another deposition, when asked if he received income from Medtronic, Durrani replied, *"No, I don't."* When questioned further if he received a fee as a consultant, he stated, *"If you do a work, there is a contractual obligation that they have to pay you. As I told you in my last deposition, they did declare it on their website, so you can actually go on the website and see how much they paid."* In another deposition, Durrani stated that he received, *"less than $10,000 in ten years"* from Medtronic.

An email dated July 30, 2008, from Medtronic Senior Product Manager Katie Stamps to Durrani states that she *"is in the process of working on the renewal of your consulting agreement."* As stated, this information is not available on Medtronic's website, nor is any information relating to Durrani's role as a consultant for Medtronic.

A Children's packet relating to its Orthopedics department indicated Durrani received $60,000 in grants, contracts, or industry agreements from Medtronic in fiscal year 2008.

Financial information concerning Durrani's relationship with Medtronic was found in Durrani's biography on the website for the Orthopaedic & Spine Institute, which Durrani currently operates in Pakistan. The biography states that *"Dr. Atiq Durrani has also received the Clinical Spine Fellowship Grant by the Department of Orthopaedic Surgery which was funded by Medtronic Sofamor Danek with a budget of $59,170 per year."*

When a request was made to Medtronic regarding its affiliation with Durrani, the Medtronic Supplier Relations Team stated that Durrani's *"name [is] not listed in our system."*

David Rattigan, Durrani's main Medtronic representative, worked for Bahler Medical. Despite our willingness to cooperate in scheduling the date for a deposition, Rattigan refused until we subpoenaed him. Mr. Rattigan's deposition took place June 5, 2015.

David Rattigan's testified his sole job was to deliver the BMP-2 to the hospitals and make sure it was inserted correctly into the patient.

In summary, our clients, with the full knowledge and intentional consent of Durrani and hospitals, became unsuspecting experiments.

This is the informed consent policy at West Chester which they never followed relative to BMP-2 or PureGen.

Informed Consent for Surgical or Medical Procedure and Sedation:

It is the responsibly of the attending physician to obtain informed consent prior to the procedure. The patient, or his/her representative, will be advised by his/her physician of:

a. The explanation of the procedure
b. The benefits of the procedure
c. The potential problems that might occur during recuperation
d. The risks and side effects of the procedure, which could include but are not limited to severe blood loss, infection, stroke or death.
e. The benefits, risks and side effect of alternative procedures including the consequences of declining this procedure or any alternative procedures.
f. The likelihood of achieving satisfactory results

Completion of the "Consent to Hospital and Medical Treatment" form to examine and treat is NOT sufficient as consent to perform a surgical procedure, invasive procedure, or for medical regimens of substantial risk or that are the subject of human investigation or research.

The hospitals never informed victims of Durrani's financial interest, conflicts of interest or consulting arrangement with Medtronic.

The written informed consent of Durrani and CAST signed by victims also lacked the disclosure of BMP-2 or PureGen's use in his procedures.

Durrani and CAST would have patients sign a form for Evolution Medical which also failed to disclose PureGen. Here is the form Durrani asked patients to sign:

ACKNOWLEDGEMENT OF POTENTIAL CONFLICT OF INTEREST
CAST

This letter shall serve as an acknowledgement that _________________ (the "Patient") has been made aware that certain physicians that will conduct spinal implant surgery on the Patient are an investor in Evolution Medical LLC (the "Distributor"). The Distributor is a company that purchases medical devices from the implant manufacturer and sells them to the Hospital in connection with their use in surgery. As a result, the investors in the Distributor receive a direct or indirect financial benefit from their use of such implants at the Hospital. By signing this acknowledgment below, the Patient certifies that it is aware of the facts stated above, and that all transactions involving the Distributor have been and will be negotiated in good faith as an arm's length transaction.

There is no mention or explanation about PureGen on the form. It's a useless consent.

We pursued lawsuits in federal court against Medtronics on BMP-2 and Alphatec Spine and Parcell Labs on PureGen. We reached a small settlement with Medtronics before the federal judge ruled against us based upon federal law passed by Congress protecting device manufacturers. We lost on Alphatec Spine, who made no settlement offer. The Sixth Circuit covering Michigan, Ohio, Kentucky, and Tennessee is not Plaintiff friendly on these issues.

Chapter 27
Julie Martin

"Never confuse a single defeat with a final defeat."
—F. Scott Fitzgerald

During Julie Martin's surgery at West Chester Hospital on January 27, 2012, Durrani used PureGen to fuse her spine without her consent. She spent two nights in the hospital and left in worse pain and could not stand or walk. "I knew immediately something was wrong," Martin said.

In the following weeks, Durrani inserted a stimulator to block the pain and put Martin on an intensive schedule of physical therapy at CAST. He recommended a second surgery, but Martin declined. During a therapy visit on February 23, a therapist tried to force her rigid legs apart. When they wouldn't budge, the therapist called the receptionist to help and tried again. "'I screamed, 'Stop!' A horrible sharp pain shot down from my back where they had operated, all the way down my leg," Martin recalls.

Five days later, Martin visited Durrani and reported what happened. He laughed it off. "Oh, those therapists. They screw up everything." He sent Martin for a scan in the mobile MRI trailer behind his office where Martin disrobed with two truck drivers sitting within viewing distance in the trailer's cab. When the results came back, Durrani declared Martin healed.

On March 21, 2012, Martin returned to work at Durrani's insistence. Martin failed to last a day and never returned to work again. "I couldn't sit for fifteen minutes. I couldn't stand for fifteen minutes. I couldn't walk for fifteen minutes."

For the next two months, Martin continued to return to Durrani's office complaining her back pain was more pronounced than before surgery. Durrani prescribed a variety of pain medications and increased the dosages, but nothing helped. During a visit on May 8, she insisted something happened during surgery to make things worse. "I kept telling him, 'There is something wrong, there is something very wrong with my back!'" Durrani turned defensive. "I didn't do anything wrong." Durrani ordered Dr. Tayeb to inject her spine with steroids. "He didn't even take an X-ray to see where to put the needle. He just had me bend over the table and that was it," remembers Martin.

Two weeks later, Martin saw Dr. Natalie Turchin, her long-time family physician. Turchin wanted Martin to see a neurologist and booked an appointment for her with Dr. David Schmerler at Riverhills Neuroscience, an independent group of neurologists and neurosurgeons. Schmerler examined Martin on June 5 and told her she needed to see a neurosurgeon immediately. The MRI did not reflect a collapsed vertebrae, as claimed by Durrani. Durrani improperly placed the screws and cage on her fused spine.

Martin suspected the original X-ray Durrani showed her of the collapsed vertebrae was not her own, but Martin had no proof. "Who looks at an X-ray to see if their name is on it?"

Schmerler referred Martin for repair surgery to Dr. William Tobler at the Mayfield Clinic. Tobler tightened and repositioned the hardware in her spine, but that's all he could do. Before her encounter with Durrani, Martin planned to work "until I dropped. I never wanted to retire." She applied for disability benefits, but it took almost a year after Durrani's surgery to begin receiving payments.

Tobler told Martin that Durrani screwed up her back. Later at trial, Tobler denied stating this to Martin. Once Durrani fled, all the tristate spine surgeons backed off Durrani. Tobler included. In a Children's case before the press conference and arrest, Tobler testified against Durrani at a deposition and his testimony helped me settle the case.

"We had to withdraw everything. The savings. The 401K. I was the one insured, so I had to keep up the insurance, too. From an excellent credit rating, my scores dropped so low. I couldn't buy a pencil on credit. And I will always be in pain no matter how much medication they put me on," Martin cried.

Martin saw a therapist "because I couldn't believe I allowed someone to scam me like that. I thought, 'How stupid could I be? This man took my life away. He took my husband's life away."

After speaking to her pain doctor, Dr. Carl Shapiro, Martin finally decided to take legal action. She chose me. She contacted me in April of 2012, one of the first dozen of my Durrani clients. For Julie Martin's trial Dr. Shapiro testified by video. Unfortunately, Judge Guckenberger edited Shapiro's blistering statements on Durrani's reputation.

Martin's case went to trial in Butler County on June 24, 2015. Judge Guckenberger presided. Matt Hammer and Ben Maraan tried it. In his pretrial Order, Guckenberger allowed me in the courtroom, but not counsel table. It made no sense. Guckenberger always conceded to Lyon on any issue. Guckenberger allowed me to be in the courtroom, sit in the back and authorized me to email and text Matt and Ben. Lyon filed a bar complaint against me on this and Ohio accepted Guckenberger's Order. Lyon the "sneaky snake" to quote Tom T. Hall.

We loved Julie Martin. She testified better than anyone prior, and we should have won. The jury deliberated nine hours. We lost 6-2 because a little twerp juror, a young male in marketing told us later, "I took it as a challenge to see if I could convince the other jurors to vote against her." It was just a game to him. After nine hours, we were so confident we won, Ben Maraan, Melissa Hammond, who helped on the case, Chuck Holbrook, Matt Hammer and I took a group "victory" photograph by the elevators. Lincoln said, "The hen is the wisest of animals. She cackles only after she lays the egg."

Another funny "overrated" Mike Lyon story occurred during the Martin trial. Karen Carroll told Judge Guckenberger she would only use five minutes in closing for West Chester and Mike Lyon would handle the main closing. Hammer, using my drafted closing, destroyed Lyon, and Carroll ended up doing an hour closing. After closings, Carroll walked over to Hammer and said, "You did a great job, Matt. I had to clean up Mike's mess."

When we picked the jury in Martin, we decided to focus on obtaining the smartest possible jurors. We liked the jury, until their verdict. Like all the juries, they couldn't believe they weren't told the truth about Durrani.

At this trial, the defense called a neuroradiologist. We called the radiologist who confirmed Durrani lied. The neuroradiologist would claim the radiologists were mistaken. I made the decision we would never go to a trial again without a neuroradiologist. The treating radiologists had no reason to lie. They read the films and did not see severe stenosis. Durrani's paid whore came in and claimed the unbiased radiologists are mistaken and these jurors bought it. Never again.

During the Martin trial, Mike Lyon snuck in the exhibits a medical record that should have never gone back in the jury room. A special judge appointed to the case after the verdict, granted us a new trial. The 12th District Court of Appeals, also based in Butler County, reversed this Judge and we lost the appeal. It is the first and only time a judge has granted a new trial in my career and the Court of Appeals reversed it. I hate Butler County.

One of my most embarrassing moments in the Durrani litigation occurred during a break in the Martin trial. Guckenberger called me, Lyon and the Court Reporter, Brenda Keyser, into his chambers. Keyser and I had been at loggerheads throughout the Butler County cases, because I once hired and then fired her lazy lawyer husband, Greg Keyser. Once inside the chambers, Guckenberger announced Keyser reported a Deters Law check bounced. Angered and humiliated, I stayed smooth and quick, I kept my cool and apologized. "Ugh, I'm sorry. My bad. Dad transferred money to the account. I guess it didn't get there in time. I'll have a cashier's check sent over first thing."

When I left the chambers, I fumed at both Keyser, for embarrassing me in front of a judge and Dad, who constantly failed to properly fund the litigation. At least in chambers I handled it well. From that time on, Keyser made us pay in advance with a cashier's check. During the entire Durrani litigation, I always kept up the front all was great, and "lawyers, guns and money" were never an issue and would never be an issue. The only ones who knew otherwise were Mary and my staff. I even bamboozled my staff from time to time. The one "fraud" I committed on everyone—defense, clients and others—is my Dad had unlimited pockets and we would never "yield the field." It was not so. My Dad lent $1.9 million and then stopped. Based upon his reputation, I used the reputation to put up a false front. It worked. Dad was paid back all I owed him.

Our days of battling our cases in Butler County were soon numbered. If we could not win the Julie Martin trial, we could not win any trial there. Guckenberger accidentally forwarded to the firm an email Lyon sent him alone, a violation of the ex parte rule that forbids a judge from communicating exclusively with one side or the other in a trial. Guckenberger responded to Lyon. It involved Lyon complaining he and his family being worried the Durrani victims may harm them. Guckenberger told Lyon to file a police report and expressed disdain towards us. In over ten years, not one time has any Durrani victim acted in violence or made a threat of violence against anyone involved in the Durrani litigation.

In addition, we transcribed a recording in Martin of Lyon screaming at Guckenberger without a response from the bench. Meanwhile, Guckenberger repeatedly warned Matt Hammer not to raise his voice. During the Martin trial, I once put my arms and hands over my head in frustration and Guckenberger threatened to throw me in jail. Lyon could literally scream at the Judge over Guckenberger's ordering Lyon to produce an expert report and not a word.

Our firm submitted an affidavit of disqualification to Guckenberger demanding he resign. Rather than deal with the legal wrangling that would follow, Guckenberger resigned, and O'Connor appointed another retired Judge, John Bessey, in his place.

After a Saturday morning case conference with Judge Bessey, we knew we were in for more of the same. Bessey planned to follow all of Judge Guckenberger's rulings and rules. We had enough. We would no longer be insane. One of the greatest ironies and paradoxes of losing those four trials in Butler County, is it would help us save $42 million in insurance coverage.

Chapter 28
I Don't Practice Law

"Musicians play their instruments. I play the orchestra."
—Steve Jobs

Because the hospitals and Durrani lawyers knew I ran the show, they always attacked me at every opportunity. It never shocked me. What shocked me is how the Court, Ohio and the KBA would "buy" their crap. We made no secret of the work I performed on a daily basis. It remains a constant, rather comical, bogus distraction.

My writing style as reflected in this book became an issue with the KBA and Ohio Disciplinary Counsel. Obsessed with me, they accused me of writing pleadings with a "This is clearly Eric Deters' style." They would question our lawyers with:

"We know he wrote this."

Our response: "Yes. Your point?"

"Why?"

"Because we admitted I wrote letters and pleadings all the time. I'm allowed to do so."

This goes on across America every day in every law office, but by golly, Eric Deters is not allowed.

The following email is an email I once sent to an attorney explaining my "not practicing law." I'm using it because it summarizes it all:

I went over to the farm after the support meeting last night to update Dad and report on our meeting yesterday.

Dad does not believe I am practicing law. Nor do I.

We are not going to stop doing what we are doing because what we are doing is not wrong. To stop what we are doing would be an admission what we were doing was wrong. It's not.

I'm a retired Ohio attorney. All the Durrani cases are Ohio cases. Ohio Disciplinary Counsel knows I retired so I could work on the Dr. Durrani cases. They approved it. They approved my job descriptions. They approved the list of what I can do. They approved the letter to the clients we sent out.

Dad is my supervisor under the rules. He does not believe I am practicing law. Also, there is NOTHING I do we would or have misrepresented to Ohio Disciplinary Counsel. They already know what I'm doing and there isn't one person on our team who would have to lie about it.

I don't sign pleadings.

I don't appear in Court.

I don't go to depositions. I don't go to court. I don't go to meetings with opposing counsel, the Court or mediation. I don't communicate in any way, shape or form with opposing lawyers or Courts by letter, email or phone. Other law firm staff here and working with opposing counsel and law firms across Ohio do all the time, every day. I went to Court two times over the past two years, sat in the back and listened. They were two large court conferences.

What do I do?

I draft. I research. I organize. I help the lawyers like any staff person does. Based upon my nearly 30 years as a lawyer and all my work on the Dr. Durrani cases, I don't lose my knowledge. I know more than a paralegal. Just the way it is. That's not practicing law.

Ohio admitted training and teaching a lawyer is also not practicing law.

In fact, I do less than paralegals and staff do in law firms all across Ohio. There are practices like bankruptcy, social security, workers comp, real estate, where non-lawyers do everything from beginning to end, but a lawyer supervises and signs everything.

Also, in this community, EVERYONE knows I'm not practicing.

I make jokes about it.

I explain it.

I joke I'm Eric Brockovich.

Our website very clearly states roles I'm allowed:

- Office Manager
- Trial Consultant
- Paralegal
- Marketing Director
- Media Relations
- Firm Spokesperson

After I retired, Dad sent out a letter informing everyone I would do these. Ohio approved the letter. We openly informed Ohio I would do these roles.

Our website clearly states I'm a retired lawyer and what I'm allowed to do.

When anyone calls for me, leaves me a voicemail, texts me or emails me, I forward the message to the attorney or staff which handles the issue or refer them to someone. In fact, I don't even talk to them and rarely respond. I simply make sure they get to the right person. It's like a "traffic manager" in an ad agency. My wife used to work in one and explained that role to me. The person directs the flow of the work internally. This is also not practicing law. Again, all day long, every day, law office staff across Ohio direct potential clients to others. Another thing I have done is after receiving a question, I'll ask a lawyer in the office the answer EVEN if I know it, then inform the person what the lawyer said and make it clear the lawyer, and not me, said what I told them. Again, this goes on across Ohio every day.

Chris McCaughey prepares replies to Motions to Dismiss all day and night. Matt approves them. Loretta files them. Chris is NOT practicing law.

Also, Dad doesn't need to weigh in on every issue. We know he wants us to respond to Motions. There are routine, everyday things everyone knows what must be done. I talk to Dad about every major issue. We talk and/or meet every day.

Anything I send Matt or any lawyer in this office, they can reject, amend, edit, decide to send or file or not. I have been doing this for three years with Matt, Bob, Ben and Stephanie.

If they don't change it and send it out as a communication or pleading, it becomes theirs. It's not mine.

Also, Matt, Bob, Ben and Stephanie do NOT use everything I prepare.

The recent disputed Order I drafted. You and Matt weighed in. I did NOT send it.

Everyone at the office, Independence and Carew, do not believe I'm practicing law.

In the Julie Martin trial, I sent emails and texts all trial during the trial with the Court's approval! And Mike Lyon complained to Ohio. We admitted everything we did. We thought it through before we did it in the first place. Ohio did nothing. They dropped it. Let that sink in. Ohio recognized I could text and email all trial long. They also know I prepared openings, exhibits, closings and direct/cross examinations because I told them. Matt using them made them Matt's.

I am also allowed to advise, as a retired lawyer, my Dad or any lawyer on our team.

We've been doing this for three years. We are still going to do it.

My input yesterday on your Notice, Order and Matt's letter was NOT practicing law.

Everyone on the team in and out of the office has functioned fine as we have for four years. There have been no issues. Dad supports, ratifies, directs and authorizes everything the law firm does through the lawyers and staff, not just me.

On July 20, 2015, Judge Tim Hogan in the *McKee* case ruled:

"Number twelve, Eric Deters has an economic interest in his law firm and is a member of the public entitled to attend this public trial should space permit. And it obviously does. He may assist trial counsel and communicate electronically. However, he may not sit at counsel table during this trial, or address the Court, I might add."

This is judicial sanctioned trial assistance.

In 2021, the Ohio Supreme Court after a year battle, fined me $6,500 on a bogus "unauthorized practice of law" on a car accident case. It involved Clinton Pangallo. I'll spare you all the details, but from October 12, 2017 to April 24, 2018, I repeatedly told Clinton and his wife I was not their attorney.

Ohio Disciplinary Counsel claimed I gave legal advice and I didn't make it clear I was not licensed.

As a result of this ordeal, I sent the email signature which follows to Joe Caligiuri for input. He never replied. This is what I now use as my email signature which goes out on every email.

Eric E. Deters
859-250-2527 (Cell)
eric@ericdeters.com
Retired Ohio Lawyer 2013
Retired Kentucky Lawyer 2021
No Current Law License
(All information Eric E. Deters provides here by phone, text or in person is either general information or the relaying of law or case specific information under the supervision of an attorney. He also may offer his personal opinion to friends on matters who have no client relationship with Deters Law.)
Office Manager
Spokesperson on Official Firm Matters
Paralegal
Victim's Advocate

It drives my enemies insane with jealous rage I'm successful without my law license. Every single day they attack me on this issue to no avail. I have become so used to doing what I do, I no longer want or need my law license. I prefer being able to speak out as I do.

My given name is Eric Charles Deters. For fifty-six years, I used Eric C. Deters professionally and personally. After a falling out with my father, Charles, and to poke the KBA, I legally changed my name to Eric Esquire Deters on January 8, 2021. Esquire means country gentleman. Lawyers adopted Esquire years ago as their label. I am now forever Eric Esquire Deters to the chagrin of the KBA.

Chapter 29
MIKE LYON

"You're no daisy! You're no daisy at all!
—Doc Holliday "Tombstone"

I justifiably loathe the defense lawyers in the Durrani litigation, and Mike Lyon is at the top of the list. They are not honorable men.

Four published Ohio cases detail Michael Lyon's misconduct. However, he's never been sanctioned or punished.

Mike Lyon sent ex parte emails to Judge Guckenberger and no doubt more judges; never a consequence.

We have a transcript and audio in which during the Martin trial, Lyon screamed at Judge Guy Guckenberger for more than a few seconds over a ruling. Guckenberger failed to punish Lyon.

Lyon represented to Judge Guckenberger in the Brenda Shell case, he was the records custodian of CAST after the DEA raid. Not thinking anyone would remember the weekend before trial, Lyon claimed there was no custodian, so he would not have to produce records. When confronted in Court with the hearing transcript, Lyon asked if he could change his mind about being record custodian.

Lyon repeatedly misrepresented attempts in the scheduling of the depositions of Tayeb and Shanti. While informing us he was "working on it," Lyon never attempted to schedule Shanti or Tayeb for depositions. We discovered this when Shanti and Tayeb advised they were never contacted by Lyon or his office to give depositions. Lyon played this same scam in scheduling Durrani's deposition.

In early trials, Lyon refused to stipulate to medical records, so we went through the time and expense of issuing a subpoena to him for the records. In open court on more than one occasion, Lyon stated he would not comply with the subpoena. The Courts failed to punish him.

Stephanie Collins, an attorney in the office at the time, served as counsel for our Durrani clients for a brief time after my retirement in Ohio. In an email to Stephanie, copied to Judge Guckenberger, Lyon insulted Stephanie's writing ability and recommended she read a book on writing. Stephanie fired back. Guckenberger made Stephanie apologize, but not Lyon.

In another trial, Lyon threatened to intentionally cause a mistrial. Nothing happened.

Medical Protective on their national website brags Michael Lyon is one of their leading trial lawyers to carry their water. These are published and reported cases and verdicts throughout the U.S. finding Medical Protective culpable for bad faith and unfair claims practices.

Not having Durrani's deposition affected trial strategies, witness arrangements, trial preparation and presentation. We had to expend extraordinary attorney time fighting a federal declaratory action. We spent extraordinary attorney time pursuing a sanction against Durrani for not giving a deposition to no avail.

Medical Protective acted in bad faith to victims in refusing to communicate a proposal to Durrani from us in which Durrani would assign his bad faith claim to the victims. The last chapter of his book details all of it. It's unprecedented in American legal history.

We are confident Michael Lyon and Ed Perry of the Rittgers law firm, allegedly Durrani's criminal defense counsel, never took a proposal to Durrani for the assignment of his bad faith claim to the victims. It was a simple deal. Durrani would assign his bad faith claim to the victims. His bad faith claim is the Medical Protective's failure to protect him from excess verdicts and punitive damages. The victims would convince the U.S. Attorney to drop the criminal charges. Durrani could return to the U.S. He would obviously never practice medicine in the U.S. again. Durrani would also be able to travel the world freely, because there would no longer be an international arrest warrant. We know Mike Lyon and Ed Perry failed to inform Durrani of this proposal as obligated to do so for several reasons, including Durrani would leap at the chance to return to the U.S. and travel the world freely.

Our proposal was detailed in a letter dated October 22, 2018 to Lyon to forward to Durrani. We allege Lyon never sent the letter to Durrani as was his legal and ethical obligation, because he was acting on behalf of the Medical Protective, not Durrani.

Chapter 30
Judge Robert Ruehlman

"Certain thoughts are prayers. There are certain moments when, whatever be the attitude of the body, the soul is on its knees."
—Victor Hugo

On the morning of December 15, 2015, every plaintiff lawyer for the victims, every defense lawyer for Durrani and every lawyer for the hospitals sat in Judge Ruehlman's courtroom. Lawyers and staff sat at the counsel tables, in the jury box and in the audience pews. Every seat was taken. I sat in the back, next to Hamilton County Prosecutor Joe Deters with whom we recently signed an agreement for legal assistance. Not related, Joe and I knew each other for years. Joe took part time status as a prosecutor to be able to work on civil cases. More on Joe later.

Judge Ruehlman summoned this contingency of lawyers to his Hamilton County Common Pleas Court. Everyone anticipated Ruehlman's upcoming ruling on whether the over five hundred malpractice lawsuits filed against Durrani would be tried in groups or one at a time. His ruling could end the litigation.

Trials in medical malpractice cases are not always grouped. However, if there is a common set of facts and a common set of damages, there is precedent in Ohio for trying the cases in groups. We argued Durrani used a common set of deceptive tactics to pressure his patients into unnecessary operations.

If Ruehlman ordered group trials, we would save millions of dollars in court filing costs, work hours, and fees paid to expert witnesses. We would be spared the hassle of tracking down and serving subpoenas to the same witnesses for each trial. For Durrani's victims, group trials would mean timely justice. If Ruehlman failed to order group trials, the cases would drag on for decades to the benefit of the defense lawyers, the hospitals and Medical Protective.

Our adversaries feared group trials for it meant a single jury would hear from multiple victims of Durrani. For the hospitals and Durrani's insurer Medical Protective, individual trials would mean paying out smaller amounts of money over a longer period of time with their hope our clients and I would give up. The defense lawyers would be more than happy if the individual trials went on forever. They would still receive their hourly rates of $400 or more per hour.

Judge Ruehlman walked out on the bench from his chambers, he looked out at everybody packed in his court and said, "Before I read this order, I want everybody to know, I don't want any faces, any rolling of the eyes, any sighs, any noise of any kind."

Ruehlman then began reading an 18-page order slowly and deliberately, his voice emphatic and strong. Every word during his twenty minute delivery seemed to be another gavel blow to the defense. None of the lawyers moved a bone. None of them made a face.

As nearly all judges in Hamilton County at the time, Ruehlman was a lifelong Republican, but earned a reputation for being sympathetic to victims. Today, nearly all Hamilton County Common Pleas judges are Democrats. Like most of the Republican courthouse machine, Ruehlman grew up in Cincinnati's conservative, mostly Catholic West Side. He was not a typical good Catholic boy, Ruehlman once said "he was the kind of kid other parents wouldn't let their kids hang around with." Ruehlman's wife once fought off a carjacker.

Months before issuing his order, Ruehlman encountered Joe Deters in a courthouse hallway and asked Joe how Ruehlman might help have the cases against Durrani in Hamilton County consolidated under his oversight. He wanted to help resolve them. On his courthouse webpage, Judge Ruehlman claimed he enjoyed mediating cases. Ruehlman's meeting and conversation with Joe was no secret. Judge Ruehlman summoned all the lawyers on both sides to his chambers one day and told them of his encounter with Joe Deters and made his pitch. We said yes. They said no.

The cases were scattered at the time among all fourteen Common Pleas judges at the courthouse. To obtain approval for the consolidation, Ruehlman needed Judge Robert Winkler, the administrative or assigning judge among the Hamilton County judiciary at the time, to sign an Order. We filed a proper motion to consolidate after Ruehlman's chambers meeting. For whatever reason, Winkler sat on our consolidation request for weeks and refused to sign the consolidation order. Had attorneys at Dinsmore & Shohl, the firm representing Children's Hospital, gotten to Winkler? A reliable source inside the courthouse told me just that. Ruehlman moved forward and signed the consolidation order himself.

Ruehlman knew from experience group trials worked in malpractice cases in Hamilton County. In the case *Suida v. Howard*, eleven patients filed separate suits in 1998 against a local eye surgeon, Dr. David Howard, for fraud and battery in performing unnecessary surgeries for cataracts and glaucoma. Ruehlman consolidated the cases into one group trial. The Court of Appeals upheld Ruehlman's' decision. The attorney for the victims in the case, Michael Barrett, would go on to be a federal judge in the Southern District of Ohio. Barrett, also a believer in group trials, applied it to the federal cases against Durrani.

In his ruling announced December 15, 2015, Ruehlman went far beyond simple consolidation of the cases under one judge. His order dramatically leveled the playing field for our clients. In summary, he ordered:

- Juries would be allowed to hear that Durrani was arrested and indicted on federal charges that included healthcare fraud and unlawful distribution of a controlled substance, that he promised a federal judge he would not flee, that sometime in December of 2013 he did flee to Pakistan and has not returned, and that he has refused to give depositions for trial.
- Jurors may consider all of these facts in their deliberations as evidence of Durrani's consciousness of guilt.
- The triggering event for Ohio's one-year statute of limitations on filing malpractice cases began with Durrani's arrest in July of 2013.
- "Increased fear of cancer" can be considered by the jury for non-economic damages to patients who were treated with BMP-2 or PureGen bone grafting material.
- All claims against all defendants will be handled in a single trial, but jurors will be instructed that they can't find against the hospitals on negligent credentialing and retention of Durrani unless they also find against Durrani.
- Testimony from treating physicians and other witnesses about Durrani's reputation in the medical community as a spine surgeon or their opinion on his character for truthfulness will be permitted.
- There will be no gag order on the Durrani cases. "The Court finds these cases by their nature, are and should be, of great public interest. The Court has experience in seating jurors in high-profile cases. Seating jurors in these cases, with or without publicity, is not a problem."

And the clinchers for us and our clients:

- Group trials are appropriate to the Durrani cases because all of them involve an allegation of unnecessary spine surgery. "The Court believes group trials save an incredible amount of time. It allows for one jury to hear the evidence avoiding countless jury selections, openings, closings, and repetitive witness testimony… Group trials save the parties time, taxpayers money, and give closure to all parties."
- The cases will be tried in three large groups on February 29, 2016; March 14, 2016, and August 1, 2016. All remaining cases will be considered in a fourth and final trial to begin on January 2, 2017 and completed, at the latest, by the end of the year.

In other words, all our Durrani victims would see their cases resolved within two years or less. I was ecstatic, but my euphoria wouldn't last long. Not to be outmaneuvered, the defense firms petitioned the following week to remove all the cases to federal court, citing a federal statute allowing the removal from county court any “mass action” suit of more than 100 clients and potential claims of more than $5 million. The removal had no proper legal basis, but it would delay matters for a year. The defense also appealed Ruehlman’s unfavorable ruling to the First District Court of Appeals, in what is called an interlocutory appeal, another delay move. They appealed first and then removed. It illustrates how much they feared Ruehlman’s Order.

In all the litigation moves the defense would make in Durrani litigation, only this move to federal court was not anticipated by me. The reason? It was ridiculous. Matt Hammer would always marvel how I predicted every move these “Super Lawyers” made. In the end, we would win the removal battle, but the delay would cost us. If we knew what would come, we would have left the cases in federal court. However, you must make decisions with what you know and after Judge Ruehlman’s Order, no lawyer representing Durrani victims would not want Judge Ruehlman. We could have never anticipated what wickedness Chief Justice Maureen O’Connor would level upon us.

Chapter 31

REINSTATEMENT

"I'm not the sort to back away from a fight. I don't believe in shrinking from anything. It's not my speed. I'm a guy who meets adversities head on."
—John Wayne

The Durrani clients know all about my battle against the Kentucky Bar Association and Ohio Disciplinary Counsel. They know I've done nothing to deserve the treatment I received. What the public doesn't realize is everyone in my "world" knows all the facts and therefore, they support me. Many reading this book do not know the facts. I want everyone to know all the facts and the truth. I've shared it all on my *Bulldog Show*, but most do not realize how evil the legal system is and how wrong they have treated me. Here is all of it. There is not one rational person who will read this and not conclude the KBA is evil for what they did to me. The Durrani clients have read it all. My "sin" has been to not genuflect to the KBA after my enemies tried to destroy me. Larry Forgy stood at the podium of the Kentucky Board of Governors and boomed with his deep voice: "Bar Counsel said lay down little catfish, we are going to gut you. And Bulldog said no. That is why we are here."

On May 17, 2016, I applied for reinstatement to the Kentucky Bar. I decided since they would not allow me to retire, I'll ask for reinstatement again. My reinstatement included a 19-page cover letter I signed under oath. It summarized my entire KBA saga. Therefore, here it is. Elizabeth Feamster was the attorney for Kentucky's Character & Fitness Committee. Here is my entire KBA story up to May 17, 2016. I'll give you the rest of the story later. Remember, I went through this crap while fighting the Durrani battle from 2013 to 2016 and counting.

RE: My Application for Reinstatement

Dear Ms. Feamster:

I believe a cover letter is appropriate for my application. I apologize for the length, but it is my entire argument. I sign this under oath. This letter is being submitted to Mr. Meyers as part of my application. My completed application with all fees and requirements has been delivered to Mr. Meyers. I'm copying all of this also to Ms. Herrick.

I know it's my burden to prove by clear and convincing evidence that I should be reinstated. I believe my application and this letter meets that burden.

I can prove by clear and convincing evidence of my character and fitness to practice law, that I am worthy of the trust and confidence of the public and that I possess sufficient professional capabilities to serve the public as a lawyer.

This is it. If I'm not reinstated, my attorney career is over.

If I read SCR 3.505 right, there does not have to be a hearing. I ask the Committee to reinstate me without one as soon as possible. If not, then under SCR 3.505, I request a hearing as soon as possible if Bar Counsel objects to my reinstatement and requests a hearing.

The burden is on me. Please allow me to attempt to meet that burden as soon as possible. The committee already possesses a file on me. I know I can meet it. If there is a hearing, my only witness, as last time, will be me. It's my life. It's my career. I will answer any and all questions honestly and forthrightly if there is a hearing. However, this letter I believe answers every question in advance.

If the Committee recommends my reinstatement, I will go forward through the rest of the process. If not, I'll stop. I'll be done. There is no way I can be reinstated with a negative recommendation. The Court followed this Committee last time. I'm confident they would again. My ENTIRE attorney future—is in the Committee's hands.

I want to stress. I'm through and been through, since 2013 fighting the Bar. When do I get let off the mat?

Under 2.300(7), my prior misconduct has been punished and I have paid a dear price. I have served two and a half years' suspension and counting (900 days) on a total of 240 days on four suspensions. The rule also states- "including the element of time elapsed." There is no misconduct past 2013 for which I have served my suspensions. This is 2016. EVERY day of this suspension I felt its pain.

There is a critical point I must make:

SCR 3.510(2) amounts to a disbarment if I'm not reinstated. There have NEVER been any requests to disbar me because there is no basis to do so. To not reinstate me is to disbar me. That is not fair.

I hope Bar Counsel does not oppose my reinstatement. I previously asked for their position because it was going to be factored into my decision to apply or not. Ms. Herrick kindly told me, and I accept, she could not comment or decide until she saw the application. I want to stress that my constitutional challenge to SCR 3.510(2) named Bar Counsel as a Defendant. Therefore, they can choose to be vindictive and object to my application, but they had to be a party to that challenge.

I would hope the Bar agrees I have been punished enough and deserve my license reinstated. There is irony that I can draft legal documents, but I can't sign them. I can draft arguments, but not deliver them. I think it gets lost that I was an attorney for nearly 30 years. From 1987 to 2012, I practiced without suspension.

What changed? I made enemies born by my successes. And, I admit I took the wrong approach with the KBA. I got arrogant and angry. I have been thoroughly humbled.

Under 2.300(6), I believe I am more than worthy of trust and confidence of the public; I possess sufficient professional capabilities to serve the public as a lawyer (I have for 30 years); although not challenged with their last objection, I exhibit good moral character on a daily basis. Every single day I put on a "brave and happy face" and battle through this. It is so hard on me physically and mentally. It's hard on my family, our staff and the firm's clients.

The three affidavits of Kentucky lawyers I am submitting are from my father, Larry Forgy and the only Kentucky lawyer besides my father at the Deters Law Firm, Stephanie Collins.

As I have explained in the past to the Committee, the Board and the Court, please don't be fooled by my "putting on a happy face" I put on, I'm dying inside. Every day. I have to fight every day to get through it all.

Under the rules:

Among the considerations to be weighted are:

The nature of the misconduct for which the applicant was suspended or disbarred.

The applicant's conception of the serious nature of his or her act.

The applicant's sense of wrongdoing.

The applicant's previous and subsequent conduct and attitude toward the courts and the practice, including the element of time elapsed since disbarment.

The applicant's candor in dealing with the Character and Fitness Committee.

The relevant knowledge of witnesses called by the applicant.

I address all of these directly in this letter.

ARGUMENT

I have been punished under SCR 3.510(2) beyond any rational basis. Because it is most important, I put my argument first and the procedural history second. I have lost my license in Ohio and Florida as a result of SCR 3.510(2). I have been financially ruined as a result of it. I had to transfer my firm to my eighty-six (86) year old father and work as a paralegal and office manager at the firm. My father pays my bills as my salary. I have lost millions of dollars. I had an 18-lawyer firm in 2013. No more. The Deters Law Firm now has two lawyers, three including my father.

I report to you that I have no pending charges against me. The day after my Sixth Circuit loss, I received a complaint which is baseless. I attach my response to that to the application. It's called Doug Hunter. I am confident Steve Pulliam and the Inquiry Commission will be satisfied with my response. I prefer revelation to the Committee rather than the Committee wondering what is pending. I have NO charges and this one complaint which I am confident goes nowhere.

The conduct relating to all my suspensions arose from 2003-2013. I stopped fighting Bar Counsel because despite having defenses, when I did, I got punished more. It makes no sense I believe for lawyers to be treated this way. But I capitulated. My bar issues involved being too overaggressive in the bar's judgement and my fighting back on refunding a few fees from a couple clients who I believe tried taking advantage of my past bar issues.

I would hope Bar Counsel and the Committee takes into consideration what I have been through and the magnitude of my punishment vs. issues.

Since 2013 and earlier, I have had NO issues on these types of issues.

My support group during my suspension has included: my wife; my father; Larry Forgy; my godfather, Larry Grause; my brother in law, Johnny Armstrong; my friend, Judy Phillips; my friend, Hamilton County, Ohio Prosecutor, Joe Deters; my friend, Bill Cunningham, 700 WLW radio and national TV show host; my friend Chuck Holbrook; my staff and the lawyers at the firm. In addition, knowing my children and grandchildren need me not to quit and give up, keeps me going. The Committee needs to understand the context of my woe. I was and am the rock for so many. Being without my license for nearly three years hurts so many. Unlike an attorney in a firm, I lost my firm.

In May 2015, I reached my worst point. In June of 2015, I began a routine of a daily hour walk on my Dad's farm with my wife, changed my diet, and began regular weekly meetings with all the above. It saved my life.

In 2013, I stopped fighting the accusations against me and ADMITTED misconduct even when I had defenses. Wanting a lawyer, especially a prideful, well-trained and experienced one, to not fight back is like asking a lion not to roar when the pride is attacked.

I have been contrite. (It is not fair to construe my legal challenge to SCR 3.510(2) as not being contrite. That rule is unconstitutional and unfair). I offered through Bar Counsel's counsel to drop my challenge in exchange for the Bar simply not opposing my reinstatement. They refused. I performed all which had been asked of me after my last reinstatement. I have not been given credit or the opportunity to return since all the ethics courses and audit of my firm. I have taken about 30 hours ethics since 2012. I had to attend CLEs all these years and to apply while not practicing. I've had to borrow money for cost and fees. My father is paying this.

I was candid with the Committee in 2013. I will be again. I think it was so unfair I had SCR 3.510(2) used on me back to back years. But it was. It has punished me beyond reason. I don't know what more Bar Counsel wants of me.

One can always find something wrong with someone. Always. Lincoln had enemies, flaws and endured attacks. I have lived my life. There is NOTHING in it I can't defend, and I'll do so with the God given talent I have to do so.

I have not committed any crimes. I have not stolen clients' money. I have not committed a dastardly deed or acted with moral turpitude. I don't have a drug, gambling or alcohol addiction. Only by exercise, diet and support have I fought off depression and ANY prescription medicine. I take none except for blood pressure.

If you have been a lawyer for 30 years like I have been, it's not fair that I have my career taken from me by a denial of my reinstatement. It's been my life. My calling. I ask for empathy, compassion and humanity from the Committee and Bar Counsel.

Going forward there is so much more I want to do as an attorney. I helped so many people and fought so many causes. I am needed by the public in my "neck of the woods." See attached summaries and details of my biography and career.

I know of so many lawyers who have been known to have done so many terrible things and have never been suspended a day. I look around and see myself where I am, and I can't believe it.

I have been scrutinized so much for so long. A futile but rational argument I have made is how could someone so scrutinized not reveal a scoundrel if I was one?

Bar Counsel can always find something I might have said or done I suppose. I'm a "sinner not a saint," but there is nothing which should deny me my license.

I do have First Amendment rights pertaining to politics and national issues. The Bar injected those in the process.

I of course don't know, but I still can't believe I was put back through the Committee back to back years after I was approved. Has that ever happened?

The reciprocity punishment with Ohio was so devastating. I tried to convince Ohio to not require it, but I failed. To be licensed in Ohio, I was required to take a three-day bar exam in 1988. They have different rules, attitudes and systems on discipline. I still think of a legal challenge, but I just want to be reinstated. If I am, I will ask Ohio to allow me to unretire. I was told when I had to retire, that can't happen.

There are so many intangible ways I have been punished. My daughter Erica became a lawyer. I told her to take the Ohio Bar and not Kentucky because I worried about her. She took a job in the prosecutor's office in Hamilton County, Ohio because my situation prevented her from practicing law in our firm. It's sad. She feels the stigma of her Dad being a suspended lawyer.

I'm so daily "frozen" in so many ways I can't do other things. I stopped writing books. This all hangs over me like waiting for a jury verdict for three years. Anyone knows who has waited for a jury verdict, that no matter what you have to do or need to do, you're paralyzed to do anything until the verdict.

The public doesn't need protection from me. I could produce thousands of letters of support. I have 30,000 social media friends. Would a thousand letters change what I have done and/or say as being all that matters? And, I don't want to have an investigation from every name mentioned like last time which delays the process.

I get attacked so unfairly by so many because they think, well he's suspended, we can say or do what we want. I had a tenant of a building I owned sue me when he defaulted on the lease and the news FALSELY reported that I ran up a bar tab of $10,000 and stiffed them. This remains on the front page of a google search! It's all not true. I attach the settlement agreement where they clear that up.

I deal with this kind of thing all the time.

Being suspended is the same as being branded with a Scarlet S. It should not be open season on the lawyer. That is exactly what has happened. No matter how many "hunters" shot and missed, they kept coming. The "punishment" is supposed to fit the "crime." The punishment was 60 days. It was not nearly a three-year suspension plus all the collateral damage. Massive media and internet coverage of my "Bar Battle" made the entire public aware of my woes and placed me in a very vulnerable position. Any enemy or client had "leverage" to go after me if they were the least bit disgruntled.

I decided to retire from Ohio to allow me to act as a paralegal on Ohio cases which required my immediate attention and involvement. I decided to retire in Kentucky simply out of the stress. But, while Ohio allowed me, Kentucky did not. They do not allow retirement if there is a single pending Bar Complaint.

The attached reflects the legal, business, professional and personal accomplishments of me before my suspension. Out of over one million lawyers tracked by Martindale Hubble in the country, I at times have been the #1 visited site by potential clients. I also have won awards from Martindale Hubble for client service.

I would like to stress I reference accomplishments solely to prove I was an excellent lawyer and a good person. I can't fathom how Bar Counsel can claim I'm not fit to practice law. These materials also reflect my style which endears me to my clients and the public. Do all attorneys need to have the same style? My style is not unethical.

These materials refute Bar Counsel's claims that I was not fit to practice law in 2013, 2014, 2015 and 2016.

There is humiliation, stress and uncountable effects from a suspension. This includes massive news coverage based upon my public figure status. The arbitrary power to extend the suspension by decree called an "Objection" increased my damages past the mere sixty-day suspension. In other words, a suspension is bad enough. To have it extended under an unfair rule is unbearable.

It is remarkable these are the rules of a lawyer organization. If any organization should have a sense of fairness, justice and due process, it is an association of those sworn to protect and defend the Constitution and advocate the rights of their clients.

The extended suspension is far more devastating than the suspension and it affects the following:

a. Client anxiety- It is wrong I have to inform a client that I had 60 days to serve, and then try to explain to them why I had more time to serve. Then explain it again and again as the suspension goes past a year on the "extended" suspension.

b. Deters Office- I solely owned my firm. Therefore, the office has been adversely affected financially from layoffs to debt. The name of the firm had to be changed. I had to transfer ownership of the firm to my father, an 86-year-old Ohio and Kentucky lawyer. The firm's income decreased nearly 90%. It survives solely on capital infusions by my father. The reason it is being maintained is the 523 Ohio cases against a Dr. Atiq Durrani who performed unnecessary spine surgeries on unsuspecting victims. I work on these cases as a paralegal.

c. Marketing- I could no longer market the firm.

Ohio has allowed me to act as a paralegal since my retirement.

I have suffered harm as follows:

1. Financial stress and great economic loss
2. Marital stress (proud it still survives)
3. Family stress
4. Office stress
5. Embarrassment
6. Less business
7. Unknown lost business
8. Increased bar issues
9. Open target
10. Could not market the practice.
11. Stress to clients transferred stress to me.
12. Clients are harmed by delay and/or I not being able to represent them.
13. Ohio retirement
14. Florida suspension
15. The unknown of not knowing if we would be reinstated.
16. Uncertainty
17. Near daily correspondence from Bar
18. Wondering what is next
19. Mental health
20. Physical health- high blood pressure for the first time.
21. Depression
22. Mood swings
23. Lack of sleep

24. Stress eating
25. Weight gain
26. Negative publicity
27. Many people assume I must have done something criminal for Bar Counsel to have objected. It's an unfair Scarlet Letter.
28. Victim of false rumors.
29. Enemies are emboldened and increase the attack.
30. I had to transfer my law firm to my father.
31. Counting 2012, I have served nearly three years in Kentucky, not ordered by the Kentucky Supreme Court.
32. The Objection to the Automatic Reinstatement also plants a seed of doubt in the Board of Governors, Kentucky Supreme Court and the Character and Fitness Committee minds that Defendants must know something really bad I must have done. It falsely poisoned and poisons me to those who have the power over my law license.

The list which follows is from the KBA and reflects all the Bar Complaints filed against me during my career and complaints defeated by me. I believe there could actually be more I defeated. Since 1987, these were produced from Bar Counsel at the request of me. Based on this list, there have been at least 67 Bar Complaints during my Kentucky legal career. However, most of these have come the last four years as a result of my rising legal career in Northern Kentucky as I became part time radio host on 700 WLW (the Cincinnati area's station with a national audience) and as I would be retained on one high profile case after another. My law firm grew to nearly twenty lawyers and thirty staff. This resulted in my enemies orchestrating serial Bar Complaints.

Of note, over 26 years since 1988, I have never had one formal charge of discipline in Ohio. I defeated 61 of the 67 of these Bar Complaints in Kentucky.

File #	12. 11594	24. 15745	36. 17997	48. 20391	60. 22126
1. 3960	13. 12186	25. 15859	37. 17941	49. 20635	61. 22217
2. 8492	14. 13442	26. 16014	38. 18005	50. 20657	62. 22300
3. 8810	15. 13993	27. 16024	39. 18131	51. 20855	63. 22325
4. 8858	16. 14217	28. 16037	40. 18809	52. 20856	64. 22342
5. 9193	17. 14836	29. 16396	41. 19343	53. 20984	65. 22501
6. 9575	18. 14838	30. 16754	42. 19366	54. 21423	66. 23077
7. 9593	19. 15535	31. 16795	43. 19711	55. 21438	67. 23124
8. 10360	20. 15613	32. 16858	44. 19964	56. 21637	
9. 10359	21. 15681	33. 17016	45. 19969	57. 21862	
10. 11026	22. 15672	34. 17094	46. 19978	58. 21980	
11. 11586	23. 15674	35. 17897	47. 20306	59. 22026	

Not one of these sixty-seven Bar Complaints involved dishonesty, fraud, theft, moral turpitude, any addiction or any dastardly deed. No lawyer in Kentucky has ever endured more punishment in defending baseless bar complaints. I have received zero benefit, credit or recognition of my having to defend and defeat 61 Bar Complaints. My approach has been hardline. It has had to be. Any disgruntled client would "blackmail" me knowing my "bar battle." They would say: "If you don't do XYZ, I'll file a bar complaint." I had no choice but to say go ahead or I would only face more "shakedowns."

MORE FACTS TO SUPPORT MY FITNESS TO PRACTICE LAW

In January 2014, I won a $1,040,000.00 jury verdict against a Dr. Durrani on behalf of a client named Crystal Pierce in a medical malpractice case in Hamilton County, Ohio. It could be the last verdict of my attorney career.

On July 11, 2013, I won a $338,000 jury verdict against a website on behalf of client Sarah Jones in a defamation case in federal court in the Eastern District of Covington, Kentucky which no one thought was winnable.

I still work 16 to 20 hours a day, seven days a week as a paralegal, the same as I did as a lawyer. As a paralegal, working with lawyers, I keep organized everything in 523 Dr. Durrani cases. I don't know any lawyer, much less paralegal, who could have done and does do, what I do. I have not had a vacation in four years. I'm too stressed to relax.

These are just a few of countless examples I could submit to illustrate my fitness to practice law.

Since June 15, 2012 I have:

A. Quit my daily radio show to focus on practicing law and later to work as a paralegal.

B. Stopped doing a daily newsletter.

C. Not publicly bashed bar counsel and the KBA. I may have made a lighthearted joke based upon the public knowing our past issues, but done nothing bad, mean or unprofessional regarding the KBA.

D. I completed 18 more CLE on top of the over 20 in 2012.

E. I provided countless amounts of free legal advice including for example, successfully trying for free a mother wrongfully accused of beginning a fight at school while she tried to protect her child from a bully. This is one of many examples.

F. I completed my anger management as ordered by the Kentucky Supreme Court in 2012. The Character & Fitness Committee determined, I argue, this entire Bar battle gave me anger issues. My anger management counselor upon hearing my "journey" actually stated—"I don't blame you. You have a right to be. Let's try our best to deal with it."

G. I did not fight the recent 2014 bar discipline involving sanctions and accepted punishment. In 2012, Bar Counsel said: "Punish him, he fights." So, in 2014 and 2016 despite having defenses, I responded with: "I accept responsibility, mercy."

Since June 15, 2012, particularly since February 2013, I was retained by over 523 individuals in state and federal cases, as well as, in the criminal prosecution of Dr. Durrani, numerous hospitals and two publicly traded companies involving unnecessary spine surgeries performed by Dr. Atiq Durrani. I and the office are successfully battling the largest law firms in Cincinnati. I and the office also have worked closely with the U.S. Government on the case. I had more medical malpractice cases and more civil rights cases than any lawyer in the entire Cincinnati area. I was the largest Plaintiff and criminal defense-based law firm in Northern Kentucky and Cincinnati. I was the third largest law firm in Northern Kentucky and won a Client Distinction Award from Martindale-Hubble. Yet, Bar Counsel used the weapon of SCR 3.510(2) to destroy me and publicly proclaim in back to back years I was not fit to practice law.

Since June 15, 2012 reinstatement, I did not have and do not have a single Rule 11 sanction and not one bar complaint/charge on the issue of a lawsuit filing without merit.

The lawyers at the office are overstressed and overburdened dealing with all the work on cases I would normally be handling. My workload was dumped on them. While less money came in, they had a bigger burden.

During suspension, the Kentucky clients were full of anxiety after I could not return in 60 days. It became a daily issue.

There is a complete disconnect with reality and humanity. Again:

1. I have not stolen money.
2. I have not committed crimes.
3. I do not have a drug problem.
4. I do not have an alcohol problem.
5. I do not have a gambling problem.
6. I do not have a porn problem.
7. I have not committed any acts of moral turpitude.
8. I have not had any more Rule 11 violations.
9. I have not committed any acts of legal malpractice.
10. I have not harmed clients.
11. I have a stable and good marriage.
12. I have a normal, wonderful relationship with my children, parents and friends.

I am no saint. I am a sinner. But I am fit to practice law. Lawyers are not a choral of angels.

I believe I am what every Kentucky person would want in a lawyer. I'm smart; I have common sense; I am personable; responsive 24/7/365; experienced; I fight for them within the confines of ethics and rules; I am honest; I work hard; I care; and I am a good person.

Even on the bar complaints I was found guilty, there was not one client who had their case hurt based upon the issue or dispute I had with them and them me.

I had what can be considered a career case in Ohio. I represented over 523 individuals who suffered the harm from unnecessary spine surgeries at several hospitals by a spine surgeon who was under federal indictment. I was their lawyer. The entire office continues working on the case as does I as a paralegal. The KBA Bar Counsel's action eliminated me as these clients' lawyer. The lawyer they chose. The lawyer who knew this case the best. The lawyer who won a million-dollar verdict.

I was the champion in the Cincinnati/Northern Kentucky area for those fighting bullying online and in the schools.

I was the champion in the Cincinnati/Northern Kentucky area for those abused and mistreated in jail or by over aggressive police officers.

I gave free legal advice and free representation to Veterans who couldn't afford it.

The 2012 ordeal put me on high blood pressure medicine for the first time and I remain on it.

Its financial, emotional, client related, staff related, family related, health related and everything related.

I would suspect never in the history of the KBA has a lawyer who has not committed any of those acts outlined earlier in this pleading has been pursued so vigorously by Bar Counsel.

Bar Counsel did not like my style of practicing or marketing. Nicknamed by the Cincinnati Enquirer, the Courtroom Bulldog, I seized upon the marketing potential and brand of being the Bulldog. I realized the public wants a Bulldog as a lawyer. I developed a logo and a brand. There is nothing about the brand which is unethical. It's obvious to me that the public wishes there were more Bulldog lawyers.

The Ethics and Professionalism Enhancement Program I completed in June 2012 meant nothing because KBA fails to consider me benefitting from it by being less aggressive.

As reflected by the attached, I have accumulated over 21 banker boxes of files. What is pictured is since 2009. I defended myself on these charges. Lawrence E. Forgy, Jr. volunteered without pay to assist. I of course receive no compensation for all my work on successful defenses. Had I paid legal counsel; it would have further bankrupted me. Millions in legal fees. To those who have said a lawyer who represents himself has a fool for a lawyer—they are a fool. I represented myself successfully 61 times and saved myself legal fees.

I have achieved the following:

a. Making full equity partner in Deters, Benzinger & La Velle, P.S.C., now Dressman, Benzinger and LaVelle. This was my father's firm.

b. Founding my own law firm, Eric C. Deters & Associates, P.S.C., now given away to my father as Deters Law Office.

c. My law firm had 18 lawyers working on my cases. I was the sole owner of the firm.

d. Sustaining marriage without divorce.

e. Raising six children who have mutual love and respect

f. I may be the only lawyer in Kentucky's history who has handled jury trials in Kentucky and Ohio in both state and federal courts, involving civil rights, medical malpractice, criminal, personal injury, employment, divorce, and nearly every area of the law.

g. While not being "fit" I never had a Bar Charge in Ohio where I have an office and more legal matters than in Kentucky. I had been representing Ohio and Florida clients during my Kentucky suspension.

h. The Ohio Justice Association (Kentucky Justice Association equivalent) asked me to join their Board. But I'm not fit for Kentucky? Then, since Kentucky extended my suspension, the Board revoked the offer.

i. I have countless published cases of legal significance, state and federal.

j. I was voted by 25,000 people who voted, the best lawyer in Cincinnati in 2010. These were average citizens who watched as I battled for my clients. I have won this award other years too.

k. I did countless hours of free legal work for the community and clients. I'm a credit to my profession, not a bane. I've won battles others thought impossible, such as the location of the jail in my county.

l. While fighting for my rights years ago against the Bar, I drew the ire of Judge Danny Reeves and endured a voluntary federal audit of my law firm by former Chase Law Dean Henry Stevens. This audit found me fit except it came with a recommendation of more care in case review. I agreed. There have been no issues since 2012 regarding our case selection. How many law firms have endured this type of scrutiny?

PROCEDURAL HISTORY

I must lay out my history and the SCR 3.510(2) issue because it is relevant to how I have been punished so past the pale.

My application is necessary because Bar Counsel used SCR 3.510(2) against me on back to back years, the latest being on October 25, 2013. As you recall, on April 7, 2014, I withdrew my application under stress and concern at the time it would jeopardize my Ohio license. I attempted to retire to avoid the stress and protect my Ohio license. It did not work.

I have served four (4) sixty-day suspensions from 2012 through now. The last two I did not fight. I have defeated nearly seventy (70) other bar complaints. It's mind boggling what I have been through. I was not allowed to retire so I had to keep facing discipline. I just stopped fighting them. My last suspension was up May 17, 2016.

SCR 3.510(2) used against me in 2013 is the objection forcing this application. Bar Counsel did not use the SCR 3.510(2) against me in my last suspensions, so it goes back to 2013. I must stress ALL those disciplines pending when they filed the objection have either been long ago: dismissed, dropped or I agreed to discipline as noted above. I believe this is important. The REASON for the last objection under SCR 3.510(2) on October 25, 2013 and the legal basis for it (other pending discipline), no longer exists.

The Committee when they reinstated me in 2012 did the right thing in that the Committee refused to consider other pending discipline because it had not been adjudicated. This signals to me that the Committee understands the flaw of SCR 3.510(2). Regardless, I stand before the Committee now with no pending discipline except one complaint under investigation which has no basis and I address it in this letter and my application.

After not being allowed to retire, I decided I might as well try to return. I decided I needed to challenge SCR 3.510(2) so it would stop being used against me. Who wouldn't in my position? It was used against me in back to back years. Why would I not think it would be used against me again?

I attach to this letter a simple summary how the rule, if constitutional is still unfair. I filed a federal challenge to SCR 3.510(2). The Verified Complaint filed January 5, 2015 details my entire KBA story. I have incorporated a significant part of it in this letter. I lost this challenge in the Sixth Circuit. I have filed an En Banc Motion. I also attach it to my application. I attach my Sixth Circuit Brief too which details my sound factual and legal arguments. Kentucky is the only state in the country with SCR 3.510(2) which does not involve a hearing first. It's one of only four states with such a rule.

I want to stress. A court deciding SCR 3.510(2) is unconstitutional does not make it fair. Also, the basis for the federal ruling is they shockingly conclude that under Kentucky law—a law license is not a property right or even a privilege which requires due process protection. This is contrary to U.S. Supreme Court case law, thus the En Banc Motion.

In 2012, as a result of Bar Counsel's objection under SCR 3.510(2) I had to apply for reinstatement in Kentucky, go through the burdensome, time consuming and expensive Character and Fitness process and I had to serve 52 more days than the 61 days ordered by the Court. In hindsight, I realize how lucky I was it moved so fast. I hope this application can as well.

In 2012, I served a sixty-one-day suspension by Order of the Kentucky Supreme Court. I received no credit for defeating fifteen of the nineteen charges. Prior to the sixty-one-day suspension ending, Kentucky Bar Counsel filed an objection pursuant to SCR 3.510(2) to my automatic reinstatement. This forced me through a reinstatement process. It began with an application and then later a hearing before the Character & Fitness Committee. The Committee voted 3-0 to reinstate me. The Board of Governors voted 13-0 not to reinstate me. The Kentucky Supreme Court on June 15, 2012, voted 7-0 to reinstate based on the Committee's recommendation.

In 2013, Bar Counsel blocked my automatic reinstatement for the second time in two years. Just a year earlier in 2012, I had gone through the reinstatement process and was reinstated. Despite the "seal of approval" by the Character & Fitness Committee and the Kentucky Supreme Court that I had the moral character and fitness to practice law, Bar Counsel "did it to me again" one year later despite there not being one new bar issue after my reinstatement. The 2013 charges preceded 2012. My finances, law practice, character and every facet of my life was reviewed in 2012 and I was reinstated. Yet, I was forced through the process in back to back years.

I believed it unconscionable to do it to me in back to back years with full knowledge nothing changed on October 23, 2013 when they filed the Objection. On October 23, 2013, Bar Counsel had no knowledge of a single fact which arose after June 15, 2012, when the Kentucky Supreme Court reinstated me, which justified the Objection.

On October 23, 2013, Bar Counsel objected to my automatic reinstatement despite my full compliance with the suspension. Attached is correspondence to Bar Counsel updating compliance and making the case Bar Counsel should not object to the automatic reinstatement. The correspondence reflects my fear Bar Counsel would do what they did in 2012 to me again.

On October 25, 2013, I sent a letter asking Bar Counsel to withdraw the Objection.

On November 6, 2013, Bar Counsel refused. They had to amend their application admitting I had completed the CLE requirements.

I applied for reinstatement again after the October 23, 2013 Objection and began the process yet again. However, unlike in 2012 when the process was expedited, the process moved slow. Unlike the fifty-two-day time period from Objection to Reinstatement in 2012, the matter before (52) the Reinstatement Committee carried into April 8, 2014 when a pretrial was scheduled. In addition, as it dragged, and the stress of the ordeal increased. I couldn't take it.

In addition, I felt growing concern of the political circumstances that if I wasn't reinstated in Kentucky, and based upon the reciprocity rules, I would never be reinstated in Ohio. I could not take that risk. Therefore, I sent written notice to the KBA clerk, the KBA executive director and Kentucky Bar Counsel that I retired effective immediately from the practice of law from Kentucky on April 7, 2014. I soon learned I could not.

I was trying to avoid Kentucky stress and to protect my Ohio law license. However, Ohio insisted on Kentucky reinstatement so I retired my Ohio license so I could work on Ohio cases which required my immediate attention and involvement. It was a terrible choice I had to make. My Ohio legal career or helping the firm's clients who needed me at least as a paralegal based upon the knowledge only I had about the cases. In the final analysis, I lost my lawyer career in three states based upon SCR 3.510(2).

I'll never understand SCR 3.510(2). It is as if the prosecutor in a criminal case, being dissatisfied with a Court's sentence, is allowed to force the Defendant to serve a longer sentence than ordered by the Court. It provides a prosecutor, Bar Counsel, the power to overrule a Kentucky Supreme Court Order before a hearing.

SCR 3.510(2) punished me twice in Kentucky for pending discipline matters before even being tried on those pending discipline matters. Subsequently, most of those matters would be dismissed before they ever became formal charges. So to make the point:

a. Non-adjudicated minor pending discipline was used under SCR 3.510(2) to punish me with the extended suspension by the Objection to Automatic Reinstatement.

b. Then, some of the non-adjudicated minor pending discipline used for the Objection is dropped. Using pending discipline which is later dropped to be used for the Objection proves in part how it violates due process.

c. Then, some non-adjudicated minor pending discipline is pursued as a charge. In my case, two of them would be used to suspend me for sixty days a year later in 2014, which means I was punished three times for this same discipline. The two 2014 matters were used in 2012 to Object to the Automatic Reinstatement. They were used in 2013 to Object to the Automatic Reinstatement. And, I was punished on them again with two 30-day suspensions. It is preposterous. How many times can someone be punished for the same conduct? Under SCR 3.510(2), I was three times.

If someone is found guilty of a felony and he is a persistent felony offender, the punishment can be enhanced. However, there are already felony convictions on those prior matters. Under SCR 3.510(2), Bar Counsel used non-resolved matters to punish me then used several of them to punish me three times. In 2012 and 2013, I had no other pending bar matters fully adjudicated through the Board of

Governors or Kentucky Supreme Court. Yet, these bar complaints were used to further suspend me before a hearing on those matters. Then, most of them would be dropped. It's a punitive and unconstitutional use of a bar complaint. It's used to extend a suspension without a hearing, but then dropped because it has no merit.

An analogy would be a prosecutor extending the sentence of a Court based upon other pending criminal charges which have not been adjudicated and then the prosecutor decides to drop the other pending charges.

The time for the Objection under SCR 3.510(2) is allowed to be up to ten days before the suspension is up. This allows Bar Counsel to leave me or anyone similarly situated with forty-nine days of anxiety followed by the despair of the objection. In 2013, by waiting for the last possible day, Bar Counsel inflicted maximum pain because it delayed me from the beginning of the reinstatement process as I did earlier 2012 from applying right away for reinstatement when they objected within the first ten days of the suspension.

They knew about the minor pending bar discipline from day one. They could have objected on day one. They chose to wait. They realized in 2012 they gave me a 50-day jump start to be reinstated. Also throughout the suspension, I repeatedly informed Bar Counsel of each step of my compliance and literally begged them not to Object to my automatic reinstatement yet again.

Under SCR 3.510(2), all Bar Counsel has to do is always keep a pending bar complaint "alive and well" against an attorney and they can use it to extend an attorney's suspension.

Because I was licensed in Kentucky, Ohio and Florida, any suspension and extended suspensions causes triple the pain because of the reciprocal discipline Ohio and Florida have enforced. I remain suspended in Florida, only thanks to Kentucky. I also have lost my right to practice in Ohio and Kentucky federal courts. The Objection to automatic reinstatement and the continued suspension actually resulted in me being suspended nearly a year in Ohio too before I decided to retire in Ohio so I could work on critical Ohio cases at least as a paralegal. This unfair rule directly ended my legal career in Ohio where I had over 500 cases at the time of my retirement and ended my career in Florida where I did have cases and planned to retire. In 26 years, I never had one formal discipline issue in Ohio or Florida. I would receive the same complaints in Ohio, I received in Kentucky. While Kentucky would turn them in to formal discipline, Ohio would receive, read and review my response and drop the matters. On a few matters, such as a fee dispute, they would be informally resolved.

I have now been punished three times for the same matters.

Bar Counsel placed in their 2013 Objection to Automatic Reinstatement that I do not "possess sufficient professional capabilities and qualifications properly to serve the public as an active practitioner." In 2012, Bar Counsel with no basis to do so, objected to my reinstatement also on a moral basis under the language of SCR 3.510(2). With zero basis, they made a morality charge against me. During the 2012 reinstatement process, they forced me to not only prove by the clear and convincing evidence I was fit to practice law, but that I was "moral." This from a profession filled with alcoholism, gamblers, prescription drug addicts and countless other addictions that are all treated better through programs than I have been treated. I want to stress this—Bar Counsel with no basis forced me to prove I was moral.

The magnitude of the harm caused to me by Kentucky by causing a suspension in Ohio in 2012 and extended suspension in 2013 is immeasurable and ongoing. Solely because of the Kentucky suspension, I was required do the following under the 2013 Ohio Order:

a. Serve 60 days in Ohio until March 27, 2014 and since not reinstated in Kentucky, I had to retire.
b. File a Notice of Disqualification in every Ohio case—(Over 350 filed cases.)
c. Send a certified letter to all my Ohio clients at a cost of nearly $3,000.
d. Not appear at depositions.
e. Not appear at hearings.
f. Not appear at Court.
g. Not practice law in Ohio.
h. Attend one CLE for every 30 day of my suspension.

CONCLUSION

My father worries that only because he has saved me from complete ruin, that Bar Counsel is not satisfied. If that's true, that's sad. I believe I have more than enough detailed the hell I have been through.

FROM THE MERCHANT OF VENICE BY WILLIAM SHAKESPEARE:

"The quality of mercy is not strained;
It droppeth as the gentle rain from heaven
Upon the place beneath. It is twice blest;
It blesseth him that gives and him that takes:
'T is mightiest in the mightiest; it becomes
The throned monarch better than his crown:
His sceptre shows the force of temporal power,
The attribute to awe and majesty,
Wherein doth sit the dread and fear of kings;
But mercy is above this sceptred sway;
It is enthronèd in the hearts of kings,

It is an attribute to God himself;
And earthly power doth then show likest God's
When mercy seasons justice. Therefore,
Though justice be thy plea, consider this,
That, in the course of justice, none of us
Should see salvation: we do pray for mercy;
And that same prayer doth teach us all to render
The deeds of mercy. I have spoke thus much
To mitigate the justice of thy plea;
Which if thou follow, this strict court of Venice
Must needs give sentence 'gainst the merchant there."

I ask for the mercy from Bar Counsel and the Committee in the form of expedited reinstatement.

I signed it under oath and had it notarized. I told the truth, the whole truth and nothing but the truth Almighty God. It meant nothing to them, and they would show no mercy.

Chapter 32

Desperation

"Iron is full of impurities that weaken it; through the forging fire, it becomes steel and is transformed into a razor-sharp sword. Human beings develop in the same fashion."
—Morihei Ueshiba, (Founder of Aikido)

By the fall of 2016, the stresses of fighting for my law license, fending off bar complaints, fighting off collateral attacks from everyone, coordinating hundreds of court cases, trying to raise millions of dollars to continue the fight against Durrani and the hospitals, keeping my team of lawyers and staff members paid and intact, and keeping alive the hopes of over five hundred clients against all delays, took a toll on me.

Thoughts of suicide out of spite and frustration began entering my mind. I'm a strong man. I'm one who doesn't need a pity party. I stopped exercising. I stopped eating right. In candor, I thought of suicide as a "middle finger" to the KBA and to lay down a guilt trip on my Dad who simply never "got it." Stupid weak thoughts.

Working late one night, I wrote this note.

> "Dad, I can't take it anymore. I have moved and directed these cases to near perfection. They couldn't be in better shape. But the stress of my Ohio suspension waits (I just want to quit) and the financial stress of the cases is just too much to take anymore. I'm sorry. I'm sorry. I'm leaving it all in your hands. I know you will figure it out."

I never sent the note. I decided to buck up, but Mary spotted it on my desk the next morning. It scared her. If she never saw it, I would have thrown it away. I regret I never tore it up that night and put it in the garbage can.

I kept guns in both my home and office. Mary hid the guns. She then called Chuck Holbrook to remove the one she knew I kept in my office. She called Dad asking him to talk with me. Typical Dad, he failed to show any emotion or consider speaking to me or express any concern. He didn't even call me. Mary told me she called him, so I called him and told him there was no issue. This is indicative of my entire relationship for fifty-six years with Dad. Me wanting to not disappoint him. Him being cold, distant and weird.

Jed figured Dad out. Dad would call his sons up on holiday summer weekends and moan about all the hay on the ground. Not one time did I ever say no. Jed told me, Eric, he's playing you. I would ask my son, Parker and his friends to help, but I had to pay them for working. Dad played me for fifty-six years.

Here is a public disclosure for the world who believes my Dad is Mr. Family Man with his eleven children. My last encounter with my Dad happened in the summer of 2020 in my driveway. He was in his truck and I was standing in my driveway, passenger side of his truck with his window down. *"Dad, how can you ever justify the pain you caused every one of your children by not one time ever telling them you loved them or were proud of them."* This is fact. Dad's Response: *"Why do they need my love or approval?"* My Reply: *"Because you are our damn father."* His reply: goofy face silence.

I wallowed in my self-misery and then decided to snap out of it. I would not let these bastards win and the victims lose. I began exercising, eating better and Mary and I began taking daily walks.

For several years, we took long walks every day after work, sometimes in the middle of the day. It helped our relationship, because when you're walking with somebody for an hour, you are also talking.

Randy McCafferty is former pastor of Independence Christian Church. McCafferty gave a sermon at St. Cecilia Catholic Church at a Thanksgiving Eve ecumenical service. He told a story about Winston Churchill. The story is Churchill dove into the Thames to rescue a small boy who played on the riverbank and tumbled in. Witnesses thanked Churchill for saving the boy's life. The next day, the boy and his mother showed up at Churchill's office. Expecting more gratitude, Churchill told his secretary to send them in. The mother walked in and asked, "Hey, do you know where his hat is?" The point: gratitude, not what else can you do for me. Impressed with Randy, I introduced myself after the service.

McCafferty and I later played in a donkey basketball fundraising game at Simon Kenton High School with community leaders pitted against the local high school athletes and cheerleaders. Randy and I proved adept at riding donkeys around a court and sinking baskets. When we looked at the score, we were behind. We realized when we scored, they gave our points to the high school team. Randy and I looked at each other and we were like, 'What the hell, man? Why didn't they tell us we're supposed to lose?'" We laughed. It didn't matter. All for fun.

Randy and I also developed a little "bit" we called *"The Lawyer and the Preacher."* The concept is viewing issues from the side of a lawyer and a preacher results in interesting conversation. I still love the concept and would love to do it with Randy. We also came up with a church concept. Hold a church service in a bar/restaurant while patrons drink and eat. Keep it short and sweet. I still love this concept to reach those who don't attend regular service. People like me.

Despite being a preacher, Randy was real. We lifted weights together in the early morning. We became best friends because we had so much in common from history, politics and life.

When the worst of my frustrations hit, McCafferty had moved to Louisiana as a Chaplain in the U.S. Air Force. He remains in the Air Force at the rank of Lt. Colonel. I called Randy, knowing he no doubt counseled others in a similar situation. Randy said, "Eric, I think you're going to be okay. Here's when I know suicide is real. When you plan it. When you literally say, 'I'm going to do X, Y, Z.' Have you planned it?"

I said, "No".

He said, "Well, you're not there yet."

If I quit, the bad guys would win. The other side would win. Too many people were depending upon me. I would not let them down. This issue never appeared again in my life and never will. Giving up is not my way. I want to include it in the story for two reasons: to encourage others and to show how much I carried on my shoulders and mind.

Chapter 33

Money

"Do not go gentle into that good night, Old age should burn and rave at close of day; Rage, rage against the dying of the light."
—Dylan Thomas

I sometimes forget the chronological order of my funds for the law firm in the Durrani battle. I believe Judy Phillips, owner of Stand Energy, lent me a large sum first. She charged no interest. After Judy, I borrowed a good sum from Christy Schoborg, who I helped when her husband died in a tragic truck accident. Christy is Sarah York's aunt. I'm lifelong friends with the entire family. Christy's loan by agreement was high interest. My brother-in-law, Johnny Armstrong, allowed me to max out one of his credit cards. We used this for filing fees and office supplies. My Dad funded after Judy and Christy. When Dad dropped out after two years, I needed another lender.

I met Dr. Lawrence Kurtzman, a prominent Cincinnati plastic surgeon, during my days at Real Talk radio, 1160 AM in Cincinnati. I began hosting radio at 1160 AM after leaving 700 WLW. While doing my radio show, Kurtzman aired commercials for his clinic. We met at the station and became friends. In January of 2015 and desperate for another infusion of cash to keep the Durrani cases going, I gathered up the nerve to call Kurtzman and invite him for lunch at *Maggiano's*, an Italian restaurant in the northeast suburb of Kenwood. "We caught up and talked, and I never saw the opening to bring up the loan request. I just got reacquainted. I hadn't seen him for a long time. But I never brought it up. I just had this sixth sense not to ask."

I followed up with a text. I said, "It was nice meeting you, blah, blah, blah." And then I said, "Hey, you know that Durrani stuff? I didn't bring this up at lunch but…" And so I brought it up. He said, "Well, let's meet again." And I met with him again, and he agreed to lend me funds to save the day.

Not long after, Kurtzman pledged more each month until I could find my next big contributor. The promise was enough to keep the Durrani battle afloat, but it would be tight, very tight. I'll always be grateful for Dr. Kurtzman being a "bridge" from my Dad to the next lender. He saved me.

Here is a funny money story. A young fan of mine from radio wanted to meet me. I met him for breakfast on a Saturday. A sharp young college student, he also had his own business. After breakfast, he asked me if there was anything he could do for me. I asked him if he had $10,000 to help me make payroll. He said sure. I borrowed the $10,000.

When you owe someone money, you should never ignore them. I never did. I always returned calls and texts. I had countless breakfasts and lunches with those who lent me money to keep them updated. I sent them constant email updates. I developed credibility with all my lenders. I gave them good news and bad news.

By March of 2015, with all the preparation for presenting the Julie Martin trial in June, our payroll grew. This forced us to reduce our staff of fifteen, laying off one employee and asking several others to begin seeking for work elsewhere.

On top of my own financial burdens, I dealt on a daily basis with clients, many of them families of the working poor who lost jobs or found themselves buried under medical debt because of Durrani's deception and butchery. They asked me for help to pay their mortgages and rent, keep their electricity on, buy medicines, even keep food on the table. In addition to outright gifts, I offered loans, free legal help defending evictions and foreclosures, and free advice on any legal issue. One client hit hard financially after his surgery and living on a small budget, I treated he and his family for a day trip to Kings Island Amusement Park to cheer him up.

Any client who lost their case, we assured them we would still include them and give them money from our attorney fees. I can assure you no lawyer ever takes care of clients who lose their case. I did. We did. It was a point of pride for me not to lose a client, and among the hundreds in the Durrani cases, the few we lost in the eight years of litigation would regret leaving us based upon their outcomes.

Much of what I do for my clients is considered unethical under American Bar Association rules, which prohibit "financial assistance to a client in connection with pending or contemplated litigation."

I have personally violated the rule a thousand times, and I don't give a damn. Durrani preyed upon the lowest social economic group. We only have like ten clients who I would consider well-healed. Durrani preyed on Medicare, Medicaid, poor people. They have foreclosures. They have evictions. We take calls all the time. We tell them, "If you start to get evicted, let us know, we'll help you." The financial blows these people have suffered is unbelievable. By July of 2020, more than forty of our clients filed for bankruptcy.

One client, whom Durrani frightened into two surgeries with a phony scan indicating a bone fracture, was arrested for shoplifting cat food. I agreed to represent him for free. Eventually, I was able to secure a pipeline of high-interest, short-term loans for needy clients through a company called Barrister Capital. Clients would pay the loan back with settlements, but these types of loans come with high interest. However, desperate people do desperate things and high interest is better than losing your home.

Nearly 220 clients took out loans, some multiple times. Each month, though, the interest grew exponentially. Sarah York kept in close touch with Barrister and the clients, tracking who had taken out loans and how much they owed, calculating the interest with each passing day. She created a spreadsheet to organize the data and to ensure each loan was paid back in a timely manner. Once the client received the settlement money, the firm paid off the client's loans out of costs so no more interest would be incurred.

During my reinstatement process, one of the issues they held against me is my willingness not to follow stupid, unfair or unjust rules. Helping desperate clients is an example.

Chapter 34
Deters Law Alone

"None of us will ever accomplish anything excellent or commanding except when he listens to the whisper which is heard by him alone."
—Emerson

With my suspension and our losing four cases in a row, I decided the time to hire a "gray haired" experienced medical malpractice lawyer arrived. I always said "I need a gray haired" lawyer. Why? Right or wrong, fair or not, a jury respected a "gray haired" lawyer more than a young lawyer. There are some exceptions. Straight out of law school, I had clients say to me, "we heard you were the best." Hell, I never tried a case, how could I be the best? Some lawyers, like some quarterbacks, have it. Most don't.

I knew Jim Triona from trying cases against him. Unlike most defense attorneys, he appeared in words, style and personality to be human. We always enjoyed our battles. He began losing his doctor group practice clients to hospital mergers. He also suffered a bitter partnership break up when David Lockemeyer and David Calderhead left him unexpectedly and unannounced while taking most the files and clients. After a couple of dinners at Brios, we discussed terms.

We soon reached an agreement on a salary plus a few other perks. What began as a promising collaboration, ended as a complete freaking flop. After six months, I soon learned Jim cared more with being friendly with his defense lawyer friends than beating them. We never tried a case with Jim. I've only done this one time in my entire life, I checked Triona's office email. Guess what I found? Jim Triona emailed opposing counsel agreeing to undermine our positions. I could not believe it. I busted him committing law firm espionage.

Outside of the betrayal, he also developed a memory problem. His short-term memory became an obvious issue.

I contacted Dad and received permission to fire Jim Triona. I drove over to the Cincinnati office and I exposed his treachery. We paid him for the rest of the year, generous considering what happened.

I want to add this. I still like Jim Triona. He's a good guy. He simply could not make the transition to our side. Unlike Hammer, Jim blew off the KBA when they contacted him about me.

On September 7, 2017, I fired Jim Triona and on September 8, 2017, Matt Hammer sent an email to inform the courts and the defense counsel. This was important, because we did not want them to believe we were falling apart.

Your Honor,

We want to advise you that as of last evening Jim Triona is no longer with Deters Law.

For several months, Jim has shown signs of dementia, which has exhibited itself with short term memory issues. Jim told us to be candid to everyone about this issue.

In addition, and we want to also inform you, Jim was also engaged from the outset, inappropriate communications with defense counsel, which could not be described in any other manner except disloyal. We suspected this for some time and were able to confirm it yesterday. We are sure he doesn't want us to inform you of this, but as the mediator we believe it's important you know.

Be advised we are good to go here on all fronts. We do not want you to perceive Jim leaving as a problem. It's not. It's a very good thing.

I am more than capable of handling motions based upon my knowledge of the cases. Jim did not handle any of the research, pleadings, motions, or related issues.

We will have outstanding trial counsel to assist me at trial. That's no issue.

Some of the defense lawyers amusingly expressed outrage we told everyone about Jim's memory issue. Jim actually saw a doctor, admitted it to us and gave us permission to inform them.

The legal profession does a lousy job with training lawyers. No profession is more mediocre than the legal profession. Law schools turn out lawyers who fear their own shadow. Lawyers do not know how to walk and chew gum. You would be shocked how few lawyers really could walk into a courtroom and try a case. I hired countless attorneys over the years, most frightened of their own shadow.

Over the course of the Durrani litigation, we tried working with several lawyers and law firms. We once approached our former partners at Deters, Benzinger & LaVelle, now DBL Law. One of our former partners, Dave Kramer had a relative with a Durrani case. I reached out to him. We arranged a meeting at our office. Jim Dressman and Dave Kramer came and met my Dad and I. After pleasantries, Jim and Dave expressed interest in becoming involved. They had so much interest they contacted St. Elizabeth Medical Center, their largest client, and obtained their permission to represent victims against other hospitals. The meeting ended amicably. My Dad and I informed Jim and Dave we would think about it. The next day, Jim called Dad. Their proposal involved their taking over and they would cut us in for a small percentage. They demanded I would have to be out because I would be "too toxic." To his credit, Dad told Jim I was too critical to the cause from the client relationships to my knowledge. We declined working with them. To this day, "too toxic" burns my ass.

I take delight in now having several class actions lawsuits against St. Elizabeth Medical Center and DBL Law.

Joe Deters recommended Joe Shay to me. Joe Deters arranged a meeting at this condo conference room with Joe Shay and Greg Hartmann, Shay's partner. I knew Greg as one of Joe's closest friends. Everyone likes Greg, me included. Glenn Feagan, Matt Hammer, Ben Maraan, Chris McCaughey and I attended the meeting. In five minutes, we all concluded we could not work with Joe Shay. He reeked of arrogance, condescension and the one idea he proposed was foolish on its face.

Tyler Thompson is a big shot and successful Plaintiff's lawyer from Louisville. A staff member arranged a meeting with him at Thad's Flying J in Walton, Kentucky. He expressed skepticism, and I had a bad vibe. He also was not an Ohio attorney.

I called my son's Godfather, Kevin Murphy, an attorney with an aggressive reputation like me. He seemed disinterested.

I met with Mike Allen, fallen former Hamilton County Prosecutor who resigned in scandal for an affair with an assistant. Mike lacked medical malpractice experience, but knew his way around the Courthouse. He rejected an arrangement.

I thought of high flying black criminal defense Hamilton County attorney, Clyde Bennett. He defended Tracy Hunter, the infamous fallen judge. Joe Deters vetoed that hire claiming the judges disliked him. To this day, I regret not hiring Clyde. I found Clyde Bennett willing, and it would have been fun. Clyde has been suspended twice by the Ohio Bar, but returned both times and still practices. His alleged sins were far worse than mine. Regardless, I like Clyde. No one has a better presence in court. He looks like an NFL safety, dressed to kill with a baritone voice and is fearless.

Mark Arnzen arranged for me to meet with Dick Lawrence, the tri-state's most reputable medical malpractice case attorney. Dick expressed willingness. I decided they would want to take over and our styles are too different. Also, I did not like Dick's daughter, Jennifer, his right hand. Based upon Jennifer, I declined. Dick and Jennifer would end up suing each other over their law firm. Dick retired. Fortunately, we never placed our cases in that mess.

Judge Barrett suggested we engage David Kamp to help us. This made me laugh. The few Durrani cases David Kamp had he malpracticed. He never sued the hospitals, not even Children's, Durrani's employer. Also, at the request of Mike Lyon, Kamp stood down on his cases and waited after Durrani fled. Then I learned Kamp's law practice received referrals from all the large law firms, including Dinsmore. Then Joe Deters told me David Kamp served as his divorce mediator. Kamp now actually practices law at Dinsmore. We threatened Kamp to save one case he handled before it came to us. Remember, Mel Gibson's nemesis in *Lethal Weapon*, Cotton Top played by Gary Busey? I nicknamed Kamp "Cotton Top" (because of his white hair) and disliked him as much as I disliked "Cotton Top."

Bill Robinson, Northern Kentucky Bar President and the Kentucky Bar President, actually won election to the President of the American Bar Association. How many lawyer asses do you have to kiss to achieve that goal? He was the epitome of a bar lawyer, not my kind of man. Bill actually law clerked for my Dad in law school. Bill would join a group of other lawyers and literally join and try to lead every possible civil organization which existed. Climbing is an understatement.

In the early 1980s, Bill's law firm actually challenged the Deters, Benzinger & LaVelle firm in a game of flag football. Bill's firm showed up in uniforms on a Saturday morning with names on their jerseys. We showed up in sweatshirts, sweatpants and ragged clothes like normal men on a Saturday. I played quarterback and we destroyed Bill's team ten touchdowns to two. The two were at the end of the game when I benched myself after it being 10-0. Bill called our managing partner the following Monday to complain about my "behavior", arguing calls with him. Gerald Benzinger, to his credit, just laughed at him.

I battled Bill once in a dental malpractice case. I won. Bill's office was told never discuss the case again. I told everyone.

To poke fun at Bill's election to the American Bar Association, I formed the United States Bar Association and made myself President. I posted it on my website and announced it. Congratulations poured in.

The following story is representative of the character of most lawyers. After Kentucky suspended me, Larry Forgy, my dear friend, told me this story. Marcus Carey served as the Northern Kentucky Bar Association Ethics Hotline lawyer. "*Have a 'sticky' issue? Call Marcus and get his opinion. Even if wrong, you're protected if you act on his advice.*" I always got along with Marcus. He spoke out on Republican causes and stayed active in politics. However, I sensed some radio envy when I filled in on 700 WLW. After my suspension and without informing me, Marcus Carey, my "friend," called Larry Forgy and asked Larry to help Marcus take all my Durrani clients. As a loyal friend, Larry reported it to me. How is that for Mr. Ethics? Marcus Carey would have sold out the Durrani victims the first week and would never be able to finance it.

Now you understand a little more why I hate the legal profession and they hate me. I carry it as a badge of honor.

Chapter 35

"The Great Migration South"

"Perseverance is the very hinge of all virtues."
—Thomas Carlyle

In November 2016, Matt Hammer and Ben Maraan phoned me at the Fox 19 building offices after the Saturday morning meeting they attended in Butler County with Judge John Bessey and all the other Durrani litigation lawyers and delivered the bad news.

Outside my office on the fourth floor, I paced back and forth in the hall on my cell phone talking to them. They told me Judge Bessey announced he would continue all of Guckenberger's rulings. Same instructions to the jury, same everything. Right then and there, an idea came to me. Let's dismiss our cases in Butler County and re-file them all in Hamilton County. This would cost us a hundred thousand dollars. I didn't care. When you're dealing with the value of these claims, what's a hundred thousand dollars? Inadvertently, the judges copied us on Monday on an email talking amongst themselves how they thought how crazy of a move this would be.

In this litigation, we adopted the golden rule. The golden rule? If the other side does not like it, it must be good for us. It's been 100% true. I also study and practice strategy from all of history's generals including Sun Tzu.

Under Ohio Civil Rule 41(A)(1), often referred to as the "one dismissal rule," a plaintiff is allowed to unilaterally dismiss a civil complaint against a defendant "without prejudice." This means you can refile the same complaint any time up to a year from the dismissal. We originally filed the West Chester Hospital cases in Butler County based on West Chester's location. I learned after the filings the parent company of West Chester, UC Health is based in Hamilton County. This gave us legal basis for what we called "The Great Migration South." We would take the unprecedented act of dismissing and refiling over one hundred lawsuits in Hamilton County. It's probably never been done anywhere or anytime in America. Dad approved my plan on my recommendation, as did all our clients.

We decided Hamilton County could not be worse than Butler County. Even more promising, Hamilton County Judge Robert Ruehlman, consolidated under his oversight the one hundred and fifty cases already filed there.

The move promised to be costly. $500 for each filing in Hamilton County for a total of $125,000. We decided to refile all 250 cases as a single lawsuit for $500, which saved us over $100,000. We also refiled ten cases for out-of-state clients in federal district court based upon what is called diversity and sparing them the Butler County death spiral.

To handle the filing and motions for our federal cases, we contracted with Robert Winter, a 65-year-old attorney who retired in 2011 from big firm lawyering to become an independent attorney. He once worked for Taft, who would represent Medical Protective on the insurance issues. An ex-Navy submariner from Pittsburgh, Winter was a big man with a 1950s politeness. He shook hands and introduced himself to everyone he met, including restaurant servers with a cheery, "Hi, I'm Bob Winter." His often used greeting when asked how he was: "Hello, my collegial friends. I am litigating my way into the hearts and minds of my enemies today." Once working for a federal judge, Bob is an encyclopedia of all the rules.

Winter became a consigliere for me. While I was a legal creative daredevil, Winter always gave me the nuts and bolts of a move. We drove each other to anger at times, but it worked and still does to this day. Bob is my friend.

I hope you have seen the Matt Damon movie, *The Martian*. I watched it when it premiered in 2015 and it really inspired me. In the movie, Matt Damon's character is stuck on Mars. He must complete incredible tasks to survive and return to Earth. After he completes a task, another problem appears that requires his conquering. He focused on each task alone as they came. He focused on what appeared before him. I learned to do that every day and simply solve the problem in front of me. For ten years and counting I have done this. Every day it would be a judge, a ruling, client issues, staff issues, money issues or the bar association. I simply fought through each one as they came. I have lived in that state of stress for ten years and I still do. The result? As Larry Forgy said, "Deters is tougher than a pine knot." I expect a "punch" every day, but I buck up and say to myself "solve it." Can you imagine the creativity, strength and speed you acquire going through life like that? Well, I have honed those skills. I have made myself a problem solver extraordinaire. I know I could run any company, run any state and even run the country. I happen to be running for Kentucky Governor. Bob Winter is running for Circuit Judge.

Based upon Dad's abandonment, I had thirty days to find a new source of money, or I would fail to meet the payroll for my staff and attorneys. This worry plagued me for many months to come. Dr. Kurtzman filled this void. In the decade, I never missed payroll one single time. I recall a couple times I delayed payroll a day. Maria Dallas and I came to call it "cash flow by bitch"; we paid debts only if a creditor or accounts payable "bitched." It required a constant search on my part for new sources of money.

At one point, I drove Dad downtown for a mediation meeting with Guckenberger. I parked at a meter on Fourth Street and put in my credit card for a two-hour session. The meter rejected my card for $1.83. I began laughing and turned to Dad and said, "This is what my life has become." Sometimes you cry, sometimes you laugh. To everyone reading this, please know that I know how each and every one of you feel to be broke, have a credit card rejected and fear where my next buck is coming from. I lived it a long time. It required me to lose my pride and embrace humility. The prize of success kept me unashamed.

Before we made the decision to dismiss and refile over 200 cases, we researched the law. What did we find? The law allowed it. In fact, there was an Appeals Court decision directly on point. So, we took the extraordinary action. The Ohio Supreme Court later ruled we were wrong on the 41(A) dismissal issue. It was and is an incredibly wrong decision. Justice Judy French wrote the decision. Maureen O'Connor voted with her. It would be French's last decision and then off she went after being defeated in her race to become Chairman of the Ohio Public Utilities Commission and make $250,000 a year. Another example of a political gangster. They claim they love "public service." Bullshit.

From day one, we argued the Ohio statute that stayed all statutes of limitations if a doctor left the state applied. Durrani left the country. It was not until a Motion for Reconsideration on the Rule 41(a) issue defeat before the Ohio Supreme Court, the Court by one vote sent it back to the First District for a ruling on the issue. Maureen O'Connor voted against the decision despite the law being clear as a deer runs fast.

The First District would then agree with us and Durrani's 2013 flight stayed any statute of limitations or statute of repose. The First District incredibly ruled it didn't apply to CAST. All of this is now before the Supreme Court at the date of publication for them to decide to allow the First District decision to stand or to decide the issue.

The statute reads:

> Section 2305.15: Tolling During Defendant's Absence, Concealment or Imprisonment
>
> (A) When a cause of action accrues against a person, if the person is out of the state, has absconded, or conceals self, the period of limitation for the commencement of the action as provided in sections 2305.04 to 2305.14, 1302.98, and 1304.35 of the Revised Code does not begin to run until the person comes into the state or while the person is so absconded or concealed. After the cause of action accrues if the person departs from the state, absconds, or conceals self, the time of the person's absence or concealment shall not be computed as any part of a period within which the action must be brought.

This meant when Durrani fled in December 2013, everything froze in time on any statutes limiting the time frames to file a lawsuit.

The First District of Court of Appeals covers Hamilton County, Ohio. Their current members are Judge Marilyn Zayas, Judge Beth Myers, Judge Pierre

Bergeron, Judge Candace Crouse, Judge Robert Winkler and Judge Ginger Bock.

Not one of them is our friend. Crouse would later write a decision upholding my contempt. It made zero sense. I publicly stated she had the mental agility of a small soap dish. The KBA used that one against me. Meyers and Winkler are part of Joe Deters' world. Meyers came from a large law firm. Pierre Bergeron possesses a great intellect and is probably our best hope.

The Ohio legislature passed a law outlining when hospitals could be liable for not properly credentialing or giving privileges to a doctor or keeping that doctor around when they should kick him out.

The part that applied to the hospitals Durrani issue is as follows:

Plaintiff may rebut this presumption against negligence by showing, by a preponderance of the evidence, any of the following:

(c) The hospital… through its medical staff executive committee or its governing body and sufficiently in advance to take appropriate action, ***knew that a previously competent individual had developed a pattern of incompetence or otherwise inappropriate behavior***

(d) The hospital … through its medical staff executive committee or its governing body and sufficiently in advance to take appropriate action, ***knew that a previously competent individual would provide fraudulent medical treatment but failed to limit***

There was no question West Chester Hospital should have never given Durrani privileges or kept him around. Children's should have never kept him around.

What did the legally challenged Ohio courts do?

The Ohio Courts simply considered this statute, despite completely different elements, the same as a medical malpractice case. It is absurd.

For a negligence/medical malpractice case, a victim must prove by the preponderance of the evidence (tip the scales/greater than 50%) that a doctor deviated from the standard of care and the deviation caused harm to the patient.

The statute has nothing to do with malpractice, but that's not what the Court concluded. The legal elements in this statute are not the same as a medical malpractice case. One of the purposes of this book is to expose how corrupt the Ohio court system has been to these Durrani victims. It's my opinion, these Judges believed they could help their healthcare friends and no one would ever learn of it or care. I hope this book leads to them being proved wrong.

Another "soap box" issue of mine for many years is simply because one obtains office or high position does not mean they are smart, fair or just. Judges are no exception. Any American "paying attention to the public servants" today know what I speak of.

Chapter 36
Stan Chesley

"Eric, remember all the dogs without the bone
want to take it away from the dog with the bone."
—Stan Chesley

In January 2014, I never saw the lobby and offices of Stan Chesley in the Union Central Tower downtown Cincinnati as empty as when Dad and I walked off the elevators of the fifteenth floor.

A lone receptionist met us and took us back to Chesley's lavish quarters. No one but Chesley still made the place their office. Chesley sat us in the living room area adjoining his desk space. Chesley looked no different than before his fall from prominence as one of the nation's leading class action lawyers. Same expensive gray suit and red tie. Same starched white shirts and cuff links. Same manicured nails. He spent the next hour regaling us with his legal triumphs.

One story Chesley failed to tell us is one Joe Deters told me. Stan and Joe tried a case against a railroad. A man became completely disabled in an accident. Stan turned down millions to settle, then lost the trial. In opening statements, Stan forgot his client's name.

Chesley became a legend in the legal world of Cincinnati and the nation as a pioneer in the crafting of class action suits. A former shoe salesman, he came to fame representing the victims and their families in the 1977 Beverly Hills Supper Club fire. One hundred and sixty-five died and another two hundred were injured long before the blaze was extinguished. Chesley blamed the fire on faulty aluminum wiring.

Chesley's Beverly Hills lawsuit was the first to create a class action by pulling together large numbers of victims in the same suit with a legal concept called "enterprise liability", which held unrelated people and corporations jointly liable if they could be tied to the resulting harm. Chesley used the electrical wiring theory to secure a settlement for victims. In recent years, mob related arson has become a more plausible reason for the fire.

Chesley also led the cause against Pan Am over the Lockerbie terrorist attack and against Dow Corning for its troubled silicone breast implants. In 1998, he served on the steering committee or "inner circle" of lawyers who negotiated the $246 billion tobacco settlement on behalf of state governments. In the 1980's when I "gophered" at Dinsmore & Shohl, Chesley battled Dinsmore in the Rely tampons toxic shock syndrome cases. I copied countless exhibits for Dr. Frank Woodside of Dinsmore & Shohl, who defended P&G.

In 2010, Chesley's illustrious career came crashing down after he negotiated the settlement in a class action suit against Wyeth Pharmaceuticals, the manufacturer of Fen-Phen diet pills. The pills spurred a national weight loss craze until they were linked to heart valve problems. Former clients in the fen-phen suit sued Chesley and three other victims' attorneys. The lawyers took more of a fee than they were entitled to and set up a phony victim's trust fund on top of the fee fraud. Two lawyers went to jail. Another lawyer won his trial with the defense that he was too drunk to know what was going on. Chesley testified. I believe the only reason Chesley was not charged is that his wife, Susan Dlott, is a federal judge.

Roy Cohn, the New York power lawyer, once said *"I don't want to know what the law is, I want to know who the judge is."* It's true. Joe Deters told me Stan Chesley had a "chamber practice" and so did Joe Deters. I asked, "what is a chamber practice?" Joe said it's when you go back in chambers and talk to the judges. As Hamilton County prosecutor, Joe got away with this all the time. In 2011, Kentucky disbarred Chesley and he chose to retire in Ohio rather than face a reciprocal disbarment.

More than an hour into our meeting, Chesley at last began dispensing the advice we sought. He simply affirmed what I already knew about the case including gather all the clients you could. "Numbers matter," he said. Why? Because hospitals fear big numbers. We had over five hundred clients and we could use that for leverage.

Chesley only wanted to control the litigation and benefit from it, not help. He refused my request for $250,000 in financial assistance. I would learn later from Joe Deters he would regret his decision. Like me as a retired lawyer, Chesley could have been an advisor to us as a consultant.

Chapter 37
Our Team

"Courage is contagious. When a brave man takes a stand,
the spines of others are often stiffened."
—Billy Graham

Winning a medical malpractice case requires competent and credible experts. I already introduced Wilkey. For the first ten trials, Dr. James Cole, a local neuro-radiologist, became a hit with juries while demolishing Durrani's interpretations of scans and X-rays. The defense never retained a local expert to defend Durrani. This fact reflects the egregious nature of Durrani's conduct. Usually, a local doctor is able to find local experts. Durrani's defense relied on "whores" they flew in from California to testify. "Whores" meaning willing to testify to anything for money.

I once used a California expert. I'll never forget Frank Benton, a medical malpractice defense lawyer saying to the jury in closing arguments: "As I sat here, I wondered how many states Mr. Deters had to fly over to find his expert: Ohio, Kentucky, Indiana, Missouri, Arkansas, Kansas, Nebraska, Colorado, Utah, Nevada and finally California." I wanted to crawl under the table. Great argument, Frank. I never used a California expert again. Durrani only used California experts with few exceptions. I told our lawyers how Frank Benton used this little bit on me and we used it too. Imitation is flattery. Frank Benton is the attorney who connected me to Dr. Cole.

Before we hired him, Cole only served as an expert once and it was for Mike Lyon defending a doctor. Cole also worked at St. Elizabeth Medical Center now. Cole, salt of the earth, could not be touched on cross examination. We could argue not only did Cole work at a Cincinnati area hospital, but even Lyon gave him the "seal of approval."

Anxiety of the battle proved too much for Cole. We replaced Cole with Dr. Ranjiv Saini, a radiologist from South Carolina and licensed in twenty-eight states, proved authoritative and effective. In addition to being paid $15,000 every time he testified, Saini insisted on being put up in luxury hotels, picked up at the airport, and reimbursed for the smallest expenses, including parking meters. I tease him he's a "prima donna," but he's our prima donna. He does a great job for us and the victims. He's an outstanding expert. He's also engaging outside of court. He's a fun LSU college football fan. Of course, all Cincinnati Bengals fans are now LSU fans.

At the suggestion of Jim Triona during his brief tenure at the firm, I hired Dr. Stephen Bloomfield, a university-based neurosurgeon who devoted himself to the health of coal miners in West Virginia for eighteen years. A New Jersey native, Bloomfield was tall, lanky and bespectacled.

In high school, Bloomfield played in a rock band. In college, he hitchhiked all over the West before settling into medical school. At *Woodstock*, Bloomfield helped run the "mushroom tent" for concert-goers on bad acid trips.

"The Wiley One" as I called him, would lull the defense into traps and endear himself to jurors. He was quick on his feet in the witness box. We became friends over steaks and fries from *Walt's* when he came to town. He's an outstanding expert.

The logistics of preparing over five hundred cases for trial would have strained the largest law firms with hundreds of employees, much less the five lawyers and ten full-time staffers at Deters Law. Filings needed to be filed on time and then carefully tracked through the court system. Defendants required served promptly with summons.

Sarah York updated lists and lists of lists, over three hundred, including contact information for clients and experts, depositions and their schedules, the status of affidavits of merits, bankruptcies and deaths of clients, and trial verdicts and schedules. Thirty to fifty discovery questions from the defense for each case had to be answered as soon as possible. Defense firms have no interest in speeding cases toward trial; in fact, with delays, they make more money. For the victims, delays mean added expenses. The burden is on us to keep the cases moving forward through the court system.

A victory at trial did not mean a case was over for us or our clients. Defendants appealed the verdicts, leading to more attorney fees and tying up the victim's compensation for years.

In every Durrani case, Defendants filed hundreds of motions with the clerk of courts. A motion is a word used for a request.

In a normal lawsuit, the court would rule on post-trial motions within a month of the jury verdict so the case could move on to the appellate court. In the Durrani cases, over our objections, the court often took more than a year to rule on post-trial motions. The long delays not only kept the victims from receiving their just award, but encouraged the defense to continue their delay tactics.

We created a system that we used in the Durrani litigation. It worked as follows:

- Office staff Maria Dallas, Mona Eldridge, Alexa Kavanaugh and Brittany Pillman requested the clients' medical records and bills from doctors and hospitals.
- Kimberly Kelly reviewed the records and prepared a chronology of each case going to trial, pulling pertinent documents. She also made lists used at trial consisting of: condition before and after Durrani, potential witnesses and a summary of the malpractice.

- Sarah York took Kelly's information and filled out a template for experts to review, then prepared a PowerPoint opening statement for trial. York indexed the medical records and exhibits, preparing them in tabbed binders for easy access, creating two copies, one for the court and one for our team. She sent them to the defense prior to trial. York printed and boxed the defense exhibits, maintaining complete organization in preparation for the trial.
- Christina Rutter went through the medical records and pulled the most critical ones.
- Shelly Bagby summarized the depositions for the lawyers.
- The experts were sent all the medical records and our clients' depositions.
- York and I prepared the experts for their testimony. York handled scheduling the experts for their trial testimony and made all their travel accommodations.
- If the defense filed a motion to dismiss a case, Jim Maus researched and responded. My first cousin, Jim, worked as a federal public defender in Guam and as an attorney in Texas and Minnesota before joining me. He's an excellent researcher and writer. He's been with us long enough to have knowledge valuable to his work.
- Sylvia Derrien, Bob Winter, and Jim Maus performed legal research and drafted the documents for filing with the clerks of court. Sylvie, Alan Statman's lawyer employee, moved to Texas but still works with us. She's an outstanding secret weapon. She can research and draft with the best of them.
- Bob Winter handled the filings and research for the federal cases and for the state appeals.
- Ben Maraan was the lead lawyer on all court filings. He reviewed, edited and approved everything the firm filed.
- Kavanaugh answered the discovery requests from the defense.
- Loretta Little, a legal secretary, kept our calendar of deadlines, filed all court documents and scheduled depositions and meetings.
- Statman and Maraan handled the trials. Alan the lead. They handled motions, arguments, and trials. Alan and Ben took the information the team prepared and used it in the courtroom.
- Sabrina Cain photographed and video interviewed the Durrani victims.
- I managed the entire operation and prepared the initial voir dire questions for jury selection, the opening and closing statements and scripts for witnesses. The trial lawyers modified them as they saw fit.

York created a template distilled with the overlapping facts of the cases against Durrani we used for opening and closing statements for each trial. We modified the templates for the case specific facts.

York ensured all trial preparation occurred on time. She contacted clients before their individual trials to make sure they were prepared. Each client reviewed their deposition testimony.

We created a well-oiled machine so efficient Alan Statman and Ben Maraan learned to trust on the first day of the trial all was in order and ready to go. They only needed to show up with the box for the case. They took it from there.

Chapter 38

Missed Opportunity

"The success of any legal system is measured by its fidelity to the universal ideal of justice."
—Earl Warren

On November 15, 2016, I picked up Dad from his home in Walton, Ky. and drove to the scheduled mediation in the office of Federal Judge Michael Barrett at the downtown Cincinnati federal courthouse. We planned a "global" mediation with lawyers for all of the Durrani defendants present: hospitals and Medical Protective. I possessed high hopes. With Ruehlman's ruling a year earlier leveling the playing field, I believed we would receive a reasonable settlement for the Durrani victims from Medical Protective.

As I exited the interstate into downtown Cincinnati, an email alert came through on my cell phone. I looked at my phone as I pulled to stop at a light. The press release came from the office of the Ohio Supreme Court. Chief Justice Maureen O'Connor pulled Ruehlman off the Durrani cases.

I pounded the steering wheel. "Fuck!"

"What is it?" Dad asked.

"They got to her! They got to O'Connor!"

The year before, the Ohio Supreme Court allowed to stand the Court of Appeals decision keeping Ruehlman on the cases. The defense filed a request to remove Ruehlman and it failed.

Having lost once on the same issue, the Durrani and hospital lawyers, filed another request to remove Ruehlman. It was absurd. The Court of Appeals agreed. On the second appeal, the Supreme Court decided to take up the case and ruled in favor of the defense. Explain that? You can't except corruption.

The Court argued Ruehlman acted improperly in signing the consolidation order because he was not the court's administrative judge at the time. It was a procedural nitpick. Administrative judges are appointed for one-year terms to handle the assignment of county court cases. Judge Robert Winkler was Hamilton County's administrative judge at the time. Winkler ignored our request from the victims to consolidate the cases. We filed a proper motion. It was not our fault Ruehlman signed the consolidation order. So after the Court of Appeals twice and the Ohio Supreme Court once ruled what Ruehlman did was fine, now it was wrong. It is completely unexplainable except corruption.

"Of all times!" I shouted. "The fucking worst!"

"I knew something would happen," Dad said. Dad was always for claiming knowledge after the fact and denying blame or fault. He is the worst person you ever want in a dog fight or in a fox hole. I have never once in my entire life heard my Dad admit he made a mistake or strengthen an ally. He always blamed someone else, too.

I slammed the steering wheel again. "Fuck!"

Just as I expected, our appearance at the mediation proved fruitless. The defense lawyers received the same press release from O'Connor.

Before I dropped off Dad at the mediation, Joe Deters called to share the same news from the Ohio Supreme Court. I insisted the mediation go forward, but it was a lost cause.

On that day five years ago, O'Connor ruined an opportunity to resolve all the cases with Medical Protective.

Chapter 39

Death and Trials Over Forty Years

"In our sleep, pain that cannot forget, falls drop by drop upon the heart, and in our own despair, against our will, comes wisdom through the awful grace of God."
—Aeschylus

Between the Kentucky Bar Association, Kentucky Bar Counsel, Kentucky Bar Board of Governors, Kentucky Supreme Court, Judge Mark Schweikert (being introduced to you soon), Judge Chuck Kubicki (a coming attraction), Ohio Disciplinary Counsel, Ohio Supreme Court and the local media who covered all their actions against me, one might conclude I was a lawless, unethical criminal. Google me. See for yourself. Fortunately, through email lists of clients, friends and fans and my use of social media, those who counted in my life knew the truth and ignored all of the attacks and efforts to destroy me. I learned to focus on my core supporters.

All of those referenced in the prior paragraph became so obsessed with me they cared more about what they perceived I was doing, had done or would do, rather than justice for the victims. It is an indictment of all of them. They hated the one person who stood in their way of a steam rolling of Durrani victims. You can ask Glenn Feagan, Jim Maus, Alan Statman, Larry Grause, Mark Arnzen, Bob Winter and any lawyer who knows our side of the story, they will all tell you no lawyer or law firm would have stayed in this battle and achieved the success we would have, but me. It is an honor.

My refusal to allow those in paragraph one to vanquish me, shut me up or accept their corruption without a fight resulted in their being more aggressive towards me.

From day one to now, I explained everything to the Durrani clients, so they knew the system was the problem, not me. The clients could care less I no longer possessed my law license so long as I kept fighting for them in the capacity allowed.

Chief Justice Maureen O'Connor knew Durrani victims were dying waiting for trials and did not care. The following are those who have died so far at the date of publication, seventy-nine of them:

Louise Bayliss, Antoinette Benjamin, Leona Beyer, Barbara Boggs, Nancy Boland, Deena Borchers, Gerald Botner, Randy Brewer, Carrie Britten, Eileen Brorein, James Brown, Patricia Bruce, Annette Buskirk, Timothy Byrd, Barbara Couch, Jackie Couch, Margaret Dailey, Ollie Deaton, Holly DeClair, Darrell Earls, Connie Ellington, Robert Ellington, Tony Falkner, Neil Favaron, Troy Fite, Donna Good, Lisa Hall, Jade Hamby, William Hayes, Heather Heffner, Evelyn

Helton, Lois Hughes, Connie Huser, Irene Hyde, Dillon Jones, Phyllis Judkins, Sarah Juergens, Linda Kallmeyer-Ward, Christopher Knauer, Adrian Lilly, Rhonda Mains, Paul Marksberry, Jeff McClure, Junior Monroe, Gary Neu, Gail Nordeman, Kenneth Pfetsch, Jeff Potts, Lawrence Pridemore, Sharon Pritchard, Marcia Quinn, Todd Ray, Jane Reeder, Holly Reifenberger, Harry Reynolds, Jason Riley, Donna Rister, Dorothy Rose, Fay Rosebery, Kathrynn Rueve, Carson Rutter, Delores Scott, Gregory Shott, Crystal Slone, Billy Spivy, Michelle Stephens, Clara Tubbs-Hill, Kimberly Underwood, Michael Watkins, Daniel Webber, Regina Wesley, Violet Whalen, Tamathy Wilder, Jetton Wilson, Terry Wilson, Teresa Worley, Leah Wright, Veronica Yeakle, Evelyn Young.

Based upon what our medical and legal team knows about each of these cases, Durrani's unnecessary surgeries and treatment played a part in their deaths. They each died never receiving the opportunity to take the stand and tell their story to a jury.

Why would O'Connor not care?

Everyone in the law business of medical malpractice and personal injury knows a deceased client's claim is not as valuable under the law as a living suffering victim. The reason is the deceased is no longer suffering and juries generally award less to an estate than a living victim. Remember John Travolta's character in the 1988 *Civil Action* movie explaining this in the beginning of the movie as he wheeled his client into the courtroom? Travolta nailed it.

The spouse and/or children or the parent of a child would receive whatever a deceased person's estate would recover.

In addition, I believe O'Connor saw it as a sick way to unfairly pressure us to take a lousy settlement by believing we would do so before more died.

Victims have a constitutional right to an expeditious trial. O'Connor trampled on this right. After ten years, hundreds of victims will still not see a courtroom until over a decade passes. It is unacceptable.

Every Judge, except Judge Robert Ruehlman, the only duly elected judge who had the cases, violated the Ohio Supreme Court rule to close a case in three years. Ohio gave us no remedy to their neglect.

In an attempt to keep the cases moving in a timely manner, we tried to fix the consolidation issue. However, Judge Ruehlman, the Chief Judge in 2016, and Judge Marsh, the Chief Judge in 2017, now feared O'Connor. My source? Joe Deters. All Judge Marsh needed to do was sign an Order consolidating the cases to Judge Ruehlman. She refused. Judge Ruehlman no longer wanted them.

The largest and most powerful law firms in Cincinnati and their clients are not only the largest and most powerful Cincinnati employers, they represent the largest and most powerful lobby in Ohio: the healthcare and insurance industry. They all contributed to Chief Justice Maureen O'Connor. Columbus, Ohio, where the Ohio Supreme Court sits is the insurance capital of the world—State Farm, Allstate and Nationwide.

After O'Connor removed the consolidated cases from Judge Ruehlman, the cases were distributed back to the active fourteen Hamilton County Common Pleas Judges who began to set them for trial.

Meanwhile, the victims suffered on every level: physically, mentally and financially. We fought their battle with extraordinary time, money, resources, risk and stress while Durrani and the hospitals benefited from tentativeness and delay. The hospitals operated their businesses without a hitch during the litigation. The law firms rewarded with incredible legal fees based upon their self-serving recommendations.

For ten years we stood with over five hundred clients calling, texting, emailing and messaging in need of our assistance with medical treatment referrals, desperation, evictions, foreclosures, collections, hopelessness, wanting to give up and take their own life, pain, medicine issues, relationship issues, divorce and death.

Justice and fairness for Durrani victims should have never been this difficult.

What follows is a lot of detail of what happened in Hamilton County, but it's worth the read to show the corruption. I also want the world to know how we have truly tried everything. We took nothing lying down.

In November 2014, we moved to consolidate the Durrani Hamilton County cases.

On January 29, 2015, a Consolidation Order as we have explained was entered and signed by Judge Ruehlman, not Judge Winkler.

On August 15, 2015, the First District Appeals Court dismissed the defense's appeal of the January 29, 2015 Order.

On August 26, 2015, the Supreme Court affirmed the First District Order by not accepting it.

On November 12, 2015, the First District Appeals Court dismissed the next attempt by the defense to remove Ruehlman. This was just another "trip up the ladder" with the same issues.

The defense filed their appeal to the Ohio Supreme Court on November 12, 2015 the same date the Appeals Court ruled in our favor. The Supreme Court granted it in November of 2016, one year later. The tragedy of that Order? It was the morning of the scheduled mediation. If the Order was a day later, the cases may have been settled. To this day, we do not believe it is a coincidence.

Judge Guckenberger, Chief Justice O'Connor's appointment, handled the cases from Butler County at the request of the Butler County Common Pleas judges and he scheduled one trial at a time.

Judge Bessey, appointed by Chief Justice Maureen O'Connor to replace Judge Guckenberger stated his intention to follow everything Judge Guckenberger ordered. We dismissed the cases to Civil Rule 41(a) and refiled them in Hamilton County. Judge Bessey transferred his remaining forty-four cases to Hamilton County, which we could not Rule 41(a) based upon the cases already being dismissed and refiled once.

After the Judge Ruehlman's consolidation came apart, we accepted the duly elected fourteen Common Pleas judges less those few who recused. Many of these judges made clear their intention to keep the cases, set them for trial and move them forward towards a resolution. Several judges told Ben Maraan this at status conferences on the cases he covered. Trials were set in April (Mann) and June (Potts) with Judge Ruehlman. Ruehlman, regardless of the consolidation issues, still had six or seven cases. He set them for trial.

On February 2, 2017, Judge Melba Marsh, out of the blue, signed an Order stating as follows:

In light of this Court's pending request to the Chief Justice of the Supreme Court of Ohio to assign a visiting judge to oversee and manage the multitude of Durrani cases currently pending in Hamilton County, it is hereby ordered that all active future court dates and all pending motions are hereby stayed and held in abeyance until the Chief Justice appoints a visiting judge or denies the request. Counsel of record will be notified promptly of the Chief Justice's decision.

This Order stopped the Mann and Potts trials going forward in Judge Robert Ruehlman's Court in April and June 2017. The Potts trial would be continued at least three times.

On February 2, 2017, Melba Marsh, after her order, wrote the following letter to Chief Justice O'Connor:

Re: Request for the Assignment of a Visiting Judge to Oversee Durrani Cases

Dear Chief Justice O'Connor:

I am writing you in my capacity as the duly elected 2017 Administrative Judge of the Hamilton County Court of Common Pleas, General Division, and as the Presiding Judge of the Hamilton County Court of Common Pleas.

As you know, you previously appointed a visiting judge at the request of the Butler County Court of Common Pleas to handle the numerous medical malpractice lawsuits that were filed in Butler County against Dr. Abubakar Atiq Durrani, the hospitals where Dr. Durrani performed surgery, and other Defendants. Hamilton County currently has 267 active Durrani cases, many of which have been transferred from Butler County or dismissed in Butler County and re-filed in Hamilton County. In addition, there are a handful of cases where hundreds of plaintiffs are included under one case number. The Deters Firm, who represents many Durrani plaintiffs, has indicated in their filings that they represent roughly 500 Durrani plaintiffs in Hamilton County cases.

Currently, three of the 15 Hamilton County Common Pleas General Division judges have recused themselves from a Durrani cases. All of the remaining 12 Hamilton County Common Pleas General Division judges are assigned Durrani cases.

Many of the motions filed in the Durrani cases that tough on consolidation reveal that attorneys for both sides agree that having a single judge manage the cases for discovery purposes and to rule on common questions of law such as the statute of repose, has merit. In my opinion, however, it would be difficult if not impossible for any sitting Hamilton County Common Pleas judge to oversee all of the Durrani cases even for preliminary purposes. Even with the Durrani cases distributed among the 12 judges who have not recused, the number of plaintiffs and potential number of trials in these matters will disrupt the court's dockets and might result in inconsistent rulings. Given the volume and complexity of the cases, the ongoing transfers of additional Durrani cases from Butler County, and to avoid inconsistent rulings, duplicate proceedings and unnecessary costs and delays, I am hereby requesting that you assign a visiting judge to manage the Durrani cases.

I have consulted with each of my colleagues who are currently assigned Dr. Durrani cases, and all 12 judges agree that the cases should be heard by and assigned to a visiting judge. For all of the foregoing reasons, I hereby respectfully request that you assign a visiting judge to oversee all of the Durrani cases currently pending in Hamilton County as well as any Durrani cases that may be filed in or transferred to Hamilton County.

We knew this to not be true. Why? Joe Deters told me Melba Marsh told him Chief Justice Maureen O'Connor called her and told her to request a Special Judge.

On February 2, 2017, Matthew J. Hammer sent a letter copied to all counsel and to Chief Justice Maureen O'Connor which states in its entirety:

Dear Chief Justice O'Connor:

On behalf of 528 Plaintiffs, we object to Judge Marsh's request. Our clients have had their justice delayed long enough: four years. We had cases moving now, as reflected by the attached calendar. Assigning a Visiting Judge would delay trials and justice for another year.

What's really frustrating is that the cases were consolidated under ONE judge for a year and they would have ALL been tried or in trial right now. The Order attached.

What is most shocking. Everything Judge Marsh states is why we asked the cases to be consolidated under ONE judge in the first place. The Defendants objected to consolidation before any judge. Also, not one Judge we have been appearing before indicated a desire to give up their cases.

The judges of Hamilton County should keep these cases. They are equally divided among the judges.

We reserve the right to supplement this. We wanted to object immediately.

On February 3, 2017, Matthew J. Hammer sent a letter to Chief Justice Maureen O'Connor, copied to all defense counsel which stated in its entirety:

Dear Chief Justice O'Connor:

This is a follow up to our letter late yesterday afternoon based upon the importance of the issue and our inability to know the Court's time frame for responding to the request.

It also is as the advocate for the 528 Plaintiffs who have filed cases with affidavits of merit. We ask for the Court's understanding of our obligation on their behalf to advocate their position regarding Judge Marsh's letter.

Before outlining the history, we want to make our main points which the history supports:

1. Any action by the Court which delays trials is not fair to the Plaintiffs
2. We strenuously object to the Court appointing a visiting judge without all the party's consent.

The Plaintiffs have a right to have their cases decided by duly elected judges by voters in Hamilton County who have been randomly selected for each case.

For the Court to appoint a judge or judges to decide major issues means the Court decides the course of the litigation by the person it chooses. We are not naïve. WHO is chosen matters. Unless the parties and their counsel AGREE, the Court should not force a judge upon the parties and counsel over the duly ELECTED judges.

There are 12 competent elected judges managing their Dr. Durrani cases just fine as indicated by the rolling calendar we keep and we provided yesterday.

Neither party was asking for Judge Marsh's request. In addition, as we stated yesterday, we were the one advocating consolidation from the beginning. After the following history, we state our suggestions and recommendations.

On February 17, 2017, Maureen O'Connor appointed retired Judge Jennifer Sargus to "hear cases involving defendants Abubakar Atiq Durrani, et al, and to conclude any proceedings in which she participated." Based upon our inquires with attorneys who practiced before her, we concluded Judge Sargus would be a fair judge to the Durrani victims. From northeast Ohio and Belmont County, Sargus is also married to a federal judge from Columbus, Ohio.

On February 27, 2017, Matthew J. Hammer sent a letter to Chief Justice Maureen O'Connor copied to all defense counsel, which stated in its entirety the following:

Dear Chief Justice O'Connor:

We met with our clients this past week. They had a lot of questions regarding Judge Marsh's request. We had copied it to them and our response. Our clients are justifiably feeling mistreated that after consolidation is dissolved and they accept going forward with twelve elected judges, there is now a request for a form of consolidation with a visiting judge.

This has failed twice before. A visiting judge is not answerable to anyone but you. They are paid by the hour and have no incentive to move the cases along. If they come from another area of the state, time and distance is an issue. Finally, they have to catch up on all the issues. Furthermore, it is hypocrisy we sought consolidation, the defense fought it, and now they don't oppose a visiting judge. The fact the defense does not object to a visiting judge further proves our point. They are for anything which delays trials.

Our clients deserve better. Their trials have been delayed for years by the defense. As we mentioned in our prior letter, there is no reason the twelve (12) judges could not meet and agree on rulings on all major issues. Or, pick from one of their midst a "lead" judge to hear the arguments and decide.

The attached list of 55 cases were not only set for trial multiple times, discovery was closed and is over in each case. There are requests in front of these twelve judges to set these for trial right away. The Mann case is set for trial on May 15, 2017. The Wright case is set for June 26, 2017. We have filed Motions to Lift the Stay on these before Judge Marsh.

We are also filing Motions to Lift the Stay on the other 53 cases which need to go to trial ASAP. The results of which will probably end this entire litigation in a settlement favorable to one party or the other.

On March 6, 2017, Matthew J. Hammer sent Judge Melba Marsh, copied to all defense counsel the following email:

Your Honor:

Based upon the attached appointment of Judge Sargus, we have a question if you know the answer. Is she handling everything to the exclusion of the Hamilton County judges or is she going to oversee the cases with the assistance of the Hamilton County Judges?

We never received one response to any of our letters to Chief Justice O'Connor and Judge Marsh. The Chief Justice had every option of communicating to all parties and express how she would ensure impartiality. She refused.

On April 18, 2017, Deters Law provided five binders of requested information on the Durrani cases to Judge Marsh for Judge Sargus.

On April 19, 2017, Deters Law provided a letter to Judge Marsh responding to Defendants' materials.

Without explanation, after six months and holding only one status conference, Judge Sargus resigned and O'Connor appointed Judge Mark Schweikert, an Ohio Supreme Court lobbyist with the state Judicial Conference that the state legislature defunded and disbanded. Schweikert was Chief Justice O'Connor's lobbyist to the state legislature. His entire career is one of Republican Party political appointments in the court system. He sat for election for a Hamilton County Common Pleas position once and won.

When Schweikert retired from the Ohio Judicial Conference, Chief Justice Maureen O'Connor stated as follows:

"On behalf of my colleagues, it is an honor to recognize his dedication and diligence on behalf of the Ohio Judicial Conference as its executive director for the past 10 years. Mark's experience and insight into the judiciary ensured his leadership of the Judicial Conference would be meaningful and effective. Not only was he a tremendous resource for judges, but also for legislators, as they sought information and understanding of Ohio's judicial system.

"Mark's experience and insight into the judiciary ensured his leadership of the Judicial Conference would be meaningful and effective," O'Connor said. "Not only was he a tremendous resource for judges, but also for legislators, as they sought information and understanding of Ohio's judicial system.

We concluded Judge Mark Schweikert was someone Chief Justice Maureen O'Connor believed she could trust to handle the Durrani cases to the advantage of Durrani and the hospitals. This became clear by the rulings on cases and the manner and method of his trial scheduling. Judge Schweikert was appointed by O'Connor. He answered to O'Connor.

The legislature O'Connor referenced in her Schweikert praise is the same legislature who passed the statute of repose.

This is a sampling of the victims' thoughts on all which took place:

Email from Durrani Victim on December 1, 2017:

"They continue to feed my fire! The way I feel now... I will never settle with this scum and I will never keep quiet. It comes from the Fed, our justice system, Medtronics, the daily suffering in a county that could care less and the complete lack of coverage by local media. This is how people with money corrupt our news and justice system. How many years does it take to get a case in court? JOKE! As far as I'm concerned, should stop wasting his time. Schedule the damn trials. Everything has been appealed! There is nothing stopping these trials from continuing. No one is on our side! How many years have you been at this? Just flat out sad! Unconstitutional."

Email from Durrani Victim on December 1, 2017:

"Doesn't seem to me that any judge wants to work very hard on anything... especially on this case. No wonder people are fed up with our judicial system. Victims of this kind of crime, and to us, it is criminal, are treated worse than any criminal. This is getting to the point of comedy, it's a shame there is nothing we can do to force these people to do their jobs. Most of us would be fired for dragging our feet in the real world. Rant over."

The Chief Justice holds broad powers to control dockets in Ohio. No one is more powerful in Ohio except the Governor. O'Connor has never used her power to help the Durrani victims.

Chapter 40

Judge Mark Schweikert

"A judicial system is corrupt if truth is denied the right to be a witness."
—Suzy Kassem

Mark Schweikert grew up on the conservative West Side of Cincinnati. He earned his law degree from Northern Kentucky University's Chase College of Law. He also earned a reputation as a weak man who often scurried home from court or "his wife would kill him" if he was late for dinner. He told this to Alan Statman in open court. I spoke to a law school classmate of Schweikert's who told me Schweikert possessed all the characteristics as a Nazi asshole even then. Schweikert was such a "boy scout" that a county prosecutor once quipped, "He's probably never peed while taking a shower." Ruehlman once shared a story from his youth. While driving his car too fast as usual, a young female passenger asked Ruehlman to stop. She exited the car filled with other teenagers and walked home. This very sensible young woman would later marry Mark Schweikert. If she preferred a boring stiff, she got one. I'm confident Schweikert has no traffic tickets.

Schweikert claimed a long history of service to the Republican machine that dominated the Hamilton County Courthouse for a century. He served as Hamilton County Municipal Court administrator from 1981 to 1995. The perfect paper pushing bureaucrat job. In 1995, he gained an appointment as a Municipal Court Judge. In 1999, he secured a Hamilton County Common Pleas Judgeship. In 2002, he won the election to that seat. Joe Deters told me once that Schweikert, after being passed over a judicial appointment, literally cried in Joe's office. Joe Deters also claimed Melba Marsh thought Schweikert would be the right man for the Durrani cases and that he "would be fair." After a failed bid to become Hamilton County's chief administrator, Schweikert retired from the bench in 2006 to become the Executive Director of the Ohio Judicial Conference (OJC), the lobbying voice of Ohio's 700 judges. Schweikert lobbied for Ohio's health care providers in that position. We made a freedom of information request and obtained all we could from the OJC on Schweikert.

Schweikert and O'Connor served on the OJC's executive committee as Ohio began enacting the toughest laws in the nation restricting medical malpractice suits. A massive industry-financed advertising campaign claimed frivolous malpractice suits responsible for soaring health care costs pushed the legislation. In 2003, Ohio's Senate Bill 281 capped jury awards for non-economic damages; added penalties if a claim wasn't filed in "good faith"; and enacted a one-year statute of limitations on filing claims. Subsequent rulings by the Ohio Supreme Court reaffirmed these laws.

In 2003, I wrote an op-ed column for *The Kentucky Post* opposing these laws from the perspective of what I satirically called a "greedy" trial lawyer: "I represent American citizens who through the negligence of others have lost children, parents, spouses and friends. Many were lost when a doctor prescribed the wrong medicine, missed a cancer on an X-ray, failed to treat an obvious life-threatening illness or simply didn't care enough to order a simple test."

As I pointed out in the piece "greedy" trial lawyers receive no pay if we lose. In a prophetic statement, I wrote: "More money is wasted in the legal system from doctors and hospitals refusing to accept responsibility for their mistakes than from 'greedy' trial lawyers."

Mark Schweikert, a career political bureaucratic hack straight from the other political hacks, took over our Durrani cases.

Chapter 41
Corrupt Ohio

"Liberty lies in the hearts of men and women.
When it dies there, no constitution, no law, no court can save it."
—Learned Hand, Supreme Court Justice

In 2003, the Ohio legislature passed a limit or "cap" on the amount of compensation a court or jury could award a plaintiff in a medical malpractice case. Ohio's cap applies only to noneconomic damages: pain and suffering, emotional distress and loss of enjoyment of life.

The healthcare industry bemoaned noneconomic damages as "subjective" because they tend to vary from plaintiff to plaintiff, and they're not so easy to capture with a dollar amount. This is bullshit. Why? These damages should be subjective. Economic damages can be calculated from loss of employment and income, past and future medical care, lost earning capacity, and other financial losses stemming from the malpractice.

Under Ohio law, noneconomic damages in a medical malpractice case may not exceed the greater of $250,000 or $500,000 if the injury is proven permanent or catastrophic.

This means that if you suffered the loss of an arm or leg at the age of twelve or became paralyzed as a result of malpractice, then a jury may not award you more than $500,000 for pain and suffering. It is absurd. Actually, juries are not told about the caps. The system allows the jury to award what they believe under the facts. The Court subtracts after the trial any amount over the caps.

With guidance from Schweikert's OJC, two key Ohio Supreme Court decisions, *Ruther v. Kaiser* in 2012 and *Antoon v. Cleveland Clinic Foundation* in 2016, upheld a new law further restricting victims to file medical malpractice claims. Ohio had a short one-year limit for filing claims that began once victims knew of their injuries. Under what is known as the Statute of Repose, victims could no longer sue for injuries after four years, regardless of whether they knew about the injury or not. The Statute of Repose had the potential to restrict a hundred of our Durrani cases in Ohio. In Kentucky, the state Supreme Court already threw out a similar law as an unconstitutional violation of victims' right. You understand this America? One state through the political make up of its Court, finds a law unconstitutional and another state finds it constitutional. The Ohio Supreme Court before O'Connor also found the statute of repose unconstitutional.

To understand the quid pro quo of Ohio's medical malpractice system, you have to follow the money. According to data from *FollowTheMoney.org*, of the

$3.8 million in campaign donations toward O'Connor's elections to the Supreme Court since 2002, O'Connor received nearly half from the large law firms and medical and insurance industries for a total of $1.8 million, including $86,000 from the lawyers defending Children's. Based at the University of Montana, the non-partisan research group tracks the voting records of elected officials across the country and their campaign donations.

The unknown are sources of "dark money" spent toward O'Connor's' elections including ads financed by groups of anonymous donors not directly involved in her campaigns. Dark money now accounts for about forty percent of all spending in Ohio Supreme Court races according to *Justice at Stake.*

O'Connor maintained over the years campaign donations do not affect her decisions. What a bunch of poppycock. In 2006, a *New York Times* study found that Ohio Supreme Court justices ruled in favor of their donors in seventy percent of cases. Unlike a dozen other states, including Michigan and West Virginia, Ohio has no system to force judges to recuse themselves from litigation in which their donors are involved. As a result, "they don't step away from cases that many ordinary people would expect that they would," said Catherine Turcer, executive of *Common Cause* of Ohio.

This is from O'Connor's *Wikipedia* page:

O'Connor's political career began out of Summit County, Ohio. O'Connor earned a bachelor's degree at Seton Hill University, Greensburg, Pennsylvania in 1973 and a Juris Doctor degree at Cleveland State University Cleveland-Marshall College of Law in 1980. In 1981, O'Connor began practicing law in Summit County, Ohio. In 1985, she was appointed a magistrate of the Summit County Probate Court. She was then elected as a judge of the Summit County Court of Common Pleas, serving on the bench from 1993 to 1995. In 1994, she was elected to the office of Summit County prosecutor and served in that office from 1995 to 1999. In 1997, O'Connor received "The Cleveland State University Distinguished Alumnae Award for Civic Achievement."

In 2002, O'Connor won her first election as an Ohio Supreme Court justice after insurance-backed campaign ads warned insurance premiums would soar if she weren't elected to control medical malpractice claims. Two years later, O'Connor was a featured speaker at a "Future of Medicine" summit sponsored by the Ohio State Medical Association. They held the summit seven months after the passage of Senate Bill 271, which set new limits on medical malpractice cases. OSMA President Tim Maglione boasted that the bill "was the most comprehensive tort reform package to pass in this country in the last twenty years." He then brought "attention to what some believe is a much more important matter. Will the Ohio State Supreme Court hold S.B. 271 to be constitutional?"

O'Connor delivered the summit's luncheon speech. She gave a reassuring message to the doctors in the audience. "What I will never forget and always want to recall in sharp focus is the support I received from physicians in the state of Ohio."

Judge Guckenberger, Judge Bessey, Judge Sargus, Judge Schweikert and all other visiting judges who worked on Durrani cases do not face election from the voters. O'Connor ages out at the end of 2022 as a lame duck who could care less about the Durrani victims.

Chapter 42

Affidavits of Disqualification

"Deliberate with caution, but act with decision,
and yield with graciousness, or oppose with firmness."
—C.C. Colton

Under Ohio law, a party or their legal counsel may file an affidavit of disqualification against a judge. It is filed with the Ohio Supreme Court. Guess who hears and decides the issue after the judge responds in writing to the affidavit? The Chief Justice. This means Maureen O'Connor would decide every affidavit against the judge she appointed, Mark Schweikert. She also would decide the affidavits against her, even though if she chose, the rules allowed her to allow another justice to rule. She would never allow this to happen. Every affidavit we filed contained justified reasons for removal. Every one denied. We filed these from December 15, 2017 to November 21, 2019. Four were against O'Connor. Thirty-six were against Schweikert. We would either obtain new information or the judges would do something egregious, which would justify yet another affidavit. What follows in no particular order are the reasons contained in those affidavits for our request. No rational person reading these reasons would not agree O'Connor and Schweikert should have been removed:

A. Judge Schweikert held ex parte communications with the defense attorneys while serving as the presiding judge.
B. Judge Schweikert's wife is either a registered nurse employed by a presently unknown doctor or hospital.
C. Judge Schweikert stated during a social engagement that Plaintiffs' cases are a "pain in his ass."
D. Judge Schweikert set numerous sets of three trials for the same day with plans to only try one of them on that day. This forced us to prepare for three trials when only one would actually be tried. The defense law firms are paid by the hour and have the staff to accommodate this directive. Judge Schweikert rejected this disparity in setting trials.
E. Judge Schweikert stated he would consult with Guy Guckenberger on the cases. Judge Guckenberger is a previously-recused judge in the cases.
F. Judge Schweikert stated he did not care what rulings had been made by the prior presiding judges during the last four years.
G. Judge Schweikert refused to sanction Durrani for his conduct.
H. Judge Schweikert denied Plaintiffs motions to amend their complaints.

I. Judge Schweikert claimed he relied upon the legislative history of a statute in making a decision, then ignored the very legislative history favorable to Plaintiffs.

J. On February 28, 2018, Judge Schweikert signed a series of decisions in several of the cases adverse to Plaintiffs and entered them on March 1, 2018, with the Hamilton County Clerk of Court's office knowing there were at least two Affidavits of Disqualification pending against him before the Chief Justice.

Other judges presiding recused themselves over allegations far less serious than those directed to Judge Schweikert. For example, Judge Steven Martin recused himself after disclosing he served as chaplain at The Christ Hospital. Judge Guckenberger recused himself arising from his handling of ex parte emails from Durrani's counsel, Michael Lyon.

The standard for recusal includes appearance of bias or impropriety. In response to our affidavits, Schweikert would claim he could be fair. Rather than consider our allegations, O'Connor simply ruled: "He says he can be fair."

If the defense filed a motion to dismiss a previous motion by us, Schweikert refused to allow any amendment to our motion in response.

Schweikert was the only judge in the Durrani cases to order our clients and Deters Law to pay a security deposit on court fees for all cases. His ruling came just a week after we had filed a federal suit challenging O'Connor's handling of the Durrani cases. In effect, Schweikert ordered Deters Law to pay $1.2 million in court fees in advance. This is a first in litigation in the history of America.

Those exorbitant court costs could have been avoided if Schweikert agreed to an earlier request by us. In early 2017, when Marsh was the chief judge in Hamilton County, we asked to have one case number to file documents related to all cases. For example, a deposition could have been filed under a separate case number and then applied to all cases rather than refiling the paperwork for every case. Marsh never ruled on the motion and Sargus suggested the separate case numbers could be used by all parties. When Schweikert took over, he vacated the proposal, then tried to stick us with the cost of the problem after rejecting our solution.

We filed suit over the security deposit order and Schweikert dropped it.

The Ohio Supreme Court Rules of Superintendence requires the cases be tried within two years of filing and if they are labeled "complex" within three years. During the Durrani litigation, the Court changed the rules to simply three years. By 2018, cases were already five years old and still being tried one case at a time. In other words, the Ohio Supreme Court when it comes to Durrani cases, ignored its own rules. It is now 2022.

This is a critical point. At any time, O'Connor held the power and to this day holds the power to solve the problem. O'Connor could order group trials or to provide the Hamilton County courts with more judges and resources to speed the cases along. Even though she had long claimed to be an advocate for timely justice in Ohio's courts, she declined. In an article for the Albany Law Review in 2013, she quoted the famous adage from William Gladstone, "Justice delayed is justice denied." She wrote, *"Delay in the courts is unqualifiedly bad. It is bad because it deprives citizens of basic public service; it is bad because the lapse of time frequently causes deterioration of evidence and makes it less likely that justice be done when the case is finally tried; it is bad because delay may cause severe hardship to some parties and may, in general, affect litigants differently; and is bad because it brings the entire court system a loss of public, confidence, respect, and pride."*

What a complete phony! She refused for ten years to apply this to Durrani victims. This article is the inspiration for the shirt I wore at the contempt hearing.

Judge Sargus wanted to sit on all motions to dismiss for statute of repose or other issues and focus on trials. Judge Schweikert focused on dismissing any case he could for a statute of repose issue. This is another way Schweikert hurt the Durrani victims.

On June 26, 2019, Judge Schweikert called Alan Statman livid someone, believing it to be me, called his son, a lawyer at a Washington DC firm. He threatened me. I shot off the following email on June 27, 2019 to Schweikert:

I fully investigated this allegation made by Judge Schweikert to Alan that someone called Judge Schweikert's son at his DC law firm from Deters Law and simply hung up.

First, no one from Deters Law made such a call.

Second, I learned my 27-year-old son Cole, did call him from his cellphone where he lives in Colorado. The reason he called was on his own without any knowledge from anyone at Deters Law or me was researching Judge Schweikert and his background and he was calling to confirm Grant was the Judge's son and then simply decided not to follow through on the call. Cole has never harmed or threatened anyone ever. He's a good kid.

I learned of this when I told my wife about the Judge's call to Alan. My wife said, "I bet Cole did, because he told me he was checking out Judge Schweikert online."

My family is kept fully updated of the Dr. Durrani litigation based upon normal family discussions about work etc. Guess what—led by me, no one likes Judge Schweikert.

Third, Cole calling and hanging up without anything more, which both the Judge and Cole confirms is not a crime and is a non-issue.

Here is what is an issue.

The Judge told Alan his son's law firm had security measures and was investigating. Really? A hang up call from a 27-year-old from Colorado? By this email

Jenner & Block and Grant Schweikert are to preserve any and all investigation they have done, and I expect a copy of it. Any destruction or editing of that investigation is a crime. And, we will prosecute.

If there is ANY invasion of Cole's privacy or Deters Law privacy or my family's privacy etc., we will sue Judge Schweikert's son and his law firm and we will prosecute.

Furthermore, based upon the Judge's comments and overreactions to Alan Statman, it is clear he once again reveals his bias and prejudice.

He needs to resign from the Durrani litigation.

We also will seek a deposition of Grant Schweikert about his work at Dinsmore during the Durrani litigation and his interaction with his father while his father has been a judge. Again, preserve all communication.

It is getting old that Judge Schweikert can keep claiming he can be fair and impartial.

We will be filing more affidavits of disqualification. We have accumulated many more reasons since the last one, including this bogus phone call issue. For example, Judge Schweikert actually took a 30-minute court break and made me and Ben wait in the Courtroom so Christ/Good Sam could serve us with contempt papers. Beyond improper. A judge assisting those wanting to hold us in contempt serve us with contempt papers to start the process which can't be started until we are served.

What really bothers me is Judge Schweikert doesn't care about our clients dying, being evicted or bankrupt. He refuses to sign an Order on our attorney fees- another basis for disqualification. But by golly, he will get upset about a meaningless hang up phone call. His words to Alan: "I'm not going to take this." What does that mean Judge? Resign. You know you can't be fair and impartial. And, that hang up phone call is important, but our clients having their trials over 40 years is no issue. Context. Perspective. Says it all about you, Judge Schweikert.

I never heard from or received any communication from Judge Schweikert on this issue.

Chapter 43

Holly DeCair

"But let judgment run down as waters, and righteousness as a mighty stream."
—Amos 5:24

On February 23, 2013, trusting my instincts from Durrani's deposition in Pierce, I named the UC Health and West Chester Hospital as defendants in the new seven cases. Durrani trained at UC and Children's Hospital and held privileges at West Chester.

The local media attention brought a private phone call from a friend, Dr. Angelo Colosimo, a local orthopedic surgeon and team surgeon to the Cincinnati Bengals and UC Bearcats. Colosimo once operated on my son, Cory and my daughter Erica. An assistant professor of orthopedic surgery at UC, Colosimo told me "off the record," Dr. Peter Stern called him into a room one day and stated: "We knew all about Durrani's issues before he came to us, but we needed the money..." '*we*' being West Chester.

Months later, Colosimo tipped me off to more. A group of spine surgeons at UC tried to send a letter to the Ohio State Medical Board warning about Durrani's unnecessary and often dangerous surgeries. On the advice of university lawyers, they never sent the letter. Colosimo claimed he did not have a copy of the letter.

Leading this advice was University Hospital's General Counsel, Charles H. Pangburn, III. This man has blood on his hands. All the lives he could have saved from Durrani. While Pangburn enjoys retirement in North Carolina, Durrani victims suffer.

Appreciative but frustrated, no matter how much I begged and pleaded, Colosimo wouldn't testify, wouldn't go on the record and wouldn't sign an affidavit. At one point, I even subpoenaed him. He called, pissed off. I simply had to drop it. We asked for this letter in formal discovery, but UC Health denied its existence. At least thanks to Colosimo I knew they lied.

Durrani would continue to leave a trail of victims: maimed for life, paralyzed, crippled and left in uncontrolled pain. Several patients died from Durrani's incompetence and deception while the hospitals protected him.

Holly DeClair, a recent widowed mother of two teenagers, found herself desperate to find relief from lower back pain caused by an inherited condition Ehlers-Danlos syndrome. EDS weakens the body's connective tissues, including the discs that cushion vertebrae in the spine. The 41-year-old Maumee, Ohio, native consulted first with surgeons in Toledo and Cleveland, both recommended she lose weight and try physical therapy.

In 2009, DeClair learned of a clinic at Cincinnati Children's specialized in the treatment of EDS for both children and adults. A doctor at Children's referred her to Durrani. By this time, Durrani's aggressive and experimental surgeries were being questioned and criticized by Dr. Mehlman. In fact, Durrani left the hospital earlier under a cloud of complaints about his professional and personal conduct. None of this would be communicated to his patients or Holly DeClair. Durrani assured DeClair "he could take care of her. It would just be a normal surgery, and it was no big deal," recalled her sister, Jodi Behrendt.

DeClair's surgery would be one of ten Durrani performed that day at Christ Hospital. Imagine if you knew you were one of ten going under surgery by one surgeon in one day. What if you were number ten? Unknown to DeClair, Durrani's plan was to fuse together the lower vertebrae of DeClair's spine using BM2.

To hold the spine in place while the bones grew together, Durrani planned to insert screws through the vertebrae. The first screw pierced the iliac artery that runs along the front of the spinal column. He removed the screw and inserted a shorter one. With the artery still bleeding, Durrani sewed up DeClair and informed Holly's family surgery was a smashing success.

In the recovery room, DeClair struggled for life. Her heart stopped from loss of blood. Rushed back to surgery, a vascular surgeon made a heroic effort to stop the bleeding. After countless blood transfusions, replacing all the blood in DeClair's body, her heart gave out and she died. Her children no longer had a father or a mother.

When her father learned of his daughter's death, he suffered a heart attack on site in the hospital.

Chapter 44
Charles "Cowboy" Mehlman

"Courage: to bear unflinchingly what heaven sends."
—Euripides

Dr. Charles Mehlman, a spine surgeon at Cincinnati Children's Hospital Medical Center, attended a wedding reception in his normal cowboy hat and boots. A lover of Midwest American values and country music, Mehlman dressed to match his tastes. For the special occasion, Mehlman added a dark suit and bolo tie. Fifty-four at the time, Mehlman's outfit and ponytail revealed outlaw, not spine surgeon. I later nicknamed him "Cowboy." I knew one of the other attendees at the wedding, a friend who will remain nameless. My friend and Mehlman by serendipity struck up a conversation at the wedding. Mehlman introduced himself. When my friend told Mehlman he knew me, Mehlman said, "He's the Durrani guy!"

"I hope they get that guy," Mehlman exclaimed. Mehlman, a straight shooter and Ohio farm boy whose two younger brothers still run the family's fifth-generation dairy farm in Bellaire, Ohio continued: "I hope they go after him and put him on the mat for everything he did."

My friend thanked him and gave Mehlman his phone number. "Give me a call if you have anything you ever want to share." He doubted Mehlman would ever contact him.

Children's Hospital and Durrani's lawyers at a later deposition of Mehlman would ask if he ever spoke to someone at Deters Law. They failed to ask him if he ever spoke to a friend of mine. You have to always ask the right question.

Two years later from the chance wedding encounter and "out of the blue," Mehlman called my friend's cell phone. Mehlman wanted to talk about Durrani. My friend jumped on it. How about dinner that night? Mehlman said he could do an early dinner and suggested the *Precinct,* his favorite hangout. The *Precinct* steakhouse and seafood restaurant is on the east side of Cincinnati and is owned and operated by Jeff Ruby.

I once asked Jeff Ruby if he could help raise publicity about our Durrani battle. He is one of the few honest men in Cincinnati on Durrani. He told me he would love to, but he made too much money from the hospitals. I appreciated his candor. No one else admitted their compromised position. To this day, I judge the entire Cincinnati business community and leaders for not intervening as a community to resolve the Durrani litigation. It is a stain on Cincinnati. It affects my view of the city in a negative manner to this day.

By this time, I knew Mehlman worked with Durrani at Children's. His name appeared in emails Probst kept. I asked for several years to depose Mehlman, but each time Children's legal team denied our request. Now my friend possessed a chance to speak to someone on the inside at Children's without lawyers around.

My friend and Mehlman met at the upstairs bar at the *Precinct* and over whiskeys and steak, Mehlman unloaded. Mehlman revealed everything I suspected. Children's knew Durrani performed unnecessary surgeries. Durrani even bragged about his revenue driven immunity.

Mehlman complained about Durrani at Children's. Mehlman's supervisors recently asked Mehlman to undergo a psychiatric evaluation and receive in-house counseling for anger management. Fearing being set up for firing in retaliation for his whistleblowing, Mehlman retained a labor law attorney, Randy Freking, the same lawyer Joe Deters once tried bringing to my team. Randy Freking actually suggested to me once I should settle the Durrani cases for a "hair cut," "get my money" and be done with it all. In other words, sell out the clients.

My friend called and told me all Mehlman told him.

Chapter 45
The Letter

"Duty is ours. Consequences are God's."
—Thomas "Stonewall" Jackson

The morning after my friend met Mehlman, I walked out to the big black mailbox at Deters Law to check on the mail. Inside I found an envelope with my name on it. It was hand delivered, not mailed. I opened it up and inside without a comment or note was the letter Colosimo told me about. I have no idea who put it there.

Drafted in October 2009 by three physicians at University Hospital who worked with Durrani, they intended to send it as a warning to the Ohio State Medical Board. They hoped to spur a medical board investigation and stop Durrani before he injured or killed more patients. On the advice of lawyers led by Charles H. Pangburn III, they never sent the letter. Pangburn told them Durrani might sue them. Once again, corporate lawyers caring more about money than what is right.

The letter deserves to be placed here in its entirety. It will astonish you.

Letter from Dr. Guanciale, Dr. Asghar and Dr. Agabegi to Ohio Medical Board

Roy H. Thomas, MD, President
Ohio State Medical Association
The Elyria Eye Clinic, Inc.
850 East Broad Street
Elyria, OH 44035-6559

Dear Dr. Thomas and Members of the Ohio State Medical Association:

I am writing to you in regards to my concerns regarding a local orthopaedic surgeon and a situation that appears to involve poor surgical indications and, therefore, poor surgical decision making. Although I am sole author of this letter, this feeling is shared by many members of the orthopaedic community and, in particular, spine surgeons within the community to a point that this concern resulted in some initial attempts at disciplinary action that I believe have failed to protect patients in our community.

The person in question is A. Atiq Durrani, M.D. Dr. Durrani is a physician who initially came to Cincinnati care through acceptance to a pediatric orthopaedic fellowship within the Orthopaedic Department at the

Children's Hospital Medical Center. Dr. Durrani then, with continued interest in orthopaedic surgery, subsequently underwent application and acceptance for a United States based orthopaedic residency training at the University of Cincinnati within the Department of Orthopaedic Surgery. I am a member of the Department of Orthopaedic Surgery along with others, including Chairman Dr. Peter J. Stern. Dr. Durrani subsequently completed his residency program at the University of Cincinnati and this was followed by a one-year spine fellowship training in Louisville, Kentucky. He then returned to the Children's Hospital Medical Center in Cincinnati as an orthopaedic surgeon specializing in tumor surgery, pediatric spine surgery, as well as adult spine surgery.

During Dr. Durrani's short tenure at Children's Hospital Medical Center and within the Department of Orthopaedic Surgery, it was recognized by the greater Cincinnati community of spine surgeons, spine surgeons within the Orthopaedic Department and orthopaedic residents that Dr. Durrani displayed a pattern of surgical indications that would, by most standards, appear to be inappropriate. In particular, it was noted by all the above that it was not infrequent that a teenage patient with only intermittent back pain would be recommended an anterior/posterior fusion for treatment of symptomatologies where radiographic imaging would display minimal to no actual disc pathology. Similar situations arrived where patients were not infrequently under the age of 18 recommended artificial disc replacements for, again, discogenic back pain. Patients were recommended fusion surgery for having completely normal diagnostic testing studies, including MRI examinations of the spine.

A recent abstract submitted to the North American Spine Society would also suggest that Dr. Durrani has been recommending operative treatment to nearly every adolescent patient that would present with back pain and some type of radiographic abnormality involving pars interarticularis region rather than conservative treatment which is effective in the majority of cases. I think it is also important to briefly note that this abstract submitted to the North American Spine Society for its meeting last November 2008 based in Toronto had to be retracted because the data was found to be falsified. It actually has been subsequently found by our own research review committee within the Orthopaedic Department at the University of Cincinnati that essentially no data existed for this abstract and its supposed results, therefore, constituting research fraud.

I would again like to reiterate that the observation of significant concerns about Dr. Durrani's surgical indications was voiced by many members of the Cincinnati medical community, all of which were relayed to our chairman, Dr. Peter Stern. This subsequently was brought up in a formal meeting and discussion with Dr. Durrani in the fall of 2008 during his employment with Children's Hospital Medical Center of Cincinnati, this including attendance by: the Chairman of the Department of Pediatric Surgery, Richard Azizkhan, MD, the Director of the Children's Hospital Orthopaedic Program, Dr. Eric J. Wall, as well as Dr. Peter J. Stern. There were actually three separate areas of concern about Dr. Durrani's practice that were discussed at the meeting of which one involved his surgical indications. The other involved concerns about research fraud where he was submitting abstracts to medical societies without data or the actual project even existing and the third involving personal issues with employees. I did not attend this meeting but had direct involvement and discussions with Dr. Peter J. Stern since I am the Director of Spine Surgery within the Orthopaedic Department. Shortly after this meeting, Dr. Durrani voluntarily resigned from Children's Hospital Medical Center.

My concern, at this point in time, therefore, involves the fact that Dr. Durrani now is in private practice within the Cincinnati medical community and is under no structure that would allow for continued monitoring of his surgical practice, clinical skills and surgical indications. My concerns are that the same adolescent and pediatric patients that were receiving recommendations for very aggressive surgical treatment, such as artificial disc replacement and anterior/posterior fusions for situations not involving instability but rather dark disc disease, will continue unabated. The same members of the orthopaedic spine community that presented their initial concerns about Dr. Durrani's surgical indications, at this point and time, remain concerned as well. It is also very concerning that Dr. Durrani is attempting to establish a spine fellowship program to teach future generations of spine surgeons. I do not believe that Children's Hospital Medical Center has in place any program to suggest observation of Dr. Durrani's surgical practice at this time nor that they actually have jurisdiction to do such. I do not believe that they have actually contacted the Ohio State Medical Association in regards to these concerns.

Finally, I am concerned about the disproportionate number of severe complications that Dr. Durrani's patients have experienced, including death and paralysis that would be deemed to be unacceptable by the orthopaedic community for a competent spine surgeon. I am troubled by what many members of the medical community consider to be irresponsible surgical care that is being delivered to patients in the Greater Cincinnati area.

I, therefore, am contacting you expressing my sincerest concerns. I, as well as others are able to provide detailed, specific evidence to support the above. Although I am sole author of this letter, other spine surgeons within the Department of Orthopaedic Surgery at the University of Cincinnati, including Drs. Ferhan A. Asghar and Steven Agabegi, share these concerns and have read and signed this letter.

Sincerely,
Anthony F. Guanciale, MD
Associate Professor
Director, Division of Spine Surgery
Department of Orthopaedic Surgery
University of Cincinnati Medical Center

Ferhan A. Asghar, MD
Assistant Professor
Department of Orthopaedic Surgery
University of Cincinnati Medical Center

Steven Agabegi, MD
Assistant Professor
Department of Orthopaedic Surgery
University of Cincinnati Medical Center
Cincinnati Children's Hospital Medical Center

This letter proved to be a proverbial "smoking gun." We now knew of a doctor inside Children's ready to "sing" and possessed a "smoking gun" letter. Hope springs eternal. My hopes soared.

Chapter 46

JOE DETERS

"The brave man inattentive to his duty, is worth little more to his country, than the coward who deserts her in the hour of danger."
—Andrew Jackson

Early in the litigation, I calculated we could use some Hamilton County "firepower." I first met Joe Deters, no relation and Hamilton County Prosecutor, at an attorney league softball game in the mid-1980's. Our team played his team at the Lunken Airport fields and my brother Jed and I kept hearing the other players shout "Deters." We met on the softball field and had a good laugh. We would occasionally interact. I would also run into Joe's brother, Dennis, at the Hamilton County Courthouse. He, too, practiced law. My grandfather checked our family tree and concluded we were no relation.

My Dad invited Joe and his family to his annual Derby Party one year. Joe came with his first wife Missy and youngest son, Patrick, a toddler at the time. The Deters family dog bit Joe. Later that evening, a car in the driveway ran over the dog and killed him. The family joke at the dog's expense: don't mess with Joe Deters.

Joe's grandfather was long time Hamilton County Sheriff and Democrat, Don Teehan. Teehan also refereed NBA basketball games. After law school, Joe began a political career that would take him from an assistant prosecutor under Simon Lies, who famously prosecuted Larry Flint; to county clerk; to Hamilton County Prosecutor; to Ohio State Treasurer; and Hamilton County Prosecutor again. He has served as the longest serving Hamilton County prosecutor than anyone in county history.

When I began doing radio shows on 700 WLW, I interacted with Joe more. Joe always gave Bill Cunningham the first interview on any high-profile case, so when I backed up Willie, I interviewed Joe.

Joe always told me, "Damn, you're better than Willie." In reality, Joe and Willie—longtime friends—were two parts of a triangle, and I was never going to make the third side. It took years for me to come to this realization. This is even more odd when Joe would constantly tell me he had few real friends and I was one.

Joe once held a fundraiser at the Montgomery Inn and asked me to introduce him. In front of an outdoor porch of judges and lawyers, I made up a funny story and everyone laughed. One of the judges there was Sylvie Hendon, a Family Court then a Court of Appeals judge and Joe's mother-in-law. Later on in our saga, she befriended me and we had lunch. She sought my help in keeping her daughter and Joe together amongst their marital problems. I tried to no avail. She would text me all the time about Joe's personal life problems. At one point, I had to choose between Team Hendon or Team Joe, I chose Team Joe. Joe is now married to WCPO Channel 9 Cincinnati news anchor, Tonya O'Rourke.

At some point, Joe decided he needed to make more money than his prosecutor's salary. The law allowed him to go to "part-time, " cut his salary in half and work in a law firm. Where did Joe decide to work? Stan Chesley's office. The man who was Mr. Class Action and hosted parties for President Clinton. The Hamilton County Republican voters became a little uneasy.

One story is worth sharing about Chesley and Clinton. Melissa Powers, an over-the-top attractive Hamilton County Judge, told me Stan Chesley once tried to pimp her out to President Clinton at a fundraiser. Chesley told Powers she could have any job she wanted including a federal judgeship. Powers told me that under the table at the event, Clinton kept rubbing her leg with his foot. All the while, Clinton kept his hands above the table. Just imagine, all the women Clinton in his political career played this game with. Judge Powers, classy as she is, declined the offer.

While Joe was still affiliated with Stan, Stan's world caved in. I described this in a prior chapter. When the Fen-Phen victims sued Chesley in Kentucky, they secured a judgment for what became I believe $40 million. The Boone Circuit Judge, J.R. Schrand, found Chesley in contempt for not appearing and issued an arrest warrant. Joe Deters issued an Order to the Hamilton County Sheriff that he could not arrest Stan on the warrant. Have you ever heard of such a thing? No. But that's power in action and power we wanted. Unfortunately, we would never receive the Chesley treatment.

While I reached out to Chesley, I also reached out to Joe. Chesley would tell me Joe didn't know what he was doing. Joe would tell me Chesley would drive him crazy.

At the first morning meeting with Joe at the Fox 19 building, it was clear from the smell, his face, his eyes, his speech and his manner, Joe was intoxicated and not just a little bit.

I informed Bill Cunningham of this fact. It was then Willie told me Joe had a severe alcohol problem, his closest friends tried interventions, he was often times publicly drunk, there were police encounters, he was in the middle of a divorce and his life was falling apart. Willie said "everyone" knew.

I decided to choose the congenial drunk Joe over the rude and abusive Chesley. Over the years I interacted with Chesley, and always found him an asshole of the highest order. He never gave a damn about anyone including his clients. Joe promised results. He also lived in the same condo complex as Judge Guy Guckenberger. I saw Joe had a friendly connection to the Republican judicial establishment.

Joe and I would embark on communication by his personal email, private phone calls and texts, meetings at his condo, meetings at Pizza Hut across from his condo, meetings at restaurants, coffee houses, and later at his town home. Joe never took anything too serious and in candor, I thought we became friends. He is very likeable.

Joe's downtown condo actually belonged to Stan Chesley. When Chesley fell on hard times, he sold it and Joe had to move. Here's a gross thought for anyone who knows Stan Chesley. Joe said Chesley used the condo for his female hookups. One of those became, of all people, Alan Statman's ex-wife. Larry Sheakley, a wealthy Cincinnatian and Stan Chesley, actually fought over Alan's wife. Sheakley once flew to Vegas and got arrested for roughing her up in anger.

Joe said one time the woman showed up to the condo with a key to meet Chesley and scared the hell out of Joe. He almost shot her. This wicked woman once took Sheakley's cuff links to his wife, rang the doorbell and said, "Here's Larry's cufflinks he left on my nightstand." When Alan divorced this piece of work, she asked for her Valentine's Day present the day before Valentine's Day. He gave her a diamond necklace. The next day she left him. She even took the loose change bowl.

Another ironic fact, Glenn Feagan worked with Stan Chesley in and after law school.

I began referring to Joe as my Air Force. I used this term because I called the young lawyers who worked on Durrani every day my Armored Division. Joe and I both liked the movie *Tombstone*. Joe wanted to be "Doc" and insisted I be "Wyatt." I also called Joe "The Breeze" because he never seemed upset about anything. Joe, an Elton John fan, also wanted to be "the Brown Dirt Cowboy" and me "Captain Fantastic." I know that I certainly should have been "Doc Holiday" and not "Wyatt Earp." Yes, we acted twelve.

Joe, Willie and the I began having weekly breakfasts every Wednesday at Bob Evans in Kenwood. Willie would tease Joe about being my father or brother. From jail, a man who cut up his wife and put her in a garbage can at the curb actually was caught on the jail phone from the jail saying he couldn't hire me because I was Joe Deters' son.

Joe Deters told me inside stories, including most personal stories about everyone: Judge Barrett, Judge Marsh, Judge Guckenberger, Judge Schweikert, Defense Lawyers, Defense Firms, Politicians, Chesley, Judge Dlott (Stan Chesley's wife), Judge Black, Alex Triantafilou, Greg Hartmann, Judge Powers, Judge Shanahan, Judge Hendon (his mother in law), Judge Mock, Judge Fisher, Judge DeWine, George Vincent, Judge Martin, Rob Portman, Justice O'Connor, Judge Winkler, Mike DeWine and Judge Kubicki, to name a few. I heard it all. All the dirty little secrets he knows, he told me.

Joe planned a huge fundraiser at the Great American Tower downtown, home of Western Southern and the Lindner companies. Governor DeWine and Senator Portman came to speak. The host list included all the power brokers, including Dinsmore & Shohl attorneys. For $10,000, you could be a host.

I decided to play a game with Joe he would lose. The game? How do you prove where someone really stands?

I told Joe I wanted to be a host and planned to send $10,000. I wanted to see how Joe would react to my name being next to his friends at Dinsmore and all the others.

You can't make this up. Joe said it was not necessary and I could come for free. From his voice, to his manner, to his words, it was clear as a recently Windexed window. Joe would be embarrassed by me being a host with the Dinsmore club.

At one point, I proposed transferring my firm to Joe Deters. Fortunately, that never happened. We actually drove each other nuts. I would guess no one has ever cussed out the Hamilton County Prosecutor like I did. I couldn't take the lack of results. Make no question about it. It's illegal for a public official to use his public influence for economic benefit. But that's the entire "thing" Joe promised me. And I wanted it for these victims. The evil bastards I knew used all their "sources." These victims deserved someone. Joe just didn't care. He overpromised and undelivered. Despite repeated requests, he never even made it to one client meeting. Then he asked Willie to be in on all our discussions as if I couldn't be trusted.

Joe's communication skills were awful. However, I soon learned the best information always came late at night on a drunken phone call.

Despite repeated pleas for action, Joe failed the Durrani victims. Willie told me he believed Joe overpromised. I become convinced Joe would take credit for something he had nothing to do with and when something didn't happen, simply act like he tried.

By April 3, 2019, I sent Joe a letter that summarized it all. It's all true and will shock you. Imagine if you hired him to help these victims and what follows is what happened:

> Dear Joe:
>
> I am a loyal and rational person. I enjoy using the Galileo example about reason. Despite his knowing the Earth orbited the sun, he had to confess to the Pope he was wrong. It is not fair to ask a rational person to accept 2 + 2 = 5. It's cruel actually.
>
> I have been good to you. I am also not Johnny come lately. I am grateful for jobs to Erica and Cooper and your assistance on several issues which arose. I keep track of everything. Thank you for having Mac meet Cameron. Also, you were a great help on that one Estate and the Cincinnati Bell issue. Also, there was the BS workers comp issue. You may have actually forgotten. I have not. I remember with gratitude.
>
> However, in Durrani, it seems we suffer more harm from your recusals than benefit. We need more.
>
> I was dumbfounded to learn at the Reds game Elyse by her own words "did a ton of research and wrote at least 10 decisions" for Judge Schweikert.

All his decisions have been against us. How could you not know this? (Elyse is his daughter. This reveal came Reds Opening Day when by serendipity my wife and I sat behind Joe and his family).

From Facebook, it's clear Elyse is very close to her mother and grandmother who hate me because I chose "team Joe." In addition, she worked for Judge Martin, who hates me. Your relationship with Judge Martin never helped us in Durrani. His few decisions were devastating.

Mary and I were speechless learning she was doing work for Schweikert. Steve Martin had to recuse himself from the cases. I'm sure he gave Elyse plenty of poison on us.

Then there is John who works for Barbiere who represents Judge Schweikert. That confuses me. (John is Joe's son.)

Then there is the following:

1. No assistance despite repeated requests with Governor DeWine on our healthcare liens and our Medical Board lawsuit. You gave us expectations.
2. Issues just sit in limbo and unknown in the First District. You gave us expectations.
3. Your relationship with George Vincent and Alex T has not helped us in the least. (Dinsmore lawyers)
4. Pat DeWine has been brutal. I feel like publicly telling the world what I know about him. I don't solely because of you which is silly because he doesn't help us.
5. Your talk to Jim Simon every week. We paid him $40,000. He got us nothing including not even Judge Schweikert's son worked at Dinsmore. I'm convinced he sold us out.
6. Pat Fisher has been horrible.
7. Robert Winkler didn't sign the consolidation.
8. Janitor (Brittingham) gets away with massive suborning perjury. You could have appointed a Special Prosecutor to shake him.
9. Dlott has not ruled on my simply going back into Court. Judge Crawford let me in this current trial.
10. I was anxious and desperate to meet you and you won't unless Willie is there. That's odd. Makes me feel yucky.

Based on all this, what rational person in my position has faith you truly want to do all you can for this cause? And, what does it mean when a friend ignores communications? Is that respect? Is that loyalty? Would Doc do that to Wyatt? I have been loyal. I remain loyal. I will stay loyal. Hell, I was willing to hand you the firm and the cases. I keep in confidence all our conversation and information. No one is receiving this letter. Just you and me. I wanted to lay it all out calmly. I need the best of you.

My letter failed. Nothing changed. Joe wouldn't even return calls to Glenn Feagan when I was in jail for contempt.

The end would come in early 2020. I warned him I reached the "end of my rope." He never responded or tried to resolve our relationship. I must assume he decided he had enough of me. I decided to abandon Joe and even support his political opponent, Judge Fanon Rucker, a Democrat. Outspent, Joe beat Rucker.

The straw that broke the camel's back was Joe ignored my repeated requests to simply obtain an Ohio state contact for help on resolving Medicaid liens. In April of 2020, I burned the bridge. I even told the public about his alcoholism and nicknamed him "Otis" from Andy Griffith's character. I decided Joe needed to pay a price for his betrayal.

A lawyer for Strauss Troy sent me a letter once asking on Joe's behalf for part of one of our settlements. I lost it. Joe dropped the request. At one time, Joe would have had a nice pay day, but he lost the right when he failed us. He blew it, not me.

"Breaking up" with Joe Deters resulted in Willie stopping communication with me. It was clear if I was not friends with Joe, I couldn't be friends with Willie. The last communication I sent Joe and Willie was a text with a photo of a burning bridge. That was in April 2020. I have not had one regret ending those relationships. It was more freedom. I always had to worry about their relationships with others. No longer. I had my own orbit and did not want to be in theirs. As you know, sometimes you do not know how you will feel about someone until they are out of your life. I am happier without Joe and Willie in mine.

In 2015, I sat at the conference room table with Matt Hammer, Erica, my daughter, and Cooper Bowen, and I said, well, let's prepare the statute of repose challenge. There's fourteen judges, maybe it'll be divine providence and we'll land Judge Ruehlman. Out of fourteen random common pleas judges, we landed Judge Ruehlman. And Judge Ruehlman ruled in our favor on the statute of repose.

I asked Joe what the likelihood of this thing holding up in the Appeals Court and he told me it would. I asked, "Why is that? He said: "Well, Pat DeWine's my friend, Judge Fisher's daughter works for my office, Russell Mock I vacation with and he gave my son his golf clubs." Ruehlman handed us a victory on the statute of repose issue and fraud exception. Mock, DeWine, and Fisher were the three judge panel who wrote a First District Court of Appeals opinion blasting Ruehlman and reversed it all. Thanks, Joe. Thanks, Air Force.

Chapter 47

Alan Statman

"I have nothing to offer but blood, toil, tears and sweat."
—Winston Churchill

On September 11, 2017, my wife and I attended the sixtieth birthday celebration of Dr. Lawrence Kurtzman at another steakhouse, *Cincinnati Prime*, in the heart of downtown Cincinnati. As always, Kurtzman asked how things were going with the Durrani cases. "Not good," I said. I'd just let go my only veteran trial lawyer, Jim Triona."

Triona's firing would have another cost as well. Matt Hammer grew close to Triona during those six months and saw Triona as his new mentor, even picking up Triona's trendy preference for using fountain pens rather than ballpoints for signatures. Hammer turned on me in part because I canned Triona. Besides the odd pen habit, Triona wore the brightest craziest ties he could find. Hammer never adopted that habit. Hammer and Triona both worked in our Carew Tower office. Therefore, I did not see them every day.

Kurtzman suggested contacting his close friend, Alan Statman. Statman built a successful practice in real estate and bankruptcy law representing creditors. His main client, Fifth Third Bank, is the second largest bank in Cincinnati and the 20th largest in the U.S.

By the early 2000s, Statman flew high like Icarus. His firm boasted thirty-five lawyers with three offices in Cincinnati, Chicago and Palm Springs, Florida. He owned a condo in Palm Springs, a dozen motorcycles, six Ferraris, a collection of guns and a private plane he flew around the country on business trips, a high-tech, single-engine Cirrus SR22 with room for three and its own colossal parachute in case of engine failure. He flew it once all the way to Jackson Hole, Wyoming to help foreclose on a mansion.

The Great Recession of 2008 to 2009 brought boom times for Statman based upon more bankruptcy cases than his firm could handle. It all began to unravel in 2015 and 2016 when Fifth Third implemented a cost-cutting reorganization, closing 100 branches. The bank's executives also decided the company would be better served by a regional or national law firm, not Statman's. With his firm's primary source of revenue gone. Alan found himself in a bad spot.

I never met Statman, but knew him by reputation. I didn't really care for him. He seemed like another asshole corporate lawyer to me. I would later joke with him I couldn't even stand his webpage photo. At the time, Statman's office was just several floors below our downtown offices in the Carew Tower. I asked if I could meet him in his office. Statman said "come on down."

We talked and I liked what I heard. Statman said he had trial experience in both individual and class action lawsuits, including medical malpractice. He said he was on good terms with both of the judges in the Durrani cases, Michael Barrett who was hearing the federal cases and Robert Ruehlman in Hamilton County.

I also liked Statman's presence. He was a big man at six feet four inches, and I assume three hundred pounds. Jurors are more likely to be persuaded by alpha males. Age fifty-nine at the time, Statman had gray hair and a beard. Statman looks like Moses. Alan is also incredibly smart. He obviously has a high IQ.

Statman also looks ten years younger than his age. He credits his good genes from both of his parents, alive and well in their mid-eighties. At age sixty-one, two years after I met him, Statman would marry a twenty-one-year-old waitress he met at *First Watch*, the downtown restaurant where our team had breakfast every morning of trial. It would be Alan's fifth marriage. They now have two children. Alan has another child with wife number four.

I don't judge him for his five marriages because the circumstance of each are quite unique. Here's another aspect of Alan I admire. While I have known him, he could be going through all kinds of hell from a divorce to whatever and he showed up undistracted to try a case.

Whether it came naturally to him or because he needed the collaboration with us for financial reasons, Statman made clear his willingness to let Dad and I be in charge. This never happened with the other half-dozen lawyers I interviewed and rejected. Statman treated us with respect. The others treated us with condescension.

Statman knew me only peripherally from my radio show. He knew I was a lawyer based in Northern Kentucky and was on WLW radio. Kurtzman, who had been a friend and client of Statman's for years, felt like we would be a match in terms of our mutual skills and personalities. Statman and Kurtzman also knew everyone in the Cincinnati Jewish community to which they belonged. They had connections I thought might be useful.

Statman liked my passion, my overall strategy for the Durrani cases and my organization. Several more meetings followed and we developed a cautious, but mutual respect. We both had egos, but we needed each other and shared a common goal of winning. I offered Statman generous compensation to be our trial lawyer as an independent contractor. With my staff and I doing all the trial preparation, Statman said yes. He would have the challenge and fun of trying cases, but not the daily grind of managing staff, assisting clients and piecing together the presentations. Durrani post-trial interviews also reveal jurors like Statman.

Alan and I began as me needing a trial lawyer and he needing money. It began with mutual suspicion. It is now one of friendship and mutual respect and trust. He's an incredible asset to our cause.

Chapter 48

Fred Johnson

"They are surely to be esteemed the bravest spirits who, having the clearest sense of both the pains and pleasures of life, do not on that account shrink from danger."
—Thucydides

I ran into Fred Johnson, a criminal defense attorney, on occasion and he always went out of his way to be friendly. I saw him at *Brio's* all the time. He always gave me some law gossip. Ten years younger than me, Fred looked just like the actor Jeremy Renner. Fred grew up hard scrabble in Newport, Kentucky. His mother left home and his Vietnam veteran father raised him. He worked and studied through all of his schooling. Fred made it through college in Indiana and law school at Chase Law School at NKU. Fred worked at several personal injury and criminal defense law firms before setting up his own practice in Covington, Kentucky. Fred was quick to laugh and full of fun. He took my truck once and videotaped this "theft" mocking the Bulldog.

Fred began feeding me information regarding lawyers and public officials. He wanted me to use my platforms to publicize the information. I obliged. Fred also began showing up at the Saturday morning breakfast at Frisch's in Independence I held every week with Bob Winter and my friend, Chris Mann. I soon learned Chuck Holbrook knew Fred from attending AA meetings. I began referring criminal cases to Fred and we spoke often. After a year, I offered Fred a job to work at Deters Law and help us on the Durrani cases. He accepted.

Although Fred possessed no experience in medical malpractice cases, I explained to him the skills of trying a criminal case translate to a medical malpractice case. Fred could try a criminal case. Therefore, I knew he could help us try Durrani cases. Comfort in the courtroom is universal. Every case is applying facts to law.

You can't make up this true story. Fred, on his first day, signed and filed a pleading in a Durrani case. Jim Brockman, Mike Lyon's partner, sent out an email to his team and inadvertently copied us. Brockman stated in a sarcastic tone there was no way Fred Johnson prepared this pleading on his first day. Two days later, Fred's phone rang and he answered. On the other end, Joe Caligiuri of Ohio Disciplinary Counsel, to question Fred about the filing. Fred and I laughed about this forever. The second day! Fred explained how he worked "off the record" for us for a year and knew all he needed to know once he joined us.

Undaunted, Fred began helping us cover hearings, depositions, attending trials and assisting Alan Statman. Al and Fred became fast friends. We gave Fred an office in both Independence and the Carew Tower in downtown.

It soon became clear, alcohol still gripped Fred. He showed up late, went home early and could be moody. We would part company and "get back together" many times. So much talent and promise, I hated to give up on him. I also simply liked him. He was one of us. Fred once said, "We aren't a law firm, we are a gang." I believe us to be both.

Chapter 49
Glenn Feagan

"One man with courage is a majority."
—Andrew Jackson

By 2018, my father wanted to bow out of the Durrani battle. He wanted to give the firm to whoever I chose and I was willing to oblige. I lost trust in him and I never trusted my brother Jeremy lurking in the shadows. The replacement needed to be tough, willing to take the heat and someone I could trust.

I first considered Joe Deters. After much thought, I decided not to trust him.

I approached others. I spoke to my cousin, Jim Maus. I trusted Jim but didn't believe he was strong enough. I spoke to Ben Maraan, whom I trusted, but didn't believe he had the strength either. I took Alan Statman to Buffalo Wild Wings in Independence and broached the subject. Alan showed interest and welcomed further discussions. Finally, I remembered an old friend, Glenn Feagan, a Cleveland attorney and a cousin of my first wife who lent me money during the firm's "cash flow by bitch" period.

I was always jealous of Feagan, because as a teenager he dated all the hot girls. From a big Catholic family like mine, all Italian on his mother's side, Feagan attended Covington Catholic High School, University of Kentucky and graduated from Chase Law School a year behind me. Glenn's just a really good guy. I could never imagine Glenn screwing over somebody. Ever.

When I called, Feagan didn't play coy. 'Absolutely," he said. "Whatever you want to do, however you want to do it." Glenn was the only one who never wanted to "think about it." So I cut a generous deal with Glenn. He didn't have to risk anything. I would continue to fund the cases. He would simply take Dad's place. Even though he resided in Cleveland, he'd fly down when needed. I would manage it all under his control, supervision and his final say. We communicate by text, email or call every day.

The other advantage to the transfer was Feagan was licensed only in Ohio, meaning the Kentucky Bar Association would no longer have any jurisdiction over the firm. We created an entirely new Ohio law firm, and all the clients signed new fee agreements.

In fact, Judge Schweikert during the West Chester settlement, openly attacked our fee agreements on the record. Why? Kentucky does not require a lawyer to sign the contract, only the client. Ohio requires the lawyer to sign, too. We used the same contract for Ohio and Kentucky, but used the Kentucky format. Schweikert made this a big deal. Think about it. It's the same agreement. The client signed. Dad or Glenn simply had not signed it. It became obvious Schweikert might void our fee agreements. We couldn't believe it. It is just another example of how evil he was and wanted to hurt us and cause problems. We came up with a solution: new law firm and new fee agreement. It's important to stress this. Schweikert, on purpose, always tried to create issues with us and our clients. The son of a bitch failed, based upon the trust and bond I formed with clients. They hated him and loved me. I hated him and loved them.

Choosing Glenn is unequivocally the best move I've made. Feagan not only supported my brand of aggressive lawyering, he's been more active in helping us with our cases. He's engaged.

Feagan's loyalty is fraught with irony given the history between our two families. Feagan's maternal grandfather and uncle were part of the mob who once controlled Newport, Ky., beginning with Prohibition in 1933. These family members included "Screw" Andrews, Glenn's Uncle and an enforcer. Glenn's mother, an Andrews, is one of the nicest women ever placed on Earth.

For decades, Newport earned the name "Sin City," a hotbed of gambling, prostitution and widespread corruption. By the 1960s, my paternal grandfather Bud, then managing editor of *The Cincinnati Times-Star*, used the power of the press to expose the mob and help bring it down. Bud served on what was called the Committee of 500. "Screw" would later be thrown out of St. Luke Hospital room window to his death. Glenn tells stories of suitcases of buried cash.

Another twist, Glenn lived next to the infamous Bill Erpenbeck, who served two decades in federal prison for housing and mortgage fraud. Bill committed fraud upon Glenn's family, too. Bill served as my finance chairman for a failed political race. He got arrested the week after he held a fundraiser for my race. Thanks Bill.

Chapter 50

HOLBROOK AND YORK

"Life is a storm. You will bask in the sunlight for a moment and be based on the rocks-the next. What makes you a man is what you do when that storm comes. You must look at that storm and say do your worse. For I will do mine. Then the fates will know you as a man."
—Edmund Dantes "Count on Monte Cristo" Birthday Toast

It seems I always hire people who are "nicked." I mean people with a troubled past or an existing crisis who need a job and a second chance.

I give those who are nicked a second chance on the belief they will work all the harder out of gratitude and to prove themselves worthy of my trust. In most of them I found "redeeming qualities." At times, I have been "burned."

Chuck Holbrook is a recovering alcoholic. My goodness his stories from grade school to now. After high school, Chuck enlisted in the Navy. The Navy expelled him two weeks before the end of his enlistment for fighting at a Jacksonville, Florida nightclub. Chuck's work on the flight deck of an aircraft carrier cost him much of his hearing. After the Navy, Holbrook worked as a creative representative for advertising agencies and film production firms in Los Angeles. Partying with stars to spending thirty days in LA County, Chuck crashed Los Angeles. In 2006, Chuck returned to Kentucky and later settled down with his wife, Rebecca. They now live in Arizona.

In 2009, Chuck and I met after Rebecca's mother suffered a horrific accident. While using an ATM machine, a young driver hit the accelerator instead of the brake and pinned Deborah Poynter's legs against the brick wall of the bank. Airlifted to University Hospital trauma unit, doctors questioned whether she would ever walk again. She would.

A Facebook friend who I never met, Chuck recommended me to his mother-in-law. Chuck sent a message simply stating, "Terrible accident. Friend and loved ones could use your help." I responded within minutes. "At your service."

Based upon Chuck's marketing experience, I offered him a job. Holbrook asked me "Do you believe people can change?" I answered with a firm "yes". He took the job and has not only remained sober, he became the most loyal and one of a kind friend anyone could ever have.

"Nicked" also means someone with a grave misfortune. I hired Joe Rutter, a Durrani client, to help Chuck. I hired Rutter's wife Christina as a nurse reviewer. Maria Dallas, my long-time secretary and office manager, is a Polish Ukrainian refugee whose family fled the Soviet occupation. Maria transcribed the secret tapes in the Gotti mobster trial in 1992 while she worked in New York. To this day, Maria refuses disclose anything under her confidentiality oath. Chuck brought me several "nicked" people, including Fred Johnson.

My assistant, Sarah York, stands out as the most "nicked" of our employees. York worked as a Northern Kentucky high school English teacher. She also became the captain of the Cincinnati Ben-Gal cheerleaders. One day in late 2011, police showed up at the high school asking her about her relationship with a 17-year-old male student at her school, Cody York. Sarah never realized the police seized text messages from Cody's phone, after someone contacted authorities. Fortunately for Sarah, both Cody and his parents refused to cooperate with the police. Sarah spent a few hours in the Kenton County jail before posting bail.

Then named Sarah Jones, she resigned from her teaching job and called me. I already represented her in a civil case against TheDirty.com. In that case, I obtained a jury verdict against the Arizona-based gossip website for running a post claiming Jones suffered from two venereal diseases and had sex with Bengals players. All vicious and cruel lies.

Friends with her entire family, I agreed to take Jones' criminal case, too. To help her through the tough times ahead, I offered her a job with the firm. At age twenty-seven, Jones was under indictment for a felony and permanently lost her teaching career. The local news as common in these teacher/student matters brutalized Sarah. It was almost too much for Sarah to handle. "I created a plan to kill myself. I wrote suicide notes to my family. My mom placed me on a 72-hour hold in a psych ward, and I just hit rock bottom. I was done," explains Sarah.

The case pursued by a special prosecutor was weak. The state could not prove when and where sex took place. In addition, the statute allowed the prosecution for a teacher being involved with a 17-year-old, but in Kentucky 16 was the age of consent. I prepared for that legal argument.

I publicly taunted the prosecutor's case. The Friday before Monday's trial, the special prosecutor offered Sarah a deal she accepted. The deal included the sealing of the text messages. Jones' plea reduced her charges from first degree sexual abuse to custodial interference and sexual misconduct. Her sentence? Seven months of house arrest and five years' probation. In her guilty plea in October of 2012, Jones confessed to having sexual contact with York. Jones later married York and they have three children together.

To keep her mind off her problems, York began a work routine that she maintains to this day. She's in the office at 5:30 a.m. on trial days and 6:00 a.m. on regular days and works until 4 p.m. when she returns home to care for her three young children, ages six, four and nine months. After dinner, she works for two more hours, then puts her children to bed and works another hour before going to bed herself. She works weekends as well. Next to me, she works the most. Bob Winter would place third.

York double majored in English and Math at Northern Kentucky University. I write freehand cursive on legal pads and I do not type. She types all my letters and emails, knows how I want everything and tolerates my constant assignments and communication.

Sarah and I meet every morning and plan the day. We accomplish more in a few hours before 8 AM than most do in a full day. She is indispensable.

The most rewarding part of her job is working with the Durrani clients. "When you see our clients and the pain they endure daily, you realize, this is something bigger. This is not just a job." I am paid to do what I do, but I also put my heart and soul into it because these victims deserve justice. They're not going to be able to go to another law firm and get what they've gotten here. It makes me proud to be a part of Deters Law. We are doing something monumental," explains York.

I have always treated the employees well. We never deny a request for family time off or challenge unemployment benefits for those who leave the firm. Many years ago, I did once and I still regret the one. We also offer small perks such as buying their lunch on Fridays and early departure times too on Fridays at 4 p.m. We give bonuses when large settlements come in and help out with any financial problems. We are family.

We demand loyalty to both our causes and our leadership of the firm. We don't expect anyone to work my hours.

Our office has our own little inside jokes and fun. This includes nicknames for all in the Durrani litigation. Durrani is "The Butcher." Lyon is "Munster" for his resemblance to Grandpa on the old TV series; "Rat" because he looks like one; and "Maestro" for his self-absorbed trial theatrics. Jim Brockman, Mike Lyon's partner, we named "Woody" from *Toy Story*. This based upon Jim being as goofy as "Woody." Paul Vollman, Lyon's and Brockman's colleague, we call "Ron" because the Judge kept calling him "Ron" before remembering his name. He also is "challenged" in court, so we assigned him "Dunce Cap."

Paul McCartney, a hothead and difficult to work with, we named "Puke." A judge who will remain nameless actually gave us the "Puke" nickname. Schweikert, we named "Reich" for obvious reasons. Guckenberger became "Fuckusberger." David Brittingham, the attorney representing Children's Hospital, was dubbed "Janitor" by Joe Deters because he said we may as well be dealing with the janitor at Dinsmore. Rob Carpenter, Children's risk manager, we labeled "Leprechaun." Jeff Hines, from Rendigs, we named "Stork" from *Animal House*.

Judge Robert Ruehlman, with his well-known love of scuba diving, was "Scuba." Judge Michael Barrett was "The Irishman." Expert neurosurgeon and star witness Dr. Stephen Bloomfield became "The Wiley One." Chuck Holbrook was "Underboss" for his work as my righthand man. Matt Bradley was "Murdoch" after the crazy character on A-Team. Alan Statman, late for a nickname, is "Moses." Fred Johnson named himself "The Hitman." Joe Rutter, tall, dark, and handsome, "Marlboro Man."

One time I sent Paul "Puke" McCartney an email where I used the good-natured man insult: "Take your purse off, Paul." He actually "told on me" to Judge Guckenberger in open court.

Chapter 51

The Cowboy "Sings"

"I may stand alone but would not change my free thoughts for a throne."
—Lord Byron

On June 15, 2018, the attorneys sat two-deep around the conference table in the downtown offices of Freking Myers & Reul. Al Statman, Fred Johnson and I attended for our team. On the defense side sat David Brittingham, for Children's Hospital; Mike Lyon and Paul McCartney for Durrani and CAST; Jennifer Mitchell, for Christ Hospital; Bill Paliobeis, Marilena Walters and Karen Carroll for West Chester Hospital and its parent organization, UC Health; Randy Freking, represented the main attraction, Dr. Charles T. Mehlman.

We subpoenaed Mehlman to give his deposition in all cases.

When I arrived, Randy Freking introduced me to Mehlman. Mehlman feared trumped up charges against him in the hospital's peer review process. Children's never used this process to remove Durrani, but used it against Mehlman. In over twenty years at Children's, not one patient ever filed a malpractice case against Mehlman.

We found it amusing Mehlman attended the deposition under force of subpoena, Brittingham attended to "represent" him, and Freking represented him against Children's. A triangular legal standoff. No one in the room knew my friend informed me Mehlman appeared ready to "spill" all he knew. I hoped he would, but until it happened, it was only hope.

Mehlman allayed my concerns out of the gate. Mehlman testified for the next four hours with both guns blazing. He even began with mocking Brittingham's representation of him. This led to an off the record break between Mehlman, Freking and Brittingham. Mehlman adopted a tone of defiance and indignation.

"Some sort of effort to protect the public should have been undertaken. People were paralyzed. People were killed. While paralysis occurs in a fraction of 1 percent of those undergoing spine surgery, Durrani had more paralysis cases than any surgeon I ever saw in his career at Children's. Four patients were paralyzed to the best of my knowledge." testified Mehlman.

According to Mehlman, the responsibility for protecting patients against Durrani rested on the shoulders of Children's Hospital and its academic partner, the University of Cincinnati College of Medicine. Dr. Alvin Crawford allowed himself to be dazzled by Durrani's charm.

"Dr. Crawford was in a sad and conflicted position with a young man who he commonly referred to as his son. He had a special liking, a special attachment to

Durrani through the years. And at the tail end of things, I have it on very good authority that he had been moved to the point of tears as he reflected on his own poor judgment with Dr. Durrani," testified Mehlman.

Prior to the first Durrani trial, when Chuck Holbrook tried to serve Crawford with a subpoena, the 80-year-old surgeon eluded Chuck by playing "hide-and-seek" in the hallways and stairwells at UC Medical Center. After repeated visits to his home, Holbrook finally caught up with Crawford and Crawford invited him inside. They sat in the solarium of his house in full view of a photo of Crawford with President Obama. Chuck would serve Crawford countless times for the Durrani trials.

"Business decision-makers at Children's built a machine around Durrani. We never had spine nurses like we did until Durrani was there. We never had schedulers, that I know of, that hung out in the clinic just to schedule the cases as they rolled out, and I sure as heck never saw a surgeon have two operating rooms three days a week. Durrani had an incredibly accommodating environment," testified Mehlman.

The special attention rewarded the hospital's bottom line. According to the hospitals records, Durrani's total billings at Children's more than doubled from $1.5 million in 2005 to $3.6 million in 2008. Durrani became the top revenue producer in the hospital's entire surgery department. Durrani bragged to nurses the hospitals he worked for wouldn't dare discipline him because he was making too much money for them.

Durrani also made money for Medtronic, the manufacturer of the controversial bone grafting material BMP-2. Even though the FDA warned BMP-2 should not be used in children, Durrani implanted it into hundreds of children. *"If you added up every single partner's use of BMP-2 in their career, I think it would be lower than Durrani did in three years. I've never used it in my entire career,"* Mehlman testified.

In 2006, when the reports of adverse reactions from BMP-2 began to hit the medical literature, the emails from Children's prove Durrani and Crawford as the only two surgeons at Children's still using BMP-2. In 2006, Medtronic and other medical device companies funded Durrani's fellowship program for advanced training of spine surgeons at Children's after Durrani replaced Crawford as head of the fellowship.

When Mehlman found out about the program's corporate funders, he declined to provide lectures or supervision to fellows in the program. *"I was aware of the research on the topic of conflict of interest" in medicine. So when surgeons become the beneficiaries of these companies that are dishing out money, it's been shown very clearly to change surgeon behavior. You use more of that company's stuff. Maybe during surgery you open up the $10,000 vial of BMP instead of the $5,000 bottle,"* testified Mehlman.

Mehlman claimed in his deposition Durrani's fellowship at Leatherman Spine Center in Louisville, exposed in 2010 as a spine surgery mill by the *Wall Street Journal*, turned Durrani into a money hungry monster. He wanted what the Leatherman guys possessed: money, planes, yachts, and homes everywhere.

Maureen Grady, a Children's nurse, testified in her deposition Durrani began in 2006 to ramp up the volume of his surgeries, as well as the workload for his exhausted staff, by persuading his patients surgery was the only solution to their problem. Victims of Durrani would include hundreds of student athletes with lower back pain caused by physical stress and a small congenital fracture in a vertebra, a condition called spondylolysis.

By the best standards of medical care, the vast majority of those young patients should be treated successfully without surgery by having them take time off from their sport and participating in physical therapy. With Durrani operating at Children's, *"we reached a point where four kids a day were having that surgery,"* Mehlman testified. *"I haven't done four in my career."* There was also *"an explosion of TLIF"* operations, a type of lower spinal fusion done primarily on adults with degenerative spinal disease. Durrani was performing them on children as young as twelve.

Mehlman testified Durrani was *"striking"* in the aggressiveness of his surgeries, *"stuff that I had never seen before. It was nothing like anybody else's practice I had ever seen in our group."* Durrani would operate on children with 30-degree curvatures of the spine when standard practice called for the use of braces. Durrani operated on scoliosis *"curves we had never done surgery on before,"* testified Mehlman. In his twenty years of practice, Mehlman never operated on a child with less than fifty degrees of curvature. Without approval from Children's Investigational Review Board, Durrani performed an experimental procedure on children called percutaneous scoliosis surgery, a minimally invasive method which used spinal fusion and metal implants to correct a curvature. Children's never took action to stop the unapproved experimental surgeries.

By 2006, Mehlman began complaining to his supervisors at Children's, including Dr. Alvin Crawford; Dr. Eric Wall, then in charge of orthopedic surgery at Children's; and the hospital's patient safety officer, Steve Muething. Mehlman openly criticized Durrani during the pre-operative and post-operative teaching conferences with surgical residents and fellows, with senior surgeons and department supervisors in attendance. Residents and fellows *"would roll their eyes"* knowing Durrani's reputation, testified Mehlman. Mehlman's comments had no impact on Durrani. Durrani seldom attended the conferences and when he attended, he was unreceptive to feedback. *"I don't know of a single situation when anybody raised an issue where he changed his surgical plan,"* testified Mehlman.

Chapter 52

Wall and Azizkhan

"A quiet conscience sleeps in thunder."
—Thomas Fuller

After a conference in 2006 in which Mehlman questioned Durrani's aggressive practices, Wall told Mehlman, *"Chuck, you've been asked to be quiet."* Wall wouldn't say by whom. Mehlman responded, *"Eric, the day that I'm quiet in this conference, you better check a pulse. Because as long as it's my job to teach these residents and these fellows, the next generation of practitioners, how to be ethical and to be evidence-based practitioners, I will continue to speak up."* Mehlman referenced the exchange with Wall as the low point of his professional career.

On October 12, 2006, Wall sent a recommendation for Durrani to UC Health, helping launch Durrani's later practice with UC Health and West Chester.

In April and May of 2007, administrators and members of Durrani's staff began sending complaints about Durrani's surgical practices to Krissy Probst, his administrative assistant. Insurance companies refused to pay unless Durrani filed his paperwork.

Meanwhile, Durrani world-hopped at medical conferences. He gave a seminar for surgeons in Bangladesh on May 31, 2007 to tout Medtronic and the benefits of its product BMP-2 in spinal fusion. More email complaints followed in June until Sandy Singleton, the surgical division's business manager, asked for a meeting with Durrani's team "*without Durrani*" to hear them out.

The email complaints continued into July of 2007 when Durrani became a fellow in the American Academy of Orthopedic Surgeons and a board-certified orthopedic surgeon. By December of 2007, Anthem insurance began rejecting payment for the use of BMP-2 for patients at Children's. More insurers followed and by June of 2008, the FDA no longer approved BMP-2 even for investigational use.

To assure his steady income from medical devices and their manufacturers, Durrani met with the president of Alphatec, a California-based company peddling another non-FDA approved fusion material called PureGen. Durrani would cash in on PureGen by setting up his own distributorship for the product to make sure hospital purchases of the material lined his own pockets.

In the era before hospitals became corporate enterprises run primarily by corporate administrators, Durrani might have been flagged and dismissed under "peer review" a process where the hospital's staff physicians review and discipline their own members. Doctors are now employees of the hospitals in which they treat patients and can no longer act independently to censure other doctors. The responsibility for monitoring and disciplining hospital physicians today lies not in the hands of their physician "peers" but in the hands of hospital administrators whose first concern is the institution's bottom line. Doctors like Mehlman who openly criticize the competence of other staff physicians face retaliation from hospital administrators.

Children's Medical Executive Committee, composed of staff physicians who ostensibly review their peers, "is a relic," testified Dr. Elaine Billmire, who served on the committee during the years Durrani was on staff. *"It's really the hospital executives and the board of directors who decide" when a doctor is disciplined or fired. The hospital has not been handling doctors the way they should be. And that means both giving them the respect they deserve, and also dealing with serious problems as they should be,"* testified Billmire.

The one person in Children's hierarchy who could have taken immediate action against Durrani was Azizkhan, then Director of Surgery. "*We were not supported by Azizkhan*," he said. "*He was a punitive, vindictive administrator.*" Azizkhan alone had the power to discipline or to fire Durrani in consultation with the hospital's chief executive, Jim Anderson. Azizkhan's salary and bonuses were based on the expansion of the surgical staff and the revenue produced for the hospital.

Nothing changed for the next two years until Durrani resigned from Children's in August 2008, claiming an "inhospitable environment" after he met privately with Wall and Stern. The announcement letter Children's sent to patients informing them Durrani resigned offered no explanation for his departure or warning about his surgical record so as to protect both Durrani and the hospital, not his patients.

If Children's officially sanctioned Durrani by revoking his hospital privileges, they would have been required by law to report him to the National Practitioner Data Bank, a federal clearinghouse designed to protect patients from dangerous doctors. If Durrani fought back, it could have opened a public window into how the hospital enabled his fraudulent and shoddy practices for years.

A study by *Public Citizen*, a non-profit consumer advocacy organization, found forty-seven percent of all hospitals in the country never reported a single sanction against their doctors to the NPDB from 1990 to 2007. Hospitals often circumvent the law by either not officially disciplining a bad doctor or by limiting any suspension of their privileges to twenty-nine days—one day short of the thirty days required by law for reporting a physician. The database is used by state medical boards and hospitals around the country to conduct background checks on doctors to see if they have been sanctioned for misconduct by a hospital, had their license curtailed by a state medical board, or have had any malpractice payments made on their behalf. The background checks are only as good as the information reported to the NPDB.

Azizkhan left Cincinnati Children's to become president of Children's Hospital in Omaha, Nebraska, where he again found himself embroiled in a controversy over the competence of a staff physician. In January of 2019, two surgeons in Omaha sued Azizkhan, claiming he had retaliated against them for questioning the performance of another surgeon. Ten physicians resigned from the staff of the hospital in protest.

In 2017 Dr. Puccioni was encouraged to hire Dr. Adam Conley. This encouragement came from Azizkhan. Omaha Children's Hospital paid Conley $50,000.00 to join Puccioni's practice. Puccioni became increasingly concerned over Conley's skill and ability to properly practice pediatric neurosurgery. He began to doubt Conley was competent. He expressed those concerns to the administration at Omaha Children's Hospital. After expressing those concerns, Conley began rumors Puccioni abused drugs. Azizkhan gave credence to these baseless charges. Despite passing drug tests, Omaha Children's insisted Puccioni take a second drug test and then face a psychological evaluation. All this was done in retaliation for Puccioni's complaint over Conley's incompetence.

In the fall of 2018, Conley operated on a seven-month-old child at Omaha Children's Hospital. The child died on the operating table. Conley lost control of the bleeding caused by his incisions. At one point he poured a significant quantity of hydrogen peroxide directly into the cranial cavity in an effort to stop the bleeding. This is not an acceptable surgical practice. Puccioni, who in seventeen years of pediatric neurosurgery never lost a patient on the operating table, was horrified by the death of the child which he reasonably believed was caused by the incompetence of Conley. Puccioni wrote a communication to the administration at Omaha Children's Hospital stating this opinion and suggesting that Conley was unfit to operate at the institution.

Dr. Jason Miller, who for many years operated alongside Puccioni on patients who required both of their specialties, was similarly shocked by the actions of Conley and also wrote a communication questioning Conley's skill. Within days of writing the letters both Puccioni and Miller's privileges to practice at Omaha Children's Hospital were suspended. Puccioni was falsely accused to be in violation of the hospital bylaws. Miller was falsely accused of placing his patients at risk.

Miller's peers pursuant to the Bylaws of Omaha Children›s Hospital reviewed his suspension and unanimously voted to immediately reinstate his privileges. Despite this vote Azizkhan and Omaha Children's Hospital refused to reinstate him and threatened it would report his suspension to the State of Nebraska, thereby causing irreparable injury to his reputation and career unless he resigned his privileges. Under this threat, Miller resigned his privileges.

After Miller's resignation, Omaha Children's Hospital engaged in deceptive practices designed to misdirect, alienate and otherwise drive away his patients for its own profit. Azizkhan and Conley participated in the effort to destroy the practices and reputations of Miller and Puccioni. Omaha Children's Hospital ratified and endorsed these wrongful actions when the Board of Directors met and failed to correct the egregious wrongs done in its name and to its shame.

Surgeons who by virtue of training, hard work, skill and compassion build a successful practice often have privileges at several institutions. Successful surgeons, like Puccioni and Miller, attract patients who during their treatment collectively spend many millions of dollars a year for hospital services. As a result, physicians employed by Omaha Children's Hospital, offer a more profitable and predictable stream of revenue.

Omaha Children's Hospital used the wrongful suspension of Puccioni and Miller to gather up their patients for themselves.

Azizkhan handled the Conley issue exactly as he handled the Durrani issue. He went after the "whistleblower" Mehlman and protected the "bad guy" Durrani. We gave Puccioni and Miller's lawyers and the Omaha news media all the information we possessed on Durrani and Azizkhan. Omaha Children's Hospital would fire Azizkhan by way of his "retirement." First a butcher, now a protector of butchers, we took Azizkhan out, too.

Chapter 53

DURRANI "RESIGNS"

"When you have to shoot, shoot. Don't talk."
—Tuco "The Good, The Bad and The Ugly"

Even after his official resignation and unofficial firing in August of 2008, Durrani continued to perform hundreds of additional surgeries at Children's until March of 2009. In the fall of 2009, Children's Business Director Peter Clayton asked the orthopaedic surgeons, *"What's happened to your spine revenue? There's a big drop off."* Mehlman responded, *"Peter, we're now doing only indicated surgery."*

In May of 2009, despite hearing complaints, UC Health recruited Durrani to their new West Chester Hospital. Durrani continued to perform fraudulent surgeries on thousands of his patients until May of 2013. As head of Durrani's residency training, Dr. Stern evaluated him as only "average," but that didn't keep West Chester from promoting Durrani as a "world-class" surgeon in its advertising. As Dr. Stern told Dr. Colosimo, *"they needed the money."*

The chorus of complaints about Durrani at Children's grew dramatically in the year leading up to his departure. Radiologists questioned his readings of patient X-rays. Other surgeons and residents raised concerns during weekly patient review sessions about his unorthodox practices, Durrani simply shrugged them off before ending his attendance at the meetings altogether. Insurance companies began refusing to pay for his unorthodox and unnecessary treatments, including the use of BMP-2.

Surgical nurses at Children's complained about the volume of surgeries and improper diagnoses of Durrani's patients. Staffing became a problem. Nurses and administrative staff at nearly every hospital where Durrani operated complained he failed to sign patient orders, dictate his post-surgical notes, or complete patient discharge records on a timely basis. Sometimes it would take him months, long past the point when any physician could expect to remember important clinical details. In one case, after performing surgery on Rebecca Applegate on January 21, 2011, Durrani failed to dictate her post-operative report for 259 days or nearly nine months later.

Those record-keeping requirements were all part of keeping a surgeon's hospital operating privileges. Hospital administrators would repeatedly suspend Durrani's privileges on paper, but allow him to continue to operate. Durrani became such a hot topic in the nursing stations and doctors' lounges that supervisors would admonish them not to talk about him. It was like "*he whose name we shall not say*," testified Mehlman.

Several nurses at Children's, fed up with the workload and Durrani's shady medical practices, simply quit working for him. Nurse Gari Ann Dunn testified the answer from department supervisors at Children's to continuing complaints about Durrani was always, "*We're trying to take care of it.*" Durrani kept on operating and kept on bringing in millions for Children's. Durrani bought expensive gifts for Children's executives, including a fur coat for Sandy Singleton, the surgery division's business director.

As part of his departure deal in 2009, Children's scrubbed clean Durrani's personnel file. When we finally obtained his file in the discovery process, the file made no mention of his repeated suspensions for failing to file his surgical reports on time or any other disciplinary action against him.

Durrani proved himself a fraud as a medical researcher by falsifying his data and exaggerating or lying about his credentials at research conferences. An abstract he submitted to the *Scoliosis Research Society* in February 2008 was later discovered to be based on experimental surgeries he performed on patients without the hospital review board's permission. Another paper he submitted later that year to a major spine conference was based on totally fabricated data.

Durrani's personal behavior also became a popular topic among nurses and doctors at Children's. He would claim particular nurses solely as his own although they worked for the entire surgical department. He hired the mother of a patient right out of the waiting room, because he was smitten with her looks.

Durrani's bedside manner left much to be desired. He met with the parents of one child after operating on their son and announced in front of the entire waiting room, "Someone needs to put this child on a diet."

Durrani nicked Steven Andrew Schultz's, artery while inserting screws and rods he didn't need into his lower spine. An emergency room trauma surgeon had to be called into the operating room to repair the damage and save Schultz from bleeding to death. Durrani told the family afterward he saved Schultz's life. While recovering in intensive care for the next eight days, Schultz asked Durrani if he should see a hematologist about his internal bleeding. Durrani told him no. "They're going to start sticking and poking you in places you don't want them to," he said.

Many patients saw Durrani as their savior. According to an affidavit by Jeff Angeline, a physical therapist who now owns his own practice, Durrani fired Angeline from doing contractual work at Durrani's clinic because Angeline urged therapy before trying surgery. *"It was his modus operandi to claim he could do what no other surgeon could do. He had his patient area walls covered with framed accomplishments. While all surgeons do this, Dr. Durrani took it to another level,"* swore Angeline.

Angeline witnessed Durrani sitting in his office reading with a waiting room full of patients. *"He wanted his patients to think, If I have to wait for him, he must be incredible,"* swore Angeline.

Durrani's final undoing at Children's would be the affair he began with his physician assistant, Jamie Moor. Durrani made no attempt to hide the affair from his staff and met privately with her in his office for sex. I was told a parent of a child walked in on them.

When a medical device sales representative, Dave Rattigan, asked Moor out for a date, Durrani instructed a nurse to inform the rep "hands off." Supervisors at Children's finally moved Moor to another department in 2008 to break up the work-hours tryst. Not long after, Durrani announced he was leaving the hospital and launching his own facility, The Center for Advanced Spine Technologies (CAST) in Mason, Ohio. Later, he would open offices in Evendale north of Cincinnati and Florence in Northern Kentucky.

Asked during his deposition why he failed to report Durrani to the state medical board, Mehlman said he feared retribution from administrators. "*Surgeons are expected to be quiet, docile Stepford Wives that come and do surgery when they're called, and then move on. So I take exception to the question because it makes it sound like I was weak or somehow not committed to fighting or talking to disinterested administrators who were all about corporate protection.*" Mehlman testified he reported Durrani to the FBI.

Children's never disciplined any of its administrators involved in supervising Durrani. "Black Monday" is the day in early 2015 that Azizkhan, Dr. Frederick Ryckman and a top public relations person, were let go by then chief executive Michael Fisher. Fisher replaced Jim Anderson at Children's not long after Durrani departed.

I discovered the pattern in Durrani's lies about the need for surgery and falsified diagnoses. Durrani would have his patients fill out a consent form describing their surgery, but he usually performed no physical exam on them even though he would often dictate in his medical report that he had. If he ordered an MRI or other radiological test, the image would show no issues requiring surgery. Durrani would send a letter to the patient's primary care physician stating the patient suffered severe stenosis and required surgery. The patients never saw the letter or the actual radiology report. The PCP assumed Durrani told them the truth. These letters to patients' PCP's are filled, too, with how well the patient is doing after the surgery. Not until litigation would patients learn of these letters. All lies. Despite the surgery being a disaster resulting in pain and misery, Durrani reported otherwise.

Like so many of Durrani's patients, Thomas Atkinson proceeded with the unnecessary surgery Durrani insisted on for his neck pain, not once but twice. "*He was a man of black and white in a system that offers you a thousand shades of gray,*" Atkinson said. "*Durrani strode into the examining room like a colossus. Your X-ray was up on the panel. He walked up to it and he went, 'That's your problem and I can fix it.'*"

Durrani scheduled Atkinson's first surgery at Christ Hospital and then switched to UC's West Chester Hospital without an explanation. Durrani and the hospital failed to inform Atkinson that Durrani lost his operating privileges at Christ for having killed his last patient there, Holly DeClair.

When Atkinson asked in the recovery room how surgery went, Durrani looked visibly shaken and told Atkinson and his wife, "*I hope I never have to do that again.*" The operations failed to ease Atkinson's pain. The surgery only made it harder for Atkinson to turn his head. Cincinnati's Mayfield Clinic later informed Atkinson both of Durrani's surgeries had been unnecessary.

Chapter 54
Cathy Beil

"Success is not final, failure is not fatal; it is the courage to continue that counts."
—Winston Churchill

With a history of neck and lower back pain, Cathy Beil's family physician referred her to Durrani and his CAST office in Erlanger, Ky. Durrani marketed himself through mailers to the tristate primary care doctors. It worked. Durrani performed a quick exam and ordered an X-ray. Durrani informed Beil that she suffered from severe scoliosis and required immediate surgery or she would end up in a wheelchair. Durrani's solution? Spinal fusion surgery. Durrani promised Beil it would be minimally invasive with three small incisions and a recovery time of four to six weeks. He failed to inform Beil he would place rods in her spine.

On November 20, 2009, Beil, underwent surgery at West Chester Hospital where Durrani used BMP-2 as the bone grafting material for the fusions. Beil would soon learn after the surgery the procedure had been far more than minimally invasive. The pain and muscle spasms in her back became so bad after three days Durrani prescribed her oxycontin and valium. Two days later, Beil's neighbor's nurse friends volunteered to help give Beil a shower. The shower is when Beil learned she had forty-four staples in her back.

On December 4, Durrani's physician assistant and mistress Jamie Moor removed the staples. Also there was Hank, Durrani's beloved German Shepherd with the MRSA infection. Beil complained to Moor her mid-section was so swollen her clothes failed to fit. Beil's right leg and foot radiated pain. Moor told her everything was normal. Moor added, "You have to remember, Cathy, you had major surgery." She advised Beil to begin her physical therapy as soon as possible.

During her first therapy visit, Beil's therapist expressed concern about her surgical wound. Once home, Beil called Moor at Durrani's office. Moor told Beil not to worry about the wound because it wasn't seeping or oozing. In the evening, Beil reached to feel her back and her hand came back wet. Before too long, her clothing soaked through. Beil's husband Wayne, tried to clean her up the best he could with Betadine and bandages. An hour later, drainage ran down her leg.

The next day, Moor prescribed oral antibiotics and instructed Wayne to clean and bandage the wound three times a day. Moor also sent Beil to the hospital for scans of her swollen leg and foot. The images showed no arterial blockage, but the infection worsened. Wayne began replacing the seeping bandages every one to two hours. Unable to reach Moor again, Wayne drove Beil to the emergency room at St. Elizabeth, The doctors recommended IV antibiotics for her infection.

In the following weeks, Beil developed cellulitis, an ugly and painful condition causing the tissue beneath her skin to erupt through her surgical wound. After several more visits with Moor, Beil finally saw Durrani on December 22 upon his return from Pakistan. Durrani told Beil she was healing nicely and she should begin physical therapy again and consider swim therapy. Beil complied with Durrani's recommendation.

When Beil complained to her family physician, Dr. Troy Schumann, about the disastrous outcome of her surgery, Schumann referred her to Dr. Michael Rohmiller, a Northern Kentucky spine surgeon at Beacon Orthopedic and Sports Medicine. In March of 2011, Rohmiller ordered scans and delivered Beil the news.

The screws Durrani inserted in Beil's vertebra were dangerously loose and could lead to a rod snapping in her spine. The grafting material also failed to fuse the spine. Durrani lied to Beil. Her scoliosis did not warrant corrective surgery at sixteen degrees curvature. Durrani falsely claimed the curvature was thirty-five degrees. The rods Durrani placed in her spine improved her condition by only a half degree. In his corrective surgery, Rohmiller tightened the screws but he couldn't remove the rods without causing further injury to her spine.

In the end, the pain in Beil's lower back worsened before Durrani's surgery and she never regained the flexibility she once had. "Small things, like rolling over in bed or wiping properly after using the restroom, have become major difficulties," she wrote in her personal narrative. There would always be the extensive scarring down her back from Durrani's "minimally invasive surgery."

Beil felt betrayed, not only by Durrani, but by Cincinnati's hospitals. Before agreeing to Durrani's surgery, she visited Durrani's website where he touted his achievements at area hospitals, including Children's. "What he does not reveal and what I did not learn until after he mangled me was that he was let go from Children's and several other hospitals. If only I had known these things before…" wrote Beil in her narrative.

Chapter 55

Rule 41(A) & Statute of Repose

"The general must be sharp, as Homer says, as a bird or as thought, darting in his swiftness of mind at every matter."
—Onasander

The trial of *Beil vs. Durrani* would be one of several firsts. The first case tried in Hamilton County after a two-year legal battle in federal court and a three-year wait following the refiling from the losses in Butler County. The first case tried by the firm's two new trial lawyers, Alan Statman and Fred Johnson. The first trial to hear expert testimony for our clients from neurosurgeon Dr. Stephen Bloomfield and neuroradiologist Dr. James Cole. The first case tried in front of Mark Schweikert, the Judge appointed to preside over the Durrani cases. *Beil vs. Durrani* would also establish trial rulings applicable for all future Durrani trials.

It was a war.

Alan Statman and Fred Johnson, with me assisting, would face four defense lawyers: Mike Lyon and Jim Brockman of Lindhorst & Dreidame for Durrani and Walt Haggerty and Bill Paliobeis of Frost Brown Todd for West Chester Hospital.

In the months leading up to the Beil trial, Schweikert proved where he stood with the plaintiffs. In December of 2017, Schweikert made a ruling that risked the dismissal of over a hundred of the Durrani cases transferred in 2015 from Butler County. He ruled in favor of the defense that the cases originally filed, dismissed and refiled, would now violate the Ohio's Statute of Repose. To this day, this is the biggest crock of shit ruling in the Durrani litigation. It was merely Schweikert's attempt to get rid of cases.

The statute of repose R.C. 2305.113 is not superior to the savings statute under Rule 41(a). Durrani and the hospitals attempted to gain a cheap and unfair win which is not consistent with the facts and law and Schweikert gave it to them. It is shocking.

The Savings Statute never mentions the Statute of Repose, likewise the Statute of Repose never mentions the Savings Statute. Schweikert ruled: Statute of Repose wins. Savings Statute loses. It's wrong. He claimed the Ohio legislature could have made the Savings Statute an exception to the Statute of Repose. He does not conclude, by the same logic, that the Savings Statute did not make the Statute of Repose an exception to the Statute of Repose.

Example of the Rule 41(A) Savings Statute vs. Statute Of Repose:

Surgery Date	Butler County Filing Date	Rule 41A Date	Hamilton County Re-Filing Date
2010	2013	2015	2016

The original case was filed within four years. Every case was also refiled within the one year of the savings statute under Rule 41a. Durrani and the hospitals claimed from 2010, the surgery date, to 2016, the refiling date, is over four years which means the case now has a statute of repose issue. All case law, legislative history, common sense and justice is on our side. The Savings Statute "saves" the case.

The entire false premise of the statute of repose is notice within four years. Durrani and the hospitals had it. The case was timely filed. There was also no surprise of the refiling. The Rule 41(a) dismissals stated the cases would be refiled.

We researched this issue before taking the action.

Antoon v. Cleveland Clinic Foundation does not apply to a properly and timely filed, Rule 41(a) and refiled case and did not decide the savings statute issue by its own admission. The trial court erroneously applied *Antoon*. In *Antoon*, the Plaintiff did not properly Rule 41(a) and timely refile.

A case timely filed, properly Rule 41(a) and timely refiled, is "saved" under the savings statute and not "trapped" by the statute of repose.

At the time we dismissed and refiled our cases, *Antoon*, which doesn't apply anyway, was not decided by the Supreme Court and no law should be applied ex post facto, meaning after the fact. It is infuriating to us that we researched this issue before deciding to make the Rule 41(a) move and the law was clearly, as it still is, on their side. Schweikert ignored the law. It's beyond shocking. At the time all the cases were Rule 41(a), despite the facts not applying, the *Antoon* case relied upon by the trial court was a District Appellate Court decision favorable to us. Its maddening. *Antoon* stated in its own words it did not decide "whether Ohio's saving statute, R.C. 2305.19, or the federal tolling statute, 28 U.S.C. 1367, properly invoked, may allow actions to survive beyond expiration of the statute of repose."

The day after Schweikert's ruling, the defense lawyers sent us a letter offering a lousy combined total settlement from Children's, West Chester and Durrani's insurance company Medical Protective.

We replied, "hell no" and counter punched. We filed an Affidavit of Disqualification to disqualify Schweikert for bias and have him removed as the presiding judge in the Durrani cases. Our filing froze Schweikert's ability to dismiss the cases until Chief Justice O'Connor ruled on the disqualification motion.

My Dad refused to sign the affidavit, but approved the move. Matt Hammer signed it at Dad's request. I told Dad as the owner of the firm the Affidavit would have more force if he signed it. Always the "scaredy cat," he demurred. This always frustrated me. My Dad no longer practiced law, except in Durrani cases. He had three sons as lawyers, four before Jed passed. In his eighties, why in the heck did he care about all our enemies in the cause?

Beil's case almost never made it to trial. Her previous attorney, David Kamp, filed the malpractice case prior to us and allegedly never notified Durrani and West Chester with an extension letter to allow more time to file. Only after we threatened David Kamp with a legal malpractice suit days before trial, did Kamp cooperate with an affidavit so Beil's case could proceed to trial. Ole "Cotton Top" did the right thing under threat.

Chapter 56
David Prater

"The most powerful weapon on earth is the human soul on fire."
—Voltaire

I felt unbearable pressure going into the Beil trial. With the four losses in Butler County, we had to win.

At least I alleviated my money woes. It happened by chance. Even with the monthly installments from Kurtzman, I struggled every two weeks to meet payroll. I again began asking for money from anyone I knew. Glenn Feagan kicked in some. My chiropractor lent money. Crystal Pierce lent some of her winnings.

In September of 2017, I spotted an over-sized glossy postcard in our office mail. It listed a toll-free number to call Barrister Capital, an investment firm that funds legal cases for personal injury, medical malpractice, nursing home abuse and other plaintiff settlements. The postcard read: "We are here, ready to help. The application is free and we do all the work because we understand that your time is important."

I thought, why not? When you're borrowing money from your chiropractor, anything is worth a try. I called the toll-free number and asked to speak directly to the owner. They gave me the number for David Prater, whose offices were based in Lexington, Ky.

"I was in Elizabethtown, Ky, south of Louisville on a business run when I got the call. I didn't know who this guy was. I didn't how he got my number. All I know is there's this guy on the other end who says he's got these cases and he needs some capital. And he had this passion in his voice," remembers David Prater.

Prater agreed to meet with me at my law office in Independence a few days later. Prater would rendezvous there again with Barrister's general counsel, Mike Fox, whose job was to review cases and recommend whether David should invest. Fox was known to be conservative in his estimates of any potential settlements or awards. Understandable in the world of lawsuits.

I took David and Mike to the "bunker" in the walk-out basement of an empty office building a few blocks south on Madison Pike from my Independence, Ky. office. The bunker is jammed, but organized well with a 1000 banker boxes. The front of each box listed the client's name or the topics. No one could go to the bunker and not be impressed. Matt Hammer and I even took Judge Barrett there once as part of a mediation Barrett conducted. The first thing I do when I want to explain the Durrani litigation is take them to the "bunker."

Later on his drive home, Prater heard from Fox on his cell phone.

"What's the value, do you think?" Prater asked.

"Dave, this is a nine-figure case," answered Fox.

David asked me to meet him at *First Watch*, downtown Cincinnati. We sat down for breakfast, and he said, "I can commit to $1,000,000 and probably more."

David Prater saved me and saved the Durrani victims. I thank him every possible chance. He is still on my team.

Chapter 57
Cathy Beil Trial

"When strength is yoked with justice, where is a mightier pair than they?"
—Aeschylus

From the first day of the Beil trial, Schweikert resented my presence. As I passed notes and whispered information to Statman and Johnson, Schweikert admonished me from the bench. He also hated I would walk back-and-forth between the counsel table and the twenty banker boxes at the back of the courtroom.

All of this would be allowed without issue by any assistant helping a lawyer in Court across America except Reich allowing me.

One document trip impressed David Prater, who sat in the back pew of the courtroom dressed in a T-shirt and shorts to avoid being noticed as the chief lender to my cause. The defense repeatedly objected to evidence in the case they insisted we never filed.

During the next break, I walked back to our twenty boxes and knew instantly where to find the evidence in dispute. "He pulls three files from two boxes and hands them to Fred. All the evidence came into the trial at that point, and the judge and the defense lawyers had to shut their mouths. Nobody knew the evidence had been entered except Eric, and he knew where to find it in twenty banker boxes," recalls Prater.

Prater believes the anecdote "exemplified to me what Eric has been able to do as basically a one-man show against people who have spent millions to defeat him. I've been involved in several hundred of these types of cases, and I'd not seen anybody like this." Prater ended up lending even more. It meant the end to my money woes for the Durrani litigation. David Prater saved me, saved the victims and my gratitude for him is immeasurable.

Schweikert hamstrung us from the outset of the trial. Like Guckenberger, Schweikert disallowed disclosure of the reason of Durrani's absence. Schweikert disallowed the jury to watch Durrani take the Fifth Amendment 101 times on the questions asked during his videotaped deposition from Pakistan. We worked for years to have our moment with Durrani's deposition and Schweikert stole it from us.

Schweikert also deprived the jury of the most humorous incident during Durrani's deposition. On his first day of video testimony from Pakistan, the Muslim call to prayers could be heard in the background when a dog began barking inside Durrani's home. Durrani apologized for the dog barking. Alan Statman asked, "Is that Hank?" Durrani knocked over the glass of water on his tabletop as he answered, "Yes."

We could not believe it. We thought Hank would be dead by now. Not only had the MRSA infected dog survived, Duranni took Hank with him to Pakistan while leaving his wife and two teenage children behind.

During the video deposition, Durrani repeatedly addressed Statman as "learned counsel," a fawning title we teased Fred Johnson never received from Durrani in later depositions. To this day, we sometimes address Alan as "learned counsel."

Durrani not only took the Fifth Amendment one hundred and one times during his deposition, but he also refused to answer over fifty other questions. Schweikert disallowed it all. Durrani testified conservative care should always be tried before surgery and timely reports are critical to patient care. Of course, Durrani failed to do either.

Under oath, Durrani lied about hospitals never suspending his operating privileges; lied about being charged with a crime; lied about only performing one spinal fusion per week; claimed departure from Children's was cordial; claimed he had been a surgeon to the Saudi royal family; claimed he never performed surgery for money.

Durrani actually insisted on placing in the record he fled to Pakistan only because "Eric Deters and his Bulldog Nation ran him out of the country."

In the Beil trial, Dr. Sigurd Berven, a handsome, charming orthopedic surgeon from the University of California-San Francisco, scored points with the jurors on behalf of Durrani. Meanwhile, two of our witnesses, Dr. Michael Rohmiller and Beil's family physician Dr. Troy Schumann, backtracked on their earlier opinions about the lasting impact of Beil's surgery and whether it worsened her back pain and limited her flexibility.

Statman and Johnson performed well, as did our new expert witnesses Bloomfield and Cole. According to Statman, "it was a firefight like I'd never been in before, and I've been in all kinds of contentious cases, including criminal trials with victims' families agitating for justice and prosecutors' intent on winning at all costs. There was constant fighting during meetings in the judge's office. I bet we had a hundred of them. Instead of sidebars where lawyers discuss things privately with the judge in the courtroom, Schweikert insisted we go into his office, and these were always free-for-alls," said Statman.

The defense moved for a mistrial five times during the two-week trial. Shockingly, Schweikert overruled them. "I've never had a mistrial in my entire career," Statman said. The bad blood between Schweikert and me continued to build. Before the end of the trial, Schweikert ordered me not to say anything to Statman and Johnson in the courtroom and to stop sending them notes and fetching files. Why? He knew this hurt our cause.

In a comedic incident I call "*The Great Potato Chip Bribe*," Mike Lyon's wife, Jacki and Bill Paliobeis' girlfriend, saw me during a break in the proceedings jokingly offering a juror a potato chip from the bag I'd purchased from a courthouse vending machine after the jury laughed at the noise of the bag opening. No potato chip exchanged hands. The women immediately reported the incident to the defense attorneys who tattled to Schweikert. Schweikert would actually take a recess and interview each juror alone in open Court over the potato chip incident.

Jacki and the girlfriend did not attend the trial in stoic silence. They attended as two animated groupies. I've never witnessed anything like it.

Jacki, Mike's second and alleged trophy wife, taught at Xavier University in the English Department. She also wrote a couple "salty" books. Jim Triona told me the funniest story of Mike and Jacki's courtship. Jacki, single at the time, dated Mike, but other men too. Distraught one night, Mike drove over to Jacki's house, but a much wealthier and prominent man who Mike knew answered the door in a robe. The man replied, "Hi Mike, I'll get Jacki."

Another bizarre scenario occurred with Mike Lyon's wife, Jacki. During court at a break, Alan and I stood outside by the elevators for privacy. Jacki actually walked over and stood right next to us. I mean literally next to us in some bizarre eavesdropping intimidation attempt. Alan and I looked at each other like, "what the hell." On an elevator once, Mike Lyon claimed Jacki planned to write a book about the Durrani cases. I've yet to see it.

I suspected at least two of the eight jurors were on Beil's side. Although I stopped my radio show in 2015 to focus on the Durrani cases, one juror told me privately walking down the hall prior to jury selection, before I knew they were a juror, that he missed the show. The jury foreman, a local union official, openly registered his reactions throughout the trial. He sat in the corner of the jury box closest to me. It was as clear from his body language he was on our side. When Statman would score a point during a cross-examination, the juror would throw his hands in the air and mouth the word "exactly." When the defense said something he thought didn't ring true, the juror would put his face in his hands and shake his head. I have never witnessed a more animated juror.

We knew the defense could not turn a 16-degree curvature of Beil's spine into 35 degrees. Once again, I prepared large charts showing the jury the differences among mild, moderate and severe cases of scoliosis. It was obvious Beil's case was only mild and never required surgery.

An eight-hour jury deliberation followed on the issue of Durrani liability. On that question, the jury returned with a $300,000 award in favor of Beil with half for fraud and half for negligence. However, the jurors made an error in their verdict. They found proximate cause for fraud but not proximate cause for negligence against Durrani. This meant an award of only $150,000 for Beil unless we asked the Court to have the jury deliberate more. We decided it too risky, because what if the jury made the mistake on the fraud causation, not the negligence causation. With the acceptance of the flawed verdict, it left the second part of the trial to be resolved of whether UC's West Chester Hospital could be held liable for negligent credentialing and retaining Durrani on their medical staff.

Walt Haggerty moved to block our expert witness on West Chester's liability, Dr. Wilkey. Wilkey reviewed hundreds of the Durrani cases and wrote more than 400 affidavits of merit to support the victims' claims. The hospitals deposed him over twenty times.

For the Beil trial, Wilkey flew in from New York to testify live for the Durrani portion of the trial and then flew back later to pick up his surgical practice.

Before the portion of the trial against West Chester began, the defense argued they never had the chance to question Wilkey about what his testimony would be against West Chester. Schweikert upheld the objection. He ruled Wilkey's testimony would be disallowed unless Wilkey flew back to Cincinnati within days to be questioned by the defense. Wilkey could not. Schweikert's decision, complete balderdash, excluded all which Wilkey knew. His ruling on this is one of the most biased, outlandish and corrupt rulings ever. The West Chester lawyers already possessed all of Wilkey's opinions and basis for them.

With Schweikert disallowing Wilkey's testimony, we knew there was no way to win the trial against West Chester. If we pursued the liability case against the hospital, we would establish a bad precedent for all future Durrani trials.

West Chester offered Beil a $50,000 settlement. We advised Beil to accept the settlement. The firm promised to compensate Beil a total of $350,000 less attorney fees and costs rather than risking a jury verdict in favor of West Chester and setting a dangerous precedent for future cases. Beil agreed. We would have lost against West Chester and she would have only received $150,000 (50%) recoverable under the policy. Fraud is not covered under the insurance. So we promised Cathy double what she would have received. We would pay it when the settlements came in from West Chester and Durrani.

Chapter 58

UNGRATEFUL

"How the hell did we get ourselves into this?"
—Wyatt Earp "Tombstone"

No good deed goes unpunished.

I spoke to the Beils throughout the trial. My text messages reflect how pleased the Beils were with our effort I'll not reproduce them here.

As in all the Durrani cases we advanced court costs. Those totaled $117,909.13 in Beil. Most law firms will not advance costs. The Beils could not afford to advance these costs.

Cathy suffered no lost income because before the surgery in question; she had already retired. We felt before trial the case was strong on liability. However, that too soon turned into a battle. Dr. Rohmiller, a subsequent treating doctor, failed to testify to what he told us off the record. I even personally went and spoke to him before his deposition. Dr. Rohmiller's surgery returned Cathy to her pre-Durrani state.

We tried the case with great preparation, diligence and care.

The jury made a mistake. The jury awarded $300,000 but decided 50% negligence and 50% fraud. They found causation on fraud, but not negligence. A debate ensued on what to do. The major question: do we ask the Court to send them back to see if they would correct their inconsistency and mistake. We simply agreed for it to be all a fraud verdict and not send it back to the jury. Why? We needed a win. Period.

If the jury returned and "corrected" the verdict as we wanted, and found causation on both fraud and negligence, Beil would have only recovered $150,000 under the Medical Protective policy, which only covers negligence. Plus, Durrani appeals all verdicts. Therefore, she would be on appeal and still not have recovered anything to date. The $150,000 is all she would have recovered. Only Crystal Pierce whose appeal is over received money from Medical Protective; not one other client has received a nickel from Medical Protective after eight years.

Our next West Chester case was going to be in federal court with Judge Barrett. We knew we had a more favorable forum to "establish the rules" for Stage II against West Chester.

So, what did Deters Law do for Cathy Beil?

We told her we would guarantee her $350,000 less fees and costs. This meant she would receive $150,000 more than the covered verdict, plus the $50,000 from West Chester.

Despite the $50,000 from West Chester, we threw her back into the settlement pool where the Special Master gave her the highest number over all our clients, $196,913.54, not $50,000. Why? Her victory put us back on track.

Because all our moves helped against West Chester, we proposed to all clients that Beil's trial costs be spread over all West Chester clients. They agreed. This netted Cathy even more money from the $350,000 promise.

We then sued the medical lien holder who paid all of Beil's medical bills. They dropped the lien. This saved Beil hundreds of thousands. If we did not do this, she would have received nothing.

Alan Statman and Fred Johnson could not believe what we did for Cathy Beil. They thought it was unnecessary and overly generous and actually thought Dad and I were nuts. Dad and I believe it the right strategy for Beil and all the other clients.

Despite all of this, Cathy Beil sued us. In the history of American law, we might be the first law firm ever sued for winning a malpractice case.

Chapter 59

Judge Michael Barrett

"Around here we have something called the Missouri boat ride."
—Josey Wales

Michael Sander held down two jobs as a truck driver and assembly worker. He walked outside on a cold winter morning to shovel the snow off his front sidewalk. He lifted one shovel full of snow and felt something give way in his back. In excruciating pain, he limped back into his house. The pain reached from his lower back all the way down both legs, causing numbness in his toes.

His family physician, Dr. Michael Gieske, gave him muscle relaxants and took an X-ray of his back. Gieske thought the problem severe enough to recommend Sander visit Durrani. Sander knew nothing about Durrani but trusted his family physician to refer him "to a decent doctor." Durrani examined Sander and took an MRI before giving him the bad news. He had two herniated discs. The good news was Durrani could fix his problem with two separate surgeries and Sander would return to a normal life in six months.

Durrani performed three surgeries at West Chester, which only made Sander's condition worse. The first surgery fused the spine around one alleged herniated disk. The second surgery removed the scar tissue pressing on the nerves from the first surgery. The third surgery fused the spine on his other alleged herniated disc.

After a month of heavy pain medications and physical therapy, Sander suffered more pain in his lower back and legs and had less flexibility in his spine than before his first surgery. In January 2011, Sander went back to CAST and Durrani told Sander there was nothing more he could do. A Vietnam-era veteran, Sander turned for help to the VA Medical Center in Cincinnati, where a neurologist told him Durrani's operations caused permanent nerve damage in both his legs. Further surgery might help. "After what I'd been through, there was no way Durrani or anybody else was going to touch my back again," said Sander. Another surgery, he feared, would leave him totally immobile.

Before being mangled by Durrani, Sander enjoyed four and five mile hikes in Kentucky's beautiful state parks with his grandkids. Sander not only had held down two jobs, but was a skilled handyman around the house, doing carpentry, painting and other chores. In January 2011, Sander qualified for Social Security disability payments. He can walk no longer than ten minutes at a time with his cane and needs a walker for support on longer walks.

Pain keeps Sander from sitting more than thirty minutes at a time and wakes him every two or three hours at night. He can no longer bend from the hip or lift objects from the floor, forcing him to give up his handyman duties. Since Durrani's first surgery in 2010, Sander believes he has not had "one day without pain." The powerful pain medications he takes have made it "hard to be intimate" with his wife.

Sander never gave a thought to suing Durrani until his wife saw a TV news story in July of 2013 about Durrani's arrest. They retained me to pursue Durrani.

After we dismissed the cases from Butler County a few cases qualified to be filed in federal court rather than state court based upon their living out of Ohio. Sander's case was one. His case would be tried before Judge Michael Barrett.

Barrett grew up on Cincinnati's prestigious Grandin Road in Hyde Park, where a century ago the wealthy of the Gilded Age built lavish estates on hillsides overlooking the Ohio River six miles east of downtown. Barrett's childhood home was a three-story, six-bedroom Gothic Revival mansion of stone block and castle-like turrets with a sweeping hilltop view as the Ohio bends north around Kentucky and west toward downtown.

Despite being a member of one of the most influential families in Cincinnati, Barrett is personable to all and possesses wit and humor. His brother John is chief executive of Western & Southern Financial Group, a Fortune 500 company based in Cincinnati. His brother William, a radiation oncologist, is executive director of the University of Cincinnati Cancer Institute, known as the Barrett Cancer Center, the area's comprehensive cancer treatment center. His brother Francis is a prominent local attorney with his own firm. In 2012, Francis was elected chair of the University of Cincinnati board of trustees. The three men's father, Dr. Charles Barrett, a radiologist, served as chief executive of Western & Southern and founder of the cancer center which bore his name.

Michael Barrett graduated from the University of Cincinnati college and law school. He became active in the Republican Party and joined Hamilton County prosecutor's office. He became partner at the law firm Graydon Head, before joining his brother Francis's firm in 1995. He served as head of the Hamilton County Republican Party and the Ohio Republican Party. In 2006, George W. Bush appointed Barrett a federal judge. Close to Stan Chesley, Chesley arranged Chuck Schumer and Hillary Clinton to sponsor Barrett's Senate hearing confirmation. Appointed by a Republican and sponsored by two powerful Democrat Senators, Barrett's confirmation sailed. It's no secret with Barrett having practiced criminal law and personal injury law, he allows Plaintiffs to put on their case without much restriction. Barrett is married to Carol Williams, a retired local TV news anchor.

Barrett's handling of the Durrani cases contrasted with Schweikert's. Barrett allowed group trials. He permitted the refiling of the Durrani cases from Butler County without imposing a new filing date for the statute of limitations. He issued no gag orders. For the first time in any trial against Durrani, Barrett informed the jurors Durrani had been indicted and fled to Pakistan.

Chapter 60

Federal Trial

"It's not enough that we do our best; sometimes we have to do what's required."
—Winston Churchill

Barrett, not Schweikert, would now be the first Judge to hear a case against West Chester. We settled Beil as part of this strategic plan.

Kimberly Kelly, a former X-ray technician at West Chester, remembers Durrani entering the operating room suite without a mask and talking to his junior surgical partner, Shanti, while standing next to the patient's sterile field. During one surgery, Durrani manipulated a patient's upper thigh with his bare hand and then touched the sterile surgical drape on the operating table.

On more than one occasion, Kelly overheard Durrani talk to other doctors about how stupid Americans are and how they would believe anything he told them. After Durrani's arrest on Medicare fraud charges, one of Kelly's supervisors attended a conference on medical terrorism and Durrani matched the profile. Kelly wrote in an affidavit: "*It is my opinion Durrani was a medical terrorist who hated Americans and wanted to harm Americans.*"

Jeff Angeline, a physical therapist owned his own practice and was fired as a contractor at Durrani's clinic for urging pre-operative therapy over surgery. In his affidavit, Angeline wrote: "*I actually remarked to others that I thought Durrani, based on what I witnessed, was a medical terrorist. He went back and forth to Pakistan all the time. He clearly and purposefully mistreated and misdiagnosed his patients. It just did not add up: Pakistan, what he was doing to patients, his general attitude. When I would mention to my friends that I thought he was a medical terrorist, I would be accused of being a racist. I am not. I truly believe to this day. I do even more so knowing he was indicted and fled back to Pakistan.*"

Like many other West Chester employees who worked with Durrani, Kelly feared losing her job if she complained about Durrani. The hospital staff was warned repeatedly via emails with supervisor instructions not to discuss Durrani, his behavior or performance. Kelly didn't bring her concerns to me until 2017 after being fired from the hospital for blowing the whistle on infection control issues.

I drove up to Butler County, Ohio and met Kelly the first time at a *Bob Evans* where she told me all she knew. Kelly impressed me so much, I gave her a job. She now prepares all the documents we use at trial from the medical records. She's an incredible asset to our cause.

According to Tayeb, Durrani would brag in the hallways of the hospital that he was West Chester's "top money-maker." In separate testimony, Shanti said

Durrani bragged he could get the hospital to do anything he asked because of how much revenue he brought in. Even the hospital's risk manager, Jill Stegman, admitted in testimony she and other administrators at West Chester knew Durrani "had issues."

The complaints about Durrani not completing records began almost as soon as he began at West Chester. On September 2, 2009, an employee email was sent to Ron Rohlfing, vice president of operations and Paula Hawk, director of medical staff services, about Durrani failing to submit his progress notes. Five days later, Rohlfing emailed Durrani: "Durrani, we have not been seeing progress notes on your patients...." On October 26, 2009, Hawk sent an email to Rohfling and two other administrators about a complaint Durrani wasn't discharging patients on a timely basis.

Inside a file we inherited from John Holschuh, Potts' prior lawyer, I found a memorandum where Holschuh's paralegal, Sandy Snapp, called West Chester for medical records. A representative from the hospital, Bryan Isaacs, told Snapp he couldn't obtain the records yet because Durrani had been suspended for not completing medical records. When Snapp called back in three months, Durrani remained suspended. We deposed Isaacs and Snapp under force of subpoena. We could prove Durrani was suspended for at least three months from August 2010 through October 2010. We also obtained the trial schedules of Durrani at West Chester. They revealed, despite his suspension, Durrani continued to perform surgeries. Thirty of our clients had surgeries at West Chester by Durrani while he was suspended and none of them were emergencies. These Atwood six cases fell in this suspended timeline.

Despite the suspension, emails among administrators reflect that Durrani was still booking up to five surgeries a day. A month later in September, an email from Cyndi Traficant, vice president of patient care services, complained to West Chester CEO Dr. Kevin Joseph and Hawks: "Durrani cases ran long and had to call in on-call team. Resulted in another doctor taking a surgery to another place. Schedulers know that they are not to take Durrani's office staff word for how long a case will take."

Insurers were refusing to pay for surgeries Durrani failed to properly document. By May of 2011, Hawk told Joseph and CFO Mike Jeffers she was badgering Durrani on a daily basis about complaints of "delinquent dictations, no clinical documentation, Aetna denial, Op notes are supposed to be dictated within 24 hours in our bylaws. My daily conversations with Durrani don't seem to be working."

To obtain the number of operating rooms Durrani needed for his surgical assembly line, Durrani pulled the same scam at West Chester he used at Children's by declaring a surgery an emergency "add on" at the last minute and after regular business hours so no one at the hospital questioned his assertion. Dr.

Thomas Kunkel, an anesthesiologist at the hospital, complained to the hospital board and management about Durrani's high number of add-on patients. They ignored him.

Emails among the hospital's administrators reflect they were more concerned about the overtime costs of staffing for the added surgeries than jeopardizing patient safety. After Durrani asked to schedule two emergency surgeries on a Saturday in July of 2010, Nurse Clinical Manager Debbie Blimline sent Joseph an email. "I do not know the symptoms these patients are having that could possibly make them emergent. I did not know he wanted to have the day scheduled tomorrow and we are not ready to grant that at this time... I know there are other surgeons who have wanted Saturday time. My concern is that if we offer it to Durrani for a few Saturdays and cover it with all the staff (including anesthesia) on OT, then other doctors will also expect this to happen them."

Joseph, who claimed in his deposition that he knew nothing about the complaints against Durrani, emailed back: "Thank you for the info. I called Durrani to discuss urgency and explain significant cost implications, logistical implications with call team and also lifestyle implications with call team. Thank you for making me aware."

The hospital reserved three to four surgical suites at a time for Durrani. While other spine surgeons performed two procedures a day, Durrani three, four, five and even six a day, according to Gerry Goodman, then the interim director of operating room nurses. Goodman complained to the hospital's general counsel, Mitch McCrate, Durrani's excesses were affecting patient care. Operating room staff worked on patients from 7 a.m. to midnight. Fatigue among staff jeopardized the standard of care. McCrate told Goodman not to worry because "the hospital had state funding and therefore was not held to qui tam rules that would require the hospital to refund the government for fraudulent surgeries." We proved that wrong.

Goodman told administrators, including CEO Joseph, about what the operating room staff called "the Shanti Shuffle." Shanti, Durrani's junior partner, was supposed to assist Durrani in surgeries, not replace him. Durrani began a surgery and Shanti would finish it on his own while Durrani went on to the next surgical patient. Shanti would illegally perform the surgeries under Durrani's government provider number. When Goodman confronted Durrani on the billing practice, she told him "Dr. Shanti and I are co-surgeons." Goodman checked the patient consent forms which never named Shanti. Shanti also dictated operative reports Durrani would illegally sign.

Durrani and Shanti would do three or four cases at the same time, moving from operating room to operating room, and bill them all to Durrani. On at least two occasions, Goodman testified, Durrani's patients were left "open" on the operating table for more than an hour waiting for him to perform the surgery.

To keep the patients' wounds from becoming infected, Durrani simply ordered the infusion of more antibiotics as they waited unconscious on the operating tables. Besides jeopardizing patient safety, the hospital was billing for unnecessary anesthesia, in increments of fifteen minutes at a time, when patients were open longer than necessary.

When Goodman complained to Chief Operating Officer George Caralis, he told her to "keep your mouth shut and go back to work, because you are just an interim." Caralis told her the hospital needed Durrani's admissions and surgeries, and weren't going to stop him. Goodman went ever higher with her complaint, to CEO Joseph, and said she couldn't work at a hospital that condoned illegal practices. She was asked to ignore them. She refused and resigned.

At a meeting with Durrani, Tayeb, University Hospital CEO Brian Gibler and Paula Hawk, Hawk told the group, "We cater to Durrani, you know, to point where we want to try to expedite and make everything easy for you guys to bring (patients) over here.... He's our partner in crime." At one point, according to Tayeb, Durrani went an entire six months at West Chester without filing any patient or surgical records. Hospital policy is to charge doctors a fine of $100 a day for records more than thirty days late. As far as Tayeb knew, the hospital never fined Durrani.

Even though West Chester officials told us Durrani left the hospital in May of 2013, he performed another surgery at the hospital on September 13, 2013, five weeks after his indictment.

In his review of over 400 patient charts at West Chester, Wilkey found more than 500 "event triggers" that required disciplinary action against Durrani by the hospital. The triggers included a wrong operation being performed, a procedure on the wrong patient, serious injury caused by a medical device, medication resulting in death, a delay in treatment resulting in serious injury or death and surgical death.

Walt Haggerty, West Chester's main attorney, told me in a cell phone call in May 2014 we would never be able to pin negligent credentialing and retention on the hospital because we couldn't prove the hospital administrators knew what was going on. I told him, "Walt, when I assign cases to a lawyer, it sometimes goes well or it doesn't go well. But every time I personally handle a case, I win. And I want you to know, Walt, we're going to get a win."

Prior to the Durrani cases, Walt and I got along on cases. In fact, I liked him as much as any defense lawyer. He lived in Fort Wright, Kentucky. He married long time Kenton County Sheriff Bill Steenken's daughter. He loved beer and golf. He was the least pretentious defense lawyer I knew. Based upon the high stakes of the Durrani cases, he proved as contentious as any lawyer. He's since retired.

From the beginning, my view of the case values would be based upon what I believed a jury would think about anyone undergoing an unnecessary spine surgery regardless of all other facts including the victims' age and prior surgery circumstances.

For example, before a patient has a surgery, much less a spine surgery, the patient must have all pre-op testing, pre-op physical, pre-op radiology. You have to obtain insurance approval. You have to line up your time off work. You have to line up someone to take you to the hospital. You're going to stay in the hospital for a few days. You have pain. You have physical therapy. You have work issues. It is unbelievable what you go through. I coached our team to focus on proving the surgery unnecessary and I said it's worth a million dollars. I know I would give a million dollars, and the average verdicts became a million dollars.

During the Federal group trial, Judge Bartlett didn't think Rebecca Brady was hurt at all after she testified. The jury gave her $741,000. During the trial, Barrett pushed a settlement in the cases against West Chester and its parent organization UC Health.

On August 21, 2018, two weeks before the Atwood trial, we invited all 430 Durrani clients with cases against West Chester to a meeting with the legal team in the ballroom at the Radisson Riverside Hotel in Covington, Ky. We shared the news West Chester and UC Health were offering a settlement of all claims. We advised the group not to take the amount because we believed they could do much better at trial. At meeting's end, the group unanimously voted down West Chester's offer.

When he heard about the rejection, Barrett ordered the victims and us to his courtroom for a pre-trial meeting the very next evening. The after-hours session at the federal courthouse included security checking in the 200-plus clients who were able to show on such short notice.

I feared what Barrett might say at the meeting. When I entered the courtroom to sit with the clients, they openly applauded me. I'll never forget the moment.

Barrett gave the victims a low-pressure sales pitch by warning them of the realities of litigation, the staggering costs, the years of appeals and delays, the risks of not winning anything at all. Barrett agreed no settlement would ever be enough to compensate all 354 Durrani/West Chester victims for their suffering. Without being pushy, Barrett asked the victims to reconsider the current offer and rethink their vote on the settlement. Barrett explained all options well.

When the floor was opened to questions and comments, the audience was decidedly split down the middle on the issue.

The following Monday, August 27, we again called all 354 clients to a meeting at the Radisson. The Durrani/West Chester clients stood their ground on settlement. The cases against West Chester were going to trial.

Chapter 61

West Chester Settlement

"In the actions of all men, one judges by the result."
—Machiavelli

On September 4, 2018, clients Sander, McCauley, Brady, Shempert, Houghton and Stanfield showed up in Barrett's courtroom for the group trial against Durrani and West Chester Hospital, known simply as "the Atwood case" for Christopher Atwood, whose name appeared first alphabetically among the ten clients on the lawsuit. These six were grouped for the first trial since all underwent surgery on their lower spine. They sat in the audience pews with their spouses. Statman sat at the victims' counsel table with Fred Johnson and Ben Maraan. I sat at a table behind them. Lyon and Brockman represented Durrani. Haggerty, Paliobeis, Carroll, Pullen and Korfhage, five lawyers, represented West Chester.

Judge Barrett would inform the jury of the following:

> "This is a civil case alleging medical malpractice, it is not a criminal case. Due to some media coverage from time to time, I am advising you that Dr. Durrani was indicted on August 7, 2013 on various counts alleging criminal conduct. An indictment is not considered evidence, it is merely the charging document that notifies a defendant of the allegations against him. Dr. Durrani is presumed innocent of the charges unless and until a criminal jury would find him guilty. Sometime after the indictment, Dr. Durrani left the jurisdiction of this Court for Pakistan. You are not to consider the indictment for any purpose whatsoever. As he has left the jurisdiction of this Court, he has removed himself from the Plaintiff's subpoena ability. It is my understanding that he will not appear in person or remotely for this case and therefore will not testify. You are to draw no conclusions from this alone but may consider the absence of his testimony in light of the other evidence and testimony presented in Court. If an additional instruction is appropriate, it will be given at the end of the case."

Group trials proceed in the same way as individual trials, but a single jury hears all of the individual cases. The opening statement references all six clients. Each of the six clients are witnesses, followed by the expert witnesses who testify to all six cases. The closing arguments cover all six clients. The jury then deliberates and determines the outcome for each client before announcing the multiple verdicts.

A group trial for six clients would normally have taken about two weeks, but the Durrani cases were slowed by a slew of defense motions and a planned week-long vacation by Barrett, scheduled before the trial for the middle of the trial. The Atwood trial would take over a month. Each trial would have taken about two weeks, for a total of three months. Even with the delays, the federal group trial wrapped up in a third of the time.

I felt good about our prospects especially with the jurors having been fully informed of Durrani's arrest and his subsequent flight to Pakistan. As the trial progressed, the victims testified well with the exception of McCauley, who would mutter "bullshit" under his breath every time he disagreed with a statement by the defense. I think the jury heard it. I heard it.

One morning during the trial, we were unaware we escaped a bloodbath. Omar Santa-Perez, 29, looking to settle a grievance with U.S. District Judge Susan Dlott, approached the entrance to the courthouse in possession of a 9-mm. pistol and numerous rounds of hollow-point ammunition. When Santa-Perez saw the U.S. marshals and other security measures just inside the door, he lost his nerve and walked across the street to the lobby of The Fifth Third Bank. There he opened fire at 9:10 a.m., killing two bank employees and a contractor and wounding two others before being killed himself by an arriving Cincinnati police officer. We never learned about the mass shooting until our lunch-time break. Thank God for U.S. Marshals and security checkpoints.

I was pleased with Statman's work throughout the Atwood trial, as well as the expert testimony from Wilkey, Bloomfield and Cole. On the drive to the airport for Wilkey's return flight to St. Louis, he and I congratulated each other on the strength of our case, including the second stage of the trial accusing West Chester of negligence in credentialing and retaining Durrani. Barrett reserved ruling on Wilkey's testimony in Stage II which we preserved by video taken in Barrett's Court. Wilkey gave the testimony by video in case it would be allowed.

To make this clear, Judge Guckenberger established the precedent of the process we followed on West Chester cases. Rather than try the case against Durrani and West Chester, we tried the case against Durrani first, Stage I, and if we won, then the jury would hear the case against West Chester in Stage II. The process was unfair to us. Why? The judge allowed the West Chester lawyers to participate in Stage I. They gave openings, questioned witnesses, called experts and gave closings. Also, the juries were not told they must rule against Durrani before hearing the West Chester case. The Marshall jury actually thought they were going to hear evidence against West Chester even though they ruled for Durrani.

The following day, Barrett summoned our lawyers into his chamber. He told them losing the trial against West Chester would be devastating. He again pressured us to settle. He stressed the impact of "res adjudicata" on all future trials in the Durrani affair. "Res adjudicata" is Latin for "the thing has been judged."

In other words, the outcome of the trial for the six federal cases against West Chester could determine the fate of the remaining four hundred. A win in federal court might open the vaults to a lot more than the settlement being offered by the hospital. But a loss could result in nothing from West Chester for all four hundred victims. When I contemplated that possibility, it made my blood run cold.

We callled another meeting of all the West Chester clients at the Holiday Inn in Covington and this time encouraged them to take the deal.

We were straight with them. We explained Judge Barrett's risk concern. The clients were ready to put some money in their pockets and we needed to refresh our funds for the continuing legal fight.

Among the two hundred or so clients who showed up at the meeting, the voice vote was in favor, but not everyone was happy with the deal. The agreement with West Chester stipulated that all four hundred clients must sign a consent form or there was no settlement. Chuck Holbrook and Joe Rutter were assigned the duty of visiting every client household in the area and collecting the signatures.

"It was hard to get a lot of those signatures, because the clients didn't know yet how much they would be getting," Rutter said. A special master would be appointed by the court to divvy up the settlement based on numerous factors. Everyone signed except Michael Crail.

Crail, sixty-four years old, left in permanent pain every time he moved his head up or down or side to side by one of Durrani's botched fusion operations on his neck. He suffered alternating leg pain following a second surgery by Durrani on his lower back. Scans showed both surgeries unnecessary. Prior to meeting up with Durrani, Crail built and managed phone systems for large business operations. When Rutter showed up at Crail's modest one-story house in the blue-collar suburb of Fairfield, Crail was impatient and irritable as Rutter tried to persuade him to sign the consent form.

Rutter made three more visits to Crail, the last one accompanied by me. I determined one client should not hold up the deal for the others. I heard Crail out for an hour.

Crail worried he would lose his Medicare disability payment for a possible one-time payout from West Chester. Crail also feared his insurance company's lien on the settlement would wipe out most of what he would have to settle for. I was sympathetic and told him "this whole deal will go down unless you agree to sign." I reminded Crail that he could still be awarded money from the suit against Durrani and Medical Protective. Crail swallowed his fears and signed.

I never blamed him or anyone for hesitancy. All his concerns were rational and legitimate.

We used Randy Freking as a Special Master believing he would help us too. It became a disaster. He put language in the West Chester settlement documents that we fought to change. He delayed checks to our clients after we resolved the liens. He made me so angry, and I tore into him bad. We agreed I would no longer have any contact with him. He charged $450 an hour to be the Special Master and he billed every minute plus of his time. It is robbery. We will never use Randy on any future settlements. He could care less about these victims. He retired so this job is his gravy train.

Here is an example of how Randy billed the victims:

1/15/21			
RHF	Emails regarding Mains	495.00	0.30
RHF	Emails - Dotson	495.00	0.30
RHF	Emails - Pridemore	495.00	0.30
RHF	Emails - Reeder	495.00	0.30
RHF	Review Emails	495.00	0.30

There is no way Randy spent that much time on these matters. Remember *The Firm* where billing fraud brought the law firm down?

Chapter 62

Medical Liens

"Anger is prelude to courage."
—Eric Hoffer

The West Chester settlement was complicated by a frustrating law few Americans know about: medical liens. When a personal injury victim wins an award or settlement, the law permits the victim's insurer to place a lien on the settlement for repayment of their medical costs. Every insurance policy you purchase has this in the contract of insurance. Both private insurers as well as Medicare and Medicaid can impose liens to get their money back, reducing and sometimes decimating the amount of money given to patients for their own expenses and suffering. A lien simply means: "right to be paid back." States have laws requiring Medicare and Medicaid liens be paid. It is an unfair curse on those who suffer jury.

In the West Chester case, medical liens reached heights of absurdity. West Chester paid back Medicare $4.1 million to settle all its claims for Durrani's unnecessary and injurious surgeries from our false claims case we filed. Medicare officials still insisted on a medical lien against West Chester's settlement with the patients. We complained the agency's demand amounted to a double payment to Medicare on the backs of our clients, all of whom were victims of the unnecessary and experimental surgeries that Medicare failed to screen and stop in the first place. Medicare wanted paid back for a surgery that should have never happened. Therefore, the client became a victim yet again. First a victim to Durrani, then a victim to the legal system by not getting their trial in a timely manner and now a victim to the insurance companies.

Despite my pleading to both an Ohio U.S. Senator Sherrod Brown and the U.S. Attorney General's office, Medicare officials refused to waive their liens despite being paid back from West Chester. I couldn't believe it. We decided to file a federal lawsuit against Medicare, Medicaid, and the private insurance companies for approving Durrani's fraudulent surgeries. We would use the lawsuit as a bargaining tool so insurers would waive their liens. For some insurers, it worked. Aetna, Anthem and Cigna agreed to waive their liens against the Durrani victims if we dropped the suit against them. Many other insurers weren't so conciliatory, including Medicare. We would finally resolve it with them with the mediation effort of Judge Barrett. This lawsuit is unprecedented. No law firm would ever file this; we named over one hundred health insurance companies, Medicaid, and Medicare in the lawsuit.

Insurers impose liens for treatments ordered by Durrani before, during and after surgery, as well as those ordered by another doctor treating a condition caused by Durrani. The liens are further complicated if the victim changed insurance companies while under Durrani's care or even years later. Sorting through and certifying all the lien claims as legitimate can take months or even years. A few of these liens are not resolved years later.

A claim waiting to be certified is called an "unknown." Until all liens are certified and paid, victims don't see a penny of their settlement. The laws on liens are written for insurance companies by corporate America and their attorneys. We have to prove that insurer's money wasn't used for a treatment caused by Durrani. It's like being guilty until you prove yourself innocent.

Alexa Kavanaugh, a paralegal, was given the unenviable task of handling the lien process. Kavanaugh, a former classmate of my son Cory, was originally hired to answer the discovery requests from the defense. Have you watched *Shameless*? Alexa looks and has the personality of Debbie. She quickly trained herself to become the office expert on liens. She compiled the contact information for all 580 clients' insurance companies with multiple insurances. Kavanaugh sent a letter of representation to the insurers to notify them that there is a lawsuit pending. Once a settlement is reached, the insurers are then notified again, asking for a full and final lien statement as well as documents to determine the rights of the insurance company. As those trickle in, Kavanaugh had to go through each individual charge on the lien and dispute any charges that don't pertain to the client's injury.

The lien settlement is supposed to be for the spine surgery in question. Other charges that don't relate to the surgery should not be on the lien. But as expected, insurers usually include other treatments to pad their share of the settlement, creating more work for the firm and introducing yet another delay to reimbursement for the client. Kavanaugh entered the insurance code for each charge into a database to determine if it related to the client's injury. And if it didn't, she wrote an explanation to the insurer as to why it should be removed from the final lien statement.

Kavanaugh challenged every charge by sending records to show the client would have needed the treatment regardless of their spine surgery. For every client, she went through scores of unrelated charges: prescriptions, pain management, physical therapy and more to ensure each client is getting as much money back as possible.

Over the course of the litigation, we have saved the clients more than $30 million dollars with our aggressive lien fight. At the same time, we have to keep in continual contact with the clients, many of whom are justifiably anxious to get their money, and the weight of their angst and frustration falls on our shoulders.

Thomas Atkinson, who had two Durrani surgeries on his neck that caused him permanent pain and immobility, is one of the clients who switched insurers between surgeries. As negotiations with insurers continue, his lien numbers keep changing, adding to the anxiety of waiting for a settlement check or even knowing if he will get one at all.

Deborah Doyle, a nurse's aide for more than twenty years, couldn't find work because of her pain and her limp after Durrani fused her lower spine and removed three of her discs in 2009. Doyle ended up with very little from her settlement after attorney fees and liens were taken. "I'm heartbroken. I wish I could be hypnotized to forget this ever happened. But the pain I feel all day, every day only reminds me! I'm grateful for Deters Law but highly pissed at the crooks who are supposed to be fair and just," Doyle wrote to us in an email.

Attorney fees for the victims in malpractice cases are paid on a contingency basis. If the victims lose their case, they pay nothing. If they win, they pay 33 to 40 percent of their award to their attorney. In other words, the attorney earns the percentage by assuming the costs and risks of filing the case. I promised our clients that if there were an early settlement of the Durrani cases, we would reduce the percentage of our contingency fee. Since that failed to happen, we charged the contract rate of 40 percent. Medical malpractice rates are higher than car accident rates because the cases are much more difficult. Some law firms charge 50% if the case goes to trial or is appealed. We don't.

"The percentage for contingency fees is based on both tradition and what the courts will allow," said Daniel Hinkle, "state affairs counsel for the American Association of Justice, the advocacy group for the nation's trial lawyers. But the contingency fee also helps ensure that the attorney will work harder and smarter to get the highest possible award for the client," he said.

The contingency fee system "gives anyone harmed by someone else access to extremely competent—the best—lawyers in the world. And that lawyer has every incentive to put in all of the hours in those cases and work them all the way through the court system in order to win because their incentives align perfectly with the client's. In some states, where they've taken away the contingency fee, there's no incentive for the lawyer to take the case and the victim can find no representation," said Hinkle.

By comparison, Hinkle said, "if you look at lawyers who work on an hourly basis in plaintiff litigation, those lawyers tend to work more hours toward settlement because they have a financial interest in working longer. So those cases take longer to resolve and they generally resolve for a lower value for the client because the lawyers aren't working as hard as they can to get every dollar for the client."

The day after the West Chester settlement was signed and completed, all five of West Chester's lawyers and their support team disappeared from the federal courtroom during the Atwood trial. Mike Lyon and Jim Brockman remained to defend Durrani and the interests of his insurer, Medical Protective. After more than a month of testimony and closing arguments, the jury began deliberations on October 12 and continued into the next day.

On October 13, I sat behind my desk at my Independence office when Statman texted me from the federal courthouse. One by one, as the verdicts for each client were announced, Statman texted me with the amounts of the awards. The jury awarded Mike Sander the largest sum of $1.4 million. For all six victims, the total came to $6 million. Only McCauley lost. He would receive part of the settlement from West Chester. McCauley lost on a statute of limitations issue.

Chapter 63

CARSON RUTTER

"Courage is of two kinds: first, physical courage, or courage in the presence of danger to the person; and next, moral courage, or courage before responsibility, Whether it be before the judgment seat of external authority, or of the inner power, the conscience."
—Karl Von Clausewitz, "On War"

On September 24, 2018, we began the Carson Rutter trial. Back to Hamilton County and the courtroom of Common Pleas Judge Mark Schweikert. Back to a gag order. Back to individual trials for the remaining cases which would take decades to resolve. Back to sealed verdicts. Back to a ban on any mention of Durrani's federal indictment on fraud charges. Back to a courtroom, void of empathy. If any couple deserved empathy, Joe and Christina Rutter deserved it. Their one-year-old son Carson, born with Spina Bifida, suffered through three fraudulent and bungled surgeries on his neck in a single week, which left him unable to communicate. An enthusiastic Bengals fan, Joe Rutter named his firstborn son after Carson Palmer, the Bengals quarterback.

Only by attending a hearing or trial can you understand how much Schweikert sucked the life out of a courtroom. He vaporizes the heart and soul out of it.

Schweikert blocked Mehlman from testifying. Schweikert ruled Mehlman's testimony not relevant to the Rutter case based upon Mehlman complaints to his supervisors about Durrani occurring after Carson's surgeries.

The Rutters, high school sweethearts, met the first day in music class at Norwood High School, a working-class town minutes north of downtown Cincinnati. A recent transfer from Florida, Joe caught the eye of Christina, two years older than Joe. She played cello and he played percussion in music class.

In 2001, two years after high school graduation, Joe served as an Army Reserve in the Iraq War for a year. While there, Joe earned a Purple Heart. Joe suffered a massive concussion and shrapnel wounds in his knee from a roadside bomb that blasted through his unarmored Humvee. As part of a transportation company delivering engine fuel, Rutter's unit suffered fifty-three ambushes in a year. Once safely home and recovered, Joe and Christina made wedding plans. When Christina became pregnant with a child afflicted with Spina Bifida, a birth defect in which the baby's spinal cord doesn't develop properly, the couple moved up the wedding date and honeymooned in a cabin in Gatlinburg, Tennessee.

Christina received her prenatal care at Children's Hospital and Carson began treatment immediately after his birth. So pleased and inspired with her son's care at Children's and the kindness and attentiveness of its doctors and nurses, Christina chose to return to school to become a nurse. Joe began training as a corrections officer with plans to become a sheriff's deputy. Joe and Christina split their schedules to take care of Carson at home. Several months later, neurosurgeons at Children's performed surgery on Carson's neck to relieve the pressure on his brain stem, which slipped down into the cervical portion of his spine, compressing the nerves and causing breathing problems.

The surgery a success, Carson healed up and began to respond to his parents like any baby, smiling and playing peekaboo. Before his first birthday, he spoke "mama" and "papa" and "bubbaflew" for butterfly. His pediatrician believed Carson would have normal mental development.

Then Carson's head began to droop forward, threatening to block his air pathway. A scan proved kyphosis or a weakening of the neck bones in the spine, caused the drooping. The neurosurgeons at Children's placed Carson in a neck brace to stabilize him. With therapy and growth, they believed Carson would gain enough strength in his neck to control the drooping. The neurosurgeons also referred the Rutters to Durrani.

By 2006, Durrani refined his fraudulent technique for frightening patients into surgery. "He told me Carson could be paralyzed without surgery. He said he could be in a car accident and his head would fly off from his neck. My husband wasn't there at the time and I was scared to death," said Christina.

Durrani pushed for immediate surgery. The Rutters persuaded him to wait until after Carson's upcoming first birthday on April 18. Durrani assured them it would be a simple procedure with a small incision and the insertion of rods for support. What Durrani failed to tell them was he planned more than just a simple spinal fusion. He designed an entirely radical and experimental surgery and would use BMP-2 too.

Durrani attached rods between Carson's upper spine and the back of his skull with bolts that would adjust every few years as he grew. Soon after the first surgery, the bolts detached from his skull. Durrani performed a second surgery to reattach them. Again the bolts detached. For the third surgery, Durrani implanted a metal halo around Carson's skull to hold his head in place until the fusion fused. Durrani performed all three of these procedures in one week on a one-year-old child.

The halo meant Carson, at a critical stage in his development would lie in traction at all times on his back or stomach, his body carefully turned every twelve hours, for an entire year. During this time, no one could hold or hug him. Carson spent his day watching children's videos from a screen placed above his bed. The year of forced bedrest stunted his emotional and mental development.

Carson failed to communicate with words or sounds again. Within the year, Durrani performed a fourth surgery on Carson. Durrani performed a cervical fusion. By the age of fifteen, Carson could not communicate to anyone. Carson began hitting himself in the face with his fist when frustrated, blackening his eyes, and even broke his nose.

During these early years in Carson's life, Joe suffered from PTSD from his war experience. Joe became a stay-at-home-dad while Christina earned her nursing degree from Christ Hospital. Once certified, Christina became Carson's nighttime nurse. The Rutters would also have two daughters, Ella and Sophie.

While working on a Hamilton County jail road crew as a corrections officer, Joe heard me on 700 WLW speaking of Durrani's arrest. He decided to contact me. From her training and experience as a nurse, Christina began to question the necessity and design of Carson's first three surgeries. I preferred to try the Rutters' case first among the Children's cases because I believed it possessed great jury appeal. I should have factored in the time frame issue so Mehlman would have testified.

Not long after the Rutters became clients, I hired Christina to review the medical records of Durrani's victims and to summarize the depositions of expert witnesses.

In the spring of 2016, the local media never bothered to cover the courtroom battles. I blame the influence of the hospitals, who are the largest employers and media advertisers, second only to car dealerships, in the region. The only daily newspaper and four television news stations ignored the Durrani saga.

Taking advantage of the shift in cases from Butler to Hamilton County and the gag order temporarily dropped because it began as a Butler County Order, Christina sent out emails to the four television stations and the *Cincinnati Enquirer.* She included details of what happened to Carson and her family, hoping to gain their attention for the upcoming trial. "I was just so angry. I just couldn't believe what had happened to these patients right under everyone's noses. But once Durrani fled the country, the media just disappeared," Christina explained.

The gag order on us always bothered us because while we were "gagged," the hospitals advertised how outstanding they were every single day.

Christina received two responses to her emails. One from a reporter at the *Enquirer* on May 18 stated, "Hi Christina, thanks for reaching out. We've previously reported on Durrani, so we'll pass this along and see what we can do with it." They did nothing. Christina received a promising response from Sheree Paolello, the news anchor at Channel 5, who wrote, "I'd love to take your story to our producers and see about doing a story." Christina responded with more details. By the time Paolello reached out to her again to say her boss was enthusiastic about the story, Christina couldn't write back because Schweikert reimposed the gag order originally put in effect by Guckenberger in Butler County.

Paolello interviewed the Rutters and met Carson at Christina's mother's house on an evening an ice storm hit. The Rutters laid out on the kitchen counter all the photos of Carson's ordeal. Carson played on the floor in the living room. I told Paolello about the other cases pending against Durrani. "I went back and told my producer," Paolello said. Mike Dardis and Sheree Paolello of News 5 showed up a few weeks later at the next monthly support group meeting of Durrani victims. "I don't want to sound insensitive, but the meeting was literally like the Land of the Walking Dead. It was so sad. There were people walking in bent over at 90-degree angles. People in wheelchairs. People using walkers. Beautiful moms with crooked necks." She talked with many of the clients after the meeting. "At that point, I knew I had to get the station aboard. But would they let us do all these stories?" Paolello explained.

Paolello's supervisors liked the idea but "they were very concerned that we wanted to take on the hospitals" which protected Durrani, she said. "I told my bosses it wasn't just about Durrani anymore. He had fled the country. But now it was about the hospitals and the claim by Eric they knew about Durrani and didn't stop him." Finally, the station's general manager and news director told her to go ahead "but you'd better get this right." The Hearst company, owner of the station and thirty-three others across the U.S., tasked its New York lawyers with vetting the stories for potential lawsuits.

Paolello and other reporters at the station, including her husband and co-anchor Mike Dardis, would do a dozen stories on the Durrani victims and the ongoing legal battle. "We really had to dot our I's and cross our T's," Paolello said. "It was a battle for every story with the Hearst lawyers. I can't tell you how many times I was crying in our news director's office." Once again, large law firms and corporate lawyers blocking the truth.

Especially disappointing, the Hearst lawyers spiked an interview with Mehlman about Children's liability in the Durrani cases. Mehlman discussed in his interview the letter the three UC surgeons wrote to warn the state medical board about Durrani, but was never sent on the advice of university lawyers. We gave News 5 the Mehlman video deposition footage. They failed to use it. Any lawyer for any news media outlet knows if you use deposition footage and court documents, there is zero liability concerns. The advertising dollars conquered all.

The twelve-story series won Paolello and her colleagues a regional *Edward R. Murrow Award,* one of the TV news industry's most prestigious honors for community service in journalism. "It was one of those few times in your journalistic career where you really feel you made an impact," said Paolello. Those stories helped the cause. The problem is after News 5 won their award, sayonara. Paolello is a down to earth sweetheart. Mike Dardis is a smart reporter. I do not blame them. I blame their news station, their news director and their New York lawyers.

Chapter 64

CARSON RUTTER TRIAL

"We are not weak if we make a proper use of those means which the God Nature has placed in our power... the battle, sir, is not to the strong alone; it is too vigilant, the active, the brave."
—Patrick Henry

Christina Rutter spent years doing her own research and thinking about her testimony for trial. Eager to testify for Children's Hospital turning against her family. "I trusted Children's completely because everyone who worked there had been so good to us. They were the ones who made me want to go into nursing." But when it came time to testify against Durrani, no one at Children's would step forward. They were against us," Christina said.

Children's lawyers at Dinsmore made it impossible to obtain honest depositions from current and even former employees at Children's because they always coached and intimidated them. Several former employees contacted us with damning information about Durrani, but later changed their stories after the hospital attorneys got to them. Only Mehlman stood up to it.

Ever heard of HIPAA? It is not there to protect patients. Do you know if someone violates HIPAA rights, you have no right to sue them? The best you can do is file a complaint to a useless board. Hospitals use HIPAA to keep their staff in fear under threat to reveal "bad things" that happen to patients. This is what HIPAA is for. Remember, it is never a HIPAA violation to report something to an attorney or law enforcement.

Ben Maraan remembered one former Children's employee showing up alone for her deposition and said her personal attorney told her she could tell Maraan anything. While Maraan took a phone call in his office and returned to the conference room, the woman disappeared. Maraan found her in the building hallway conferring with a Children's attorney. Maraan asked what was going on. "I represent this person," the Dinsmore lawyer said. When the woman sat for her deposition, her story completely changed from what she told Ben Maraan.

On March 22, 2013, Deborah Faris called us. We recorded the call. She reported how Durrani lied about scoliosis measurements at Children's to justify surgery. When we deposed her, she played stupid.

Another witness not intimidated was Maureen Grady, a Children's nurse who married a trial attorney who represented her. When she began her deposition, one of Children's lawyers objected to Maraan's line of questioning. Grady asked the Children's attorney what he was doing there. "I'm still your attorney," he said.

"Oh, no, you're not," she insisted. "Grady was one of our best hospital witnesses," Maraan said.

The Dinsmore attorneys went to great lengths to ensure the hospital's witnesses stayed silent. Dr. Alvin Crawford, Durrani's mentor and chief protector at the hospital, was overheard at a party claiming the Dinsmore attorneys would rehearse each witness for their deposition with every possible question we might ask. They videotaped the rehearsals and then told the witnesses how to "better" answer the questions.

With Statman still in the Atwood trial, Fred Johnson broke off from Atwood and would try the Rutters' case. I spent months preparing the script for the arguments and the questions for the witnesses in the trial.

Later in the trial, we brought Carson into the courtroom so the jury could see his condition. For several hours, he sat next to our counsel table breathing through his ventilator and hooked to an oxygen monitor. His suctioning equipment was attached to the back of his wheelchair in case he needed it to clear his ventilator.

Schweikert decided Carson's appearance wouldn't happen again. The whooshing from his ventilator and the beeping of his monitor he found too much, he told Johnson.

Schweikert ruled Christina couldn't read from the baby book she kept when Carson was little, tracking his progress before and after the surgeries with Durrani. Schweikert called it "hearsay" and inadmissible as evidence. This ruling is absurd because Christina wrote it.

Schweikert would permanently ban me from his courtroom based upon a pretrial hearing in the Cotter case, which took place in a break of the Rutter trial. Fred Johnson failed to show at the early morning hearing, so I had to on the spot help Ben Maraan on the sues.

Schweikert shouted from the bench. *"Mr. Deters, stop that talking!"*

Angry and not wanting to lose control and shout back, I got up and walked out of the courtroom while stating, "Judge, let the record reflect that Eric Deters is leaving the courtroom."

"Maybe that's a good idea," responded Reich.

"Yes, it is," I answered before exiting.

"He's not allowed in here anymore," Schweikert told Maraan and backed it up the next morning with a written court order on October 4, 2018.

Schweikert wanted me out of the courtroom, because he knew I contributed well to our cause. In time, Alan, Ben and Fred would not need me in trial. At this point, they did not know what I knew, so it was important for me to be there. Schweikert knew of this and therefore, loved banning me.

Fred's alcohol issue raised its head during the Rutter trial. In fact, we fired him over a weekend in the middle of the trial and Glenn Feagan made plans to fly down and finish the trial. The Rutters even accepted and approved the move. After contrition, we decided to allow Fred to finish.

Despite the victims' many obstacles during the trial, including the absence of any mention of Durrani's arrest and flight, I was optimistic about the outcome for the Rutters. We assumed the six women jurors would be sympathetic to the Rutters and their child's plight. The unknown, the male jury foreman, a retired diesel mechanic from Pittsburgh. After three weeks of testimony, the jury deliberated for eight hours. Their verdict, 7 to 1 in favor of Durrani and Children's. The one juror in our favor, a young male artist.

The verdict crushed Christina.

I never faulted the Rutters, Fred Johnson or anyone involved with the presentation of the case. I faulted Schweikert's rulings and a callous jury. Never underestimate how cold jurors can be. They can be indifferent when they're deciding someone else's fate other than their own. In a malpractice case, a victim's lawyer is not permitted to ask a jury to imagine themselves in the position of the victim. It's stupid because I believe every juror should have to ask themselves or would ask themselves: "What if this happened to me or my loved one?"

A weird jury dynamic can occur in personal injury trials. Jurors don't like to do something for someone else because they're not getting anything for their own issues. They're sitting there thinking, "This is what I'm dealing with in my life, and I'm not getting anything for what I'm going through. Why should they get any money?"

A survey of the jurors after the trial found two of the women thought Christina exaggerated the damage Durrani inflicted on Carson and believed she wasn't that "put out" by his care. A complete crock. Women can be harshest on other women. The male jury foreman days later actually showed up in a photo store where Sabrina Cain worked and she asked him about the verdict. She actually recorded the comments. "Durrani didn't do anything so bad. The kid was already messed up anyway," said the ass from Pittsburgh.

The law allows damages when malpractice worsens a condition and Durrani destroyed Carson. In essence, the argument of the defense lawyers during the entire trial: "Yeah, so Carson was born with a lot of issues. Let's go and finish him off." Paul McCartney, "Puke" himself, compared Carson during jury selection and opening to a "dead tree."

On January 13, 2021, Carson Rutter passed away. Christina and Joe will never recover from this unimaginable loss.

Chapter 65

Jacob Cotter

Patience and perseverance have a magical effect before which difficulties disappear and obstacles vanish."
—John Quincy Adams

After the defeat in the Rutter trial, we needed a comeback against both Durrani and Children's. Scheduled for trial next, Jacob Cotter was born with abnormally fused spinal bones in his neck. Durrani performed his first surgery on Cotter in late 2008 when Jacob was eleven. Durrani improperly inserted a screw which to this day remains dangerously close to Jacob's spinal cord and can't be removed.

After the surgery, Cotter developed a life-threatening infection and suffered a forced quarantine at Children's. Doctors wanted to discharge him after three days of IV antibiotics, but his mother, Melissa Morgan, objected. It turned out to be MRSA, the same bacteria afflicting Durrani's dog Hank. Morgan was unable to reach Durrani for assistance in blocking Jacob's discharge.

When Morgan returned the afternoon from the hospital cafeteria to Jacob's isolation room, she found Durrani talking to her son without a protective gown or mask. She overheard him bragging to Jacob about how he bought a sword dating back to medieval times at an auction. Morgan confronted Durrani outside Jacob's room and screamed expletives in his face. Several nurses came rushing to Durrani's rescue. Morgan complained to hospital supervisors and the head of patient relations removed Durrani from Jacob's case.

Cotter, now in his early twenties, is in constant pain as a result of his surgeries and on so much medication that he sleeps twenty hours a day. A history enthusiast who hoped for a career as a professor, Cotter dropped out of college because he couldn't stay awake during classes, due to constantly being in pain. Jacob would make a good witness at trial. I found him engaging and talkative. Jacob looks like the poster child for St. Jude's Hospital in their television commercial.

We would also win the Dana Setters trial before Jacob Cotter's trial. Dana Setters, a young mother, saw Durrani complaining of lower back pain. Setters suffered from Ehlers-Danlos syndrome. Never mind Setters' symptoms were in her lower back, Durrani resorted to his usual frightening lie that Dana risked losing her head in a car accident without fusion surgery. Without Setters' consent or FDA approval for the use of BMP-2, Durrani performed another sloppy fusion and left Dana's head permanently tilted to one side and her neck immobilized.

"He told me all of that was normal," Setters said. Dana can no longer drive or walk her dog and needs the help of her mother to raise her young daughter. The jury awarded her just under a million dollars.

Many of the jurors interviewed after the Durrani trials in Hamilton County felt deceived and guilty when they learned only after deciding their verdict Durrani had been indicted and fled to Pakistan to escape prosecution.

Heather McCann injured her back at work. McCann rode by ambulance to the hospital with a broken tail bone. Durrani talked her into an unnecessary fusion of her cervical spine, causing her neck to be permanently immobilized and in pain.

After two days of infighting, the jury awarded McCann $208,000 for Durrani's negligence. "I really felt guilty about the amount that she received," Juror Andrea McDonald said. "It was pocket change after the attorney fees. But it was either that or nothing." One juror who could not be removed worked in the insurance industry. I hope that juror enjoys this book.

In the Carson Rutter case, Schweikert blocked Mehlman's testimony because Carson's surgeries took place in 2005 before Mehlman began complaining about Durrani. Mehlman should have been allowed to testify as to Durrani's credibility and reputation. Jacob Cotter underwent his procedure in September of 2008, a month after Children's forced Durrani to resign. Durrani would perform hundreds of surgeries on unsuspecting patients at Children's after his resignation through March 7, 2009. For Children's to allow Durrani to perform over 200 more surgeries after concluding Durrani needed to go is unforgivable.

Dr. Wilkey suggested I find a pediatric spine doctor on our Children's cases. For Cotter, we would use Dr. Errol Mortimer as an expert who also testified in Rutter. I found Mortimer at the University of Massachusetts Medical School in Worcester where he worked as an assistant professor of orthopedics and pediatrics. Mortimer, clear and confident in his testimony, proved to be a strong witness in all the Children's Hospital cases.

At one point, Jacob's health deteriorated so badly I arranged for his video testimony in the event he should die before trial. I want everyone to realize these five hundred Durrani clients have lives with all the same issues everyone has. Daily, on top of everything else, I had to navigate through their issues. It's life.

Meanwhile, Schweikert mildly pressed both sides in the case for mediation. During a mediation conference call, Children's attorneys offered Jacob $50,000 to settle, while claiming they might be willing to go as high as $200,000. Morgan hung up the phone on them and we went to trial.

As Statman tried the Dana Setters case, we decided to go again with Fred Johnson as the attorney in the Cotter case rather than prepare a new lawyer for the fight against Children's. Morgan lacked faith in Johnson. She found his unwillingness to communicate with her frustrating. "During breaks, he would go outside and smoke. He'd never go to lunch with me and tell me how he thought things were going with the trial. I couldn't do this with him anymore. I didn't feel like he was fully vested in Jacob's case," Morgan remembers.

A week into the trial, Morgan wanted to settle for the $250,000 being offered by Children's. At the group lunch that day, we talked her off the cliff. We told her we had a good chance of winning Jacob's case against Children's and for a good deal more than $250,000. We also reminded her that accepting an offer now would limit all future settlements against Children's. "On behalf of all the other clients, we have to set the bar high," We told her. To Morgan's credit, she listened.

The trial lasted weeks with numerous delays caused by objections and sidebar conferences with Schweikert. Schweikert announced once in the courtroom, "In my forty years as a judge, I have never seen so much squabbling." Schweikert caused the squabbling by his weakness.

When the jury returned with their verdict after nearly eight hours of deliberation on December 19, they awarded Cotter $1.2 million against Durrani. We won Stage I.

The jury's Stage II deliberation would decide whether Children's had been negligent in credentialing and retaining Durrani on its staff. The hospital's lawyers scrambled to make a settlement with Morgan before there was a second jury decision. David Brittingham, Children's attorney, warned Johnson "that no jury is ever going to find against Children's" because of the hospital's reputation. Brittingham offered Morgan $800,000 at the courthouse and pointed out a jury award would be delayed by appeal.

The amount Children's offered Jacob for Durrani's lifelong injury to her son was a little more than a tenth of what it spent in 2016 on a $7 million rebranding campaign. According to a business page article in the *Cincinnati Enquirer*, the millions would be spent on "a new logo and tagline, signs, an inspiring video and a marketing campaign that could include innovative advertising."

Based upon our encouragement, Morgan rejected the offer. I couldn't blame Morgan for being interested in a settlement for Jacob. She loved and looked out for him. Fortunately, she trusted me. In Stage II of the trial, we only called Mehlman. The straight-shooting Cowboy held "court" on the stand just as forcefully as his deposition six months before. He told the jury Durrani performed unproven and dangerous surgeries on children who didn't need them, leading to paralysis in some patients and even death. He pointed out the hospital built a money-making machine around Durrani to accommodate his assembly-line surgeries. He faulted the administrators at Children's who knew for years Durrani performed unnecessary procedures but loved the revenue.

The jury hung on every word. They openly sighed. They shook their heads. They cried. Brittingham never asked Mehlman a single question on cross examination. Mehlman was the only witness called in Stage II. After deliberating only an hour, the jury announced their second verdict. Their award to Cotter was twice what Children's offered: $2 million. Jacob won a total verdict of $3.2 million.

The Cotter verdict is the first-ever jury award against a hospital in Ohio for negligent credentialing and retention of a doctor. I assume it remains the only one. In interviews after the trial, jurors said they would have given Cotter even more money, but feared at his young age, he couldn't handle the money responsibly.

Fred took a photo in the elevator with all the jurors, and our entire office celebrated at *Cincy Prime*. I look forward to the Children's lawyers finding out a secret I kept from everyone. I'll wait until the litigation is over. It's hysterical.

The Cotter verdict finally brought Children's Hospital to the negotiating table with a serious offer. Five years earlier after Durrani had been indicted and fled the country, Children's attorney David Brittingham approached me after a hearing in Guckenberger's court. We were standing at the fourth floor elevators, when Brittingham spoke to me about settlement. For years, Brittingham simply just played with us and never acknowledged the risk Children's faced.

It changed after the Cotter verdict. The hospital insisted on a confidential settlement, but they tripled the amount of their original offer. I can't reveal the figure. In April of 2019, we took the offer back to our clients and all but two signed off on it. Children's paid the undisclosed amount in March of 2020 to all 185 Children's clients.

Mark Arnzen helped mediate the settlement. Because he is my friend and his son works for Dinsmore, Brittingham asked if we would agree to Mark, as the mediator, and we did.

Chapter 66

Fred Johnson Leaves

"For us is the life of action, of strenuous performance of duty; let us live in the harness, striving mightily; let us rather run the risk of wearing out than rusting out".
—Theodore Roosevelt

To help Fred out and because he knew so much about the Children's cases, we made him the Special Master of the Children's settlement.

On March 24, 2020 Fred Johnson sent the following email to Glenn Feagan:

> Dear Glenn, today I expressed to you my concerns about the litigation I am involved in with you and the issue of giving that information to Judge Reece in light of his questioning during the recent telephone conference. Upon further reflection, I thought it prudent to contact my ethics advisor and explain the situation. He recommended that I inform the Court and counsel for the Defendants to make sure that we are following our ethical duties of candor to the tribunal. You and I discussed that we do not think my work on the three non-Durrani cases raises a conflict I am sure you agree with me and my advisor that informing the Court of this is required as well as the responsible and prudent thing to do. Neither of us want this to come up at a later date and cause any issues relating to independence. Thanks, Fred

On March 24, 2020 Fred Johnson sent the following email to the Court and Defense Counsel:

> Dear Judge Reece and counsel, upon reflection after the phone conference, I wanted to make sure that everyone is aware that I am co-counsel with Deters Law on three non-Durrani cases. These are Kentucky civil cases and are not related to the Durrani litigation. I have my own independent law office and malpractice insurance. I am not an employee of Deters Law, but I do receive some compensation for my work on those Kentucky cases.

On March 27, 2020, I sent Fred Johnson the following email:

> Glenn and I discussed this and, on my recommendation, he agrees that effective immediately you are off all non Durrani cases: Lynn. Kent. Sex-

ton. Hanson. Any others. The reason is based on the amount of work you're doing on the cases we can't justify what we are paying you. Your pay stops as of yesterday.

On March 27, 2020, I sent Fred Johnson the following email:

Effective immediately, Glenn, on my recommendation is relieving you as special master. We will handle the change with the Court. Randy Freking is being re-appointed as West Chester Special Master. We will substitute him for you in Children's too.

On March 27, 2020, Fred Johnson sent an email to the Court and Defense counsel regarding his termination:

Dear Judge Reece, please be advised that today I was terminated by email and text by Eric Deters from my independent contractor work and as Special Master on Children's Hospital. Allegedly Glenn Feagan is in agreement although I have not heard from Glenn directly. I find this baffling as all I have done is disclosed my work on three non-Durrani cases as I was ethically bound to do. I am told that Attorney Randy Freaking will be taking over as Special Master in both the Children's case and the West Chester case. I will forward the two emails I received today regarding my termination. If you would like to discuss this further I would be happy to do so, my cell phone number is 859-250-XXXX.

Best Regards,
Fred Johnson

On March 27, 2020 Glenn Feagan sent an email to the Judge in response to Fred Johnson's email to the Court and Defense:

Your honor:

I just saw Fred Johnson's email regarding his termination. I can assure you that it was my decision to terminate Fred Johnson and Eric Deters carried out that decision on my authority. We were assured by Fred Johnson that his battles with alcohol were behind him and that we would have no problems with his diligence and work ethic. Over the last week it became very apparent that he is still battling these issues and we have no faith in his ability to carry out the duties of a special master or be counsel on any of our non-Durrani files. Obviously, this is a sensitive matter and I would request that it stays between all of us. Randy Freking has agreed to take over as

> Special Master on the Children's cases as well. We are all familiar with his excellent work as Special Master in WCH and I'm sure this court knows he can bring that same work ethic to the Children's settlement. We are preparing the appropriate Motion and Order to have Mr. Freking appointed as Special Master in the Children's cases and I hope to have them filed no later than Monday. Thank you for your attention to this matter.

On July 5, 2019, Alan Statman called me. His first words: "Fred's dead." I couldn't believe it. On July 4th, Fred drove to his law office to meet a client. He never came home. His wife Heather kept calling him and Fred would not answer. The next morning, Heather drove down to his office looking for him and found him deceased. The police launched a criminal investigation, which I believe remains open. All I know, Fred died, and I believe someone murdered him. At this time, I'm not at liberty to discuss the details. One day I will. It is unrelated to the Durrani cases.

We miss Fred. It's simply tragic. He left behind a wife, son and daughter.

Chapter 67

Evil Reich

"There are two kinds of people. Those with loaded guns and those who dig."
—Blondie "The Good, The Bad and The Ugly"

Judge Schweikert refused to allow pleadings applicable to all cases be filed under one assigned number as Judge Sargus set up. He failed to solve the problem when we proposed the solution. Even Judge Sargus realized the solution. Schweikert drove up the court costs then blamed us.

Schweikert proved oblivious to the victims' plight of their delayed justice including dying victims. Schweikert, when learning Jim Brown died the eve of trial, failed to express one word of sympathy or empathy, he simply said, "who's next?"

The Ohio Rules of Superintendence require cases be tried in three years. This never happened.

Schweikert refused every motion to amend our lawsuits. This decision has no basis in law, the opposite is true. Amendments are readily granted.

Schweikert refused to allow reputation, credibility and impeachment witnesses. He actually followed a standard that if it's bad for Durrani, it's not fair. He will not even allow Mehlman to testify as to these issues.

Schweikert threatened to dismiss cases with prejudice over court costs, which we challenged.

Schweikert threatened contempt for court filings he claims not warranted—a standard he only applied to us.

Schweikert never expressed concern for Durrani's victim's pursuit of justice while always being concerned about Durrani's "rights."

Schweikert constantly "coddled" Durrani at every turn.

Schweikert never properly sanctioned Durrani for his flight to Pakistan.

Schweikert took no action against Durrani's counsel for five years of games on scheduling Durrani's deposition.

Schweikert never considered any sanction or contempt motion of ours, but always set the defense sanction motions for hearings.

Schweikert made erroneous rulings on countless issues which left Durrani victims the long road of appeal as their own recourse.

Schweikert insisted on mediations, knowing Durrani's insurance carrier made no offers. Our lawyers are not paid by the hour. Defense lawyers are. They can attend baseless mediations all they want.

Schweikert's son worked at Dinsmore up until his appointment in 2017, meaning Dinsmore was handling Durrani litigation in 2015 and 2016 while Mark Schweikert's son worked there.

Schweikert allowed Durrani and the hospitals to supplement experts and not us.

Schweikert allowed them to amend answers six years after the lawsuits.

Schweikert publicly proclaimed he doesn't know if Durrani is a "bad guy."

Schweikert canceled trials January 7, 2019 and stated he wanted to slow down trials. This only helped Durrani and the hospitals and discouraged a just settlement.

Schweikert took at least four extended month-long vacations each year. The defense "wins" on any slow trial course—one at a time, etc.

Schweikert maliciously managed his docket. He scheduled mass hearings in the middle of trials.

Schweikert declared the McCann trial would begin on a Monday. On Monday the trial was moved to Tuesday. This cost us $5,000 for an expert witness, and McCann drove 2.5 hours from Wilmington for nothing. This is an example of what occurred all the time.

Schweikert ignored repeated misconduct by defense attorneys even in his presence including:

A. Mike Lyon threatening to cause a mistrial on purpose.

B. Paul McCartney calling Fred Johnson names. Fred threatened once to deck "Puke" while they both stood at the podium.

Schweikert held us in contempt for $62,000 in court costs for filings he arbitrarily deemed unnecessary Imagine the unnecessary fillngs made by defense lawyers who bill all they can.

Mehlman became a once in a lifetime witness for us. Schweikert mocked his significance and mocked the UC letter you have now read. Schweikert mockingly stated in court one day: "Your big letter."

The recusal process to deal with a judge like Schweikert is corrupt, so he smugly knew he could hide behind the immunity of the system and the blessing of Chief Justice O'Connor while he personally harmed the victims of Durrani.

Schweikert dismissed several cases filed before the victims turned age twenty-two which legally could not be dismissed. Despite a filing in the record of each of the cases, he claimed he still made the right decision. Children's and Durrani lawyers even admitted they shouldn't have been dismissed. He reluctantly vacated his Order. This resulted in another Affidavit of Disqualification.

Based upon all of the above, no Durrani client and no attorney representing them would ever believe the Durrani victims are being treated fairly. Not one single citizen of America would not be appalled how Durrani's victims have been treated by the system and those in it while Durrani is coddled by the same system.

On August 6, 2019, Judge Dale Crawford at a hearing for one of Durrani's cases he tried, put on the record that 99% of Ohio Judges would disagree with Judge Schweikert's rulings. Judge Crawford said he's tried more trials than any Judge in Ohio.

Then there is the failed leadership of the Ohio Supreme Court led by Chief Justice O'Connor, who allowed it all to happen. She refused to remove Schweikert. She put him in his position.

Besides the courtroom battles for clients, I fought the Kentucky Bar Association over my license suspension, the Ohio Supreme Court over the long-delayed justice, and biased judiciary in the Durrani litigation, and Schweikert's handling of the cases.

On May 17, 2016, I applied for reinstatement of my Kentucky license. A Kentucky Bar investigation into my application alleged I forged Matt Hammer's name on an affidavit accusing O'Connor of bias in the Durrani cases, a lie Sarah York and I would prove by Hammer's own emails.

Matt Hammer, the young attorney I hired straight out of law school and trusted with three of the Durrani cases lost in Butler County, turned against me. Our relationship grew strained after Triona left. He also seemed upset Alan Statman would take over as our trial lawyer. Hammer also suffered from a mental health issue he claimed as post traumatic distress from his assisting a high school classmate who died. His newlywed wife, Katie, discovered an Asian porn site on Hammer's computer. She left Hammer and Hammer called me.

At my request, Ben Maraan took the fall for Hammer's Asian porn, apologizing to Hammer's wife and saying he accessed the site. All not true. Rather than thank Ben and I for bailing him out, Hammer complained about Ben. Hammer would sleep in his office and the stress of his rocky marriage affected his performance at work. Hammer claimed he had medication adjustment issues. He became so bad, we would not allow him to even talk on the phone with a client or opposing counsel without someone else present. I even told him he could go home, work from there and get better.

Hammer resigned from Deters Law in February of 2018 not long after we fired Jim Triona. To prove Hammer lied under oath, we produced emails and other documents from Hammer corroborating the validity of his signature on the affidavit. I then sued Hammer for defamation, a suit that was dismissed by a federal court based upon Hammer having absolute immunity as a witness in my disciplinary proceedings. Instead of turning on Hammer, the bar association faulted me for "intimidating a witness." The Court ruled that even if a lawyer or witness intentionally lied, there is nothing you can do. Tell me that is fair? Every lawyer or person who wants revenge is free to falsely accuse any lawyer all they want to the bar association.

The Ohio Disciplinary Counsel, the ethics watchdog under control of O'Connor, likewise pressured me. The affidavit Hammer denied signing in

December of 2017 was part of the firm's lawsuit in federal court to remove O'Connor and her appointee Schweikert from the Durrani cases. The suit argued the two were biased in favor of the defense because of the millions of dollars the health care industry, insurance companies, and defense lawyers had contributed to O'Connor's campaigns.

Six days after Deters Law filed suit against O'Connor on August 23, 2018, Maraan received a letter of investigation from the Ohio Disciplinary Counsel demanding a justification for the suit. Their attempt at intimidation failed. The firm filed a countersuit within three days against the Ohio Disciplinary Counsel for violating Maraan's right to due process in the courts. Soon after, disciplinary counsel sent an email withdrawing their investigation. There is only one reason Ben received a letter so quickly, O'Connor told disciplinary counsel to do so.

By the time of the March 2019 lawsuit and six years after the first Durrani cases were filed in 2013, more than fifty of the Durrani victims died waiting for trials. At the date of this publication, it is now up to seventy-nine. One of them is sixty-four-year old Donna Rister, who died in 2017 of a massive infection after a series of radical operations left her wheelchair-bound. From 2010 to 2012, Durrani performed four separate surgeries on Rister for back pain, including multiple fusions of her spine and the insertion of rods. Each surgery further compromised her spine until she was stooped over and could no longer walk or drive. Durrani placed so many wires into her spine they could be seen poking through the skin of her back.

Her husband Gordon said he couldn't talk his wife into a second opinion. Rister called Durrani "another Mengele," the infamous Nazi physician who performed deadly experiments on Auschwitz prisoners. Another Cincinnati spine surgeon, Dr. Kahn, used the Mengele reference to one of our clients.

From his appointment by O'Connor in August of 2017, Schweikert tried only three Durrani cases in twenty months. During this time, Schweikert took a three month-long vacation to his second home in The Villages, Florida. While being paid $100,000 a year as a visiting judge on top of his retirement pension, Schweikert golfed.

On a Friday at a hearing to discuss the upcoming trial on the following Monday, of the next Durrani victim, James Brown Jr., Schweikert was informed that Brown had died. His only response was, "Who's next?"

Brown wasn't just a name on a court docket. Sabrina Cain, my videographer, said his living conditions were among the saddest she witnessed among all the Durrani clients she interviewed and recorded. Brown saw Durrani in 2011 complaining of burning, itching, and throbbing pain in his lower back and right leg. Durrani told Brown he could do a minimally invasive surgery which had a ninety percent chance of success and would return him to his home remodeling job in just two to three weeks. Durrani performed two separate laminectomies on Brown in 2011 and 2012, removing parts of his spinal canal with the aim of reducing the pressure on his spinal nerves. The first surgery only spread the pain to Brown's neck and the second sent it shooting down his left leg. Unable to lift, bend his back or work again, Brown fell into a deep depression that required psychiatric care.

In 2014, Cain visited Brown in his small home in the neighborhood of Cincinnati's Walnut Hills. Brown's house was in disrepair and sparsely finished. Brown spent his days sitting mostly by the window of his front room in a beat-up computer chair. Brown told Cain he could no longer bathe or cook for himself. He simply used his microwave. When he began to rise from his chair to show her the rest of the house, "he was trembling so badly I thought he would fall over," Sabrina said. He had to place the flat of his hand on the walls to steady himself as he moved about the house. When Cain told me about Brown's living situation, I had furniture delivered to the home. On September 18, 2018, Brown died at age sixty of a heart attack, three weeks before his scheduled trial. This is the man Schweikert simply asked: "who's next?"

Our clients and I grew increasingly frustrated with the trial delays. I turned to organized protests and media publicity as a way to try to have the cases moving again. The first protest in January of 2016 was held in front of the three major hospitals involved in the Durrani cases at West Chester, Children's and Christ on the second anniversary of the last case heard in Hamilton County.

Finding victims of spine surgery to walk a picket line is challenging. I asked Chuck Holbrook to visit Northern Kentucky drug and alcohol rehab center called "The Grateful Life" and hire dozens of its clients at $50 a person to hold up signs for several hours at the protest. Mary and I supported Grateful Life's work. I'd always explain to Chuck, "You got to get at least ten people with signs or it's a bust. Twenty-five makes for a successful protest."

In April of 2016, we staged a protest in front of the Duke Energy Convention Center in downtown Cincinnati, the night of Children's Hospital annual gala ball and fundraiser. We forced everyone attending to pass our massive group of protestors.

We protested more than once at West Chester Hospital, University Hospital, Christ Hospital, Children's Hospital and the Hamilton County Courthouse. We also took a bus trip to Columbus to protest outside the Ohio Supreme Court. The Columbus police made us move and threatened me with arrest. It was funny. We took a bus to Columbus. I gave a five-minute speech in the cold. We took photos and videos and went home. I just wanted O'Connor to know, we were there.

We were soon "blackballed" by the KBA, Northern Kentucky Bar Association, Chase Law School at NKU and UC Law School. Despite requests for resumes for law clerks and lawyers, they never send us resumes. Either all law students and new graduates have jobs or we were "blackballed?" Easy answer. Blackballed.

We also faced what's called vexatious litigation lawsuit before the Ohio Supreme Court. This is an accusation we file too many lawsuits. Jim Brockman filed it. The Court has never ruled on it.

What may be the funniest story of this saga occurred when Alex Petraglia, a public defender who lost his job after a work day encounter with a prostitute, began work at our office. I hired him at the request of Chuck Holbrook who knew him. For two years, I trained him, let him try a couple of Durrani cases and I thought he would be a "keeper." Another "nicked" person added to the team. Then one week after being licensed in Kentucky, he received a bogus KBA complaint about his working with me and he quit. Guess he wasn't a keeper.

During a deposition of a female witness, the witness told Alex he looked familiar. Alex recognized her too but denied it to her. Alex would later confess to me that he once hooked up with her in a "street" encounter. In the history of law, I wonder how many times a "john" unwittingly participated in the deposition of his "gal."

During his deposition, William Hamilton, a Children's case client, chafed under the bombardment of questions from an attorney at Dinsmore & Shohl. Hamilton stepped outside the deposition room during a break and flipped the bird through the glass wall at the Dinsmore & Shohl lawyer. The lawyer stated, "Let the record reflect your client is giving me the middle finger." The court reporter dutifully put it in the transcript.

Chapter 68
Patricia Adams

"Dripping water hollows stone."
—Lucretius

We made a breakthrough against the hospitals that protected Durrani. Four of the eight healthcare facilities where Durrani operated eventually settled for confidential amounts for the victims. In 2019, Children's settled with 185 clients; in 2018, UC West Chester settled with 354 clients; in 2016, Deaconess settled with twelve clients; and in 2016, Journey Lite Surgery Center of Cincinnati settled with forty-three clients.

Continuing their legal battles remain Good Samaritan Hospital in Cincinnati, where four Durrani cases survived Ohio's statute of repose time limitation; Christ Hospital in Cincinnati with forty cases; and Riverview Health Institute with twelve cases in Dayton, Ohio, where Durrani went after West Chester. We have over 400 cases against Durrani and CAST and thirty new cases against Children's. Lots of Durrani litigation remains.

Thanks to their defense lawyers, more interested in collecting billable hours than reaching a reasonable settlement, the hospitals overplayed their hands. Hoping to outlast us with their deep pockets, the hospitals spent millions more on legal fees and settlements to the victims than if they accepted responsibility and put the cases behind them out of the gate.

In March of 2019, we tried the Adams' case. Patricia Adams, a West Virginia dental assistant, traveled by car four-and-a-half hours to Durrani's CAST office with symptoms of lower back pain. Adams heard Durrani was "the best spine surgeon around." At her first appointment, Durrani told her it was her neck, not her back, which placed her in danger. Relying on his usual scare tactic, Adams could be paralyzed or her head would fall off if she didn't have surgery, Adams agreed to surgery.

In a 2011 surgery, Durrani fused Adams' head to her neck using the unapproved grafting material PureGen. Adams never saw Durrani after the surgery. When her husband Larry inquired why, an office staffer told him it Durrani's policy not to see patients after an operation. Adams recovered enough to go home, but she couldn't stand the pain of sitting on the dental technician's chair and was forced to quit her twenty-six-year career. She can no longer turn her head.

In 2013, Adams had a second surgery that resulted in a botched fusion of her lower back. Adams never saw Durrani before or after the operation. From West Chester Hospital, Adams returned to West Virginia and for the next four days was "lying in bed and screaming from pain." Unable to reach Durrani by phone, Larry drove her the four-and-a-half hours back to CAST, where office workers gave her an IV infusion of pain killers.

During her trial before visiting judge, Dale Crawford, Adams moved the jury. Before the verdict, Judge Crawford wrote down on a piece of paper $900,000 as what he thought the award would be. He shared it with the attorneys. On April 4, 2019, after seven hours of deliberation, the jury awarded Patricia Adams $1.1 million. On January 12, 2022, the First District Court of Appeals upheld the verdict. Durrani will now appeal to the Ohio Supreme Court.

Chapter 69
Judge Dale Crawford

"I care not what others think of what I do, but I care very much about what I think of what I do: That is character."
—Theodore Roosevelt

For a first in the history of American law, Schweikert ordered the verdict in the Beil case and all Durrani verdicts sealed from public view. Schweikert ruled it was necessary to prevent any bias toward the defendants in upcoming trials. This defeats the purpose for punitive damage awards, to publicly shame those who are responsible for harm to victims.

During a hearing in Hamilton County, Judge Dale Crawford, no relation to Dr. Alvin P. Crawford, reversed Schweikert's seal decision and scorched Durrani attorney Paul Vollman for disregarding the U.S. Constitution.

CRAWFORD: For the purposes of the record, it's my understanding that Judge Schweikert on previous cases has determined that the verdict forms shall be under seal. I don't know any authority to do that. And it's my position that all verdict forms, as with the courtroom, will be open to the public and they are public records. I have no authority to seal them, so they will not be sealed.

VOLLMAN: I would just like to maybe formally move to have the records sealed on the grounds that've — it's protection for — you know, there are 400 pending cases, and we believe that it's protection for the other cases.

CRAWFORD: Who am I protecting?

VOLLMAN: Well, in all fairness to the defense, to seal the verdicts.

CRAWFORD: Well, the beauty of the American justice system is that it is an open public system, and it's set forth in the Constitution that these things are public hearings.

MR. VOLLMAN: Uh-huh.

CRAWFORD: And we only have private hearings to protect under certain circumstances young children or whatever it is.

VOLLMAN: Right.

CRAWFORD: Nobody is going to be protected one way or another by me. That's not my job to protect the defense.

VOLLMAN: Uh-huh.

CRAWFORD: MY job is to have an open public courtroom and invite the entire public to see and hear what we do. And jurors are public. They've made their determination.

VOLLMAN: Well...

CRAWFORD: Bring them in.

VOLLMAN: I just want — there is precedent for sealing verdicts, especially in cases of complex litigation and numerous plaintiffs against one defendant.

CRAWFORD: I've never heard of such a thing.

Neither had I. When Johnson & Johnson got nailed for its baby powder causing cancer, were those verdicts sealed? No. The judge doesn't seal those verdicts just because there will be other trials against Johnson & Johnson.

Schweikert reversed Crawford's Order.

Chapter 70

Middendorf

"Courage is being scared to death... and saddling up anyway."
—John Wayne

Medicare investigators found that ten percent of the nation's spinal fusions that the agency paid for in 2011 weren't necessary, translating to $157 million in wasted payments for just one procedure. In an investigation conducted by *USA Today* in 2013 based on data from the American Board of Internal Medicine, Consumer Reports and Medicare, the newspaper reported the following percentages of unnecessary surgeries for eight common procedures: 20% of cardiac pacemakers, 43% of colonoscopies, up to 37% of Caesarian sections, 70% of hysterectomies, 12% of cardiac angioplasties for stents, 17% of spinal fusions for back pain, 26% of total hip replacements, and 38% of total knee replacements.

The larger problem is neither doctors nor patients have good information available to them when deciding to choose one type of surgical procedure over another or over a non-surgical alternative. Unlike drugs and medical devices, which are regulated by the FDA, surgery in America has no direct state or federal regulation and no central database of information where risks and outcomes can be compared.

State medical boards can discipline surgeons who fail to meet professional standards, but only if they are reported. Likewise, hospital peer review committees and administrators can withdraw operating privileges from surgeons who are deemed dangerous, but only if other doctors on staff have the courage to report them and press their case.

Without regulatory standards or even a database for comparing one surgeon's work to another, aggressive surgeons like Durrani perform dangerous, unproven and unnecessary surgeries on patients and claim they are being "innovative" rather than greedy. With backing from his respected mentor at Children's Hospital, Dr. Crawford, Durrani was able to hide his fraud for years behind a veneer of medical sophistication. At the height of his career at Children's, the hospital launched an ad campaign around Durrani as an innovative leader in scoliosis treatment.

Durrani often performed surgery on patients with mild scoliosis who would have been better treated with braces rather than surgery. Without the permission of Children's investigational review board, he performed experimental surgeries for scoliosis as well. A brief that Durrani published in *The Spine Journal* in 2011 touting the success of his minimally invasive surgery for scoliosis had to be withdrawn when it was discovered he had done the forty-five surgeries without the approval of Children's IRB or the adult patients themselves.

At least one of the patients in the study, a twenty-four-year-old woman, suffered severe pain in her lower back and right buttock three years after the surgery when the rod Durrani had inserted into her spinal column broke free of its screws and dropped down to her tail bone. Crawford and two other spine surgeons at Children's published a paper on the case in the *Journal Spine Deformity* in 2015 but failed to mention Durrani performed the experimental surgery without patient or hospital consent.

Durrani operated on young patients whose bones and skeletons were still immature. Lyndsey Middendorf, then fourteen years old, was referred to Durrani in 2009 for shoulder and neck pain after being involved in a car accident.

At her first visit, Durrani took three different scans of her entire spine and diagnosed her with mild scoliosis. Lyndsey suffered from scoliosis since age eleven. With no further testing, Durrani declared her cervical spine unstable and she would need a fusion on her neck as soon as possible or her head would fall off. Without performing a genetic test, he told her she was suffering from Ehlers-Danlos syndrome.

"It was scary," said Middendorf, now 25. "He told my parents if somebody so much as bumped me in the school hallway, I would end up being paralyzed or dead. My parents were terrified to drive me anywhere." For the next two to three weeks before the operation, Middendorf left her middle school classes under escort five minutes ahead of the rest of the students. "We took everything he said as gospel because we thought he was the best of the best," Middendorf said.

Crawford told the Middendorfs he "loved Durrani. He is like a son to me. I trained him," Lyndsey recalled. Crawford agreed with Durrani on the surgical plan. Crawford's surgical approach differed from Durrani's, in that he would enter the neck from the rear rather than from the front. Nor did Crawford guarantee perfect results as Durrani promised. Durrani "told us I would have the strongest neck in the family afterward and everything would return to normal," Middendorf said.

Following the early morning surgery at UC's West Chester Hospital, Middendorf woke up later in the night in pain and with her throat in spasms. She felt she couldn't breathe. They placed her on oxygen, Durrani arrived and began to examine her. He poked her lower legs and feet with a needle repeatedly. Middendorf felt nothing. "He started screaming at me, 'Yes, you can! Quit faking it! Yes, you can!' My mom said Durrani was literally dripping in sweat at the time," recalls Middendorf.

After ordering an MRI, Durrani diagnosed Middendorf with an infection and treated it with antibiotics. An expert at Middendorf's trial would later read the same scan and testify the problem had been a blood clot from Durrani's surgery pressing against her spinal cord. Genetic testing showed Middendorf did not have Ehlers-Danlos syndrome as Durrani claimed.

Middendorf spent five days in the intensive care unit before returning home, but her young life would never be the same. She had to learn again how to use her feet and to walk without falling. Because she couldn't turn her head or keep her balance with any sudden movement of her skull, she had to give up dance lessons and her position on the school volleyball team.

After she grew to her full height, the neck fusion Durrani should have never done on an immature patient had dire repercussions. Middendorf suddenly lost her vision at times and developed blinding headaches and shooting pains from the back of skull, down her neck and into her arms. The screws Durrani placed in her spine backed out. Other surgeons told Lyndsey any repair would be too risky.

The same examination also found Durrani's fusion blocked the growth of the rest of her spinal column, pulling on the ligaments between the vertebrae and throwing her spine out of alignment. The pressure from the misalignment on her optic nerve caused the sudden blindness and shooting pains. Injections to loosen the ligaments helped reduce the frequency of her symptoms, from every other day to about once a month. The pain of sitting for longer periods, however, forced Middendorf to quit her office job. She now works in medical sales and is on her feet.

"I'm more fortunate than some of the other Durrani victims," she said. "But I'm also one of the youngest of his patients. We don't know how it will work out in the future," Middendorf worries.

Middendorf would win her trial and it is now on appeal.

Chapter 71

Schweikert's Huckleberry

"We are all honorable men here; we do not have to give each other assurances as if we were lawyers."
—The Godfather

I have difficulty in not confronting my enemies. In the Durrani litigation, when I dwell upon all the unnecessary hell we have been through by everyone on the "other side," it's downright near maddening. I believe Durrani, his lawyers, the hospitals, their lawyers, Medical Protective, their lawyers, the KBA, Maureen O'Connor, Schweikert, Ohio Disciplinary Counsel, all of them, deserve hell. Hell as in the biblical sense and hell as in from me.

On February 14, 2019, I got in the faces of Mike Lyon and Jim Brockman. Schweikert threatened me over it. My letter the next day on February 15, 2019 to Judge Schweikert summed up what happened and how I felt. I just needed to tell off Schweikert every chance I could for me and the victims. You will enjoy the letter:

> Dear Judge Schweikert:
>
> I am writing to you to make several things clear. First, I resent ALL your unjustified comments and actions toward me past and current. Second, always know I am my own legal counsel and as such I DEMAND to be present and heard whenever any of my rights are being discussed. Third, I will triple down on my words and actions on Wednesday. Do you and the defense lawyers actually expect me to accept in silence all which you and they do to me and the Durrani victims?
>
> I was present in the hall, eager to testify on your baseless and unjustified contempt motion against Fred Johnson. (Why don't you allow us to submit all the baseless filings the defense has filed? Why didn't you allow the Miscellaneous Case Number that Judge Sargus set up?) Mr. Brockman walked out at a break and as he walked by me gave a smirky smile and half wave. This resulted in me walking up to him and while not laying a hand or touching him getting very close to him and "telling him off" verbally. I told him I was going to sue him and why. I never physically threatened him.
>
> He has slandered and defamed me for the past six months and more. He has falsely spread I assaulted and threatened him which he is now doing again. He has called me names behind my back. He has told lies about me to both the Ohio and Kentucky Bar Associations. I can prove it all. I am

and will be suing him and others on Tuesday as is my right to do. It has nothing to do with lawyering but a man to man honor code. It's actually no one's business but mine and his except he has chosen to make it more. Fine with me. As I spoke to him, I also used plenty of expletives for what he's said behind my back. That's the way I roll which is my style and right. Straight up. Not cowardly and phony like all the defense lawyers in the Durrani litigation.

As I was letting Mr. Brockman have it, which is my right to do as a man and in the public hallways of a courthouse, Mr. Lyon was watching on as if he had something he wanted to say. I asked him if he did. He cowardly demurred. Mr. McCartney was watching as well with his arms crossed and also with a look as if he had something to say. I asked him if he did. He too cowardly demurred. Finally, Mr. Brittingham earlier had walked out, and based upon this being the first time I saw him since the $3.2 million Cotter verdict, the collateral estoppel issue, the Dr. Azizkhan issue and the deposition issue, I merely asked him how he was doing. He too cowardly demurred.

Every defense lawyer in this litigation has libeled and slandered and held me in false light by falsely accusing me of practicing law in Ohio while retired. Every one of them and their law firms are being sued by me for defamation in federal court based on diversity. I'll be representing myself pro se. The attached text from my daughter, an assistant county attorney, proves my point about the value of my defamation case. I hope my verdict bankrupts at least the smaller firms.

Later Wednesday as I was standing in the first-floor lobby with our lawyers, Mr. Lyon, who is the biggest lawyer scoundrel I have EVER known and I have kept a running list of his criminal, unprofessional and unethical conduct in this litigation since 2013 for proof, walked out of the elevator with Mr. Brockman. They were lamenting about me. I proceeded to walk over to Mr. Lyon and let him know I was coming after him too. He is going to be sued by Deters Law clients for his conduct which will be detailed in upcoming lawsuits. He's being sued by me. As I walked and talked next to him, I never touched him. Furthermore, I never threatened any violence against him or Mr. Brockman.

You don't get it. I say what I mean and mean what I say. There is always purpose. It is always in control. Do not mistake my passion as being out of control. I know what I can and can't do.

On the first floor, Mr. Brockman the petulant wimpy cowardly man he is, asked the two bailiffs to intervene with my giving Mr. Lyon a piece of my mind. Neither bailiff did anything. The taller one clearly recognized it was nothing. The shorter one told me not to get in Mr. Lyon's face. I told him I was not in his face and also told him I was exercising my rights under the first amendment. I would like to see a criminal code about being in someone's face even though the video reflects I was not. I can't wait to hear what lies Mr. Brockman told them.

The video of these incidents supports my position 100 percent. I am no fool. As I stated, I know what I can and cannot do. Furthermore, my life's record is one of NEVER physically threatening or striking another lawyer. I state that for these drama queen's benefit as they attempt to use this to some advantage, not realizing I shall use it for my own.

I loathe and hate these men as I am allowed to do and state quite simply in my opinion, they are the lowest form of attorneys and humans. Feigned as just representing their clients they have chosen the irrational path detrimental to their clients of their billing for six years over a rational fair settlement. As the victims' advocate and spokesperson for the Dr Durrani and hospital victims, I have the right and obligation to hate and loathe them. We have successfully battled these large law firms for six years and now have Medical Protective Durrani's insurance carrier and Children's hospital in the worse possible shape they have been in since the litigation began. And NONE of it has anything to do with you. It has been despite of you which makes it even more epic.

Now let's turn to you.

You are without a doubt the biggest disgrace of a judge and person in the history of the Ohio Justice System. You are lazy. You are petty. You are not bright. You are not competent. You are mean. You are biased and prejudiced against the Durrani victims and against Deters Law. You are the classic bureaucrat not answerable to voters. You are greedy. You are apathetic towards the victims. You coddle Dr Durrani and the hospital. You have a double standard towards our lawyers and their lawyers.

Even if I was a lawyer, there is a Sixth Circuit decision allowing a lawyer to say what he wants about a judge based upon facts. All I say about you is based upon facts and is my opinion based upon those facts. I also attach for emphasis the Sixth and Seventh Affidavit of Disqualification. All truth.

You and the defense lawyers will never get or understand someone like me because of the pathetic people you are. You can't stop me from writing this. You can't stop me from sending this. You can't stop me from what happened Wednesday. You can't stop me from social media. You can't stop me from the press. You can't stop me speaking the truth. I will do anything within the law and ethics I can do in this fight. You, nor anyone, can punish me for it, because I'm allowed to do it. I am a retired Ohio lawyer. I am a man with a just cause. I can speak my mind so long as I don't threaten violence.

Al Statman, Fred Johnson and Ben Maraan are NOT my supervisors, Dad is. And, they have no power or obligation or duty over me. Regardless nothing I have done is wrong and I know they stand with me too. I feel their pain having to deal with you in the Courtroom without me.

You're pathetic. I have the record how you worried I caused the defense lawyers "anxiety" in Beil. Laughable. Why do I ? Because in Beil when they were lying about Dr Wilkey's deposition on damages I found it and our lawyers used it in chambers to prove them liars. So, they say to you: "He has to go." You capitulated eventually to aid their cause. Thus, my lawsuit against you which I will win.

You go to Florida for months on end. You're such a prima donna and don't even check your email. You don't set group trials. You seal public verdicts. You threaten us with contempt. You threaten our clients with costs. You golf and sun while there is work to do. You make clearly erroneous decisions forcing us to appeal those issues. You ignore defense attorney contemptuous behavior including Mike Lyon twice threatening to cause intentional mistrials. It goes on and on and on. You just don't care at all about the victims of Dr. Durrani. It's sickening.

Everything you do aids the defense, extends the litigation and make settlement impossible because it allows the defense to drag it all out Judge. Deters Law and Plaintiffs are NOT going to do what they and you want us to do: quit and take an unfair settlement for these poor victims.

You should never have been appointed. You should be recused. You should resign. You should stay in Florida and golf.

Let the record reflect this:

1. You went out of town December 20.
2. You returned this week for a few days.
3. You're leaving for Florida again until March 20. You plan to be here a few days and leave another month.
4. You complained before Wednesday's hearing that it was too cold, and you had consternation about being here. Well Judge, Deters Law clients have been suffering incredible pain from unnecessary spine surgeries since 2005 through 2013 and you won't give them their trials! You disgust me!
5. You on the record yesterday (we will have it) asked for a telephone hearing coming up to be held in the afternoon because you were golfing in the morning.

Meanwhile, Judge Robert Ruehlman would have had ALL these cases resolved by the end of 2017.

For the Chief Justice to defend you, protect you and not to remove you, is equally shameful. For the record, I do not fear her either. I would welcome a public hearing in front of her too. She deserves public scorn for her role in this.

The unprofessional conduct of the defense attorneys you ignored while worried about me "telling off" Jim Brockman and Mr. Lyon includes:

1. Their lying for five years about Dr. Durrani's deposition.
2. Threatening to cause mistrials.
3. You refused to make Paul McCartney apologize to Fred Johnson for calling him names in a deposition.
4. Lying repeatedly about facts and law.
5. Mike Lyon actually assaulted Fred Johnson in open court. Touched him.
6. You do nothing to them ever for anything.

Furthermore, you have NO jurisdiction to hear anything about me from Wednesday. I won't be charged with any crime because there wasn't any. You're not the hall monitor. And trust me when I say I relish a court hearing. I can't wait to take the stand. Be advised I will invite the media there. I crave to testify in Court or speak on my own behalf in a public forum against you.

Also just like your gag order you forced on us doesn't cover our lawsuits against you and the Chief Justice, they don't cover Wednesday's controversy. This letter is going to the news media and as many relevant parties as possible. I don't care where it goes or who it goes to. I stand by all of it. It's the truth. It's justified.

What Deters Law has done in fighting injustice and biased power in the Durrani litigation is epic. I am proud to be its leader in the capacities I am allowed. We and I am the antithesis of everything the defense and you are. I don't fear even jail in the cause, although I will never go there because I have committed no such offenses. I don't love money or country club memberships. I do NOT have any insecurity issues. I walked away from political power I held as a leader in the Republican Party in my 20s and a partnership in a large firm to fight for the little guy. Thus, I do. I had to give up my Ohio license unfairly because of Kentucky to help these victims. And I did. In fact, I ponder all I'll be able to do if I am unshackled from the bar completely. If you think this letter contains candor your wrong. It's restrained.

And I have come to learn I don't need a law license to do what I do so long as there are lawyers willing to fight this cause with me. I am willing to sacrifice EVERYTHING in this cause for these poor beaten butchered broken victims of THE BUTCHER OF PAKISTAN.

With no respect for you or the defense lawyers and the defendants because you deserve none,

Eric "Bulldog" Deters

Judge Schweikert, after the potato chip incident, would also falsely accuse me of jury tampering at another trial.

I inadvertently left an email about Judge Schweikert on a courtroom hall bench from a stack of papers. A juror found it and turned it in. In the email I tell of Schweikert again. The jurors told the Court they never paid it any mind.

It caused me to send another email on November 7, 2019 to the Court and all Counsel:

Glenn asked me to go to Court yesterday and wait out in the hall to communicate to him if he needed to make any decision.

The hearing was going to be I thought at the east end courtroom. The lawyers all went there too. Unable to be in Court, I sat on a bench outside.

When it moved to the other West courtroom, I moved and sat outside.

If I inadvertently left a few papers I had behind on a bench it was certainly not intentional.

I would not want to cause a mistrial.

I would not want to "tamper" with a jury.

And, as we all know, I know there are video cameras in the hall.

I take great offense to be accused of intentionally leaving behind papers to tamper with a jury. Its defamation.

There have been jurors inadvertently seeing names on boxes, etc. There have been lawyers and witnesses inadvertently saying names.

Once again, Reich moved on. From the Cole phone call, from the Lyon and Brockman incident, from the "potato chip" to the left behind paper, Schweikert always cowered when I stood up to him.

Protest at the courthouse demanding trials on behalf of Durrani victims.

Alan Statman and Eric Deters at the depositions of the University letter writers.

Billy and Katherine Walls

Chuck Holbrook and Harry Reynolds

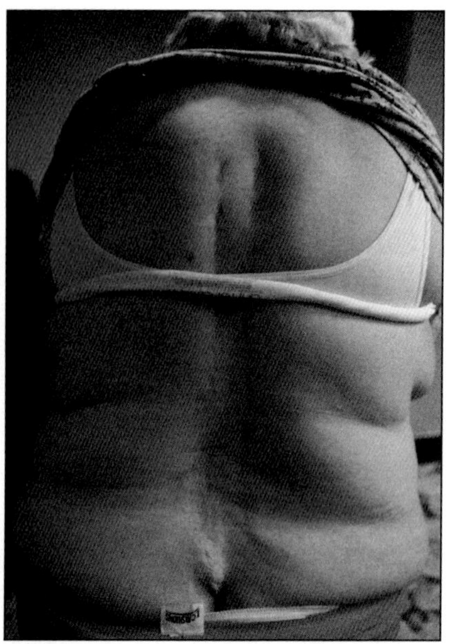

Donna Rister's back following the Durrani surgery.

The staff of Deters Law, l-r: Alexa Kavanaugh, Sarah York, Brittany Pillman, Eric Deters, Chuck Holbrook, Maria Dallas, and Loretta Little.

Dr. Kevin Joseph, CEO of West Chester Hospital during the Durrani surgeries.

Dr. Richard Azizkhan

Dr. Alvin Crawford

Dr. Charles "Cowboy" Mehlman waits in the hall to testify in the Cotter case.

Dr. Eric Wall

Dr. Keith Wilkey, Orthopedic Spine Victims Expert, with Eric Deters.

Brad and Teresa Nichols

Dr. Lawrence Kurtzman and Eric Deters

Dr. Errol Mortimer, Pediatric Spine Surgeon Victims Expert, with Eric Deters.

Judge Robert Ruehlman

Dr. Stephen Bloomfield, Neurosurgeon and Dr. Ranjiv Saini, Neuroradiologist, both Durrani victims experts.

Durrani victim, Todd Ray.

Durrani and his girlfriend, Beth Garrett, from Pakistan.

Durrani giving testimony from Pakistan.

Eric Deters holds a meeting with Durrani victims.

Eric Deters and Glenn Feagan

Eric Deters in trial.

Eric Deters being arrested for contempt of court.

Eric Deters and Alan Statman at the bunker.

Federal Judge Michael Barrett

Fred Johnson and Alan Statman celebrating the Beil verdict.

Mary and Eric Deters

Elaine Waxler and Bill Wolder with Eric Deters

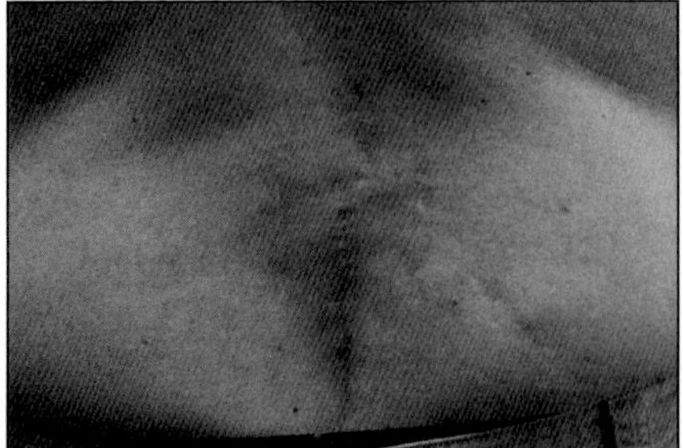

The back of Jeff Potts after the Durrani surgery.

Judge Guy Reece

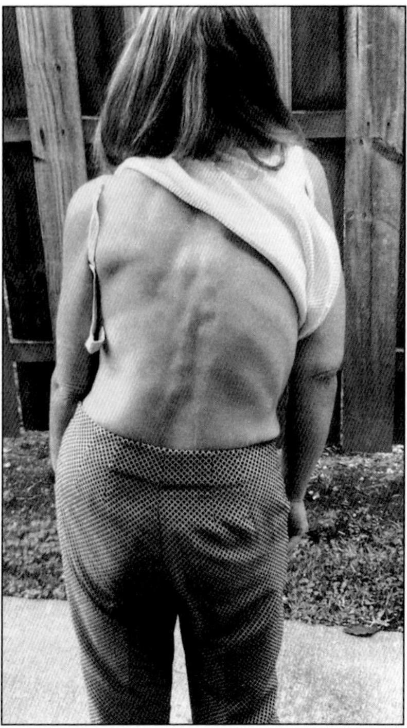

The back of victim Karen Johnson following the Durrani surgery.

Fred Johnson with the Cotter jury after the verdict.

Ohio Chief Justice Maureen O'Connor

Patricia and Judy Adams

Larry Grause and Eric Deters

Mike Lyon, Durrani's Attorney, and Judge Mark Schweikert

Paying back David Prater

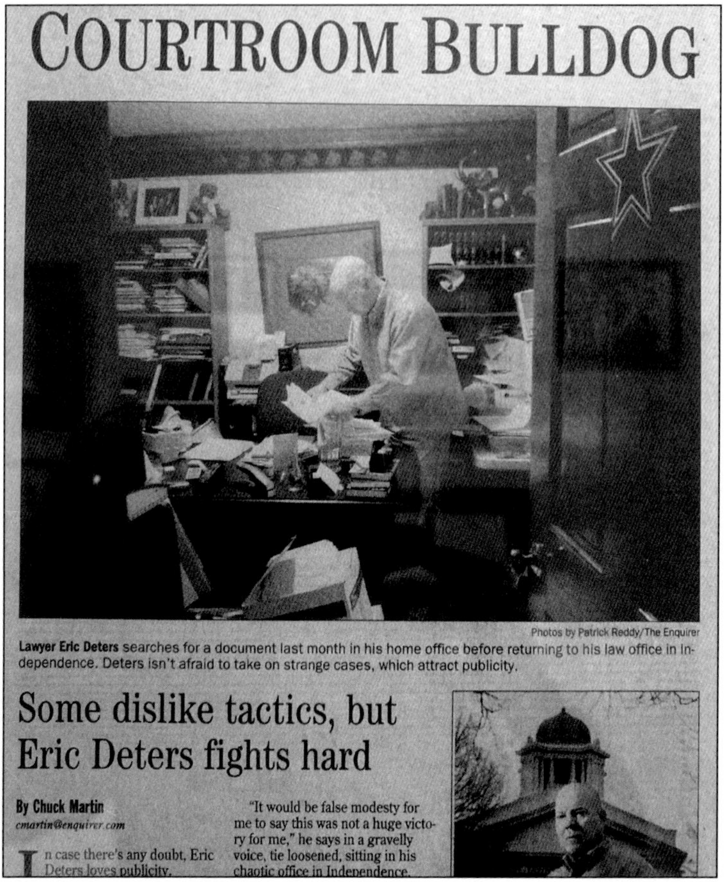

COURTROOM BULLDOG

Photos by Patrick Reddy/The Enquirer

Lawyer Eric Deters searches for a document last month in his home office before returning to his law office in Independence. Deters isn't afraid to take on strange cases, which attract publicity.

Some dislike tactics, but Eric Deters fights hard

By Chuck Martin
cmartin@enquirer.com

In case there's any doubt, Eric Deters loves publicity.

"It would be false modesty for me to say this was not a huge victory for me," he says in a gravelly voice, tie loosened, sitting in his chaotic office in Independence.

The article that gave Eric Deters the name "Bulldog".

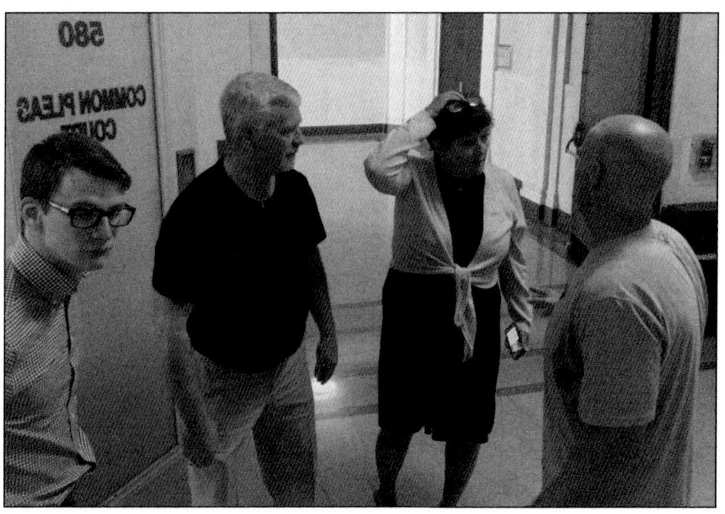

The Potts family before the Ohio record verdict.

Protest at the Children's Gala.

Theresa Woods, Durrani Victim, and Eric Deters.

The Bunker where all the Durrani victims files, hospital and Durrani case materials are kept.

The Deters Law trial team, l-r: Alan Statman, Joe Rutter, Debbie Worley (client), Chuck Holbrook, Eric Deters, Fred Johnson, Ben Maraan, and Matt "Murdoch" Bradley.

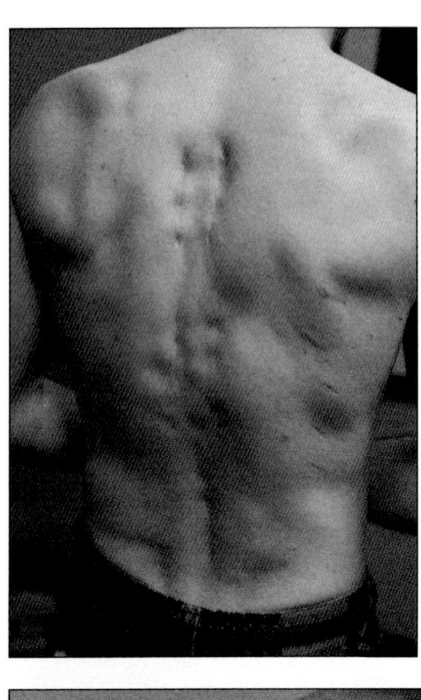

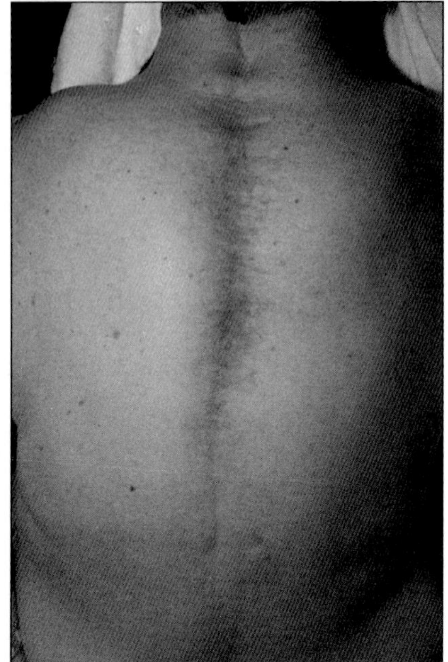

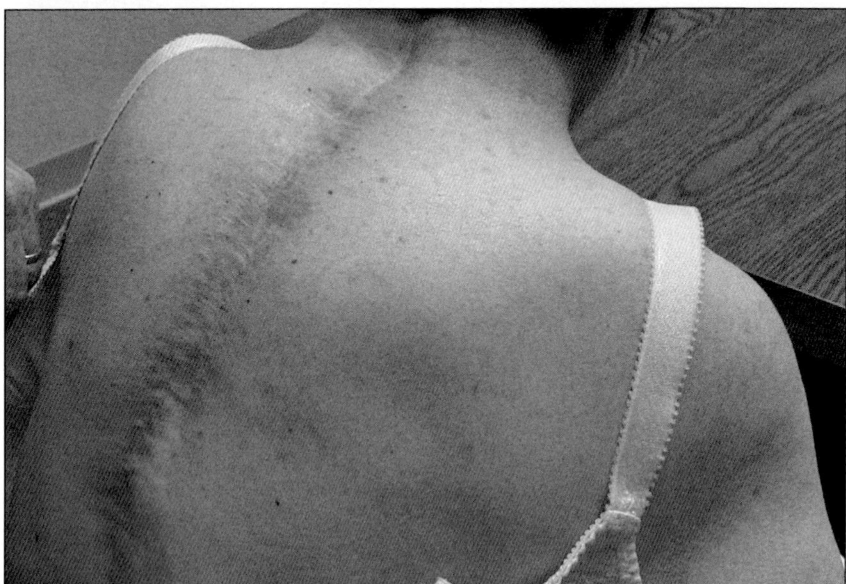

Victim Scars

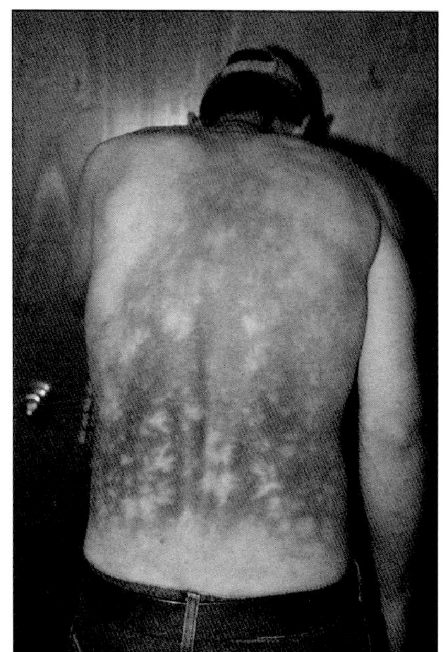

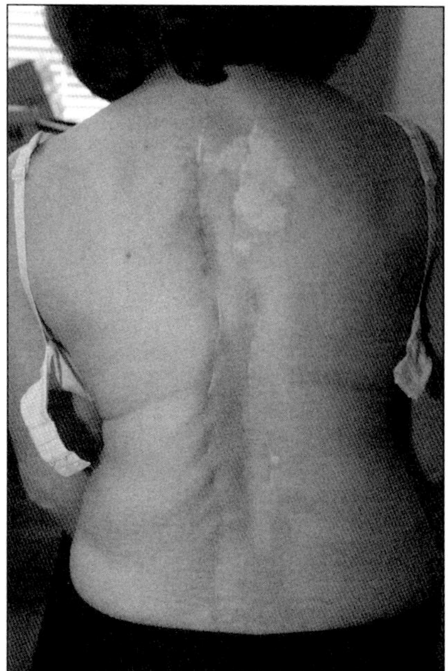

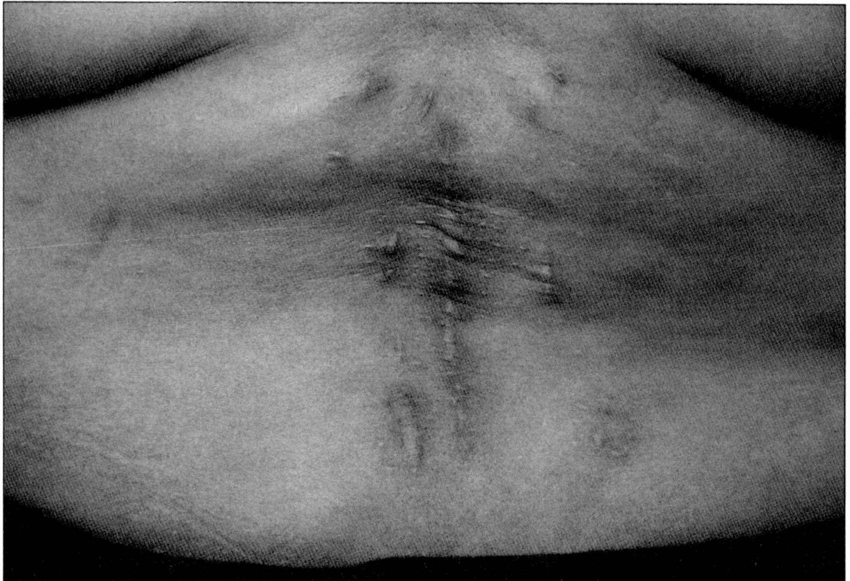

Victim Scars

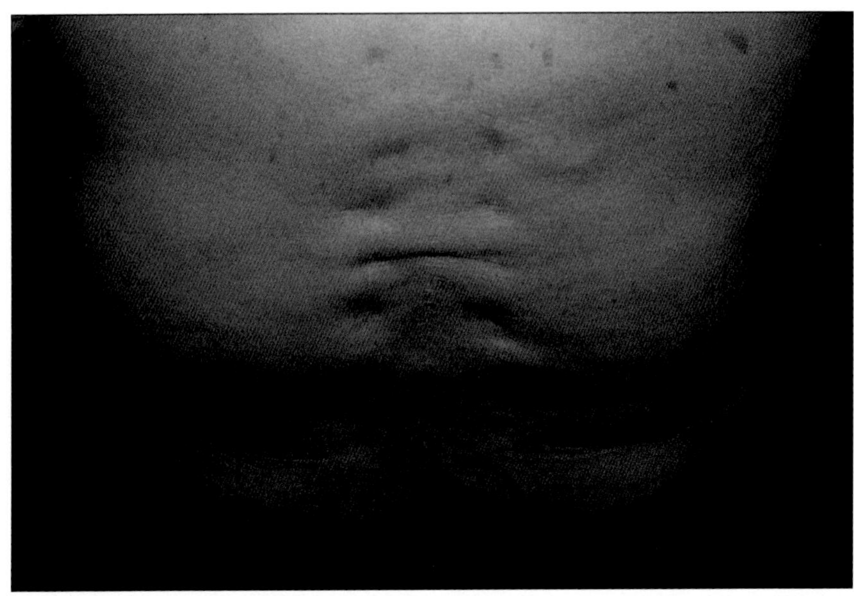

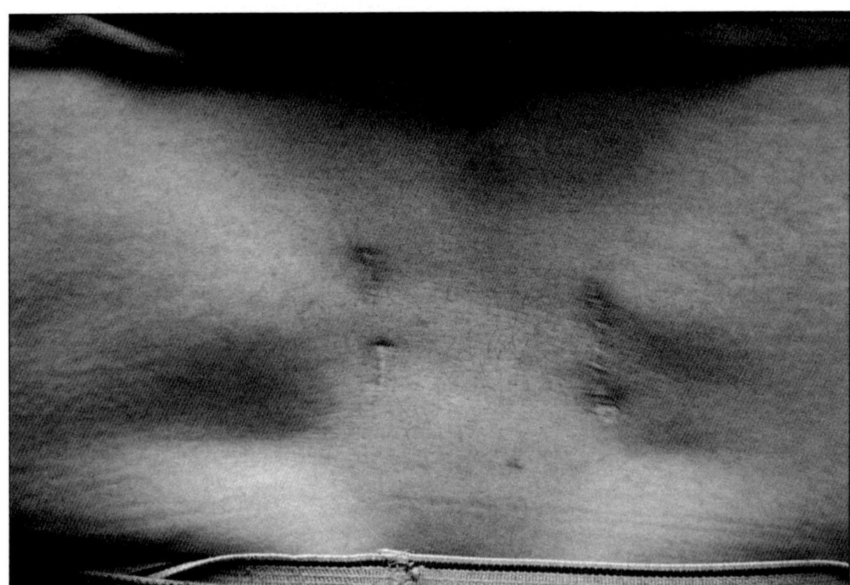

Victim Scars

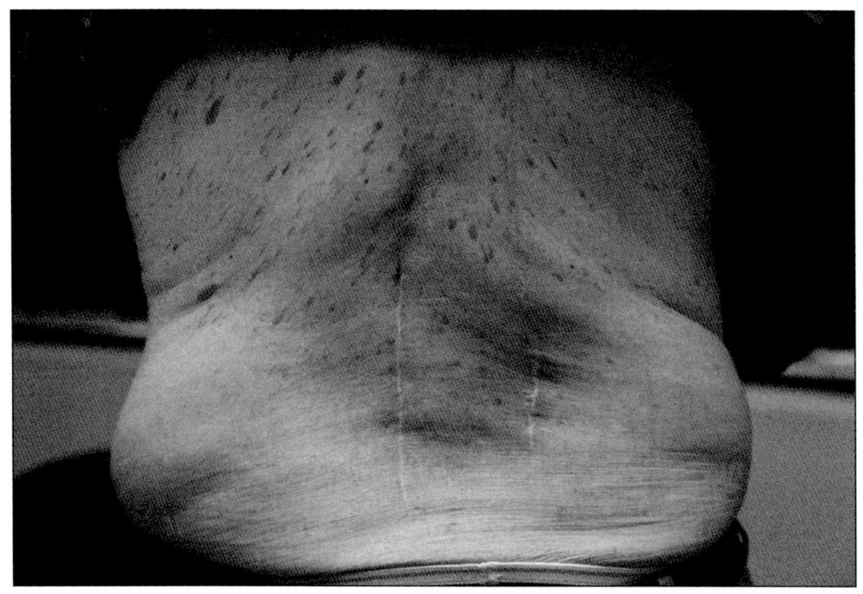

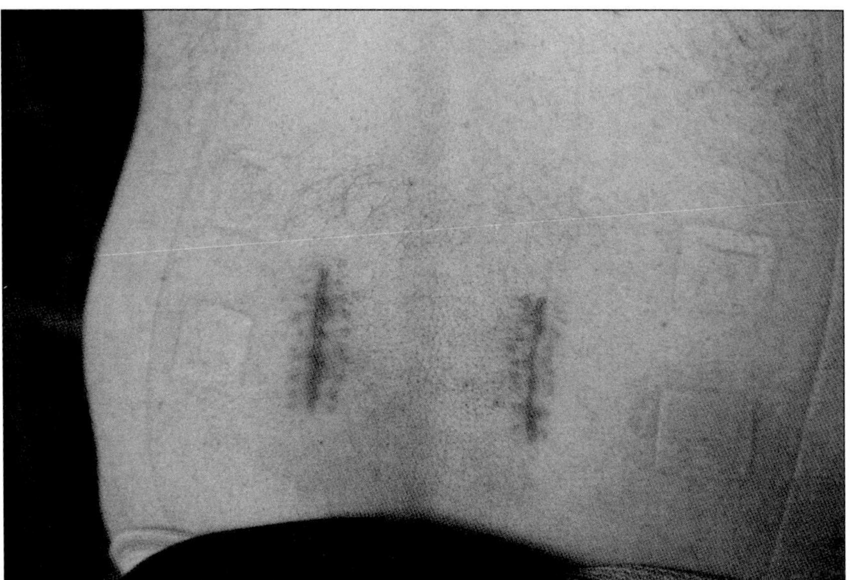

Victim Scars

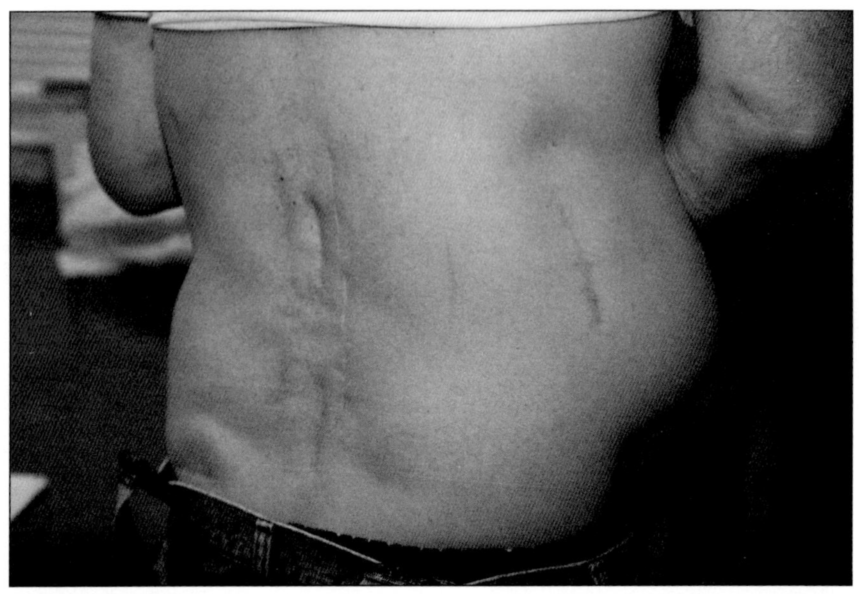

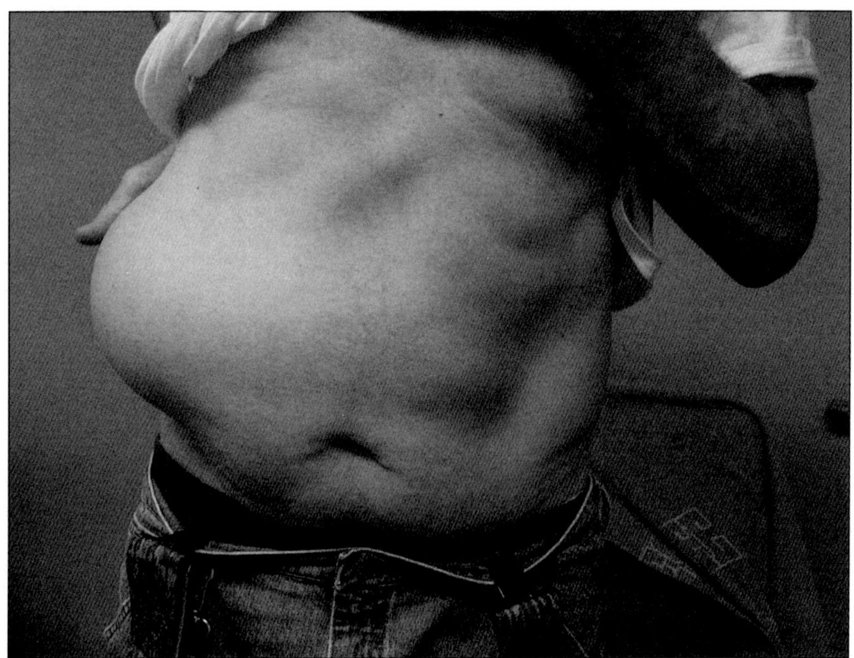

Victim Scars

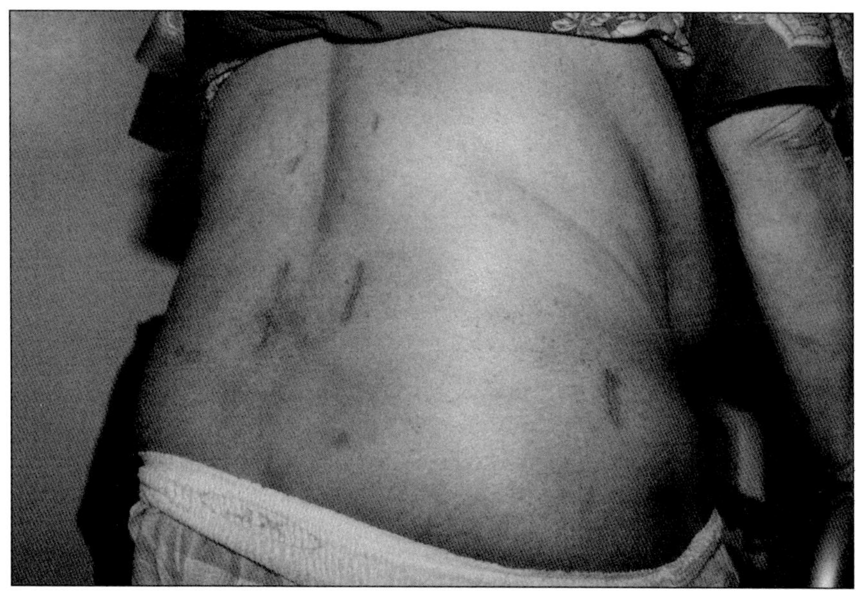

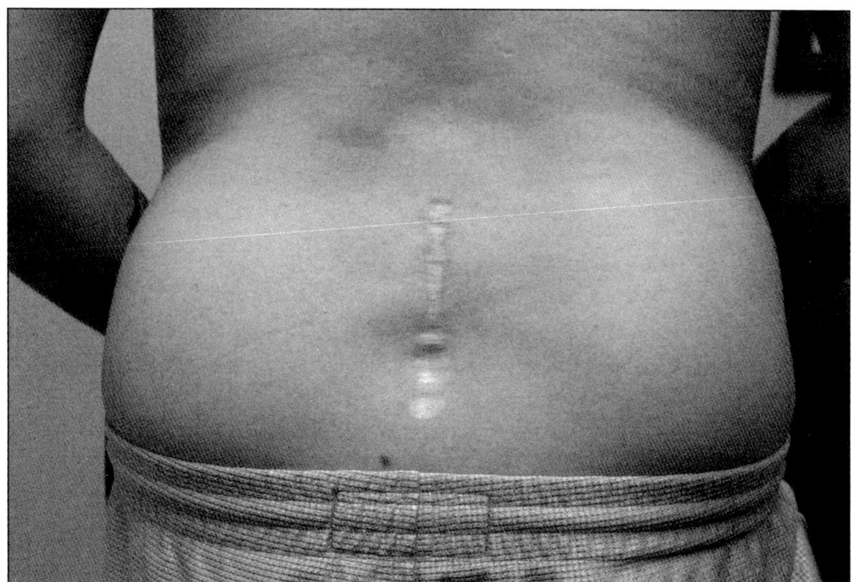

Victim Scars

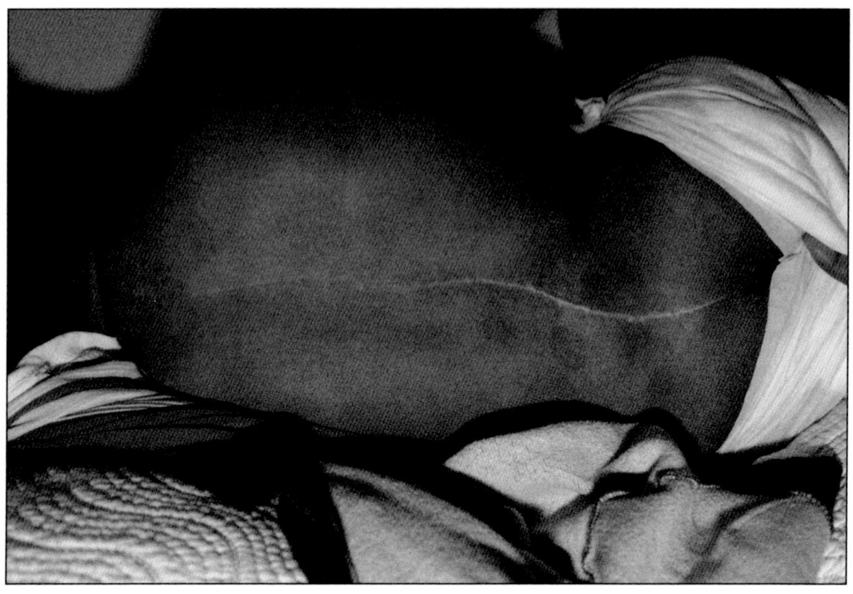

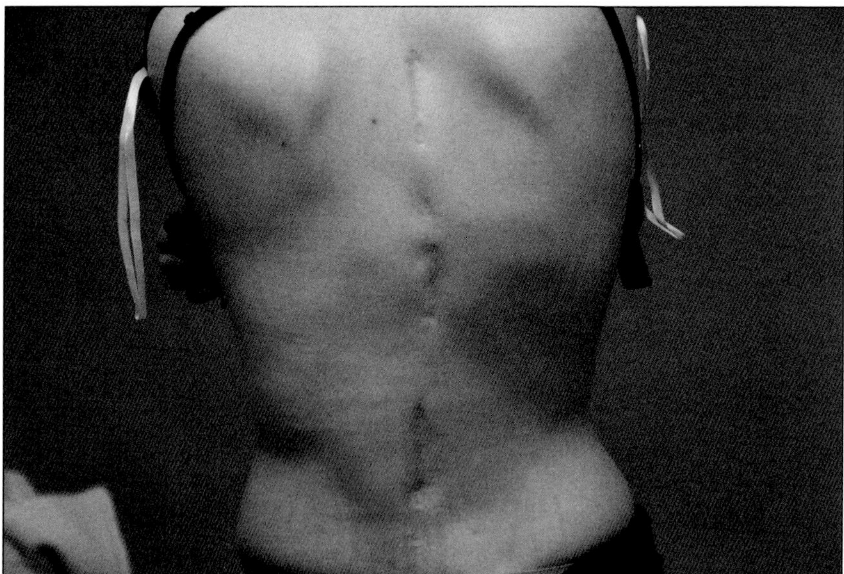

Victim Scars

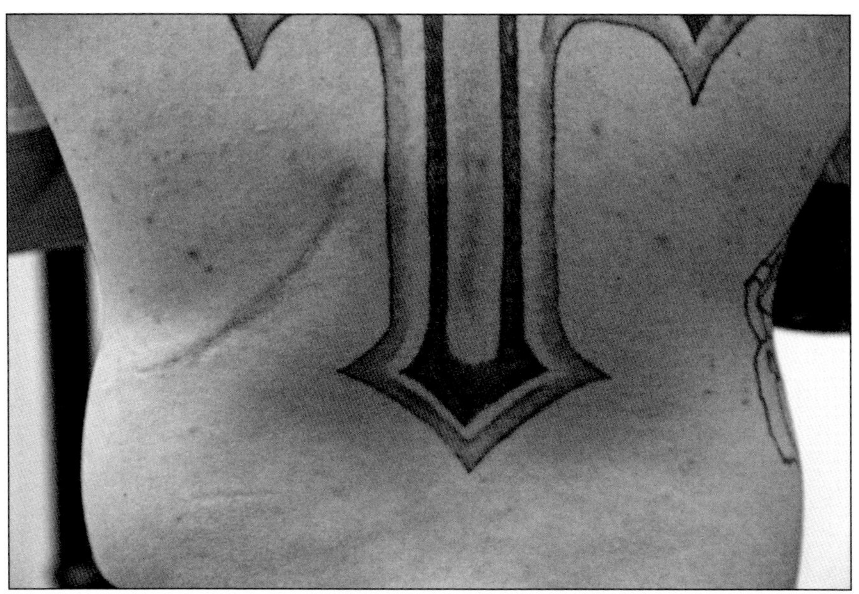

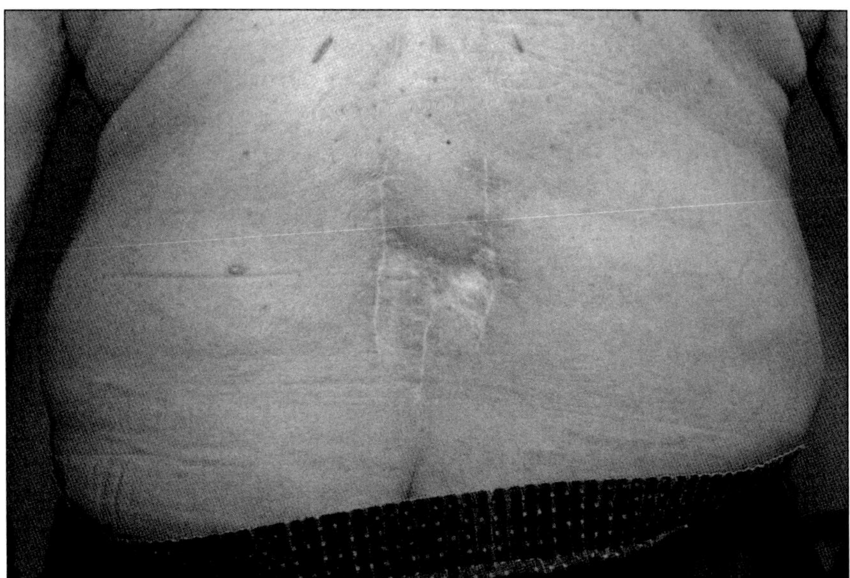

Victim Scars

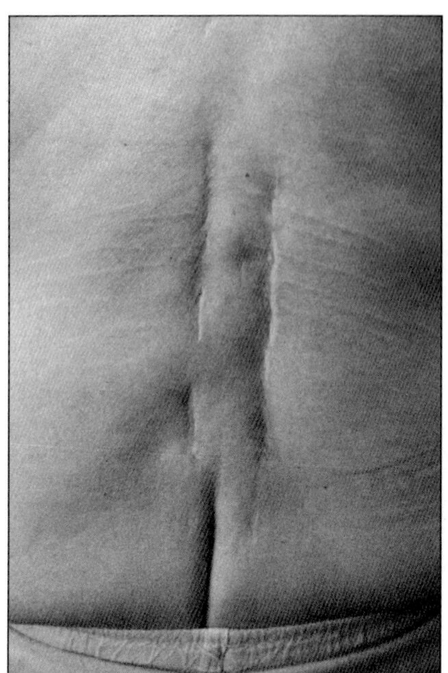

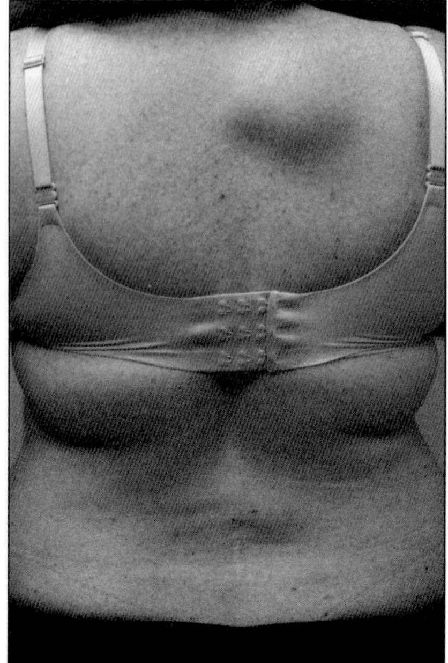

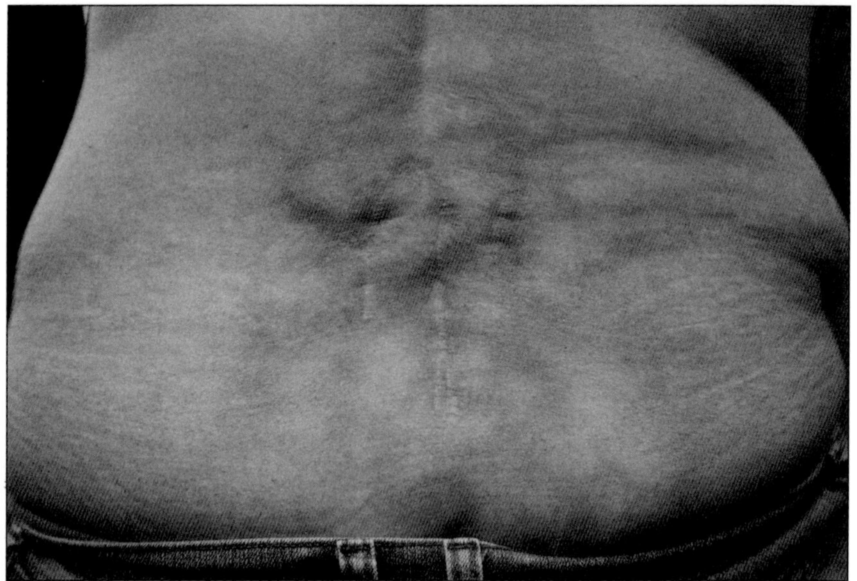

Victim Scars

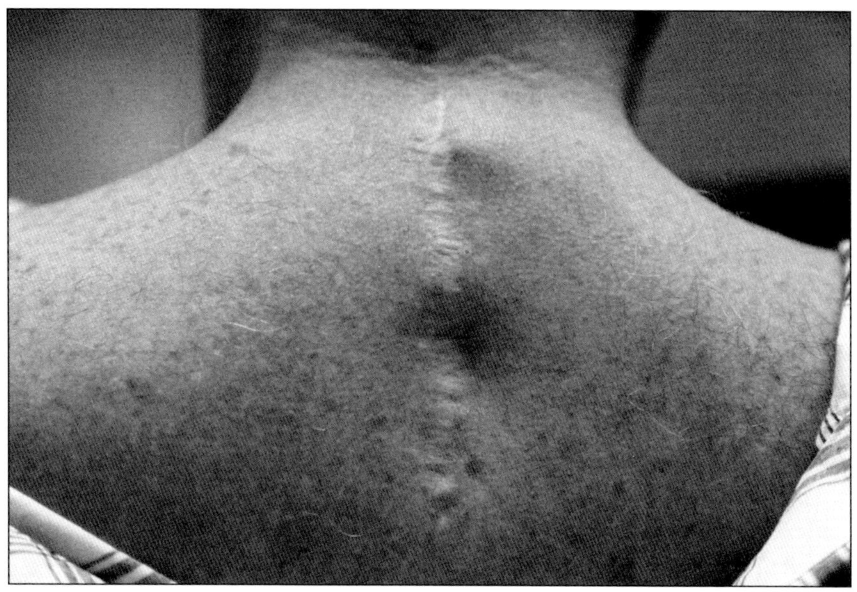

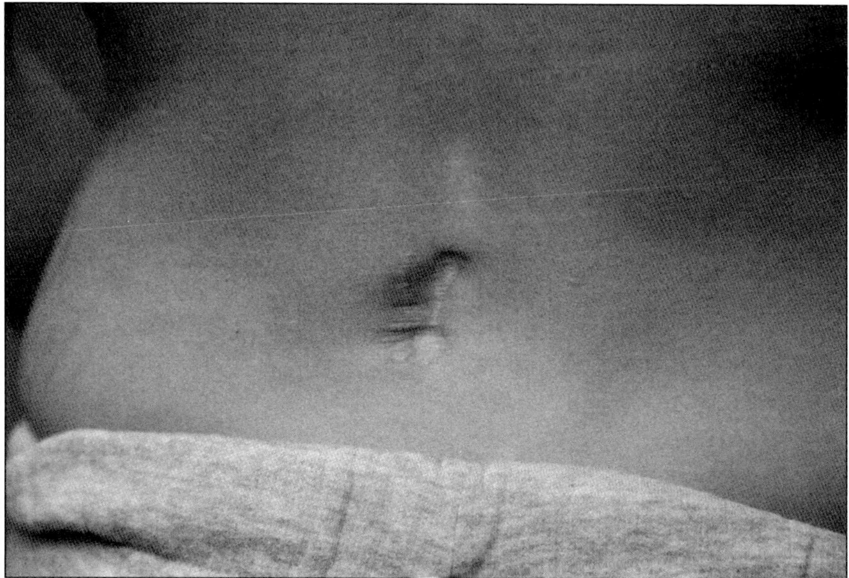

Victim Scars

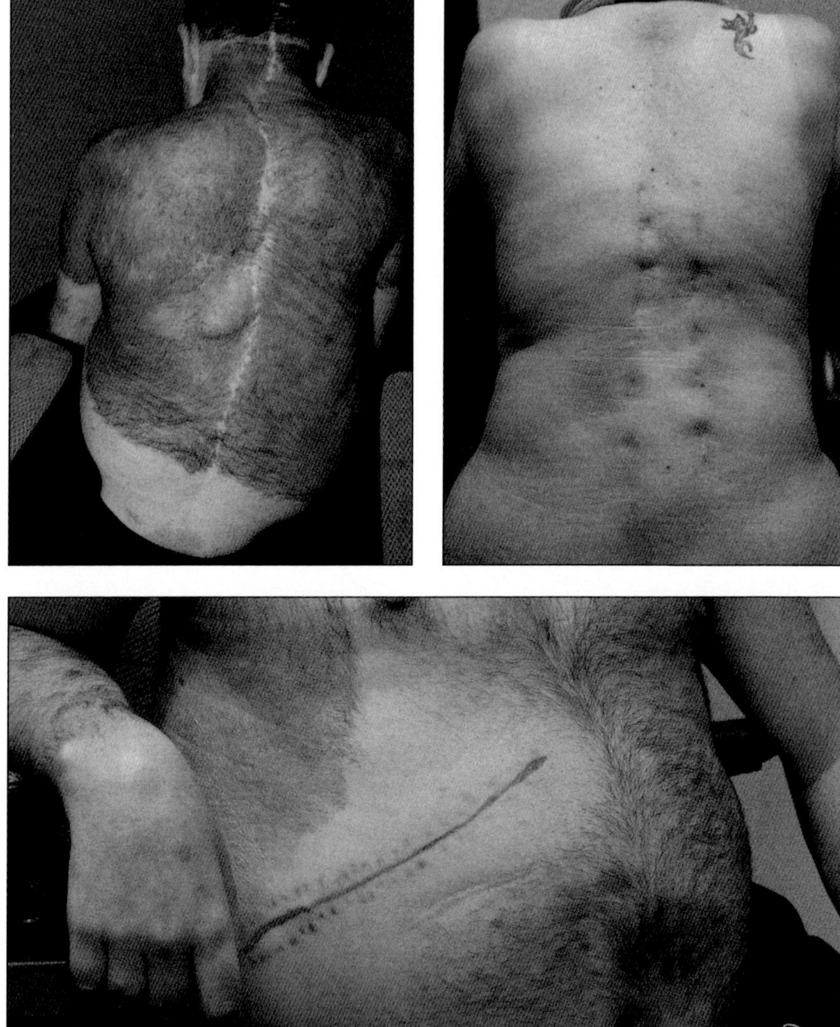

Victim Scars

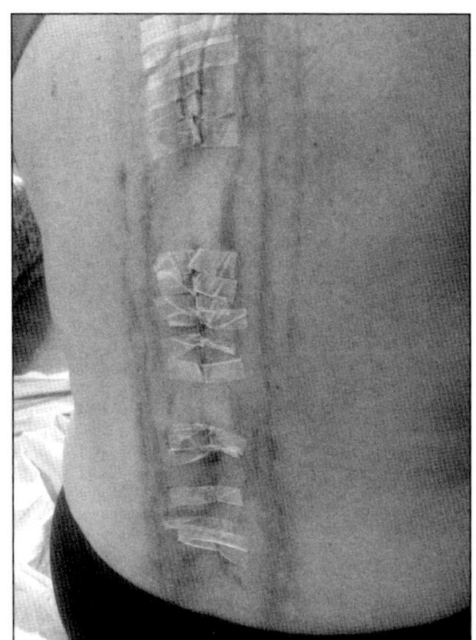

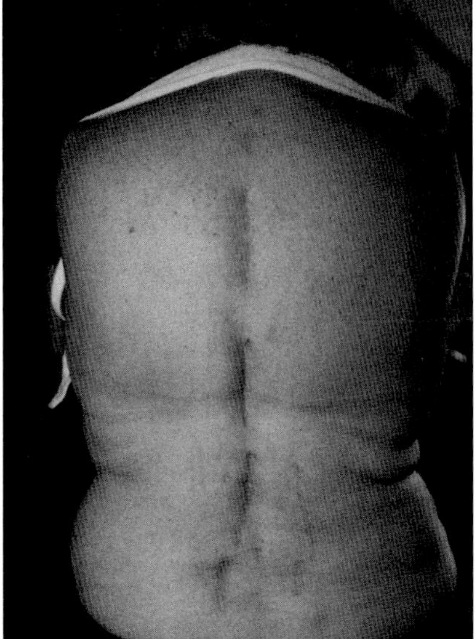

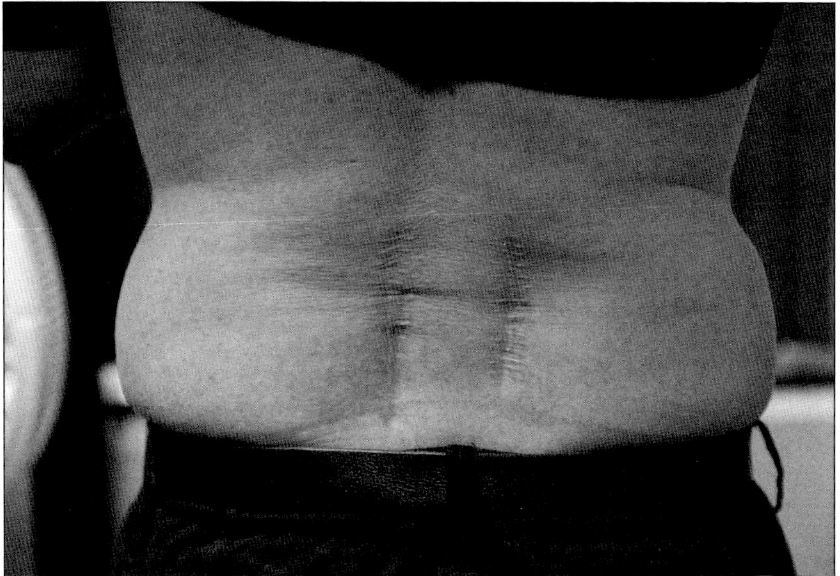

Victim Scars

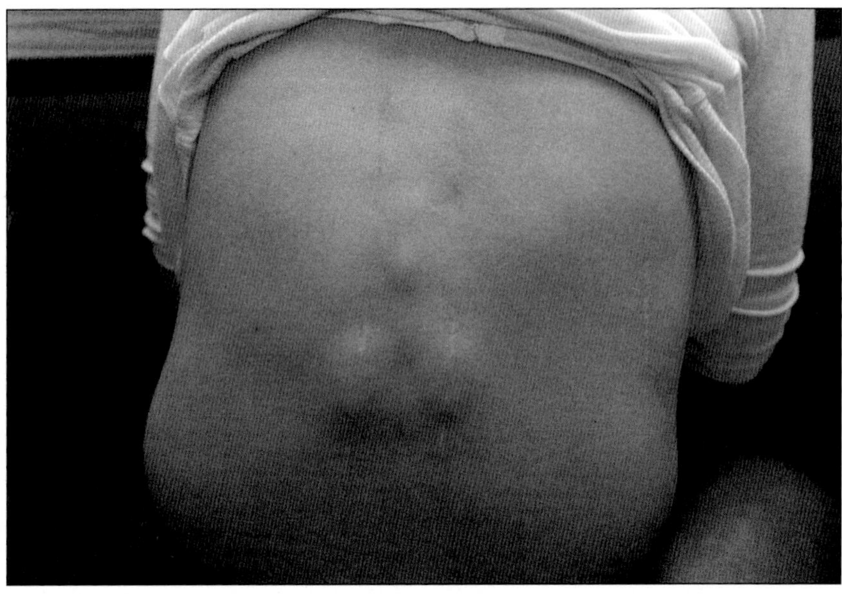

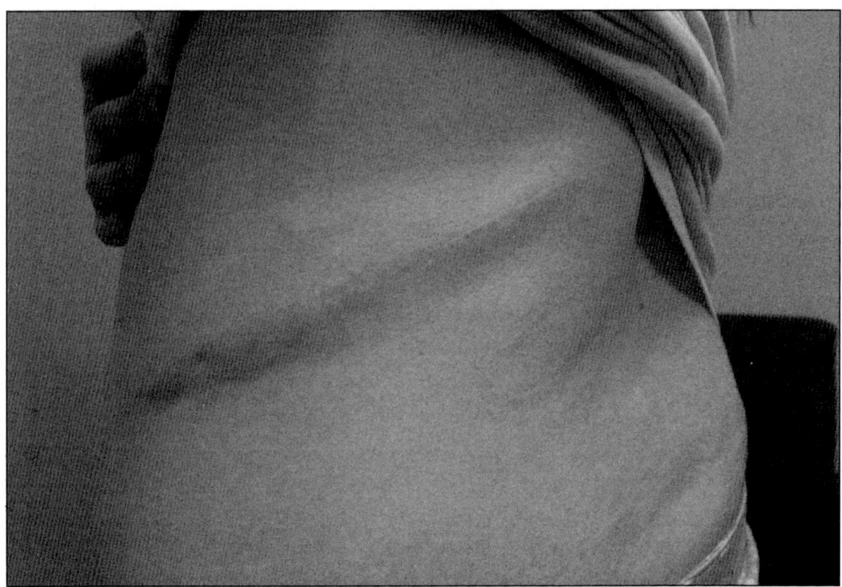

Victim Scars

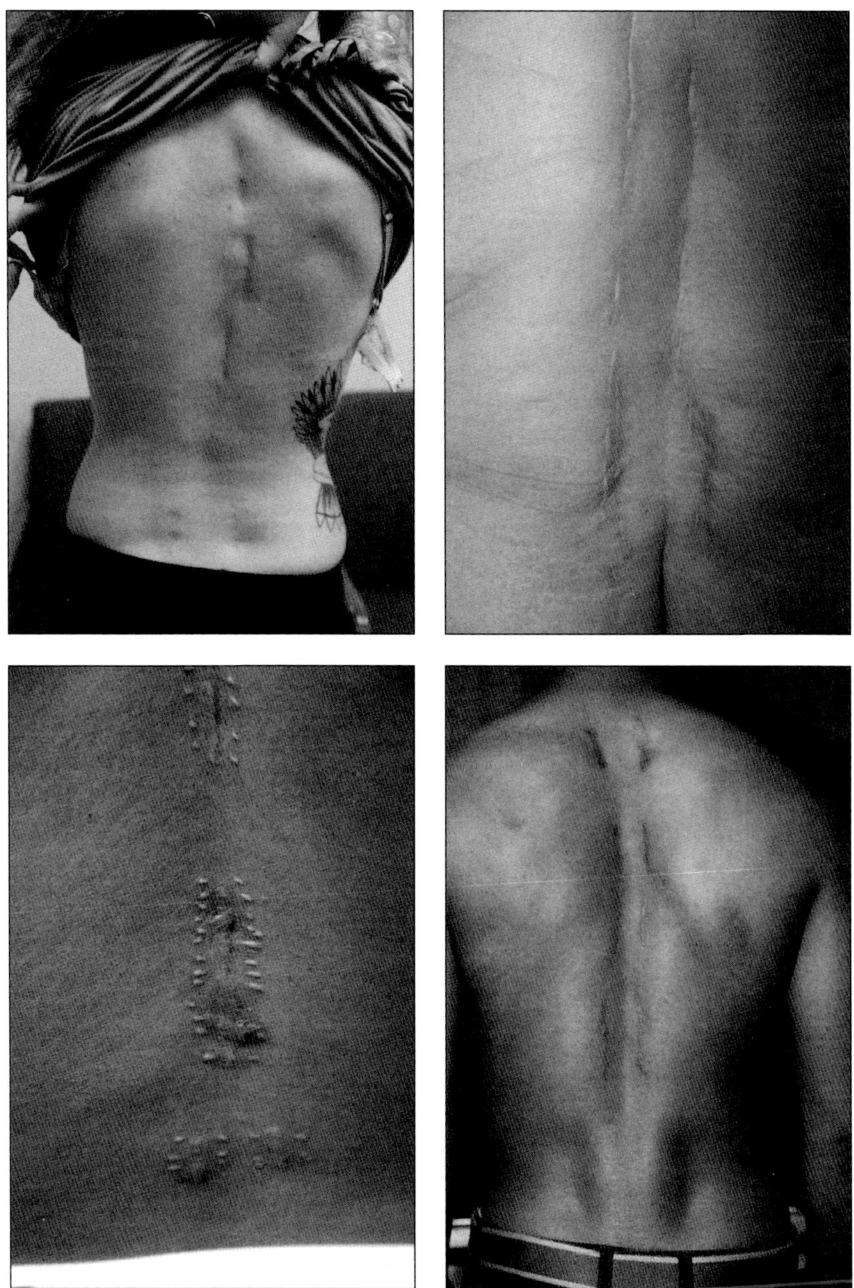

Victim Scars

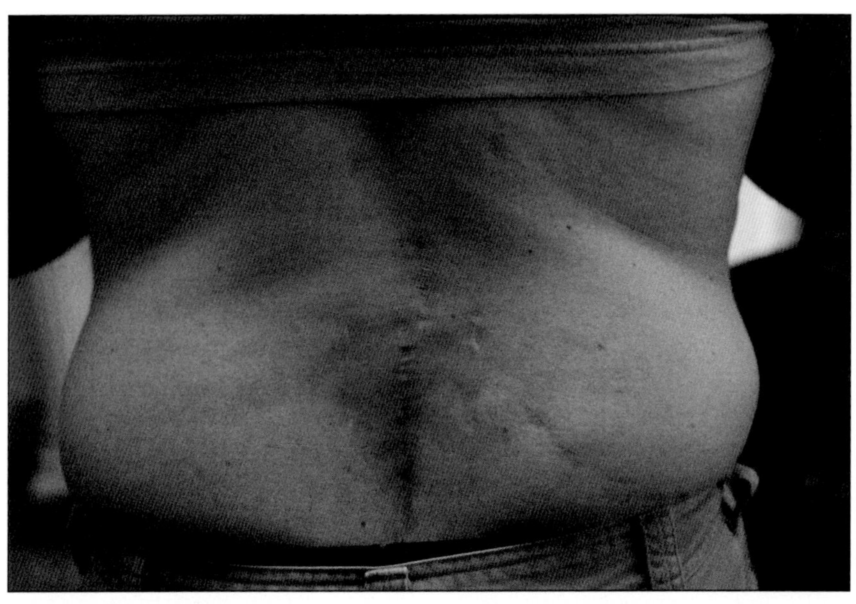

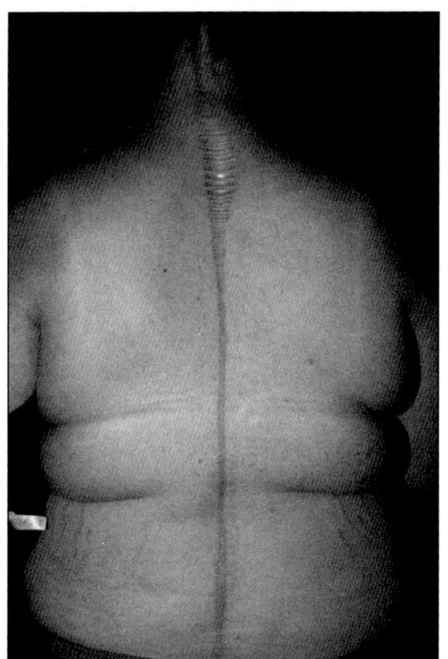

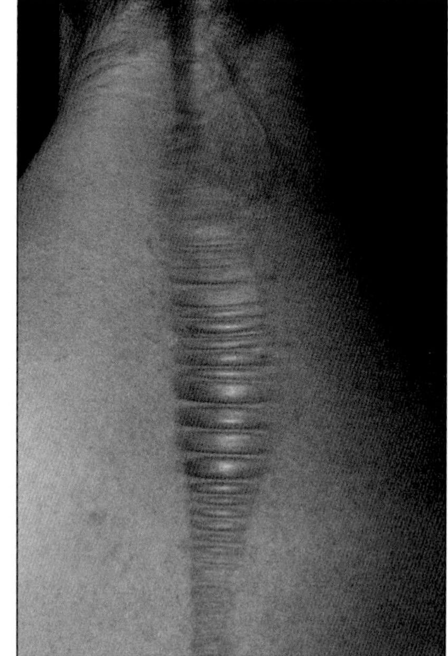

Victim Scars

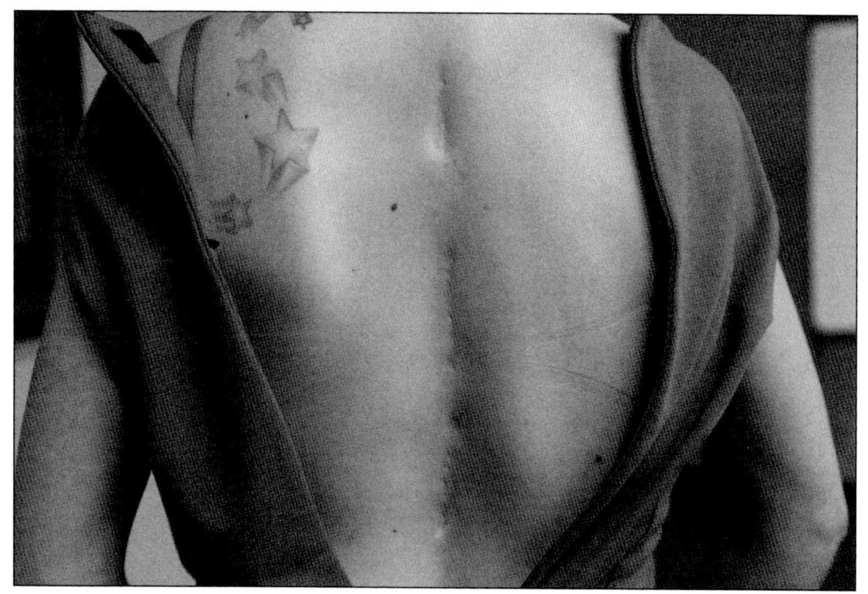

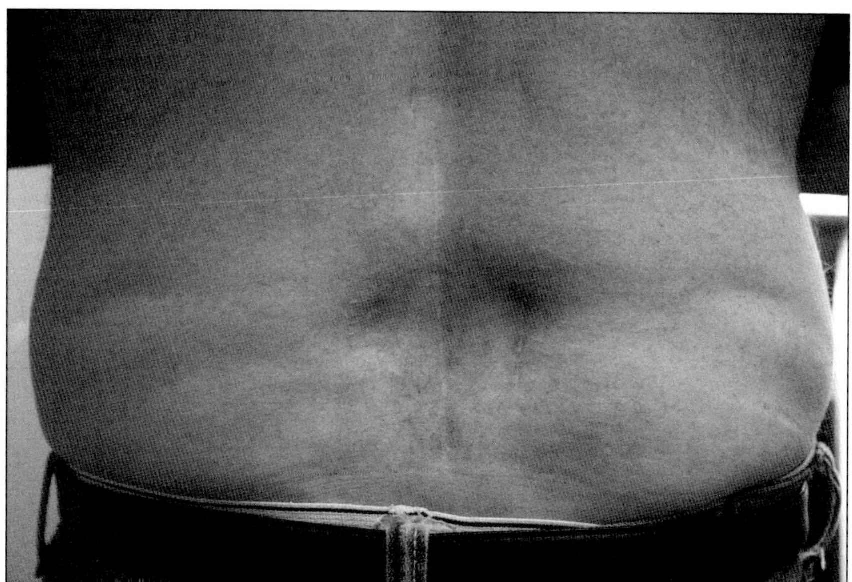

Victim Scars

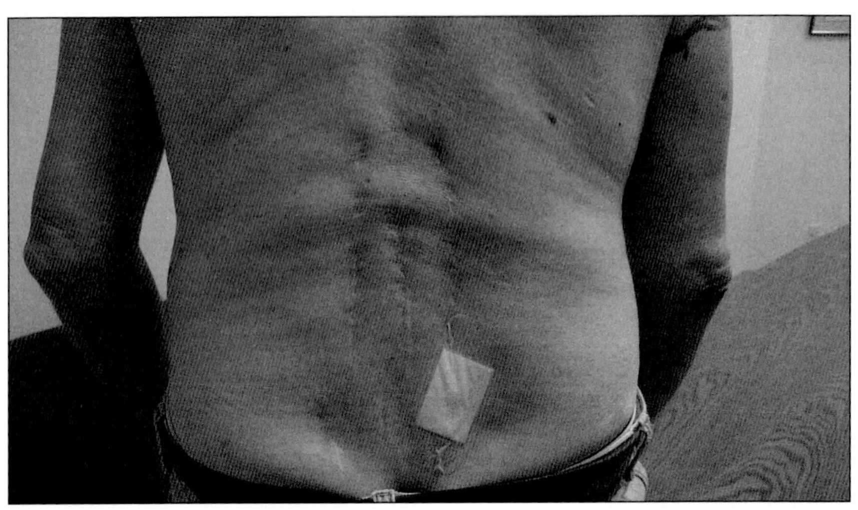

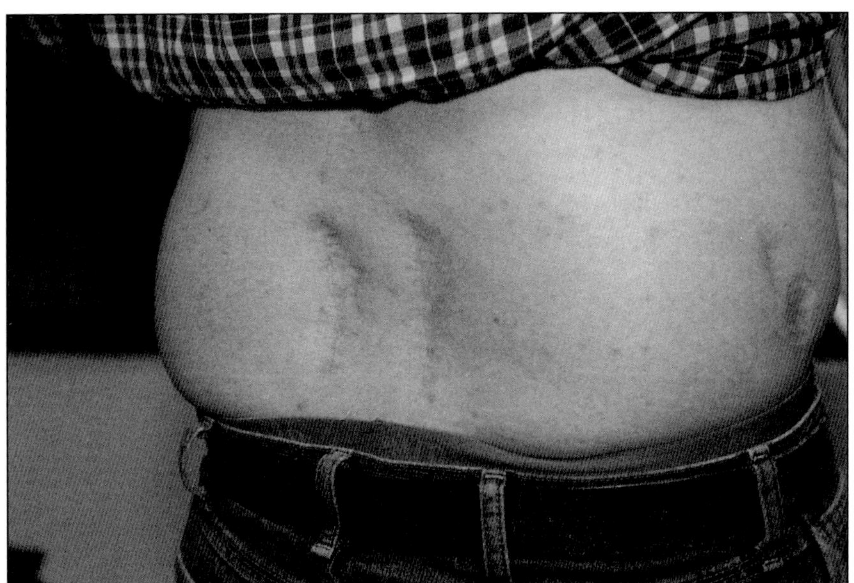

Victim Scars

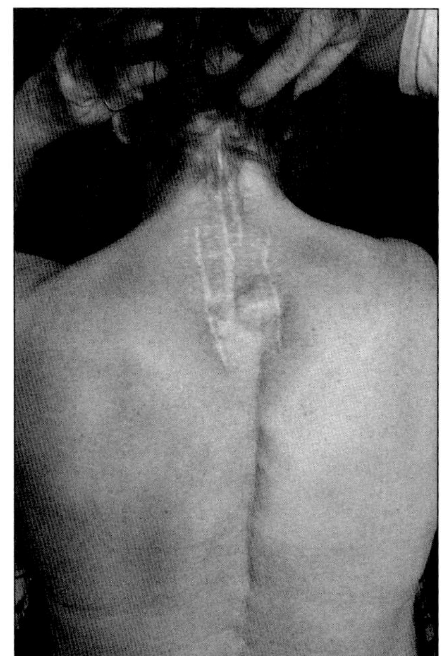

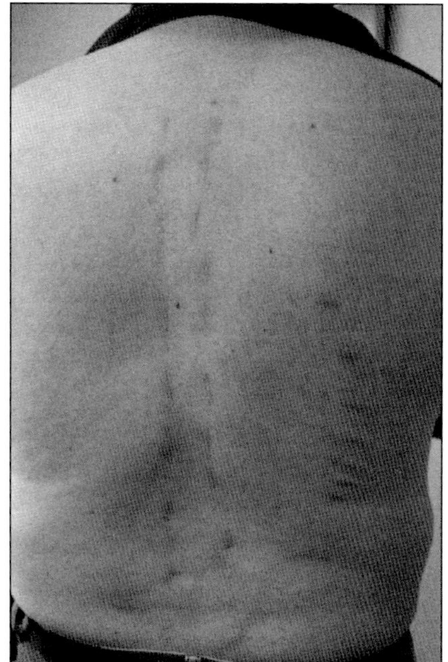

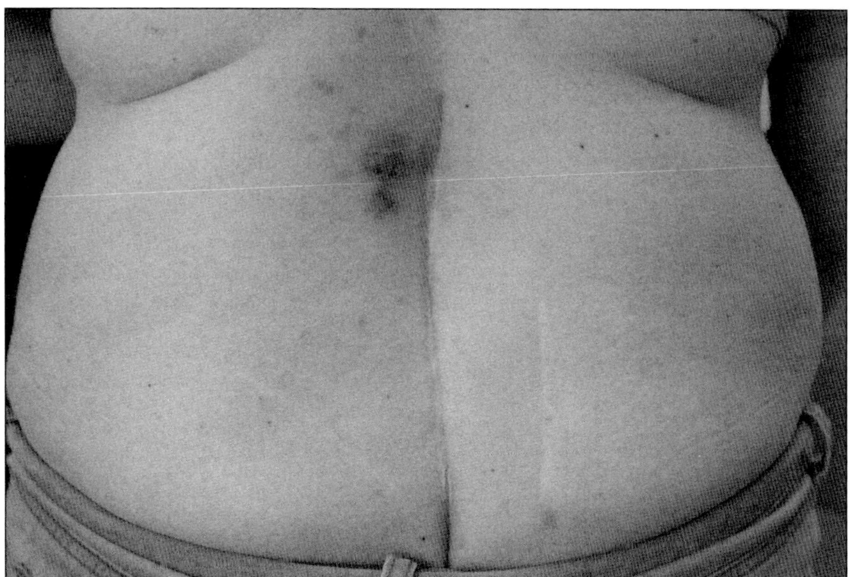

Victim Scars

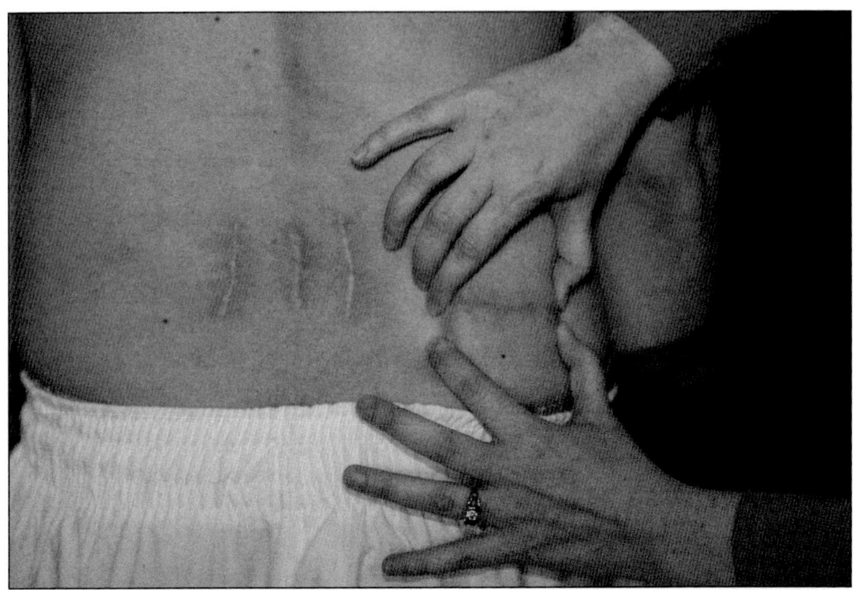

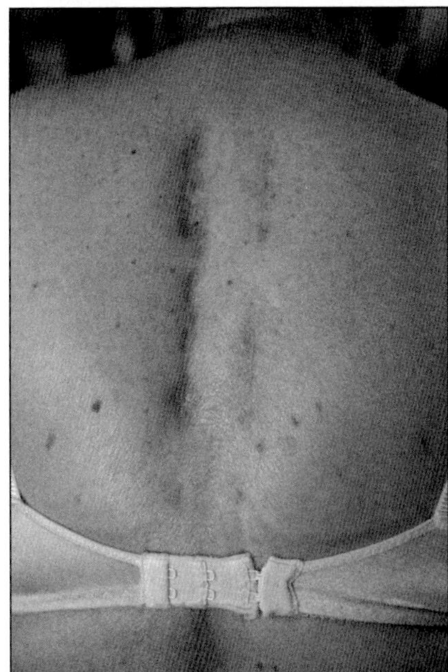

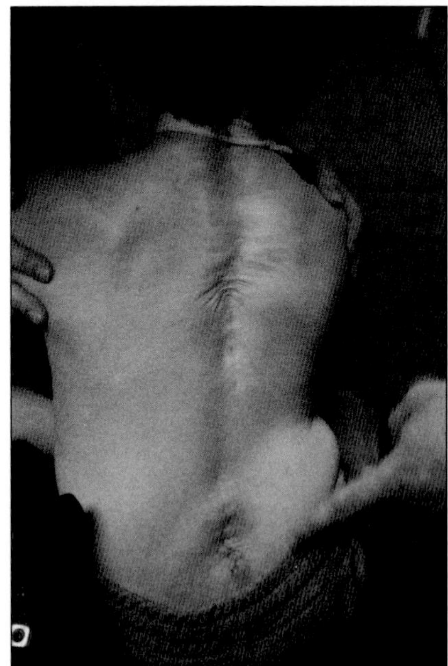

Victim Scars

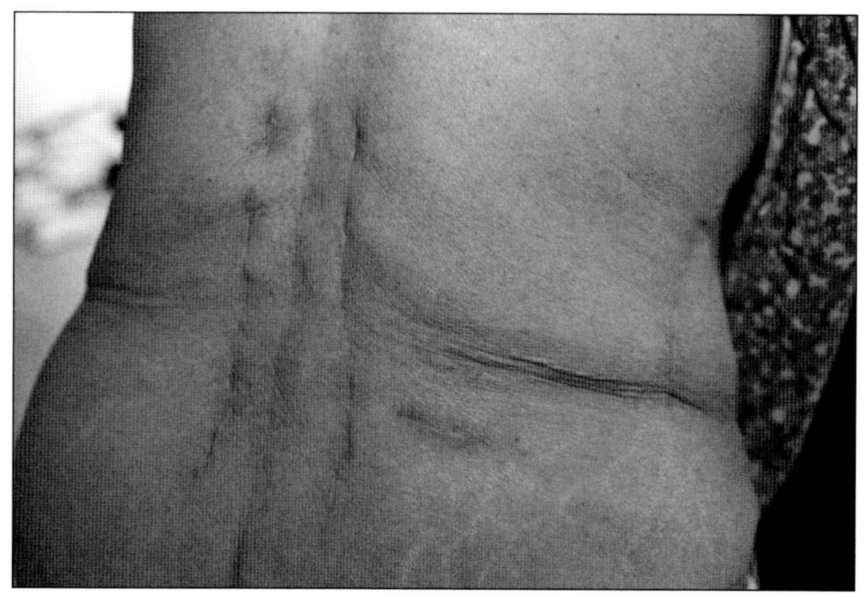

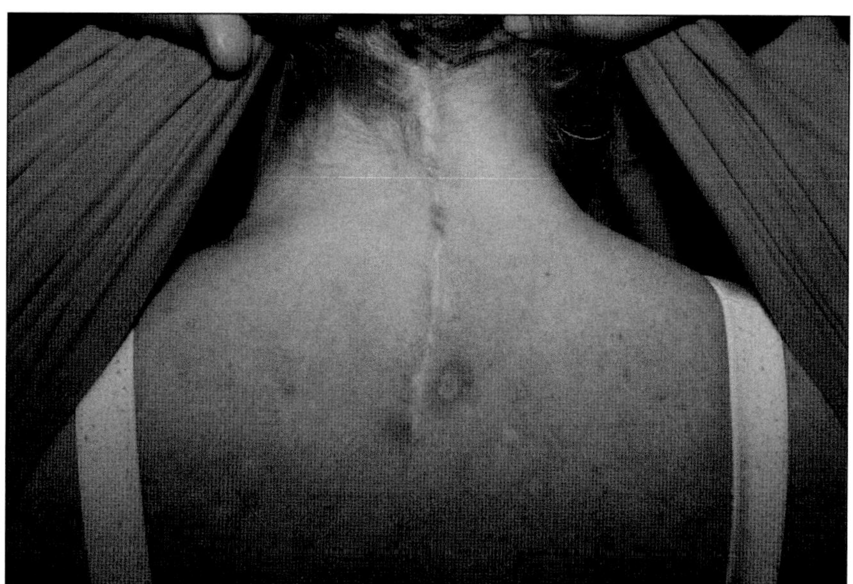

Victim Scars

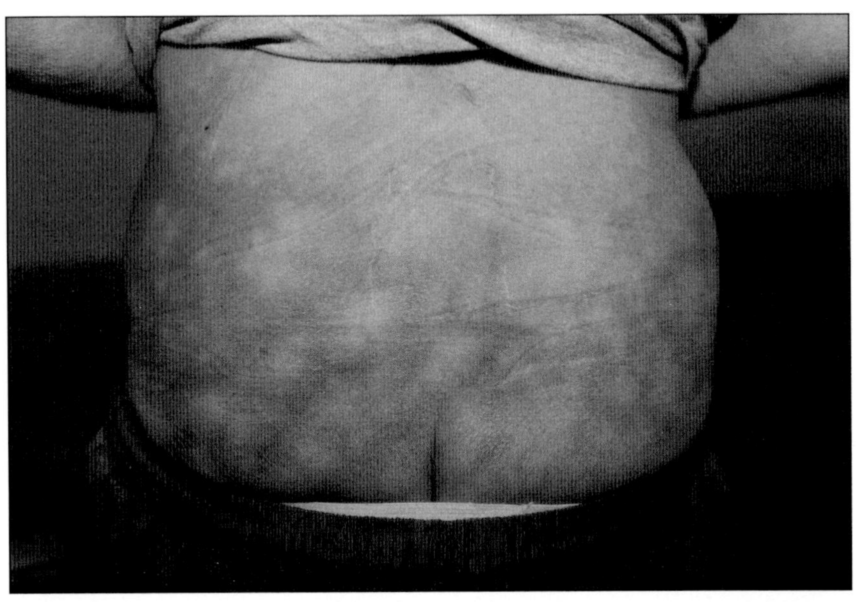

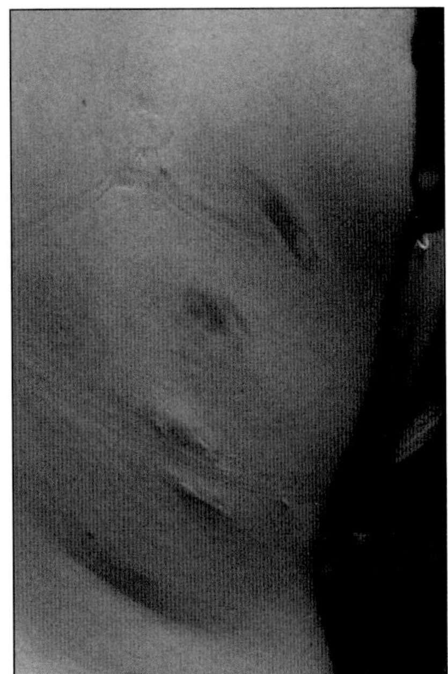

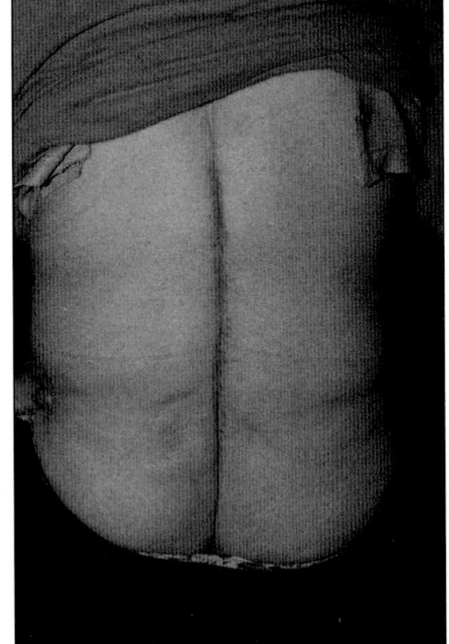

Victim Scars

Chapter 72

Walls and Nichols

"True hope is swift and flies with swallow's wings;
Kings it makes Gods, and meaner creatures kings."
—William Shakespeare

In 2012, Katherine Walls saw Durrani complaining of pain in her lower back and legs. Without trying other alternatives, Durrani pressed Walls into surgery at West Chester Hospital. Post-surgery, Walls suffered more pain and lost all flexibility in her spine from the hardware and bone grafting material Durrani implanted. Katherine is now permanently bent forward from the hips and walks perpendicular to the floor with the aid of a walker. Her back is parallel to the ground.

Of all our clients, she is one of the most outwardly affected by Durrani. The before and after surgery pictures shown to the jury reflected the transformation of a healthy, attractive Army veteran transformed into a stooped, prematurely aged woman, dependent on her teenage son for much of her care.

The visiting judge, Michael Jackson of Cleveland, allowed me to sit at the counsel table during the trial. Judge Michael Jackson served in Vietnam as a leader of troops. He is a most impressive man and like Judge Crawford, treated the victims as a victim should be treated.

At a break before jury selection, Walls needed to use the restroom. All the lawyers were in chambers with Judge Jackson. Attempting to grab the walker for Katherine, which she placed in front of our counsel table, I stepped into a banker box and tripped. I almost fell to the ground. The entire jury panel laughed out loud with me, not at me.

As I helped Walls out of the courtroom, silence from the jury. With her 16-year-old son Billy close by, Walls took one slow step at a time, her head and torso perched over her walker, plodding past the jurors seated in audience pews and out the door. The ordeal took several minutes, and the jurors sat reverently silent. We won trials with jurors who showed good humor and empathy. The Walls' jury panel's laugh and silence proved both. I left the trial before voir dire and never returned. I texted Ben and Al what happened and told them no need for my input on the jury. After deliberating an entire day, the jury awarded Walls over four million dollars in compensatory and punitive damages.

After Walls, we tried Teresa Nichols, an active mother who loved dancing. When she saw Durrani in 2010 complaining of chronic back pain, Durrani told her she had herniated and bulging disks in the thoracic or middle portion of her spine and she risked paralysis if she didn't undergo surgery to relieve the pressure on her spinal cord. He performed an extensive fusion procedure in December, which only worsened her pain. Afterward, Nichols tried multiple forms of physical therapy for months at a time. In June of 2012, Durrani ordered additional scans and told Nichols her problem moved to her lower spine with more bulging discs were pinching the nerves leading to her legs. Durrani performed a second, even more radical surgery on her lower spine. As a result, Nichols' pain spread through her back, hips, and legs.

Durrani blamed Nichols' issues on a fluid build-up in her spine from the second surgery. Durrani inserted a shunt to relieve the painful pressure, but it failed. Nichols continued to suffer from severe pain in her back, neck, hips, legs and suffered headaches. It all relegated Nichols to bed and sofa. Nichols lost her job as a claim's processor for Anthem Blue Cross and Blue Shield. In 2016, she suffered a stroke when a blood clot in her leg traveled to her brain. A stroke is a common risk in patients bedridden for long periods of time. Walking became a challenge for Nichols. On four separate occasions, she fell at her home, once breaking a wrist and another time an ankle.

As a wife and mother of four children and only in her forties, Nichols generated sympathy from the jury. The jury saw before and after photographs of Nichols from a vibrant, tanned, attractive blonde prior to surgery and now someone drawn, drained of energy and color. Her testimony proved challenging, especially on dates and time frames. Statman told me after her testimony he thought we would lose.

I told Alan no worries, Brad Nichols, Teresa's husband, would be a star on the stand. I called Brad that evening and said, "Brad, tomorrow when you take the stand, be yourself and let it rip." Brad told me he was more than willing. Judge Brogan told Alan Statman and Ben Maraan after the trial that Brad gave the most compelling testimony he's ever heard.

The jury returned with a mindboggling verdict of $26 million. Defense attorney Rick Weil, who tried the case for Medical Protective, told me in a post-verdict text and phone call, he didn't understand why Medical Protective continued to fight the Durrani cases.

Rick Weil, an attorney from Reminger & Reminger, is a former FBI agent. He would actually fare better in the Durrani cases than Mike Lyon. Mike Lyon would lose so many cases, he stopped trying them. He let "Woody" and "Ron" take the beating. We believe Lindhorst has now probably lost more jury trials than any medical malpractice defense firm in Cincinnati law history.

Chapter 73

Jeff Potts' Trial

"You called down the thunder. Well now you got it."
—Wyatt Earp "Tombstone"

On July 24, 2019, the morning of the third day of his trial, Jeff Potts used his cane and walked with his right foot dragging along the floor to the witness box. Potts sat down in the witness box. Nervous his testimony might falter under cross-examination. Potts would ask Schweikert if he could stand up in the middle of his testimony to relieve the agonizing pressure on his back.

Durrani's operation perforated Potts' bowel in two places, leading to a massive infection. Durrani tore Potts' dura, the covering around the spinal cord beyond repair so that it would always leak spinal fluid and cause intense headaches. Without Potts' consent and against FDA guidelines, Durrani fused together the vertebrae of his lower spine with BMP-2. Wilkey testified this caused Potts' breast cancer. On the top of all the Durrani hell, Potts drew a short straw for breast cancer. After the surgery, Durrani left behind contaminated hardware screwed into Potts' vertebrae, which couldn't be removed and would make further infection an ever-present risk. Durrani based it all on a fake diagnosis and a fake scan.

Potts could no longer help around the house with basic chores while his wife Cheri worked sixty hours a week to support the family and pay their staggering medical bills. Potts could no longer travel on vacations. On many days, Potts skipped meals and stayed in bed. He slept in a separate room from Cheri based upon his not sleeping and her needing sleep. Sexual intimacy was over.

Many of the jurors displayed emotion as Potts testified. Photos of his condition after Durrani's surgery passed from juror to juror. The jury glanced upon the jagged pattern of stitches running the near length of his back. The jury saw the infected wound in his right flank where Durrani inserted his surgical scope. The jury grimaced looking at the withered legs. One juror asked for a box of tissues and passed them around to the others.

After Potts' testimony, Alan Statman and Ben Maraan called me to lament Potts incoherent recollection. I always good naturedly complained they were "Debbie downers." I told them: "Cheri is going to kill it." Cheri Potts came to nearly every meeting. She always understood our strategy. She's smart, supportive and simply an all-around wonderful person. She even attended other victims' trials in support, even the ones in Butler County.

Cheri Potts' testimony the next day would be as emotional as Potts'. Several times during the three to four hours on the stand, she broke down crying. As a hospital nurse for the past twenty-five years, she drew on her knowledge in the medical field to withstand the toughest questions from the defense. Her testimony wasn't just authoritative, it was sympathetic.

Alan Statman told Cheri before she took the stand "to be the wife, not the nurse." She was both. She told the jurors how it devastated her to watch her husband, a man's man who once ran his own HVAC company, in so much pain after his surgery and witness him cry. After Potts was sent home, Cheri changed his dressing in the afternoon and found gas, stool and pus draining from the incision in his right flank, all signs of serious infection.

Cheri couldn't reach Durrani by phone and Durrani failed to return her calls. By early morning, Potts began complaining of pain all over his body. He couldn't be moved from bed. Cheri called 911 to have Potts taken to emergency at Good Samaritan where they immediately started IV antibiotics to fight his raging infection. Durrani later showed up at the hospital and insisted Potts probably suffered a burst in his bowel from his long narcotic use. Durrani blamed drugs. The exploratory operation by the attending surgeon at the hospital found the perforated bowel and he repaired it. A later scan found the torn dura.

More than three weeks later, after two stays in intensive care and seventeen days in rehab learning to walk again, Potts was sent home with IV antibiotics for the next six months to battle the simmering infection in his abdomen. He lost thirty pounds. Cheri used her vacation time from work to care for him including bathing, dressing, and feeding him, getting him out of bed to go to the bathroom, giving him his medications and changing his dressing. After Potts fully recovered from surgery, Cheri witnessed his battle with pain keeping him from doing the simplest chores, from taking part in the daily life of his family, from taking any satisfaction from who he was as a father and a husband. These curses are representative of all Durrani victims.

Potts would be our twenty fifth Durrani trial. Our experts honed their testimony to perfection. Wilkey testified by video Durrani never received the training to perform, a "lateral" fusion of the spine by inserting instruments through a hole in the side of the abdomen. Wilkey testified the diagnosis was a lie in order to obtain the insurance coverage. Wilkey in his reviews of Durrani cases learned the reason Durrani always claimed spondylolisthesis, slipped disc, is Durrani knew insurance always covered the condition. No reasonable surgeon would have operated on Potts. His spine X-rays showed no pinched nerves as Durrani claimed. The surgery was sloppy and rushed. Durrani cut twice into Potts' bowel, and tore his dura, and either failed to notice or ignored the damage before closing Potts up. Durrani's use of BMP-2 was not only without Potts' consent, but its presence near the torn dura also resulted in nerve damage.

Because of an error in editing his video, Wilkey also blamed the use of BMP-2 for the breast cancer Potts developed. Immediately, the defense called for a mistrial. Schweikert ruled prior to the trial Potts' cancer could not be mentioned in testimony, nor the fact BMP-2 increases a patient's chances of developing cancer. This is contrary to an Ohio case called *LaVelle*. Schweikert overruled the objection but struck the testimony from the record. Schweikert also admonished the jury the cancer information could not be considered as evidence in determining their verdict.

Do you know why a lawyer moves for a mistrial? They believe they will lose.

Cheri cried when Bloomfield's presentation showed a scan of Potts' lower spine that couldn't possibly justify the surgery. The image showed no collapsed vertebrae and no pinched nerves to the legs. The scan is not the scan Durrani showed the Potts.

Almost to the point of embarrassment, the defense experts struggled to explain and support Durrani's diagnosis and treatment against Statman's battery of questions. "Alan knew how to beat their experts. He knew he wasn't going to beat up a doctor on medicine. They're doctors, he's not. But what he would do get them to agree to certain facts, to agree with what our experts were saying. The defense expert would either have to suck it up and agree or look like a fool disputing what an objective radiology report says," said Ben Maraan.

I have a maxim. On cross examination, you want a witness to either admit something which helps you or deny something obvious which destroys their credibility and makes them look like a fool. This would always be easy with their California whore experts.

I know the unpredictability of juries. After the series of defeats in the four Butler County cases and the defense verdict for the Rutters, the previous three trials in Hamilton County produced two of the biggest awards for Durrani victims. I never understood how any jury ever voted for Durrani. Could the Potts' jury vote for Durrani?

Chapter 74

The Record Book

"I firmly believe that any man's finest hour, the greatest fulfillment of all that he holds dear, is that moment when he has worked his heart out in a good cause and lies exhausted on the field of battle — victorious."
—Vince Lombardi

On July 30, 2019, the jury in the Potts trial began its deliberations. Statman, remained a pessimist and a worrier. This is simply Alan's defense mechanism. He faced pressure to win. He did not want to disappoint me. He preferred the "prepare to lose, be happy you won" angle. I remained optimistic about the outcome. Waiting for a jury verdict is the very worst for a criminal defense attorney and a Plaintiff's attorney. It's excruciating. A client's freedom and a client's economic future are at stake. One blessing of my retirement, Alan and Ben waited for verdicts, not me. I do not miss it.

The jury continued its deliberations late into the evening and decided to start again in the morning. A good sign. Later that night, I sent Cheri a text stating we would win based upon the length of deliberation. Did I not learn the Martin lesson?

The Potts wouldn't allow themselves to be too excited. After all, the Rutters thought they would win. Still anxious, the Potts arrived at the courtroom with their son Jesse the following morning at 10:30 a.m.. Statman, Maraan, Chuck Holbrook and Joe Rutter were all there. I came later but found myself relegated to the hallway based on Schweikert's ban.

The afternoon came and the jury deliberated more. Later in the afternoon, the bailiff came into the courtroom with questions from the jury about the limits on loss of consortium. Not long after, I showed up at the courtroom door and motioned for Cheri to come outside. I gave her a hug.

"Congratulations, you won," I said.

"How do you know?" she asked.

"Because of the jury questions. If they didn't find for Jeff, they wouldn't have questions about consortium," I told her.

"Oh, my God!" Cheri cried.

Any lawyer will tell you, they hate and love jury questions. They hate them when they indicate trouble. They love them when they are favorable.

Cheri went back into the courtroom and gave the news to her husband and son. "Still, I needed to hear it from the judge. I was still too nervous. I mean, I thought we would win but I was nauseous waiting for the official reading," Cheri recalls.

When the jury delivered the verdict to Schweikert, the reading had to be delayed until the defense lawyers returned to the courtroom from their office.

The minutes of waiting seemed like hours for the Potts family. "My heart was pounding and pounding," Cheri said. "It was hot in the courtroom, and Jeff and Jesse and I were sitting at the counsel table and holding hands, just sweating." Cheri recited "Hail Marys" in her head. Jeff prayed the "Our Father."

The jury filed into the jury box with poker faces. The foreman handed the thick, 23-page verdict to the bailiff, Judy Walters, who handed it to Schweikert on the bench. Before reading it aloud, Schweikert glanced through the documentation. He then motioned the lawyers to approach the bench for their own look. Maraan saw the first page and started to tear up. Statman flipped eagerly through the rest of the pages before returning it to Schweikert.

Jeff, Cheri, and Jesse held each other at the counsel table when Schweikert read the Plaintiff's verdict. "My feelings were of glorious validation," Cheri said. "Jeff said he was like a cartoon character melting down out of his chair. But it was the money amount that was the big shock for us."

After Schweikert announced the verdict on liability and compensatory damages, the lawyers argued punitive damages to the jury and the jury returned to deliberate punitive damages. In short order, the jury returned with their punitive damages award.

The jury awarded Potts $9.1 million in compensatory damages. The jury awarded Cheri $4 million in consortium damages. They awarded punitive damages of $26 million for a total verdict of $39.1 million.

It is the largest single malpractice award in Ohio history. It's never been reported by the Ohio news or Ohio lawyer bulletins.

Although state caps on non-economic damages and insurance coverage limits reduce the award, the jury sent a powerful message, Durrani is the Butcher of Pakistan.

Reflective of the quality person Cheri is, the Potts were overwhelmed with gratitude. Cheri's thank you note is framed and hanging on my office wall.

> *Eric,*
>
> *We thank you for ALL that you have done for us. We know that we would never have gotten here today without you. You have orchestrated a beautiful campaign for us. And we will be forever grateful!*
>
> *With much gratitude, Cheri and Jeff Potts*
>
> *God bless you now and always!*

I treasure it. I treasure them.

Schweikert sealed the verdict and again the community would not know the extent of another jury's outrage against the Butcher of Pakistan. Cheri, from the counsel table, thanked Schweikert for presiding over the case. He looked at her and never replied. Another anecdote to sum up Reich.

We now won the largest medical malpractice case in Ohio history in Potts and the only negligent credentialing case against an Ohio hospital in Ohio history in Cotter. The Ohio Justice Association, the so called Plaintiffs' organization, and the Ohio Bar Association, the general/defense organization, ignored it all. If any other law firm won these awards, they would be asked to speak at seminars throughout the state. Alan Statman, Fred Johnson, Glenn Feagan, Ben Maraan and I never received any such request.

Chapter 75
Defiance

"Make no mistake. It's not revenge he's after. It's a reckoning."
—Doc Holliday "Tombstone"

I hired Cincinnati detective Jim Simon, owner of Business Intelligence, on a $40,000 retainer to investigate any conflicts of interest or other matters that might disqualify Schweikert from presiding over the Durrani cases. This is not illegal or unethical. I would later learn, Simon "laid down" at the direction of Joe Deters. Simon, prior to these events, told me he spoke to Joe every day on investigations he performed for Joe. Joe told Simon to stay away from Schweikert and the system. It was a $40,000 con. I called Simon out on it and he has not dared to challenge me on the issue. He knows he's a son of a bitch scoundrel. Simon never even prepared a report. He called me one day and said, "Found nothing." He failed to even find and report the Dinsmore connection. Wonder why? Joe's relationship with the Dinsmore lawyers.

The continuing protests organized by me and posted to my public Facebook page brought Schweikert's wrath upon me. A demonstration on the Hamilton County Courthouse steps on February 22, 2018 demanded the removal of Schweikert and O'Connor from the Durrani cases. I posted a video of the demonstration on Facebook and the defending hospitals fired off a complaint that I violated the gag order. At a hearing before Schweikert on April 27, I argued Schweikert's order applied only to a public discussion of Durrani and the defending hospitals, which might prejudice a future jury, not to criticism of the judges handling the cases.

Schweikert dropped the charges. He insisted I remove the offending Facebook video and expanded his gag order to be inclusive to no talking to the media, no social media postings, no podcasts, no public demonstrations or communication of any kind or in any way related to the Durrani cases.

What does this prove? How my use of social media hurt the "bad guys"? This was not about jury integrity. It was about keeping negative publicity from the hospitals.

Schweikert informed Alan, Ben, and Fred as our trial attorneys in the Durrani cases, they were responsible for my behavior. He warned them they would be charged with contempt if they failed to notify him in advance of any plans I might have to violate the gag order; all absurd and not consistent with the law.

In January of 2019, Schweikert cancelled an upcoming trial and called for a slowdown in the Durrani cases. I attacked him on my Facebook page for his indifference to the Durrani victims. During a hearing, Schweikert again warned me and the legal team we could be jailed for posting about the cases on social media. He advised me no more "foolish antics." Schweikert imposed another gag order, barring any public discussion or social media posts about the Durrani cases and their merits. He made all the lawyers sign it, but I never signed it.

On August 6, 2019, Schweikert responded to another request for group trials by claiming he wouldn't be available "in the near future for trials." I lost it. After two years as the presiding judge, Schweikert personally heard only three Durrani cases. In total, just twenty trials in six years. Meanwhile, fifty of the victims died waiting for their day in court.

We filed another suit in federal court petitioning for O'Connor to approve group trials and to set up a schedule that would resolve all of the remaining Durrani cases within the limit required under Ohio's Rule of Superintendence of three years. To publicize the filing, we planned to show up with picketers on the courthouse steps for a press conference on August 22, demand group trials and mourn the deaths of the fifty Durrani patients. Alerted by unknown parties, we assume Durrani lawyers, Schweikert issued a written warning a day ahead of the protest.

Undeterred, I showed up with twenty protestors holding our usual neon-colored signs at 4 p.m. We waited until the courthouse closed for the day to hold the press conference and demonstration. Filling in for Schweikert, who was vacationing at his Florida home, retired Judge J. Howard Sundermann observed the press conference. I conferred with Sundermann beforehand and Sundermann told me we were allowed to criticize the Courts. Sundermann is a levelheaded man. He tried several Durrani cases as a visiting judge.

WKRC Channel 12 interviewed several Durrani victims at the protest. "We would like the group trials to happen ASAP," Theresa Woods told the reporter. "It's not like we have forty years to give for this. Do the math, you know what I'm saying?"

I pointed out all other non-Durrani Hamilton County cases filed in 2015, 2016 and 2017 had been resolved, but not the Durrani cases, even though nearly all of them had been filed in 2013. "Our plea is rational and logical," I told the reporter. "Why should all litigants have their trials, but not Durrani victims?"

I also posted a video of the press conference on my Facebook page. This time Schweikert ordered all Deters Law attorneys to appear in his courtroom on September 3 and explain why we shouldn't all go to jail. The Order covered Glenn, Alan, Ben, and yours truly.

The hearing order summarized all the alleged gag order violations of the previous year, pointed out the most recent offense on the courthouse steps occurring five days before the jury selection in the next Durrani trial. "*Such acts appear reasonably likely to prejudice these proceedings and inhibit the right of the parties to a fair and impartial jury. Such acts appear to be a mockery of the Courts' authority … and is disrespectful of the administration of justice. Such action requires remedial action as soon as possible…"*

Schweikert making statements as these ran hollow for me.

I relished the opportunity to tell Schweikert exactly what I thought of him on the record and in front of an audience of supporters and news cameras. I must explain the contempt hearing gave me mixed emotions. On one hand, I hated my actions put Glenn, Alan, and Ben in peril. I love them for bearing with me. On the other hand, I craved the confrontation.

Chapter 76
Contempt

"We all have it comin' kid."
—William Munny "Unforgiven"

On September 3, 2019, at 3 p.m., fifty Durrani victims and representatives from every Cincinnati news media outlet appeared for the much-anticipated contempt hearing in Schweikert's courtroom. Everyone in my camp, including my wife Mary, wore black T-shirts embossed in front with the quote "Justice Delayed is Justice Denied" and on the back the names of all fifty plus Durrani victims who died before their cases could heard. The quote is a William Gladstone quote Justice Maureen O'Connor cited in a law review article.

With the exception of Channel 5 News, the local media ignored the major issues of the Durrani cases, the debate over O'Connor's appointment of a special judge, the legal battle over group trials, the long delays in the trials, and the impact of all of it on Durrani's 580 victims. "But, by God, if Eric Deters is going to jail, we'll cover the hearing," I quipped.

The hearing would not happen in front of my supporters. Schweikert kept the assemblage waiting for more than an hour in his courtroom with no message or word to explain his absence or delay. Schweikert sat on the bench in the courtroom next door in the middle of a Durrani trial. Ben and Alan were with Schweikert in the trial. Glenn and I waited for the hearing together. Schweikert never gave us the courtesy of a message. After 4 p.m., with the courthouse set to close for the day, I told the crowd they should simply leave. I assumed Schweikert would reschedule the hearing. Everyone headed for the elevators including Glenn and I.

Glenn and I headed for steak dinners at *Walt's Hitching Post* when Alan called my cell phone. Schweikert told Alan he was ready for the hearing. "If you guys don't come back, he's going to issue a bench warrant for your arrest," Alan said.

Glenn and I held a short debate on what to do, all while laughing, and then decided we would return and face ole Reich. We contemplated the fun of being fugitives from Reich, hiding out somewhere such as Glenn's mom house. Glenn and I talked our way past security to re-enter the courthouse after hours. Schweikert could now hold his hearing without fifty of my supporters in the room. The media of course stuck around. Schweikert glared from the bench as Glenn and I arrived.

Schweikert began by claiming he had been tied up in a trial and unable to take a break until after 4 p.m. Then why schedule the contempt hearing at 3 p.m.?

Reich offered no apology or explanation as to why he never sent word to the 50-plus people waiting an hour in his courtroom. He then asked if I represented myself. I replied I had no choice since he issued his order on Thursday before Labor Day weekend. I never had time to arrange for a lawyer or to subpoena Sundermann as a witness I explained. Statman showed up with a lawyer, his friend John Smith. Ben, Glenn and I, no counsel. Scheduled as a hearing for all four of us, Reich chose to focus on me.

Reich sarcastically claimed I had time to write a 157-page objection to the hearing and file it in court over the weekend. Of course writing the objection was easy because I already had all the materials and the 157 pages included over 100 pages of exhibits. Schweikert offered me the opportunity to confer with the other lawyers present and I declined. I refused to waive my rights as a defendant, including legal counsel. Why would I? I jousted with Reich for sport. Schweikert asked me to sign a waiver of counsel. I declined. He then actually ordered me to sign it. I signed it and wrote "under protest." Imagine if this happened to any other citizen in the United States. A judge demanding you sign a waiver of legal counsel, a constitutional right.

"But if this Court says you're going to hold this hearing anyway no matter what my rights are, then I'm going to represent myself pro se without a lawyer," I said. "I haven't had the opportunity..."

Schweikert interrupted. "Mr. Deters, we've had this conversation before. You do not need to scream. If you continue to scream at this Court, you'll be held in contempt again."

But I wasn't screaming, I used my natural loud voice. Schweikert knew a transcript only would record his words, not my decibel level. So he used "screaming" to attempt to disparage me in the transcript.

Schweikert cited his April 27, 2018 gag order and listed my offenses, then asked how I wanted to plead.

"Not guilty," I responded.

Schweikert asked if I planned to call any witnesses in my defense.

"I had witnesses here at three o'clock who couldn't stay until four o'clock," I said.

That also didn't matter to Reich. Imagine if that happened to any other citizen in the United States.

I called Michael Dreyer, one of the sheriff's deputies present at the press conference, to testify. Dreyer confirmed I spoke to Sundermann before the press conference, but he couldn't confirm or deny whether Sundermann gave me permission to go ahead with the press conference. Dreyer testified he attended the protest to make sure we held a peaceful protest and confirmed it was a peaceful protest.

Reich, as he enjoyed doing, secured the security camera footage and I stipulated to its contents. I was like "duh." I know there are security cameras and they confirm my version of events. Tip for you. Assume every place you go, except maybe your home, is captured by video.

I testified in my own defense. I explained the agreed upon gag order signed by my father, owner of the firm at the time before Glenn had nothing to do with Judge Schweikert. It had absolutely nothing to do with the issue of these clients receiving their trials, the only issue brought up at the press conference.

"Judge, 50 people have died—it's on the back of my shirt. Fifty people have died waiting for their trials. And there's more that are about to die. And there's at least 50 that have filed bankruptcies. And they suffer. And despite all their suffering, this court doesn't care. Chief Justice O'Connor doesn't care. So, therefore, we are going to raise some hell about it. And as was testified by the deputy, it was a peaceful protest. It's my testimony right here under oath that Judge Sundermann approved what I did. When I told him what I was doing, he very clearly said, "You're allowed to criticize the courts." And I said, "Thank you very much," I testified to Reich.

So you understand the significance of Sundermann, Sundermann attended the press conference at the request of Schweikert. So if the representative of Schweikert blesses our press conference, how can Schweikert complain? Imagine how tyrannical this is. Schweikert knew Sundermann as one of his judges trying Durrani cases. Schweikert could have simply called Sundermann on the phone and said did you tell Deters he could criticize the Court?

I then took aim at Schweikert. *"You worry more about Durrani than you do the victims. And, in fact, the record will reflect under oath that, to this day, Judge Mark Schweikert has never acknowledged and spoken to a single plaintiff during a hearing or during the course of a trial. And even when Cheri Potts, after winning the largest medical malpractice claim, (Schweikert again warned me to restrain my voice), in the history of Ohio, said, "Thank you," you refused to even acknowledge her. Cold. Without public pressure, nothing will happen. These victims need this compelling story told."*

"I also want to put on the record that you said I violated the sealing of the verdicts. It's not true. I posted on social media the Deters Law Firm verdicts. I took out the client's name of every verdict. It doesn't mention Durrani at all. And I put the amounts on those verdicts, totaling $89 million in 14 months to put this on the record in our defense."

"So here I am ready to go to jail, ready to go to jail fighting for these people. And you're anxious to make me the bad guy like I'm a contemptor. It blows my mind that I'm the bad guy. No, Judge. You're the bad guy. Chief Justice O'Connor is the bad guy."

"Disrespectful of the administration of justice? Five hundred sixty people waiting 50 freaking years for a trial? That is disrespectful of the administration of justice, your Honor."

"If I have to go to jail, I'll go to jail. But Judge, you know the extraordinary work and effort that we put forth for these victims. You know that. You also know the critical nature that I play in that."

Schweikert heard enough. *"Mr. Deters, you're starting to repeat yourself."* He then asked if I was calling any other witnesses. I replied no.

"Well," Schweikert said, *"there are so many inaccuracies and misrepresentations in what you just said that I don't know that I can take the time to go through all those because 90 percent of it is not relevant. Tell me about that shirt you've got on."* He was full of crap. It was all accurate.

I told him they were the idea of Christina Goldstein, one of the Durrani victims. *"She suffered a great deal — she's just really devastated and messed up. In support of our battle, why don't we have shirts made up with all of the 50 names of those people that died on it? That's not a bad idea, Christina. We could put on the front of the shirt Justice O'Connor's quote, 'Justice delayed is justice denied,' where she quotes William Gladstone in her law journal article,"* I testified.

Schweikert was unmoved. *"You didn't think maybe that the news media would have their cameras on your back the whole time you were making your presentation today?"*

I never thought of that one, but glad it worked. I responded, *"I wore the shirt with the other people. That was not the-"*

Schweikert interrupted. *"See, I don't think you're irrational. I think you intend everything you do. And I think there's a purpose to it."*

He got that right.

"Well, there is, your Honor, you're correct," I said. "There is a purpose of my wanting to get you and Chief Justice O'Connor to do something to help these people and give them their trials. Thus, the press conference. Thus, we hope the press would shed light on the issue."

For Schweikert, my side of the hearing was over.

"I'm going to ask you to return to your seat. I'm not going to argue with you about these things. But I've made some notes about some of the things that you commented on because I think it's necessary for the record.

"This group trials argument, I gave great consideration to. And I wrote a decision. That decision is a legal decision. And, at some point in time, some court will review that and determine whether I'm right or not. You haven't talked about that. But that's how I work. I follow the law."

Again, total crap.

"And I explained to you that you don't decide what the gag order says. I decide what the order says. And I offered you the opportunity in the event that you wanted to avoid a violation to come to the Court and seek guidance. You've never done that.

"Mr. Deters, I have made great efforts in this situation to preserve the jury pool. One of those is this gag order. Another is the careful jury selection that we go through to try to make sure that all parties get a fair jury. And in every jury selection process we've gone through, we've encountered jurors whose perspectives have been poisoned by the things that they've seen in the media...

"And your commentary about the chief justice and me are not general criticisms. They're criticisms about this particular case. Ordinarily, about me. If you think I care what you say about me, you've got a very inflated perspective of yourself. I care about giving a fair and impartial trial to the parties in this case. And I'm going to do it as long as I continue to be involved."

More crap.

"You and I agree on one thing. And I said this from the beginning when I took over these cases. We've got a great challenge in this situation with all these cases. And I said from the beginning that mediation and settlement needed to be a part of this process. I've made every effort to try to get the parties to the table. I had a meeting this morning on that issue that delayed us getting started on the trial today."

Every time Medical Protective came to the table, their lowball offers for settlement were only insults. In all the years of the Durrani litigation up to this point, we held twenty mediations, usually arranged by a judge involved in the cases. None were productive. Why? Because Judges never did anything to move Medical Protective.

I tried to explain my own understanding of the gag order, but Schweikert cut me off.

"You called the news media in," Schweikert said. "Channel 12 accepted the bait. And they reported on the Durrani litigation. They reported on Durrani. That's what you expected. That's what you intended. That's what you expected from this rhetoric that you provided before the Court today. It's your hope that they'll go back and they'll deliver this to their editors and they'll play this today. I don't know. They may be streaming it live right now. That's what you hope. You want to be a martyr here."

"No," I said, *"I want to bring attention to the issue of these people."*

"It's my turn," Schweikert snapped.

"Do I get a rebuttal?" I asked.

"No. You've had your opportunity... From your statements today, there is no question in my mind that your attitude and your intent is to disrupt this court's efforts to provide fair and impartial justice to these parties. It's your intention to try to influence this jury pool."

Total crap. And, his "you've had your opportunity" reminded me of Dean Werner in *Animal House* talking to Hoover on "point of order."

"Based on all that, I find you guilty and in contempt of court. I further find that this Court is required to take remedial action to ensure that this doesn't happen again and that these matters are taken down from your Facebook page and the Internet."

"I'm not interested in hearing your arguments on the facts any further. I'm not interested in hearing your arguments about how this Court has conducted its proceedings. I'm only interested in whatever you have to say that might mitigate this Court's sentence."

My turn again.

"Your Honor, how do I want to put this?" I said. "I say what I mean, and I mean what I say. And I'm not a coward. But I'm not a martyr. When you said that my intention was to bring attention, admitted. Correct. I wanted the attention on the plight of these people getting their trials.

"Your Honor, if you watch that 26-minute press conference, I did not talk about the merits of the cases. I didn't. This shirt doesn't talk about the merits of the cases."

"I ask that you consider what I was trying to do to help these people. You've acknowledged that forty years of waiting for trials is too long. Now, you don't like what I did, but I don't make any excuses that I try to get the media to do it."

"You've been a judge. People have had to serve thirty days for physically beating up somebody. As I'm standing before you, your Honor, I've never physically assaulted anybody. I've never been in a fight."

"If you consider a sentence, I'd like a suspended sentence. I think that's your prerogative. Hang 30 days over me and tell me you don't want to hear a peep out of me with the press ever again. I'll take that. I ask you to be creative."

"I'm not afraid to ask for mercy, your Honor. I'm a good person fighting for these people… These people are dying. They're filing bankruptcy. Every day, your Honor, we get e-mails -- evictions, heating and air conditioning turned off. I'm the victims' advocate. I deal with these 560 people every day. Think about that. Five hundred and sixty people and their plight. And Durrani preyed upon the low socioeconomic group."

"So I ask for mercy. I just want to do my job."

This completed my sentencing argument.

"We've been through this before, Mr. Deters," Schweikert said. *"You take these things down. You say you're not going to do it again—"*

I interrupted. *"This was about group trials, your Honor. It wasn't the merits of the cases. I kept my word on the merits of the cases."*

"It's my turn. It's my turn," Schweikert barked. *"See, that's your argument. That's your justification. That's your rationale. I don't buy it. You want to twist your argument that way, but your intent, your intent is to draw the media in, to draw attention to Durrani and these cases and to effect an impact on the jury pool."*

"So it's the order of the Court that you serve a period of fifteen days in the Hamilton County Justice Center. And further that you remain there until these things are removed… And, further, you need to agree in writing that you understand the

order of this Court as it's reflected in that transcript and you will comply with that order and that you understand that if you violate it again, I'm going to treat this as a misdemeanor of the first degree."

Schweikert directed Dreyer to take me into custody and hold me in the jury room until escorted to the county jail.

I did not beg, yell, cry, or fuss as I leaned forward and put my hands behind my back. Dreyer placed the cuffs around my wrists and led me away. I accepted my fate with pride.

"All right, buddy," Glenn Feagan told me quietly. *"I'll see you in two weeks."*

A week after I was sent to jail, Schweikert held a contempt hearing for Feagan, Maraan and Statman. Schweikert fined each $250 for their responsibility in "allowing" me to violate my gag order.

Their contempt would be overturned by the Appeals Court. We were right on the law. They could not be responsible for me.

Chapter 77

JAIL

"I have been driven many times upon my knees by the overwhelming conviction that I had nowhere else to go. My own wisdom, and that of all about me, seemed insufficient for that day."
—Abraham Lincoln

It surprised me Schweikert sentenced me to jail. I expected a suspended thirty-day sentence with the promise to fly straight or maybe a night in jail as shock treatment. Most judges handled these situations in that manner. My knowledge of this guided my actions. But not Schweikert. I now faced fifteen days in jail. We immediately filed an appeal with the state Court of Appeals, but a ruling could take longer than my fifteen day sentence.

The first night in jail, I slept alone on a mat on the cold concrete floor in a large room. I have no idea where, except it was in the Justice Center. In the morning, they walked me to my "permanent home."

I determined to make the most of my stay in jail. Blend in. Get along with my cell block mates. Work on my appeal. Find a way to communicate with the firm and the clients. Keep the Durrani cases moving forward without missing a beat.

In the end, my time in jail proved a blessing. The Durrani clients loved I fought so hard for them. It would strengthen my marriage. It gave me the incredible stories I'll share for the rest of my life and in this chapter. I became a hero of sorts among the inmates when word spread quickly I "told off" a judge.

They placed me in the G Pod, one of three cell blocks on the north end of the Hamilton County Justice Center's fourth floor. Each two-story pod held ten to twenty men with six cells on the bottom and six on top accessed by stairs and a balcony. The two-person cells surrounded a small common area where the inmates ate their meals on steel tables and chairs attached to the floor. When not confined to the cells, we sat on the benches and watched a 24-inch TV hanging from the ceiling. Rather than crane your neck, you could stand on the balcony for a better view.

They allow inmates one fifteen minute visit each day behind glass with friends or family. Inmates receive unlimited visits from attorneys. I used this rule to schedule a steady stream of visits from attorneys to keep my hand on the Durrani cases. Dominick Romeo and Rachel Siekman would come every day. Alan and Ben would stop by. To stay in touch with clients, I wrote out messages in long hand on a legal pad and delivered them by lawyers to Sarah York who sent out emails.

In a September 5 email to the clients, I wrote:

"I am in protective custody based upon my "celebrity" status, as they've explained to me. I have been in here now 24 hours covering two days so I have served two of my 15 days. The deputies have been extraordinarily nice to me. I have a cell to myself. I have a toilet, desk, and a bed with my jail issued sheets and blanket. (I) use one blanket for my pillow. I have a sink, a towel, soap, a toothbrush, and toothpaste. They issued me my "uniform"—gray stripes and two right-footed sandals—one of which I wear on my left foot.

"There are two phones in here and there are many times day and evening we get to use them, making calls 20 minutes apart. I have been calling out as much as possible to my wife and office. I have also called Chuck and my son Parker who was worried about me. We get woken up at 6:30 a.m. and end for the night at 10:00 p.m. From 1:30 to 5:00, we have to be in our cells [for "quiet time"] as well as other times. It really doesn't make much sense.

"The 10 to 12 men in here are men from probation violations to much more serious crimes, one for murder. I have told them who I am and they have accepted me. I respect them. They respect me. I have followed the hierarchy of who goes first on the phone, etc. One by one, they have begun to ask me about their legal woes and I have offered assistance from my connections. This has resulted in their giving me first dibs on the phone. LOL.

"Each of them has vowed to have my back and the head guy, who I was worried about, informed me this evening that he won't let anything happen to me. I feel like a protected Godfather now. LOL.

"I have not once been scared or worried until the new guy yesterday wanted to ask the jail to be my bunk mate because he didn't want to be in the cell with a black man. I told him I did not think the jail would put anyone in my cell. And, to be candid, if they did, this guy scares me. LOL.

"Half of these guys are black and half are white—no issues—they all get along. The guy who wanted to join me in my cell I think is the only racist.

"One of the young black men, I'll remember for life. He's told me the rules, helped me out, looked after me and truly is a new friend. I didn't have toilet paper, he gave it to me.

"The food is so bad that I would not even give it to a dog. I'm sure I'll lose 10 more pounds. The water is awful and I am forcing myself to drink it because I don't want to get dehydrated.

"I have plenty of money on my commissary (account), but they only deliver on Friday. I have a purchase in for gym shoes, 10 packs of peanuts, 5 Snickers, and a thermal shirt. I'm going to double my peanut and Snickers order since it will have to last a week."

Breakfast in jail? A cheap Danish washed down with a sugary, tang-like beverage. Lunch? A dry sandwich on white bread and a piece of tasteless fruit. Dinner?

A casserole with mystery meat. I lost ten pounds. I would have lost more weight if lawyers never brought me sandwiches and snacks to me at their visits.

Inmate Stone, a tall, handsome black man who awaited transfer on a bond issue, told me he worked in the jail cafeteria and the food is actually expired food from the Cincinnati Free Store that they give to the jail.

As bad as the food was, a tall, skinny pod mate in his twenties couldn't seem to get enough of it. I often gave him my meals. Learning more about the young man's impoverished background, I asked if I could help him. The man gave me his sister's address and I had $200 mailed there. He told me the money would change his life. For $200 his life was changed? He planned to buy new pair of tennis shoes and still have money for the halfway house. It helped put things in perspective for me during my stay.

I soon learned everything in jail happens by barter. I often traded my mystery casserole with another pod mate for the fresh carrots served with the evening meal. Unhappy with my cheap, uncomfortable Converse knock-offs ("Chinese Chucks") I'd purchased on my first day, I paid for $10 in commissary items to trade for another inmate's size ten tennis shoes.

On my fifth day in jail, I wrote to assure my clients nothing changed in the handling of their cases:

"I'm receiving and reviewing everything. I'm drafting, reading, calling, etc. It's truly awesome how we have this set up. I have piles of organized papers everywhere in my cell. Myself, all attorneys and staff are doing our jobs the same as if I was at the office or home - just a little slower and under harsher conditions.

"I want to express something here important. We have fought not just the Defendants and their lawyers, but the entire system. It is without a doubt an inexcusable blemish on the soul of American justice. They want to break us. They want to break me because they know I'm the leader. I'll NEVER break. I'm willing to spend all my money, spend all my time and fight them until we don't capitulate and give up but WIN."

I then offered more details about my life in jail:

"I have settled into a groove in my cell. I'm doing my stretching, chin ups, walking up and down the pod stairs, going through the old karate routines in my cell, thinking, reading, writing, calling, meeting, playing spades with my cellmates (me and my partner are the Kings LOL), helping out each of my cellmates from food to legal (issues) and looking forward to getting out of here."

One inmate, a house framer, was in for growing and selling marijuana. Can you imagine? An intelligent house framer serving time in the Hamilton County prison system for growing pot and making pot brownies while corporate America is allowed to sell all the pot they want across the country.

After this house framer expressed how difficult it was to get in touch with his public defender, I had our office take over his representation.

I went five days without a shower. I did not want to use the open-door facility on the second tier of the pod. When I could no longer live with my own personal hygiene, I woke at 3 a.m. and took a sink bath in my cell. Unable to rinse properly, I itched for the remainder of my time in jail.

Missing my five-year-old granddaughter Raygn's birthday party on a Friday night was my low point. It was the first time "Pop Pop" missed one of my four grandchildren's birthday parties. Statman asked Schweikert for a temporary release for the day. He refused.

Sweet Rylee sent me the following letter:

Dear Pop Pop,

My first day of school was great. Zeke signed 6 years to the Dallas Cowboys. I love you so much. —Rylee, Raygn, Rhett

Here is a stupid rule. No books unless they are shipped by Amazon. I would have loved one book. You weren't supposed to have a pen. I had a pen and pad to write memorandums.

My scariest episode occurred on a Tuesday morning when the power went out for several hours. A squirrel hit a piece of electrical equipment, tripping the fire control system and shutting down electricity throughout much of the building. The squirrel did not survive. The inmates didn't fare well either. We remained locked in our cells for the duration of the day with the only source of light the six-inch strip of glass on the back wall of the pod.

It scared the heck out of me. I'm claustrophobic. With the ventilator fans not working, the heat in the cells began to build. I felt as if I was being cooked.

I admittedly faked a heart issue to try to get out, but the jail nurses never fell for it even though my blood pressure rose to a high level.

Bill Cunningham, still a friend of mine at the time, stopped by on a Sunday. "So let me get this straight," he said. "You have to serve fifteen days, and Durrani has never served a day?" Let that sink in.

Mary visited twice. It was the only time I ever cried in jail when I saw her across the glass.

When I arrived in cellblock G, I became low man on the totem pole. I didn't know anyone. Two phones are in the cellblock. I noticed they took turns on the phone and they controlled turns. I sat and waited. I wasn't about to rock the boat. It drove me crazy only one phone call every twenty minutes. Once you used the phone, you had to wait twenty minutes to use it again. You used a code. You could imagine me without my cell phone. I needed to use the phone so I found out the biggest, baddest dude in my cellblock was Red, a young, handsome black man with facial tattoos. I had my people from the outside pay Red's $300 bond. The lingering unpaid bond kept him from transferring back to Kentucky. He returned my favor by informing everyone I would be first in the phone line.

I played the game. When you're in jail or prison, you need to make friends, get along, do favors, and it pays off. Everything's a commodity. Knowledge, time, everything. I had my own cell. Everyone else was bunked up together. Then one guy decided on his own he wanted to become my cell mate. He moved all his stuff up into my cell without even announcing or asking his move. The other bed in my cell he took served as my desk.

The young man came into my cell and yelled, "Deters, this is not your office. This is prison." I told him I didn't want a cell mate and who told him to become mine. I gave him ten packs of peanuts and he left. The great peanut bribery.

I only had one night with a bunkmate. He looked like a nice young clean cut man. We exchanged pleasantries. I gave him my name and the man replied, "Oh my god, you're my lawyer, I am a Durrani client." What are the odds that I'm in the Hamilton County Justice Center serving time for contempt and my cell mate is a Durrani victim? His crime was petty baloney. We talked half the night from A o Z.

On Sunday, an African American church group from *New Hope Missionary*, came to the cell block. Five inmates, including me and Red, participated in the prayer service. We're all in our grey stripes. They came in singing hymns. The older pastor delivered a great message. I was ready to sob during the whole hour service. It was wonderful. One of the songs included lyrics: *"And all the angels bow down, and all the saints bow down."* So here I was singing in the middle of his cellblock *"all the angels bow down,"* bowing in my gray stripes. When in Rome, do as the Romans do.

One of the ladies from *New Hope* came up to me before she left and she said, "There's something about you. I don't know what it is, there's something about you and when you get out of here, you keep doing what you're doing." I never met her. She didn't know who I was. It was a very moving moment for me.

I orchestrated lawyers continuously visiting four times a day. It got me out of my cell. They gave us quiet time from 1:45-3:30, as if you're a kindergartener. Sometimes I got to go up to the law library to meet with the lawyers visiting. The lawyer would leave and no one knew I was still in there and I wasn't anxious to go to tell them I was ready to go back. So several times, I jogged for an hour around the law library. The law library is like a big conference room and I just jogged for an hour around in my jail stripes. I worked out in the cell block. I did chin ups and pull ups on the stairs at the cell block. I walked back and forth in my small cell for an hour.

Coming out of the law library one day, I ran into Tracy Hunter, the Hamilton County Judge convicted of misconduct. She looked at me in shock and said, *"What are you doing here?" "Justice, Tracy. Fighting for justice,"* I replied.

I also ran into David Fulcher, former Bengals safety, who has a jail ministry for men. He asked if I would speak to his group and I readily agreed. I met

Fulcher and several other teammates of his at celebrity softball games. David, Jim Breech and company are good guys.

The so called "murder pod" was next to our pod; there were tough men in there. Everyone in the pod knew I was in for telling off a judge. So they held me in high regard. They all wanted legal advice and passed me notes throughout my time there. I never replied to any of them.

One man in my cellblock was in for murder. He was a little, short guy, glasses, beard, wimpiest looking guy in there. No one knew the details of the murder. It must have been a poisoning.

I like to point out to all you hard asses about jail, about my new perspective now that I've experienced it. Jail is hard enough with your liberty being taken. People don't realize how bad it is. At the Hamilton County Justice Center, you don't have crap. You might as well feed them some decent food. I realize inmates are in there to suffer consequences, but their liberty taken is enough. You don't need to compound it with making it just completely, utterly miserable. The men I served time with explained to me the system is all about breaking them down and destroying their pride as a man.

The man I bribed with peanuts had a pair of tennis shoes. He asked me if I wanted to buy tennis shoes and told me he would sell them to me for three bucks. I didn't want to take advantage of the guy. I asked him what size they were and sure enough, they were my size. I offered him ten dollars for the used shoes. He was adamant about only taking the three dollars, but after I insisted, he wanted the ten dollars put toward his commissary account, so I did with the help of another inmate. Now I had a decent pair of tennis shoes to jog in the law library.

While inside the jail, I paid unpaid bonds to help out my fellow inmates. I later heard Maureen O'Connor had the audacity to go to Columbus and speak at the National Judiciary Conference regarding the bond issue. She spoke how people can't get out because they can't afford the bond, resulting them being stuck in jail and how the judiciary has ruined people's lives. She said the system needs to examine their conscious about this bond issue. She put on an act, playing the role as a crusader for the "little guy" while she sits idly by and does nothing for the Durrani victims. She pontificated with the news cameras a bunch of bullshit about the bond problem, as I actually paid several bonds for them. Another example of politician v. someone who does something.

After eight days in the Justice Center, Appeals Court Judge Russell Mock ruled I could be released while my appeal was being considered, a good sign Schweikert's ruling on the gag order would be reversed. I was called out of my cell and given the news.

Jim Maus, my cousin, delivered the Order. Sheriff Jim O'Neal insured I remained safe in the jail. He would later lose his election as a Democrat because he supported Donald Trump. He's now switched to the Republican Party.

Dominick Romeo drove me home. The drive home seemed surreal. It was if I was in jail a year. Mary and I embraced in the front yard, followed by my having a most needed shower and then a steak at *Walt's*.

The twelve fellow inmates I shared cellblock G with all preferred to be in the Ohio or Kentucky state prison system than Hamilton County. They told me they would take any jail, any prison, state or federal prison, over the Hamilton County Justice Center.

I still ponder the many facets of my jail stay. I won the legal side, but I still served eight long days. I won the practical side. I accepted I was stuck there and "played the game." I made the most of it by exercising and getting along with the inmates. I failed the emotional part, but everyone fails. Time seems to stop while you're in jail. It's slow moving and torturous. Unlike some of the other inmates, I had legal hope. If one doesn't have legal hope, it would be psychologically crippling.

Jail doesn't just affect those inside the walls. Those outside the walls suffer their own turmoil. Mary said the time away felt like I died. When I got out, she said it was like I had come back to life. She only was able to see me two times behind glass for about fifteen minutes each time due to the limit they put on non-lawyer visits. My time in jail actually strengthened our marriage.

My time in jail taught me many lessons and allowed me to put life in perspective. Some people just read the headlines in the news and assumed I deserved jail. What some people miss is I was in jail for doing something good in fighting for those who deserved my fighting. I continued the legacy within the walls of the jail cell. I stopped worrying about enemies who assumed the worst of me. As my wife visited me in jail, she told me many people shared with her they stood behind me and admired me for my not backing down in my fight for the victims. A trades worker came to our house while I was in jail to work on cabinets. He asked Mary if I was her husband. She said yes. He said, "You tell him the people are behind him." Nothing feels better than those moments. It makes it all worth it.

Chuck Holbrook wrote me a note my first day in and reminded me that all civil rights leaders spent time in jail. His point? I now had "street cred" in the battle for justice.

Chapter 78
Warren Buffett

"Who bravely dares must sometimes risk a fall."
—Tobias George Smollett

One day I decided maybe if we could reach Warren Buffett, we could settle the Durrani cases. I came up with the idea to send Chuck Holbrook to Omaha.

Multi-billionaire Warren Buffett, the fourth richest man in the world last I checked, lives in a quiet neighborhood in the city where he grew up, Omaha, Nebraska. He lives in the same house he built in 1958 for $31,500. The five-bedroom classic home of beige brick, slate roof, and rounded gables is surrounded by a simple ornamental metal fence. The only security is an intercom system at the end of the home's driveway.

On January 23, 2020, Chuck Holbrook flew to Omaha and took a cab to the Buffett residence. On the cold winter morning, Chuck pushed the buzzer button.

A woman with a high-pitched voice sounded polite but annoyed responded.

"Hello?"

"Hello, I'm here to deliver a book to Mr. Buffett," Chuck replied.

It was a coffee table book about the battle against Durrani my office staff and clients put together for me as a sign of appreciation. Tucked inside the book, I placed a copy of the legal complaint against Medical Protective and a handwritten note from me to Buffett:

Mr. Buffett-

Please intervene on behalf of these 540 victims of Dr. Durrani insured by Medical Protective. We believe it's in your company's best interest to.

Eric Deters

"I didn't write this book," Holbrook told the woman on the other end of the intercom. "It's about a spine surgeon insured by Medical Protective. We're quite sure Mr. Buffet knows nothing about this, but if he did, we're certain he would do something about it."

"I'm sorry. He's not here, "I'm his wife," she said.

It was Astrid Menks, Buffett's second wife whom he married in 2006 after the death of his first wife of fifty years, Susan, in 2004.

Holbrook held up the book cover to the camera. He could see she was looking.

"If you don't mind. I'll just leave it atop your mailbox here." Chuck said.

"No. Please take it to his office," she replied.

Holbrook thanked her and walked back to his waiting cab. The drive to the headquarters of Berkshire Hathaway is a straight shot down Farnam Street into downtown Omaha, less than two miles from Buffett's home.

Over ninety years old, Buffett still drives himself to work every day in his thirteen-year-old Cadillac Seville. His wife leaves change for him in the car's ash tray each morning, the amount determined by how well the stock market has done the day before. Buffett uses the money to buy his sausage-and-egg biscuit at McDonald's, just off 40th Street, on his way to the office.

In less than five minutes, Holbrook arrived at the Berkshire Hathaway headquarters, a fourteen-story cement office tower as simple as Buffett himself. Holbrook walked inside the big rotunda-like lobby, his usual smiling and positive self.

At the reception desk, he found a crewcut security guard in a dark suit who could have been a moonlighting Navy SEAL. Holbrook is five foot ten, but the guard towered over him and was built like a linebacker.

Holbrook raised the book cover for the guard to see. "Sir, do I have an important book for you."

The guard gave it a close look, all business. "So what have you got there?"

Holbrook flipped through the pages. "It's about a spine surgeon that did unnecessary surgeries on all kinds of people. I'm talking about children, too. Our law firm is representing about 500 of them. But the insurance company hasn't offered us anything. They won't negotiate. Warren Buffett owns this insurance company and I'm sure he doesn't know about it."

Holbrook leaned in close as he continued with the Durrani story. The guard warmed up. "I could tell he cared about what I was telling him," Holbrook said.

The guard called upstairs and, within minutes, someone in a suit walked off the elevator.

Holbrook identified himself as an employee of Deters Law, then gave the man his card, the book, and the Medical Protective complaint with the cover note from me. The man said nothing and returned to the elevator.

Holbrook walked back to the cab and off to the airport for the return trip to Cincinnati with no way of knowing if Buffett would receive the book or read its pages. We must assume he never did.

When Warren Buffett bought Geico, he stated he loved the insurance business because Geico received premiums like clockwork, but could delay the payment of claims. It's the old: deny, delay and defend. I've read Buffett's biography. I once admired him. No longer. He is the epitome of corporate profits and stock values regardless of all else. I'm for both of those too, but not at the expense of all else. The next and the last chapter describes the magnitude of Medical Protective fraud on Durrani victims.

Chapter 79
Medical Protective

"Time brings all things to light. I trust it so."
—Willie Stark "All King's Men"

Medical Protective, based in Fort Wayne, Indiana, is the nation's leading provider of healthcare liability insurance, collecting more than $1 billion in annual premiums from more than 240,000 covered health care providers. Since its inception in 1899, Medical Protective has defended doctors and hospitals against more than 400,000 malpractice claims. The company boasts on its website that it offers "peace of mind" to physicians through its "pure consent provision that gives you control to refuse to settle a claim," not to mention its "90% trial win rate (and) 80% of claims closed without payment."

Mike Lyon, one of Medical Protective's stable of defense attorneys, is quoted on the company's website touting the insurer's tough stand against settling claims: *"A lot of companies hire lawyers to settle cases—they hire lawyers to make sure they never really go to trial because there is too much risk, they just want to get them to settle. But Medical Protective is just the opposite. They hire the best trial lawyers, not litigators, trial lawyers, who have tried cases to verdict because they want experienced tough trial lawyers available to try these cases. We are able to be strong, courageous and give the plaintiffs' bar the kind of battle they need.»*

In one of our earliest attempts at mediation with a hospital in 2015, a leading national mediation firm, JAMS, mediated. After the initial meeting with the defendants, the mediator, Jerry Roscoe, came into the room where our team sat. He wrote a figure on a folded post-it note and I caught a glimpse of it. I thought the figure a fair sum for the victims. After all, the hospital had insurance coverage. When Roscoe read the figure on the note, the offer represented another insult. I read the number wrong. This hospital would later settle.

In February of 2017, attorneys from Medical Protective agreed to a mediation at my Independence office to be mediated by a well-known attorney the insurance company chose from Columbus. The mediator, Frank Fay, spent nearly half an hour informing us how great he was. Glenn, Ben and I became nauseated. When Steven Janik, the Cleveland lawyer representing Medical Protective, arrived at the meeting, the best he would offer was $2.1 million for all 400 clients when the insurer was sitting on $42 million in coverage for Durrani and his private clinic CAST. I immediately ended the meeting and sent Janik packing back to Cleveland. Glenn gave me the honor. I walked into the conference room and sat down on one side of the table. Steve Janik, a Kansas City lawyer and Robert

Ignasiak were sitting on the other side of the table. In a calm and strong voice I stated: "On behalf of all the Durrani victims and Deters Law, you can go fuck yourselves." Meeting over.

Now many of you may find my talking to them like this intemperate. It must be placed in context and I'll explain the purpose. I believe in sugar and honey in talks. However, there comes a time when someone's disrespect is so great, you must deliver a message you do not fear them, do not respect them and will fight them "to the death." Early in this litigation we tried "honey" with Lyon, the hospitals and everyone. It gained us nothing. In the law game, if the lawyers on the other side like you, it may be because they do not fear or respect you and you do what they want you to do.

On Glenn Feagan's flight back to Cleveland, Steve Janik was on the same flight. Glenn told Janik that was a waste of time. Janik replied: "If Deters didn't tell us off, we would have gone higher." Feagan thought yeah right to $3 million. This is all the bullshit games they play. Nothing stops anyone from making a fair offer at any time. Here's my favorite "rule" the defense has. If your demand is "too high" they won't respond because it's a "non-starter."

In January of 2020, Deters Law sued Medical Protective in federal court for "bad faith." The 133-page complaint accused the company and its lawyers of a conspiracy to defraud the Durrani victims by persuading the surgeon to flee the country, by refusing for five years to allow Durrani to testify in his defense, and by failing to make a reasonable offer to settle the hundreds of claims against Durrani during the seven-year period of the litigation. The last chapter of this book details all of it. This chapter is a brief overview.

The tactics were all part of Medical Protective's "scorched earth" policy based on their own perception the defendants couldn't win their cases at trial. During the Patricia Adams trial, Lyon told Statman even "a monkey" could win the plaintiffs' cases. If the defense couldn't win, they could try to void their coverage of Durrani or spread out the trials over many years until we went bankrupt in the fight or settled for practically nothing for our clients.

After Durrani fled, at the urging of Lyon and Medical Protective, Lyon argued that Medical Protective was off the hook in its insurance coverage because their client wasn't cooperating with his defense. On February 3, 2014, Lyon claimed Durrani declined to give any depositions. Three weeks later, Lyon told a judge that "recent efforts to communicate with him have been fruitless." A week earlier, Durrani gave medical advice to one of his patients in Cincinnati via email.

Lyon and Medical Protective didn't want Durrani to testify for two reasons. First, it made their case Medical Protective could void its coverage because he wasn't cooperating and second, they knew from Durrani's previous testimony he made a disastrous witness who turned jurors against him.

The defense dithered to their own advantage on whether they were able to communicate with Durrani or not. On May 13, 2014, before the trials of two more Durrani patients, Deters Law asked if the defense informed Durrani of the notices to depose him. Claiming it was a matter of attorney-client privilege, Paul McCartney, one of Durrani's attorneys, replied: "You are not entitled to know how or if we have communicated to Dr. Atiq Durrani about the notices."

Lyon then simply claimed he never heard from Durrani. On May 21, 2014, Lyon cancelled the scheduled depositions with Durrani. During this time, Durrani was working at Doctors' Hospital in Lahore, Pakistan, and owned a cell phone, a home phone, work phone and email.

The defense lawyers always made jokes about Durrani. During a discussion at a deposition, Walt Haggerty made a joke about serving papers on Durrani by camel. During a break in the Julie Martin trial, Lyon sat on the witness stand and with only the trial lawyers in the room, broke into a heavily-accented impersonation of his client. "My name is Atiq Durrani. I don't like Chuck Holbrook running around the bushes of my house every night trying to serve me. I have drones that will come and watch you and get you."

Lyon then claimed he reached Durrani. "We have advised Dr. Atiq Durrani of this. He advises he will not be available." And in the same statement: "In light of this advice... we shall not insist that you go through the formality of arranging for a court reporter in Pakistan, having the court reporter there and you personally attending the deposition to prove he is unavailable."

Finally, the depositions from Pakistan scheduled for June 6, 2014 were cancelled by the defense since Durrani was "unreachable." Another deposition set for November 24, 2014 was cancelled by the defense without an explanation.

Of the ten judges to handle the Durrani litigation over the years, only two sanctioned Durrani in any meaningful way, Hamilton County Common Pleas Judge Robert Ruehlman and federal Judge Michael Barrett. If a plaintiff refused to give a deposition, their case would have been dismissed. One more way the system is stacked against the victims.

In the meantime, Medical Protective attorneys filed a motion in federal district court arguing Durrani's flight to Pakistan and his refusal to cooperate in his defense meant he forfeited all his rights under his insurance policy. Our position is they never asked Durrani to assist in his defense.

On October 21, 2016, Medical Protective's strategy failed when Federal District Judge Timothy Black ruled Medical Protective would have to prove whether Durrani's lack of cooperation made a difference in their defense. In effect, the ruling said the trials must go forward, but we would have to try every case, secure a verdict and demand payment from Medical Protective for each of the 400 clients.

In the four weeks which followed Black's ruling, we sent Medical Protective a series of settlement demands, beginning with $42 million on November 8 and ending with an undisclosed sum on January 18, 2019. Medical Protective ignored all of them. A deposition scheduled for March 31 never happened. An email response from McCartney simply stated: "He will not be appearing." McCartney also refused to agree to an on-camera review to prove Durrani received the notice to compel the deposition.

On May 3, 2017, Barrett entered a contempt order against Durrani to comply with the deposition notice. A similar court order was sent out for all the state cases on May 23, 2019. Finally, on June 1, 2017, for the first time since 2014, Lyon sent a letter to Deters Law saying Durrani would give a deposition with restrictions, one per month for each of the 500-plus cases, a process which would take more than forty years. We rejected the ridiculous offer.

Chapter 80

Deposed From Pakistan

"Questioning is an indispensable instrumentality of justice."
—Justice Robert H. Jackson

In a June 26, 2017 pre-trial hearing, Hamilton County Common Pleas Judge Jennifer Sargus took up the issue of sanctions against Durrani. McCartney tried to elicit sympathy for the fugitive by noting his Pakistani medical license had been revoked because of "events in the U.S." He told the judge Durrani "still needs to make a living." McCartney then asked Durrani face the same trial sanctions he did in the Butler County cases where jurors were never told why he was absent from the courtroom. But, he added, "perhaps with instruction that Dr. Atiq Durrani has refused to give a deposition and maybe they can draw a negative inference from it."

Sargus indicated a willingness to instruct the jury Durrani fled the country to escape criminal charges. Lyon assured her Durrani would give depositions. The back-and-forth between plaintiff and defense attorneys continued until the two sides agreed on three days of depositions, ten hours each, for all 500-plus cases. We agreed to the compromise only because it proved Durrani's cooperation and prevented Medical Protective ever again having an excuse for voiding the insurance coverage.

Durrani gave six depositions in individual cases before he fled the country. He gave a deposition on February 24, 2018 for all West Chester cases and one on March 10, 2018 for all Children's cases. He would also give video depositions for the Beil case and a few other cases.

The highlight was in the February 24, 2018 deposition by video conference, where Durrani pled the Fifth Amendment 101 times and refused to answer countless other questions. Schweikert would not allow any jury to know this fact. During this deposition, Durrani's dog would bark, the call to prayers could be heard and Durrani repeatedly referred to Alan Statman as "learned counsel." Mike Lyon would roll his eyes at the call to prayers and dog barking as if, "you've got to be kidding me."

Some more highlights included:

1. Conservative care should always be used first. (Durrani never used it.)
2. You can live with pain. It's not cancer and it's not going to kill you. (Durrani always used pain as an excuse to operate.)

3. He lied about his privileges ever being suspended.
4. He lied he was ever charged with a crime.
5. He claimed any procedure that could cause retrograde ejaculation should not be used. (Durrani always used BMP-2 which caused this condition.)
6. He claimed if the MRI shows perfect anatomy, no surgery should take place. (Durrani lied about radiology findings.)
7. Differential blocks are the best way to diagnose pain. (He never used them.)
8. He claimed he only did one fusion a week. (Durrani performed multiples surgeries every day, usually a fusion.)
9. He claimed he never faced a peer review committee. (This is true and sad.)
10. He claimed he was wealthy from a family business empire in textiles. He did not know the name of the company. He then said: "Durrani Holdings."
11. He denied ever doing a surgery for money.
12. He never had to defend his privileges to a medical executive committee. (Sad, but true.)
13. He denied every being suspended at West Chester. (West Chester suspended him all the time.)
14. He admitted documentation is critical. (He never dictated reports.)
15. He admitted an operative report should be dictated in 24 hours. (He rarely dictated a report in this time frame.)
16. He claimed his departure from Children's was cordial and based upon contract negotiations. (He was fired by "resignation.")
17. He claimed to get privileges, you just fill out the application and send it in. (Sad, but true.)
18. He denied ever being a Prince or telling the clients that. (He told everyone this.)
19. He claimed he was the surgeon for the Saudi royal family. (Not true.)
20. He denied ever knowing about a complaint. (Not true.)
21. He claimed CAST was a business and financial decision.
22. He reviewed his own radiology.
23. He denied ever threatening or scaring patients. (He always used fear.)

This laundry list contained two principal facts: Durrani lied about nearly everything and Durrani failed to assess and perform surgery as he claimed.

We scheduled Durrani for depositions on February of 2018 and March of 2018. We noticed his deposition in every single case and spent over twelve hours on those two days, asking him only information about his background, credentials, education, training, lies, credibility, so we could use it every single case. No case specific questions were asked to ensure we could use his answers in all cases.

At every trial, an edited version of these deposition are played. The jury is able to see Durrani lying about his background. In recent trials, we do not play the video. The Judge trying the cases now gives the jury an instruction against Durrani:

The Defendant Dr. Durrani has not attended these proceedings in person. He is represented here by counsel. You shall not speculate on why is not present or consider his absence for any purpose, except as instructed below:

Dr. Durrani has voluntarily left the jurisdiction, removing himself from Plaintiffs' ability to subpoena him to trial.

When a party, such as Dr. Durrani, has relevant evidence or testimony within his or her control and the party failed to produce that relevant evidence or testimony, that failure gives rise to an inference that the evidence or testimony is unfavorable to that party.

Judge Brogan once told Durrani lawyers "I don't know how you guys win any trials when a jury watches that." Defense switched things up at one point and called Durrani to testify in individual cases by video. They lost those trials so they stopped using that tactic.

One of the most hysterical occurrences during the litigation is the statement Durrani would state on the record before any deposition at Mike Lyon's request.

Durrani blamed me and my "Bulldog Nation" for running him out of the country.

Here is his statement:

Almost about a decade ago now Mr. Deters filed hi fit- — - one of his frivolous lawsuits against me.

He offered us to settle, which was refused.· He eventually ended up losing the lawsuit (not true)*, at which time he sent a letter threatening us that I will spend the rest of my life defending cases filed by him.*

He then started a malicious radio and social media campaign urging anyone who had surgery by me to contact his law office to file a claim against me.

He called me the Butcher of Pakistan, a Muslim terrorist, a Taliban supporter, and that's all I can remember so far, who came to this country to maim the Americans. (I never called him Muslim or Taliban.)

All this was done to ignite racially-motivated Islamic-phobic hysteria. He then proceeded to file several malpractice lawsuits against me.

Instead of capitulating to all of this, we decided to face them in the courts, and we continue to do so to date.

It was my practice at that point that I visit Pakistan about two to three times a year to do charity surgeries.

During one of these trips in 2013 while I was in Pakistan I was informed that I was under federal investigation. I returned to the United States and asked my attorney to reach out to the US attorney and offer all possible help from our side. An offer was not reciprocated.

Meanwhile, Mr. Deters was announcing my imminent arrest by the feds on his Bulldog Nation, on his social media blog.

My attorney at that point reached out to the US attorney and was supposed to meet him at 8:00 a.m. in the morning.

At 6:00 a.m. in the morning my home was raided by the federal agents with the media present outside.· I was arrested, put in a jail cell.· My office was raided the same day by the FBI who took our computers, some of our charts, interviewed our employees, emptied all of our drawers.· And this was done right in front of our patients in the building area.

As I sat in that jail cell I wondered what did I do so wrong to deserve this.

Eventually, the indictment was handed over to me. And the indictment stated that I have done unnecessary surgery on five patients with a very rare disease called the Ehlers-Danlos Syndrome, abbreviated as EDS.

Honestly, it was shocking to me that how can a federal agent determine the necessity or the unnecessity of a surgery in such a rare disease for which there truly are just a handful of experts in the country. And I just happen to be one of them.

When we review the charts—when we review these charts further, it showed that out of the five that were named, two of them have never been operated on. None of these patients were dead, paralyzed, or maimed.· This was clearly shocking to me.

Then the Court ordered me to send every patient of mine, whoever was going to come and see, any new patients, a letter stating that I had been indicted for Medicare fraud. And to me, this clearly was an attempt to destroy my livelihood

I, at that point, decided that I'm going to fight these charges and requested a speedy trial within 90 days—as per the rules. (He never requested a speedy trial. He waived a speedy trial.)

A trial date was set. And for the reasons that are still unknown to us, the assigned judge recused herself and a new judge was assigned.

At the pretrial the US attorney informed the judge that he intended to bring a superseding indictment and asked for the trial to be delayed.· His wish was granted.

In the meantime, the Ohio Medical Board suspended my license citing that during the raid they found signed scripts in my office, which was against the law.

I was simply shocked. This is a very, very common practice in every medical office where surgeons will leave signed scripts with their nurses who authorize refills on patients' medications while they were in the operating room or out of town for any reason after they give approval for those refills.

This could have been simply dealt with a simple warning, but to take away someone's license over this seems extremely unfair.

This meant that I had to shut down my practice in Ohio. And this was all over signed scripts for genuine patients for genuine medication refills.

Soon after that, the Kentucky board, due to the reciprocity clause in between the two boards, filed suit at the behest of Mr. Deters.

This effectively meant that I had to shut down my practice and I had no means left to practice my profession or earn a livelihood.

A superseding indictment was then subsequently brought which included twenty-six counts of me authorizing medication refills on my patients while I was on my charity trip to Pakistan and unnecessary surgeries on the EDS patients.

I was simply shocked.· But I absolutely refused to yield to this intimidation.

Once again, I requested a speedy trial and the date was set for December of 2013. At the pretrial hearing the US attorney asked for a further delay of the trial since he needed more time to prepare for prosecution.

To my total shock and dismay the judge delayed the trial again until 2014.

Meanwhile, Mr. Deters and his collaboratives in the media continue to stir racially-motivated Islamic-phobic hysteria on the social media and the airwaves and urging folks to contact his office to sue me.

Being branded as a terrorist, a butcher, et cetera, et cetera, the hysteria reached to the tipping point when followers of his Bulldog Nation started posting life threats on his blogs. It was truly disconcerting and despicable.

As I faced all of this, my dad had been diagnosed with cancer of the oral cavity. That is the mouth. Every week I would tell him that this will soon be over and I will be there to take care of him.

His condition took a turn for the worst as cancer literally ate through his left cheek. He was unable to eat or drink anything. Dad was declared terminally ill.

With the trial delayed, I asked the Court to allow me to be with my dying father and offered to furnish any bond that the Court deemed appropriate.

Unfortunately, at the objection of the US attorney, the Court denied my request.

Ladies and gentlemen, my repeated requests for a speedy trial were denied and the trial delayed time after time. (He never asked for a speedy trial. He waived it.) *My license has been taken on a practice that is carried out of necessity by every doctor's office in this country, thus leaving me no means to practice my profession and earn a livelihood.*

I had not done any unnecessary surgeries on any patients and was willing to defend any and all of my actions.

The airwaves and the social media were being poisoned every day with racially-motivated Islamic-phobic hysteria by Mr. Deters and his media collaboratives.

I was being branded as a terrorist, a money launderer, a butcher who came to this country to maim Americans. This hysteria had reached a point where life threats were being held by despicable people.

I was convinced that in the environment and from this criminal—and from this criminal justice system I would never ever get justice. All of this was being done, forced me to capitulate and accept the terms of surrender and plead guilty to something that I have never did.· I could never ever do that.

So I decided to leave and be with my dying father, knowing very well the consequences of my actions.

I would be branded as a fugitive who fled from justice because he was guilty and couldn't defend the charges against him.

Ladies and gentlemen, the truth could not be further from that. Why would I be sitting here today participating in my defense week after week, case after case if my aim was to evade justice?

This despite the very harsh reality that I have already lost everything that I hold so dear in my life. And literally, no verdict will ever undo the loss that I've already suffered. I will never be able to regain what I have lost.

But still, I sit here week after week, case after case simply because someone needs to stand up to this injustice and we cannot let this injustice win.

Ladies and gentlemen, I did not become a fugitive from law.· I am following the law right now to fight this injustice. I simple left the US, at a very great personal cost, to continue my battle against this grave injustice rather than accept the terms of surrender.

There you have it. Durrani, the unfairly persecuted and misunderstood surgeon, ran out of the country by Bulldog Nation.

On February 24, 2018, Durrani's first deposition in nearly five years quickly revealed his lawyers had been using delay tactics all along:

STATMAN: Did you ever tell Medical Protective that you would be unable to cooperate in the defense of the medical malpractice cases filed against you?

DURRANI: No.

STATMAN: So you never sent a letter or an email that would say something to that effect, is that correct?

DURRANI: Not – not to my – not my knowledge. I have always maintained that I would like to participate in the defense of these cases.

STATMAN: You never received any letters to that effect?

DURRANI: I got letters, or emails, correspondence from Medical Protective. And I've always said that I will likely be participant in the defense of those cases… I have no problem whatsoever being deposed in every single case that you're referring to defend my medical decision-making. I have absolutely no issue with that.

STATMAN: And you've been asserting that position since 2013, correct?

DURRANI: I've always maintained that position.

STATMAN: Were you aware, though, that requests for your depositions have been occurring since 2013?

DURRANI: No.

STATMAN: So you're unaware of deposition requests until the deposition today, is that right?

LYON (TO DURRANI): I'm going to instruct you not to answer that.

STATMAN: Were there problems prior to now giving depositions between 2013 and today?

DURRANI: I've always maintained that as long as the depositions are limited to the medical decision-making of any individual pertinent cases, I'm more than happy to be deposed and defend myself. That has been my constant decision since Day One.

STATMAN: Were the requests (for depositions) sent to you in the mail?

MCCARTNEY: Objection. Don't answer that.

STATMAN: How did you communicate with counsel to work on your discovery requests?

LYON: Objection. Do not answer.

STATMAN: Was there a time in 2014 that you stopped communicating with your counsel?

MCCARTNEY: Objection. Don't answer that.

STATMAN: Your counsel informed us that recent efforts to communicate with you had been fruitless. Were you aware they sent that correspondence to the Deters Law Firm?

LYON: Objection. Don't answer that question.

STATMAN: If I understand your testimony about wanting to defend yourself, had you known about the deposition dates that had been previously set, you would have wanted to be there to defend yourself, correct?

LYON: Objection: I instruct him not to answer that.

Depositions would have allowed the plaintiffs' lawyers to cross-examine Durrani on all the issues related to each victim's case as well as his credibility, background, and misleading resume. Not having Durrani's deposition for five years affected trial strategies, witness arrangements, and trial preparation and presentation. It cost us extra time and money fighting the federal declaratory action in which Medical Protective argued Durrani's lack of cooperation freed the insurer from any coverage.

Crystal Pierce, Brenda Shell and Tim Marshall suffered through trials in which the Court instructed the jury only that "Dr. Atiq Durrani elected not to be here." In the Julie Martin and Laura Kranbuhl McKee trials, the judges simply instructed the jurors that "Dr. Durrani left the country" with no mention of the criminal fraud charges pending against him. At least in the Pierce case, Durrani gave a deposition, one that worked to his disadvantage, leading to a $1.04 million verdict.

The double-speak on Durrani's defense continued into April of 2019 during a pretrial hearing when Judge James Brogan asked Lyon if Durrani had asked to settle the cases.

LYON: I can assure you that he would testify that he wouldn't want to settle. He didn't do anything wrong. He thought it was the right thing to go to trial.

BROGAN: What if he had said—assuming he had said, I told them to settle the case.

LYON: Oh, then we would have to consider that... If Dr. Durrani in any of these cases said to me, "Hey, I want to settle. I'm demanding you to settle this case." Believe me, I would have put that in writing to the insurance company and we would have conferenced it and gone from there.

Minutes later, Brogan reiterated his question.

BROGAN: We're trying to decide whether Dr. Atiq Durrani made a rational decision not to settle the case. And you represent to us that he told you in this case not to settle, is that right, or you can't—well, you can't—

LYON: I can't tell you what he told me (under client-attorney privilege).

BROGAN: I understand.

LYON: Let me put it this way. I can represent to you the court that he didn't tell me not to, but I don't want to—I don't want to misrepresent to the court, either. I didn't tell him to settle it.

BROGAN: Right.

In the end, Lyon admitted that it's the insurance company, not Durrani, who makes the call anyway.

LYON: When it comes to resolution and money and settlement and decisions, judge, the insurance company makes that decision.

In other words, after years of insisting he represented Durrani, Lyon acknowledged he actually represented the interests of Medical Protective, the company that pays him.

"Bad faith" is simply a legal term for dishonest dealings. For insurers, it can mean denying a claim without giving a reason, offering less money than a claim is worth, lying about coverage limits or delaying payment of a valid claim.

In 2006, a Pennsylvania federal court upheld a $7.9 million award against Medical Protective for its bad faith in hiding the full limits of its policy from a dermatologist who failed to properly screen a patient for skin cancer. It was then the largest bad faith award in Pennsylvania history. In 2009, a Kentucky woman won a $2.5 million bad faith judgment against Medical Protective for refusing to settle a $200,000 claim against a doctor who severely damaged her inner ear, even after the doctor admitted he had made a mistake. In 2018, a high school counselor in Georgia facing a lawsuit for allegedly harming a student sued Medical Protective for denying coverage of his claim.

Medical Protective built its marketing brand by assuring the 240,000 health care providers they cover they will fight their malpractice cases to the bitter end even if it means spending far more on legal fees than settlement of their cases. Since 2013, I estimate Medical Protective has spent $20 million in legal fees to fight the Durrani cases in court.

Medical Protective totally miscalculated in their belief they could wear us out and beat us down.

In the forty Durrani cases tried between 2014 and March of 2020, juries awarded more than $94 million in economic and non-economic damages to the victims. With Ohio's limits on non-economic damages, those not related to medical bills or the loss of a job or income, the $19 million in verdicts were covered by insurance.

Even with Ohio's limits on medical malpractice damages, Medical Protective is on the hook for $19 million. There are still hundreds of cases to be tried.

Chapter 81

More Death & Group Trials

"And did you exchange a walk on part in the war for a lead role in a cage?"
—Pink Floyd, "Wish You Were Here"

By March of 2020, sixty-four, Durrani victims died waiting for justice. Chuck Holbrook and I visited many of our dying clients before they passed. After each death, an estate had to be set up with the family in probate court and an administrator appointed. The estate then had to be substituted as the party in the Durrani case. It added legal work. Phil Cameron handled all our probate matters for us. He's an indispensable member of our team.

One of the deceased who never made it to trial was 81-year-old Ollie Deaton. Her son called us to let us know she had been placed in hospice. The rod Durrani placed in her spine protruded from her tailbone and caused a serious infection. She died less than a week later.

In 2019, Daniel Webber died in a car accident when Durrani never properly fastened the cervical screws from the surgery and Webber's spinal cord was severed upon impact by the screws.

In 2016, Robert and Connie Ellington, both older patients of Durrani, died before their trial and two weeks apart. Surgeons removed a cantaloupe-sized mass from Robert's side caused by Durrani's sloppy incision.

Neil Favaron, a Marine veteran, passed away before his trial. In 2008, Favaron suffered in an auto accident and a neurosurgeon told Neil he didn't need surgery. After continued back pain, a family member referred Neil to Durrani. At his first appointment, Durrani told Neil he needed immediate surgery on a disc in his neck or he would be paralyzed for the rest of his life. "He put the fear of God in me," Favaron claimed.

Durrani performed three surgeries on Favaron's neck in seven months leaving him in more pain than ever. "He suffered for four years. From the time he had the surgeries to the time he passed away. Every single month that went by, it would get worse," his mother Linda explained.

Favaron grew dependent on pain medication and suffered intense bouts of guilt "about who he had become and how much he had to rely on others," Linda said. "He felt he was useless and couldn't work and was a financial burden." Embarrassed to attend his best friend's wedding because of his impaired ability to walk and his financial status, Favaron tried ending his life with an overdose of pills. He later died in his sleep from congestive heart failure.

Countless friends, family members and primary care physicians carry guilt from their referrals of loved ones to Durrani.

In 2017, Leah Wright died before her trial. Still living at home and in fear that she might end up in a nursing home, she often called my office just to talk. She's the only client who ever told me she prayed for Durrani. Durrani performed several surgeries on her. Her son Ron said he tried to tell her the last surgery in 2012 wasn't necessary "but she had it anyway, because he was always dressed so nice." She came out of the surgery "looking like a corpse." Ron said Leah passed out and fell several times before her death.

Justice delayed is justice denied is an antiquated, but truthful legal tenant which has never been more applicable than to Durrani cases. We filed a federal lawsuit to have trials ordered under the Seventh Amendment in the same manner criminal defendants receive a speedy trial under the Sixth Amendment. The Court refused to Order them based upon jurisdiction grounds only. We have literally tried everything. Lawsuits, protests, contempt, jail… what else are we to do? I decided to write a book and see what happens.

The system must do something under the law and under the facts and circumstances for justice for the victims who have been waiting for their trials now for over seven years. Courts have the power to do so. It should also have the will.

I have a maxim: Be a marine and adapt, adjust and overcome. Chief Justice O'Connor and the Ohio court system are no marines.

Group trials would expedite justice for victims, who by 2022 sought trials for eight years. Group trials would bring pressure to bear on Medical Protective. Durrani's Medical Protective lawyers claimed on the record there needed to be a few trials to determine the value of the cases. There have been fifty-four trials. The total verdicts have been $120,754,790. The amount covered under the $42 million dollar policies is over twenty million dollars. Yet, Medical Protective's last global offer was $7 million. They now face a federal bad faith and unfair claims practices claim covered in detail in the last chapter. When will the Courts realize the coddling of Dr. Durrani must end?

The parties stopped deposing experts and recently both parties and the Court agreed to forget about discovery scheduling orders. Why? Everyone knows the "drill."

The system must do something. It is not fair some victims receive their trial before they die, and others don't. All cases have an Affidavit of Merit since 2014. Written discovery has been completed in each case and medical records obtained over seven years ago.

Our expense and Medical Protective's expense of trying cases one at a time is astronomical. They don't care. We do. Medical Protective has made no offers on individual cases because they want to try one at a time, appeal and cause as much pain on the victims and us as possible. The Ohio justice system does nothing about it.

Imagine how for nearly a decade, we've had to explain all this delay to our clients over and over? These are lay people. How are lay people supposed to understand how this could happen? Be the way it is?

Seventy-nine clients have died. More will. Many have cancer, many face foreclosure, eviction, repossession and financial catastrophe. Over forty have filed bankruptcy.

We hired lawyers to try two and three trials at once, as Judge Guckenberger planned. We hired a fulltime videographer for court. It never happened. We were left with lawyers hired to try cases helping try a case. This means over twenty years to try cases resulting in:

a. Most clients dying
b. Experts dying
c. Lawyers dying
d. Judges dying

Surgeries from 2009 through 2013, have lawsuits filed in 2013 and won't be tried for twenty years. Group trials are the solution to limited judicial resources. It saves time and money for both parties. Experts can testify to more than one case each trip.

Cases can be grouped rationally. This involves by location of surgery and/or type of surgery and/or time frame of surgery. The first six Atwood cases Judge Barrett tried were all lumbar lowest levels and during same time frame. The next two which Barrett tried were thoracic and the next two were cervical. We prepared groups over and over. Judge Schweikert claimed we never did. He lied. We presented Judge Schweikert our list over and over again.

On December 15, 2015, Judge Robert Ruehlman set all cases for trials in groups in 2016 and 2017. He not only did so, he set up a rational plan to prepare for them. It's all spelled out on page 15 of his Order:

"The Court believes group trials saves an incredible amount of time. It allows for one jury to hear the evidence avoiding countless jury selections, openings, closings and repetitive witness testimony. Experts can testify at length, even a week or more, on all cases they are an expert. Group trials save the parties time, taxpayers money and closure to all parties."

Judge Ruehlman gave the parties four months to prepare for the first group trial, eight for the second and one year for the third. He waived pretrials. He planned to restrict length of testimony. It was a rational and appropriate plan.

After Judge Schweikert took over in August of 2017, right out of the gate, we asked for group trials with great specificity and consistent with what Judge Ruehlman proposed. Judge Schweikert did not hold a trial until June 2018 because of Durrani and West Chester lawyers complained about their schedules despite cases being ready for trial in August 2017. We lost another year.

On November 6, 2018, we filed a Motion to Set Group Trials. On January 7, 2019, Dr. Durrani's legal counsel opposed it. On January 8, 2019, we filed a response. On January 15, 2019 we filed a Supplemental Response.

On May 24, 2019, the Court made a "decision" on group trials. Judge Schweikert denied our Motion. He admitted group trials were allowed. He claimed we failed to present specific groups and grounds for group trials. A complete lie. We had been doing so for four years and what we submitted the same formula used by Judge Barrett to hold a federal group trial of six in September 2018. The Court ridiculously claimed, "if all parties to an action agree, "the court will attempt to accommodate that." He gave Durrani veto power over group trials.

On June 7, 2019, we sent the detail again to the Court including:

The Court's Order on group trials, while welcomed, claimed we have never been specific about what cases could be in groups. We have documentation from 2013 through 2018 that has specifically addressed the issue. Instead of resending it all again we will address it here. Based upon cases not tried, we gave groupings of cases which could be tried together. Without group trials, our clients continue to suffer and be denied a reasonable trial date in which to address their claims. They are entitled to this and it is unfair to not have group trials and move these cases forward, as opposed to one at a time. We have made our arguments in support of group trials over and over for eight years and they are as relevant now if not more so, in light of the fact that one, so many victims have died and forever been denied their day in court, and two, the verdicts over the last year support the validity of their claims. As previously asserted, group trials save time, money and resources. One jury. Open opening. One closing. Same experts. Multiple cases."

We want to stress that last point. With group trials, we would have one voir dire, one jury, one opening, one closing and experts could cover all the cases in one or two days.

On July 15, 2019, we filed an Updated Group Trial Report in federal court. We also sent it to Judge Schweikert's legal counsel and Chief Justice who were parties to that action. On August 7, 2019, Schweikert entered a Case Management Conference Order. On August 14, 2019, before even seeing the August 7, 2019 Order we sent an email to the Court.

The August 7, 2019 Order is the last Order on the issue of group trials. It reflects Schweikert's incompetence, bias and lack of empathy to the victims. We have clamored for group trial for five years. Judge Robert Ruehlman scheduled them in 2016 and 2017 for all cases. They would all be over. Judge Schweikert refused from 2017 through 2019 to do anything regarding this issue. It is wrong. It is evil based upon people dying waiting for trials.

Judge Schweikert's last Order continued his failure:

"Regarding the Plaintiffs' continuing request for group trial. I am not available for an extended trial in the near future. The similarities and efficiencies need to be more refined regarding a specific proposed grouping than what was submitted in order to persuade this Court to develop and adopt a group trial procedure against the will of a defendant. Perhaps the Plaintiffs' Trial Attorney and the Defendants' Trial Attorney could come to some agreement on a defined group and such a procedure with evidentiary and procedural limitations."

He was not available? Who is available? We gave countless "similarities" and "efficiencies." "Against the will of a defendant?" Judge Schweikert knew Durrani, the only Defendant in the ongoing trials, through his insurance company and Lindhorst is never going to agree to group trials. He knew they oppose group trials. It says it all. Once again, Schweikert accommodated Durrani, not the victims. Schweikert expressed concern about Durrani not his victims. It's sickening.

We sent an email to Defendants' counsel on Friday, August 16, 2019 regarding group trials. No response to our email on group trials ever came. In other words, to prove the absurdity, we did as Schweikert suggested to make our point. It made it. No response.

It is inherently unfair any victim, after over seven years of litigation, must wait for their trial over forty years while others are allowed to be tried. They each have a severe injury from an unnecessary surgery. The system's disregard of this reality is shameful. Durrani victims are cheated and delayed because there were too many victims and too much harm? It makes no sense. The opposite is true. The court system must treat them equal and it can through group trials.

How does Ohio justify how an active federal judge, Michael Barrett, can try group trials simply based upon the location of the surgery- thoracic, cervical or lumbar and that standard is not good enough for Ohio?

The Ohio Court system in the Durrani matter has proven to be a joke. It certainly does not reflect the inscription on the U.S. Supreme Court building. "*Equal Justice Under Law*" or the motto of the Ohio Supreme Court: "*With God, All Things Are Possible*" or the inscription on the Hamilton County Courthouse: "*What Doth the Lord Require of Thee But To Do Justly and to Love Mercy.*"

There is no legal, ethical or rational basis for all which the Ohio Court System has done except the following:

1. They don't give a damn.
2. They are "bought and paid for" and controlled by the medical and legal establishment.

We filed a federal challenge for group trials under the Seventh Amendment. We lost based upon the federal court believing they did not have jurisdiction.

We protested on the steps of the Ohio Supreme Court in Columbus. We protested on the steps of the Hamilton County Courthouse.

We have written letters to county officials. We have used social media to protest.

I went to jail.

No one cares. No one does anything.

After hours of searching nationwide, not one case can be found where anything like this has happened. Over five hundred cases assigned to one judge who simply cannot complete the trials within his lifetime and many if not most of the plaintiffs will never see their day in Court. This is not speculation. The defense has repeated often they will not settle or even make an offer. Therefore, group trials are all the more critical because all the cases must be tried.

In 2013, Chief Justice Maureen O'Connor wrote a law review article for Albany Law School. She espoused how it's a shame the low opinions the public has regarding lawyers. She told a story about General Ulysses Grant. Ironic that while Grant helped win the Civil War in four years for the Union and O'Connor can't give the Durrani victims a trial over forty years. She "pondered" "when I consider the question what makes the Ohio Supreme Court great on its forty-fifth anniversary" she claimed it was "the Modern Courts Amendment." She even mentioned how it elevated the Supreme Court judges to "justices." She called the Rules of Superintendence the "most significant central feature." What follows are her words:

"Here, I would like to examine in detail, three areas where the court has been very successful in improving the administration of justice through exercising its authority of superintendence: caseflow management, access to court records, and language interpretation.

Article I, Section 16 of the Ohio Constitution states that "every person . . . shall have justice administered without denial or delay." The importance of this provision is reflected in the Preface to the Rules of Superintendence for the Courts of Ohio, which states:

[t]he foundation of our government rests upon the confidence of the people in the ability of their courts to achieve liberty and justice for all under the law. The fair, impartial, and speedy resolution of cases without unnecessary delay maintains this confidence, safeguards the rights of litigants to the just processing of their causes, and earns the trust of the public.

One will notice a common thread running through these two passages—the word "delay." As the British statesman, William E. Gladstone, said in the nineteenth century, "[j]ustice delayed is justice denied." His quote is today a common refrain understood by those both in and outside of the legal community—delay is the foe of an effective judicial system. As Dr. Ernest C. Friesen, a nationally recognized educator in court management, argues, delay undermines the very purpose of courts.

In fact, a 1961 report of the Ohio Legislative Service Commission that served as a precursor for the development of the Modern Courts Amendment identified delay as one of the major issues facing Ohio's courts and calling for reform. "The oldest and most publicized problem facing the courts of the state is delay," the report found:

[d]elay in the courts is unqualifiedly bad. It is bad because it deprives citizens of a basic public service; it is bad because the lapse of time frequently causes deterioration of evidence and makes it less likely that justice be done when the case is finally tried; it is bad because delay may cause severe hardship to some parties and may in general affect litigants differentially; and it is bad because it brings to the entire court system a loss of public, confidence, respect, and pride.

It is this judicial delay that brings into focus the importance of caseflow management. Although it may be misunderstood as a mere bureaucratic concern, caseflow management is in fact a key element in combating judicial delay and, ultimately, achieving the very purpose of our judicial system.

The Supreme Court of Ohio plays a significant role in overseeing caseflow management throughout Ohio's local courts. Pursuant to Rules 35 through 43 of the Rules of Superintendence for the Courts of Ohio, the supreme court, through its Case Management Section, exercises a variety of caseflow management oversight powers, all with the goal of reducing delay and ensuring the effectiveness of the judicial system.

These include:

- Setting case time limits;
- Collecting, analyzing, and monitoring statistical caseflow data from the state's local courts;
- Conducting audits of the state's local courts;
- Assisting and training judges, court administrators, clerks, and other court personnel in caseflow management areas.

Chief Justice O'Connor never applied her words to the Durrani victims. Why? Healthcare money.

Judge Dale Crawford claimed he's tried more trials than any Judge in Ohio. On August 6, 2019, Judge Dale Crawford at a hearing put on the record that 99% of Ohio Judges would disagree with Judge Schweikert's rulings. Yet, we were stuck with Judge Schweikert. Think about Judge Crawford's statement. The most experienced trial judge in Ohio believes 99% of judges would believe Schweikert's rulings wrong and this is the judge assigned to Durrani cases.

From our Founding Fathers, Abraham Lincoln, abolitionists, Martin Luther King, Jr., civil rights leaders, the history of this country, the United States of America has been about standing up to injustice and wrong even if it's against foolish law or rules. On a conference call with the Court on group trials, what was Mike Lyon's response? "It's not fair." Really? Not fair to who? Durrani. The guy who fled from an indictment. The guy who lives in Pakistan. The guy who doesn't attend trials.

Chapter 82

Larry Grause

"Good men must not obey the laws too well."
—Emerson

Larry Grause is my Godfather by the Sacrament of Baptism in the Catholic Church. He helped me as much as anyone during the Durrani litigation battles by giving me unconditional support. He gave me the love and support of a father. We developed a regular schedule of lunches several times a week at *Brio's* in Newport, Kentucky. I often visited Larry at his condominium on Western Avenue in Covington just off Interstate 75 because it was on the way to and from our Cincinnati office and the Hamilton County Courthouse. Larry listened. He offered sage advice. He encouraged. He supported me.

To those of you who do not know the legend of Larry Grause, I'll share a brief history. Larry grew up in Newport, Kentucky, the son of a self-employed tile man. Larry attended Newport Catholic High School and his family later moved to Ft. Thomas, Kentucky. During summers, Larry Grause worked as a lifeguard and studied his vocabulary while he sat in his lifeguard chair.

The following news article sums up Larry's brilliance:

Law Student Excels in Scholastics and Activities
The Kentucky Kernel
April 29, 1966
By: Carolyn Williams

Larry Grause, retired editor-in-chief of the Kentucky Journal, has been said to be a "once-in-a-generation law student."

Throughout his career in UK Law School, he's managed to gain the admiration of his instructors and the respect of his fellow students.

"Larry is one of those rare once-in-a-generation law students who manages to excel in every phase of law school activity," says Dr. Paul Oberst, professor of law and a member of the UK Board of Trustees.

This year Grause was named the outstanding graduate of the year by the UK Breckinridge Inn of Phi Delta Phi. The award is given annually only if there is a deserving graduate. It is based on scholarship and leadership.

Just recently Grause received notice that he was selected as the Law Graduate of the Year from Province 14, including such schools as Vanderbilt, University of Mississippi, and University of Alabama, besides Kentucky.

He will now vie for the National Graduate of the Year title which will be announced in June.

Another distinguishable characteristic about Grause is the fact that he has participated in Moot Court, somewhat unusual for many Law Journal staff members because of the rigors of both programs.

Yet he doesn't merely "participate." This year he won a position on the team that won the regional meet in the annual nationwide competition. The team tied for sixth place in the national competition held in New York.

How has he managed to keep so active and still retain his numerical overall of 82.55 (the highest in the class from a possible 85, or A?

"I simply grapple with each challenge as it arises as though life itself were hanging in the balance," explains cum laude graduate of Villa Madonna with an A.B. in history. "You have to learn to channel all your energies toward the immediate hurdles."

Grause's lists of accumulative activities is indeed impressive. To name a few, he has received 11 book awards, was runner-up for the McEwen Award for the outstanding oral advocate and received the Clarence Darrow Award, another leadership and scholarship honor which is only awarded each year when there are qualifying recipients.

Another recent award was the Order of Coif, somewhat similar to Phi Beta Kappa, which is said to be the pinnacle of law school success.

"I think my wife Libby deserves some consideration, too." Admits Grause. "She's not only helping me through school, but at the same time, she's been a student, teacher, housewife and mother of our seven-month-old daughter."

Despite all of the extracurricular activities and the average 45 hours a week on the Law Journal, Grause has been employed part time. He is working as a special assistant to President John W. Oswald and is compiling an administrative manual regarding governing regulations of the university.

"From my observations of many students as both President of UK and as a vice president at UCLA," Oswald points out, "Larry is possessed of distinguishable leadership qualities."

My father represented Larry's father. After law school, Larry received an offer to teach law school at UCLA. My father offered him a partnership. Larry chose a local law career over UCLA. Larry and I discuss this choice from time to time, and I believe it the wrong decision. Larry could have become a U.S. Supreme Court Justice or the head of a national law firm.

Larry not only possessed a photographic memory and brains, God blessed Larry with the looks of a movie star. In fact, Larry and Elizabeth, an intelligent teacher with looks of a model herself, made quite the couple.

Deters & Grause formed and Larry became the work horse and trial lawyer of the firm. With all his attributes, Larry never lost a trial. He won and then won some more. Larry soon grew tired of "just being a lawyer" so he dove into the restaurant business. He left the law partnership. *The Conservatory* and the *Glass Menagerie* became abundantly successful. The common concept: restaurant on one side and night club on the other. While restauranting, Larry continued to practice law with several attorneys including one of my few attorney friends, Mark Arzen.

Larry lived large. For decades in the 1970s and 1980s, a six-foot seven man who packed heat, named Marvin, chauffeured Larry around town in a white stretch limousine. This may have been passe at the time for LA or New York, but not in Northern Kentucky and Cincinnati. Everyone noticed and knew. Larry's lifestyle cost him his marriage and he would marry twice more. He remains close to Elizabeth and their two daughters, Tammy and Tara. He built a magnificent home on the side of the hill in Kenton Hills, Kentucky staring at the Cincinnati skyline. Randy Michaels, founder of *Clear Channel*, bought the home from Larry.

Larry invested profits in his restaurants in the stock market. When the market crashed on Black Monday, October 19, 1987, Larry lost half the value of his stock portfolio. Someone advised him to place his money in something safe such as Macy's bonds. He did. Macy's filed bankruptcy. Fortunately, Larry still saved millions, so he quit law and he quit life. Depression took over. He became a recluse for a decade.

I reached out to Larry. He responded and he and I began to meet regularly for lunch. Larry claims I saved his life. I don't know if I did or didn't, but our relationship is an important one to me and the Durrani battle.

The last ten plus years we have shared some of the best times including some of the funniest. My goodness the stories. For both Larry's and my own sake, I will keep most of them between he and I. I plan to write one hilarious screenplay called "Larry."

Larry lent me money once to make payroll and again to assist paying for my daughter's wedding. All of this during my Durrani battles when I found myself strapped for cash. I paid back the undocumented no interest loans after the first settlement.

At my request, Larry reviewed pleadings in Durrani from time to time to give me his "two cents."

The proudest honor Larry bestowed upon me is he attended the entire *Sarah Jones v. Dirty.com* trial and afterwards told me that as good as he was, I was better. I don't believe it, but honored he told me so. Larry also wrote an incredible letter for my KBA for me. The National Law Student of the Year recognized my talent, just not the KBA.

Chuck Holbrook and I watched the 2016 Presidential Election results at Larry's condo. What a time we had late into the night rooting for the impossible Trump victory as we ate the prime rib Larry cooked.

I arranged for Larry to have his first cell phone on my phone plan. Chuck and I taught him to text. We also helped him on other issues from pharmacy visits to nursing home visits to see his brother. He helped me. I helped him. No one kept score.

Chapter 83

Judge Guy Reece

"Never be afraid to raise your voice for honesty and truth and compassion against injustice and lying and greed. If people all over the world... would do this, it would change the earth."
—William Faulkner

In a court filing to all parties on December 3, 2019, Judge Mark Schweikert announced his retirement from the Durrani cases and all court work effective on January 1, 2020.

When he announced his decision, he claimed he made it with his wife in June 2018.

What I believed caused Judge Mark Schweikert to decide in June 2018 to leave at the end of 2018 is my ruse of a protest at his Florida home at the *Villages*. When our local protests failed to help the cause, I came up with a "fake" Florida protest.

I first sent an email to all the clients to play along with a fake Florida protest. I then announced on Facebook that I was organizing a protest outside Schweikert's Florida home in the *Villages*. I announced buses were being procured. I announced we may charter a plane. I asked the clients in the Facebook comments express their enthusiastic support. They claimed they would go. Many claimed they would have Florida family and friends help, too.

I knew all our enemies follow me on social media. Sure enough, Joe Caligiuri, Ohio Disciplinary Counsel, contacted me a few days before the protest and stated he thought the protest would violate ethical rules. I informed him we disagreed, but we were canceling it for other reasons without informing him what those reasons were: it was a ruse.

I'm convinced Schweikert's wife, hearing of this event, no doubt told her husband—enough! We are not going to have a "mob" outside our Florida home. I believe this is what led to Judge Schweikert finally leaving the cases. Alan Statman told me he always tells lawyers: "The thing about Eric is, he comes up with some crazy ideas, but half of them work." This one worked.

I also believe it no coincidence Reich held a contempt hearing in September 2018 after the June decision. Reich wanted a parting shot at me, knowing he planned to retire.

In Reich's place, O'Connor appointed Judge Guy L. Reece, a retired African-American judge from Columbus. We represent thirty-six black victims of Durrani. It angers me while on a daily basis in 2020, 2021 and 2022, its race, race, race, but Durrani victims, black and white, do not receive their justice. At first,

Reece appeared not much different than Schweikert. He followed the Schweikert rulings. For the trials, he wouldn't allow plaintiffs to claim a pattern of fraud on the part of Durrani and his hospital enablers, refused to lift the gag order and continued the unprecedented action of sealing the verdicts. In the beginning of his tenure over the cases, he refused to consider group trials. He would later agree to two at a time in June 2021 when trials resumed after Covid. He now is entertaining three at a time beginning in June 2022. Progress.

Judge Reece is also not mean and punitive like Schweikert. Judge Reece possesses good judicial temperament.

I have often used this story I believe is attributed to President and Chief Justice Howard Taft. It makes no difference to me because regardless, it is truth. Everyone looks at a judge as they would at God. Every judge plays God. Therefore, every judge should act as God would act: compassionate, emphatic, just, forgiving and other virtues based upon the facts and circumstances. Is this too much to ask? What would God do in the Durrani cases? Not how O'Connor and Schweikert handled them.

The trial for Kimberly Jenkins, in February of 2020, didn't turn out well. The defense attorney stalked Jenkins' Facebook page and retrieved photos from her posts to use against her. In one photo, she stood on a hoverboard with her granddaughter holding her steady with her arms. In another photo, she posted she shopped all day. She failed to mention in the post she shopped online all day. Regardless, the defense seized on the photos as proof she could withstand a day of shopping. In the end, the jury gave her nothing for the damage Durrani inflicted upon her. Again, I'll never understand how a jury ever votes for Durrani.

In early 2020, the coronavirus "panic" began to spread throughout Ohio. By March 8, 2020, Gov. Mike DeWine issued orders closing barbershops, beauty salons, tattoo parlors, hair and nail salons, and more than 180 Bureau of Motor Vehicles offices. Businesses still open were asked to take the temperature of every employee prior to the workday.

On May 1, Hamilton County courts followed suit by delaying all civil trials until at least August 1 and possibly until January 1, 2021. The covid delay would last to June 1, 2021.

In late July of 2020, with the request for group trials pending, we went on the offensive again. We filed a suit against Supreme Court Chief Justice Maureen O'Connor in federal district court for obstructing justice and fired off letters to President Trump, U.S. Attorney General William Barr, FBI Director Christopher Wray and local U.S. Attorney David Devillers asking for a federal criminal investigation of O'Connor. No one responded.

"We suspect some of you may think we are crazy, and like so many things we've tried, it won't work. But we will never stop trying," we emailed clients July 28, 2020 regarding our above actions.

Even more puzzling to our clients and me, Hamilton County officials decided to reopen the courts in July for landlords who wanted to evict their tenants during the pandemic, but not for Durrani victims, who waited seven years for justice.

I rallied our clients to contact Beryl Love, executive editor of the *Cincinnati Enquirer*, by email and pressure the city's only newspaper to cover the Durrani trial delays. The effort resulted in a brief story on July 31 on page 6A which mostly recapped the long-running case. A similar push by clients to have the *Enquirer* to try to overturn the sealed verdicts in the Durrani cases, a legal action unheard of in civil or criminal trials, was futile.

The newspaper sued to unseal the divorce records of Dawn Gentry, a Kentucky family court judge accused in a juicy scandal which made national news. Gentry allegedly retaliated against lawyers and their clients who denied her campaign donations. I think Dawn Gentry got a raw deal and I publicly defended her. The *Enquirer* could fight to unseal her records, but never for the Durrani victims. I actually gave Dawn Gentry a job. She resigned, believing working for us hurt her chances not to be suspended. She later accepted a three year suspension from the KBA.

In August, with no movement by Hamilton County Courts on the issue of group trials, I turned to social media, railing against the delays on my Facebook page. "This ought to scare the shit out of you. One day I might lose it... And when I burn down the courthouse in Hamilton County, everybody will say, 'Well, I can't believe Bulldog burned down the courthouse in Hamilton County'... Does it take violence and destruction of property to be heard in Hamilton County?" I said in the video. "I should be at their (judges') homes. I should take up arms. We should riot. We should burn down the damn courthouse... We're not doing enough obviously because they're not listening."

Why did I say all of this? Because as cities burned down across America, Black Lives Matter received all the attention. I made the point: is that what we have to do? Everyone knew the point I was making.

The next day, Judge Charles Kubicki, the administrative judge for Hamilton County, signed an order restricting my access to the courthouse. "Given Mr. Deters' history, I have no choice but to take these threats seriously," Kubicki wrote in his order. I was barred from being anywhere near the courthouse.

While Kubicki banned me from the Hamilton County Courthouse, Judge Barrett sent out three federal Marshals to check on me. It was a truly funny and friendly visit. When they appeared in the lobby, Sarah came back to my office concerned. I just woke up from a nap. When they came into my office, I stood up to greet them and they noticed not one, but both of my guns on my desk. They smiled and asked if I could put them away. I replied with compliance. We would talk for over thirty minutes, and they left. One gave me a Marshal's keychain, which I use. They told me Judge Barrett simply wanted to check on me out of concern. Barrett did not ban me from the federal courthouse.

I would mock Judge Kubicki by calling him "Little Bitty Chuck Kubicki" and claimed the Order was no doubt the work of Joe Deters, Judge Kubicki's closest confidant. How comical. "Given Mr. Deters' history." What part of my history included violence and arson? It is believed I am the only person in history banned from the Hamilton County Courthouse. Judge Kubicki would be one of the judges to lose election and Joe laid off my daughter and son-in-law to make room for him in his office.

Less than a week later, Reece agreed to group trials in a ruling on August 21, 2020. He rejected our proposal for ten cases per trial, but said the court was willing to start with two or three at a time and increase the numbers if the trials went smoothly.

I would be part of the fight against all the tri-state hospitals regarding vaccine mandates. We filed the lawsuits for those who refused to be vaccinated. We fought the same law firms and same hospitals as we fought in Durrani. You should know no part of the American system is more "woke" than the Court system. We lost our request for injunctive relief and the U.S. Supreme Court by a 5 to 4 vote ruled against healthcare workers. Deters Law is the only law firm in the Cincinnati area who tried, from August 2021 to the present, to help all the workers we could for no charge.

State and Hamilton County court officials delayed all trials again until at least June of 2021, another setback for Durrani's victims. The federal courts in Ohio followed suit. "Pain and suffering is prison to us every day," Brenda Conley told a local TV news station. "You know, I've got grandkids I'd love to do things with, but I just can't." Brenda Conley is a gem. She comes to all our meetings and sits in the front row.

With no new Durrani trials or a settlement with Medical Protective in sight, I was soon borrowing $65,000 every two weeks to meet payroll. In October of 2020, we announced the firm was laying off six people by year's end. In addition, Holbrook, my righthand man, moved to Arizona while Maria Dallas, my longtime secretary and office manager, retired.

"These cuts are necessary to continue the Durrani battle," I wrote in an email to the staff. "We have had no trials for a year. Yet, we laid off no staff."

We changed our minds in a few days, and we laid off no one. I just couldn't do it. Each person made their case why they should not be laid off and Glenn and I accepted their arguments.

On June 30, 2020, the Court of Appeals for Hamilton County upheld the fifteen-day jail sentence Schweikert gave me for violating the gag order, meaning I still have another seven days to serve on his sentence.

The fourteen-page ruling signed by all three judges was as tortured in its logic as it was long. The panel of judges acknowledged my contempt during the courthouse protest was indirect, not direct, because it never occurred in front of Schweikert.

Direct contempt is when you are in the presence of a judge, like in Court, say: "F you, Judge!" Indirect contempt is outside his presence. Schweikert was in Florida. How could Schweikert and the Appeals Court consider my contempt direct?

But the appeals court judges ruled Schweikert was permitted to "loosely follow" the procedure for indirect contempt because I repeatedly defied his gag orders and had shown up at the contempt hearing without witnesses. All not true. They also ignored the waiver of counsel issue.

I appealed to the Ohio Supreme Court, but they refused the appeal. Even if I turned myself in to serve out my remaining seven days in jail, I would have been sent home immediately during the coronavirus epidemic. Low-risk, non-violent offenders were no longer being held in jail to avoid the spread of the infection.

However, at any moment, I could go back to serve seven more days. I guess it is Judge Reece's decision. Alan and Ben told me Judge Reece does not seem too concerned about me, sending me to jail or any gag order. I hope not.

Chapter 84

The Process

"The will to do, the soul to dare."
—Sir Walter Scott

We ask every client when they signed up to write a written narrative of what happened to them. We answer all the written discovery Durrani's lawyers send us. The defense takes the deposition of the Durrani clients under oath. The clients ultimately have a "microscope stuck up their colon" throughout the process. By filing a lawsuit, they have to answer every question about their past, their work history, their medical history, their personal lives, all under oath at a deposition.

The defense use to depose our experts. The experts provide their opinions in written reports. To prepare a case for trial, we have to prepare jury selection, request medical records of the client going to trial, prepare an opening with client's specific medical records, prepare scripts for the client and experts. When requesting the medical records, it can become overwhelming because most of the clients have extensive medical history, including their primary care physician, back doctors, pain doctors and therapists.

York puts together all the clients' trial exhibits. Alexa Kavanaugh, now Nickie Hatfield, totals up the medical bills to show how much the client has paid in bills. It is an extraordinary amount of work. All medical records have to be reviewed by our experts. Our experts do trial video depositions or testify live at trial. It is necessary to prepare the client for their upcoming trial. Their deposition is sent to them for their review to refresh their memory.

Imagine the work it takes doing that, then you pick one jury and you have to do this over and over again, one at a time. If it was done through group trials, you'd have one jury and one opening statement. The expert could fly into town and testify on several cases and then leave, instead of one at a time.

For the trials, we hired a company to assist in running the technical aspect at trials. We hired Matt Bradley away from them, because as cases were being tried, the amount to pay this company became astronomical. Matt Bradley, who we nicknamed "Murdoch" from the crazy guy on the A-Team, became our main technical support at trials. He does a great job for us. We bought a gigantic screen and all the equipment. Matt grabs the client exhibits from Sarah, and has them readily accessible during opening, testimony, cross-examination and closing arguments.

As Abraham Lincoln said, "Give me six hours to chop down a tree and I will spend the first four sharpening the axe," preparation is key to success. Knowing cases were going to be tried back-to-back, we had to come up with a system to ensure cases were being handled sufficiently and adequately. We owed it to our clients to treat each one as individuals.

I spent time preparing voir dire, scripts for the experts, direct testimony scripts for the clients, opening and closing documents, exhibits, trial binders and preparing the clients. After I prepared the blueprint and foundation of what needed to be done, York took over trial preparation, as my focus shifted to other aspects of the litigation. York used her organization skills and created a system to always complete everything on time.

York contacts each client before their individual trial so they feel prepared, and goes over pertinent trial documents with them. As a prior client herself, York wants the clients to know what it's like on the stand and wants them fully prepared for direct questioning and cross examination, and to be an advocate for their own case. The attorney contacts each client closer to trial to answer any follow-up questions. Until Covid slowed things down, trials were being held every other week with an excruciating time frame, but we never missed a beat. When Covid closed many businesses, we stayed open and prepared the cases for when the Courts would open back up. The staff is always ready to handle whatever comes.

There are a thousand traps for a plaintiff when you file a lawsuit. A plaintiff's lawyer has to file the case on time. You have to have an affidavit of merit from an expert. You have to make sure you serve the parties with the summons and that included Durrani in Pakistan. When they send you discovery, you have to answer all their questions. If you don't, information can be excluded at trial. There are deadlines to amend the complaint. There are deadlines to disclose experts. There are deadlines for your experts to be deposed.

For trial, you must disclose all your witnesses and all the exhibits. As the plaintiffs, we have to move the case forward. All the burden is on us. We are proud that during this whole process, representing over five hundred cases, we never screwed one of them up. We never missed a deadline.

Some of the clients filed bankruptcy. Fortunately, Alan Statman is a top bankruptcy lawyer and handled this for us.

We answered 4,000 sets of written discovery from Durrani and the hospitals. This is something any lawyer will tell you is burdensome. They send you a set of questions: all the places you've worked, all the places you have treated for a doctor from birth until now. Thirty to fifty questions you have to answer in writing, and we had to answer those for over 500 clients. Guess who sends you questions? The hospital sends you questions, Durrani sends you a set of questions. We always answered them on time. The amount of work is unbelievable. Alexa Kavanaugh handled this under my and the lawyers supervision before she turned to the liens battle.

When we first signed up the Durrani cases, I told all the clients we would discount our 40% fee if there's a quick settlement which at the time I thought certain to happen. I was wrong. By dragging it out, defense took even more money out of our client's pockets because if we didn't have to fight them for ten years and borrow millions, we could have discounted our fee. Now we need the 40% to handle our costs and expenses.

Schweikert actually made us set aside money for court costs, too. He's worried more about the clerk getting paid their court costs, than clients receiving their money. Americans do not realize how much a plaintiff or victim goes through and what they "net" is far less than they ever win or settle.

Once Durrani left Pakistan, there's a requirement you have to serve him with summons every time he is sued. We researched and filed a request for Judge Guckenberger to allow the firm to serve him by regular mail or email. In addition, the same attorneys were representing him, so they could accept it on his behalf. Lindhorst and Dreidame loved getting new lawsuits, as it allowed them to tally up billable hours.

Guckenberger ordered us to simply mail the lawsuits to Durrani by regular mail at his last known address. We complied.

In our new lawsuits, the law firms do not accept service. We have followed Guckenberger's Order and have an outstanding motion or request before Judge Reece on the issue.

Judge Reece would reverse the one and only favorable ruling we received from Judge Schweikert. On February 1, 2019, Schweikert ordered we could depose members of the hospital's Medical Executive and Credentialing Committees and Board of Trustees of Children's Hospital. The Order would apply to all hospitals. Judge Reece reversed this decision. If we won, they could appeal right away. If they won, we could not. We have to wait. It's unfair. Schweikert got this one right. Judge Reece did not.

Chapter 85

Durrani in Pakistan

"It is natural to man to indulge in the illusions of hope.... For my part, whatever anguish of spirit it might cost, I am willing to know the whole truth; to know the worst, and to provide for it."
—Patrick Henry

In July 2013, Durrani turned in his passport as part of the condition of his release on bail. This worthless condition failed to stop Durrani's fleeing the U.S. to his native Pakistan sometime around December 13, 2013 using a fake passport.

Upon arriving in Pakistan, Durrani worked at Pakistan's elite Doctors Hospital in Lahore, where in January of 2015 they listed him on the hospital's website as a spine surgeon and director of the hospital's Center for Spine Disorders. He brazenly posted on his Facebook page Cincinnati is his hometown and he had been in a relationship since October 2011 with Beth Garrett, who continued to visit him in Pakistan.

Eventually, Durrani's U.S. past caught up with him. *DAWN*, Pakistan's oldest English-speaking newspaper, published a story in December of 2017 about the federal criminal charges Durrani faced in America. The story reported Doctors Hospital suspended his operating privileges after the Pakistan Medical and Dental Council suspended his medical license. The Council stated it would not reinstate Durrani's license until he could resolve the charges in the U.S.

Durrani found a way to work around the system and continue to butcher patients. A year later, *The News International*, Pakistan's largest English-speaking newspaper, reported Durrani remained one of the busiest and highest-paid surgeons in Lahore even though his license was still under suspension by the Pakistan Medical and Dental Council.

Complaints surfaced in Lahore reflecting Durrani never changed his scam from his years in Cincinnati. *The News International* cited the example of Dr. Rozina Haroon, a doctor, who consulted with Durrani about pain in her back and leg. He recommended immediate surgery and warned any delay would result in complete paralysis.

A day after the procedure, Haroon worsened with pain reaching to her unaffected leg as well. Haroon showed all the signs of a serious infection with the surgical wound oozing blood-tinged pus, she suffered headaches and shivered from a high fever. She returned to Durrani who gave her an injection and sent her home. On her third trip back to his office, Haroon slipped into critical condition. Durrani performed more surgery, but Haroon continued to deteriorate. Twenty days after her first surgery, she died.

Haroon's sister blamed Durrani's "poor clinical judgment, incompetence and negligence" for the death. Durrani told the newspaper Haroon aspirated fluid during an epileptic seizure prior to the second surgery and died of pneumonia. The family said Haroon had no history of seizures.

According to *The News International* story, the Punjab Healthcare Commission, which oversees medical facilities in the region, asked Doctor's Hospital for an explanation of why Durrani still operated at its facilities.

In 2019, we decided to hire a Pakistani attorney to keep tabs on Durrani and for help with contacting him. I found Salim Ur Rahman, a former legal advisor to the *Pakistan Medical and Dental Council* and a current Advocate Supreme Court. The title means that Rahman is an experienced lawyer who has been certified by the nation's highest court.

Rahman left a message for Durrani's two Pakistani lawyers that Durrani should cooperate with us in the U.S. because his insurer, Medical Protective, had exposed him to nearly $80 million in insurance uncovered verdicts. When Rahman called Durrani's lawyers, they put Durrani on the phone and Rahman told Durrani personally about his $80 million in potential liability. Durrani told Rahman he would speak to his American attorneys. We never heard a response. What do you believe Lyon told him?

In crazy irony, Durrani has a whopper of a lawsuit against Medical Protective for failing to protect him from the verdicts, including massive punitive damages verdicts. We wish he would assign his claim to the victims. If he assigned his claim to the victims, we could end all the litigation against him and nail Medical Protective. We also would ask for criminal charges be dropped. He's not coming back anyway, so the current criminal charges mean nothing. Durrani could also travel again. It makes no sense Durrani doesn't do one of these options either sue Medical Protective or assign the claim to us. The answer remains. Why? Why is Durrani so loyal to Mike Lyon and Medical Protective? It makes no sense except to question what they paid Durrani.

On June 9, 2020, Durrani was scheduled for a hearing on his medical license before the Pakistan Medical and Dental Council. The hearing was canceled at Durrani's request upon his claim he had contracted Covid. "I admit it. I hope he gets it. But I'm sure he's lying to play whatever game he has going on," I told our clients in an email.

Let me be clear. I hope Durrani dies a miserable, horrible death and I hope he does soon. I believe spine cancer would be perfect. I make no apologies for the sentiment. All our clients deserve a few minutes alone with him.

Chapter 86

IRS

"The harder the life. The sweeter the song."
—From "Crazy Heart" Movie

In June 2021, imagine my shock when I heard the IRS out of Lexington, Kentucky U.S. Attorney's office, opened a criminal investigation and issued subpoenas to my former secretary, Maria Dallas, my retired secretary, and my accountant, Gary Collier. No one contacted me prior to any of this news.

Susan Lawson, Chairman of the Kentucky Character & Fitness Committee, no doubt began this. If not her, Jane Herrick, Kentucky Bar Counsel. If not her, some other enemy. Their hatred and obsession for me has no boundaries. This included their belief I should not be paid for work.

I learned of the IRS investigation when Maria Dallas called me and said: "Hey, two investigators just left my house." Maria informed me all they asked.

Then, my accountant, Gary Collier, called and said they contacted him, too.

How did I respond? Unlike all the bad lawyers out there who would advise me to do nothing, I followed my own advice. If you're innocent, fight back. After they also met with Gary Collier, I sent the following:

Gary told me about your meeting with him.

I want to provide some more information.

The loans which came from Charles Deters, Deters Company, Judy Phillips, Dr. Kurtzman and Barrister Capital never came in big one-time amounts. They came as we needed money. Dad would write checks, Deters Company would write checks, Judy would, Kurtzman would, Barrister Capital would wire as they still do. The $65,000 every two weeks you see from the bank records you no doubt have reflect this. Maria was supposed to tell Gary they were loans.

I was and am personally obligated for all these loans. I'm the only one obligated. No one else. From 2013 through now. Not the law firm. Me.

All the Durrani clients were signed up for the most part before my Ohio retirement. We have kept them happy for one reason – ME. If you ask anyone connected to Deters Law from lawyers to staff, they will tell you – Eric is the key to all. I hope you paged through the book I sent. (I sent them the picture/story book that the staff put together for me with the clients.)

I'm allowed to be paid what my value is. The KBA wants to ignore that fact. And, I make no secret that we kept the KBA in the dark on purpose. I refused to turn over my 2019 and 2020 (not done) tax returns to them NOT because anything wrong, but to avoid their stupidity in reviewing.

When ____________ settled in ______, I was paid $_____________. That's all the money you have seen go in my accounts and out to places. I will be reporting all of it on my 2020 tax return in October.

Also, I have to put money back into the firm on a regular basis. Loans from me. This will continue.

Barrister Capital covers payroll on loans from me. I cover the rest, plus a few cases. We just got a $______fee.

From 2013 to 2019, it truly was survival week to week.

Our bank accounts will reflect huge checks going in 2019/2020 from those two settlements and checks going out to creditors, experts, etc. In 2019, Dad was paid back $2 million.

I also must assume this began as a criminal investigation because I was accused of "embezzlement" and "tax evasion."

I have NEVER embezzled money. Again, the money was my money or borrowed by me.

Someone, the KBA I assume, made you think I was a crook. If the KBA told the IRS I was a crook, I understand why you would take that serious.

The lawsuit against my Dad involved my getting another $____________ which you see in my accounts. That will be addressed on my 2021 tax return.

The activity in accounts involve my concern about inflation/cash. So I have been putting money in real estate and beginning some other businesses. All are properly set up, tax ID, sub-S selections and taxes will be paid. I need to protect my money to have it to continue helps the victims in this $2 million a year cost litigation. This could go on for years. If I don't finance it, it falls apart.

Eric C. Deters & Partners, Inc. (Associates) has been kept open. Why? To resolve any loan issue when Durrani is over. Susan Lawson just can't accept this. Look at the Kentucky Secretary of State. It's still active. Only ONE reason, the loan issue. When Gary suggested we close it, I reminded him we needed to keep it open to pay back the loans when it was ALL over.

We also created the present Ohio law firm if you wondered not for any tax reasons, but ONLY because the evil judge, Mark Schweikert, attacked our fee agreements. Therefore, we created a new Ohio law firm to correct all our fee agreements. Every client signed again. We also wanted to get out of the jurisdiction of the KBA. The KBA can't hurt Glenn Feagan and me operating in Ohio.

Everyone is obsessed with me and what I'm doing in the Durrani cases rather than how bad the Durrani victims are getting screwed by everyone.

I enclose what the pitch is to Netflix. I'm even sending the episode with the request you please watch and delete. We can't have it getting out. (I actually sent them the first episode.)

I'm trusting you.

Don't worry, if you need later we still have.

Our story now includes a criminal investigation of me.

Finally, please reserve all external communication you have received from the KBA and anyone else including all forms 211 and others used by "whistleblowers" etc. Why? One day when this is over, I want to see the defamation of me by those people. (I received this advice from a tax attorney friend.)

I have a mantra for all my former clients who are innocent. Shout it from the mountain tops. Do interviews. Fight back.

I'm following that advice.

I'm sure you guys are sharp as hell. I also will and must assume you're decent human beings.

I hope as you review this matter and investigate further, you use your discretion to determine either I'm innocent (my belief) or if we have innocently or negligently screwed up something – it's civil and we can reach an agreement to remedy.

I forgot to include these two Memos and I wanted to add a few more thoughts.

I was, am and always have been personally obligated on all loans and debt of the law firm.

The fact we considered from 2013-2019 these as advances, I believe, should be revisited by us in the form of possible amended tax returns because I borrowed the money, it went into the firm and the firm paid my bills.

Also, during this entire time 2013-2019, Dad owned the law firm. Not me. But I was the one obligated on all the loans, not him.

Finally, Gary Collier has been my accountant nearly my entire career. He's experienced. I trust him. He's taken the checks every month and he's prepared my taxes. There has never been ONE time where I demanded or attempted to influence anything he's done. In fact, he dealt directly with Maria, not me.

I'm all for legal tax avoidance, but I would NEVER attempt to tax evade. EVER.

If something is disagreed upon, it is most certainly a civil and not a criminal matter.

For this to BEGIN as a criminal investigation is plain and simply wrong.

I'm no fool.

Susan Lawson, Chairman of Character & Fitness, was obsessed with how I was paid and my taxes.

She acted like a know it all.

Of course, she's from Lexington where you are.

In addition, they hated my taunts that I now HAD money. Well, that's in 2020! And as I stated, that tax return is coming in October. (I reported all income on my 2020 tax returns.)

And of course, my politics run contrary to all my enemies in the system.

I know there is no basis for a criminal investigation or charge. If it comes, I'll be more than willing to represent myself, tell my story to a jury and they will be like: WTH are they picking on this guy! Thank God a jury would get to decide my fate!

I saved thousands from Dr. Durrani's scalpel.

I have recovered millions for his victims.

I have saved $42 million in insurance coverage.

We have won $98 million in verdicts that we have to fight on appeal.

I have had to do it all with me borrowing money from anyone and everyone and being constantly under attack. Now, from the IRS.

It's all bullshit.

This must be a first. A criminal investigation where the target borrowed money and paid himself.

Also, I have now established that I called you. No return call.

I have emailed you information.

I have offered full cooperation and have been ignored.

That may be your IRS policy, but that doesn't make it right.

I'm giving you all this information because I'm confident you did not have it and I hope it alters your perspective and discretion.

The agent contacted me and told me he would be in touch when ready to do so. At the time I sent this in for publication in February 2022, I haven't heard anything since June 2021. It would not shock me if they file something. If they do, I'll fight back. Gary claims they move slow.

The year before the IRS criminal investigation, my own father attempted to steal my 15% ownership in the Deters Company, which I owned with my father for nearly forty years. We owned Snappy Tomato Pizza, Wendy's franchises, convenient stores called "Blue Pantry", and real estate.

In April of 2020, in the middle of building a house on eight acres on the northern edge of the family farm, I suffered a permanent betrayal by my father and brother, Jeremy. They refused to give me the promised deed for the eight acres after the house was half built. I sued them. The next week I received the deed. My Dad then attempted to convert an old loan of $300,000 I paid back over twenty years ago as a stock sale.

It would result in my having to sue them and the Deters Company. I represented myself with Alan Statman as my co-counsel. A settlement was reached which included confidentiality. The details of the lawsuit can be found at Kenton Circuit Court Case No. 20-Ci-01009. I will simply say I "won" the settlement.

Also in 2021, Glenn Feagan and I discovered "out of the blue" Ohio Disciplinary Counsel, Joe Caligiuri, actually subpoenaed without any proper notice to us all the law firm's banking records. We immediately filed a federal lawsuit against him. A party to a subpoena is supposed to receive notice so they have the opportunity to object to the subpoena.

After Ohio Disciplinary Counsel subpoenaed our bank records, I sent the following email directly to Joe Caligiuri:

This is my "two cents," not Glenn's response which he will still do.

First and foremost, every check paid out of the IOLTA account was my money or my money lent to the firm.

Not one dollar was a client's money or theft.

As is common knowledge, I finance the Durrani litigation. I'm allowed to do so.

Despite the filed lawsuit, I want to respond in the strongest of terms because I resent not only how the subpoena was improper, but the implication the law firm has done anything illegal or wrong.

The law firm's contracts allow us to hire independent contractors. The law firm doesn't "share" fees.

Nor are fees "shared" with me.

Maria retired. Loretta took over. They handle the check writing, not me. I'm on the account for only if they were out or on vacation. It's totally normal for office staff to be on bank accounts.

Also, it must be stressed, we don't hold any of the Durrani settlement money of our clients. All of that is held by the Special Master.

The worst-case scenario is my money was "co-mingled" with the firm's money, which is really "my money" since I lent it to the firm.

I enclose the reason for each check. Every bit of this was the firm's money or mine.

The obsession with me just never ends with the KBA, Ohio Disciplinary Counsel and enemies from every corner. Every attack, every time, over ten years required me to stay strong and fight back. Everyone wanted to destroy me. If they destroyed me, the Durrani victims would lose. If the adage what does not destroy you makes you stronger, then I am steel.

I can relate to Donald Trump. For six years, he's been under attack by the law, politicians and media for matters always going nowhere. The only way he's survived is fight. I do the same. Only by accepting the fight can I survive and thrive.

Look at this chapter: IRS, father betrayal and bank subpoenas. All false attacks and attempts to harm me. Open season on Eric Deters.

Chapter 87
SYSTEM FAILURE

"I have lived my life, and I have fought my battles, not against the weak and the poor - anybody can do that - but against power, against injustice, against oppression, and I have asked no odds from them, and I never shall."
—Clarence S. Darrow

"The whole enforcement network is supposed to protect patients failed abysmally in this guy's case," said Max Mehlman, a professor of law and director of the Law-Medicine Center at Case Western University in Cleveland and no relation to Dr. Charles Mehlman of Cincinnati Children's Hospital.

Research by consumer advocacy groups and the news media show hundreds of bad doctors like Durrani escape scrutiny each year while continuing to harm patients. The patient protection system is broken.

In the Cincinnati area, countless physicians, nurses and hospital administrators knew for years Durrani performed thousands of unnecessary surgeries but no one reported Durrani to either of the watchdog mechanisms meant to protect patients: the Ohio State Medical Board and the National Practitioner Database.

Medical boards in every state possess the authority to discipline and revoke the licenses of doctors found incompetent, negligent or fraudulent, but the boards investigate only if alerted by others. Physicians who fail to report an incident of malpractice can also be disciplined by the board, but that has never happened in the history of Ohio's medical board which is governed by other physicians.

Lawyers blocked the three University of Cincinnati doctors from sending a warning to the Ohio Medical Board about Durrani.

None of the six hospitals in Cincinnati where Durrani performed surgeries reported him to the National Practitioner Database, even though two of them, Children's Hospital Medical Center and UC's West Chester Hospital, disciplined him repeatedly for failing to produce timely records on his patients and surgeries.

The federal government launched the NPDB in 1990 as a national clearinghouse for adverse reports on doctors. The purpose is to stop dangerous doctors from moving from hospital to hospital or from state to state undetected. The database includes medical malpractice payments, Medicare or Medicaid exclusions, licensing sanctions or any action taken against a physician's hospital privileges or professional society memberships.

Hospitals check the NPDB on physicians who apply for clinical privileges or staff membership and vet all their physicians with staff privileges every two years. State laws require hospitals to notify the medical board of any sanctions reported to the NPDB to determine if licensing action against the doctor is appropriate.

In 1986, when Congress passed the legislation creating the NPDB, it touted the databank as a way to improve health care and reduce fraud and abuse. To pass the measure, Congress appeased the powerful health care lobby, the American Medical Association, by withholding the databank's information from patients. Anyone outside the health care industry, including attorneys, have no access to the database.

The NPDB is only as useful as the information received and as powerful as the willingness of state medical boards and hospitals to act on its information. In 2000, the General Accounting Office, the investigative arm of Congress, found the database riddled with duplicate entries, inaccurate data and missing information.

By 2007, according to *Public Citizen*, two decades after the inception of the NPDB, nearly half of all hospitals in the country never reported a single privilege sanction against a doctor to the NPDB. In the first seventeen years, an average of only 650 sanctions a year were reported to the database. Prior to the opening of the NPDB in 1990, the government estimated 5,000 reports per year and the health care industry itself estimated 10,000 reports.

Also according to *Public Citizen*, state medical boards often fail to discipline doctors facing hospital sanctions. From 1990 to 2009, of nearly 11,000 physicians in the databank with one or more actions taken against their hospital privileges, 55% escaped any state licensing discipline.

Public Citizen found more than a 35% of those physicians who escaped punishment had been reported to the NPDB for serious behavior and performance issues such as sexual misconduct, unsafe practices, insurance and Medicare fraud, licensing fraud and narcotics violations. Two thirds of the doctors who made ten or more medical malpractice payments, the most egregious offenders were not disciplined by their state boards at all.

Hospital peer review committees failed patients as they failed Durrani's victims. Composed of hospital's physicians, the committees used to provide oversight of hospital staff and help ensure quality care by monitoring physician performance and suspending or revoking the clinical privileges of doctors delivering substandard care. With the growing dominance of hospital administrators in medical affairs and the corporate emphasis on hospital revenue over patient safety, peer review committees no longer have any real power to discipline physicians. At least two members of Children's Hospital's peer review committee, its medical executive committee, knew of Durrani's transgressions and never brought them before the committee.

Case Western's Mehlman said the Durrani cases prove Ohio learned little from the infamous case of Dr. James C. Burt and his "love surgery" during the 1970s and 1980s. Burt, a gynecologist at St. Elizabeth Medical Center in Dayton, Ohio, maimed thousands of female patients with experimental surgical techniques he claimed enhanced their sexual responsiveness. In his 1975 book, *Surgery of Love*, Burt claimed his surgery to reconstruct women's genitalia could make them sex crazed. The opposite happened. Most of his patients suffered from sexual dysfunction along with "extensive scarring, chronic infections of the kidney, bladder and vagina, and the need for corrective surgery in many cases."

Burt began to experiment on his patients without their knowledge or consent. *The Dayton Daily News*, printed a flattering article on his "revolutionary" techniques. Burt became a media darling, appearing on the *Donahue* TV talk show and featured in an article in *Playgirl* magazine. By 1978, hundreds of women sought his "love surgery." Burt and St. Elizabeth Medical Center made millions.

The insanity continued for twenty-two years even though doctors and nurses at St. Elizabeth knew Burt butchered patients. When a critical 1988 article appeared in The *New York Times*, malpractice lawsuits followed, including one in which thirty-three women reported they never agreed to have their genitals reconstructed. Many plaintiffs claimed intercourse caused them "excruciating pain" based upon Burt's alterations. In 1989, Burt finally lost his medical license. Malpractice awards against him totaled $21 million. Burt declared bankruptcy and in 2012, Burt died in his hometown of Dayton, Ohio. One would believe a Burt scenario would never happen again. It always happens again.

In the Durrani fiasco, the country's legal system for protecting patients is as broken as its medical system. In Ohio and twenty-seven other states, victims of malpractice and their lawyers can't file a malpractice suit against a doctor unless they first obtain an affidavit of merit from a relevant physician certifying their case has merit. The cost of finding a suitable expert physician to review a patient's records and write up an affidavit can cost up to $10,000 and that's just the beginning of fees paid to experts in the case. Total expert fees run from $50,000 to $100,000 or more. Unless a lawyer is willing to advance the cost of the fee, like we did for Durrani victims, most patients lack those funds, especially when there is no guarantee they will win their case. The thirty-two states that don't require an affidavit of merit set minimum standards for the expert witnesses supporting the patient's malpractice claim.

Many states passed medical malpractice "reform" measures in recent years which restrict when patients file a suit and how much they can collect for damages. States like Ohio, under pressure from health care and insurance lobbyists and their advertising campaigns, passed laws restricting the amount of money juries can award for non-economic damages in malpractice cases as well as the time window when patients can file their claims. Non-economic damages in Ohio are limited to $250,000 or $500,000 under special circumstances. Case Western's Mehlman points out that Ohio's limits are based on a California law passed in 1978. In today's dollars, $250,000 is equivalent to $1.2 million. Ohio has made no adjustment.

"Caps penalize victims who don't have jobs or income and have few economic damages they can claim," said Daniel Hinkle, state affairs counsel for the American Association of Justice, the advocacy group for America's trial lawyers. "The cap systematically discriminates against those who do not have economic damages—children, a stay-at-home parent, the elderly, anyone that you can think of that doesn't have a lot of income. They're not losing wages because they were injured. Even though they're physically in pain and have had that harm done to them, the amount of damages that are available are capped at such a level that an attorney might not even look at their case."

Most states allow two to four years from the time a patient discovers their injury to file a malpractice claim. Ohio and Kentucky two states requiring patients to file in a year from the time of discovery. In many instances, that's not enough time to collect all the patient records and witness depositions to determine who was responsible for the patient's injury. Mehlman said the one-year statute of limitations leads to "shotgun" lawsuits where patients and their attorneys name "everyone and anyone" involved in their treatment as part of their claim in order to meet the deadline and still hold to account those responsible.

In addition to the statute of limitations, Ohio is unique in imposing another recent malpractice "reform" called a statute of repose limit of four years. The statute provides a patient just four years from the time of their injury to file suit against a physician or hospital—regardless of when they first discover the malpractice.

I once handled a case in which a woman discovered ten years after the fact she never required a career ending, life altering open heart surgery. She only found out after ten years when a new cardiologist reviewed the scans from the surgery. Why should this woman not have a claim? I filed it, not knowing about the statute of repose in Ohio. When I learned of this injustice, we argued for a fraud exception, a tact we took in the Durrani cases too, with no success. In other words, why should someone who fraudulently conceals their malpractice benefit from the delay in discovery? The statute of repose rewards those able to conceal their malpractice.

Passage of the laws constraining malpractice claims in Ohio and other states in 2008 and 2009 followed a massive lobbying and advertising effort by the health care and insurance industries falsely claiming "frivolous" malpractice suits were driving up the cost of health care. A 2007 study by *Public Citizen*, titled "*The Great Medical Malpractice Hoax*," revealed medical malpractice payments actually declined since 1990, based on data from the NPDB.

From 1991 to 2005, the number of individual medical malpractice payments dropped more than fifteen percent and the annual average of those payments, based on inflation, fell eight percent. Million-dollar verdicts were less than three percent of all payments in 2005. And nearly two-thirds of all payments involved death or major injury. So-called "frivolous" suits, or payments for insignificant injuries, accounted for less than one-third of one percent of all payments in 2005.

The "frivolous" lawsuit argument is bogus. No lawyer wants to file a lousy lawsuit.

Public Citizen concluded in its report "the real medical malpractice crisis continues to be inadequate patient safety, rather than the legal system. Instead of being distracted by business lobby myths about the court system, health care providers should improve patients safety and better protect the health of patients."

Hundreds of thousands of Americans die every year from medical mistakes. Most never become lawsuits. Most never know about the mistake.

Beyond the laws restricting the timing and awards in malpractice suits, states like Ohio which elect their judges also give a judicial advantage to hospitals, insurers, physicians, and their lawyers over their less wealthy constituencies. The health care and insurance industry pour millions of dollars into judicial campaign coffers, electing those judges who are more certain to share their point of view. With the U.S. Supreme Court's 2010 ruling in *Citizens United*, they pour millions more into advertising campaigns without revealing their identities. In Ohio and most other states, judges who are assigned cases involving major campaign donors decide for themselves whether to step aside and let another judge preside.

The hospitals in the Durrani cases deserve criminal prosecution. Case Western's Mehlman believes so, especially at Children's Hospital and UC Health's West Chester, where both doctors and administrators were aware of Durrani's crimes. Both hospitals shared in the millions of dollars in revenue Durrani brought into their coffers through unnecessary surgeries. Why shouldn't they share the criminal liability as well? "Their medical staffs should have been on top of this. They have a legal responsibility to assure the quality of care. They have a duty to investigate," Mehlman said. We pushed the U.S. Attorney and Joe Deters, Hamilton County prosecutor, to file criminal charges against the hospitals. Nothing. In the middle of his "assistance" of our cause, Children's Hospital honored Joe Deters at their annual dinner.

The authors of a paper published in 2017 in the medical journal *Clinical Orthopedics and Related Research* argue there is legal precedent for prosecuting hospitals which benefit financially from unnecessary surgery under a doctrine called "willful blindness." In its ruling in a 2011 patent dispute case, *Global-Tech Appliances v SEB,* the U.S. Supreme Court stated that "a willfully blind defendant is one who takes deliberate actions to avoid confirming a high probability of wrongdoing and who can almost be said to have actually known the critical facts." The authors conclude that "willful blindness, invoked in Global-Tech, may expose hospitals to health-fraud prosecutions."

Many patient advocates claim the first step is to improve the reliability and completeness of the National Practitioner Database and to provide the public access to its information. "You can find out more information about whether your toaster is bad than whether your physician is a hatchet," said Robert Oshel, a former official of the NPDB, told *Public Citizen*. "It's just nuts."

Data sent to the NPDB should be standardized into a national format to eliminate discrepancies and confusion among state reports. Loopholes which allow hospitals not to report offending physicians should be closed. This includes eliminating the requirement that a physician face at least a 30-day suspension of hospital privileges before being reported to the bank. Likewise, hospitals should not be allowed to make malpractice payments for physicians without naming them in order to hide their identity from the database. The trick hospitals play on reporting is ask a victims' lawyer to dismiss the doctor from the lawsuit and the hospital will settle. Every victim's lawyer agrees to that term in order to settle, including me. No lawyer wants to block his client from a fair resolution with just compensation by being adamant who pays the money.

While state medical boards report their own actions against physicians to the database, they often fail to check the records of physicians who apply to work or are already practicing in their state. Although it costs a mere $2 per physician to search the NPDB data bank, thirty state medical boards used the database fewer than 100 times in 2017, according to the federal Health Resources and Service Administration. Thirteen state boards never consulted it once. Even though states have the option of receiving automatic updates from the NPDB every 24 hours, only 13 of them subscribe to the service.

It's all a scam to protect doctors and hospitals, not patients or the public.

State legislators should push for stronger actions by state medical boards or create more oversight. They could begin by changing the makeup of those governing the medical boards so they aren't dominated by physicians and their sympathetic view toward other physicians facing discipline. Although I suspect friends of physicians would gain the appointment.

In Ohio, the governor appoints twelve members of the board, nine of whom are physicians and three who are non-physicians representing the public. "State legislatures have completely fallen down on the job," Sidney Wolfe told *MedPage Today* in 2018. Wolfe is founder and senior advisor of Public Citizen's Health Research Group. "There is not a state that can't find cases, just from the newspapers. Why aren't they having hearings and demanding information from the boards? We need to put medical boards on the hot seat."

State legislatures should insist medical boards put more information on their websites which is accessible and meaningful to the public. In Ohio, the medical board website has no direct link to a list of doctors facing disciplinary charges.

Instead, consumers must look up the status of an individual physician's license, and the disciplinary information is incomplete and full of legalese.

Durrani's license is now listed as permanently revoked by Ohio's medical board. The website page lists only Durrani's alleged prescription abuses and nothing regarding his unnecessary surgeries, his harming of patients or his bilking of Medicare for millions of dollars. To find those details, you have to click on the page's "view" link and download the documents filed there by the Kentucky Board of Medical Licensure. As in many states, Ohio's medical board rarely disciplines doctors for substandard care or for dangerous and deceptive practices. Information which would alert patients who might seek their treatment.

The one physician in Cincinnati who cared enough about patients to go on the legal record against Durrani, fellow spine surgeon Mehlman, proved his fears justified. In September of 2020 Children's Hospital suspended his admission and operating privileges. A month later, he sued the hospital for seizing "every opportunity to… take unjustified disciplinary action" against him in retaliation for his whistleblowing and open criticism of Durrani. The lawsuit is active at the time of publication. The lawyer representing Cincinnati Children's against Dr. Mehlman? You guessed it. David Brittingham of Dinsmore & Shohl. The lawyer "representing him" at his Durrani deposition. Alan Statman demanded Brittingham and Dinsmore remove themselves from the Mehlman lawsuit with a clear conflict.

Although the hospital received no complaints about Mehlman in his first fourteen years with the hospital, the lawsuit alleges his problems with the hospital's administration began in 2012 when he first testified in a medical malpractice case against Durrani. The suit alleges the harassment and retaliation continued for the next eight years and culminated in his suspension in 2020 for refusing to leave his established practice on Children's main campus and move to the hospital's new Liberty Township facility twenty-two miles away. Children's is on a mission to punish Mehlman and he's fighting back.

Not one of the bogus complaints about Mehlman that Children's alleges involves patient care.

Chapter 88

Juries & Verdicts

"I returned, and saw under the sun, that the race is not to the swift, nor the battle to the strong, neither yet bread to the wise, nor yet riches to men of understanding, nor yet favour to men of skill; but time and chance happeneth to them all."
—Ecclesiastes 9:11

It is difficult to comprehend how any jury listens to a case that includes Durrani not being present, hear our experts testify for our clients, listen to our clients testify and then vote for Durrani. Any rational person would have to know something is up. The fact we lost 30% of the cases proves how cold jurors can sometimes be and you also never know what agenda a juror may have. Despite the jury selection process, jurors often lie and you never know when a "friend" of the defense is selected just like the defense never knows if a "friend" of ours makes it on.

Also, despite admonitions from the Court, I believe jurors google information, but do not announce it to other jurors. If I sat on one of these juries, I would have the same temptation.

A jury heard our case for Bunnavuth Chhun in which he testified he walked across Cambodia as a child to escape the Khmer Rouge. He is such a good man. Even the pessimist Alan Statman thought we would win his case. We lost.

In Hamilton County, Ohio, 95% of medical malpractice cases are won by the defense at trial. This doesn't count cases which settle before trial. We have won 70%. This is 165% swing to us. No one can question the merit of the Durrani cases.

The total amount of the verdicts we won to date is $120,754,790 against Durrani and CAST. Out of that amount, over $20,000,000 is recoverable under Ohio law and under the Medical Protective insurance policies of Medical Protective.

As of the publication of this book, Medical Protective refused to pay any verdict. Every verdict is on appeal. The Setters verdict appeal is final, but Medical Protective still won't pay the verdict. A federal lawsuit is pending to force Medical Protective to pay it. Judge Barrett has the case and has sat on Medical Protective's fully briefed Motion to Dismiss for a year. He grants it, we appeal. He overrules it, we could take discovery and depositions and have a trial. It's my opinion, Medical Protective will never allow the trial to happen.

Dr. Wilkey once insured by Medical Protective, went to trial in St. Louis on a case because he refused to settle. He won. Yet, Medical Protective agreed to pay a large sum during the trial. It baffles him Medical Protective refuses to pay these victims when their claims have merit, unlike the one against him.

Medical Protective has not made one offer on one single case. We have made a million-dollar demand on each one. We reduce it to $500,000 at trial. Not one offer is made despite their ceaseless losing.

$42 million would be only $100,000 per victim with a claim under the policy. The policies are broken down by year. They have failed to even offer a year under the policy for those harmed during that year.

The reason for Medical Protective's position?

Our entire team believes it is for two reasons: they simply can and choose to be cruel and their hatred for me. Their hatred for me is because I have waged this war and not "sold out" the clients. If one is judged by one's friends and/or enemies, I am honored Medical Protective, all these hospitals, all the defense law firms and Durrani hates me. They hate me because I have kept the battle going for a decade and refuse to allow them to crush me and the victims.

Our team is also puzzled by Judge Barrett's refusing to rule on the Motion to Dismiss in the bad faith and unfair claims practices case. He entered an Order advising the parties to conduct discovery and not wait for his ruling. He then reversed course and instructed both sides to wait for a ruling.

We believed Judge Barrett's ties to the "well heeled" in the community hurt us when it came to the hospitals because he has friends who serve on those boards. But Medical Protective? Why does he not let them have it? He has before all the facts you have in Chapter 92. Those facts come from the lawsuit.

In a deposition, Durrani claimed it took lengthy counseling in Pakistan to "get over" his hatred for me. I'm confident his hatred remains considering I'm the one who pushed for his prosecution and sued him over 500 times. I drove him out of the United States and he lost the life he lived here.

Every jury loss is painful. It hurts me for each client who loses. However, we appeal and fight to the end. If Medical Protective won't pay our victories, we won't allow their wins go easy into the night.

When hundreds of millions of dollars are paid out within a year or two in the Michigan State, Ohio State and Olympic sex cases involving many who were improperly touched (that too is evil, wrong and devastating), and the Durrani victims suffered unnecessary spine surgeries, it is agonizing as a comparable to the Durrani victims both in settlement amounts and swiftness in resolution.

The cost to defend, try and appeal all these cases over ten years has cost Medical Protective near what they could have paid to resolve it. On top of the attorney fees and expect fees they have paid, they now face over $20,000,000 in collectible verdicts. Medical Protective chose to pay lawyers, experts and lose over and over again rather than compensate victims they know deserve it. It's all pure evil. Lawyers and law firms have collected hourly rates on these cases for ten years. These large law firms have seen the Durrani litigation as a money-making billing bonanza.

Before 2013, all of these large law firms' medical malpractice departments slowed down. How do I know? We heard of their layoffs. In addition, Walt Haggerty, West Chester's counsel, asked me before all the Durrani cases: "Eric, why don't you file some medical malpractice lawsuits, we need the business."

We will not stop trying these cases. Judge Reece is awarding prejudgment interest and attorney fees where relevant on our wins. Even after the $42 million is accounted for, prejudgment interest and attorney fees will make trying all these cases worthwhile for all our clients and Deters Law and we will. Those two items are payable on top of the $42 million under the policies.

As of the publication of this book, since April 2020, Judge Michael Barrett has a fully briefed Motion to Dismiss on our unfair claims and bad faith practices lawsuit. Whether he does the right thing or not is in his hands. All he needs to do is overrule it, allow us to conduct discovery against Medical Protective and set it for trial. What do you think happens? Medical Protective will never allow a jury to hear what they concocted as described in Chapter 92.

I promised the Durrani victims I will spend every dollar I have and die broke and living in a barn if I must before we stop pursuing these evil doers. I mean it.

From day one, the solution to this entire litigation was simple. The Courts should have properly lowered the boom on Durrani and Medical Protective. They did not. They have not. They should have at least given us our trials. It is easy. They could have set aside a room somewhere in Hamilton County to try Durrani cases. They could have tried them even through Covid by testing and other measures. They could have tried them in groups. Judge Ruehlman understood this with his December 15, 2015 Order.

No judge has ever ordered the President of Medical Protective to his chambers for a mediation. Judges, especially federal Judges, do this all the time. No judge in the Durrani cases ever has. While I live the maxim, where there is a will, there is a way, the judges in the Durrani matter do not.

We have signed up thirty more clients against Children's after the settlement with them. These cases are still timely because Durrani fled the country. In 2021, Glenn Feagan sent the following letter to Rob Carpenter and David Brittingham:

Is there any interest to have a mediation of our current cases with Mark Arnzen or another mediator?

A few points that we want to stress:

1. Regardless of the coming ruling on flight, which we expect to win, we have cases which will survive because they were filed in time regardless. If we win, nearly all or all will survive.
2. Dr. Charles Mehlman will be one of our experts in every one of these cases. In the history of malpractice in America, we suspect no Plaintiff has had an expert who:

A. Has never been sued and,

B. Works at the Defendant Hospital and,

C. Has a lawsuit going forward against the Defendant for being punished for complaining about the doctor subject of the malpractice.

3. Cotter proved the strength of our negligent credentialing claim. And, we have cases whose surgery dates follow that date and August 2008 when Durrani was forced to resign. Durrani performed over 200 surgeries at Children's after being forced out.
4. We are now in possession, even though we didn't need it, of even more damaging evidence against Dr. Duranni from the countless Children's employees who have emailed our office.

Let us know if Children's would like to end their Durrani issue once and for all. I believe our track record proves we are capable of litigating these cases as long as we need to.

They ignored it as always. Arrogance and evil is are a helluva combination.

Many of these children endured surgeries with Durrani after Children's fired him in August of 2008. This means they involve the Cotter time frame and juries will award massive sums when they are tried.

In the history of malpractice cases, I suspect no hospital has had one of their own serve as an expert against them, while he works there, while suing them for their punishing him for complaining about the doctor the Defendant in the malpractice case. If they fire Mehlman, all the better for his lawsuit and ours.

Chapter 89
KENTUCKY RETIREMENT

"Be more concerned about your character than with your reputation, because your character is what you really are, while your reputation is merely what others think you are."
—John Wooden

After my reinstatement request, Character & Fitness sat on my request for a year, doing nothing to advance it through the process. After I complained, they conducted a half-hearted investigation then sat on it for another year. When they finally held my hearing, I played the game as counseled by Jason Nemes and Joe Lambert, two connected lawyers I hired to help me. Jason is a Louisville attorney and legislator who sits on the committee funding the Courts and Joe Lambert served as the former Chief Justice of the Kentucky Supreme Court. It made no difference. The committee unanimously recommended against me, followed by the Board of Governors.

In December 2019, the Kentucky Supreme Court ordered me to have a psychological examination and ordered a new hearing before Character & Fitness. This obviously signaled hope. I heard the Court deadlocked and this was a compromise. I rolled with it. I took the exam with Dr. Paul A. Ebben in Lexington on January 28, 2020. The report was completed on February 11, 2020. The highlights: I passed with a perfect score on the MMSE-2 test. I had a normal profile under the PAI test. I passed the MCMI-III. I had no mental issues. The report concluded: *"So to address the Supreme Court's question, it is the undersigned's opinion and conclusion, within reasonable psychological certainty, based on information provided, that Mr. Deters does, in fact, possess the "capacity" to follow all legal and ethical guidelines relevant and pertinent to the practice of law in the state of Kentucky, but as far as his willingness to do so, that remains to be seen, as he has not practiced law in quite some time. The bottom line is, he is capable of ethical conduct if he chooses that path."*

As each year passed from my initial reinstatement, the KBA would add on anything and everything from my life. I refused to live my life to appease them because I found it impossible to appease them. They now added my courtroom and courthouse ban. When Character & Fitness scheduled another hearing, I decided no more kicking me around and no more begging and pleadings. I showed up in my Bulldog Mafia T-Shirt and gave it back to them. From *Shawshank Redemption*, I gave them the Morgan Freeman treatment. They changed the question not whether I could follow the rules since I passed my exam, but whether I would follow the rules. Of course the answer is, who knows, but I told them if they reinstated me, I would follow their rules. And, I would have. Their changing the question simply proved nothing mattered to them when it came to me.

The committee, all masked up and socially distanced, even arranged a Fayette County police officer as security to "protect" them from me. The Board of Governors hired police security at every hearing I had with them over this process. The message to the Board by Bar Counsel: this lawyer is so bad we need security. Complete bullshit. Susan Lawson, Chairwoman, remained obsessed with how I earned money. I refused her middle of the hearing request for my tax returns. They never properly asked for them prior to the hearing. I stressed my efforts for the Durrani victims proved myself more than fit to practice law. They concluded I simply could not be trusted to follow their rules. I would refer to the Character & Fitness Committee, all lawyers, as "human excrement." I meant it.

They failed to grasp an argument I made regarding how in history, Martin Luther King, Jr., Rosa Parks and others broke rules that deserved breaking. They also concluded I simply failed to respect them. Yes, I don't. Imagine if you could not work in your profession if you failed to respect others in your profession. Hey painter, unless you respect all other painters, you can't be a painter.

Character & Fitness unanimously rejected my reinstatement, followed by the Board and followed by the Kentucky Supreme Court. Jane Herrick, Bar Counsel, wrote the scathing report that soon found its way to all my enemies.

Months later, Jane Herrick, Kentucky Bar Counsel, filed a Motion for Contempt against me to the Kentucky Supreme Court. At the date of publication, the motion has not been heard.

I told the Kentucky Supreme Court the following:

Applicant. Pro Se, submits this Brief on his reinstatement. I do not seek oral argument. This Court remanded me to Character & Fitness to have a psychological exam to determine if I was capable of following the "rules." It's taken a year since I had such exam to get back before this Court. I "passed" the exam.

So what did Bar Counsel and Character and Fitness do? They changed the question to: will I follow the rules. I have made it clear I will follow the rules if reinstated.

I also made it clear that after eight (8) years of being in limbo and the mistreatment endured by me by Bar Counsel and Character & Fitness and their desire to "keep me out" no matter what that I was not about to beg and plead with them because I have had enough of them.

I'm mad. I have a right to be based upon the process I endured. But, I will follow the rules if reinstated.

I am no risk to the public.

I seem to be a risk to the KBA not having every lawyer walk, talk and act the same.

I have committed no crimes.

I have not stolen money.

I have not committed any frauds.

I have not been dishonest.

I have committed no acts of moral turpitude.

I have no alcohol, porn, drug or gambling problem.

I have committed no dastardly deed.

Yet here I am.

It is simply wrong.

I attach the 21-page Oral Argument before the Board of Governors.

It summarizes the gist of this matter.

I have been punished enough. I passed my exam. To not reinstate me because Bar Counsel, Character & Fitness and the Board of Governors believe I won't follow the rules is barring me on some form of anticipatory breach. Remember, I am being "disbarred" by this reinstatement process, yet Bar Counsel has never moved to disbar because there is no basis.

They have NEVER said do ABC and we will reinstate you. It is the general vague desire on their part, I guess, that I'm not supposed to be angry and speak out about the system and HOPE they would reinstate me one day. It's absurd.

This is for the record. The Court's decision is an example of how the fact someone such as a Supreme Court justice acquires a high position does not mean they are wise, competent or "get it right."

This Court sanctions corruption through its Supreme Court Rules. For example, allowing bar counsel to object to the automatic reinstatement and force me to go through reinstatement in back-to-back years is the same as a prosecutor being allowed to object to the automatic release of a prisoner and forcing the prisoner to convince a Court he will not reoffend. It's absurd. It's wrong. And this Court allows that rule to exist. What's worse, it was allowed to be used against me by the disgraced Thomas Glover. I was suspended eight years on 180 total day suspensions under this rule. All from an organization in which due process should be important. (Thomas Glover abruptly resigned as Bar Counsel. They held no party and made no announcement. I heard there was misconduct. The KBA gave him the sole authority to put me through hell.)

Then there is the absurd rule that an attorney can't "retire" with pending discipline. Only a lawyer in Kentucky can't retire as he chooses. That rule can never pass constitutional muster. For the record, I have retired, quit or whatever you want to call it. Then the Court allowed my reinstatement process to take four years and says, "so what?" Then the Court by rule doles out immunity to everyone in the process on the "prosecutor" side. Immunity means you get away with a wrong. It doesn't mean you don't do wrong. I will always fight immunity laws.

But MOST egregious is how this Court tries to apply SCR 3.120(5.7)(b) to me. That rule was adopted just a year or two ago and long after my suspension. It can't be applied to me not only because of that clear fact in the record, but that rule can't apply to me because I don't work in the law firm from when I was suspended. I believe the rule was adopted from Ohio just for me. I work in an Ohio law firm created two years ago, under an Ohio lawyer, working on Ohio cases with the express consent and guidelines of the Ohio Supreme Court. This Court thinks it's the Court of the world? You're not. And reciprocity doesn't apply to an Ohio retired lawyer. So this Court has no authority under number 2 of its Order and its simply further proof the corruption of this Court that the Court can get it so wrong from the record. Seven Justices. All their staff lawyers. How could they get this so wrong? Corruption.

Also, there was nothing inappropriate about my compensation. I'm allowed to be paid what my Dad wanted to pay me. Period. And I filed proper tax returns. Of course, the Committee waited until the hearing to ask for my 2019 and 2020 tax returns and I said, "hell no." They knew Jason Nemes no longer represented me and they sent the request to him, not me. Last I checked there were no legal ceilings what a law firm could pay its staff. I am a most valuable employee.

The Court got one thing right. I do not respect this Court, the KBA, the system and the legal profession or the Ohio Court system, all for good reasons. They are corrupt. I prove it every day with facts. Also, I am completely self-aware. And I am now this Court's worse nightmare being free of any lawyer rules. Enjoy all my broadcasts which will be constant and relentless under my First Amendment rights. The entire legal system is a joke. And I'll spend the rest of my life sharing facts with the public. Also, enjoy the documentary coming out soon which will show the world how corrupt you are.

Also, this Court has no authority whatsoever over me to promote Deters Law, an Ohio law firm, individually, all I want. I could spend money singing the praises of any law firm I want, including Deters Law and I will. Any member of the public can promote any law firm he or she wants under their First Amendment rights.

How long it takes for a case to move through the Kentucky appeals court process is preposterous. How this Court takes so long to do anything proves its laziness and inability to manage.

This Court as reflected by its decision upholding unconstitutional orders of the Governor locking down this state during the phony Covid epidemic proves this Court needs a remedial class on Constitutional Law. Anarchy? The political party of this Court majority has proven it supports anarchy. This Court talks about the Constitution when the Court has ignored it over and over again. I always embrace the Constitution and Bill of Rights, as I do here again.

This Court takes months and months off every year. This Court is lazy. This Court is political biased and shameful in the process. This Court is disconnected from how the public knows and feels how justice is being dispensed in this state. The entire discipline process is biased towards the small practitioner. The entire legal profession and court system preys upon the public. Large law firm lawyers control the KBA as they do the Bar Associations across the country, and they therefore rarely face discipline.

The legal system and this Court protects itself by its rules relating to criticism of itself. It's beyond comical that the system and the Court tries to restrict free speech rights of lawyers. If you ask lawyers who don't work in big law firms what they think of the legal profession and Court system and bar process they will tell you it sucks. Yet, does anyone ever hear lawyers say that publicly?

The Court has rules designed solely to protect the Court from shame when the Court and system deserves all the shame it gets. It brings shame upon itself. I'll be publicizing through advertising and all my platforms how disgusting this Court and the system is for the rest of my life.

I have done more free legal work and fought harder to help the little guy in this state and Ohio than any lawyer I have ever met. This Court's members couldn't do what I do every day for my entire career because it's too lazy , doesn't care and has the mental agility of a small soap dish.

Every ill of this country can be traced to big law firms who control the American bar, control Congress, controls state legislature, controls the judges and are employed in all the state and federal swamps writing the complicated laws that they get rich off in their practices while destroying the country. Yes. As Al Pacino said in "Devil's Advocate" there is a reason Satan chose the legal profession.

Then there are the rules this Court makes on elections. You mean the world should not be allowed to know which political party you're in and your position on political issues? For example, in Northern Kentucky, every voter needs to know Michelle Keller supports Joe Biden and abortion on demand.

Meanwhile an attorney who admits whether truth or not he has a porn, alcohol, drug or gambling problem can escape any consequences. It's absurd.

I'm just getting started against this Court and the KBA and the legal profession.

This Court is disconnected from reality. I hold my head high not in shame of my words and actions against this profession. This Courts attempt to harm me not only fails, it strengthens me. This court is not omnipotent. It rules wrong every day. Courts bring shame upon themselves and then punish those who shout shame. I do not respect this Court, the legal profession or the KBA because it deserves none, so therefore I give it none.

The Court wants contrition for what? Being abused by Ms. Herrick and the Character and Fitness process over a course of a decade.

Matt Hammer committed perjury by under oath defaming me and accusing me of forging his signature. Yet, the Court uses my actions against him, justified as they are, against me. The legal issue I'm battling is immunity NOT whether he lied under oath. That's a fact we proved.

I proudly went to jail fighting for the Durrani clients to get their trials by protesting the Ohio system's failures. You seven legal dwarfs would never go to jail for a righteous cause.

I never threatened to burn down the Hamilton County courthouse. What I said is: "Is that what Durrani victims have to do to get their trials?" Yet, out of all the miscreants in Hamilton County, I'm the only person in history banned from the Courthouse. What an honor.

If I am guilty of the unauthorized practice of law and I'm not, a prosecutor can charge me. I welcome the jury trial.

I am allowed to work in this building. I own it.

The Conclusion by Bar Counsel is taken completely out of context. I DO make sure everything is done and completed. I do so by making sure attorneys meet deadlines. It's my job. Lawyers approve and sign ALL filings. Unfortunately, I do have to work through and with lawyers when I once did it myself.

I work for Deters Law and Glenn Feagan is my supervisor.

I informed Jane Herrick I retired. On July 2021, Loretta Little sent an email asking to confirm this too. There was no response. I do know this. Everyone has a right to retire. Period.

I never got a copy of the August 13, 2021 Order.

Regardless, EVERYTHING until that Order is not final. So ANYTHING prior to that is a moot issue too.

The KBA acts as if they control me for the rest of my life. They don't.

In addition, I have retired.

I am NOT a suspended lawyer.

I am a retired lawyer.

Bar Counsel also doesn't make it clear whether they are asking for criminal or civil contempt, direct or indirect.

I most certainly have done nothing direct or criminal.

In addition, since the Ohio unauthorized issue where I told Ohio make it clear what I can or can't do. I adopted the attached. This is so there are no misunderstandings. Ohio knows this is the basis of what I can do. It's the same for Kentucky. I'll place it here for emphasis:

Eric E. Deters

859-250-2527 (Cell)

eric@ericdeters.com

Retired Ohio Lawyer 2013

Retired Kentucky Lawyer 2021

No Current Law License

(All information Eric E. Deters provides here by phone, text or in person is either general information or the relaying of law or case specific information under the supervision of an attorney. He also may offer his personal opinion to friends on matters who have no client relationship with Deters Law.)

Office Manager

Spokesperson on Official Firm Matters

Paralegal

Victim's Advocate

The firm name is the Ohio law firm's name. The sign depicts the name.

As reflected by Covid, lawyers and law firms can practice anywhere.

The firm website is the same because it's the firm's name.

Jane Herrick, the KBA and the Court, have no right to tell me what I can do in an Ohio law firm under the supervision of the owner of that firm. The KBA has successfully kept me from being reinstated. I can't practice law. I can't sign pleadings. I can't take depositions. I can't appear in Court. I can't try cases. Why is this not enough for the KBA? I will never shut up about the KBA and the legal system and I'll always work in law. No one can stop me from doing that.

Rather than simply recuse herself on my contempt issue, Justice Michelle Keller chose to file a disclosure. She disclosed her doctor husband works at St. Elizabeth Medical Center, against which Deters Law fought for the unvaccinated and her daughter works for the law firm defending St. Elizabeth, DBL Law. Here is my response to her disclosure:

The disclosure is an example of what the public abhors about the legal system. There is not a single American Citizen who would read what Justice Keller disclosed and want her to sit in judgment of them if they were where I sit. Rather than just recuse, she wants to see if I object and then decide?

DBL, where I once was an equity partner, are my sworn enemies and everyone knows it. And the Democrats there are no doubt some of Justice Keller's best "buddies." She knows who I'm talking about. They defend St. Elizabeth Medical Center where Deters Law has multiple "battle royales" raging, not just on the vaccine mandate, which Justice Keller also publicly supports.

Her daughter works at DBL Law, her husband works at St. Elizabeth and she's a liberal Democrat. I'm an ardent Trump supporter, and I'm supposed to be "cool" with her sitting in judgment of me? I don't think so. I object to her sitting in judgment of me.

Then in January of 2022, I received an email from Andy Wolfson from the *Courier Journal*. He informed me the Kentucky Judiciary Committee passed out of committee by a 14-2 vote an amendment making a second conviction of the unauthorized practice of law a Class D Felony, not a misdemeanor. This means on a second offense someone could serve five years, not one. Jason Nemes, my prior lawyer, was one of the two no votes. I told Wolfson I could care less because I don't unauthorize practice and the legislature should have more important issues to solve. Just as the Kentucky Supreme Court and KBA passed "Eric Deters" rules, now the legislature passed an "Eric Deters" rule. I know this. If any prosecutor tries to charge me, I'll represent myself and am confident I will never be convicted.

Chapter 90

Children's & University

"Whoever causes one of these little ones who believe in me to sin, it would be better for him to have a great millstone hung around his neck and be drowned in the depth of the sea."
—Jesus

This is a long chapter for a good reason. It relates the entire story and case against Children's and University Hospital. It is all in the public record of the lawsuits filed. It is the compilation of all the evidence and testimony. It might be too much for the casual reader of the story, but I want the world to know all the evidence against these two hospitals. It is more detailed than prior information. Italics indicate a witnesses' affidavit or testimony.

Dr. Zeeshan Tayeb, Durrani's pain doctor, signed an affidavit on August 22, 2017 for the victims.

The content of that affidavit is as follows:

A. I worked for Dr. Atiq Durrani as I have detailed in several depositions in the Durrani malpractice cases for Deters Law.

B. What was not covered in these depositions was the issue I am addressing in this affidavit. I do so based upon personal knowledge from working with Durrani's patients and reviewing patient charts after-the-fact.

C. No matter their medical condition or what the outcome of the surgery, Durrani, after his patient's surgeries, would always inform those patients it took time to heal no matter the condition or the reason for the condition. I learned after-the-fact from discussions with patients, reviewing patient charts and from investigations that he would make misrepresentations to his patients to keep them from going to other doctors or leaving his care. I believe Durrani may have done this so his patients would not learn of any malpractice or fraud on his part in performing the surgeries. However, I did not know this until after-the-fact based on discussions with his patients, reviewing patient charts and from information obtained from investigations.

D. As a post-surgery pain doctor employee on his staff, he used me to treat his post-surgical patients, I believe from my conversations with patients, review of those patient charts and information obtained from investigations that his patients did not suspect Durrani did anything wrong.

E. I believe based upon my conversation with patients, review of those patient charts and information provided from investigations after-the-fact that patients of Durrani were left in poor medical condition following surgery. Additionally, I believe these patients may have been deceived by Durrani into believing that "all was fine." I believe Durrani to avoid any issues, attempted to and in some cases successfully, convinced patients to believe that he had not done anything wrong, which may have resulted in post-surgery issues experienced by many of his patients.

F. While treating Durrani's patients, none of the patients ever brought up BMP-2 or PureGen to me. I am unaware whether Durrani informed his patients that these devices were placed in them. It could be discovered if the patient reviewed the intraoperative reports, but I am uncertain if patients ever did this.

Durrani and Children's Hospital intentionally deceived victims and concealed information in an attempt to avoid civil liability by creating a statute of limitations and/or statute of repose defense.

The statute of limitation and statute of repose issues are all about notice. Durrani and Children's Hospital had notice of what was going on and concealed it from Plaintiffs.

From January 12, 2005 to March 7, 2009, Durrani performed 645 spinal surgeries at Children's.

Mehlman made formal complaints within Children's about Durrani. Mehlman made complaints to "*everybody in the room*" in the pre-op and post-op conferences and Dr. Steven Muething, safety officer. Mehlman told Dr. Wall "the only thing worse than taking this to Dr. Azizkhan is not to take it to him." Dr. Wall, Dr. Crawford, Dr. Ray, Dr. Tamai, Dr. Twee Do were present at the meetings and heard Mehlman's concerns. Mehlman believes these doctors shared his concerns.

Azizkhan served on the Medical Executive Committee at Children's. Mehlman also served on the MEC at Children's a couple years in the late 1990's.

Mehlman believed it was Wall, Rychman and Azizkhan's responsibility to report Durrani to the medical board. "*Surgeons are expected to be quiet, docile Stepford Wives that come and do surgery and come when they're called, and then move on. So, I take exception to the question because it makes it sound like I was weak or somehow not committed to fight to talk to disinterested administrators who were all about corporate protection.*" Azizkhan once refused to culture a house fly for Mehlman when the fly landed on an exposed surgical field. Mehlman saw this as an example of the attitude of management.

In 2006, Wall, the division director, told Mehlman at a pre-op/post-op conference: "*Chuck you've been asked to be quiet.*" This pertained to Mehlman speaking up about Durrani. Mehlman saw this as the low point of his professional career. With emotion, Mehlman responded: *"Eric, the day that I'm quiet in this conference you better check a pulse, because as long as it's my job to teach these residents and these fellows, the next generation of practitioners, how to be ethical and to be evidence-based practitioners, I will continue to speak up."* Mehlman believes Peter Clayton, Azizkhan or Rychman are the source for Wall's "shut up."

Alex Taylor, our client, became Mehlman's and Dr. Rohmiller's patient after Durrani treated him. Taylor's kyphosis could have been treated non-operatively. Mehlman brought it to Wall's attention. At one point Guanciale informed Wall about Durrani issues. Guanciale informed Wall residents were presenting concerns about surgeries being performed by Durrani's. *"I had more conversations with Dr. Wall about that as a result."* Guanciale once called Wall from Toronto on the research issue of Durrani's.

Agabegi held conversations with Wall about Durrani. With respect to Wall, *"I remember in one conversation that I directly had with him that he was concerned and frustrated.* Wall expressed frustration about the alleged external review. Agabegi also spoke to Mehlman and Wall about Durrani.

Stern spoke to Wall and they arranged a Saturday morning meeting in Azizkhan's office. *"I raised the concern that Dr. Guanciale raised to me in his letter. I believe that I shared the letter with Dr. Azizkhan. I had previously shared the letter with Dr. Wall, and Dr. Azizkhan told me that he would look into matters,"* said Stern. Stern first contacted Wall. Stern relayed to Wall what Guanciale wrote. Stern told Wall this must be looked into. *"He was a little reluctant at first, and I told him that if he didn't look into it, I would contact legal counsel at Children's Hospital and ask them to look into it."* Wall never stated the reason for his reluctancy.

In an October 3, 2008 email, Stern wrote to Wall: *"Dr. Mehlman has raised some serious issues here. I believe Durrani is fully entitled to due process, but also think this apparently aggressive behavior might warrant some type of independent evaluation. I believe as a profession we must exercise some oversight, especially when it involves patient well-being."*

Between 2005 and 2008 at the indication conferences at Children's, Wall acknowledged Durrani's indications were discussed. Wall was aware of the research fraud issue. Wall denied ever informing Mehlman he's been told to be quiet. Wall denied Guanciale informing him orthopedic residents were expressing concerns about surgery indications by Durrani. This is a serious credibility issue for Wall based upon Guanciale's and Mehlman's sworn testimony.

Wall claims not to know who from Children's would handle the NPDB reports. This is absurd. More alarming are Wall's answers to the following questions. Do you know why Durrani was able to continue to perform surgeries after his resignation at Children's Hospital Medical Center? *"No."* Were you aware that he was continuing to do surgeries? *"Yes."* Did you have an issue or problem with that? *"Yes."*

West Chester/UC Health, their staff and management, and their executive committee, knew Durrani had issues at Children's before he applied for privileges there in 2009 because they trained him in his residency and Stern. *"How could they not know,"* testified Mehlman.

Wall made a comment once to Mehlman regarding finding a certain number of sociopaths in every category of humans. He made the comment in direct reference to Durrani. Children's knew they harbored a sociopath and chose money over protecting children.

Wall admitted conversations with Durrani in July 2008. The conversations were about personnel issues, research data and surgical indications. Wall called Jamie Moor a *"serious inappropriate sexual relationship. It was brought to my attention by Durrani's wife."* HR addressed the Moor situation, but never resolved it. An action plan was set up, but Durrani failed to comply. Durrani's HR problems were an issue with his employment because it violated policy.

At the meeting referenced in the October 20, 2009 letter was Stern, Azizkhan and Wall. The topics included were the sexual relationship and the research fraud Guanciale referenced. Guanciale was the instigator on the surgical indications issue. It related to something new and spondylolysis. Durrani never recommended non-operative treatment as others would have and recommended doing more surgeries. Wall admits the serious concerns raised by Guanciale about Durrani led to the meeting with Wall, Stern and Azizkhan. Surgical indications and exhausting non-operative means were discussed at the meeting.

Mehlman believes Durrani resigned within several days of the meeting referenced in the October 20, 2009 letter. Mehlman did not know Durrani resigned and kept working at Children's. *"And based on that letter I felt that I needed to- in my capacity as chair, I needed to discuss his concerns with the individuals at the Children's Hospital Medical Center,"* testified Stern. It happened ten days after the meeting. Stern believed Durrani's resignation came from the meeting.

According to Wall, Durrani grew unhappy at Children's over compensation, Jamie Moor and complaints.

Wall doesn't know if Durrani resigned or Children's terminated him. Wall testified he did not want Durrani in the department anymore. This is an unexpected and critical admission by Wall. *"I didn't want to be taking care of him."* He admitted surgical issues were part of it too. *"I would say it was all of the issues."* Wall has no regrets how he handled Durrani at Children's. Wall testified he would never rehire Durrani.

After Durrani's resignation, Stern saw Durrani at a social function. They never spoke about the issues. *"I don't believe I ever spoke with him about the concerns."*

Mehlman testified during board collections period an orthopedic is extra careful. This is where cases a surgeon perform are gathered for review. Mehlman noticed in Durrani an aggressive pattern even during board collections. After he cleared boards, it was *"even more striking."* By aggressive, Mehlman meant *"stuff that I had never seen before."* Mehlman evaluates surgeons and educates surgeons on what is the standard of care. Children's has a very intense and academic experience. Thirty to forty plus fellows come from around the country every year. They have organized educational conferences where cases are presented and discussed. There is a lot of transparency. According to Mehlman, disciplinary action can be taken against a physician under the bylaws outside the peer review process. *"One of the most horrible cases is one of the very last patients who suffered permanent paralysis at our hospital,"* testified Mehlman.

Mehlman is on the editorial board of the *Journal of Pediatric Orthopedics.* Mehlman testified a review of 600 Durrani surgeries by a board-certified orthopedic spine surgeon would be the same as an external review. Our expert, Wilkey performed a review of over 1,000 Durrani surgeries. *"The principle was that I saw behavior and support offered to him that was striking. People like Peter Clayton, Sandy Singleton and other business decision-makers built a machine around him. We never had spine nurses like we did until Durrani was there. We never had schedulers, that I know of, that hung out in the –in clinic just to schedule the cases as they rolled out, and I sure as heck never saw a surgeon have two ORs three days a week,"* testified Mehlman.

In 2008, Sandy Singleton and Beth Stautberg, tried to help Durrani obtain his permanent U.S. residency. Mehlman refused to sign Durrani's permanent U.S. residency given to him by Sandy Singleton.

In 2005, Mehlman doesn't know if Children's knew Durrani was doing fraudulent surgeries. He does believe in 2006, 2007 and 2008 the administration did know. Sandy Singleton, business director, was quite pleased about the money rolling in from Durrani. She received prominent gifts from Durrani including a fur coat. Children's told Mehlman, other doctors and nurses, not to talk about Durrani. It was like *"He whose name we shall not say,"* testified Mehlman.

Mehlman believed Azizkhan was *"incompetent and a punitive vindictive administrator."* When Azizkhan and Rychman were fired, there was *"jubilation amongst many of my surgical colleagues,"* testified Mehlman.

Mehlman did not report Durrani to state medical board *"because of an atmosphere of fear and retribution within my institution, and a fear for my job and fear for retaliation."* Mehlman did not have the power to report to the NPDB. UC lawyers told them not to send the letter. *"I told Guanciale then I was sad that I was unable to sign on to it at that time because of the environment that I worked within,"* testified Mehlman. Mehlman worked in a punitive, vindictive environment where he feared for his job. His *"chief of surgery was no longer agreeing to participate in the process across the street. We were not supported by Azizkhan."*

Mehlman respects Crawford. But, *"he's not perfect. I think Alvin is a reasonably good judge of character and competence, most of the time."* Obviously not when it came to Durrani. *"Dr. Crawford was in a sad and conflicted position with a young man who was commonly referred to as his son."* Dr. Morley from the United Kingdom was the initial Crawford connection to Durrani. Mehlman has it *"on very good authority that Alvin has been moved to the point of tears as he reflected on his own poor judgment with Durrani."*

Peter Clayton is the former business director over all the surgery at Children's Hospital. Months after Durrani left Children's, at an administrative meeting, Peter Clayton asked all the orthopaedic surgeons, *"What's happened to your spine revenue. There's a big drop off."* Mehlman responded: *"Peter, we're doing only indicated surgery."*

"Durrani had an incredibly accommodating environment. I never saw another orthopedic surgeon in my entire career get that treatment. Durrani met with three to four industry representatives a week. So, when surgeons become the beneficiaries of these companies that are dishing out money, it's been shown clearly to change surgeon behavior," testified Mehlman.

Before Durrani left Children's, Mehlman anonymously contacted the FBI about Durrani. Mehlman is unaware of any action.

Wall served on committees at Children's between 2005 and 2008. He knows he's reviewed cases at Children's. He doesn't know the names. He has been involved in root cause analysis committees so he believes he has been involved in peer review committees. Root cause analysis means if there's a serious safety event they will look at the root cause of the permanent injury. He has served on a quality assurance committee. In the early 1990's, he served on the Medical Executive Committee. MEC was a monthly meeting in which they discussed how the hospital is doing and various issues. He's never served on a credentialing committee, but he has participated in the credentialing of physicians for Children's.

Wall admits Crawford considered Durrani as one on his children. Wall claimed to be unaware of complaints from other employees at Children's. Suspended surgeons are not allowed to perform elective surgeries, but Durrani simply claimed they were emergencies.

In 2013, Crawford left Children's. Crawford claims he can't remember Mehlman making allegations against Durrani. This is not believable. Crawford also denies knowing anything about Dr. Mehlman's email allegations. This too is not believable.

While working at Children's full time, Crawford claims he never interacted with other spine surgeons. This is also not believable. He claims he was clueless. This is not believable. He stated: *"I have no knowledge of it."* Regarding all the allegations about Durrani.

On July 1, 2014, Wilkey, a board-certified spine surgeon, performed a review of Children's cases for us and issued a report. The report included the following:

A. "It is important to look at these cases as a whole as they show the lack of supervision of Durrani by this facility during the five years that he was on staff."
B. "From my previous medical experience, being a member of a peer review committee at two other facilities and serving as a former orthopedic department chairman, I am appalled by the lack of supervision from this facility."
C. "Taken as a whole, it is beyond my comprehension that this surgeon was allowed to operate as long as he was given the poor patient selection, complication rates, and use of contraindicated medication. There appears to be a complete failure of the peer review process with respect to Durrani."
D. "Durrani performed novel surgeries in which he was inadequately trained with regards to their indications."
E. "Alarmingly, greater than 100 percent of the patients reviewed had been exposed to Infuse during their surgery which is contraindicated due to their young age."
F. "One has to ask why this was allowed to happen at an institution such as Cincinnati Children's Hospital."

Children's Hospital admits they collected the following sums from Durrani's billings:

2005 – $1,508,555.83	2007 – $3,154,595.72
2006 – $2,202,192.13	2008 – $3,610,137.58

These extraordinary billings by Durrani is why Children's Hospital allowed Durrani to do as he chose, regardless of patient harm. The motive? Money and greed. It is all the more troubling when one considers Children's makes an exorbitant amount of money and would survive without Durrani's stained revenues.

Durrani "resigned" from Children's in an August 8, 2008 resignation letter to Azizkhan Durrani referenced "*inhospitable working environment in the division.*" Azizkhan claimed this was because they moved Jamie Moor from Durrani. In his deposition, Durrani lied and claimed he left for a financial opportunity. It's important to note, Children's never "fired" Durrani. He resigned.

Until the victims saw the news of Durrani's arrest in 2013, they had no idea what Durrani might have done at Children's. It was rational or reasonable for them, upon seeing Durrani arrested for unnecessary surgeries, to retain us at that time.

On November 25, 2005, Children's employee Powell sent an email complaining about unsigned orders of Durrani. This is the first evidence of this problem with Durrani which he never corrected. It is never known by the victims. Children's never released this to any victim and it was concealed by Children's. It is not discovered until discovery and emails are produced.

On December 28, 2005, Children's employee Robinson emailed Probst, Durrani's administrative assistant, regarding Durrani needing to dictate an operative report. Durrani is never made by Children's to correct this practice of not dictating an operative report or dictating it timely. It jeopardized the victims' health in post-operative medical care.

In 2006, the FDA began releasing adverse reports and studies pertaining to BMP-2. As of 2006, the hospitals knew there were issues relating to BMP-2. Despite this knowledge, Durrani and Children's still used BMP-2 in countless patients.

Based upon our statistics from our patients, 72.8% of Durrani's patients at Children's had BMP-2 used in their surgery. Considering BMP-2 is not indicated for minors, this is shocking. All of this happened with Children's full knowledge and consent, but not the knowledge and consent of the children and their parents.

From 2000 through 2009, Children's Hospital settled Durrani cases and never reported them to the NPDB.

On April 23, 2007, there is a Children's email reporting Durrani's failure to do reports.

On April 25, 2007, there is a Children's email regarding problematic issues regarding Durrani.

On May 21, 2007, there is a Children's email reflecting Durrani needs to send a note to Peter Clayton, Children's management, regarding an issue.

On May 31, 2007, there is a Children's email reflecting a problematic issue regarding Durrani.

On June 5, 2007, there is a Children's email reflects a problematic issue regarding Durrani.

On June 11, 2007, there is a Children's email reflecting a problematic issue regarding Durrani.

On June 12, 2007 there is a Children's email reflecting a problematic issue regarding Durrani.

On June 16, 2007, there is a Children's email reflecting a problematic issue regarding Durrani.

On June 21, 2007, there is a Children's email which reflects Children's management wanting to meet with Durrani's *"team"* without Durrani to discuss his problematic issues.

On June 29, 2007, there is an email where Probst states: *"Oh my gosh. Such a man."* This is regarding Durrani.

On July 11, 2007, there is a group of Children's emails that includes Durrani and Probst referencing many issues about Durrani.

On July 16, 2007, Williams and Probst exchange emails regarding complaints about Durrani.

On November 2, 2007, an email at Children's states Durrani missed without reason an important conference at Children's.

In December 2007, Probst stated her and Durrani relationship changes based upon Durrani's personal conduct.

On December 13, 2007, there is a Children's email exchange including Durrani and Probst about surgery scheduling issues.

On December 20, 2007, there is an email at Children's stating Anthem is rejecting BMP-2 as experimental. Children's never informs the victims or any patient or stops its use at Children's.

On January 16, 2008, Dr. Tim Cripe, Children's doctor, complains to Durrani regarding patient issues.

On January 17, 2008, there is an email at Children's stating Anthem is rejecting BMP-2 as experimental.

On January 22, 2008, there is a Children's email regarding Durrani missing an important meeting.

On January 24, 2008, there is a Children's email regarding an issue with Durrani and his patients.

On April 24, 2008, there is a Children's email including Durrani stating BMP-2 is being denied for payment as investigational.

On April 25, 2008, there is a Children's email reporting BMP-2 is denied for surgery by insurance. The email reports Crawford and Durrani were the main users of BMP-2 at Children's.

On May 2, 2008, there is a Children's email reporting BMP-2 is denied for surgeries by insurance.

On May 28, 2008, a lawsuit filed by Alexander Ranus against Durrani is settled by Children's. It is never reported to the National Practitioner Data Bank.

On May 28, 2008, a Children's email reflects problematic issues with Durrani.

On May 30, 2008, billing manager at Children's, Singleton, is "blindsided" by more Durrani issues.

On May 30, 2008, Krissy Probst resigned as Durrani's administrative assistant based upon Durrani having an affair with Jamie Moor, his physician's assistant. Probst testified Durrani would begin surgeries, leave the surgery and allow unsupervised fellows to perform the surgery while Durrani would be in his office with Jamie Moor. Probst gives Children's this as the reason her resignation. Probst saved Durrani information on her Children's Q drive. Most of the information referenced here is from her saved information.

The victims had no idea Durrani allowed a fellow unsupervised resident or fellow to perform their surgery and would have never consented to such.

On June 25, 2008, Durrani is suspended by Children's for not properly completing and signing medical records. Without disclosing this to the victims or any patient, Durrani still does surgeries at Children's.

On June 26, 2008, in an email, Durrani refers to Probst as "a piece of crap."

On June 27, 2008, there is a Children's email reflecting an issue of Jamie Moor seeing his patient's post-op rather than him.

On July 22, 2008, Durrani is still suspended at Children's. Children's allowed Durrani to do surgeries on June 27, June 28, June 30; July 5, July 6, July 7. No patient is told of the suspension.

On August 7, 2008, Durrani resigned from Children's for "*inhospitable atmosphere.*"

On August 12, 2008, an email by Probst details Durrani mistreatment of her.

On August 18, 2008, an email at Children's references patient letter "*turn arounds*" are twelve days for Durrani, not the required forty-eight hours.

On September 17, 2008, Wall sent a letter to Durrani patients informing them Durrani is leaving Children's. He fails to inform them of any of the Durrani issues.

On November 24, 2008, there is a letter to Children's patients from Durrani announcing his departure and welcoming them to follow him to his new spine center for care. It's on Children's letterhead. Most Durrani patients, including the victims, follows Durrani to CAST not knowing any issue of Children's.

January 1, 2009 is the effective date of Durrani's resignation and Durrani opens CAST.

Krissy Probst was Durrani's professional and personal assistant handling professional, academic, travel, surgery scheduling, his journals, his Boards, his credentialing, his personal affairs and his bills.

Krissy Probst worked as Durrani's assistant for three years at Children's Hospital from 2006 to 2008.

Krissy Probst reported Durrani to Sandy Singleton, the Business Director at Children's for his having an affair with Jamie Moor, his physician assistant.

Krissy Probst resigned in 2008 from Durrani and remained working for three other surgeons in the Orthopedic Department.

Krissy Probst worked in the Orthopedic Department for eleven years from 2002 to 2013. She retired in May 2013.

Krissy Probst confirmed Durrani claimed being a Prince.

According to Krissy Probst, Crawford, an icon in pediatric orthopedics treated Durrani "*like a son.*"

According to Krissy Probst, Crawford unconditionally supported Durrani no matter the issues and problems Durrani faced.

Durrani's patient care at Children's Hospital dropped off considerably after Jamie Moor became his physician assistant and they began their affair.

Durrani was the only orthopedic spine surgeon at Children's who would perform a dangerous high volume of surgeries.

Agabegi would do one spine patient a day at Children's because it takes normally eight hours for a full fusion. Durrani would schedule two, three or more spine surgeries a day at Children's Hospital.

Durrani would repeatedly have the Business Director, Sandy Singleton, or OR Director allow him to add surgeries claiming they were emergencies.

There is also a Dr. Peter Sturm, not to be confused with Peter Stern, who is an orthopedic at Children's who also had "no use" for Durrani.

Durrani chose his own codes for Children's billing which he manipulated with the full knowledge of Children's Board and management.

While doing research at Children's, Durrani would misstate facts regarding his research. Children's knew.

Durrani's last date as employee of Children's Hospital was December 31, 2008, yet he performed spine surgeries there through March 2009.

Durrani used his relationships with Children's officials to purge his Children's file of all patient safety and legal issues which had occurred as part of his departure "deal" which Children's hides with privilege. Only Probst saving so much, saved us.

On January 3, 2001, Durrani received a notice called Physician Notification Letter, from Ellen Witsken, Associate Director, Health Information Management Department... It lists two cases: one is 80 days late and one is 72 days late. The letter states: "Failure to complete these records within 30 days will result in automatic suspension of all non-emergency admitting and clinical privileges."

On November 11, 2006, 9:13 AM, Mehlman emailed Rick Brilli of Children's regarding industry support for the orthopedic spine fellowship. It is a long 9-point email with a conclusion expressing concerns of the conflicts involved with industry sponsoring the fellowship. Mehlman cites many articles in support of his position.

November 20, 2007, 10 PM, Mehlman emailed Wall *"are you aware of the fact what would seem to have been an experimental procedure was performed at our hospital? Are there policies/procedures to deal with such things???"*

On November 21, 2007, 8:30 AM, Wall responded to Mehlman. Wall explains he believes it is just a surgical technique but states: *"is a more radical departure from traditional fusion and is off-label." "What do you recommend for modifications to surgical procedures?"*

On November 26, 2007, 12:40 PM, Mehlman responded to Wall. He states per his research at Children's and call with Kathie Hays, there is no policy on FDA approved implants at Children's. He states Wall's examples in prior emails were already adopted and supported by literature. He stated Durrani did a *"spot fusion."* Mehlman concludes with this: *"Therefore, I would suggest to you that when a procedure deviates significantly from existing standard of care, when it has no identifiable literature support, and when it benefits are theoretical and its outcomes UNKNOWN- this might be a procedure that some would label EXPERIMENTAL... and this is why God created Institutional Review Boards and Ethics Committees and the like."*

On December 14, 2007, 5:48 PM, Mehlman emailed Wall titled, *"at least the 2nd complication like this I am aware of."* He states: *"Two of something is just dif-*

ferent than one of something." He expresses patient safety concerns. He suggests a referral to Steve Muething's, patient safety. "*The same patient I am showing you now also has one thoracic pedicle screw that is super close to the aorta.*"

On December 20, 2007 5:02 PM, Mehlman emailed Wall and attached a previous email and images. He states there are at least two instances of "adjacent segment disease" in the form of upper thoracic spondylolisthesis occurring following pedicle screw instrumented kyphosis. He references he can't find other examples of the complication except a St. Louis paper says patients over 50 are higher risk. He states "*Our CCHMC cases are clearly much less than 50 years of age- one was at least transiently paralyzed by the complication.*" He also states: "*I would recommend to you that a root-cause analysis be undertaken regarding these cases- this would be aimed at PATIENT SAFETY. I would further suggest a moratorium on this technique until results of a review are in hand. This is prompted by the fact that it gets my attention when I see a complication twice in relatively short period of time- especially a complication that I had not previously seen or heard about.*"

In 2008, Dr. David Stern became Vice President for Health Affairs at University of Cincinnati. From the College of Medicine website: "*His focus was on building collaborative programs, especially with Cincinnati Children's Hospital Medical Center... and providing a foundation for the university's health system (UC Health).*

On February 7, 2008, 2:03 PM Mehlman emails Durrani requesting a moratorium on a procedure called upper thoracic spondylolisthesis above kyphosis constructs Durrani performed on kyphosis patients. Mehlman references Larry Lenke agreeing with Mehlman.

On February 7, 2008, 4:34 PM, Dr. Twee Do responded by saying "*This is a very nice way to put it.*"

On February 7, 2008, 6:21 PM Durrani responded to Mehlman disagreeing with the moratorium.

On February 8, 2008 3:51 PM, Mehlman emailed Durrani referencing a new complication, calling it a patient safety issue, requesting a "*root cause analyzed*" and seeing how to prevent this from happening in the future.

On February 8, 2008, 5:48 PM, Durrani responded to Mehlman stating, "*I do not think this needs to be root cause analyzed.*" He also states: "*To make this a patient safety issue is inappropriate.*"

On February 8, 2008, 6:13 PM Mehlman emailed Durrani stating Larry Lenke as agreeing with him on the issue of the upper thoracic spondylolisthesis above kyphosis constructs.

On February 8, 2008 6:37 PM Durrani emailed Mehlman regarding the upper thoracic spondylolisthesis above kyphosis constructs. Durrani complains about addressing the issue by email and defends his conduct and claiming, "*Just because Larry Lenke said it does not make it a scripture.*"

On February 15, 2008, 4:00 PM, Mehlman emailed Dr. Crawford and Durrani and copied to Dr. Do, Dr. Tamai and Wall regarding unsolicited feedback peds ortho fellows and residents regarding inability to participate in cases in the OR setting.

On March 6, 2008, 9:46 AM, Dr. Mehlman emailed Wall complaining Durrani performed an experimental procedure on a minor at Children's. The email closes with *"the only thing that concerns me more than taking a big issue like this to Dr. Azizkhan is not taking it to him."*

On March 6, 2008, 2:02 PM, Mehlman emails Durrani withdrawing as a faculty member for the Children's Spine Fellowship. Mehlman refuses to participate in a corporate influenced program.

On March 21, 2008, 6:08 PM, Mehlman emailed Wall. He references percutaneous scoliosis fusion surgeries. He believes it requires IRB approval protocol. He believes it is experimental. He believes legal should be consulted on consent. He states there is no human or animal subject literature in support and no IRB approval. He states: *"To the best of my knowledge- this procedure is a dramatic departure from nearly 100 years of scoliosis spinal fusion evidence." He also states, "Scientific misconduct has already occurred in relation to this study insofar as a "preliminary report on the technique" ABSTRACT was submitted to IMAST/SRS."*

On March 21, 2008, 11:36 PM, Cassi Kirby emailed to Mehlman titled Percutaneous Scoliosis Study. *"CTM, Just as an FYI... This was Lisa's response... which pretty much confirms that nothing has been submitted to the IRB (problem report, protocol submissions, etc.). My interpretation of the response is that AAD is pushing to get his approved as a "retrospective stay. CASH. AAD is Durrani.*

Durrani attempted to have an experimental procedure approved by the IRB after the fact.

On April 3, 2008, 8:37 AM, Mehlman emailed Dr. Frenck, *"I would appreciate it if you are able to treat this as privileged communication. I am an abstract reviewer for the Scoliosis Research Society. Attached is the original abstract of the study in question- which as a reviewer "caught my eye." I later confirmed that the abstract came from my own institution and in fact no IRB existed. My PUBMED search shows no literature precedent for such a scoliosis procedure in animals or humans.*

On April 7, 2008, 9:51 PM, Dr. Bob Frenck, IRB Chairman, sent an email to Durrani, informing Durrani to rescind his abstract submission because IRB is not allowed retrospective approval for projects. He cautions if there are others, same applies. He copies Wall, Jamie Bailey and Jeremy Corsmo.

On April 11, 2008, 2:10 PM, Mehlman emailed Wall *"I wish to continue to raise concern regarding children undergoing spondylolysis surgery at our institution."* He references two patients by name. He references four patients by name who are scheduled. He lists 13 more patients by name. He suggests outside reviewers. He suggests an internal review by Peter Stern, Guanciale and Asghar.

On April 12, 2008, 3:46 PM, Wall emailed Mehlman and states: *"I am most concerned about the patients who were recommended surgery without being given a trial of PT or bracing 1st. Do you have those names still? I had a similar case."*

On April 12, 2008 at 5:10 PM, Mehlman emailed Wall and stated: *"I do not have a sub-list of suspected "little or no effort" at non-operative care. In my opinion, proper peer review of actual patient records would be necessary to make such a determination."*

On April 12, 2008, 5:19 PM, Mehlman emailed Wall and requested Wall look at Article I of Children's bylaws regarding *"Actions Affecting Medical Staff Members."*

On October 1, 2008, 5:50 PM, Mehlman emailed Wall detailing Alex Taylor course of treatment with Durrani. Dr. Rohmiller agreed with Mehlman surgery for kyphosis was not necessary. He asked Wall to *"review the case on your own."*

On October 2, 2008, 11:42 AM, Mehlman emailed Wall with more cases and names of questionable procedures.

On October 2, 2008, 12:52 PM, Mehlman emailed Wall regarding two kyphosis patients with complications, patients with the procedure referenced in the abstract and other cases. One was brought to his attention by Dr. Twee Do.

On October 2, 2008, 3:11 PM, Mehlman emailed Wall and provided 24 names of patients which Durrani did spondylolysis repair. He provided three names of patients who had *"pedicle screws and some type of flexible implant that connects the screws."* He gave the names of two others with questionable procedures.

On October 2, 2008, 3:18 PM, Mehlman emailed Wall another case which came through the pre-op/post-op conference.

On October 3, 2008, 6:01 AM, Stern emailed Mehlman and Wall: *"Dear Eric: Dr. Mehlman has raised some serious issues here. I believe Durrani is fully entitled to due process but also think this apparently aggressive behavior might warrant some type of independent evaluation. I believe as a profession we must exercise some oversight; especially when it involves patient well-being. Peter"*

On October 10, 2008, 5:51 PM, Mehlman sent an email to Dr. Tamai in which Mehlman speaks of his work with Board of Certification, debates about standards of care, difference between standard of care and style of practice.

On October 11, 2008, 7:04 AM, Stern emailed Mehlman: *"Chuck: Interesting dialogue. It is important for us to remember that there is usually more than one way to skin a cat. I use the 3 standard deviation rule: when you run a problem by 3 colleagues and they all agree that the selected treatment is 'out of bounds' it may be time to be openly critical."*

We came into possession of a letter on May 8 that had been authenticated even in its absence at the time by Guanciale at his deposition on July 12, 2017. The letter proves that in 2008, Children's Hospital and their orthopaedic department, which included University and UC Health physicians, knew Durrani was a danger to any patient.

Durrani resigned from Children's on August 7, 2008, but it was not effective until January 1, 2009. He cited *"inhospitable working environment."* He addressed his letter to Azizkhan but failed to mention the facts contained in the October 20, 2009 letter. On September 17, 2008, Wall, as Director of Pediatric Orthopaedic Surgery of Children's sent a letter to Durrani's patients announcing Durrani's departure from Children's. There was no warning or disclosure of the meeting and facts described in the October 20, 2009 letter to any Durrani patient, the public or any regulatory agency.

On November 24, 2008, Durrani sent a letter to his patients announcing his departure from Children's on Children's letterhead. There was no disclosure of the facts described in the October 20, 2009 letter to any Durrani patient, the public or regulatory agency.

On November 24, 2008, on Children's letterhead, with University of Cincinnati logo on it, sent a letter to *"Dear Valued Patients and Families"* advising them December 31, 2008 was his last day as an employee at Children's Hospital. He included a form for them to complete if they wanted to follow him.

On February 12, 2009, 1:27 PM, Azizkhan emailed Durrani informing him if his patients are admitted at Children's, he is responsible as attending, but stated Children's can provide consultations and support as requested, and residents and fellows help out.

On February 13, 2009, 10:21 AM, Durrani sent an email including Dr. Azizkhan: *"Hi everyone."* It appears it also went to Wall and Durrani's staff. It is a coordination of patient care with Children's. This after his resignation.

On February 15, 2009, 4:22 PM, Wall emailed Durrani making sure Children's and nurse stations have *"proper contact numbers for you and your team at CAST.* This after resignation.

On February 16, 2009, 5:34 PM, Durrani replied to Wall and copied Mehlman, Dr. Tamai, Sandy Singleton and Julie Hartmann he had given the numbers.

May 30, 2008 letter from Guanciale to Stern:

Dear Dr. Stern:

I am writing this letter to you as a brief reference to my concerns about the clinical competency of Dr. Atiq Durrani. As we have discussed, I have had, I would consider, the unfortunate experience of seeing several of Dr. Durrani's patients as a non-referred second opinion after receiving fairly what I would describe as radical opinions about surgical treatment for their children. I believe there have been five or six of these to date over the past approximate year and a half. These have all involved extensive surgical procedures either involving recommendations for anterior fusion procedures or artificial disc replacement procedures in patients who are less than 20 years of age. None of these patients have involved any actual deformity or instability of their spine and have essentially had activity-related back pain, typically not constant pain, but rather with playing a particular sport. None of these had significant abnormalities on numerous radiographic studies including MRI's, as well as often bone scan, CT scans, even possibly CT discography tests, which would be an extremely uncommon test ordered in a young person or adolescent. The predominant portion of these patients simply had disc desiccation and some early discogenic changes on their radiographic studies, which I believe consistently throughout the country would be treated nonsurgically.

One recent such evaluation involved a patient, Caitlyn Figgins, who is a 17-year-old local high school student/athlete playing basketball and I believe soccer, who has back pain only after sports participation, and who has early disc desiccation changes and a small disc protrusion. Caitlyn was specifically recommended an artificial disc replacement by Dr. Durrani. An artificial disc replacement in a 17-year-old with intermittent back pain that's non-debilitating would certainly lie outside of the standard treatment recommendations by I believe almost any spine surgeon in the country. Another such patient was a 14-year-old patient, who is a figure skater or attempting to be a figure skater, who was having difficulties with back pain symptomatology and rare leg pain, who had a disc herniation, who at most would've possibly benefited from a lumbar microdiscectomy type surgery.

She, however, in seeing Dr. Durrani was recommended an anterior and posterior lumbar fusion procedure with pedicle bone screw instrumentation for her intermittent ice skating related back pain. Her pain subsequently resolved with undergoing physical therapy, albeit over many months (greater than 6 months), and epidural steroid injections. Her pain has completely resolved at this time and she's returned back to figure skating without requiring any surgery.

I have provided these examples with one patient's name being included and I can provide other patient's names if necessary in order to attempt a convey information that establishes a pattern by Dr. Durrani of being overly aggressive in regards to surgical treatment suggesting very serious surgical procedures that have often high complication rates for underlying pathology that is very minimal in nature and often is treated nonsurgical. I believe this is a very serious concern, this clearly shows some difficulties in judgment in regards to clinical decision making. As we all know, just because we're surgeons, it doesn't mean that every patient needs a surgical procedure, let alone an extensive surgical procedure. As you know, and I believe as you practice, certainly most of our patients are treated non-surgically. I believe that this pattern of treatment is a concern for the residence of the Greater Cincinnati area and long term do not provide the treatment that they all desire and deserve.

Sincerely,

Anthony Guanciale

***This letter is very powerful and gives specific examples. Of note, it's May 30, 2008. It took months for the meeting.**

July 8, 2008 letter from Stern to Guanciale:

Dear Tony,

I am in receipt of your letter dated May 30, 2008 regarding your concerns of Atiq Durrani, MD. As you will recall, we have informally discussed your concerns voiced and I have also spoken with Dr. Asghar and John Roberts, MD (both informally). Finally, I met in my office with Eric Wall, MD about a month ago regarding the withdrawal of Richard Owens' thesis presentation.

With your permission, I would like to setup a meeting with yourself, Dr. Richard Azizkhan, Dr. Eric Wall and myself.

I am very concerned about Durrani's activities and his indications for surgery. I also strongly believe that he is entitled to due process and I would think that a formal discussion is outlined above would be appropriate starting point.

I look forward to hearing from you and hope you are willing to meet with Drs. Azizkhan and Wall.

Sincerely,

Peter Stern

July 14, 2008 letter from Stern to Wall:

Dear Eric,

This is a follow-up letter to our conversation in my office regarding Atiq Durrani on July 12, 2008. Three items were discussed in detail:

A. Durrani's indications for spine surgery appear to be overly aggressive.

B. Possible research misconduct (re PARS defect)

C. Human Resource issues.

We agreed that all three of these issues are potentially very serious. We further agreed that we will discuss these issues with Dr. Azizkhan in the presence of legal counsel to insure proper action and due process.

Sincerely,

Peter Stern

July 29, 2008 letter Stern to Azizkhan and copied to Wall:

This is a delayed follow-up letter to our meeting two weeks ago regarding Atiq Durrani, MD. I received a phone call from a community spine surgeon who also expressed concerns regarding the aggressive nature of Dr. Durrani's indications for spine surgery in children. He told me that there are several other members of the Orthopaedic community that have seen patients for a second opinion who have voiced similar concerns. He told me that a list of names could potentially be produced.

Granted, this is hearsay. Nevertheless, I remain concerned about Durrani's indications for spine surgery in these young individuals. I appreciated the opportunity to speak with you and Dr. Wall and am encouraged that you will take the necessary steps to look into my concerns.

Sincerely,

Peter Stern

Email October 23, 2009 at 11:46 PM from Guanciale to Agabegi and Asghar:

"Here is a copy of the Durrani letter.

Keep in mind as you get all these comments from "people" about him this needs to be reported, that the ultimate responsibility should have come from the director of orthopedics at Children's and from the chairman of the dept of orthopedic surgery.

This letter is CONFIDENTIAL and to be shared with no one if it is to be effective!!"

*Significant they want the director and chairman on the letter.

Email October 24, 2009 12:52 AM from Asghar to Guanciale and Agabegi:

"I commend you for restraining the tone of your letter more than I would be able to...

I'm happy to cosign this with you and anyone else. I do wonder if this will simply get buried somewhere in the State offices, and agree that PJS and Wall need to get involved too. A letter from the Chair of a department about a person who he trained (and who he would usually stand up for) a former president of the AOA- will carry more weight.

Do you think specific cases should be included at this stage? A list of ten cases will show that we aren't just a bunch of disgruntled former colleagues who have a bone to pick with him. Perhaps they should be reminded that this is not the first time they have been contacted about him.

It's absolutely amazing how long this has been allowed to continue.

FAA"

*Who had contacted the Board earlier and when?

Email October 26, 2009 at 11:16 PM from Agabegi to Guanciale and Asghar:

"I made a couple of minor additions. Hope you don't mind. I added a small paragraph about complications... don't know if you want to include it. I think mentioning his complications gives the letter more "urgency"... that patients are at risk."

Agabegi added the following to the letter:

second page... bracing removed and added "which is effective in the majority of cases."

He added the final two paragraphs on page three:

"Finally, I am concerned about the disproportionate number of severe complications that Dr. Durrani's patients have experienced including death and paralysis, that would be acceptable by the orthopedic community for a competent spine surgeon. I am troubled by what many members of the medical community consider to be irresponsible surgical care that is being delivered to patients in the greater Cincinnati area."

He added this to the final sentence and final paragraph:

"I am able to provide detailed specific evidence to support the above. Although I am the sole author of this letter, other spine surgeons within the Department of Orthopedic Surgery at the University of Cincinnati, including Dr. Ferhan Asghar and Steven Agabegi, share these concerns and have read and signed this letter."

He added Dr. Asghar and himself at the end to sign.

Email November 16, 2009 9:45 PM to Teri Lyons, Guanciale and Asghar:

"I think it should be sent to the Ohio State Medical Board. I think Dr. Stern meant the board and may have mistakenly said "association." Board address would probably be better.

What is the status of the attorney reviewing the letter?

I spoke with Dr. Mehlman and he is on board with us... he knows one of the physicians on the board—this may be a good resource.

Dr. G: Any word from Roberts/Kahn/Rohmiller? Will they sign the letter? I know the letter was emailed to them, but did you want to ask them directly if they will sign? Do you want one of us to talk to them? Please advise. The more people involved the better."

-Steve

November 16, 2009 After 9:45 PM- email from Guanciale to Agabegi and Asghar:

"I agree with the note about sending to the medical board.

I received the email back from Kahn, Roberts and Rohmiller however no offer to cosign.

I think at this time instead of further delay it is best to just send the letter in a confidential status and allow the board to proceed.

I don't think an attorney needs to review any letter sent to the board as this is our responsibility.

I also found out at NASS that several people were unaware that Durrani's false research paper sent last year was indeed false and represented research fraud."

On July 26, 2013, 11:00 PM Agabegi sent an email to Stern, copied to Mehlman, Dr. Kuntz and Asghar where he copied an article about Durrani being sued for unnecessary surgeries and stated: "Looks like UC Health and CCHMC got some splainin' to do... Can't help but remember our meeting in the dean's office in 2011."

This is a lawsuit we filed.

Email September 3, 2013 at 12:06 PM from Jared Camper to Asghar and Rob Kotarski (FBI)

"Hi Dr. Asghar. I hope you had a great, long weekend. During our meeting last week, you mentioned 2 prior Dr. Durrani patients you saw on whom you likely would not have performed surgery. From my notes, you saw one patient 2-3 years ago and the other patient just 1 week ago. Would you provide us the names and DOBs of these 2 patients?

Thanks, Jared

Jared Camper

Special Agent

DCIS Dayton RA

Email September 3, 2013 at 2:43 PM from Asghar to Jared Camper:

"Sure, will do.

I'm in the office tomorrow so should be able to get this to you. If I don't get back by the end of the week, please call/email me again to make sure it didn't fall through the cracks on my "to-do list"

FAA

Email September 4, 2013 from Jared Camper to Asghar:

"Dr. Asghar, just a friendly reminder to send me the names of those 2 patients... thanks."

Email September 10, 2013 at 8:55 PM from Asghar to Jared Camper:

"The patient I saw a couple of weeks ago is ___________. As mentioned, I didn't see her presurgical MRI so can't say it was entirely unindicated surgery. Some of the notes did look questionable though- radiology note made mention of grade 1 spondylolisthesis (mild and the most common) but his note said (severe spondylolisthesis) Also op note was dictated over 4 months later.

Second patient is _______________. She had a lumbar fusion surgery and says that he told her he would be doing a disc replacement, not a fusion. Also, have not seen pre-surgical MRI scans but doubt there was much pathology that warranted an operation.

How does it work in terms of patient confidentiality that I provide this info to you without patients' permission? I imagine they would be willing to speak to authorities about their experience, but I don't want them to be taken aback by a phone call without notice.

Stern is Chairman of the Department of Orthopedic Surgery at University of Cincinnati, so he is Mehlman's academic boss. UC Logo has been on Children's letterhead. University and Children's share training. Children's is the pediatric academic arm of the university. University of Cincinnati oversees us all.

"Some sort of effort to protect the public should've been undertaken," testified Mehlman. The announcement to patients from Children's when Durrani resigned should have included a warning. Mehlman remembers the secretaries in the office stuffing the letters about Durrani's practice location changing. Mehlman believes Children's had a lot of explaining to do in 2006, 2007, 2008 and today. *"They should be explaining why they didn›t protect the public."* Based upon his experience with Durrani from the years he worked with him at Children's, Mehlman's opinion about Durrani's reputation for truthfulness and honesty in the community is... *"he's an unethical sociopath."*

Guanciale is employed with the department of orthopedic surgery through University of Cincinnati Physicians. He is also employed by University of Cincinnati Medical Center as *"far as my educational role and research role."* He's a faculty member in the department of orthopedic surgery. He's an associate professor. He teaches residents and does research. His academic appointment is through the University of Cincinnati. His surgical appointment is through University of Cincinnati Physicians. In 2008, he was director of spine surgery in the orthopedic department. In 2008, he reported to Peter Stern. In 2008, Guanciale had privileges at Children's. Crawford asked him to occasionally assist in some scoliosis surgeries. Guanciale first met Durrani when Durrani was a resident at University. Durrani was an orthopedic resident.

Guanciale supervised himself, Asghar and Agabegı. The only adult spine surgeons at University. Guanciale knew Mehlman and Wall as faculty members. His private practice was Cincinnati Spine Institute with Dr. Kahn, Dr. Roberts and Dr. Kramer.

"Durrani did surgeries here as well. He even took call here, spine call," testified Guanciale. This is a reference to University. Stern did annual reviews for everyone in the department.

Agabegi is a licensed Orthopaedic since 2008. He became board certified in 2010. He was at Children's from August 2008 until March 2009 full time, then part time until 2015. He spoke to Asghar, Guanciale and Stern about his deposition. They have discussed Durrani many times over the years. The letters summarize it. Agabegi had experiences with Durrani at Children's and UC before Durrani left Children's. Agabegi began his residency in 2002 when Durrani was chief resident. Agabegi treated two Deters Law clients who had claims against Children's. He's employed by College of Medicine and UC Physicians. Hospitals under UC Health. Durrani helped Agabegi get his Children's position.

Agabegi left Children's because he wasn't doing enough surgery. Durrani told him Durrani left Children's for the better opportunity of private practice.

Asghar is an employee of UC Physicians. He's an assistant professor of Orthopaedic surgery. He works at West Chester. Children's and University have a common resident program. They have meetings and research. "Their residency program is what brings us together." His first true job in 2005 was at University. He was in residency a year or two before Durrani.

Stern has been on staff at Children's his entire time in Cincinnati. He does one or two cases a year there. As Chairman, he has responsibility for the practice of the individuals within the department and the education of the residents that are training at the University of Cincinnati in Orthopaedic surgery.

Stern didn't recall the five lawsuits against Durrani during Durrani's residency. At the time Durrani became resident, it was not common to invite foreign medical graduates for interviews. It was not common to accept foreign medical graduates. They mostly came from the Midwest. The program never accepted an applicant from Army Medical College in Pakistan. American Board of Orthopaedic Surgery is twenty Orthopaedic surgeons involved in certification. It's stated mission to ensure safe, ethical and effective practice of Orthopaedic surgery for the benefit of the public.

Durrani was Chief Resident from July 1, 2002 until June 30, 2003. Every resident becomes a chief resident. On the technical side, I *"would say he was average to above average and on the brash side."* Being a Chief Resident is no big deal. Every resident becomes chief resident.

Wall is current director of sports medicine at Children's. He's been at Children's for 26 years. In 1993, he was an assistant professor. In 2005, he became an associate professor.

In 2005, he became division director of orthopedics and he held that position for about five years which would have been the entire time Durrani was employed at Children's. He is now, a full professor of orthopedic surgery. All the professorships were and are affiliated with the University of Cincinnati.

No one at West Chester contacted Wall to provide information for the credentialing of Durrani at West Chester. This is a direct violation of West Chester's credentialing rules which specifically require the department head to weigh in. Wall provided no information to West Chester. If asked, at that time Wall would not rehire Durrani due to all the issues. He has no personal knowledge of West Chester contacting Children's to credential Durrani. They didn't.

He claims Stern was part of peer review process, despite Stern not being employed at Children's.

Crawford is now employed at UC Health. He is Professor Emeritus in Orthopaedic Surgery. Clinical practice is part of his Professor Emeritus position. *"I didn't do adult surgery at all. He did adult surgery. He was part of their triangular fellowship of University, Children's and the Mayfield Clinic,"* testified Crawford. Crawford claims to not know Durrani left Children's. He claims his conversation with Durrani was merely *"I see you're leaving. Yes, I'm leaving."*

Asghar's concerns in 2009 regarding Durrani were regarding the indications for surgery and the appropriateness of surgery. Concerns remained the same from 2009 to 2011. He heard there were other investigations done at other hospitals. He thinks West Chester did a review 2011 or 2012. In 2013 they formed a committee at West Chester to review his practice. Dr. Joseph, CEO was involved. This of course was after we filed 150 lawsuits.

Multiple physicians were on the committee. The findings were he failed to disclose he had pending legal issues on his recredentialing application. *"I'm sure there were other things."*

In not those many words, were they told UC would not stand behind them if Durrani sued. There were *"things in that letter I cannot personally testify to, but I was—I had concerns. So, I was willing to put my name on there as well, but we all contributed to it,"* testified Asghar.

In 2009, Asghar was on the MEC at University Cincinnati Medical Committee. Pertaining to the April 2011 letter. UC administration *"expressed concerns and we were supported in our concerns."* He's covering for his current employer. There were concerns how it would be received. Durrani would claim they were competitors. Durrani would claim conflict of interest and bad faith. Other than complications and code section, he agrees with everything in letter is true. He heard regarding Children's meeting *"research irregularities," "personal relationship with staff member," "someone had reported him to the board," "the board said they were going to investigate him." "If you investigate me, I'm going to resign."* They said, *"We have to investigate you"* and so he resigned. *"But that was before any formal investigation was ever launched, so nothing ever got reported to NPDB,"* testified Asghar.

UC counsel was present at the Dean's meeting. He doesn't know if it was Dr. Boat. He claims University of Cincinnati Medical Center indicated a willingness to take action besides the one 150 case study. *"I believe internal investigations were performed."* He does not know so. *"The results were such that there was enough concern to require an outside investigation. The concern was that anyone doing an internal investigation was conflicted because we were competitors of his."* TGL on the letter was Teri Lyons, Angelo Colosimo's administrative assistant.

Other spine doctors in the community were spoken to. When asked, Dr. Rohmiller said UC said they would not stand behind them if Durrani sued them.

Testimony of Asghar:

Q: *"Is there any – any doubt in your mind that West Chester Health knew about the issues that you were raising in your 2009 letter in or around that time?"*

A: *"They knew because we were raising issues to them."* Asghar practiced at West Chester from the outset. From 2012 to 2013, he's been on West Chester MEC. *"I was on at the time that he left. "Prior to his indictment there wasn't any conversation at MEC about him. It wasn't until his indictment that it became the subject of conversation."* It proves they were "deaf, dumb and blind" or ignored for the money. *"This was not a subject of conversation at the MEC level. MEC deals with multiple things ranging from golf outing and – and policies for consults and such, and we are doing all of that, and any disciplinary action against a doctor gets brought up to the MEC, if there is one. And that was – that happened after the indictment."* MEC rules cover more than golf outings.

Asghar thinks UC Health West Chester was *"in a difficult situation" because their take on it was that other surgeons are complaining about another doctor."* Durrani defended himself by saying I'm taking care of people no one will. Asghar said Kevin Joseph had knowledge about Durrani. *"The MEC only gets what certain things that are on the roster for the conversation of that evening." "There would have been, potentially maybe, before I was on MEC, some discussions about him, but it's not like Durrani comes up every month that we meet at MEC."*

Discussions with spine surgeons included surgeons at Children's. He was not at Children's meeting. He *"had mixed feelings about it"* regarding the alleged UC Health external investigation. *"I think people put together an effort, people who didn't have to, they put a lot of time into it. Yet, we didn't really get anywhere, so I was frustrated by that."*

Asghar was the first surgeon at West Chester. Half his practice is there now. There is no pre-operative review at West Chester. UC Health did not revoke Durrani's privileges until 2013. West Chester never acted against Durrani until I began filing countless lawsuits. Durrani would not accept advice or criticism. There were unhappy Durrani patients. Dr. Chunduri said there was a review. They were worried about good faith and a claim they chased him out of UC.

Stern claims he saw October 20, 2009 letter for the first time ten days before his deposition. He agrees with each paragraph. He doesn't know if Azizkhan got back to him. He thinks so. The April 19, 2011 letter was never sent. The letter was never sent because: *"Dr. Kuntz, who worked for Mayfield, was—my understanding was – was asked not to sign the letter."*

"We had spoken with Kevin Joseph, who was the CEO of the West Chester Medical Center, and he promised us to do an independent peer review investigation. And finally, quite frankly, we were concerned about potential retribution as Durrani was assumed to have fairly deep pockets," testified Stern. Joseph claimed he ordered an independent review from Boston and *"said the review was essentially clean."* It allayed concerns, but not completely. We have never seen this so called external review. Best case review is chart review. Stern can't recall ever telling Colosimo in a private meeting in 2013 that UC Health knew all about Durrani, but "they" needed money. Stern and Colosimo operated on the same day on Fridays so it's certainly probable they had conversations about Durrani. Stern spoke to Joseph. He can't recall if Joseph mentioned how important Durrani was to West Chester financially. Stern admits you don't need a statute to report a physician conducting unethical practice or inappropriate practice and harming individuals.

"I only know that Durrani resigned very shortly after that meeting. It was quite precipitous," testified Stern. These allegations against a peer is pretty serious. Asked about alleged 2011 external review. *"It helped allay some concerns."* The alleged external review did not completely satisfy his concerns. *"I had continued concerns,"* testified Dr. Stern. He feared retribution from Durrani.

"Dr. Asghar, Dr. Agabegi and Dr. Kuntz were above reproach," testified Stern.

"You never know what course a resident takes. I believe sometime during the first two to three years at Children's his reputation became increasingly tarnished," testified Stern.

Why was the letter not sent? Concern of retribution. Concerns Dr. Kuntz not sign. Durrani bragged about his wealth. The main reasons is UC Health general counsel, Charles H. Pangburn III, convinced them not to send the letter. All those from the date of the letter through 2013, butchered by Durrani should curse the name, Pangburn.

Guanciale worked at Christ Hospital fairly routinely and he knew two deaths that occurred at Christ Hospital. And they were Durrani patients. Guanciale was in private practice operating at the Mercy Health System and Christ. Guanciale scrubbed in on a Durrani case at Christ.

As a resident, Agabegi did one surgery with Durrani at Christ. It was his first week. Both he and Agabegi did this at Christ early 2000's and both backed out of the surgeries based upon Durrani's surgical plans.

Dr. Chunduri told Asghar there was a Good Samaritan investigation. Asghar scrubbed into five surgeries at Christ.

"He had a serious complication and ended up resigning from Christ," testified Asghar. He believes Durrani had a serious complication at Good Sam and they conducted an investigation. He does not know the result of the investigation. He is not aware of any other hospitals in the 2009 through 2013 time frame which conducted investigation.

Chapter 91

West Chester

"Both parties deprecated war, but one of them would make war rather than let the nation survive, and the other would accept war rather than let it perish, and the war came."
—Abraham Lincoln

West Chester and UC Health from the outset of their opening in May 2009, through their Medical Executive Committee (MEC) and administration under the MEC bylaws:

1. Failed to "govern the affairs of the Medical Staff."
2. Failed to enforce their rules upon Durrani.
3. Failed to provide oversight of Durrani.
4. Failed to properly evaluate Durrani.
5. The Orthopedic and Surgery Departments abdicated their responsibility under the MEC bylaws to review, investigate and supervise Durrani.
6. Failed to properly discipline Durrani including summary suspensions and revocation.
7. Failed to properly discipline Durrani.
8. Ignored the information readily available pertaining to Durrani before credentialing and granting him privileges.
9. Failed to act on Durrani's disruptive behavior, unprofessional behavior and clinical performance placing patients at risk and causing harm.
10. Certified and approved the unnecessary procedures of Durrani knowing they were unnecessary, knowingly allowing the improper use of BMP-2 and knowing there was not proper informed consent.
11. Failed to act on Durrani's failure in medical record documentation.
12. Failed to require Durrani to follow the rules for off label experimental procedures.
13. Allowed Durrani to use undisclosed and unqualified surgeons to perform his surgeries.
14. Allowed Durrani to do multiple surgeries at once.

Why? Why would West Chester/UC Health allow all this? Money.

Durrani details his arrival at West Chester at a deposition:

A. 2009, okay? So 2009, you know, I went there at that point. You know, it was like any other hospital. I was operating in a lot of hospitals so—

Q. I would like for you to take me through the process, as a surgeon, what you have to do to obtain privileges at West Chester Hospital.
A. There's a privileges application. You fill it and you send it. That's all I know.

Q. All right. So you prepare—you fill out the application, you send it in. Do you know who reviews that?
A. I do not.

Q. Do you know how long it takes from the time you submit that till you get word?
A. Don't know.

Q. Is there any personal interviews or anything like that?
A. No.

Q. It's like a college application, then.
A. Yeah, you send an application and you're good.

Q. When you left Children's in 2009 and then before you applied at West Chester in 2009, where did you have privileges? And if I asked you that last time, I apologize.
A. You did.

Q. But I feel pretty good I'm not covering too much.
A. That's fine. I had privileges at Good Samaritan, I had privileges at Christ Hospital, University Hospital; I think even at Jewish at that point.

Q. Did you ask to join the staff—or excuse me, did you ask to have privileges at West Chester, or did you have any conversations with anybody at West Chester where they recruited—for lack of a better word—they recruited you to come there?
A. No. They never recruited me.

Q. When you became privileged at West Chester Hospital, did you give up privileges at any other hospitals?
A: A. No.

Q. Have you ever, while you were at West Chester Hospital, have you ever had to face any board of inquiry of some type on any case?
A: No."

Durrani faced no scrutiny joining West Chester despite all which happened at Children's and despite all that happened at West Chester, no scrutiny there either.

Carol King served as the Senior Vice President at West Chester from prior to opening until April 7, 2010. Why did she leave? All we know from King is "they didn't want me there anymore."

Carol King knew JCAHO standards and the bylaws. She knew this meant ongoing monitoring and supervision. Carol King testified: "What we wanted was a very transparent organization, where staff could raise their hand if they identified an issue. Those would be followed up on."

Carol King claims she never knew Durrani used BMP-2 and PureGen without the patients' consent. Investigations on these issues were left the physicians. *"Q: Did you personally have any concerns about anything Durrani was doing while he was at West Chester? A: Nothing was brought up that would be a concern that would need follow up."*

Carol King heard rumors about Durrani being kicked out of Children's, but she never investigated. Carol King claims to be unaware of scheduling issues with Durrani. We believe Carol King's vision of patient safety first is why she was "kicked to the curb." On Durrani's lack of dictation of operative reports, Carol King knew the bylaw requirements. She also knew privileges were supposed to be suspended if they did not comply, yet: *"I am not aware, while I was there, that his privileges were ever suspended."* They had a tracking system for delinquent records. Carol King claims no knowledge of other surgeons concerns about Durrani.

Karen Carroll instructed Carol King not to answer this question: *"What do you believe could have been different to protect patients from a surgeon like Durrani?"* However, Carol King testified: *"The processes are in place to look at complications, sudden events, anything that would be out of the ordinary, and those are, you know, things that all hospitals look at and focus on to look at what can be done differently."*

Carol King testified that if a surgeon wanted to perform *"a new procedure something that's brand new to that physician beyond what they had applied for in their privileging process, they would need to reapply for those credentials. Time in surgery, return to surgery, complications, all of those indicators are something that all hospitals look at and measure for patterns and trends."*

Dr. Brian Gibler is Dr. Kevin Joseph's partner. Joseph served the CEO of West Chester. Gibler is immediate past President of University Hospital. He remarkably claimed he never held a conversation with Dr. Joseph about Durrani. Dr. Gibler claims the biggest challenge is: *"Decreasing reimbursement that's coming from all aspects of medicine."* Interpretation? Money is an issue. Dr. Gibler claims a physician is a good choice to run a hospital because they understand how patient care is delivered. This is significant because Dr. Joseph, as CEO of West Chester, is supposed to know and understand patient care, yet allowed the wholesale ignoring of Durrani's version of "patient care."

David Schwallie is part of the risk management team for UC Health involved also in West Chester. He was made aware of concerns about Durrani at West Chester: *"I would say prior to 2011 sometime."*

Thomas Brown, MD served as director of radiology at West Chester from the time the hospital opened until January 2013. He served on the MEC during this time frame. He participated in the credentialing of Durrani. He testified many doctors liked Durrani and in part: *"There are other surgeons I know in the community that don't think highly of him in terms of his, maybe his judgment as to who he operates on and who he doesn't."* Who he operated on is the heart of the issue against Durrani. Brown claimed if he knew one surgeon performed surgeries in another surgeon's name, he would report it to other members of the MEC or administration. Brown knows the MEC makes decisions on termination or revoking privileges.

Paula Hawk served as the director of medical staff. Durrani approached her to join the staff at West Chester. She admits patient safety is the number one goal. She maintains mid-year 2013 the time Durrani left, they began a policy called "Stop the Line": *"It's called Stop the Line, but like if anybody notices just even a single thing that isn't quite right, you're supposed to be noisy about it and stop the line, just to make sure that whatever—you just need to make sure that we pay attention to safety."* This of course begs the question what was the policy before the "stop the line." Hawk claimed money and profits should never trump patient safety. She and Ron Rohlfing made the initial interviews for doctors seeking staff privileges. The National Practitioner Data Bank (NPDB) is relied upon in the credentialing process. Hospitals protect peer review data "to protect each other." West Chester ignored Durrani's issues based on Durrani's volume. Hawk claimed the only complaints she ever heard about Durrani was in peer review context. Hawk claims not to remember telling Durrani West Chester and Durrani were "partners in crime."

Mike Jeffers served as director of Finance at West Chester from February 2008 to end of January 2012. Durrani's name came up in monthly budget and financial meetings. This confirms informant's Elizabeth Dean's testimony which is summarized later. Durrani's name would come up as a top revenue generator. Jeffers tracked it monthly. They called it a monthly accounting support document from the West Chester finance director. They held budget meetings with every department manager. He claims no complaints about Durrani. Jeffers claims hospitals should look at the best interests of the patients. Jeffers admits Durrani helped West Chester in their time of need: *"Describe profit, since we lost money most months. So in many cases it was probably more beneficial to have him there than not."*

Orthopedics and spine surgeries rose to the highest revenue source at West Chester 2008 to 2012 with Durrani as the volume leader. West Chester tracked occupancy for their 162 beds by floor. West Chester billed BMP-2 and PureGen for more than they paid. Jeffers heard "rumors" of Durrani being assigned more than one surgery room at once. Bonuses were paid to administrators based on financial performance. Durrani's surgeries were expensive relative to revenue.

Jeffers prepared spreadsheets to track volume of surgeries. Jeffers had surgery schedulers put together patients' revenue, supply costs, insurance for monthly reports. It was an excel spreadsheet. He would send it to corporate. Annette Willenborg and other women did this for him. Jeffers verified Durrani cranked money into West Chester and used BMP-2 even after the July 2008 FDA warning.

Dr. Peter Stern, the head of orthopedics for UC Health for twenty-two years, supervised Durrani's residency at UC in which the best Stern could muster in praise is Durrani was "satisfactory." In 2013, Stern told Colosimo another UC orthopedic that UC Health knew about Durrani's "issues" but that "they" needed the money and they should have gotten rid of him long ago. Stern does not "remember" the conversation nor the meeting or the content of the conversation. He never denied telling Colosimo Durrani was a problem. He did not deny claiming they "should have gotten rid of him long ago." He did not deny that " Durrani made so much money for the hospital, because of the volume of his surgeries that everybody looked the other way."

Credentialing begins with an application, followed by verification of the information in the application, followed by review and approval of the Credential Committee, followed by review and approval of the MEC, followed by review and approval of the Board. Ms. Shelley, a UC Health employee involved in credentialing claims if any information not provided on the application, but public knowledge would be reviewed. The NPDB and state medical boards would be checked.

Dr. Eric Schneeberger, Durrani's employee, served on the West Chester MEC. This begs the conflict question. Employees at West Chester complained about long hours from so many surgeries performed by Durrani. This created an obvious patient care issue.

When West Chester opened Elaine Kunko served as the daily operations coordinator for the operating room. She later became assistant nurse manager. West Chester then assigned to data analysis tracking surgeon activity and reported to Tom Harris. Then she became a coordinator in quality management. Kunko reported Durrani frequently late and often needed reminding about completing medical records. Kunko's job included ensuring the surgeons completed the OR reports. She became clinical coordinator for OR from March 2009 to March 2011. She remembers Scott Rimer, Vickie Scott and Gerry Goodman , three informants for us. Ms. Kunko denies receiving complaints from Gerry Goodman. Goodman remembers otherwise. Kunko admits Durrani scheduled many emergency surgeries. "She knew Shanti would finish for Durrani. Ms. Kunko denies hearing about extended periods of anesthesia and sexual harassment. It is "possible" Kunko claims Vickie Scott made complaints about Durrani.

Kunko recalls the nurse staff meeting when documentation regarding what surgeons were in the rooms at what time was discussed. This verifies our informant's testimony. Durrani become the volume spine leader at West Chester. Administration received a monthly volume analysis for all surgeons. She heard "locker room" talk West Chester needed the money from Durrani surgeries. Kunko heard this from nursing and anesthesia staff who worked with Durrani. This is an incredible admission. Kunko served as a member of the special quality committee which discussed statistics of surgeries, quality measures and compliance with quality measures. Kunko verified Vickie Scott's email comment regarding the meeting on documentation. Kunko denied Vickie Scott brought it to her attention that Durrani made it appear he performed all the procedures when Shanti performed them. Kunko denied ever hearing about unnecessary spine surgeries.

Lisa Davis worked as an access representative at West Chester's inception. In May of 2010, she became the department manager. Authorization for the procedures was Durrani's responsibility. Nursing handled the surgical consents at bedside. Davis doesn't recall hearing anything "bad" about Durrani.

Jill Stegman served as the Director of Risk Management at West Chester. Her duties as Director of Risk Management involved handling claims, completing and assisting with insurance applications for the hospital, reviewing Midas incident reports, participation in various committees, and taking general calls related to any questions units may have in regard to power of attorney and living wills. At West Chester she is on the patient safety committee, the environment of care committee, performance improvement committee, service excellence committee, grievance committee, and a member of a corporate committee that's a subcommittee of a quality corporate meeting and they review incident reports throughout the organization, the whole system. She can't "recall" any complaints against Durrani.

Stegman remembers Gerry Goodman coming to her. Gerry Goodman came in to meet with her in her office. Goodman asked why Durrani worked there, and Goodman mentioned he had been kicked out of other facilities. Stegman doesn't recall Goodman complaining to her about Durrani working in conjunction with Shanti or Durrani having patients in more than one room at one time. She doesn't remember having discussions with Goodman about other surgeons performing significant portions of Durrani's procedures. The meeting between Goodman and Stegman was brief and less than fifteen minutes.

Stegman took no action as a result of the conversation with Goodman. Jill Stegman claimed it hearsay from the community, but did pass it on to her supervisor, Gary Harris. Goodman knew Durrani was kicked out of other facilities and not allowed to practice other places, but Stegman claimed to have never heard it. Stegman passed it along to her supervisor Harris, an attorney. Stegman said Goodman failed to complain about any specific practices or procedures Durrani performed at West Chester. Goodman never complained about surgeons to her other than Durrani. Stegman never spoke with Goodman about Durrani at any other time.

Gerry Goodman and George Caralis worked at Insight Health Partners under a contract with UC Health at West Chester in 2010. She was the Interim Director of OR nursing and he was the Interim COO. Caralis doesn't "recall" or deny anything Goodman claims she reported to him.

Kathy Hays worked as the perioperative director at West Chester at the recommendation of Durrani who knew her at Children's. Hays insured Durrani and surgeons had the supplies and implants requested. Deanna Griggs, the spinal coordinator, also helped in that regard. Hays testified if BMP2 was used in a patient of Durrani, West Chester knew it based upon how the product would be ordered and the reps. The same would apply for the use of Puregen by Alphatec.

If Durrani planned to use Puregen in a patient, representatives of West Chester Hospital would know based upon the process she described. As the perioperative director, she never became involved in making sure a product being used by Durrani in a spine patient was approved by the FDA. That responsibility fell under MedAssets. This indicts the hospital on the BMP-2 issue. From the time she came to West Chester, Dwayne Brown was in charge of MedAssets and is the MedAssets liaison for UC Health. She used to report to Dennis Robb. Regarding the original consent by the patient, Hays stated she played no role because they do an acknowledgment of informed consent.

Kathy Hays' role is to make sure the nurses interact with the patient to make sure the patient agrees with the procedure that is documented or the surgery that's scheduled and that they have no questions. Their role is to make sure that all questions have been answered before that patient signs the acknowledgment of informed consent. The nurses simply obtain an acknowledgement of the informed consent that the surgeon's staff obtains. The nurses aren't informing the patients of things, they're asking the patient for questions. According to Kathy Hays, informed consent is a conversation between the physicians and the patient. The team of nurses would not be giving all the information to the patient to make sure they were fully informed. The surgeons give the details.

If a nurse wanted to make a complaint about Durrani under the protocol at West Chester Medical Center, they would file a complaint with the OR manager. They would come to her, and they would funnel that on up through senior leadership. The OR had forty percent growth in volume after Durrani came to West Chester.

Thomas Harris became perioperative director in 2010 through September 2012. Harris claims Durrani and Shanti averaged six surgeries per week. This is off by 80%. No one ever told Harris whether or not Gerry Goodman ever reported anything about Durrani or expressed concerns about him.

Since West Chester opened, Dr. Tim Kremchek served as director of the orthopedics department. He denies telling Bill Cunningham of 700 WLW radio West Chester should have gotten rid of Durrani long ago. Bill told me Kremchek said that to him. The orthopedic department ran loosely. Kremchek states he never took any concerns about Durrani to anyone at West Chester Hospital while Durrani practiced there. In his opinion, the purpose of the orthopedic committee and on orthopedic department is to make sure that the nursing floors are going well. It was mostly when the hospital was opening, make sure the operating room was doing well, the surgeons happy, the staff given things that they need, and how they could recruit other physicians.

The bylaws claim the purpose is to supervise the surgeons, not what Kremchek claims. Only a few orthopedic surgeons would ever show up at the meetings. However, the administrators and staff attended. Durrani attended a couple meetings. Kremchek had an idea Durrani was very busy and performed many surgeries because they would show them at our orthopedic section meeting. Kremchek denies anyone coming to him with any specific complaints about Durrani. He heard Durrani might have been "sloppy." Imagine having a "sloppy" spine surgeon for your surgery. Kremchek claims being unaware Durrani used BMP on his patients and never held any discussions with anyone about the use of BMP at the West Chester OR. He is not familiar with Puregen and is not aware if Durrani used it. He's the Chief of Orthopedics and despite Jeffers tracking BMP-2, Kremchek claims he doesn't know.

In 2008, Ron Rohlfing became VP of hospital operations at West Chester. He worked with Mike Jeffers on budgets. He remembers Gerry Goodman. He does recall providing her, at her request, reports on the use of BMP2 manufactured by Medtronics as it was used in the OR and states reports about BMP would either come from supply chain or possibly the pharmacy. Kevin Brooks ran the pharmacy at West Chester from January 1, 2009, all the way through to May of 2013. Kevin Brooks' job would to be compliant with all regulations and state laws; to oversee the pharmacists; to make sure that quality, safety are adhered to; to maintain an accurate inventory and correct dispensing of the medications. Rohlfing admits BMP was used, but he's not aware of the profitability of BMP.

Dr. Kevin Joseph became the President of West Chester since April 2010 when he took over from Carol King. He also served as Senior VP of UC Health. He's since left both. He's taken over quality assurance at another healthcare system. It is scary he is. Joseph testified he had minimal involvement in the operations of the surgery suite at West Chester Hospital. The medical staff is responsible for oversight of surgeons and physicians in the OR. Joseph agrees a hospital must protect patients from unnecessary harm "as much as they can." He is familiar with "stop the line" policy. They stress throughout West Chester everyone should speak up if something doesn't sound right, smell right, look right. Joseph states that it's just part of the West Chester culture and has been the case since he got there. He has promoted and encouraged that policy from the time he took over his duties as President and CEO. Joseph states experimental surgeries are not performed at West Chester unless it goes through an Investigative Review Board.

According to Joseph, there is no mechanism in place at West Chester Hospital that would perform any type of surveillance or oversight to try to determine if a physician performed experimental procedures. This is scary. The CEO ignores the MEC bylaws. Dr. Joseph doesn't see any plausible or realistic way to create an oversight body when they have 900 physicians and thousands of different types of procedures, and for each procedure there's thousands of different medications and treatment options.

Gina Witko is the coordinator in West Chester Hospital that is responsible for the joint commission. The results of a joint commission survey are provided to the hospital and then it's voluntary whether the hospital publishes those or makes those available to the public and Joseph wouldn't have any issues volunteering it. The primary goal of joint commission standards and accreditation is bettering the care and improving the quality and service and safety of the patient. Joseph believes behaviors which undermine a culture of safety in healthcare include intimidating and disruptive behaviors, includes verbal outbursts, physical threats and sexual intimidation. As will be reflected in Vickie Scott's testimony, this is an issue. Joseph claims West Chester Hospital has a policy of discouraging any such behavior. There is a written policy with regard to what is considered inappropriate behaviors or disruptive behaviors.

Joseph sits on West Chester Hospital's credentialing committee process and is a non-voting member. At the time Durrani applied for privileges, Joseph served as a voting member of the credentialing committee. Joseph denies that West Chester Hospital violated its duty to some of its patients with respect to patient safety through Durrani's actions. Assuming that Durrani performed procedures he should not have performed at West Chester Hospital, Joseph would not agree that West Chester Hospital is responsible for harm that would come to patients for surgeries performed here that were unnecessary. A very arrogant and false claim.

Joseph denies knowing what capacity BMP was used in the hospital and doesn't know who is using it. He claims this despite his financial officer tracked it. He is unsure if it is still being used in the hospital. Assuming there's a request for a product such as BMP by a physician, West Chester relies on that physician to use it for an appropriate purpose. He refuses to acknowledge it's the MEC responsibility. The hospital, if it's for the operating room, would request that product pursuant to the physician's or surgeon's request. Joseph stated that it would not be possible to review an off-label use, assuming a surgeon wants to use a product for an off-label use and it hasn't been approved specifically by the FDA for the specific purpose that the surgeon is using it for. Joseph is not familiar with PureGen. Yet, Durrani used it at will at West Chester.

In his role as President and CEO, Joseph claims he never heard any complaints by anyone in the OR about Durrani. Joseph denies Gerry Goodman raised concerns Durrani in the operating room. Joseph denies any complaints raised here at West Chester with Durrani's use of either BMP or Puregen. He denies any complaints about Durrani's patients being subjected to prolonged and unnecessary anesthesia. Joseph was aware that Durrani being assigned to more than one operating room at a time and states it is a standard practice in many hospitals. It is not common, but it happens a surgeon to have more than two operating rooms assigned at the same time. Joseph states a surgeon being assigned patients in more than two operating rooms at the same time depends on the processes and operations.

Joseph denied being aware of Durrani making any sexual overtures or any staff in the operating room. Joseph denies Shanti was permitted to assist Durrani with any cases before Shanti was actually granted privileges and states that no one can operate at West Chester and practice without having privileges. Joseph denies being made aware that Shanti was performing procedures on patients who had consented for Durrani to perform their procedures.

Joseph states it is true that West Chester profited financially as a result of the procedures that Durrani performed. There is a bonus incentive in his role as President and CEO. Finances are part of the corporate, so it depends on not how well West Chester does, it depends on how well UC Health does, finances. Joseph received a bonus for each year he served as CEO and President. Regarding documentation which tracks the sources of revenue which makes the West Chester profitable, each source is gone through. They look at programs like the GI program to see if it's doing well. They'll take a look at it, see what the revenue is, see what the expenses are and see if there is an opportunity for efficiency. On a monthly basis, he would receive some type of accounting reports from the finance department and receive income and balance sheets.

There is an email exchange with Joseph and staff that appalls Wilkey. Joseph is upset about Durrani's record keeping, not based on patient care, but to bill workers compensation.

Mark Tromba is the OR manager since April 2012. Mark Tromba became aware Durrani used BMP for procedures because it is an approved product that MedAssets approved. Mark Tromba was a circulator. He acknowledged informed consent required the patient to have information they need that Durrani or Shanti or any surgeon should have provided to them. They would confirm with the patient they know everything or have any questions, and as long as they don't, they come back to surgery.

In February 2010, Cynthia Trafficant became the permanent Chief Nursing officer for West Chester. She remembers Gerry Goodman as a contractor. She remembers Shauna O'Neal as being a consultant for there and doesn't recall her being the Director of Nursing while she was there. Shauna was a Compass Clinical Consulting person, to get them ready for Joint Commission readiness. Cindy has no recollections of ever receiving a letter from Shauna. Shauna O'Neal sent her a letter complaining about Durrani. It's a fair statement to say she doesn't mean she did not send it, but just that she can't recall it. She does not recall any nurse, technician, staff employee ever complaining about Durrani, but it could be that she does not remember. Traficant agrees it would not be quality of care if a surgeon performed an unnecessary spine surgery on someone. She states it would be atypical if Shanti performed procedures under Durrani's name and agrees that would not be good quality of care.

Jeff Drapalik from May 2011 to past Durrani's departure, was the Director of Finance, CFO, for West Chester Hospital. His job description involved managing the financial operations for West Chester Hospital; preparing budgets, capital planning, doing financial analysis, and doing monthly closes for the financial operations related to West Chester. Also included direct reporting or management of admitting, medical records and finance. He had a dual reporting relationship to the CEO of West Chester Hospital and also the Vice President of Financial Operations for UC Health. Joseph was the former. The latter would have been Doug Arvin, who is the director of VP of Financial Operations for UC Health. The senior leadership team involved Drapalik, Kevin Joseph, Daskalakis, Baker, Rohlfing, Paula Hawk, Talbot, Grant Whitzel and Chip Washienko that had scheduled meetings on Mondays and Fridays, and then would have other periodic ad hoc meetings as needed. Doug Arvin would secretly provide me information during the litigation.

West Chester performed evaluations on physicians. Drapalik agrees during the time he was CFO at West Chester the orthopedic service provided more cases for West Chester Hospital than the other services. Orthopedics ranked number one and spine number one within orthopedics.

Dr. Lesley Gilbertson served as a member of the MEC and director of anesthesiology at West Chester 2008 to 2009. Gilbertson witnessed concerns from Goodman Durrani would do multiple spine surgeries at the same time. She witnessed patients of Durrani left open under anesthesia for extended periods of time and it concerned her.

Dennis Robb worked as Senior BP of Operations and Chief Supply Officer for UC Health. He decided spending of $369 million. On a daily basis Robb's responsibility was to look for contracting opportunities, to negotiate contracts, to coordinate contracts with the Office of General Counsel, compliance, privacy and to work with the physicians as groups and one-on-one to see where they could leverage contracts by reducing the number of vendors or moving to a better price opportunity based on utilization. This would include Medtronics and Alphatec.

Robb is familiar with BMP-2 and acquired it for the health system. They kept an inventory and supply of it for the hospitals out of a warehouse. They placed orders with Medtronic. Medtronic delivered BMP-2 to the warehouse which is in the UC Health Business Center. BMP-2 would be distributed on a daily basis, five to six times a week to the sites based on their inventory demand.

From March 2010 to July 2012, Karen Ghaffari served as Director of Nursing at West Chester. Karen resigned out of a different philosophy than her manager, Patrick Baker. The difference in the philosophy is she believed in working with employees, receiving feedback and incorporating their ideas into the plan that is her philosophy as a transformational leader. She developed concerns regarding Durrani's documentation. Durrani used post-surgery notes. Nurses complained. They prepared an audit of charts. She spoke to her Chief Nursing Officer, Cindi Traficant. She testified Joseph knew about any complaint about Durrani. Yet, Joseph claims to know nothing.

Melissa Helmer worked as Clinical Program Director West Chester 2008 to April 2012. She remembers Durrani having a higher volume of surgeries.

In 2011, Patrick Baker became CNO at West Chester and in November 2011 he became VP of Patient Care Services and CNO. His job is to make sure of quality, patient safety, make sure that people have the resources and tools to do their job, to provide guidance and instruction. On a day-to-day basis through different meetings, committees, initiatives, problem solving. When he began, they saw 50 to 60 patients a night and by 2013 up to 120 to 140. His main job is problem solving, operation efficiencies, and then through these operations and efficiencies and growth, the safety and quality aspects and service excellence like with the accommodations we make for our patients. Baker's direct supervisor is Tom Daskalaskis and the CEO is Joseph. They held meetings on a regular basis as the leadership team. When he began at West Chester the surgery department and management structure was in turbulence with high staff turnover.

Vickie Scott worked from September 2008 to September 2012 at West Chester as a coordinator in endoscopy and a circulating nurse. She interacted with Denise Evans, Cindi Traficant, Melissa Helmer, Mark Tromba and Kathy Hays. She spoke to risk management about Durrani. She participated in surgeries in Durrani's surgery rooms. The issues with Durrani at West Chester hospital is the reason she reported him to risk management. She spoke to Jill Stegman, the risk manager. She spoke to Ron Rohlfing. Jill asked her to talk to Ron. Vickie Scott told Rohlfing of the Durrani problems in the OR. Vickie told Stegman the patients did not know who was doing surgery on them despite the schedule claiming Durrani. Staff would not know Durrani or Shanti until right before surgery. She would take that patient to the OR. The surgeon would come into the room and do the procedure. It wasn't listed on the schedule who specifically was doing the surgery. It appeared Durrani was doing them all, but that was noy true.

Sometimes Shanti would do a surgery from the beginning to the end and Durrani was not involved at all. Patients would not know who performed their surgery. One morning, Durrani came in and marked a patient, but Vickie knew Shanti was going to be the surgeon in the room. She asked the patient if they knew who Shanti was and the patient told her they've never heard of him. She reported this to Jill Stegman.

Scott was responsible for keeping accurate records as to what personnel was in the operating room suite at what point and time. It was her understanding at the time she had that position, that she had that responsibility. In the procedures in which she was involved, where it identifies who the physicians was in the particular procedure, she was the person who entered that information. If Shanti, Durrani, Dr. Wolf or Dr. Husted was in the room for X amount of time, it was her responsibility to document whatever time period they were in the room. She also presented to Jill Stegman other issues like physician's treatment of staff.

Vickie Scott gave information to Elaine Kunko in writing. All of the circulators went to Elaine and said there were issues with who's going to be in the room and charting. The report would be generated with Durrani being the surgeon. It's regenerated in the computer when the scheduler puts it in there. All of the cases would have Durrani as the primary surgeon. She would have to literally go in and do a lot of changing to take him out. The procedure record is the circulator's responsibility and they identified what surgeons were in the room. The information was pre-generated and was already in there. So in order to take Durrani out, there was several things she had to do. She had to go in and pick another surgeon, pick the procedure, and those procedures weren't necessarily listed in the charting for her to select all the different things Durrani was doing. There was a lot of major changes which needed to take place in order for the circulator to change the primary surgeon.

If there was a time frame listed for Durrani, it didn't always mean he was in the room during that time frame. There may have been a time he was listed as a primary surgeon and may not have even come in the room. If that happened, there would be no times next to his name in and out possibly. The purpose of changing the primary surgeon's name was because that was who was actually doing the surgery. She doesn't have any information to suggest the billing is done by West Chester as opposed to the surgeon. She recalls Elaine making a comment Durrani was billing for all of the procedures.

The perioperative director, Kathy Hays, was from Children's and Durrani got her the job. Vickie Scott had a problem with Kathy Hays. Most of the staff had a problem with Mark Tromba. Scott said Tromba didn't know anything, was very immature and didn't know how to manage. Scott saw Patrick Baker is a wolf in sheep's clothing and a "bad guy." A number of the staff had issues with Baker. Baker took an OR nurse alone in a room and she felt very intimidated. She had a discussion with Patrick Baker about the problems in the OR when he first got there. Every time a new person came onboard, they hoped that this person was here to fix the problems in that hospital. But every time someone came, and you would go to them, nothing would happen. The same problems consistently went on every day.

Shanti would be doing the entire procedure and Durrani didn't show up at all. There would be times that Durrani would stick his head in the room and ask if things were going good and then say see you later. Durrani signed off on the operative note indicating he did the entire surgery, in many cases that wouldn't be correct, and Shanti did the entire surgery. The operative note that was prepared at the hospital is something to rely on for who actually did the surgery. They had something called Midas, a system for complaints. Scott filled out Midas forms.

Durrani called everyone an asshole. Scott never heard anyone else ever call an individual an asshole or dumb at work. She never heard anyone speak to staff the way Durrani did. She never heard any surgeon speak to staff in the OR room like Durrani did.

Vickie Scott was part of the staff that started West Chester and when she became involved with the project, along with a lot of other key staff people, they were told that the hospital was going to be like no other in Cincinnati, where quality patient care was going to be the most important thing and bad doctors were not going to be tolerated. She has not seen or experienced things she experienced at West Chester. West Chester represented themselves as something that is world class healthcare and they weren't. It was a challenge at times because of the management and the lack of knowledge. She thought that she was going to die before she got out of that building. She had been trying so hard to get out of there because of the way the place was.

In her entire nursing career, Vickie Scott never witnessed a doctor or heard information and witnessed things like you did with Durrani. He was more than just a bad doctor. It was like a "war zone." There was always something going on. That's the kind of atmosphere it was in that building. Jill Stegman would not return her phone calls. There was maybe a couple of attempts to contact and it became very clear that people that spoke up became the problem and then you were gone. Some of her coworkers were afraid to speak up and knows this from personal conversations with them.

It was common knowledge the reason they tolerated Durrani was the volume of surgeries and the money he brought in. Everyone knew it was all about making money.

In February 2009, Elizabeth Dean began at West Chester. She worked as a patient access representative. In Elizabeth's position as a patient access representative for registering patients for radiology studies or other diagnostic studies, she did not interact with Durrani on a regular basis but only saw him when he arrived to do back injections. This meant all the injections had to be prepared before Durrani came in because he had so many patients. Preparing the injections wasn't complicated, but the entire room was filled with patients that had to be squeezed into a small amount of time. Elizabeth was responsible for registering those patients. Durrani, to the best of her knowledge, was the only physician who sent patients to West Chester for steroid injections.

Elizabeth was responsible for registering patients for diagnostic studies. She also completed spreadsheet for Mike Jeffers, the CFO. Mike Jeffers would email the information for the spreadsheets to Elizabeth. She was also called into the meeting to find out the process and the flow of how to bill the injections without them going out incorrectly or kicking out of the system. The information on the spreadsheets contained patient name, medical record number, date of service, probably a CPT, amount charged, how much was paid and how much was contractual. Elizabeth added that up for Mr. Jeffers.

When Elizabeth spoke about how much was paid and how much was contractual, she spoke about what the insurance paid. After the insurance paid, the remainder was written off. The information giving the amount of insurance payment and what was written off was gotten from the Last Word system. The Last Word system gave all of the information: Name, Medical Record number, date of service, CPT code and the amount charged. It also listed the doctor and all of them were Durrani patients. Elizabeth never had responsibility for collecting the information for any other physician. She only did the spreadsheet for Durrani's patients. Mr. Jeffers sent this information to her and the section that was blank was the amount paid and the contract amount. Elizabeth Dean stated that she was responsible for filling in the amount paid. After filling them in, she would send them back to Jeffers. She did this biweekly until she left. Her last day at West Chester was July 2010.

Elizabeth also attended most corporate meetings regarding the process for the injections performed by Durrani. When asked about the name/type of meeting, Elizabeth did not remember the name of the meeting that she was involved in, but the group met weekly. She would attend these weekly meetings on a weekly basis, if she was invited. Between February, 2009 and July, 2010, she probably attended two or three of those corporate meetings. She called them corporate meetings because Ron Rohlfing, the vice president was the person leading the meetings. Elizabeth states that Mike Jeffers was present in that meeting, along with Ron Rohlfing and Lisa Davis. She couldn't remember other names.

Elizabeth was the one that was actually doing the whole process, how to get his patients in and get everything correct and how it could be done in a timely manner. If she could figure out how to get things done faster/quicker, they would ask her. Elizabeth was asked to the meetings to discuss the process of getting patients registered in a timely manner, how to get that patient flow to keep moving so that the waiting room didn't get backed up.

Elizabeth was the actual patient access rep who registered and spoke with all of the Durrani patients, all of those that registered for testing and pre-op or other procedures. The only Durrani patients Elizabeth interacted with that were registered for inpatient or surgery were the ones that were a direct admit. She did a few of those. She was known as "mobile". She wasn't always sitting at a desk. If there was a patient who needed a direct admit and she was available, Elizabeth did that. Elizabeth stated that West Chester was not picking up revenue like it should have. Her basis for making that assumption was that there were no patients. It was like a ghost town.

Elizabeth states that there was a lot of commotion where people were new. It was chaotic. The reason for the changeover for the new CEO is that they wanted to have the hospital run by physicians and that's what they were told. Elizabeth says that Joseph was named CEO because he was a physician. In her opinion, the visions of honesty and integrity were gone. The talk of the hospital and everyone was whispering it was Children's kicked out Durrani. When a doctor walks in and has a slew of patients no other doctors has, it raises red flags. It began to make her wonder, why is nobody questioning it and why does he have so many patients? Elizabeth stated that it was like a conveyor belt, one after the other.

Elizabeth asked Jeffers why Durrani left Children's to come to West Chester, because the rumor was that he was kicked out. Mike said that he didn't know why. Elizabeth said she estimated she prepared 10-20 reports for Mike Jeffers and the only info she added to the reports was the general information, the amount, the insurance amount and the contract amount. Elizabeth heard many of Durrani's patients' stories firsthand. They sat in front of her and talked to her while she was checking them in. It made her sad that she couldn't help them or tell them to find another doctor. Elizabeth said that if you've ever talked to someone with back pain, that's all they talk about. Elizabeth wanted to help get them relief, maybe go somewhere else, get a different opinion, but she says that she couldn't. As checking in, patients would discuss their pain. She didn't have access to the treatment that they had up to that point. Elizabeth didn't have access to tell if they had prior surgeries unless the patient told her. Some of the patients told her that they had prior surgeries. Whether the surgeries were done by Durrani or another physician, she did not know. She had one patient, an older woman, come in as a direct admit and she stated when she came in, "I'm back" and Durrani had just performed surgery on her. Elizabeth had a direct admit patient who leaked spinal fluid after his surgery.

Elizabeth felt like it was about the money. Durrani did it all for money and the patients were just numbers. Elizabeth didn't have any other doctors that would re-present and re-present the same patient. There were patients who had more than one admission related to Durrani. Elizabeth was not aware of other doctors who had re-admissions of the same patient. Elizabeth said that in the magnitude that Durrani did multiple surgeries, she didn't feel that other doctors did that many. There were emails between Elizabeth and Mike Jeffers about Durrani. When Jeffers saw the spreadsheets that showed the amount of revenue that was being generated by Durrani, he would be excited to see the revenue. He would want to see the numbers. He wanted to review it with Elizabeth to confirm that the numbers were correct.

Before Durrani, Jeffers would say things were just not picking up. There were not enough patients coming in. Elizabeth testified the emergency room would pick up every once in a while, and all of the floors of the hospital were not all open. This changed after Durrani began doing his procedures at West Chester. There was discussion around the hospital about Durrani and even concerns about what he was doing. Although there were questions, Elizabeth was not aware if anyone spoke to administration or upper management about these concerns while she was there. People wondered how Durrani was at West Chester, what was going on, and how he was able to practice there. Durrani once held discussions with West Chester to lease the entire fourth floor for CAST and physical therapy.

Scott Rimer worked at West Chester from April to July 2010 as a circulating nurse. The leadership team of West Chester, including Joseph and Traficant, held a meeting of the OR staff because of issues in the OR. No one spoke up. A second meeting was held, and Scott Rimer decided to speak up. He recalls Joseph talking about profits. Rimer described an incident in the OR. The next day, he was called into a room by management and the process of removing him from employment began. Durrani was dishonest in the consent/surgery process: "*Yes. But he's the only surgeon that I was told not to fill out the procedure until the end. No other surgeon had that—no one came to me and said, wait until the end of the procedure to find out what he did. We used the consent form; this is what we're doing. And that's the procedure performed. So when the patients asleep and I'm their advocate, this is the procedure they're having. When you come to me and say, don't write the procedure out until we're done and it's not what the consent form says, I had a problem with that. I had a big problem with that from a director ethical standpoint. I had a big problem with that. It's not my job to stop them, but it is my job to watch out for that patient. Was he doing back surgery? Yeah. Did the patient have back surgery? Yeah. Was it exactly what they consented for? No. Do I have a problem with it? Yes. It's an ethical issue.*" Scott Rimer witnessed Durrani during a spine surgery go in and out of a surgery bidding on a Lamborghini and bragging about it. Surgical teams often switched in and out of surgical fields. Scott Rimer also believed it was inappropriate PureGen was being used at the hospital.

Tom Blank is an independent sales representative working with Medtronics/BMP-2 and Alphatec/PureGen and West Chester/UC Health and Durrani. Becky Griggs, the ortho/neuro coordinator at West Chester would contact Blank and arrange for the BMP-2 or PureGen product. Durrani would also contact him. "*So then my main role is to basically facilitate the ordering of the product and making sure that it got to the hospital and it was available for surgery.*" West Chester knew PureGen and BMP-2 was being used. He also dealt with Dwayne Brown. PureGen was an alternative to BMP-2. "*No. I know that the hospital was concerned about the safety and efficacy of BMP, as well as, you know insurance companies who were deciding to cover it.*" West Chester and UC Health knew the problem about BMP-2.

We sued Tom Blank. He called me. I said give us information and we will drop you. He came to the office the same day and told us all the BMP-2 and Puregen information, which is detailed in this book.

Chapter 92
Bad Faith

"Such is the avarice, such the insatiate thirst for gold of these ecclesiastical harpies, that they would snatch the last hoe cake from the widow and the orphan."
—Patrick Henry

This, too, is a lengthy chapter and is last on the Durrani subject for a reason. You will be appalled at what you read. It's all still pending at the date of publication before Judge Michael Barrett. He will decide if we have our day in Court against the massive evil committed by Medical Protective. We must share the complete story.

Medical Protective's conduct involves egregious behavior of unprecedented magnitude relative to the handling of malpractice claims. Verdict amounts covered by the insurance policy now exceed twenty million dollars. Medical Protective makes no offer on any case, even after a verdict against them is returned. Medical Protective made statements on the record "we will never settle." This means we must and will litigate every case until the end when they will have to pay. They once claimed they based their denials on an algorithm. After we destroyed the algorithm by our winning 70% of the cases, they ignored the algorithm. Their lawyers use every delay tactic known to law in the misguided belief we will fold. Meanwhile, their lawyers simply make more money.

These claims involve more than just not settling. Medical Protective aided, abetted, and encouraged Durrani to flee the United States. They orchestrated this with the intent to deny coverage based on non-cooperation. They attempted every possible tact including the deception over five years regarding Durrani's unwillingness to give a deposition. For years, the lawyers claiming to represent Durrani at trial claim no contact with him.

Medical Protective's wrongful conduct goes far past simply not making offers on undeniably valid claims. This is further proof of their malicious bad faith. Medical Protective attempted to avoid coverage through nefarious means, manipulating Durrani into fleeing, fraudulently failed to produce Durrani for deposition while making decisions without communicating with Durrani.

In Medical Protective's Claim File for Rita Hounchell, Medical Protective acknowledged Durrani agreed to give testimony in ten cases on top of the two depositions. Medical Protective lost those trials. After losing these trials it is no coincidence Durrani stopped giving depositions and testimony. Mike Lyon told Durrani not to testify or failed to tell Durrani of the depositions and trials at all. Despite Durrani's willingness to testify via Skype or Zoom, Medical Protective continued their charade claiming, "once again we face the reality of Durrani's refusal to participate in this case as a witness, whether live or by video conferencing." There are references to experts in claims files which Medical Protective hired who after reviewing a case informed Medical Protective they can't defend the case. Medical Protective instead tries to hide the negative reports behind privilege logs.

In claims files, Mike Lyon references Alan Statman as inexperienced in medical malpractice and average ability. Despite Alan Statman's alleged inexperience in medical malpractice or average ability, Alan continues to win record breaking victories. Instead of acknowledging either the extreme talent of our team or the absolute weakness of their cases, Medical Protective's claims files are filled with sarcasm directed towards me, Alan Statman, and Glenn Feagan who together as a team racked up over $100 million dollars in verdicts against Durrani. Medical Protective refuses to offer or counteroffer on any Durrani case and obviously views the massive verdicts and suffering of Durrani's victims as a joke.

Medical Protective provides no correspondence in their claims file after verdicts reflecting they are unwilling to offer to settle cases even as they are on their way to appeal or adjust their strategy of "no deals." Medical Protective views Judge Reece as "plaintiff oriented" in these files. They make no offers despite stating they have a "plaintiff oriented" judge for their cases. As far as their allegation, I wish Judge Reece was plaintiff oriented. He's not. He's down the middle.

Medical Protective knew at the outset of this massive litigation in 2013 and prior to trials, Durrani breached the standard of care and committed negligent acts, criminal acts, and fraudulent acts involving unnecessary spine surgeries which would require Medical Protective to defend Durrani and provide coverage for the negligent acts. Medical Protective knew Cincinnati Children's Hospital terminated Durrani in 2008 after his colleagues produced undeniable evidence he engaged in unnecessary surgeries, unauthorized experimental surgeries and fraudulent surgeries. Medical Protective also knew Durrani's colleagues drafted a letter to the Ohio Medical Board describing Durrani's frauds and erratic behavior and warned he is a clear and present danger to patients.

Durrani and CAST operated both Kentucky and Ohio locations where patients visited, called, received information from, billed from, marketed from and treated and interacted with them. In 2013, prior to trials, Medical Protective knew Durrani had been arrested and indicted on over thirty federal charges related to unnecessary spine surgeries and prescription fraud and then fled from the United States to Pakistan to avoid a federal criminal trial and civil litigation. Medical Protective actually chose a bad faith and unfair claims scorched earth defense for Durrani who faced all of this. It defies logic. It is bad faith and unfair claims practices per se, which means it speaks for itself.

Medical Protective, including their legal counsel, encouraged and participated in Durrani's flight to Pakistan. Medical Protective attempted to use Durrani's flight to void coverage under their policies of medical malpractice insurance under the so-called non-cooperation clause found within each policy and cheat Durrani victims from Medical Protective's coverage.

Following his flight to Pakistan, Medical Protective obstructed victims' counsels' efforts to depose Durrani for over five years of pending civil litigation, claiming Durrani refused to give depositions when Medical Protective knew Durrani wanted to be deposed in cooperation of coverage. Medical Protective used their scheme to void coverage and thwart litigation against Durrani in flagrant violation of KRS §304.12-230 ("Misrepresenting pertinent facts or insurance policy provisions relating to coverages at issue"). Medical Protective claimed they could not contact him and/or he refused a deposition, when Medical Protective never asked him to give more depositions. Medical Protective and Mike Lyon actually use the phrase referencing Durrani: "before he allegedly left the country" as if they still do not know he left. It's all absurd.

Medical Protective sent Durrani the same bogus form letters clearly attempting to "set up" the lack of cooperation on each case. Lindhorst and Reminger placed in reports that Durrani's "lack of cooperation" is why they might lose. A total scheme.

Medical Protective Claims Files reference a letter from Durrani to Attorney Lyon in January 2019 "stating no longer to participate in defense." Medical Protective refuses to produce this letter. Medical Protective also references our proposal to Durrani and claim it should be referred to his criminal defense lawyer Ed Perry who schemes with Mike Lyon.

Despite knowledge of the magnitude of their liability and exposure from 2013 to the present, there has never been a single rational good faith proposal of resolution by Medical Protective to resolve the Durrani litigation. If the facts in this matter do not support a claim against Medical Protective, no set of facts ever will.

Medical Protective issued a policy of medical malpractice liability insurance to Durrani, effective January 1, 2009 to January 1, 2010, which was thereafter renewed on an annual basis through December 31, 2013 with the policies in effect from January 1, 2009 to December 31, 2010, having limits of $1,000,000 "one occurrence" and $3,000,000 in the aggregate and policies in effect from January 1, 2011 to December 31, 2013 having limits of $5,000,000 "one occurrence" and $7,000,000 in the aggregate.

Medical Protective issued a policy of medical malpractice liability insurance to CAST effective January 1, 2009 to January 1, 2010 which was thereafter renewed on an annual basis through December 31, 2013 having limits of $1,000,000 "one occurrence" and $3,000,000 in the aggregate.

The aggregate amount of the coverages under Medical Protective's policies of liability insurance issued to Durrani and CAST referenced above is $42,000,000.00.

Timothy Kenesey is the President and Chief Executive Officer of Medical Protective from 2001 through today. This covers the entire time frame of the litigation. From 2013 through now, he held direct decision authority on Durrani victims' claims.

Robert Ignasiak is Senior Vice President, General Counsel and Claims Leader for Medical Protective from 2012 through now. He also holds direct decision authority on all of Durrani claims. He is the Medical Protective official who came to my law office and offered $2 million dollars.

Medical Protective does a high volume of medical malpractice insurance business in Kentucky and Ohio. They insure the medical malpractice risks of countless physicians and other medical professionals.

Richard Marcello is the Division Claim Manager of Mideast Division of Medical Protective located in Louisville, Kentucky and in his position is over Medical Protective's claims in Ohio, Indiana and Kentucky, including all of Durrani claims. He held this position since September 2013. Prior to this, he served from 2002 through September 2013 as a Medical Malpractice Claim Specialist at Medical Protective and St. Paul Companies from 1986 to 2002. He is an alleged expert on medical claims against doctors. From 2013 through now, he held direct decision authority on all Durrani claims.

MacKenzie Walter is now a former employee of Medical Protective, who worked out of Louisville, Kentucky under the supervision of Richard Marcello. She monitored Durrani cases from the courtroom and through communication with the other Medical Protective representatives, the trials and litigation against Durrani. She only recently left Medical Protective.

Steven Janik is an attorney in the law firm Janik, LLP. They act as agents of Medical Protective and participated in the unfair claims practices on behalf of Medical Protective.

Rick Marcello and MacKenzie Walter handled every Durrani file out of Louisville, Kentucky where Kentucky requires compliance with their Unfair Claims Practices statute.

On December 19, 2013, Durrani emailed a former patient while in Pakistan. This reflects how Durrani maintained contact with persons located in the United States and is accessible to even a former patient.

On December 19, 2013, Marvin Benson, Sr. Claim Specialist for Medical Protective, in an email to Durrani referenced a letter he needed a reply to regarding the upcoming trial of *Pierce* scheduled January 6, 2014.

On December 19, 2013, Marvin Benson, Sr. Claim Specialist for Medical Protective, sent Durrani a letter in the *Pierce* case and copied it to Michael Lyon and David Bendel, VP/Regional Manager of Medical Protective and stated: *"It has come to Medical Protective's attention that you will not be in attendance at this trial as you are no longer in the United States and have returned to Pakistan."* How did that come to his attention? Michael Lyon. The fact this letter was copied to Michael Lyon is significant.

On December 23, 2013, Durrani sent an email to Marvin Benson: *"Mr. Benson. Thank you for the letter. At this time, I will not be able to return back to the U.S. and unfortunately will not be able to assist in any way in defense of these civil cases. I regret the inconvenience caused in this regard. AD."* This email is legalese. Civil cases? Of note, it's not copied to Michael Lyon like Marvin Benson's December 19, 2013 letter. We believe Michael Lyon wrote this for Durrani and purposefully failed to copy himself. This is one of the many questions at Durrani's deposition in 2018, Michael Lyon actually instructed Durrani not to answer solely to protect himself. Even Schweikert questioned it, but of course took no action.

On January 2, 2014, Medical Protective's legal counsel, Steven Janik, filed a Complaint for Declaratory Judgment in the United States District Court, Southern District of Ohio. In the lawsuit, Janik states: *"Medical Protective retained the law firm of Lindhorst and Dreidame, LPA to defend Durrani and CAST in the Underlying Lawsuits."* By email of December 23, 2013 to Medical Protective, Durrani advised, *"I will not be able to return back to the US and unfortunately will not be able to assist in any way in defense of these civil cases." "Durrani and CAST have failed to cooperate with Medical Protective and assist in the preparation and trial of the Underlying Lawsuits."* The significance? Medical Protective is represented in federal court, Durrani is not assisting in his defense. This would later to be proven a scam by Durrani's lawyers.

Medical Protective in this lawsuit requested a Court ruling Durrani's lack of cooperation voided or canceled all of the insurance coverage.

Medical Protective admits Durrani gave fourteen hours of depositions in 2018 for all cases.

The federal court scheduled Durrani's criminal trial date for January 3, 2014. An Overview of Federal Criminal Cases: Fiscal Year 2012," a report produced by the United States Sentencing Commission's Office of Research and Data, reflects that in 2012, there were 84,360 federal criminal cases in which the defendant was sentenced. Of those convicted defendants, 97% pleaded guilty, with fraud being the third largest category of criminal cases during 2012 at 10.5%. The rate of conviction overall remained at over 90%, as it has since 2001.

Based on the above referenced statistics, if Durrani remained in the United States and not fled to Pakistan, there is a 97% probability that he would have been convicted of or pleaded guilty to the criminal charges pending against him. Once convicted of a felony, if Durrani were present at any of the state civil actions against him, he would have had to admit he was a convicted felon. The jury would know Durrani is a felon. This fact alone proves Medical Protective benefitted from Durrani's flight and was not prejudiced. The flight avoided a certain conviction to be used at every trial.

On January 6, 2014, the *Pierce* trial began. Michael Lyon called Durrani by previously taken discovery deposition. Durrani did not attend the trial. As noted earlier the jury returned a verdict of $1.04 million dollars.

Medical Protective then engaged in a lengthy appeal process of the *Pierce* verdict. The Ohio First District Court of Appeals affirmed the judgment on July 15, 2015. Although we firmly established liability with competent evidence and knowing Durrani's abominable past actions, Mike Lyon appealed to the Ohio Supreme Court to delay payment. On February 9, 2016, the Ohio Supreme Court allowed the verdict to stand. Most verdicts do stand. Medical Protective with full knowledge there was no reasonable basis to deny the claim, denied it and made no settlement demand.

From 2014 to 2018, as Mike Lyon lied about Durrani giving depositions, we could not ask Durrani questions on countless relevant topics. The proposed questions cover his background, liability, causation, damages, credibility, his privileges at hospitals and more. We only deposed Durrani in six cases before he fled. After his arrest, informants gave Deters Law volumes of information we never knew, and we obtained the Kentucky and Ohio Medical Board files. We were not able to depose Durrani with the benefit of this newly obtained information. At trials, Durrani's legal counsel conducted voir dire, gave an opening, cross examine witnesses, called witnesses, made motions and gave a closing. We would do the same without Durrani's deposition or testimony.

Just after *Pierce's* trial, on January 17, 2014, Glenn Whitaker filed a Motion to Withdraw as Counsel for Durrani in the Criminal Case and stated: *"As the defendant fled the United States... communication between Vorys and the defendant has ceased, and the defendant has failed to fulfill financial obligations to Vorys for its services."* Of note, while Durrani is not communicating with his criminal defense lawyer, Michael Lyon claims he is communicating with Durrani in Pakistan during this time.

The victims are entitled to Medical Protective's entire claims file. In 2013, we requested it be preserved for production. At the date of publication, we have not received the file.

On January 22, 2014, we requested a telephonic video deposition of Durrani in the *Cory Wright* case and all cases scheduled for trial. I took the extraordinary step to set the deposition up from Lahore, Pakistan at Doctors Hospital where Durrani practiced as its chief of spine surgery.

On February 3, 2014, Paul McCartney, one of Durrani's lawyers not being paid by Medical Protective but another insurance company, sent us a letter regarding Durrani's deposition in Wright: *"This is in response to your letter of January 22, 2014 requesting the deposition of Durrani. Durrani has indicated that he is unable to give a deposition at the present time in this case or in any other case."* Durrani's legal counsel made it clear. There will be no depositions. Who benefited? Durrani, the hospitals and Medical Protective.

On February 5, 2014, we asked Paul McCartney for proof Durrani responded with a refusal to participate in the deposition. Paul McCartney never responded.

On February 17, 2014, Durrani gave medical treatment direction to the same patient he emailed in December 19, 2013. This patient became a client of ours.

On February 25, 2014, Durrani's lawyers stated: *"As opposing counsel and the Court are aware, Durrani has allegedly fled the country. Recent efforts to communicate with him have been fruitless."* The "alleged flight" of course is a lie because Michael Lyon told me Durrani fled and the U.S. Attorney's office confirmed it. In a response to a Motion to Compel, Michael Lyon claims: *"Dr. Durrani's attorneys, as officers of the Court, assured that they have properly communicated with their client."* We do not believe this. Medical Protective and Michael Lyon navigated a fraud for Medical Protective. They knew if Durrani gave depositions Medical Protective would have to provide coverage. They also know Durrani would be destroyed at his deposition based upon all which had been revealed after his arrest.

On February 28, 2014, Durrani's legal counsel answered discovery in the Shell case with this statement: *"As opposing counsel and the Court are aware, Durrani has allegedly fled the country. Recent efforts to communicate with him have been fruitless."*

On May 7, 2014, we requested Durrani's counsel to advise us whether or not they informed Durrani of the notice to depose him in Romer and Feltner. Paul McCartney replied: *"You are not entitled to know how or if we have communicated to Durrani about the notices."* Not only is Paul McCartney's statement legally wrong, it was clear his response is to protect him, not Durrani. Under ethics rules, Paul McCartney can't reveal what was communicated to his client, not how or if.

On May 13, 2014, we acknowledged a dispute regarding Durrani's discovery answers. Durrani is supposed to sign the answers. He never does, because Medical Protective lawyers never show it to him.

On May 13, 2014, we asked if Durrani will appear at his deposition. Michael Lyon responded by letter: *"As requested, we have notified Durrani at his deposition that you recently noticed. As of May 13, 2014, we have not received any word from Durrani regarding the deposition."*

On May 21, 2014, Jim Brockman, Michael Lyon's partner, to Deters Law: *"I know I had not had any reply from Durrani regarding the deposition. I have now heard from Messrs. Lyon and McCartney. They haven't either. If we do hear something from him, we'll be sure to advise you as soon as we can."*

On May 21, 2014, we cancelled the depositions of Durrani based upon the representations above.

On May 28, 2014, we noticed Durrani for ninety-nine depositions.

On May 30, 2014, Michael Lyon wrote us in response to the new notices for deposition. They state: *"We have advised Durrani of this." "He advises he will not be available."* He also stated: *"In light of this advice, as was the case in the previously noticed deposition, we shall not insist that you go through the formality of arranging for a court reporter in Pakistan, having the reporter be there and you, personally attend the deposition to prove he is unavailable."* The significance? It contradicts previous statements that attempt to communicate with Durrani have been fruitless. Durrani's lawyers always alternated between claiming communication with him and not, as it suited Medical Protective's needs. During all his time in Pakistan, Durrani worked at Doctors Hospital, had a cell phone, home phone, work phone and email. He's never been unreachable.

Cincinnati attorney of note, Chris Finney, flew to Pakistan for a client. He gets in a cab. Finney jokingly asks the cab driver, "Ever hear of Dr. Durrani?" The cab driver says sure, and they drive past Durrani's office. For kicks, Finney asked the cab driver to stop and wait. Finney goes into Durrani's office and Durrani is there. Finney takes a picture of Durrani and himself and sends it to Joe Deters, who sends it to me. Real unreachable.

On June 3, 2014, the discovery answers state: "... *since Durrani has, apparently, fled the country."* They still claim "apparently."

On June 6, 2014, Durrani was scheduled for depositions from Pakistan in ninety-nine cases. These depositions too would not happen.

On August 18, 2014, Durrani's federal criminal trial came and went while Durrani is in Pakistan.

On November 25, 2014, Paul McCartney sent an email to Deters Law: *"Dr. Durrani will not be appearing on Wednesday, November 26th for his deposition in the cases for which you sent notices. As before, it is not necessary for anyone from Plaintiff's to make a record. Please let me know if you have any questions. Paul"* Again, his lawyer informed Deters Law to not waste time. And note the word choice of Paul McCartney: *"will not be appearing."* Why? Because he never even told him about the deposition. He did not want to lie and chose his words carefully.

The November 26, 2014, the scheduled deposition of Durrani never took place based upon Paul McCartney's representation.

It must be stressed why Deters Law kept trying to take Durrani's deposition. To receive a sanction under Ohio Civil Rule 37, a deposition must be noticed and attempted. One of the greatest injustices to the victims is that despite what is being laid out here, the Courts never hammered Durrani, his lawyers or Medical Protective.

On August 31, 2015, Steven Janik, Medical Protective counsel, filed a Motion to Consent to Settle Cases. In that pleading, Steven Janik wrote: *"By leaving the country and stating that he will not return or otherwise assist in the defense of the civil cases pending against him, Durrani has breached his duty to cooper-*

ate, which is a material condition of the Policies, and as a result Durrani has forfeited his rights under the Policies. Durrani intentionally left the country in response to his indictment in the Criminal Litigation, and has expressly refused to participate in his defense. This voluntary and intentional conduct warrants the conclusion that Durrani has relinquished all rights under the Policies, including the right to consent to settle. Durrani has expressly stated that he will not return or otherwise assist in the defense of the civil cases pending against him. As Durrani has fled the country and refused to cooperate with Medical Protective in the preparation of his defense and trial." The significance? Medical Protective is representing in federal court, Durrani is not assisting in his defense. By 2018, Deters Law would learn of the scam to prevent Durrani's cooperation by Medical Protective.

In addition, Medical Protective obtained the Order. This means Medical Protective controls settlement. They do not need Durrani's consent. Yet, no settlement.

Medical Protective and their lawyers actually use the phrase referencing Durrani: *"before he allegedly left the country,"* despite their active assistance in his flight from justice.

On January 29, 2016, Medical Protective proposed as a stipulated fact in a federal filing: *"Since Durrani's email of December 23, 2013, Durrani has, in fact, not cooperated with Medical Protective with respect to the Underlying Litigation and has neither attended nor assisted in preparation and trial of the Underlying Litigation."* Medical Protective intentionally refrained from asking him to attend or assist. We refused the self-serving stipulation.

On February 5, 2016, Steven Janik, Medical Protective counsel, filed in a pleading in federal court: *"Since Durrani's email of December 23, 2013, Durrani has not cooperated with Medical Protective with respect to the Underlying Litigation and has neither attended nor assisted in preparation and trial of the Underlying Litigation."* Medical Protective intentionally never asked him to.

On July 25, 2016, West Chester/UC Health in a federal filing, Motion for Appointment of Receiver, asserts CAST and Durrani have failed *"to cooperate in the defense of more than 400 underlying civil cases against Durrani."* Medical Protective intentionally never asked him to.

On July 25, 2016, Medical Protective in a pleading seeking a receiver stated: *"Since that time neither Durrani nor CAST have participated in the defense of the Underlying Cases."* Defendants intentionally never asked him to.

On October 21, 2016, federal district court Judge Timothy S. Black entered an Order in favor of the victims on the Medical Protective attempting to void coverage. The crux of the decision is Medical Protective is not prejudiced at all by Durrani's absence and "so called" lack of cooperation. Assisted by their tactic of having Durrani flee, Durrani actually won four trials in Butler County.

Judge Black ruled in essence: "How can you claim lack of cooperation harmed you when you won trials?"

On October 27, 2016, based upon the Judge Black decision, we demanded the policy limits.

On October 28, 2016, George Jonson, Michael Lyon's lawyer, responded with their position: *"In light of Judge Black's decision, each of your clients are required to try their case, secure a verdict and demand payment at which time Medical Protective must refuse to pay and then you will be required to institute suit against Medical Protective and litigate the prejudice that Durrani's absence caused the defense, if any."* He is wrong. However, this issue would resolve itself in 2018 when Durrani gave a deposition in every case.

Also, only one jury could decide whether or not Durrani's absence made a difference, the jury who heard the case. Not one time has Durrani's lawyers requested the trial judge to allow the jury to decide this issue after the verdict. They have waived the issue.

On November 8, 2016, we demanded $42 million of Medical Protective. No response.

On November 21, 2016, we made another demand. No response.

On December 29, 2016, we made another demand on Medical Protective. No response.

On January 9, 2017, we made another demand to Medical Protective. No response.

On January 16, 2017, we made another demand to Medical Protective. No response.

On January 18, 2017, we questioned the game Medical Protective played with coverage, cooperation and depositions.

On January 18, 2017, we asked attorneys Michael Lyon and Paul McCartney the following:

"Before we file something on the issue, we are giving you an opportunity to explain something. We ask for a response by 5:00 pm on Friday, January 20, 2017. It's not a difficult question. Are you communicating with Durrani and receiving his assistance and input on what you prepare and file as pleadings; answering discovery; and on all decisions that are made on a daily basis? We are not asking for the substance, just whether you are or not. If you are or are not, we simply want to know. If you are, we want to schedule his deposition. If you are not, please explain to us how you can ethically represent Durrani and file pleadings, conduct discovery, answer pleadings, assert defenses, file motions, make decisions etc. on his behalf when he is your client, not Medical Protective or River City Insurance. We are asking you for the legal and ethical authority you are doing so. Again, by 5:00 pm Friday, January 20, 2017 we are asking for a response. If you ignore this request, we will take the action based upon the answer being either/or for both."

They never responded.

On January 23, 2017, we questioned attorney Thomas Glassman, Paul McCartney's co-counsel, about Durrani's deposition.

On January 23, 2017, Paul McCartney responded by letter and ignored the simple request whether he and Michael Lyon received communications and input from Durrani?

On February 8, 2017, we sent another demand to Medical Protective. No response.

On March 16, 2017, we questioned the communication of Durrani's lawyers with Durrani.

On March 21, 2017, Michael Lyon by letter stated to Deters Law:

"I have consulted with my client and as a result thereof, I am authorized to inform you that he will not attend the deposition or depositions noticed in either notice, copies of which are contained herein. Furthermore, I am authorized to inform you that he will not participate in discovery depositions or trial depositions in these cases."

Again, Durrani's lawyers made representations of no depositions now or ever.

On March 21, 2017, we confirmed the upcoming depositions as canceled. We tried again and failed based upon Durrani's lawyers' representations no depositions now or ever.

On March 24, 2017, Paul McCartney by email stated: "He will not be appearing." Again, Paul McCartney, not the brazen Michael Lyon, again uses the careful phrase *"not be appearing."* He doesn't claim communication or refusal. Why?

On March 31, 2017, Durrani's deposition never happened.

In a letter dated April 26, 2017, to Paul McCartney from Deters Law, reflects Deters Law explaining why Paul McCartney had the culpability in the Durrani deposition issue. Paul McCartney is obviously worried. Of significance, Paul McCartney refused to agree to give an in-camera review proof to Judge Barrett of proof Durrani ever received the Order to compel the deposition.

On May 3, 2017, in the Atwood cases, Judge Barrett entered a contempt Order. As of June 2, 2017, Durrani is in contempt of that Order. Durrani never complied.

In a Notice of Filing Recent Discovery Answers of Durrani and CAST in Support of Rule 37 Sanction is discovery was answered by David Williamson, Mike Lyon's associate. The requests were sent in every state case. Durrani did not verify the answers. Williamson claims Durrani assisted in Interrogatory #1. Every question was objected to #2-25 under privilege even though it was not privileged except #18: Are you willing to give a deposition in this case to defend your treatment of the Plaintiff? Answer: "No." This is May 9, 2017. Again, a representation by Durrani's lawyers that Durrani is not cooperating. This would be proven a complete lie.

On May 23, 2017, an Order circulated as in *Atwood* for the state cases. Not one defense lawyer responded or signed it. They ignored the request. They did not want another Order to compel entered against them.

It is no coincidence after that Order circulated, on June 1, 2017 a letter from Michael Lyon is the first and only time from 2013 through June 1, 2017, where there was a communication to Deters Law in which Durrani would give a deposition with restrictions including one a month which would take forty years.

Think about that for a moment. After four years of "no deposition," now a deposition, but one a month.

The letter dated June 2, 2017 details Deters Law response to Michael Lyon's deposition parameters and outlines the recent deposition history and rejects the restrictions.

The June 8, 2017 email exchange between Michael Lyon and victims' counsel reflect Michael Lyon's anger his forty-year scheduled deposition proposal was rejected.

On June 9, 2017, Deters Law informed the judges there would be no deposition based upon Michael Lyon's preposterous plan. By this point, Deters Law simply wanted a sanction for Durrani "refusing" to give a deposition for four (4) years.

On June 26, 2017, Judge Jennifer Sargus held her first and only hearing and made it about sanctions. Of note, Michael Lyon's representation on page 32 line 25 to page 33 line 10:

"Well, what do we have here? We have a situation where they have asked for Durrani's deposition for three and a half years, and during which time, for the most part, he said, I'm not going to do it. Okay. But now, your Honor is in this litigation, and now Durrani says he will do a deposition in every single case. That's the state of the evidence right now; that's the state of the situation right now."

For the most part? According to Michael Lyon and Paul McCartney for four years, he was never giving one. Michael Lyon avoided a deposition for five years. He now attempted to delay trials further by offering Durrani for depositions, one a month for five hundred plus cases, a forty-year process. It was absurd.

At this hearing, Judge Sargus wanted to focus on trials, not dispositive motions. This sounded great to us. It would be her last hearing.

At the June 2017 hearing before Judge Sargus, Paul McCartney stated as to Durrani: *"He still needs to make a living."* As if Durrani deserved sympathy. Deters Law learned Durrani's Pakistan license had been suspended based upon the U.S. events.

Paul McCartney also claimed, *"Because Mr. Lyon had more of the communication than I did."* There is no question in this entire story: Michael Lyon was and is the only contact with Durrani. He's the "handler."

Paul McCartney also asked juries be told the same sanction used at Butler County trials with: *"perhaps with instruction that Durrani has refused to give a deposition and maybe you can draw a negative reference from it."* On July 10, 2017, we sent a letter to Michael Lyon proposing five-day long depositions alone for all cases.

On July 14, 2017, Michael Lyon informed Deters Law that Durrani rejected five days of depositions for all cases. This defied all logic. Durrani and his lawyers would prefer over five hundred depositions to five depositions. The reason is clear. Delay. Delay. Delay.

On July 24, 2017, Judge Sargus entered an Order pertaining to possible sanctions and the potential depositions of Durrani.

On October 26, 2017, Deters Law made a demand on George Jonson, Michael Lyon's legal counsel. There would be no response.

On October 30, 2017, Deters Law sent a letter to Michael Lyon to Paul McCartney and copied it to the Court. Deters Law requested video depositions of Durrani.

On January 22, 2018, Deters Law accepted the first three dates offered for deposition offered by Michael Lyon.

On January 30, 2018, Deters Law informed Michael Lyon and Paul McCartney the deposition would be on all cases. This was a purposeful and strategic decision by Deters Law on behalf of the victims, which I thought of. By noticing and taking the deposition in all cases, Medical Protective could never claim then or in the future that Durrani failed to cooperate.

In addition, during these depositions we focused only on Durrani's background and credibility. Why? These applied to every single case. It would prove a wise decision.

Of interest, after refusing this option of on all cases for months, Michael Lyon never responded to our declaration the deposition would be in all cases. Why? Because he did not care. He knew his delay game was up and his delays served their purpose.

Deposition notices in the ten federal cases in Judge Barrett's Court and all state cases were sent out.

By letter, Michael Lyon attempted to unilaterally cancel the deposition of February 17, 2018 based upon Durrani needing to talk to his criminal lawyer, Ed Perry, of Rittgers & Rittgers. Imagine, after all the years, this was the excuse given.

The on the record transcript of the February 17, 2018 deposition did not happen. We did not consent to the cancellation.

The February 24, 2018 deposition did happen. However, it was promised for ten hours. After six hours, Durrani claimed he was tired. It only went seven hours.

Now take all that has been detailed regarding Durrani allegedly not cooperating and refusing a deposition and compare to the following excerpts from his testimony at the February 24, 2018 deposition on pages 35-37, 57-58, 60-69 and 93-95:

Q: Did you ever tell Medical Protective that you would be unable to cooperate in the defense of the medical malpractice cases filed against you?

A. No.

Q. So you never sent a letter or an email that would say something to that effect, is that correct?

A. Not – not to my – not to my knowledge. I have always maintained that I would like to participate in the defense of these cases.

Q: You never received any letters to that effect?

A. I got letters, or emails, correspondence from Medical Protective. And I've always said that I will like be a participant in the defense of these cases.

A. I have no problem. I have no problem whatsoever being deposed in every single case that you're referring to defend my medical decision-making. I absolutely have no issue with that.

A. I said I have absolutely no issue in defending my medical decision making in each and every single case. And I have time and again reiterated my position that I will be happy to defend myself and in the defense of these cases as far as the medical decision making is concerned in these cases. I have no issue whatsoever with that.

Q. And you've been asserting that position since 2013, correct?

A. I've always maintained that position.

Q. Were you aware that the Deters Law firm has been asking for your deposition numerous times since 2013?

A. I've always – as I said, I will maintain that as long as – as long as the deposition only relates to medical decision making, I'm very happy to participate in the defense of these cases."

Q. Were you aware though, that requests for your depositions have been occurring since 2013?

A. No.

Q. So you're unaware of deposition requests until the deposition today, is that right?

Mr. Lyon: I'm going to instruct you not to answer that question.

Q. Were there problems prior to now giving depositions between 2013 and today?

A. I've always maintained that as long as the depositions are limited to the medical decision-making of any individual pertinent cases, I'm more than happy to be deposed and defend myself. That has been my constant position from day one.

Q. Were the requests sent to you in the mail?

Paul McCartney: Objection. Don't answer that.

Q. How did you communicate with counsel to work on your discovery requests?

Michael Lyon: Objection. Do not answer.

Q. Various answers have been filed in the lawsuits that were filed by the Deters Law Firm. Did you have an opportunity to review those answers before they were filed?

Mr. Lyon: —answers to the pleadings?

Mr. Statman: I said the answers to the lawsuits –

Mr. McCartney: I'm going to instruct you not to answer that, Doctor.

Q. Did you approve the answers that were filed in the lawsuits against you?

Michael Lyon: Objection. Do not answer, Atiq.

A. Okay. I will always maintain that I will participate in the defense of these cases from day one. And that has been my constant position.

Q. I asked you if you received any letters from Medical Protective. Do you recall whether you responded to any letters from Medical Protective?

Michael Lyon: Objection. Don't answer that question.

Q. Were you aware that your deposition was once scheduled for November 26, 2014?

A. You know what, I don't – I don't recall it.

Q. Do you recall that your deposition was once set for January 22, 2014?

A. Don't recall.

Q. Was there a time in 2014 that you stopped communicating with your counsel?

Mr. McCartney: Objection. Don't answer that.

Q. Your counsel informed us that recent efforts to communicate with you had been fruitless. Were you aware that they sent that correspondence to the Deters Law Firm?

Michael Lyon: Objection. Don't answer that question.

Q. If I understand your testimony about wanting to defend yourself, had you known about the depositions dates that had been previously set, you would have wanted to be there to defend yourself, correct?

Michael Lyon: Objection. I instruct him not to answer that.

None of the above questions asked for privileged information. The attorneys' instructions not to answer were not proper. The instructions to Durrani not to answer were to protect the lawyers' conduct over the last five years, not Durrani.

It is impossible to reconcile all which Michael Lyon, his partners and associates, Medical Protective and their counsel claimed from 2013 to June 2017 and the above testimony of Durrani.

Based upon the February 24, 2018 deposition, Durrani is a witness against Medical Protective and his lawyers for bad faith.

Not once until June 2017 did Michael Lyon offer a "limited deposition to specific case." This was something Michael Lyon concocted and clearly why Durrani stated it in his testimony. This was his position since June 2017 based upon Michael Lyon's decision not for prior years. There was never any "specific case" deposition offered to us in 2013, 2014, 2015 and 2016 and half of 2017. Since 2013, Durrani's testimony under oath is clear. He wanted to cooperate in his defense and defend from day one. Depositions were no issue.

At his February 24, 2018, Durrani proved everything Michael Lyon and Medical Protective had claimed for five years pertaining to Durrani's lack of cooperation and refusal to provide a deposition as false. On February 24, 2018, Durrani repeatedly made it clear, under oath, he wanted to cooperate in his defense to use his words "from day one" and he was willing to give depositions "from day one." His words. For five years, Michael Lyon and Medical Protective represented to Deters Law and to every Court hearing any part of the litigation that Durrani was unwilling to give a deposition. They made those representations in writing and in open Court. It is a serious consequential fraud of epic proportions. It is also bad faith and unfair claims practices. The Ohio Disciplinary Counsel ignored it all. Judge Schweikert ignored it all.

Medical Protective and Michael Lyon claim Durrani and CAST are Michael Lyon's clients, not Medical Protective. Yet, Medical Protective insured Durrani and paid Michael Lyon and his firm.

Deters Law has had to fight a federal insurance coverage battle against Medical Protective based upon the fraudulent lack of cooperation claim. The issue was used against Deters Law and victims in settlement discussions. The issue delayed trials in 2015, 2016 and 2017 in front of Judge Ruehlman. The victims who had a trial were cheated out of the deposition.

Michael Lyon, his partners and associates involved, and Medical Protective officials must be placed under oath and forced to produce correspondence, documents, emails, phone records on the issue of Durrani's cooperation and deposition. We have all the information here and we still have not conducted any discovery in the bad faith case.

Medical Protective attempted to take advantage of Durrani's flight by feigning lack of cooperation by Durrani and challenged coverage in a federal lawsuit.

The lawsuit failed, so Medical Protective then attempted to defend the cases by Durrani cooperating by giving depositions in 2018.

In February and March 2018, Durrani sat for two long depositions noticed for all cases. We noticed for all cases so Medical Protective could never again claim lack of cooperation. There would be sworn testimony by Durrani in every case. Durrani's counsel failed to ask Durrani a question at these depositions. They had every opportunity to do so, especially knowing his bogus "cooperation issues." At these depositions, Durrani revealed he always wanted to give a deposition. For five years, Medical Protective claimed he would not or could not reach him.

Medical Protective and its agent, Michael Lyon, after the deposition scam, then tried Durrani testifying by video depositions for each case, which went to trial.

When Durrani lost those trials, they decided to stop having Durrani give trial video depositions. By doing so, they limited adverse evidence and testimony.

All these decisions were made wholly by Medical Proective. Durrani never made these decisions.

In a March 13, 2020 email to Durrani, Richard Marcello continued Medical Protective's charade of non-cooperation, writing that because Durrani refuses to cooperate, he is in breach of his policy. However, Durrani adamantly denied ever not wanting to testify in any case or deposition. When Durrani did testify in February and March of 2018, Medical Protective did not ask him even one question.

In the Durrani letter Marcello cites but does not provide, Durrani allegedly wrote, "*After considerable thought I feel my participation so far in this process has actually hampered the overwhelming scientific evidence in these cases due to the prevailing bias. So it is my decision that I will recuse myself from further participation in these cases.*" Interestingly, Lindhorst Attorney Mike Lyon uses the same language on the record in case after case.

On April 30, 2019, on the record at a preliminary hearing on prejudgment interest on our verdict before Judge Brogan, Michael Lyon detailed the manner in which Medical Protective decided to defend every case. Mike Lyon outlined the very bad faith and unfair claims practices they have been engaged. It also reflects how Michael Lyon claims Medical Protective is not making offers based upon the advice of Michael Lyon and lawyers. Michael Lyon, the great oscillator, enjoys telling us he has no authority and only Medical Protective decides offers. Yet, he also claims he tells us he can defend the cases and should not settle. Yet, he has told Al Statman a "monkey" could win the cases for victims. Yet, no offers are made, and we are forced to try cases a "monkey" could win. It's all one big bad faith, unfair claims practice by Medical Protective.

In April 30, 2019, on the record with Judge Brogan, Michael Lyon stated as follows:

MR. LYON: Judge, I can cite twenty-five instances over thirty-four years where I've had my clients/doctors say to me, Please settle this case, I want you to settle this case. They get personal counsel. They write me a nasty letter saying, If you don't settle the case, blah, blah, blah.

MR. LYON: And we try the case twenty-five times. The other side of the coin is normally what happens is we evaluate the case, the doctor signs a note saying I don't want to settle, the company agrees and we try the case, and then there's times when we say, Maybe we should resolve this, they sign it, but then the fourth category, we've had situations where we've begged the doctor, You got to settle this case. No, I want to go to trial. We go to trial. So there's four different versions of this. But I want the Court and the record to reflect that's not an issue in this case. Durrani's consent or willingness or not was not the impediment, was not taken into consideration.

MR. LYON: So we do a literature search and see if it matches up, see if there's sound literature supporting what the physician did. Then we interview our doctors. We go over the case with them. Then we go to our—we find—we go to the experts. Experts, all they're doing is giving you opinions. Again, those opinions can match up with the literature or they cannot match up with the literature.

To me, the objectivity of this analysis has to do with—the bottom line is, is it in the literature? Is it supported? Is it not? Do we talk—you know, do you talk to your client about the risk, the benefit? I call it legal informed consent. We absolutely do.

And here's how I discuss it with doctors. I say, Okay, we can try this case one hundred times. This is where I live, in the courtroom. If we try this case one hundred times in Hamilton County, Ohio, we're going to win eighty-five out of a hundred, but that means we're probably going to lose fifteen out of a hundred. Okay? And then I say, Okay, the ones we lose, the fifteen out of a hundred, what's the verdict range? And I give them a verdict range of the fifteen out of a hundred. And that's the best I can do prospectively as a trial lawyer. I do this statistically because doctors understand that, and that's the analysis I give them. Now, if I may go to this case, I think I'll take this a step at a time and I'll show you how we went about it. First, fully cooperated in discovery proceedings. I'll get the Court the exact dates that they asked for Durrani's deposition, but I do submit that I think the trials that were set, there was no delay. Durrani ultimately gave a long seven—or eight-hour deposition that was represented to be the one and only discovery deposition they needed in all of the cases, which is fine. He did do that.

MR. LYON: I just don't think the law in Ohio, Judge, is that we are required to make an offer simply by virtue of the fact that the plaintiffs have made a demand.

I think that once we've satisfied ourselves that, in our opinion, that it's defensible, it's a solid defense in terms of based on the medicine, whether we use the articles of court not as a tactical decision, I think it has to do with our analysis.

MR. LYON: I can assure you that he would testify that he wouldn't want to settle, he didn't do anything wrong, he thought it was the right thing to go to trial.

THE COURT: What if he had said—assuming he had said, I told them to settle the case—

MR. LYON: Oh, then we would have to consider that.

MR. LYON: Well, you're leaving a step out. I can assure you, particularly in the context of this, if Durrani in any of these cases said to me, Hey, I want this settled, I'm demanding you to settle this case, believe me I would have put that in writing to the insurance company and we would have conferenced it and gone from there.

MR. LYON: But my point is, like Judge Barrett's cases, there's no way I would have paid a penny on any of those cases knowing that Judge Barrett was going to read these indictments to the jury because I felt it was so egregious, whether I'll be justified in an appeal or not, I don't know. So the fact that things are happening in these courtrooms that are making it much, much more difficult to prevail on cases on behalf of Durrani doesn't preclude me from still arguing strenuously in his behalf. Why? Because half of these verdicts are personal to him, and I have a duty to prevent, not only a compensatory judgment, but this fraud, all of the intentional torts that are being mixed in here. So I can'—I have that duty to him. And I know the idea that if they can't collect, they can't that, that still doesn't alleviate my duty.

THE COURT: We're not here for a malpractice case. We're here as if on a prejudgment interest.

MR. LYON: Right.

THE COURT: And we're trying to decide whether Durrani made a rational decision not to settle the case. And you represent to us that he told you in this case not to settle, is that right, or you can't—well, you can't—

MR. LYON: I can't tell you what he told me.

THE COURT: I understand.

MR. LYON: Let's put it this way, I can represent to you the Court that he didn't tell me not to, but I don't want to—I don't want to misrepresent to the Court either. I didn't tell him to settle it.

THE COURT: Right.

MR. LYON: I didn't say that you need to settle this case based on what I'm seeing here.

MR. LYON: That happens, but believe me, I don't have the bottom—when it comes to resolution and money and settlement and decisions, Judge, the insurance company makes that decision.

MR. LYON: Oh, absolutely. Most importantly, the thrust of my position, as I started out saying, I evaluate the cases, Judge, from a medical standpoint, Can I defend this case by the medicine? That's what I stand by. That's what I tell the doctor. Listen, there are cases where I say, we can't defend this case. The medicine—nothing supports us. I can't find an expert, you know.

Lindhorst allegedly continues to try cases without any communication and input from Durrani.

On July 3, 2019, by letter, Ben Maraan asked Rick Weil of Reminger & Reminger (a new law firm retained to defend Durrani along with the Lindhorst firm): *"Can you contact Durrani directly and determine whether or not he will give video testimony at trial? Thank you."* There was never a response.

On July 3, 2019, another letter was sent to attorney Rick Weil from Ben Maraan:

When you communicate with Durrani about testifying, can you ask him about this attached proposal? We were unable to obtain a response. We can't imagine Durrani would not be interested in assigning his bad faith claim in exchange for all criminal charges being dropped and his ability to travel freely in the U.S. and the world. We ask you not address this with Ed Perry and Mike Lyon because we believe they purposefully blocked it.

There was never a response.

Reminger & Reminger later admitted they are not communicating at all with Durrani. They only communicate with Mike Lyon and Medical Protective.

Now, a third defense firm from Dayton, Ohio is involved in representing Durrani, paid for by Medical Protective, and they refuse to answer the question if they have any communication with Durrani. This firm is Bieser, Greer & Landis, LLP. Their lead lawyer upon losing another trial told Alan Statman, *"Why am I here? Why are we trying these cases?"*

The above represents a charade and games played by Michael Lyon and Medical Protective on settlement issues. It's enough to make one dizzy: Is it Durrani? Is it Michael Lyon? Is it Medical Protective? Medical Protective picks and chooses who makes the call that suits them at the time.

From the time of trials to the present, Medical Protective has never made one offer on one individual case. As further evidence of its unfair claims practices and bad faith, Medical Protective has made few group offers, $2,000,000 and in 2018 they offered $4 million. All to settle over 400 cases. This amounts to $10,000 a case when the verdicts are averaging over one million dollars. The cost to defend the cases exceeds $100,000 each. This alone justified a limits offer of $42,000,000.

Despite the verdicts, Medical Protective has never offered more than $7 million to settle over 400 claims against their policies. Medical Protective repeatedly claimed verdicts would be necessary to assess the value of the claims. The victims obtain a million dollar verdicts and nothing changes.

The amount of their coverage of $42 million, rounded down to $40 million, would be only $100,000 a case. This amount is far less than what Medical Protective pays Durrani counsel and experts to defend a case through trial. Michael Lyon told me in 2013 it was about $125,000 to defend a case through trial. Medical Protective has failed to even offer a cost of the defense to these cases.

There have been confidential settlements with West Chester Hospital and Children's Hospital, which will be used as a comparable in support of bad faith under sealed conditions. In other words, those settlement amounts help prove the egregious bad faith and unfair claims settlement practices of Medical Protective. For example, to reach West Chester/UC Health liability, we had to obtain a verdict against Durrani first. Despite this burden, West Chester/UC Health settled, and the settlement helps prove egregious bad faith. While West Chester/UC Health and Children's conducted discovery, took into account trials and their results, nothing matters to Medical Protective.

If we ever have our bad faith trial we deserve, the evidence will include all the above plus more. What do you think a jury will do? I believe a verdict from $500 million to $1 billion will be returned.

An exhibit at trial will include a February 20, 2013 letter to Michael Lyon from me after the filing of the second seven lawsuits. This letter was sent while the *Pierce* case was still at the pre-trial phase. No response.

An exhibit at trial will include a March 20, 2013 letter to Michael Lyon from me making claims against coverage. From that date to now. No response.

An exhibit at trial will include a June 13, 2013, letter to Medical Protective's counsel from me detailing the massive plan of discovery. No response.

An exhibit at trial will include an August 21, 2013, letter to Michael Lyon from me regarding Durrani's personal exposure. No response.

An exhibit at trial will include January 20, 2014, letters to Michael Lyon from me representative of letters sent on all cases making demands. No response.

An exhibit at trial will include a March 25, 2015, Order for Mediation by Judge Guckenberger. No offer at mediation.

An exhibit at trial will include an August 30, 2015, letter from Eric Kennedy, a Cleveland lawyer we hired to help us mediate, to Steven Janik outlining the value of the cases. No response.

An exhibit at trial will include an October 27, 2016, letter to Steven Janik from Deters Law requesting the limits of insurance. There was no response. It shows that Unfair Claims Settlement Practices was Medical Protectives strategy from the beginning.

An exhibit at trial will include an October 27, 2016, letter to George Jonson, Michael Lyon's counsel, from Deters Law demanding the limits of insurance. No response. Their strategy from the beginning. They knew even before Pierce filed her lawsuit the extent of Durrani's liability.

An exhibit at trial will include a November 1, 2016, letter to George Jonson from Deters Law. No response.

An exhibit at trial will include a November 7, 2016, letter to Steven Janik from Deters Law making a demand on the *Crystal Pierce* jury verdict. No response.

An exhibit at trial will include a November 8, 2016, letter to Steven Janik from Deters Law demanding the insurance limits. No response.

An exhibit at trial will include a December 29, 2016, letter to Defense Counsel from Deters Law outlining demands in all cases. No response.

An exhibit at trial will include a January 11, 2017, letter from Deters Law to Steven Janik making a demand in the *Potts* case. No response.

An exhibit at trial will include a January 16, 2017, letter from Deters Law to West Chester Counsel outlining bad faith. The same bad faith is applicable to Medical Protective.

An exhibit at trial will include a January 23, 2017, letter from Walt Haggerty to Deters Law referencing Medical Protective offering $2 million to settle all cases.

In Medical Protective's claim file, they tried to claim this two-million-dollar global offer was "in good faith" despite being woefully low, and lie about Deters Law Firm responding.

An exhibit at trial will include a June 2, 2017, letter to Michael Lyon from Deters Law outlining our position against Medical Protective. No response.

An exhibit at trial will include an October 23, 2017, letter to the mediator and John Cruze from Deters Law outlining a target of $30 million from Medical Protective. There was never any offer. That is no longer an option.

An exhibit at trial will include a December 20, 2017, email from Deters Law detailing our position. No response.

An exhibit at trial will include a January 30, 2018, letter to Michael Lyon from Deters Law regarding Durrani deposition after five years of intentional sabotage of the depositions.

An exhibit at trial will include a May 11, 2018, letter to Michael Lyon from Deters Law requesting a proposal. None came.

An exhibit at trial will include a July 6, 2018, letter from Deters Law to Michael Lyon outlining coverage and cases by year. There has never been a single offer or tender of limits by year.

An exhibit at trial will include a July 11, 2018, letter to Michael Lyon from Deters Law demanding the limits and explaining why. There was no response.

An exhibit at trial will include a September 21, 2018, letter to Michael Lyon from Deters Law rejecting the $4,000,000 oral offer.

An exhibit at trial will include an October 22, 2018, letter to Michael Lyon from Deters Law explaining how Medical Protective was exposing Durrani to excess coverage judgments. Durrani's personal lawyer was copied. There was no response.

An exhibit at trial will include a January 8, 2019, email from Deters Law to Mediator John Cruze regarding Medical Protective's $4 million global offer.

An exhibit at trial will be an email from Michael Lyon to Alan Statman in 2019 stating when Mr. Lyon returned from vacation, they need to meet with Rich Marcello, the claims handler operating out of Medical Protective's Louisville, Kentucky office. That meeting never took place. Mike Lyon constantly makes these types of statements and never acts on them.

In early 2018, there were individual written demands sent out on every case. Medical Protective ignored every one of them without a response.

In total, there have been over 500 ignored letters and emails pertaining to resolution of the victims' cases by Medical Protective.

Not only does the so-called Professional Responsibility Code of Conduct and Ohio Disciplinary Rules require lawyers respond to lawyers, the lack of response is also evidence of bad faith and unfair claims practices.

A history of the trials is important in support of the claims. It is shocking and is probably unprecedented both by the success of Deters Law and the refusal to resolve claims in the face of verdict obliteration.

On January 12, 2017, Glenn Feagan met with Steve Janik at Janik's Cleveland office. Defendant Robert Ignasiak attended.

At this meeting, Glenn Feagan communicated Deters Law would never recommend less than $21 million to their clients. The plan at the time was for Deters Law and victims to settle with Medical Protective at a bargain and focus on West Chester/UC Health. Our clients agreed to the plan.

At the meeting Janik and Ignasiak, with the prior authorization of Kenesey, related the following to Glenn Feagan:

A. Janik and Ignasiak claimed only $27 million in coverage. This was a mistake. They left out coverage on CAST too. This misrepresentation is also an unfair claims practices violation.
B. Janik and Ignasiak broke down the number of claims by years:

2009 - 103	2012 - 75
2010 - 115	2013 - 30
2011 - 91	

C. Janik and Ignasiak claimed after a trial, Deters Law would have to win another trial on coverage. That is no longer true after Durrani's February and March 2018 depositions in all cases where he fully cooperated.
D. Janik and Ignasiak claimed they were using a model with Deters Law winning only 20% of the trials. Deters Law is winning 70% of the trials.
E. Janik and Ignasiak factored an average verdict of $300,000. Deters Law is averaging over $1,000,000 a verdict and nearly all of the aggregate award

is covered by policies. Over $20,000,000 is covered by the policy.

F. Based on the above, Janik and Ignasiak factored in a 20% success rate in the coverage trials after the trial. Coverage trials are no longer needed so this is 100% in the victims' favor. And, it's ridiculous to place this at 20% when a judge or jury who decided the underlying case in favor of a victim would likely also rule in their favor on coverage. Regardless, this is no longer necessary.

G. Janik and Ignasiak summarized 400 cases at 20% is eighty cases at $300,000 or $24 million with 20% success rate insurance equals $4.8 million. They rounded this up and suggested the value of the victims' claims were only $5 million.

H. Janik and Ignasiak stated at the meeting that if they doubled their $5 million, it would be only $10 million.

I. Janik and Ignasiak rejected the idea of summary trials.

All of A-I is important because it all has been proven untrue and Defendants have never altered their position and models since 2017.

Medical Protective on their website brags they have managed over 400,000 claims since 1899, they win 90% of their insured trials and 80% of claims are closed without payment. This, while they are losing 70% of the Durrani trials.

Medical Protective claims they have advisory boards of experienced healthcare professionals who review claims and offer insights. In the Durrani cases, they did not and are not reviewing, falsely reviewed or ignored their reviews.

Medical Protective makes a $1 billion in annual premiums and has more than 200,000 clients and $5.4 billion in assets.

Medical Protective brags their average payout on a medical malpractice claim is only $90,000.

Medical Protective representatives attended trials and others.

Judge Dale Crawford actually questioned MacKenzie Walter during the *Adams* trial why there were no offers. This is the only trial Judge Crawford presided over. We wish he took over all of them.

MacKenzie Walter actually complained to Paul Vollman and Michael Lyon that Judge Crawford "mistreated her." He did not. Judge Crawford could not understand the lack of offers in light of the evidence he was hearing and the case he was presiding over. Judge Crawford stated Medical Protective should be happy settling for one dollar under the $42 million. It is also another act of bad faith and unfair claim practices. Medical Protective ignored Court orders to respond to demands and make offers.

Medical Protective has the right to defend Durrani and CAST. However, the law requires them to follow the law. They do not. They are not allowed to defend indefensible claims a "monkey" could win as claimed by Michael Lyon and ignore the Unfair Claims Settlement Practices Act.

The following, featuring Michael Lyon, is taken from Medical Protective's current website:

"Here's what our legal defense team has to say about our claim's philosophy, the legal environment and how Medical Protective really makes a difference in your defense.

Michael Lyon has more than 30 years of courtroom experience, 20 of those defending Medical Protective healthcare providers. He believes Medical Protective›s Claims Supervisors and philosophy make the difference for healthcare providers.

"Medical Protective's professional Claim Supervisors are without a doubt the most sophisticated, intelligent, savvy, tough claims people I've met. They know their medicine, they know doctors, they know how doctors think and they understand lawyers and the law. These people are second to none. They recognize that every physician is different – intellectually, emotionally, psychologically and economically. We don't just talk about the liability, the causation, the damages and the medicine. We also talk about the doctors. How are they doing? Are the families supportive? These are the things we talk about and it doesn't happen anywhere else. The reason that is so important is because if you are able to support, comfort and give strength to your physicians, you are so much stronger in the courtroom. Medical Protective knows that. The company is run by the most professional and intelligent people.

"They hire and work with attorneys that share their philosophy. A lot of companies' hire lawyers to settle cases—they hire lawyers to make sure they never really go to trial because there is too much risk, they just want to get them to settle. But Medical Protective is just the opposite. They hire the best trial lawyers, not litigator, trial lawyers, who have tried cases to verdict because they want experienced tough trial lawyers available to try these cases. We are able to be strong, courageous and give the plaintiffs' bar the kind of battle they need."

And Medical Protective has applied all that to Durrani, federally indicted fugitive from the law, despite all the facts.

In January 2014, a Hamilton County jury awarded *Crystal Pierce* $1,040,000. Medical Protective never made an offer before or after the trial. After losing the appeal, Medical Protective had to pay the statutory reduced verdict.

After the verdict, in 2014 and 2015, Durrani won four straight verdicts in Butler County. However, those are no longer relevant.

Since those four verdicts, the following circumstances changed:

A. All cases were moved to Hamilton County when Deters Law learned UC Health owned West Chester, and UC Health headquarters was in Hamilton County.

B. Plaintiffs added a neurosurgeon and neuroradiology expert to their orthopaedics spine expert.

C. Deters Law retained more experienced trial counsel in the absence of me who tried the Pierce trial. First and second year lawyers tried the Butler County cases.

After Medical Protective participated in delays of failed federal removal and appeals and challenges to consolidation which delayed trials for three years from 2015 to 2018, trials finally resumed in 2018.

In 2018, the Cathy Beil trial was held in Hamilton County. There was no offer before the trial. Cathy Beil won. There has been no offer since the verdict.

In 2018, six cases were tried together in Federal Court in Hamilton County with Judge Michael Barrett. There was no offer before the trials. The verdicts were as follows:

Brady – $741,000	Sander – $1,375,221
Houghton – $1,285,080	Shempert – $831,200
McCauley – Defense on Statute of Limitations	Stanfield – $943,440

There has been no offer since the trial. Medical Protective is appealing.

In 2018, the Dana Setters case went to trial in Hamilton County. There was no offer before the trial on a $1,000,000 demand. The jury awarded Dana Setters $984,906. There has been no offer since the verdict. Defendants are appealing.

In 2018, the Heather McCann case went to trial in Hamilton County. There was no offer before the trial on a $1,000,000 demand. The jury awarded Heather McCann $208,076.40. There has been no offer since the verdict.

In 2019, the Billy Wolsing case went to trial in Hamilton County. There was no offer before the trial on a $1,000,000 demand. The jury awarded a decision in favor of the defense.

During the Wolsing trial, Paul Vollman, Durrani co-counsel, informed Matt Bradley, court video support for Deters Law, Medical Protective was "never going to settle" any of the cases.

In 2019, the Patricia Adams case went to trial in Hamilton County. There was no offer before the trial on a $1,000,000 demand. The jury awarded Patricia Adams $1,100,000.00. There has been no offer since the verdict. Medical Protective is appealing. Judge Dale Crawford ordered Medical Protective to make an offer before trial and during trial, and Medical Protective ignored his orders. Judge Crawford has awarded prejudgment interest.

In 2019, the Fay Rosebery case went to trial in Hamilton County. There was no offer before trial on a $1,000,000 demand. The jury awarded Fay Rosebery $900,000.00. There has been no offer since the verdict. Medical Protective appealed.

In 2019, the Mackenzie Bender case went to trial in Hamilton County. There was no offer before trial on a $1,000,000 demand. The jury awarded Mackenzie

Bender $568,000.00. There has been no offer since the verdict. Medical Protective appealed.

Medical Protective's Claim File incorrectly estimated a 50% chance of defense verdict in the Bender trial.

In 2019, the Sophia White case went to trial in Hamilton County. There was no offer before trial on a $100,000 demand. The Judge granted a Directed Verdict motion for the defense. We appealed the Directed Verdict.

In 2019, the Katherine Walls case went to trial in Hamilton County. There was no offer before trial on a $250,000 demand. The jury awarded Katherine Walls $6,316,344.00. Medical Protective appealed.

Only July 3, 2019, a jury awarded Veronica Yeakle $700,000.00. There was no offer on the case before, during or after the trial on a $1,000,000 demand. Medical Protective appealed. All $700,000.00 of this is covered under the Medical Protective policy.

On July 18, 2019, a jury awarded Teresa Nichols $26,200,000.00. There was no offer on the case before, during or after the trial on a $1,000,000 demand. Medical Protective appealed. Nearly all $8,700,000.00 of the compensatory damages are covered under the Medical Protective policy.

On July 31, 2019, a jury awarded Jeff Potts $39,000,000.00. There was no offer on the case before, during or after the trial on a $1,000,000 demand. Medical Protective appealed. Approximately $2,146,091.00 of the verdict is covered under the Medical Protective policies.

In August 2019, a jury found against Durrani and CAST for negligence but not proximate cause in the Estate of William Hayes trial. Mr. Hayes was an 85-year-old man with cancer who Durrani operated on.

On September 20, 2019, a jury awarded Tammy Mann $500,000.00. There was no offer on the case before, during, or after the trial on a $1,000,000.00 demand. Medical Protective appealed. All the $400,000.00 awarded for compensatory damages are covered under the Medical Protective policies.

Medical Protective estimated a 50% chance defense verdict in Mann, even though Plaintiffs had won over 70 percent of trials at the time.

On September 23, 2019, the Bunnavuth Chhun case went to trial in Hamilton County. There was no offer before the trial on a $1,000,000 demand. The jury awarded a decision in favor of the defense. We appealed.

On October 14, 2019, the James McCain case went to trial in Hamilton County. There was no offer before the trial on a $1,000,000 demand. The jury awarded a decision in favor of the defense. We appealed.

On November 13, 2019, a jury awarded Lyndsey Middendorf $100,000.00. There was no offer on the case before, during, or after trial on a $1,000,000.00 demand. Medical Protective appealed. All the $100,000.00 awarded are covered under the Medical Protective policies.

On November 21, 2019, a jury awarded Sierra Stratman $1,358,847.26. There was no offer on the case before, during, or after trial on a $1,000,000.00 demand. Medical Protective appealed. $950,000 awarded are covered under the Medical Protective policies.

On December 6, 2019, a jury awarded Rita Hounchell $964,000.00. There was no offer on the case before, during or after trial on a $1,000,000.00 demand. Medical Protective appealed. $500,000.00 awarded are covered under the Medical Protective policies.

On January 13, 2020, a jury awarded Gloria Greene $1,768,468.62. There was no offer on the case before, during or after trial on a $1,000,000.00 demand. Medical Protective appealed. $1,100,000.00 awarded are covered under the Medical Protective policies.

On January 13, 2020, the Joetta Nafe case went to trial in Hamilton County. There was no offer before the trial on a $1,000,000 demand. The jury awarded a decision in favor of the defense. We appealed.

On January 14, 2020, the Paul Marksberry case went to trial in Federal Court. There was no offer before the trial on a $1,000,000 demand. The jury returned the verdict of $150,000.00. Medical Protective appealed.

On January 14, 2020, the Carol Ross case went to trial in Federal Court. There was no offer before the trial on a $1,000,000 demand. The jury returned the verdict of $1,500,000.00. Medical Protective appealed.

On January 27, 2020, the Candi McKinney case went to trial in Hamilton County. There was no offer before the trial on a $1,000,000 demand. The jury awarded a decision in favor of the defense. We appealed.

In 2020, the Kimberly Jenkins case went to trial in Hamilton County. There was no offer before the trial on a $1,000,000 demand. The jury awarded a decision in favor of the defense. We appealed.

On February 18, 2020, the Patrick Stephenson trial was held. On February 28, 2020, the jury returned the verdict of $820,014.00 covered under the insurance and $500,000 of punitive damages for a total verdict of $1,320,014.00. Medical Protective appealed.

On March 2, 2020, the Rhonda Mains case went to trial in Hamilton County. There was no offer before the trial on a $1,000,000 demand. The jury awarded a decision in favor of the defense. We appealed.

On June 14, 2021, the Robert Densler trial was held in Hamilton County. There was no offer on the case before, during, or after trial on a $1,000,000 demand. The jury returned the verdict of $162,021.20. Medical Protective appealed.

On July 6, 2021, the Christopher Atwood trial was held in Federal Court. There was no offer on the case before, during, or after trial on a $1,000,000 demand. The jury returned the verdict of $1,891,208.99. Medical Protective appealed.

On July 6, 2021, the Jennifer Hickey trial was held in Federal Court. There was no offer on the case before, during, or after trial on a $1,000,000 demand. The jury returned the verdict of $4,687,819.62. Medical Protective appealed.

On July 19, 2021, the Dana Conley trial was held in Hamilton County. There was no offer on the case before, during, or after trial on a $1,000,000 demand. The jury returned the verdict of $420,331.82. Medical Protective appealed.

On July 19, 2021, the Joan Jones trial was held in Hamilton County. There was no offer on the case before, during, or after trial on a $1,000,000 demand. The jury returned the verdict of $280,133.28. Medical Protective appealed.

On August 3, 2021, the Christopher Clark trial was held in Hamilton County. There was no offer on the case before, during, or after trial on a $1,000,000 demand. The jury returned the verdict of $700,000.00. Medical Protective appealed.

On August 16, 2021, the Jane Reeder trial was held in Hamilton County. There was no offer on the case before, during, or after trial on a $1,000,000 demand. The jury returned the verdict of $2,600,000.00. Medical Protective appealed.

On August 16, 2021, the Lawrence Pridemore trial was held in Hamilton County. There was no offer on the case before, during, or after trial on a $1,000,000 demand. The jury returned the verdict of $2,600,000.00. Medical Protective appealed.

On September 7, 2021, the Michael Koelblin trial was held in Hamilton County. There was no offer on the case before, during, or after trial on a $1,000,000 demand. The jury returned the verdict of $1,379,791.92. Medical Protective appealed.

On September 7, 2021, the Eric Courtney trial was held in Hamilton County. There was no offer on the case before, during, or after trial on a $1,000,000 demand. The jury returned the verdict of $1,087,804.88. Medical Protective appealed.

On September 20, 2021, the Thomas Lantry case went to trial in Hamilton County. There was no offer before the trial on a $1,000,000 demand. The jury awarded a decision in favor of the defense. We appealed.

On September 20, 2021, the Charlann Shepherd case went to trial in Hamilton County. There was no offer before the trial on a $1,000,000 demand. The jury awarded a decision in favor of the defense. We appealed.

On December 6, 2021, the Thomas Meyers trial was held in Hamilton County. There was no offer on the case before, during, or after trial on a $1,000,000 demand. The jury returned the verdict of $5,325,000.00. Medical Protective appealed.

On December 6, 2021, the Lenora Haggard trial was held in Hamilton County. There was no offer on the case before, during, or after trial on a $1,000,000 demand. The jury returned the verdict of $5,295,000.00. Medical Protective appealed.

On January 24, 2022, the Tara Brown trial was held in Hamilton County. There was no offer on the case before, during, or after trial on a $1,000,000 demand. The jury returned the verdict of $6,850,300.00. Medical Protective will appeal.

On January 24, 2022, the Dawn Brown trial was held in Hamilton County. There was no offer on the case before, during, or after trial on a $1,000,000 demand. The jury returned the verdict of $5,940,100.00. Medical Protective will appeal.

Medical Protective claimed in 2018 the $4 million offer for 400 cases was based upon their "algorithms" and their winning 4 of the first 5 trials in a venue different from where the cases are presently venued.

Despite all the verdicts since then, there has been no settlement proposal reflecting any "algorithm" adjustment based upon all their losses.

Michael Lyon informed a Deters Law attorney, before the Rosebery and Bender trials, "if I can win these cases maybe I can change the algorithm." He lost both. This was an admission by Michael Lyon the "algorithm" had been blown up. Yet, no offers.

Lindhorst and Reminger always report the "probable" verdict as defense or law such as $50,000-$100,000. Yet, Medical Protective has never made an offer on a single case.

Lindhorst's position as expressed by Mike Lyon and Jim Brockman is always "totally defensible" on every file, even Potts, one of the largest Medical Malpractice verdicts in Ohio history.

These jury losses by Medical Protective cover every imaginable fact scenario: young Plaintiffs, old Plaintiffs, deceased Plaintiffs, disabled Plaintiffs and not disabled Plaintiffs. There cannot be a better sample of verdicts.

These jury losses by Medical Protective involve recoverable amounts under the policies for negligence and for lack of informed consent, for lost wages, medical bills, pain and suffering and attorney fees and costs where relevant. The verdicts are not just fraud verdicts. They are exposing Durrani to fraud and punitive damages verdicts too.

These jury trials are being held also under the oversight of various judges and various rulings: Judge Barrett, Judge Brogan, Judge Guckenberger, Judge Hogan, Judge Crawford, Judge Sundermann, Judge Jackson, Judge Reece and Judge Schweikert.

All of the above reflects the following statistics:

A. 56 Total Trials
39 Plaintiff Wins
69.6% Total Win Rate

B. 40 Total Hamilton County Trials
28 Plaintiff Wins
70% Total Hamilton County Win Rate

C. 38 Hamilton County Medical Protective Related Cases
27 Plaintiff Wins
71% Win Rate in Hamilton County Medical Protective Related Cases

These statistics are reflected in Medical Protective's claims files, but Medical Protective still state the cases are defensible and provide a low range.

Juries are awarding significant sums for pain and suffering to the Ohio limit maximum of $500,000 and past and future medical bills too, all covered by the Medical Protective policies. 75% of the damages being awarded is for coverable non-economic damages under the policy.

In addition, Durrani has been exposed over and over to significant punitive damages awards, all of which will follow him to Pakistan and reflects Medical Protective's bad faith related to him. We are going to certify these verdicts to Pakistan.

In addition, attorney fees are being awarded by juries where punitive damages are awarded, and they too are covered by the Medical Protective policies.

The following chart reflects the verdict amounts covered under the Medical Protective policies. These are the collectible economic and non-economic damage reduced by Ohio law on limits that totals $24,303,074.70 on only thirty-seven verdicts when there are over 400 cases against their insureds, Durrani and CAST

Pierce	$350,000	Nichols	$4,450,000	Conley	$420,331.81
Brady	$441,000	Potts	$2,146,091	Jones	$280,133.28
Houghton	$535,000	Mann	$400,000	Clark	$495,000
Sander	$625,221	Middendorf	$100,000	Reeder	$103,519
Shempert	$331,200	Stratman	$950,000	Pridemore	$94,483
Stanfield	$643,440	Hounchell	$500,000	Koelblin	$629,781.92
Setters	$984,906	Greene	$1,100,000	Courtney	$337,804.88
McCann	$208,760	Marksberry	$100,000	Meyers	$325,000
Adams	$616,533	Ross	$1,025,000	Haggard	$295,000
Rosebery	$649,410	Stephenson	$1,320,014	Brown, T.	$550,300
Bender	$318,150	Densler	$62,021.20	Brown, D.	$440,100
Walls	$516,640	Atwood	$608,608.99		
Yeakle	$700,000	Hickey	$650,019.62		

These amounts do not cover prejudgment interest and attorney fees covered under the policy when punitive damages are awarded.

Medical Protective knows every case has the required affidavit of merit by a qualified spine surgeon. Therefore, they know these cases will "get to a jury."

On the record and "off the record," Judge Sunderman, Guckenberger, Brogan, Crawford, Jackson, Reece and Barrett, all having tried one or more case, have commented to Mike Lyon and his associates and partners, their dismay and surprise at Medical Protective's scorched earth defense with no settlement offers.

On September 25, 2020, Alex Petraglia sent this email to Mr. Porotsky regarding Medical Protective discovery:

Mr. Porotsky,

I appreciate that you are looking into turning over the Master Claim file in 7 days. In the interest of completing discovery so we can have these hearing, may you please provide the following that we have thus far not received:

1. Durrani's original January 2019 letter referenced in every claim file, but not provided;
2. The original algorithms and the input data (critical to understanding if MedPro was reasonable in their calculations of the cases);
3. Any of the post-trial correspondences regarding the claim files;
4. Internal emails pertaining to the claim files;
5. The expert reports, which are conspicuously absent from the claim files; and
6. Some agreement to hold in-court testimony of Ignasiak, Marcello and Walters

Once we have this information and have the depositions, we move these cases along to the appellate court.

I will get with you about some of the technical issues we are having with the native format emails as well.

Sincerely,

Alex

They have not provided the materials.

Medical Protective knows the evidence juries are reviewing in every trial including Durrani's video testimony focused on his credibility is insurmountable against them.

Medical Protective and Michael Lyon are choosing to spend hundreds of thousands of dollars a case on the following:

A. Review
B. Answering
C. Answering Discovery
D. Sending Discovery
E. Taking Depositions
F. Hiring Experts
G. Preparing Exhibits
H. Preparing for Trial

All on a case they think they would lose to a "monkey."

All of the large punitive damages verdicts against Durrani reflect the strength of the cases, which Medical Protective refuses to make an offer.

On August 6, 2019, Judge Dale Crawford, assigned Hamilton County Common Pleas Judge retired, to the Patricia Adams v. Durrani case, held a hearing on prejudgment interest under Ohio law, Ohio Revised Code §1343.03, on the $1,100,000 verdict.

Ohio Revised Code §1343.03 allows prejudgment interest when "the court determines at a hearing held subsequent to the verdict or decision in the action that the party required to pay the money failed to make a good faith effort to settle the case and that the party to whom the money is paid did not fail to make a good faith effort to settle the case."

Stipulations were placed on the record on August 6, 2019, for the prejudgment interest hearing.

The stipulations clearly apply to all cases including this claim against Medical Protective as placed on page 4 of the transcript. McKenzie Walter, a Medical Protective representative told Judge Crawford in 2018 as placed on the record by Judge Crawford: *"she further advised the Court we are not making offers on any of these cases."* It was repeated on page 5 of the transcript. Mike Lyon, lead Medical Protective and the Durrani and CAST lawyer, agreed to the stipulation on the record. This was the same strategy that was used in Plaintiff's case.

On pages 6 and 7 of the transcript Paul Vollman, Mike Lyon's associate, told Judge Crawford "his client," the insurance company (Medical Protective), was not making any offers." Judge Crawford found Mr. Vollman's declaration troubling. Lyon adopted the declaration on page 7 of the transcript. Again, incredible evidence supporting what is pled, that Lindhorst is not simply Durrani's counsel, but Medical Protective's, and it all supports the conspiracy to defraud the victims of coverage.

On page 13 of the transcript, Mike Lyon begins his argument opposing prejudgment interest. He argued figuratively "we had experts so too bad." Durrani's experts, paid by Medical Protective, are being paid for helping Medical Protective in their conspiracy of fraud. Their experts know the cases can't be defended, so for money, they just do it. The juries actually openly scoff at their experts during trial and give them zero credibility in post-trial interviews.

The records Medical Protective produced often redact the opinions of experts are often redacted, showing Medical Protective knew the cases were indefensible, but shopped for new experts that would "play ball."

Judge Crawford also put on the record MacKenzie Walter of Medical Protective told him Medical Protective does not care about paying attorney fees to Lindhorst. She told Judge Crawford Medical Protective doesn't care if the attorney fees exceed even the $40 million in coverage. Medical Protective would rather pay their attorneys in a lost cause than the victims.

Lindhorst always estimates the cost of trial at $150,000, Reminger estimates the cost of trial at $25,000.

Based on Lindhorst's low numbers, if 280 cases went to trial it exhausts 42 million by the cost of the defense alone. With prejudgment interest and attorney fees the price of trying only half the cases is much larger than the 42-million-dollar policy limit.

Judge Crawford, then on pages 22 and 23 of the transcript, after stating he had tried more trials than any judge in the state of Ohio declares Medical Protective's conduct "bad faith."

Judge Crawford awarded over $125,000 in prejudgment interest in the Adams case. However, what was stipulated to on the record has applicability to all the cases.

From the beginning of victims' claims to the present, there has never been one written offer to settle these cases.

Judge Guckenberger as early as August 2013, would go off the record at case management conferences and ask why limits had not been tendered by Medical Protective. Michael Lyon would state every time he needed discovery and trials first to assess our risk and exposure. Of course, that was not true. It was lie.

From 2013 to the present, the only "concrete" oral offer has been $4,000,000 to settle over 400 cases or only $10,000 a case. There was one $2,000,000 written offer only through another Defendants' counsel or $10,000 a case. This predated the $4,000,000 oral offer.

Medical Protective knows they are losing nearly 70% of the trials, all held in the state of Ohio where statistically over 90% of the time the defense wins.

From 2013 to 2017, there were no offers, including on Plaintiff's case. In 2017, there was the above referenced $2,000,000 offer. In 2018, Medical Protective made a bad faith and insulting $4 million global offer to resolve over 400 cases.

Based upon the years of delay, in 2017, Plaintiffs attempted to settle for $21 million or half of the $42 million. They were ignored. They received a $2.1 million offer at the Kentucky mediation after they thought they would receive an opening offer of $10 million. The $2.1 million was millions less than the $4.8 million they previously claimed was in their algorithm.

Medical Protective has also acted in bad faith to their insured Durrani by failing to protect him from excess coverage verdicts and judgments including punitive damages.

There are over 400 cases against Durrani and his Center for Advanced Spine Technologies or CAST and covered by Medical Protective.

Based upon these verdicts, it is bad faith and unfair claims practices for Medical Protective to make no offers.

Bad faith and unfair claims practices are supposed to avoid "low ball" offers. In these matters, these are "no ball" offers.

Feigned assessment and evaluation of every case by the defense resulting in no offers in the face of repeatedly significant jury verdicts is bad faith and unfair claims practices.

In pleadings in McCann arguing against prejudgment interest, Michael Lyon has argued the following:

A. "Defendants did in fact rationally evaluate their risks and potential liability."

B. "Defendants were represented by experienced trial counsel and they were firm in their actions in this case were medically indicated and appropriate."

C. They claimed their "conviction was based on science and expert testimony."

D. They claimed, "ongoing settlement discussions for years to resolve this and other related litigation on a global basis."

None of this has any credibility at all and further reflects bad faith and unfair claims practices. In addition, the expert credibility gap between victims' experts and Medical Protective's experts at trial is wide in favor of the victims. Every trial, Medical Protective's experts "don't touch" our experts. All of this has been witnessed and known by Medical Protective. In Summary, the following reflect overwhelming bad faith.

1. Encouragement of and/or assistance in flight from the U.S. making false and misleading statements regarding the same to Court, victims, and others.
2. The improper use of Durrani's flight by Medical Protective to attempt to mislead and state coverage would be void based upon lack of cooperation with the hope that Plaintiff would walk away.
3. The coaching and manufacturing of Durrani claiming he would not participate in trials including the drafting of Durrani's emails to Medical Protective.
4. The intentional refusal to communicate to Durrani a proposal of assigning his bad faith claim to Plaintiffs.
5. Refusal to make a single offer on a single case from 2012 through now in the face of overwhelming evidence of Durrani's liability and not attempting in good faith to effectuate prompt, fair and equitable settlements of claims in which liability has become reasonably clear.
6. Refusal to make a single global offer to settle over 400 cases from 2013 to 2017.
7. Making a global offer of only $5,000 a case at the end of 2017.
8. Making a global offer of only $10,000 a case in the middle of 2018.
9. Misrepresenting the amount of coverage.
10. Losing the majority of trials with large verdicts significant portion covered by coverage and still no offers.
11. Knowing they will lose cases, not making offers, forcing victims to try them and Deters Law to spend money on experts and both victims and Deters Law to incur the stress, expense and cost of trials. Despite the

victories, trials are stressful, including jury deliberations. Scheduling trials takes time. The victims continue to suffer through Medical Protective's delay in settling.

12. Misrepresenting Durrani's desire to testify at trial.
13. Not even offering a cost of defense settlement on the cases.
14. The delays caused by Medical Protective have affected the memories of the victims based upon the time from surgery, to lawsuit to trial. Loss of memory and many deaths equals loss of evidence and severe prejudice to cases. It is part of the intent and strategy of Medical Protective's bad faith and unfair claims practices.
15. Ignoring their own algorithm.
16. Using experts they pay well to attempt to defend indefensible cases.
17. Not communicating with Durrani while defending him through trial.
18. Not informing Durrani they have exposed him to over $80 million in uncovered verdicts.
19. Not communicating an assignment of his claim.
20. They did not appeal for Durrani the Beil verdict because it was not covered under the Medical Protective policy. This proves what they care about. It's not their "claimed client" Durrani.

Any rational and objective review of all the above would result in the conclusion Medical Protective acted in egregious bad faith and unfair claims practices.

On January 12, 2022, in the Bender and Nichols cases, Judge James Brogan ordered as follows:

At the conclusion of the January 10, 2022 evidentiary hearing, this Court received the material filed under seal. This Court reviewed the material filed under seal. After examination of the material, this Court now requires that Robert Ignasiak and Tim Kenesey of Med Pro Group Inc. disclose to this Court whether Med Pro Group Inc.'s decision not to make any offers to settle the underlying litigation involving Dr. Durrani and CAST was influenced by their belief that they will prevail in a subsequent declaratory judgment action that it need not provide insurance coverage to Dr. Durrani and CAST because of their "noncooperation." Mr. Ignasiak's and Mr. Kenesy's disclosures shall be provided under oath by affidavits. These affidavits shall be provided to this Court by January 21, 2022.

They refused to comply with this Order.

Epilogue

"Every man dies. Not every man lives."
— Braveheart

Since this is an ongoing story, from the time I sent this to the publisher until the book is released, six months will have passed. An update will be in order. I'll do so by video on my *Bulldog Show.* When the cases are over, I anticipate writing a sequel which will take the story current again and add the anecdotes I am unable to share now.

It's sad more victims will die. I hope we will be able to pursue the bad faith and unfair claims practices claims.

I hope I won't be living in a barn, but I'll prepare to do so.

So what do you think of our story? How does it happen?

Please share the story and spread the word.

It will happen again, because greed is a powerful addictive narcotic. They sell their soul, their conscious and their humanity for a prescription of Ambien so they sleep at night. When it happens again, we will be ready, willing and able to fight the next battle.

580 Victims

Here is a brief summary of all the Deters Law 580 clients' Durrani surgeries:

Frieda Aaron's case involves no signed hospital consent; elderly; BMP-2; AxiaLIF; hardware malfunction; and one unnecessary surgery.

Macy Acord's case involves eight unnecessary surgeries; suffered paralysis; suffered vocal paralysis; BMP-2; and broken hardware.

Patricia Adam's case involves no hospital consent; BMP-2; Puregen; two unnecessary surgeries; operative report was dictated 101 days late; and false diagnosis.

Michelle Agee's case involves two unnecessary surgeries; failed hardware; PureGen; revision; hardware malfunction; emergency surgery; and operative report was dictated late.

Laura Aker's case involves five unnecessary surgeries; BMP-2 contraindicated; cancer; failed hardware; nonunion; revision; false diagnosis; and a minor.

James Albers' case involves unnecessary spine surgery; and false diagnosis.

Jimmy Allen's case involves one unnecessary surgery; threat of paralysis and wheelchair.

Katrina Allen's case involves BMP-2; one unnecessary surgery; operative report was dictated late; no hospital consent; victim of Shanti Shuffle; and blank signed office consent.

Sherri Allen's case involves surgery while Durrani was suspended; two surgeries; BMP-2; AxiaLIF; operative report was dictated sixty-three days late; false diagnosis; and a revision.

Alex Anderson's case involves unnecessary foot surgery and blank operative informed consent form.

Rebecca Applegate's case involves BMP-2; an unnecessary initial surgery; failed hardware; three unnecessary surgeries; victim of Shanti Shuffle; operative report dictated 229 days late; and a serious complication.

Brad Arnold's case involves one unnecessary surgery; exposed to Hank; and false diagnosis.

George Arnold's case involves PureGen; and one unnecessary surgery.

Diana Ashcraft's case involves operative report was dictated 61 days late; false diagnosis; and one unnecessary surgery.

Brian Atkins' case involves BMP-2; threat of paralysis; two unnecessary surgeries; failed hardware; victim of Shanti Shuffle; nonunion; broken screw; and a revision.

Thomas Atkinson's case involves two unnecessary surgeries; C1-C2 fusion; EDS; loss of side to side mobility; and arthritis.

Jonathan Atwell's case involves BMP-2; wrong cage; one unnecessary surgery; and a victim of Shanti Shuffle.

Chris Atwood's case involves surgery while Durrani was suspended; BMP-2; one unnecessary surgery; failed hardware; operative report was dictated 141 days late; and false diagnosis.

Thomas Augst's case involves two unnecessary surgeries; victim of Shanti Shuffle; and BMP-2.

Joshua Ault's case involves one unnecessary surgery; BMP-2 contraindicated; false diagnosis; and a minor.

Amanda Ayres' case involves one unnecessary surgery; BMP-2; and operative report was dictated late.

Gayle Bachmann's case involves surgery while Durrani was suspended; BMP-2; Puregen; hardware left in; AxiaLIF; nine unnecessary surgeries; and no operative report.

Caidan Bailey's case involves BMP-2 contraindicated; failed hardware; two unnecessary surgeries; nonunion; revision; and a minor.

Nicole Baker's case involves failed hardware; BMP-2; and three unnecessary surgeries.

Paul Baker's case involves one unnecessary surgery; disabled as a result of Durrani's surgery; and threatened wheelchair if no surgery.

Jennifer Ballinger's case involves one unnecessary surgery; BMP-2; AxiaLIF; and operative report was dictated late.

Thomas Barth's case involves one unnecessary surgery; no WCH informed consent; and incomplete CAST consent.

Cindy Bartlett's case involves surgery while Durrani was suspended; BMP-2; failed hardware; dural tear; operative report eighty-nine days late; nonunion; four unnecessary surgeries; overgrowth of bone; and a serious complication.

Laura Batsche's case involves two unnecessary surgeries; PureGen; failed hardware; exposed to Hank and contracted MRSA; false diagnosis; and operated on asymptomatic pseudo.

Nick Battista's case involves three unnecessary surgeries; BMP-2; PureGen; operative report dictated 125 days late; and false diagnosis.

Jody Bauer's case involves one unnecessary surgery; BMP-2; surgery while Durrani was suspended; AxiaLIF; false diagnosis; and operative report was dictated 108 days late.

Joseph Baumgardner's case involves threat of paralysis and wheelchair; two unnecessary surgeries; BMP-2; false diagnosis; operative report was dictated 58 days late.

Louise Bayliss' case involves surgery while Durrani was suspended; one unnecessary surgery; BMP-2; wrong cage; operative report was dictated 150 days late; and false diagnosis.

Michelle Beavan's case involves one unnecessary surgery; and Durrani's signature forged.

Phyllis Bechtold's case involves BMP-2; two unnecessary surgeries; no hospital consent; failed hardware; victim of Shanti Shuffle; false diagnosis; AxiaLIF; and Baxano.

Judy Beck's case involves BMP-2; one unnecessary surgery; breast cancer; operative report was dictated 204 days late; false diagnosis; and nonunion.

Troy Beckelhimer's case involves one unnecessary surgery; BMP-2; threat of paralysis and wheelchair; and false diagnosis.

Nancy Begley's case involves BMP-2; victim of Shanti Shuffle; blank CAST consent; dural tear; operative report was dictated 52 days late; false diagnosis; revision; incorrect procedure on WCH consent; and two unnecessary surgeries.

Cathy Beil's case involves failed hardware; one unnecessary surgery; BMP-2; AxiaLIF; operative report was dictated 70 days late; and nonunion.

Mackenzie Bender's case involves exaggerated diagnosis; one unnecessary surgery; and a minor.

Denise Benge's case involves one unnecessary surgery; no CAST consent; BMP-2; and operative report was dictated late.

Nicholas Benge's case involves one unnecessary surgery; BMP-2; and operative report was dictated late.

Antoinette Benjamin's case involves one unnecessary surgery and BMP-2.

Shawnda Benton's case involves three unnecessary surgeries; BMP-2; exposed to Hank and contracted MRSA.

William Benton's case involves two unnecessary surgeries; operative report was dictated late; and missing informed consent.

Denise Bess' case involves BMP-2; wrong cage; threat of paralysis; one unnecessary surgery; false diagnosis; and nonunion.

Leona Beyer's case involves BMP-2; wrong cage; two unnecessary surgeries; operative report was dictated 272 days late; false diagnosis; and a revision.

Trey Billing's case involves one unnecessary surgery; BMP-2 contraindicated; and a minor.

Edythe Bishop's case involves BMP-2; Atelectasis; failed hardware; threat of paralysis; no hospital consent; victim of Shanti Shuffle; blank signed office consents; false diagnosis; hardware malfunctions; missing screws; and six unnecessary surgeries.

Joel Blair's case involves an unnecessary surgery; and exaggerated diagnosis.

Anthony Bode's case involves one unnecessary surgery; and false diagnosis.

Barbara Boggs' case involves one unnecessary surgery; and nonunion.

Kaitlyn Boggs' case involves BMP-2 contraindications; operative report was dictated 121 days late; three unnecessary surgeries; failed hardware; revision; false diagnosis; and a minor.

Nancy Boland's case involves BMP-2; three unnecessary surgeries; false diagnosis; and AxiaLIF.

Jennifer Bookman's case involves one unnecessary surgery; operative report was dictated 88 days late; and false diagnosis.

Patricia Boone's case involves BMP-2; one unnecessary surgery; and operative report was dictated 110 days late.

Deena Borchers' case involves BMP-2; two unnecessary surgeries; dural tear; operative report was dictated 219 days late; AxiaLIF; and a revision.

Doris Botner's case involves two unnecessary surgeries; BMP-2; cancer; and operative report was dictated late.

Gerald Botner's case involves surgery while Durrani was suspended; five unnecessary surgeries; BMP-2; failed hardware; contracted MRSA; operative report was dictated sixty-eight days late; false diagnosis; nonunion; revision; and broken rods.

Arletta Bowling's case involves PureGen; victim of Shanti Shuffle; one unnecessary surgery; and no operative report.

Nancy Bowman's case involves BMP-2; exposed to Hank; failed hardware; two unnecessary surgeries; operative was dictated late; and a victim of Shanti Shuffle.

Penny Brackett's case involves one unnecessary surgery; BMP-2; AxiaLIF; operative report was dictated late; failed hardware; false diagnosis; and hardware malfunction.

Latoya Bradshaw's case involves surgery while Durrani was suspended; Puregen; operative report was dictated seventy days late; three unnecessary surgeries; revision; and false diagnosis.

Rebekah Brady's case involves surgery while Durrani was suspended; one unnecessary surgery; BMP-2; AxiaLIF; operative report was dictated sixty-four days late; and false diagnosis.

Christina Brashear's case involves BMP-2; four unnecessary surgeries; false diagnosis; surgery during Durrani being suspended; and operative report dictated seventy-six days late.

Katrina Bratten's case involves unnecessary surgeries; threat of paralysis; and surgery was discussed in initial visit.

Melissa Braucher's case involves Baxano; two unnecessary surgeries; operative report was dictated 325 days late; failed hardware; false diagnosis; and a revision.

Dominique Bray's case involves one unnecessary surgery; facet fusion; hardware malfunction; and false diagnosis.

Lindsey Bray's case involves one unnecessary surgery; AxiaLIF; and nonunion.

Brittany Brewer's case involves one unnecessary surgery; BMP-2; and a minor.

Randal Brewer's case involves one unnecessary surgery; PureGen; and a victim of Shanti Shuffle.

Sharon Brice's case involves two unnecessary surgeries; operative report was dictated 167 days late; revision; BMP-2; and Baxano.

Carrie Britten's case involves one unnecessary surgery; false diagnosis; and Baxano.

Michael Brophy's case involves two unnecessary surgeries; BMP-2; failed hardware; hardware malfunction; false diagnosis; revision; screw near aorta/penetrated; and operative report was dictated late.

Eileen Brorein's case involves PureGen; failed hardware; nonunion; revision; a victim of Shanti Shuffle; and two unnecessary surgeries.

Calvin Brown's case involves an unnecessary spine surgery.

Dawn Brown's case involves one unnecessary surgery; exaggerated diagnosis; BMP-2; and dictated by Shanti Shuffle- Durrani did surgery.

James Brown, Jr's case involves exposed to Hank and contracted MRSA; two unnecessary surgeries; false diagnosis; Baxano; and revision.

Tara Brown's case involves one unnecessary surgery; and exaggerated diagnosis to meet surgical requirements.

Patricia Bruce's case involves two unnecessary surgeries; BMP-2; operative report was dictated late; and false diagnosis.

Jonathan Brunner's case involves BMP-2; one unnecessary surgery; a victim of Shanti Shuffle; and false diagnosis.

Angela Buechel's case involves exaggerated diagnosis; collapsed lung; and one unnecessary surgery.

Dwayne Burchett's unnecessary surgery; BMP-2 not on operative consent form; conservative treatment was discarded; and threat of paralysis and wheelchair.

Kayla Burton's case involves one unnecessary surgery; no CAST consent form; a minor; BMP-2; and no dictation by Durrani.

Vicki Buschur's case involves one unnecessary surgery; and no operative report.

Kathleen Bushelman's case involves BMP-2 contraindicated; dural tear; false diagnosis; operative report was dictated forty-five days late; minor; and three unnecessary surgeries.

Annette Buskirk's case involves BMP-2; one unnecessary surgery in two parts; and wrong cage.

Brenda Butler's case involves one unnecessary surgery; and operative report was dictated late.

Michele Byar's case involves BMP-2; two unnecessary surgeries; PureGen; contracted MRSA; insurance denial; and false diagnosis.

Timothy Byrd's case involves BMP-2; one unnecessary surgery; and operative report was dictated late.

Doug Callahan's case involves BMP-2; wrong cage; one unnecessary surgery; failed hardware; operative report dictated 164 days late; and false diagnosis.

Patrick Calligan's case involves one unnecessary surgery; billing issue with BMP; BMP-2 contraindicated; revision; and a minor.

Jan Campbell's case involves one unnecessary surgery; and BMP-2.

Robert Campbell's case involves BMP-2; no CAST consent; victim of Shanti Shuffle; WCH consent doesn't mention Shanti; one unnecessary surgery; Shanti dictated report not Durrani; and revision surgery.

Nina Capetillo's case involves unnecessary surgery and exaggerated diagnosis.

Andrew Carr's case involves three unnecessary surgeries; BMP-2; failed hardware; operative report was dictated late; false diagnosis; and nonunion.

Ashley Casey's case involves two unnecessary surgeries; and exaggerated diagnosis.

Renecia Cherry's case involves an unnecessary epidural injection.

Bunnavuth Chhun's case involves one unnecessary surgery; Baxano; false diagnosis; and wanted to do infusion, WC denied.

Tonya Chisman's case involves BMP-2; cancer; one unnecessary surgery; operative report was dictated fifty-four days late; nonunion; and a revision.

Sherri Cinquina's case involves two unnecessary surgeries and victim of Shanti Shuffle.

Chris Clark's case involves two unnecessary surgeries; Baxano; dural tear; and a revision.

Jena Bushelman Clark's case involves three unnecessary surgeries; insurance denial; exaggerated diagnosis; and no conservative treatments.

Jessica Cochran's case involves six unnecessary surgeries; BMP-2; CAST consent from missing doctor signature; operative report was dictated 145 days late; false diagnosis; revision; nonunion; hardware malfunction; and Baxano.

David Coleman's case involves unnecessary spine surgery; initial visit surgery was suggested; no conservative treatment; threat of paralysis; and exaggerated diagnosis.

John Collins' case involves one unnecessary surgery; BMP-2 contraindicated; failed hardware; false diagnosis; revision; threat of paralysis; and a minor.

Terry Collins' case involves unnecessary spine and neck surgeries.

Elizabeth Compo's case involves BMP-2; Baxano; exposed to Hank and contracted MRSA; failed hardware; AxiaLIF; operative report was dictated late; and six unnecessary surgeries.

David Conger's case involves BMP-2; six unnecessary surgeries; a victim of Shanti Shuffle; operative report was dictated 75 days late; and false diagnosis.

Kenneth Conger's case involves three unnecessary surgeries; BMP-2 contraindicated; false diagnosis; and a minor.

Brenda Conley's case involves BMP-2; seven unnecessary surgeries; failed hardware; victim of Shanti Shuffle; false diagnosis; nonunion; operative report was dictated 132 days late; and a revision.

Dana Conley's case involves two unnecessary surgeries; PureGen; and false diagnosis.

Lisa Conley's case involves three unnecessary surgeries; and BMP-2.

Francene Cook's case involves BMP-2; and one unnecessary surgery.

Michael Cook's case involves BMP-2; four unnecessary surgeries; operative report was dictated late; and a victim of Shanti Shuffle.

Gary Coots' case involves BMP-2; no hospital consent; one unnecessary surgery; operative report was dictated fifty-two days late; and false diagnosis.

Janet Cornett's case involves one unnecessary surgery; and Baxano.

Jacob Cotter's case involves BMP-2 contraindicated; one unnecessary surgery; false diagnosis; contracted MRSA; revision; and a minor.

Barbara Couch's case involves one unnecessary surgery; BMP-2; PureGen; and operative report was dictated late.

Jackie Couch's case involves surgery while Durrani was suspended; BMP-2; one unnecessary surgery; and false diagnosis.

Eric Courtney's case involves one unnecessary surgery; Baxano; and false diagnosis.

Krista Cox's case involves two unnecessary surgeries and exaggerated diagnosis.

Michael Crail's case involves Baxano; two unnecessary surgeries; operative report was dictated 113 days late; and false diagnosis.

Karen Crissinger's case involves three unnecessary surgeries; BMP-2; operative report was dictated late; failed hardware; and no CAST intake sheet.

Joi Crowe's case involves four unnecessary surgeries; operative report was dictated late; BMP-2; wrong cage; Baxano; and PureGen.

Kali Crowe's case involves two unnecessary surgeries; hardware failure; and cementation was not on consent form.

Amber Croxson's case involves two unnecessary surgeries; and false diagnosis.

Joy Cullins' case involves one unnecessary surgery; BMP-2; and operative report was dictated late.

Kathryn Curley's case involves spinal cord injury; BMP-2 contraindicated; hardware failure; and a minor.

James Cuzzort's case involves two unnecessary surgeries; and exaggerated diagnosis.

William Dabney's two unnecessary surgeries; BMP-2; Baxano; dural tear; failed hardware; operative report was dictated late.

Margaret Dailey's case involves one unnecessary surgery; and BMP-2.

Tammy Dale's case involves BMP-2; operative report was dictated 119 days late; infection; wrong cage; three unnecessary surgeries; false diagnosis; and malposition.

Scott Daniel's case involves one unnecessary surgery; BMP-2; and false diagnosis.

Joseph Davis' case involves PureGen; one unnecessary surgery; misdiagnosis; no WCH informed consent; and hardware issue.

Nellie Davis' case involves BMP-2; cancer; two unnecessary surgeries; and false diagnosis.

Ralph Dawson's case involves BMP-2; one unnecessary surgery; false diagnosis; and nonunion.

Brianna Dearing's case involves unnecessary spine surgery; threat of paralysis; and exaggerated diagnosis.

Ollie Deaton's case involves six unnecessary surgeries; BMP-2; AxiaLIF; failed hardware; operative report was dictated late; and a victim of Shanti Shuffle.

Stefanie Deaton's case involves five unnecessary surgeries; no operative report; revision; and nicked bladder during surgery.

Holly DeClair's case involves severe bleeding; coding during surgery; an unnecessary spine surgery that resulted in her death.

Damon Deck's case involves BMP-2; failed hardware; no hospital consent; one unnecessary surgery; a victim of Shanti Shuffle; and blank signed office consents.

Sandra Dennis' case involves BMP-2; PureGen; Baxano; failed hardware; five unnecessary surgeries; screw near aorta penetrated; and blank consent form.

Robert Densler's case involves PureGen; contracted MRSA; and one unnecessary surgery.

Kristine Dority's case involves BMP-2; and one unnecessary surgery.

Carolyn Dotson's case involves PureGen; failed hardware; and one unnecessary surgery.

Deborah Doyle's case involves BMP-2; operative report was dictated thirty-two days late; AxiaLIF; false diagnosis; one unnecessary surgery; and incomplete consent.

Amanda Dradt's case involves one unnecessary surgery; and exaggerated diagnosis.

Doug Drafts' case involves one unnecessary surgery; operative report was dictated eighty-four days late; and false diagnosis.

Patrick Dugan's case involves BMP-2; wrong cage; one unnecessary surgery; operative report was dictated fifty-seven days late; and false diagnosis.

Billy Dugger's case involves BMP-2; AxiaLIF; three unnecessary surgeries; a victim of Shanti Shuffle; and false diagnosis.

Paul Dumais' case involves unnecessary spine surgeries; and exaggerated diagnosis.

Dawn Dunklin's case involves BMP-2; one unnecessary surgery; and a victim of Shanti Shuffle.

Deja Dunlap's case involves unnecessary spine surgery; medical records missing; and exaggerated diagnosis.

Jacob Durham's case involves two unnecessary surgeries; BMP-2 contraindicated; false diagnosis; hardware malfunction; revision; and a minor.

Darrell Earls' case involves PureGen; Baxano; dural tear; failed hardware; no operative report; no consent form; false diagnosis; revision; two unnecessary surgeries; confined to wheelchair; and nursing home at the age of fifty-three.

Chris Ebbing's case involves two unnecessary surgeries.

Mona Eder's case involves insurance denial; one unnecessary surgery; and exaggerated diagnosis.

Dana Edwards' case involves unnecessary hip surgery.

Leslie Egbo's case involves unnecessary spine surgery; exaggerated diagnosis; BMP-2; and threat of paralysis.

Kevin Elfers' case involves two unnecessary surgeries; BMP-2; operative report was dictated forty-nine days late; failed hardware; AxiaLIF; false diagnosis; nonunion; revision; and PureGen.

Jasmine Elkins' case involves unnecessary spine surgery; exaggerated diagnosis; and no conservative treatment.

Connie Ellington-McClure's case involves BMP-2; insurance denial; one unnecessary surgery; failed hardware; threat of paralysis and wheelchair; AxiaLIF; operative report was dictated fifty-three days late; false diagnosis; hardware malfunction; and screw near aorta.

Robert Ellington's case involves BMP-2; three unnecessary surgeries; AxiaLIF; revision; operative report was dictated ninety-nine days late; and false diagnosis.

Richard Elliott's case involves one unnecessary surgery; contracted MRSA; BMP-2; AxiaLIF; and false diagnosis.

Kelly Engle's case involves one unnecessary surgery; exaggerated diagnosis; AxiaLIF; and incomplete dictation.

Brenda Errgang's case involves one unnecessary surgery; a victim of Shanti Shuffle; false diagnosis; and a revision.

Tracy Esselman's case involves two unnecessary surgeries; and hardware failure.

Marjorie Eversole's case involves two unnecessary spine surgeries; and exaggerated diagnosis.

Arlene Fait's case involves BMP-2; failed hardware; AxiaLIF; threat of paralysis; operative report was dictated seventy-eight days late; two unnecessary surgeries; and a victim of Shanti Shuffle.

Tony Falkner's case involves one unnecessary surgery; PureGen; exaggerated diagnosis; and no operative report.

Neil Favaron's case involves surgery while Durrani was suspended; BMP-2;

no hospital consent; three unnecessary surgeries; operative report was dictated 141 days late; and false diagnosis.

Jacob Feltner's case involves one unnecessary surgery; BMP-2 contraindicated; failed hardware; osteolysis; minor; and a revision.

Karen Feltner's case involves two unnecessary surgeries; exposed to Hank and contracted MRSA; BMP-2; hardware failure; and operative report was dictated late.

Angela Ferrell's case involves one unnecessary surgery; and exaggerated diagnosis.

Damian Fields' case involves unnecessary spine surgery; threat of paralysis; BMP-2 without consent; PureGen; and a revision recommended.

Caela Finnell's case involves three unnecessary surgeries; failed hardware; false diagnosis; revision; and a minor.

Troy Fite's case involves one unnecessary surgery; BMP-2 contraindicated; false diagnosis; and a minor.

Mary Fitzpatrick's case involves four unnecessary surgeries; BMP-2; and exaggerated diagnosis.

Alyssa Flatt's case involves two unnecessary surgeries; BMP-2 without consent; threat of paralysis; and exaggerated diagnosis.

Josh Fogel's case involves six unnecessary surgeries and exaggerated diagnosis.

Francine Ford's case involves two unnecessary surgeries; no operative report; and false diagnosis.

Shamyia Ford's case involves one unnecessary surgery; BMP-2 contraindicated; false diagnosis; and a minor.

Lennie Fossett's case involves BMP-2; wrong cage; infection; three unnecessary surgeries; a victim of Shanti Shuffle; Baxano; false diagnosis; revision; and cancer.

Angelina Foster's case involves one unnecessary surgery; and exaggerated diagnosis.

Amanda Franks' case involves three unnecessary surgeries; BMP-2; operative report was dictated 141 days late; AxiaLIF; and false diagnosis.

Joann Frazier's case involves PureGen; BMP-2; Baxano; and one unnecessary surgery.

Julie Freeman's case involves one unnecessary surgery; BMP-2; and operative report was dictated late.

Amy Fuller's case involves two unnecessary surgeries; BMP-2; AxiaLIF; false diagnosis; and a revision.

Mark Funk's case involves unnecessary spine surgery; threat of paralysis; exaggerated diagnosis; and surgery was recommended at initial visit.

Judith Gardner's case involves Baxano; failed hardware; one unnecessary surgery; BMP-2; operative report was dictated 117 days late; and false diagnosis.

Christine Geralds' case involves BMP-2; wrong cage; two unnecessary surgeries; operative report was dictated 394 days late; false diagnosis; hardware malfunction; and a revision.

Erma Gilbert's case involves BMP-2; wrong cage; cancer; AxiaLIF; no hospital consent; one unnecessary surgery; a victim of Shanti Shuffle; operative report was dictated twenty-four days late; false diagnosis; nonunion; and a revision.

Sara Godby's case involves two unnecessary surgeries; exaggerated diagnosis; PureGen; surgery recommended at initial visit; and a revision.

Christina Goldstein's case involves surgery while Durrani was suspended; BMP-2; PureGen; five unnecessary surgeries; operative report was dictated 139 days late; false diagnosis; and a revision.

Donna Good's case involves two unnecessary surgeries; PureGen; threat of paralysis; and no hospital consent.

Greg Graber's case involves one unnecessary surgery; no CAST consent; infection; and BMP-2.

Maurice Grabow's case involves BMP-2; one unnecessary surgery; operative report was dictated fifty-five days late; AxiaLIF; and false diagnosis.

Erin Greelish's case involves BMP-2; wrong cage; PureGen; threat of paralysis; two unnecessary surgeries; and false diagnosis.

Brittany Green's case involves unnecessary spine surgery.

Todd Green's case involves exaggerated diagnosis; one unnecessary surgery; BMP-2; reaction to the BMP; and operative report was dictated late.

Gloria Greene's case involves an unnecessary surgery; and PureGen.

Robbie Gregory's case involves one unnecessary surgery; Baxano; false diagnosis; and operative report was dictated late.

Carla Griessman's case involves one unnecessary surgery; BMP-2; penetrated aorta; failed hardware; and hardware malfunction

Susan Griffin's case involves two unnecessary surgeries; BMP-2; AxiaLIF; no hospital consent; a victim of Shanti Shuffle; blank signed office consents; and operative report was dictated 95 days late.

Jenny Grimm's case involves BMP-2; two unnecessary surgeries; and false diagnosis.

Melissa Habermehl's case involves one unnecessary surgery; BMP-2; threat of paralysis; and false diagnosis.

Lenora Haggard's case involves one unnecessary surgery; Baxano; and false diagnosis.

Paris Halbert's case involves BMP-2; one unnecessary surgery; failed hardware; and a minor.

Lynn Haley's case involves BMP-2; two unnecessary surgeries; failed hardware; operative report was dictated fifty-two days late; revision; and nonunion.

Alyssa Hall's case involves one unnecessary surgery; BMP-2; and false diagnosis.

Lisa Hall's case involves BMP-2; wrong cage; and one unnecessary surgery.

Ruhama Hall's case involves BMP-2; one unnecessary surgery; operative report was dictated forty-four days late; hardware malfunction; and a revision.

Jade Hamby's case involves severe spinal cord injury due to surgery; paralysis; severe bleeding; lost bowel and bladder function; became wheelchair bound; unnecessary surgery that resulted in her death.

Dorothy Hamilton's case involves BMP-2; no hospital consent; operative report was dictated ninety-seven days late; two unnecessary surgeries; blank signed office consents; and false diagnosis.

Samantha Hamilton's case involves five unnecessary surgeries; BMP-2; failed hardware; operative report was dictated late; and false diagnosis.

William Hamilton's case involves one unnecessary surgery; CAST consent is not signed by doctor; and a minor.

Courtney Hammons' case involves one unnecessary surgery; BMP-2; AxiaLIF; operative report was dictated eleven days late; and false diagnosis.

Gerald Hammons' case involves two unnecessary surgeries; and exaggerated diagnosis.

Ryan Handorf's case involves one unnecessary surgery; and operative report was dictated late.

Timothy Hannon's case involves PureGen; Baxano; two unnecessary surgeries; and false diagnosis.

Briana Harris' case involves unnecessary spine surgery; and exaggerated diagnosis.

David Harris' case involves exaggerated diagnosis; one unnecessary surgery; incomplete informed consent; operative report was dictated late; and BMP-2.

Malik Harrison's case involves unnecessary spine surgery; exaggerated diagnosis; threat of paralysis; no conservative treatment; and a minor.

Adam Hartman's case involves two unnecessary surgeries; incomplete/no consent; BMP-2 contraindicated; operative report was dictated late; and a minor.

Kevin Hartness' case involves two unnecessary surgeries; BMP-2; operative report was dictated sixty-eight days late; false diagnosis; nonunion; and surgery while Durrani was suspended.

Jessica Hastings' case involves one unnecessary surgery; and no operative report.

Wayne Hatfield's case involves BMP-2; two unnecessary surgeries; failed hardware; and operative report was dictated seventy-five days late.

Sara Hauenstein's case involves unnecessary spine surgery; AxiaLIF; and surgery was recommended at initial visit.

Douglas Hayes' case involves one unnecessary surgery; and a victim of Shanti Shuffle.

William Hayes' case involves victim of Shanti Shuffle; PureGen; two unnecessary surgeries; Baxano; cancer; no hospital consent; operative report was dictated eighty-seven days late; false diagnosis; a revision; and missed cancer diagnosis.

Emily Haynes' case involves BMP-2; one unnecessary surgery; and a minor.

Kenneth Haynes' case involves two unnecessary surgeries; exaggerated diagnosis; and no conservative treatment.

Minuet Healy's case involves one unnecessary surgery; exaggerated diagnosis; and a revision.

Cameron Hedrick's case involves one unnecessary surgery; minor; threat of paralysis; and no conservative treatment.

Heather Heffner's case involves five unnecessary surgeries; BMP-2; failed hardware; revision; Baxano; and false diagnosis.

Jack Heist's case involves unnecessary spine surgery; no conservative treatment; threat of paralysis; surgery scheduled on initial visit; BMP-2; and exaggerated diagnosis.

Denise Helton's case involves one unnecessary surgery; contracted MRSA; and surgery completed by Dr. Curt.

Evelyn Helton's case involves BMP-2; two unnecessary surgeries; false diagnosis; operative report was dictated sixty-seven days late; nonunion; and a revision.

Theresa Helton's case involves one unnecessary surgery; BMP-2; and exaggerated diagnosis.

Debra Henderson's case involves BMP-2; one unnecessary surgery; and a victim of Shanti Shuffle.

Kelly Hennessy's case involves BMP-2; PureGen; four unnecessary surgeries; failed hardware; operative report was dictated eighty-one days late; and false diagnosis.

Barbara Hensley's case involves BMP-2 and one unnecessary surgery.

Ryan Hensley's case involves BMP-2; three unnecessary surgeries; failed hardware; operative report was dictated fifty-seven days late; false diagnosis; nonunion; and a revision.

Emily Herbert's case involves BMP-2 contraindicated; operative report was dictated late; one unnecessary surgery; and a minor.

Kathy Hersley's case involves BMP-2; operative report was dictated thirty-nine days late; false diagnosis; and one unnecessary surgery.

Jennifer Hickey's case involves surgery while Durrani was suspended; two unnecessary surgeries; BMP-2; failed hardware; operative report was dictated 188 days late; false diagnosis; hardware malfunction; and a revision.

Karen Higgenbothan's case involves BMP-2; four unnecessary surgeries; no operative report; a victim of Shanti Shuffle; false diagnosis; and a minor.

Alissa Hightchew's case involves BMP-2 contraindicated; one unnecessary surgery; consent form altered; false diagnosis; and a minor.

Kortney Hill's case involves unnecessary spine surgery; threat of paralysis; infection; minor; and hip procedure without consent.

Michael Hillard's case involves PureGen; insurance denial; two unnecessary surgeries; false diagnosis; and a victim of Shanti Shuffle.

Dirk Hitchcock's case involves one unnecessary surgery; and PureGen.

Celeste Hoffman's case involves BMP-2; five unnecessary surgeries; Baxano; failed hardware; a victim of Shanti Shuffle; and false diagnosis.

Luke Holcomb's case involves BMP-2 and one unnecessary surgery.

Loretta Hon's case involves BMP-2 contraindicated; one unnecessary surgery; failed hardware; operative report was dictated 256 days late; false diagnosis; and a minor.

Chelsea Hortman's case involves one unnecessary surgery; operative report was dictated 125 days late; and false diagnosis.

Robert Houghton's case involves surgery while Durrani was suspended; BMP-2; two unnecessary surgeries; nicked bowel; operative report was dictated 160 days late; and a revision.

Robert Houghton, II's case involves BMP-2 contraindicated; one unnecessary surgery; false diagnosis; and a minor.

Ricky Hounchell's case involves BMP-2; failed hardware; two unnecessary surgeries; operative report was dictated seventy-two days late; false diagnosis; and a revision.

Rita Hounchell's case involves PureGen; no hospital consent; a victim of Shanti Shuffle; one unnecessary surgery; and false diagnosis.

Kathryn Howell's case involves one unnecessary surgery and exposed to Hank.

Lois Hughes' case involves BMP-2; one unnecessary surgery; no operative report; and false diagnosis.

Tammy Hughes' case involves BMP-2; blank signed office consents; AxiaLIF; failed hardware; operative report was dictated 354 days late; false diagnosis; hardware malfunction; revision; and three unnecessary surgeries.

Kevin Hunley's case involves BMP-2; one unnecessary surgery; operative report was dictated sixty-five days late; and false diagnosis.

Carolyn Hursong's case involves surgery while Durrani was suspended; BMP-2; cancer; failed hardware; two unnecessary surgeries; operative report was dictated 135 days late; false diagnosis; hardware malfunction; and a revision.

Connie Huser's case involves AxiaLIF; BMP-2; one unnecessary surgery; cancer; and false diagnosis.

George Hutchinson's case involves BMP-2; one unnecessary surgery; threat of paralysis and wheelchair; AxiaLIF; failed hardware; operative report was dictated forty-seven days late; nonunion; and a revision.

Martha Hutton's case involves BMP-2; two unnecessary surgeries; and no CAST consent.

Irene Hyde's case involves BMP-2; four unnecessary surgeries; failed hardware; no operative report on last surgery; operative report was dictated late; nonunion; hardware malfunction; and a revision.

Jeffrey Hyde's case involves two unnecessary surgeries; BMP-2; and operative report was dictated late.

Elsa Ieraci's case involves one unnecessary surgery; BMP-2; AxiaLIF; operative report was dictated 128 days late; false diagnosis; nonunion; and a revision.

Alyssa Jackson's case involves two unnecessary surgeries; BMP-2; and a revision.

Damion Jackson's case involves unnecessary ankle surgery; minor; infection; and sepsis.

Tracy Janson's case involves one unnecessary surgery; failed hardware; operative report was dictated 199 days late; nonunion; and BMP-2.

Kimberly Jenkins' case involves three unnecessary surgeries; PureGen; no operative report after last surgery; Baxano; false diagnosis; a revision; required fusion; and required spinal cord stim.

Sarah Jessee's case involves one unnecessary surgery; misdiagnosis; and a minor.

Stephanie Jobe's case involves BMP-2; wrong cage; exposed to Hank; infection; failed hardware; threat of paralysis; one unnecessary surgery; false diagnosis; nonunion; and a revision.

Amber Johnson's case involves seven unnecessary surgeries; and failed hardware.

Chelsea Johnson's case involves surgery while Durrani was suspended; five unnecessary surgeries; BMP-2 contraindicated; failed hardware; operative report was dictated sixty-one days late; false diagnosis; revision; infection; nonunion; hardware malfunction; hardware malposition; and a minor.

Karen Johnson's case involves exaggerated diagnosis; threat of paralysis and wheelchair; no operative report from Durrani; PureGen; two unnecessary surgeries; revision surgery; and all hardware had to be removed.

Roger Johnson's case involves two unnecessary surgeries; BMP-2; PureGen; operative report was dictated sixty-one days late; AxiaLIF; false diagnosis; revision; and insurance denial.

Sara Jonas' case involves BMP-2; one unnecessary surgery; hardware failure; operative report was dictated late; nonunion; hardware malfunction; and a revision.

Dillon Jones' case involves one unnecessary surgery; BMP-2; minor; operative report was dictated late; grossly negligent surgical techniques; and false diagnosis.

Joan Jones' case involves one unnecessary surgery; PureGen; and false diagnosis.

Rachel Jones' case involves BMP-2; PureGen; two unnecessary surgeries; a victim of Shanti Shuffle; operative report was dictated late; AxiaLIF; false diagnosis; nonunion; and Durrani was not present during surgery.

Sydney Jones' case involves BMP-2 contraindicated; one unnecessary surgery; and a minor.

Tammy Jones' case involves one unnecessary surgery; PureGen; failed hardware; false diagnosis; hardware malfunction; and revision.

Jacqueline Judkins' case involves no CAST consent; BMP-2; three unnecessary surgeries; victim of Shanti Shuffle; and operative report was dictated fifty-two days late.

Phyllis Judkins' case involves two unnecessary surgeries; BMP-2; cancer; operative report was dictated ninety-nine days late; and false diagnosis.

Sarah Juergens' case involves surgery while Durrani was suspended; a victim of Shanti Shuffle; BMP-2; no hospital consent; AxiaLIF; three unnecessary surgeries; blank signed office consents; hardware malfunction; and a revision.

Linda Kallmeyer-Ward's case involves BMP-2; cancer; blank consent form; two unnecessary surgeries; surgery while Durrani was suspended; failed hardware; and operative report was dictated late.

Joshua Kauffman's case involves BMP-2 contraindicated; failed hardware; false diagnosis; hardware malfunction; minor; and a screw near aorta/penetrated.

Katelyn Kauffman's case involves surgery while Durrani was suspended; threat of paralysis; one unnecessary surgery; a victim of Shanti Shuffle; and false diagnosis.

Thomas Kellison's case involves two unnecessary surgeries; and exaggerated diagnosis.

Michelle Keplinger's case involves three unnecessary surgeries; misdiagnosis; exaggerated diagnosis; no conservative therapy; missing CAST consents; blank consent for procedure; BMP-2; PureGen; failed hardware; post-op infection; operative report was dictated late; and a revision surgery.

Martha Kibler's case involves two unnecessary surgeries; BMP-2; PureGen; no conservative treatment; exaggerated diagnosis; and missing CAST consent.

Deborah Kidd's case involves BMP-2; PureGen; dural tear; exposed to Hank; failed hardware; operative report dictated late; insurance denial; three unnecessary surgeries; victim of Shanti Shuffle; false diagnosis; and surgery while Durrani was suspended.

Sherry Kidd's case involves four unnecessary surgeries; BMP-2; false diagnosis; exaggerated diagnosis; and operative report was dictated four months late.

Vivian Kiefer's case involves one unnecessary surgery; false diagnosis; surgery scheduled at initial visit; and exaggerated diagnosis.

Charlotte King's case involves BMP-2; three unnecessary surgeries; and false diagnosis.

Christopher Knauer's case involves BMP-2; one unnecessary surgery; failed hardware; and operative report was dictated late.

Maggie Knauer's case involves BMP-2; and one unnecessary surgery.

Amanda Koch's case involves surgery while Durrani was suspended; Baxano; infection; no hospital consent; three unnecessary surgeries; blank signed office consents; false diagnosis; revision; and operative report was dictated forty-four days late.

Rose Koehler's case involves BMP-2; threat of paralysis and wheelchair; false diagnosis; completely normal C spine MRI; and operative report was dictated late.

Shannon Koehler's case involves BMP-2; four unnecessary surgeries; operative report was dictated forty-eight days late; and false diagnosis.

Mike Koelblin's case involves one unnecessary surgery; no CAST consent; Baxano; and false diagnosis.

Valarie Kopp's case involves BMP-2; lung cancer; failed hardware; threat of paralysis; insurance denial; six unnecessary surgeries; victim of Shanti Shuffle; operative report was dictated fifty-five days late; false diagnosis; and a revision.

Shelia Krabacher's case involves BMP-2; threat of paralysis and wheelchair; and failed hardware.

Laura Kranbuhl-McKee's case involves unnecessary surgeries; failed fusion; hardware failure; and removal of hardware.

Larry Krech's case involves BMP-2; PureGen; two unnecessary surgeries; operative report was dictated sixty-seven days late; AxiaLIF; false diagnosis; and a revision.

Brandon Lacinak's case involves one unnecessary surgery; BMP-2 contraindicated; failed hardware; false diagnosis; and a minor.

Natasha Lainhart's case involves BMP-2; PureGen; two unnecessary surgeries; operative report was dictated 119 days late; false diagnosis; revision; rod removed; and failed hardware.

Sara Lane's case involves one unnecessary surgery; threat of paralysis and wheelchair; surgery recommended in initial visit; and exaggerated diagnosis.

Hailey Lang's case involves two unnecessary surgeries; failed hardware; exaggerated diagnosis; no conservative treatment; minor; and false diagnosis.

Nicholas Langford's case involves three unnecessary surgeries; failed hardware; and a minor.

Victoria Landrum's case involves one unnecessary surgery; false diagnosis; contracted MRSA; and operative report was not signed by Durrani.

Tom Lantry's case involves one unnecessary surgery; false diagnosis; and no CAST informed consent.

Patricia Legendre's case involves one unnecessary surgery; BMP-2; failed hardware; threat of paralysis and wheelchair; foot drop; no hospital consent; operative report was dictated late; nonunion; false diagnosis; and a revision.

Karen Leger's case involves BMP-2; wrong cage; operative report was dictated late; one unnecessary surgery; and false diagnosis.

Beth Leisring's case involves one unnecessary surgery; incomplete consent form; false diagnosis; nonunion; revision; and a minor.

Sandra Lemmel's case involves one unnecessary surgery; and false diagnosis.

Katie Lehmkuhl's case involves one unnecessary surgery; BMP-2: some levels without consent; not able to lift chin since surgery; exaggerated diagnosis; and no conservative therapy.

Ailene LeVan's case involves PureGen; and two unnecessary surgeries.

Hillary Levandofsky's case involves one unnecessary surgery; BMP-2; false diagnosis; and removed bone from hip but not listed on operative report.

Adrian Lilly's case involves BMP-2 contraindicated; nonunion; a revision; paralysis after fixation loss; and a minor.

Derek List's case involves BMP-2; false diagnosis; one unnecessary surgery; and operative report was dictated late.

Lynne List's case involves false diagnosis; nonunion; revision; one unnecessary surgery; and failed hardware.

Tammie Little's case involves BMP-2; wrong cage; three unnecessary surgeries; false diagnosis; and operative report was dictated 121 days late.

Tamala Lovette's case involves BMP-2; wrong cage; threat of paralysis; one unnecessary surgery; operative report was dictated ninety-eight days late; and false diagnosis.

Kimberly Luse's case involves one unnecessary surgery; revision surgery needed; false diagnosis; BMP-2; and no conservative treatment.

Kenneth Mahlenkamp's case involves one unnecessary surgery; Baxano; exaggerated diagnosis; missed diagnosis; dural tear encountered during surgery; and operative report was dictated late.

Rhonda Mains' case involves BMP-2; five unnecessary surgeries; PureGen; failed hardware; operative report was dictated seventy-three days late; a revision; false diagnosis; nerve complications; and nonunion.

Shirley Mains' case involves two unnecessary surgeries; AxiaLIF; BMP-2; blank consent form; failed hardware; operative report was dictated fifty-seven days late; false diagnosis; and nonunion.

Vicky Mains' case involves one unnecessary surgery; failed hardware; hardware loose; and required hardware removal.

Tammy Mann's case involves one unnecessary surgery; BMP-2; failed hardware; Baxano; false diagnosis; and a revision.

Jack Marcheschi's case involves BMP-2 contraindicated; false diagnosis; nonunion; one unnecessary surgery; and a minor.

Paul Marksberry's case involves surgery while Durrani was suspended; BMP-2; two unnecessary surgeries; a victim of Shanti Shuffle; operative report was dictated 129 days late; false diagnosis; and AxiaLIF.

Timothy Marshall's case involves an unnecessary surgery; loss of blood; false diagnosis; septic; and kidney failure.

Julie Martin's case involves PureGen; exposure to Hank (Durrani's dog) who had MRSA; failed hardware; one unnecessary surgery; Shanti Shuffle; and complication of hardware malposition.

Marsha Martin's case involves two unnecessary surgeries; BMP-2 without consent; and exaggerated diagnosis.

Stacy John Martin's case involves one unnecessary surgery; and informed consent doesn't match operative report.

Robert Masters' case involves two unnecessary surgeries; BMP-2; and failed hardware.

Traci Mathews' case involves one unnecessary surgery; PureGen; and exaggerated diagnosis.

Alan Matthews' case involves one unnecessary surgery; second surgery was recommended; exaggerated diagnosis; and failed hardware.

Brandon Mathis' case involves BMP-2 contraindicated; one unnecessary surgery; and a minor.

Mary Mauntel's case involves exaggerated diagnosis; minor; one unnecessary surgery; BMP-2; and became nonverbal after surgery.

Kimberly Mayer's case involves one unnecessary surgery; AxiaLIF; BMP-2; a victim of Shanti Shuffle; false diagnosis; nonunion; and Baxano.

Derek Mayfield's case involves one unnecessary surgery; BMP-2; contracted MRSA; and operative report was dictated late.

James McCain's case involves one unnecessary surgery and false diagnosis.

Jenna McCall's case involves BMP-2 contraindicated; no hospital consent; one unnecessary surgery; operative report was dictated 244 days late; false diagnosis; AxiaLIF; nonunion; and a minor.

Heather McCann's case involves AxiaLIF; one unnecessary surgery; false diagnosis; nonunion; and a revision.

Hiram McCauley's case involves surgery while Durrani was suspended; a victim of Shanti Shuffle; one unnecessary surgery; BMP-2; wrong cage; blank office consent; operative report was dictated 129 days late; and false diagnosis.

Kyra McClendon's case involves two unnecessary surgeries; BMP-2 contraindicated; operative report was dictated sixty-three days late; false diagnosis; and a minor.

Jeff McClure's case involves PureGen; Baxano; failed hardware; three unnecessary surgeries; a victim of Shanti Shuffle; false diagnosis; and a revision.

Kevin McDonald's case involves no operative report; minor; false diagnosis; surgery performed after Durrani required to leave Children's; and four unnecessary surgeries.

Marcella McDonald's case involves one unnecessary surgery; and PureGen.

Grant McKenney's case involves four unnecessary surgeries; failed hardware; and a minor.

Whitney McKenzie's case involves two unnecessary surgeries; minor; exaggerated diagnosis; no conservative treatment; and false diagnosis.

Madison McLaughlin's case involves one unnecessary surgery; minor; exaggerated diagnosis; threat of paralysis; additional procedure done without consent; and no conservative teatment.

Candi McKinney's case involves one unnecessary surgery; PureGen; operative report was dictated late; and false diagnosis.

Tyler McKnight's case involves BMP-2; false diagnosis; one unnecessary surgery; and a minor.

Teresa McMillen's case involves a victim of Shanti Shuffle; three unnecessary surgeries; BMP-2; PureGen; and operative report was dictated late.

Mark McMurren's case involves BMP-2; PureGen; four unnecessary surgeries; no operative report completed on first surgery; and failed hardware.

Kameron McNeal's case involves BMP-2 contraindicated; false diagnosis; nonunion; revision; two unnecessary surgeries; and a minor.

Kerry McNeal's case involves incomplete informed consent; four unnecessary surgeries; failed hardware; false diagnosis; operative report was dictated sixty-six days late; hardware malfunction; revision; and BMP-2.

Tonia McQueary's case involves surgery while Durrani was suspended; BMP-2; PureGen; failed hardware; ten unnecessary surgeries; hardware left in; operative report was dictated 98 days late; false diagnosis; nonunion; a revision; and Baxano.

Tiffany Meadows' case involves one unnecessary surgery; and exaggerated diagnosis.

Chris Merida's case involves one unnecessary surgery; minor; no conservative treatment; and false diagnosis.

Dawn Merland's case involves one unnecessary surgery; operative report was dictated 34 days late; AxiaLIF; false diagnosis; and BMP-2.

Tiffany Messerschmidt's case involves one unnecessary surgery; BMP-2; threat of paralysis and wheelchair; failed hardware; and false diagnosis.

Angel Messinger's case involves one unnecessary surgery; minor; no conservative treatment; and false diagnosis.

Randall Metcalf's case involves BMP-2; failed hardware; one unnecessary surgery; a victim of Shanti Shuffle; AxiaLIF; operative report was dictated 60 days late; and false diagnosis.

Diane Meyer's case involves threat of paralysis; one unnecessary surgery; and false diagnosis.

Tom Meyers' case involves one unnecessary surgery; PureGen; and pain management.

Lyndsey Middendorf's case involves BMP-2 contraindicated; one unnecessary surgery; minor; operative report was dictated forty-one days late; and false diagnosis.

Karen Miller's case involves BMP-2; one unnecessary surgery; failed hardware; AxiaLIF; and nonunion.

Ryan Miller's case involves blank CAST consent form; one unnecessary surgery; BMP-2; AxiaLIF; failed hardware; and operative report was dictated late.

Jill Millis' case involves one unnecessary surgery; recommendation of a second surgery; and false diagnosis.

Samantha Mink's case involves BMP-2 contraindicated; one unnecessary surgery; AxiaLIF; operative report was dictated 157 days late; nonunion; and a minor.

Vera Moffitt's case involves one unnecessary surgery; BMP-2; failed hardware; operative report was dictated seventy-two days late; and false diagnosis.

Junior Monroe's case involves one unnecessary surgery; BMP-2; and operative report was dictated two months late.

Billie Moore's case involves BMP-2; one unnecessary surgery; operative report was dictated 86 days late; false diagnosis; and revision.

Debbie Moore's case involves one unnecessary surgery; failed hardware; and hardware malfunction.

Donald Moore's case involves BMP-2; wrong cage; PureGen; two unnecessary surgeries; victim of Shanti Shuffle; false diagnosis; and nonunion.

Robert Moore's case involves one unnecessary surgery; and PureGen.

Stephanie Moore's case involves an unnecessary surgery; and false diagnosis.

Tim Moore's case involves Baxano; and one unnecessary surgery.

William Moore's case involves one unnecessary surgery; BMP-2; and operative report was dictated late.

Reba Morgan's case involves one unnecessary surgery and false diagnosis.

Robert Mounce's case involves one unnecessary surgery; operative report was dictated ninety-five days late; Baxano; and false diagnosis.

Sarra Mueller's case involves an unnecessary surgery; no hospital consent; false diagnosis; and a minor.

Stephanie Mueller's case involves one unnecessary surgery; PureGen; and BMP-2.

Jennifer Myers' case involves one unnecessary surgery and no informed consent.

Joetta Nafe's case involves cancer; PureGen; one unnecessary surgery; and false diagnosis.

Tonya Neal's case involves BMP-2; penetrated aorta; infection; failed hardware; AxiaLIF; two unnecessary surgeries; and operative report was dictated late.

Charles Nelson's case involves one unnecessary surgery; BMP-2 contraindicated; and a minor.

Gary Neu's case involves three unnecessary surgeries; BMP-2; incorrect procedure listed on consent versus operative report; CAST consent missing; operative report was dictated by Shanti; failed hardware; surgery while Durrani was suspended; and operative report was dictated late.

Marjorie Newman's case involves BMP-2; one unnecessary surgery; failed hardware; blank office consent; nonunion; false diagnosis; and operative report was dictated 5 days late.

Teresa Nichols' case involves BMP-2; PureGen; two unnecessary surgeries; no CAST consent; and operative report was dictated late.

Rahman Nisbett's case involves one unnecessary surgery; threat of paralysis and wheelchair; cancer; operative report was dictated forty-seven days late; nonunion; false diagnosis; and BMP-2.

Michelle Noble's case involves one unnecessary surgery; no CAST consent form; Baxano; and incorrect hospital consent form.

Gail Nordeman's case involves two unnecessary surgeries; BMP-2; hardware failure; cancer; and operative report was dictated late.

Ruvimbo Nyemba's case involves BMP-2; one unnecessary surgery; operative report was dictated forty-seven days late; false diagnosis; hardware malfunction; and surgery while Durrani was suspended.

Wendy Oberlander's case involves four unnecessary surgeries; BMP-2; operative report was dictated eighty-two days late; false diagnosis; revision; and Baxano.

Michael Odulana's case involves one unnecessary surgery; BMP-2 contraindicated; false diagnosis; nonunion; and a minor.

Timothy Osborn's case involves five unnecessary surgeries; BMP-2; threat of paralysis; operative report was dictated 114 days late; nonunion; Baxano; and a revision.

Dannie Mae Owens' case involves two unnecessary surgeries; BMP-2; false diagnosis; and a revision.

Rusty Patrick's case involves one unnecessary surgery; minor; threat of paralysis and wheelchair; and no conservative treatment.

Haley Payne's case involves BMP-2 contraindicated; one unnecessary surgery; operative report was dictated fifty-three days late; false diagnosis; revision; nonunion; and a minor.

Jeff Peddicord's case involves BMP-2; wrong cage; failed hardware; one unnecessary surgery; operative report was dictated fifty-nine days late; and false diagnosis.

Duane Pelfrey's case involves PureGen; two unnecessary surgeries; Baxano; operative report was dictated twenty-five days late; and false diagnosis.

Angela Pennington's case involves BMP-2 contraindication; one unnecessary surgery; threatened death if she didn't have surgery; and a minor.

Kenneth Pfetsch's case involves one unnecessary surgery; BMP-2; lung cancer three months after; operative report was dictated 214 days late; AxiaLIF; and false diagnosis.

Clarence Phillips' case involves one unnecessary surgery; BMP-2; failed hardware; AxiaLIF; and operative report was dictated late.

Heather Pickett's case involves an unnecessary surgery, and BMP-2.

Crystal Pierce's case involves BMP-2; unnecessary surgery; threat of paralysis/wheelchair, failed hardware; and false diagnosis.

Jeffrey Poff's case involves one unnecessary surgery; no procedure on CAST consent; WCH procedure performed does not match procedure on WCH consent; BMP-2; operative report was dictated late; and surgery while Durrani was suspended.

Jeff Potts' case involves one unnecessary surgery; BMP-2; cancer; nonunion; perforated bowel, sepsis, dural tear, exaggerated diagnosis, and false diagnosis.

Antoine Powell's case involves BMP-2; blank CAST consent form; hardware failure; and exposed screw piercing through his back.

Bryan Powers' case involves one unnecessary surgery; exaggerated diagnosis; BMP-2; AxiaLIF; and a revision.

Katie Prater's case involves BMP-2; one unnecessary surgery; and false diagnosis.

Lawrence Pridemore's case involves PureGen; a victim of Shanti Shuffle; AxiaLIF; revision; and false diagnosis.

Sharon Pritchard's case involves BMP-2; infection; one unnecessary surgery; and false diagnosis.

Sherri Puckett-Morrissette's case involves one unnecessary surgery; PureGen; and false diagnosis.

Carol Pummell's case involves BMP-2; wrong cage; screw near aorta; failed hardware; operative report was dictated ninety-three days late; seven unnecessary surgeries; PureGen; false diagnosis; hardware malfunction; and a revision.

Marcia Quinn's case involves surgery while Durrani was suspended; BMP-2; wrong cage; PureGen; no hospital consent; three unnecessary surgeries; operative report was dictated 56 days late; false diagnosis; and a revision.

Sandra Radeke's case involves one unnecessary surgery; AxiaLIF, BMP-2 and failed hardware.

Margaret Radenheimer's case involves BMP-2; threat of paralysis; two unnecessary surgeries; operative report was dictated ninety-three days late; AxiaLIF; and false diagnosis.

Mary Ravenscraft's case involves PureGen; and false diagnosis.

Todd Ray's case involves surgery while Durrani was suspended; BMP-2; three unnecessary surgeries; operative report was dictated 134 days late; and false diagnosis.

Samantha Redrow's case involves BMP-2 contraindicated; failed hardware; two unnecessary surgeries; false diagnosis; nonunion; revision; and a minor.

Danielle Reed's case involves BMP-2; infection; failed hardware; two unnecessary surgeries; a victim of Shanti Shuffle; operative report was dictated 61 days late; false diagnosis; nonunion; hardware malfunction; and a revision.

Mark Reed's case involves an unnecessary surgery; and Baxano.

Jane Reeder's case involves Baxano; two unnecessary surgeries; and false diagnosis.

Valerie Reeves' case involves victim of Shanti Shuffle; BMP-2; Baxano; exposed to Hank and contracted MRSA; failed hardware; threat of paralysis; seven unnecessary surgeries; operative report was dictated seventy-nine days late; revision; false diagnosis; and a graft extrusion.

Holly Reifenberger's case involves two unnecessary surgeries; operative report was dictated late; Baxano; PureGen; and false diagnosis.

Jeffrey Remley's case involves BMP-2; two unnecessary surgeries; and AxiaLIF.

Derrill Reynolds' case involves PureGen; two unnecessary surgeries; false diagnosis; and infection.

Harry Reynolds' case involves three unnecessary surgeries; PureGen; BMP-2; surgery while Durrani was suspended; and cancer.

Kent Reynolds, II's case involves an unnecessary spine surgery.

Lisa Reynolds' case involves BMP-2; and two unnecessary surgeries.

Jordan Ribariu's case involves BMP-2; one unnecessary surgery; and a minor.

John Richardson's case involves PureGen; three unnecessary surgeries; and failed hardware.

Jason Riley's case involves BMP-2; wrong cage; contracted MRSA; two unnecessary surgeries; AxiaLIF; operative report was dictated 43 days late; false diagnosis; nonunion; and a revision.

Donna Rister's case involves BMP-2; PureGen; three unnecessary surgeries; failed hardware; operative report was dictated seventy-eight days late; victim of Shanti Shuffle; and false diagnosis.

Deborah Roark's case involves one unnecessary surgery; incomplete informed consent; and operative report was dictated late.

Theresa Robbinson-Woods' case involves BMP-2; wrong cage; kyphosis; no hospital consent; one unnecessary surgery; false diagnosis; and nonunion.

Kelly Robinson's case involves BMP-2; one unnecessary surgery; operative report was dictated 366 days late; false diagnosis; and hardware malfunction.

Debbie Rodriguez's case involves surgery while Durrani was suspended; BMP-2; failed hardware; eight unnecessary surgeries; operative report was dictated 106 days late; false diagnosis; nonunion; and a revision.

David Rohling's case involves one unnecessary surgery; no signed surgical consent form; exaggerated diagnosis; and BMP-2.

Jason Romer's case involves Baxano; one unnecessary surgery; false diagnosis; and a revision.

Dorothy Rose's case involves PureGen; penetrated aorta; elderly; failed hardware; two unnecessary surgeries; victim of Shanti Shuffle; operative report was dictated 175 days late; false diagnosis; and hardware malfunction.

Fay Rosebery's case involves surgery while Durrani was suspended; BMP-2; two unnecessary surgeries; hardware malfunction; nonunion; superior screws into disc space; and false diagnosis.

Carol Ross' cases involves surgery while Durrani was suspended; threat of paralysis; two unnecessary surgeries; PureGen; operative report was dictated late; and failed hardware.

Sandra Roundtree's case involves one unnecessary surgery; BMP-2 and false diagnosis.

Ronald Rowley's case involves surgery while Durrani was suspended; BMP-2; operative report was dictated sixty-eight days late; one unnecessary surgery; and false diagnosis.

Joshua Roy's case involves two unnecessary surgeries; minor; failed hardware; and exaggerated diagnosis.

Kathrynn Rueve's case involves one unnecessary surgery and PureGen.

Robert Runtz's case involves BMP-2; two unnecessary surgeries; operative report was dictated 102 days late; and false diagnosis.

Carson Rutter's case involves five unnecessary surgeries, left under anesthesia for hours at a time prior to start of surgery, BMP-2; false diagnosis; failed hardware; immobilized in a halo for one year; surgical wound infections; and a minor.

Mike Sand's case involves BMP-2; one unnecessary surgery; operative report was dictated 190 days late; and false diagnosis.

Mike Sander's case involves BMP-2; AxiaLIF; three unnecessary surgeries; operative report was dictated 104 days late; false diagnosis; revision; and surgery while Durrani was suspended.

Chris Scheper's case involves PureGen; one unnecessary surgery; a victim of Shanti Shuffle; and false diagnosis.

Robin Schiller's case involves BMP-2; wrong cage; cancer; one unnecessary surgery; operative report was dictated forty-three days late; AxiaLIF; and false diagnosis.

Joseph Schimmel's case involves two unnecessary surgeries; PureGen; and failed hardware.

Kim Schmidt's case involves threat of paralysis and wheelchair; and exaggerated diagnosis.

Kevin Schmit's case involves Baxano and false diagnosis.

Patrick Schmit's case involves one unnecessary surgery and Baxano.

Brandon Schoborg's case involves BMP-2 contraindicated; one unnecessary surgery; and a minor.

Susan Schock's case involves BMP-2; wrong cage; failed hardware; two unnecessary surgeries; operative report was dictated 128 days late; false diagnosis; nonunion; revision; AxiaLIF; and cancer.

Paul Scholz's case involves an unnecessary surgery; and BMP-2.

Steven Andrew Schultz's case involves BMP-2; two unnecessary surgeries; false diagnosis; nonunion; hardware malfunction; revision; and operative report was dictated two days late.

Timothy Schulze's case involves PureGen; and one unnecessary surgery.

Ronald Schuster's case involves BMP-2; one unnecessary surgery; victim of Shanti Shuffle; operative report was dictated late; false diagnosis; and nonunion.

Delores Scott's case involves an unnecessary surgery; operative report was dictated 51 days late; and BMP-2.

Rhonda Scott's case involves three unnecessary surgeries; BMP-2; failed hardware; and operative report was dictated late.

Ali Scully's case involves BMP-2 contraindicated; false diagnosis; hardware malfunction; minor; two unnecessary surgeries; and informed consent was not correct.

Ruthie Sears' case involves one unnecessary surgery; BMP-2 contraindicated; false diagnosis; hardware malfunction; minor; and consent form incorrect.

Sarah Selm's case involves five unnecessary surgeries; contracted MRSA; and false diagnosis.

Dana Setters' case involves PureGen; Baxano; failed hardware; insurance denial; two unnecessary surgeries; and false diagnosis.

Glenna Shafer's case involves PureGen; two unnecessary surgeries; operative report was dictated 106 days late; false diagnosis; nonunion; and a revision.

Asia Shannon's case involves BMP-2 contraindicated; threat of paralysis and wheelchair; false diagnosis; minor; one unnecessary surgery; and spinal infusion bleed.

Kevin Shaw's case involves one unnecessary surgery; minor; and no conservative treatment.

Brenda Shell's case involves unnecessary surgeries; threat of wheelchair/paralysis; foot drop; infection of incision; twenty-three days in hospital; dural tear; wound care; and falsc diagnosis.

David Shempert's case involves surgery while Durrani was suspended; BMP-2; wrong cage; one unnecessary surgery; victim of Shanti Shuffle; operative report was dictated late.

Charlann Shepherd involves an unnecessary surgery; and false diagnosis.

Greg Shott's case involves nonunion; BMP-2; pancreatic cancer; one unnecessary surgery; operative report was dictated late.

Shandon Simmons' case involves two unnecessary surgeries; BMP-2; and operative report was dictated late.

Karen Sisson's case involves one unnecessary surgery and BMP-2.

Michelle Sizemore's case involves two unnecessary surgeries; no CAST consent; WCH consent incorrect; BMP-2; and failed hardware.

Heather Slayback's case involves BMP-2 contraindicated; false diagnosis; failed hardware; minor; and one unnecessary surgery.

Crystal Slone's case involves an unnecessary surgery, BMP-2; AxiaLIF; false diagnosis; nonunion; revision; broken screw; and surgery while Durrani was suspended.

Donna Smallwood's case involves BMP-2; failed hardware; one unnecessary surgery; operative report was dictated sixteen days late; false diagnosis; nonunion; and a revision.

David Smith's case involves Baxano; one unnecessary surgery; victim of Shanti Shuffle; operative report was dictated 121 days late; false diagnosis; and nonunion.

Donald Smith's case involves BMP-2; operative report was dictated late; nonunion; revision; hardware malfunction; and surgery while Durrani was suspended.

Staci Smith's case involves an exaggerated diagnosis.

Orris Smoote's case involves BMP-2; failed hardware; elderly; and one unnecessary surgery.

David Snider's case involves an unnecessary surgery; BMP-2; and operative report was dictated late.

Sherrie Spangenberg's case involves BMP-2; wrong cage; AxiaLIF; infection; failed hardware; three unnecessary surgeries; operative report was dictated forty-nine days late; false diagnosis; hardware failure; and a revision.

Billy Spivy's case involves surgery while Durrani was suspended; BMP-2; three unnecessary surgeries; no informed consent; failed hardware; operative report was dictated fifty-nine days late; false diagnosis; and a revision.

Zachary Stacy's case involves two unnecessary surgeries; threat of paralysis; BMP-2 without consent; and false diagnosis.

Eddie Stallings' case involves one unnecessary surgery; no hospital consent form; PureGen; and false diagnosis.

Earl Stamps' case involves one unnecessary surgery; BMP-2; no CAST consent form; and no operative report was dictated by Durrani.

Rick Stanfield's case involves surgery while Durrani was suspended; one unnecessary surgery; BMP-2; and false diagnosis.

Michelle Stephens' case involves BMP-2; wrong cage; one unnecessary surgery; and false diagnosis.

Patrick Stephenson's case involves BMP-2; no hospital consent; four unnecessary surgeries; victim of Shanti Shuffle; operative report was dictated late; blank signed office consents; false diagnosis; and surgery while Durrani was suspended.

Tempie Stephenson's case involves a victim of Shanti Shuffle; two unnecessary surgeries; no CAST informed consent; BMP-2; surgery was contraindicated; and no conservative therapy.

Darlene Sterling's case involves one unnecessary surgery; BMP-2; missing CAST consent; procedure missing on consent; failed hardware; required revision surgery; and operative report was dictated 181 days late.

Bert Stidham's case involves one unnecessary surgery; exaggerated diagnosis; and operative report was dictated late.

Deon Stigall Jr's case involves one unnecessary surgery; BMP-2 contraindicated; a minor; and false diagnosis.

Sierra Stratman's case involves BMP-2; threat of paralysis and wheelchair; false diagnosis; hardware malfunction; nonunion; and a revision.

Deborah Sturdivant's case involves one unnecessary surgery; no conservative treatment; surgery recommended in initial visit; failed hardware; and BMP-2 without consent.

Ryan Tackett's case involves one unnecessary surgery; BMP-2 contraindicated; hardware malfunction; insurance denial; and a minor.

Ryan Tanner's case involves one unnecessary surgery; incomplete consent form; and a revision.

Alex Taylor's case involves BMP-2 contraindicated; a minor; and one unnecessary surgery.

Karen Taylor's case involves BMP-2; penetrated aorta; failed hardware; threat of paralysis; a victim of Shanti Shuffle; false diagnosis; hardware malfunction; and a revision.

Kathleen Telscher's case involves operative report was dictated 63 days late; false diagnosis; and one unnecessary surgery.

Ben Thaeler's case involves BMP-2; threat of paralysis and wheelchair; failed hardware; false diagnosis; and infection.

Brittany Theilman's case involves one unnecessary surgery; minor; BMP-2 without consent; and exaggerated diagnosis.

Brian Thien's case involves BMP-2; wrong cage; threat of paralysis; one unnecessary surgery; operative report was dictated 194 days late; and false diagnosis.

Edward Thiessen's case involves failed hardware; one unnecessary surgery; false diagnosis; and nonunion.

Adricnnc Thomas' case involves two unnecessary surgeries; and false diagnosis.

Clara Tubbs-Hill's case involves two unnecessary surgeries; no consent; BMP-2; contracted MRSA; and revision surgery.

Connie Underwood's case involves surgery while Durrani was suspended; BMP-2; four unnecessary surgeries; operative report was dictated 110 days late; AxiaLIF; false diagnosis; and a revision.

Kimberly Underwood's case involves BMP-2; wrong cage; PureGen; screw near aorta; failed hardware; two unnecessary surgeries; operative report was dictated late; false diagnosis; hardware malfunction; nonunion; and a revision.

Jacklen Upchurch's case involves BMP-2 and one unnecessary surgery.

Jordan Vance's case involves threat of paralysis; five unnecessary surgeries; all ribs broken during surgery; four ribs removed; exaggerated diagnosis; and operative report was dictated late.

Brooke Vandervort's case involves two unnecessary surgeries; missing CAST records; BMP-2; and operative report was dictated late.

Ashley Walker's case involves one unnecessary surgery and BMP-2 without consent.

Daphne Wallace's case involves an unnecessary surgery.

Shannon Wallace's case involves BMP-2 contraindicated; insurance denial; failed diagnosis; and a minor

Vicki Wallace's case involves BMP-2; false diagnosis; one unnecessary surgery; and no consent form.

Katherine Walls' case involves one unnecessary surgery; operative report was dictated late; and Shanti did surgery.

Lindsay Walsh's case involves BMP-2 contraindicated; false diagnosis; insurance denial; minor; and one unnecessary surgery.

Madison Walsh's case involves four unnecessary procedures; minor; and no conservative treatment.

Tracey Walsh's case involves BMP-2; three unnecessary surgeries; failed hardware; and operative report was dictated late.

Michelle Walters' case involves Baxano; blank office consent; two unnecessary surgeries; operative report was dictated 104 days late; false diagnosis; and nonunion.

Helen Ward's case involves two unnecessary surgeries; BMP-2; failed hardware; elderly; false diagnosis; operative report was dictated 3 days late; and a revision.

Michael Watkins' case involves PureGen; operative report was dictated 84 days late; and two unnecessary surgeries.

Elaine Waxler's case involves seven unnecessary surgeries; PureGen; operative report was dictated 158 days late; false diagnosis; nonunion; revision; and hardware malfunction.

Cathleen Weber's case involves BMP-2 contraindicated; minor; false diagnosis; threat of paralysis and wheelchair; incorrect consent form; and one unnecessary surgery.

Daniel Webber's case involves PureGen; no hospital consent; insurance denial; failed hardware; false diagnosis; nonunion; and a revision.

Brandon Webster's case involves BMP-2 contraindicated; false diagnosis; incorrect consent form; one unnecessary surgery; and operative report was dictated late.

Laura Weisbecker's case involves Baxano; false diagnosis; revision; and one unnecessary surgery.

Kirstin Weisman's case involves BMP-2; two unnecessary surgeries; false diagnosis; nonunion; and a minor.

Regina Wesley's case involves cancer; four unnecessary surgeries; PureGen; BMP-2; contracted MRSA; failed hardware; and operative report was dictated late.

Timothy Whalen's case involves PureGen; two unnecessary surgeries; and operative report was dictated late.

Violet Whalen's case involves one unnecessary surgery; and false diagnosis.

Lonnie Wheeler's case involves BMP-2; Baxano; failed hardware; cancer; four unnecessary surgeries; a victim of Shanti Shuffle; operative report was dictated 54 days late; AxiaLIF; nonunion; and a revision.

Sophia White's case involves one unnecessary surgery.

Tamathy Wilder's case involves BMP-2; PureGen; wrong cage; five unnecessary surgeries; failed hardware; operative report 200 days late; and false diagnosis.

Troy Wilder's case involves BMP-2; failed hardware; no hospital consent; two unnecessary surgeries; false diagnosis; operative report was dictated 123 days late; nonunion; and a revision.

Ben Williams' case involves BMP-2; wrong cage; AxiaLIF; one unnecessary surgery; failed hardware; false diagnosis; and operative report was dictated late.

Kelly Williams' case involves one unnecessary surgery; and operative report was dictated late.

Patrick Willoughby's case involves one unnecessary surgery; operative report was dictated 113 days late; and false diagnosis.

Carol Wilson's case involves BMP-2; three unnecessary surgeries; victim of Shanti Shuffle; failed hardware; Baxano; false diagnosis; nonunion; and a revision.

Jetton Wilson's case involves BMP-2; one unnecessary surgery; failed hardware; Baxano; and false diagnosis.

Joseph Wilson's case involves two unnecessary surgeries; wrong arm listed on operative report; and a minor.

Paul Wilson's case involves two unnecessary surgeries; no hospital consent; PureGen; false diagnosis; operative report was dictated 11 days late; and a revision.

Paula Wilson's case involves BMP-2; PureGen; AxiaLIF; three unnecessary surgeries; a victim of Shanti Shuffle; operative report was dictated 55 days late; and nonunion.

Robert Wilson's case involves BMP-2; failed hardware; threat of paralysis; three unnecessary surgeries; victim of Shanti Shuffle; operative report was dictated 130 days late; false diagnosis; nonunion; and a revision.

Terry Wilson's case involves one unnecessary surgery and Baxano.

Vicky Wilson's case involves one unnecessary surgery; operative report was dictated sixty-six days late; and false diagnosis.

Dawn Wingert's case involves one unnecessary surgery and Baxano.

Priscilla Wittmeyer's case involves BMP-2; PureGen; failed hardware; AxiaLIF; insurance denial; four unnecessary surgeries; operative report was dictated late; false diagnosis; nonunion; and revision.

Bill Wolder's case involves BMP-2; two unnecessary surgeries; PureGen; and operative report was dictated 152 days late.

Jared Wolfe's case involves one unnecessary surgery; no conservative treatment; infection; and failed hardware.

Billy Wolsing's case involves Baxano; one unnecessary surgery; false diagnosis; and a revision.

Carla Wooten's case involves two unnecessary surgeries; PureGen and false diagnosis.

Amber Work's case involves two unnecessary surgeries; BMP-2; PureGen; and false diagnosis.

Debbie Worley's case involves BMP-2; infection; operative report was dictated 126 days late; four unnecessary surgeries; and a revision.

Teresa Worley's case involves four unnecessary surgeries; no CAST informed consent; no hospital consent; BMP-2; failed hardware; and operative report was dictated late.

Cory Wright's case involves one unnecessary surgery, BMP-2 contraindicated; threat of paralysis and wheelchair; failed hardware; false diagnosis; hardware malfunction; and a minor.

Leah Wright's case involves three unnecessary surgeries; elderly; BMP-2; PureGen; and operative report was dictated late.

Cheryl Wyatt's case involves false diagnosis; nonunion; revision; and one unnecessary surgery.

Emanuel Wyatt's case involves one unnecessary surgery; BMP-2 and false diagnosis.

Veronica Yeakle's case involves Baxano; contracted MRSA; a victim of Shanti Shuffle; and one unnecessary surgery.

Evelyn Young's case involves BMP-2 and one unnecessary surgery.

Joann Young's case involves PureGen; infection; two unnecessary surgeries; false diagnosis; dural tear; and hardware malfunction.

Judy Young's case involves BMP-2; wrong cage; two unnecessary surgeries; a victim of Shanti Shuffle; operative report was dictated 144 days late; AxiaLIF; and nonunion.

Keith Young's case involves BMP-2; one unnecessary surgery; operative report was dictated 203 days late; AxiaLIF; and false diagnosis.

Corrine Zachry's case involves BMP-2 contraindicated; wrong cage; PureGen; failed hardware; threat of paralysis; two unnecessary surgeries; operative report was dictated late; false diagnosis; nonunion; revision; and a minor.

Zachary Zaerr's case involves three unnecessary surgeries; minor; and exaggerated diagnosis.

Hannah Zmyslo's case involves false diagnosis; minor; and one unnecessary surgery.

Mary Zureick's case involves one unnecessary surgery; PureGen; false diagnosis; cancer; and no date on operative report.

INDEX

H

N

R

S

T

Y

Z